LATINO
HISTORY AND CULTURE

Volume One

LATINO
HISTORY AND CULTURE
AN ENCYCLOPEDIA

Volume One

David J. Leonard and Carmen R. Lugo-Lugo, editors

SHARPE REFERENCE
an imprint of M.E. Sharpe, Inc.

SHARPE REFERENCE

Sharpe Reference is an imprint of M.E. Sharpe, Inc.

M.E. Sharpe, Inc.
80 Business Park Drive
Armonk, NY 10504

Library of Congress Cataloging-in-Publication Data

Latino history and culture: an encyclopedia / David J. Leonard and Carmen R. Lugo-Lugo, editors.
p. cm.
Includes bibliographical references and index.
ISBN 978-0-7656-8083-9 (hardcover: alk. paper)
1. Hispanic Americans—Encyclopedias. I. Leonard, David J. II. Lugo-Lugo, Carmen R.

E184.S75L3622 2009
305.868'07303—dc22 2008047796

Cover photos by Getty and the following (from top left corner): Doug Collier/AFP; Alex Wong; Bob Parent/Hulton Archive; Tim Boyle; Kevin Mazur/WireImage.

Printed and bound in the United States of America

The paper used in this publication meets the minimum requirements of American National Standard for Information Sciences Permanence of Paper for Printed Library Materials, ANSI Z 39.48.1984.

(c) 10 9 8 7 6 5 4 3 2 1

Publisher: Myron E. Sharpe
Vice President and Director of New Product Development: Donna Sanzone
Vice President and Production Director: Carmen Chetti
Executive Development Editor: Jeff Hacker
Project Manager: Laura Brengelman
Program Coordinator: Cathleen Prisco
Assistant Editor: Alison Morretta
Text Design: Carmen Chetti and Jesse Sanchez
Cover Design: Jesse Sanchez

Contents

Volume 2

Topic Finder

Puerto Rican Studies
Samora, Julian
Spanish Language
Third World Liberation Front
Tracking

Geographic Locations
Aztlán
Chávez Ravine
Chicago
Crystal City, Texas
East Los Angeles
Farmingville, New York
Los Angeles
Miami
New York
Vieques, Puerto Rico

Government Programs, Bodies, and Initiatives
Bracero Program
Congressional Hispanic Caucus
Immigration Enforcement
Mariel Boatlift
North American Free Trade Agreement
Operation Bootstrap
Operation Wetback
Resident Commissioner, Puerto Rico
Sterilization

Health Care Issues and Organizations
AIDS/HIV
ASPIRA
Gay and Lesbian Organizations
Health and Health Care
LLEGÓ
National Boricua Latino Health Organization
Sterilization

Historical Events and Incidents
Alamo, Battle of the
Bay of Pigs Invasion
Bear Flag Revolt
Blair House Attack
Conquest of the Americas
Farah Strike
Grape Strikes and Boycotts
Grito, El
Mariel Boatlift
Mexican-American War
National Chicano Moratorium
Southwest Voter Registration Education Project
Spanish-American War
Taos Rebellion
Vietnam War
Zoot Suit Riots

Immigrant Groups, Nationalities, and Cultural Identities
Afro-Latinos
Afro-Mexicans
Argentines
Balseros
Bolivians
Boricua
Brazilians
Chicano/a
Chileans
Cholos
Colombians
Costa Ricans
Coyotes
Cubans
Dominicans
Ecuadorians
Gangs
Gringo
Guatemalans
Hondurans
Identity and Labels
Latino/a
Lowriders
Marielitos
Mestizo/a
Mexicans
Migrant Workers
Military, Latinos in the
Mulataje
Mulatto/a
Nicaraguans
Nuyorican
Pachuco
Panamanians
Paraguayans
Peruvians

Prison Gangs
Puerto Ricans
Race
Salvadorans
Spanglish
Spanish Language
Tejanos
Tex-Mex
Uruguayans
Venezuelans
Women
Young Lords
Zapatistas

Laws, Legislative Initiatives, and Court Rulings

Cuban Adjustment Acts (1966, 1996)
Del Rio Independent School District v. Salvatierra (1930)
Foraker Act (1900)
Foreign Miners' Tax (1850)
"Greaser Act" (1855)
Immigration Act of 1924
Immigration Act of 1990
Immigration and Nationality Act of 1965
Immigration Reform and Control Act of 1986
Jones Act (1917)
Lemon Grove Incident
McCarran-Walter Act (1952)
Medrano v. Allee (1972)
Mendez v. Westminster School District (1946)
North American Free Trade Agreement
Platt Amendment (1901)
Proposition 187 (1994)
Proposition 209 (1996)
Proposition 227 (1998)
Sleepy Lagoon Case
Sotomayor, Sonia
Treaty of Guadalupe Hidalgo (1848)

Literature and Literary Figures

Acosta, Oscar
Algarín, Miguel
Alvarez, Julia
Anaya, Rudolfo Alfonso
Anzaldúa, Gloria
Arenas, Reinaldo
Castellanos, Rosario
Castillo, Ana
Cisneros, Sandra
Cofer, Judith Ortiz
Flores Magón, Ricardo
Galarza, Ernesto
Garcia, Cristina
Gonzales, Rodolfo "Corky"
Guagua Aérea
Hijuelos, Oscar
Levins Morales, Aurora
Moraga, Cherríe
Muñoz Marín, Luis
Muñoz Rivera, Luis
Nuyorican Poets Café
Pérez, Emma
Puerto Rican Literature
Rodríguez, Luis J.
Rodriguez, Richard
Rodríguez de Tío, Lola
Ruiz de Burton, María Amparo
Santiago, Esmeralda
Thomás, Piri
Yo Soy Joaquín

Media: Film, Newspapers, Radio, and Television

Ferrer, José
Film
Guagua Aérea
Lopez, Jennifer
Morales, Iris
Moreno, Rita
Norte, El (1983)
Opinión, La
Popular Culture
Prinze, Freddie
Salazar, Rubén
Telemundo
Television
Univision
Valdez, Luis
West Side Story
Yo Soy Joaquín

Music and Musicians

Corridos
Cruz, Celia
Estefan, Gloria

Organizations and Institutions

Political Movements, Groups, and Personalities

Social Movements, Activists, Activist Groups, and Protests

General Editors

David J. Leonard
Washington State University

Carmen R. Lugo-Lugo
Washington State University

Contributors

Erika Gisela Abad
Washington State University

Aidé Acosta
University of Illinois, Urbana-Champaign

Jaime R. Aguila
Arizona State University, Polytechnic

Bernardo Aguilar-González
Prescott College

José M. Alamillo
California State University, Channel Islands

Bretton T. Alvaré
Temple University

José Anazagasty-Rodríguez
University of Puerto Rico, Mayaguez

David Arbesú
Amherst College

Jillian M. Báez
University of Illinois, Urbana-Champaign

Brian D. Behnken
University of California, Davis

Ellen Bigler
Rhode Island College

Mary K. Bloodsworth-Lugo
Washington State University

Annalisa V. Burke
University of Chicago

Erika Busse
University of Minnesota

Ted Butryn
San Jose State University

David M. Carletta
Michigan State University

Catherine Carrison
Evergreen School District

Diana Castilleja
Facultés universitaires Saint-Louis, Brussels, Belgium

Jason Oliver Chang
University of California, Berkeley

James Ciment
Independent Scholar

Cary Cordova
University of Illinois, Urbana-Champaign

Vibrina Coronado
Independent Scholar

Heather E. Craigie
BorderLinks

Cheris Brewer Current
Walla Walla University

Agnes B. Curry
Saint Joseph College, Connecticut

Anita Damjanovic
University of Chicago

Michael Alvar de Baca
Harvard University

Juan Declet
Arizona State University

Frank DeLaO
University of Texas, El Paso

Joann E. Donatiello
Princeton University

Jessie L. Embry
Brigham Young University

Gisela Ernst-Slavit
Washington State University

Jesse J. Esparza
University of Houston

Ruben Espejel
Columbia University

Aurelio Espinosa
Arizona State University

Michael Faubion
University of Texas–Pan American

Aurora Fiengo-Varn
Mississippi Valley State University

Glenda M. Flores
University of Southern California

Irma Flores-Manges
Austin Public Library

Justin D. García
Temple University

Timothy P. Gaster
University of Chicago

Billie Gastic
University of Massachusetts, Boston

Paola Gemme
Arkansas Tech University

Ellen M. Gil-Gómez
California State University, San Bernardino

Nelly S. González
University of Illinois, Urbana-Champaign

Susan Marie Green
California State University, Chico

Lisa Guerrero
Washington State University

Nova Gutierrez
Village Community School

Daniel Guzmán
University of Texas, El Paso

Tom Head
Edith Cowan University

Linda Heidenreich
Washington State University

Sarah Hentges
Washington State University

Marisa Hernández
University of California, San Diego

Rita D. Hernandez
Museum of Mexican Culture and History, Chicago

Alberto Hernández-Lemus
Colorado College

Juan Carlos Hernández-Lemus
Independent Scholar

Servando Z. Hinojosa
University of Texas–Pan American

Jeremy Hockett
Central Michigan University

Jessica Hulst
Independent Scholar

Matthew Jennings
University of Illinois

Vickey Kalambakal
Independent Scholar

Anil Kalhan
Drexel University Earle Mack School of Law

Douglas R. Keberlein Gutiérrez
Dominican University

Patricia Kim-Rajal
Sonoma State University

C. Richard King
Washington State University

Robert O. Kirkland
Claremont McKenna College

Dan LaBotz
Independent Scholar

Robert F. Lewis, II
University of New Mexico

Diana L. Linden
Independent Scholar

Lenny Lopez
Harvard Medical School

Madeleine E. López
Hamilton College

María Pabón López
Indiana University School of Law, Indianapolis

Paul López
California State University, Chico

Robert O. Marlin, IV
University of Houston, Clear Lake

Vanessa Esther Martinez-Renuncio
University of Massachusetts, Amherst, and Holyoke Community College

Nicole Martone
Naugatuck Valley Community College

Jennifer R. Mata
University of Texas–Pan American

Lena McQuade
Sonoma State University

Molly Metherd
Saint Mary's College of California

Gregory M. Miller
University of Toledo

Gina Misiroglu
Independent Scholar

Brian Montes
University of Illinois, Urbana-Champaign

Kristal T. Moore
University of North Carolina, Chapel Hill

E. Mark Moreno
Washington State University

Tischa A. Muñoz-Erickson
Arizona State University

C. Alison Newby
New Mexico State University

Caryn E. Neumann
Miami University of Ohio

Dinorah Caridad Nieves
Fordham University

Mariana Ortega
John Carroll University

Roberto Carlos Ortiz
Independent Scholar

Judith A. Pérez
Fordham University

Lorna Perez
Buffalo State College

Sara Z. Poggio
University of Maryland Baltimore County

Amy Meschke Porter
Georgia Southwestern State University

Lisa Y. Ramos
Texas A&M University

Susana Rinderle
University of New Mexico

Frank A. Salamone
Iona College

Jorge Abril Sánchez
University of Chicago

Rachel Sandoval
University of California, Irvine

Dorsía Smith Silva
University of Puerto Rico, Río Piedras

Grant Joseph Silva
University of Oregon

David Slavit
Washington State University

Rosa E. Soto
William Paterson University

Sarah Stohlman
University of Southern California

Heather Marie Stur
University of Southern Mississippi

Katherine Sugg
Central Connecticut State University

Stefanie Tacata
California State University, Fresno

RuthAnne Tarletz de Molina
Mountain of the Lord Fellowship, U.S. Center for World Mission, Pasadena, California

Rebecca Tolley-Stokes
East Tennessee State University

Madeline Troche-Rodríguez
Harry S. Truman College

Karina R. Vega-Villa
Washington State University

Victor Villanueva
Washington State University

E. Sue Wamsley
Kent State University, Salem

John Weber
Southern Methodist University

Howell Williams
Indiana University Southeast

Melissa-Ann Yeager
University of California, Riverside

Stephen Zafirau
Tulane University

Manuel X. Zamarripa
Texas A&M University

Acknowledgments

Putting together an encyclopedia is a laborious task. In our case, the difficulty has been lessened by the wonderful contributions of our writers and amazing support we received from a spectrum of people.

First and foremost, we would like to thank everyone at M.E. Sharpe, especially Jeff Hacker, Cathleen Prisco, Stacey Victor, Laura Brengelman, and Jeanne Marie Healy for not only their hard work and assistance with the encyclopedia, but for their consistent support and encouragement over the years. We also would like to thank Jim Ciment, who brought us all together, and whose wisdom and experience proved invaluable during each step in the process. Gina Misiroglu, Jessica Hulst, and Heidi Harting-Rex deserve many thanks, as each contributed greatly to the publication through their editing work.

Of course, the work before you is the result of the commitment, scholarly insights, and passions of our writers. We thank them for their dedication to the project and their willingness to join us on this important journey. We also would like to thank our colleagues at Washington State University for their continued support and, of course, our families for their patience, love, and guidance.

Lastly, we would like to acknowledge and dedicate this work to that diverse group known as Latinos/as, whose contributions to this country should always be acknowledged and whose strength in the face of adversity has been an inspiration to us both.

Preface

In creating this encyclopedia, we have sought to provide a reference resource that is, at once, suited to middle school and high school students conducting library research; appropriate to more specialized audiences—college students, graduate students, academics, and librarians—interested in the history and culture of Latinos/as in the United States; and engaging for general interest readers and public library users. The need for a comprehensive new work on the role of Latinos/as in U.S. history and culture was made clear both by the continuing increases in the population and the influence of the Latino community and by the ever more apparent fact that these two aspects of society are inextricably linked and profoundly influential in the evolution of the nation's ideologies, belief systems, values, and treatment of its people.

As editors, we bring to bear very different backgrounds and experiences that, in a strange way, complement and inform each other. David is a child of Los Angeles, California, politically progressive schools and parents, and innovative curricula. Despite his progressive upbringing, he, like so many of our students, had little exposure to the histories, cultures, and voices that have defined the Latino experience in the United States. Despite growing up in Los Angeles, an immensely diverse metropolis with long-standing and dynamic Mexican American and Latino communities, his privileges and social location served to insulate, isolate, and distance him from these groups and their cultures. Much like the many students who express dismay at never learning about the Brown Berets or the Spanish-American War, at never reading Piri Thomás's autobiographical *Down These Mean Streets* or Rodolfo Gonzales's epic poem *Yo Soy Joaquín* (I Am Joaquín), and at never being exposed to the many multiracial and multicultural histories that define a broader U.S. history, David's pedagogical engagement with Latinos/as was limited to the "4fs": "food, fun, festivals, and fashion."

Carmen, by contrast, is a product of Puerto Rico's educational system and a curriculum dictated by and derivative of mainstream U.S. standards. Thus, despite being separated by 4,000 miles and a vast cultural divide, she was taught much the same American history as David was. The result was a set of common understandings and perspectives, the most branding of which was a lack of appreciation for—or even recognition of—the role of Latinos/as and other minority groups in the shaping of U.S. history, society, and culture.

For all intents and purposes, the textbooks to which we were both exposed characterized the history of the United States and its culture as the direct and exclusive result of the ingenuity, initiative, and hard work of Anglo-Saxon settlers and their descendants. Almost unfailingly, when people of color were discussed at all in these books—which David read in English and Carmen read in Spanish translation—they were portrayed as obstacles or threats that intrepid Anglos were forced to overcome. Such were the portrayals of Native Americans, African Americans, Latinos/as, and mixed-race peoples alike.

Beyond that, people of color were largely invisible from the pages of U.S. history textbooks. Absent only until recently were the slaves of "founding father" Thomas Jefferson, for example—the ones who did the hard labor that allowed him the time and space to reflect on the Enlightenment values, democratic principles, and governing institutions of the fledgling American republic. Likewise absent from those pages were the myriad Native Americans slain under the policies of President Andrew Jackson, called the "great father," and the number of Indian scalps he sent to his son as gifts. Completion of the transcontinental railroad connecting the East Coast and the Far West was hailed as a triumph of American industry and an expression of America's Manifest Destiny to control the entire continent, largely ignoring the fact that it was constructed by the hard labor of Chinese and Mexican immigrants.

David's curriculum taught him more about *taquitos* and sombreros on Cinco de Mayo than about Latino artists, political figures, and social activists. He learned more about holidays, foods, and music than he did about the histories, social contributions, and cultural legacies of the diverse Latino communities burgeoning in Southern California. Carmen's curriculum taught her none of this at all, as the U.S. Department of Education mandated strict adherence to standard textbooks in Puerto Rican schools. Not even taquitos, sombreros, nor Latino holidays (the latter were not officially sanctioned by the U.S. government) were mentioned in these texts.

The fact that we received similar historical narratives and cultural portrayals in such far-flung and different locations underscores the pervasiveness of American ideology. It also tells us of the need to disrupt that ideology, recast the historical narrative, and broaden the perspective. To whatever extent people of color have been included in more recent classroom histories of the United States—the slaves of Jefferson, the slain or displaced Native Americans, the Chinese and Mexican laborers on the transcontinental railroad—the unique perspectives and contributions of many groups still are given a less than full accounting. Those roles and reciprocal influences, moreover, continue to expand and evolve with the continuing influx of Spanish-speaking immigrants, the emergence of each new generation of resident Latinos/as, and new inroads in politics and government, business, the media, science, education, the arts, and popular culture.

This publication thus represents our effort to provide a more inclusive and contemporary history: one that paints a more accurate picture of the notable events, people, groups and movements, ideas, issues, and cultural expressions of Latinos/as in America, giving voice to their histories and experiences.

We hope that the three introductory essays and nearly 300 A-Z entries in this encyclopedia, along with the supplementary research materials and recommended further readings, challenge readers to explore the full diversity of America's Latino community in terms of national and racial identity, cultural experience, historical influence, class dynamics, and gender relations. Building on our individual backgrounds, our shared experiences, our collaboration as scholars, and everything we have learned from our students, we seek to introduce readers everywhere to the erased histories and silenced voices of a past that finds pervasive expression in the United States today. This undertaking certainly has deepened our own understandings and appreciation.

Some may argue that an encyclopedia focused exclusively on Latinos/as and Latino culture hardly represents a balanced, inclusive picture. Indeed, it may not. Rather than offer this work as a comprehensive study of U.S. history and culture, we hope that—along with other information resources and academic undertakings aimed at breaking down restrictive views and ideological perspectives—this text highlights and enhances a fuller historical narrative by shining a light on an original, defining, yet long ignored element of the American canvas.

With that in mind, *Latino History and Culture: An Encyclopedia* offers a detailed retrospective, social and cultural portrait, and conceptual examination of Latino life in the United States, from Columbian contact to the present day. The sheer volume of information made possible by this format allows us to explore the complexity of the Latino experience in America in hundreds of concise, information-intensive, accessibly written articles on historical events and periods, national and ethnic communities, notable figures, social issues, cultural practices, organizations and institutions, artistic and pop culture expressions, and areas of demographic importance. Entries are written and signed by scholars from a broad range of disciplines, including history, sociology, cultural/ethnic studies, English, and anthropology.

The reader can find at least five kinds of articles in this work: (1) introductory overview essays covering three broad historical eras—1492 to 1900, 1900 to 1965, and 1965 to the present day; (2) alphabetical entries on influential Latinos/as in all walks of life, in all periods of history; (3) entries on specific national and ethnic communities in the United States (Cubans, Puerto Ricans, Venezuelans, and so on), covering their histories, demographics, and special characters; (4) entries on institutions, organizations, groups, and movements in the Latino community and mainstream American society; (5) and a wide range of entries on social issues, concepts and theories, forms of expression, and other aspects of Latino identity.

A selection of more than 100 photographs and captions helps bring the subject matter to life. A detailed timeline of events puts this rich history in chronological perspective. "Further Reading" lists at the end of every article and an extensive master bibliography direct the interested student to authoritative publications in his or her area of interest. The table of contents, topic finder, "see also" lists with every article, and index help users explore and connect the various elements of this encyclopedia and its essential themes: community, cultural identity, socioeconomic opportunity, political influence, immigration, assimilation, globalization, sexism, racism, and class.

As you may have observed from the title, we favor the term "Latino" over "Hispanic." We do this for admittedly political reasons, as the latter designation was coined by the U.S. government and imposed on a group of people who did not all identify with the cultural connection to Spain. We think of "Latino" as a more populist term, referring directly to peoples and cultures with roots in Latin America; we regard it, therefore, as less politically loaded and polemical, as well as more widely used today.

As we openly address the ways in which Anglo-European racism, xenophobia, and nativism have helped shape the Latino experience in the United States, our preference of "Latino" over "Hispanic" also reflects a particular historical perspective and academic orientation. While meeting the standards of objectivity and accuracy essential to a reference work of this kind, we have attempted to produce an encyclopedia that recounts history in unflinching terms and that gives voice to the everyday experiences and sensitivities of real people, past and present.

We hope above all that you find this encyclopedia to be a resource that both engages your interest and supports your current classroom studies, while inspiring further research in a field that is admittedly too vast to be covered adequately in any single work. Beyond that, we harbor a wish that the research, insights, and analysis of the many authors included here help promote a transformation in educational curricula from Los Angeles and Pullman, Washington, to New York City and Puerto Rico, whereby students everywhere will gain broader exposure to the rich history and culture of Latinos/as in the United States of America.

David J. Leonard and Carmen R. Lugo-Lugo

ESSAYS

History: 1492–1900

Latinos and Latinas in the United States have two sets of "founding fathers": the North American revolutionaries of the eighteenth century and the earlier monarchs and conquistadors of the Spanish Empire. While the Anglo "fathers" founded a nation, the Spanish established the foundations of Latina and Latino identity. The Catholic faith, Spanish language, and Spanish legal and cultural traditions that they brought to the New World continue to have a lasting presence, sustaining a powerful collective memory.

The origins of this collective memory began with the Spanish explorations in the New World and the implementation of Spanish political and social policies in the late fifteenth century. King Ferdinand II of Aragon (r. 1479–1516), Queen Isabella I of Castile (r. 1474–1504), and Charles V (Holy Roman emperor, r. 1519–1556; king of Spain, r. 1517–1556) established the mechanisms of colonization in the New World. Their platform of multiculturalism in the Americas—formed by the policy of *mestizaje* (racial mixing)—was the genesis of Latina and Latino identity. The crown encouraged the development of Spanish colonial institutions, and the establishment of those institutions in the Americas facilitated the integration of diverse religious and cultural groups.

Unlike other settlers in the New World, Spanish immigrants were not escaping religious or political persecution; they came to the New World to found communities. In their efforts to create new cities, the Spanish forged enduring bonds with indigenous groups. The Spanish believed that American Indians were but one of many peoples who belonged to a single world community, and that the Indians, while in the process of being Christianized, were nonetheless sovereign. The Spanish crown sought to enlarge the royal domain by advancing the founding of Indian municipalities, and native peoples were declared free subjects by Queen Isabella in 1495.

Beginning in the late fifteenth century, then, the Indians were Spanish subjects. Being a subject of the Spanish crown entailed privileges of political liberty and the freedom to form municipalities. Later Spanish theorists described the royal policy of political freedom for the American Indians. In his *Política Indiana* (1680), for instance, envoy Juan de Pereira emphasized the royal proclamation that the natives of the Indies were free vassals. He described the Crown's tradition of providing the privilege of self-rule to the American Indians, who elected their own law officers, judges, and governing councilmen.

Charles V did not change the precedent Isabella had established regarding Indian policy, which consisted of Indian liberty. Charles wrote to magistrates that the Indians had to rule themselves by means of municipalities in the same manner that the Spanish governed themselves. Indians and Spaniards had to elect municipal officers every year. Indians were considered royal subjects and, as such, were not to be stripped of their rights or removed from their established towns. "They are free," Charles added, "and not to be subjected nor divided up, but rather they must live freely in the same way that all our subjects live in the kingdoms of Spain." Also, in *Las Leyes Nuevas para la governación de las Indias* (1542–1543), Charles issued laws stipulating that uncultivated land, pastures, and water within all municipal boundaries had to be shared as commons, for the free use of the citizens who inhabit them.

The Anglo System of Settlement

The Anglo-Protestants who settled North America beginning in the seventeenth century operated under very different religious and economic systems from those of the Spanish monarchy. Many of the English men and women who first settled in North America were Protestants evading persecution for their religious and political beliefs. Another major difference between the Latino and Anglo traditions was a stark economic fact: whereas Spanish immigrants, living before the industrial revolution, were entrepreneurial adventurers, English-speaking immigrants of the eighteenth century were victims of a growing industrialization, seeking economic relief because they were exploited by the elites who controlled capital in Europe. The North American settlement was the recreation of an Albion (early British) system for Anglo-Protestants, meaning that the Anglo conquerors did not believe in the accommodation of indigenous populations. There was no program for religious and cultural multiculturalism.

Not only was there an immense time gap between the Spanish and Anglo founding fathers, but entirely new political structures had appeared during the Enlightenment that were not part of the Renaissance world of the Spanish monarchs. By the late eighteenth century, medieval kingdoms had evolved into modern nation-states with standing armies and complex bureaucracies. Industrialization had begun to revolutionize society, transforming agrarian, self-reliant communities into national economic systems with mechanisms of economic growth based on slavery and sophisticated labor exploitation systems.

All of the European monarchies engaged in the slave trade, because slavery was deemed acceptable. It was generally held that slavery was allowed by God: The institution was mentioned in the Hebrew Bible, tolerated by the first Christians, and justified by Christian theologians. Although Christians could not enslave fellow Christians, they could and did enslave infidels captured in a "just" war. All Christian societies bought slaves from merchants who acquired them from the sub-Sahara, the eastern Mediterranean, and the Black Sea region. The major difference between Renaissance and eighteenth-century Europe in this regard was that the Renaissance (and medieval) economic system did not produce wealth on the backs of slaves, whereas in the late eighteenth and early nineteenth centuries all of the imperial states developed major programs in agriculture, manufacturing, and industry that were connected to slavery. The profits of colonization and slavery fertilized every branch of national production and the overall capitalist system of England and the North American colonies.

Industrialization and capitalism were crucial elements in the formation of the North American empire, whereas the economic forces of black slavery and Indian exploitation were small-scale operations during the Spanish colonial era. By the nineteenth century, the Anglo system had the appropriate framework of institutions and production capable of converting wealth into capital, and such a framework required a steady supply of labor. American economic expansion entailed vast expenditures on infrastructure and large-scale investments in canals, roads, harbors, docks, shipping, mines, agricultural drainage, and heavy industry. In North America, the overall slave population of African origin or descent grew geometrically, from about 330,000 in 1700 to more than 3 million in 1800.

Spanish Conquest

In contrast to the English conquest of North America, the earlier Spanish conquest of Central and South America was different in several key respects. Industrialization was not a contingent factor facilitating colonialism, and slavery was not yet large-scale enough to generate major advances in national production. The exploitation of natural resources was marginal in the sixteenth and seventeenth centuries, as the combustion engines, factories, transcontinental railroads, and other forms of industrial capitalism did not yet exist.

While the Spanish mestizaje policy called for the political and religious integration of diverse groups, the Spanish did establish mechanisms of control and exploitation, implementing desegregation policies, instituting local liberties for all communities, both Spanish and American Indian, and undertaking the spiritual conversion of indigenous groups—especially the Aztecs, who were actively engaged in cannibalism and human sacrifice.

Enduring traditions from the period include a flexible and syncretic Catholicism based on local cults and devotions, Visigoth names such as Roberto and Ricardo, and local grassroots organizations. Perhaps the most important tradition imported by the Spanish was a unique form of municipal life. The central feature of the Spanish community since the Roman period was the plaza, with its market, town houses, and surrounding wall. The same features can be seen today in Latin American colonial cities, as well as in the architectural features of haciendas (typified by geometric designs, arches, and tile work). The Romans had also been responsible for the advance of organized Christianity, the Latin language, and government based on a mixed constitution. The Hispanic principle of mixed constitutional government continued from the same tradition, based on the simultaneous and coordinated functions of three jurisdictional mechanisms: an executive and two representative institutions, a senate of aristocrats and a locally elected body.

Just as the Romans implanted their civic traditions and religion in Spain, so the Spanish introduced to the New World elements of their civilization that transformed both Spaniards and American natives. The Spaniards revolutionized the medieval system of doing business. Prior to the discovery of the Americas, Europeans had relied on two models of commercial expansion: Italian-style business consortia and Portuguese maritime monopolies. When Columbus returned to Spain in 1497, having failed to obtain a secure passage to and from China and India, Queen Isabella told him that he was no longer in charge of the transatlantic project to establish a trade monopoly with the great empires and cities of the Far East. Instead, the Castilians would continue living the way they had for centuries, with free towns, privately owned farmland, commons, and a free marketplace. Nevertheless, exploration continued. By 1503, eleven voyages led by Spanish commanders had mapped the coast of South and Central America. In that same year, Isabella made free trade the policy for all Spaniards, and in 1505 Ferdinand opened the Americas to free trade as well.

The resulting Columbian Exchange—cross communication between the Old World and the New—was at once environmental, cultural, and economic. New staples were established, as tomatoes, potatoes, chocolate, tobacco, and chili became part of the daily diet of peoples all over the world. In return, Native Americans may have appreciated the benefits of domesticated livestock and cereals, musical instruments, and architecture, but they surely suffered tremendously from the innovations of metallurgy and the exposure to a range of diseases.

Religion and the Conquest

One of the most enduring legacies of the Spanish conquest of America was the transformation of medieval Christian devotions and Native American religious practices. A number of beliefs and rituals are held dear among Latinos/as, such as the devotion to the Virgin Mary, the cult of the saints, home altars, the sacraments, and their associated festivals and celebrations. These devotions have a long history, but this is not to say that they do not change and acquire new aspects. The richness of Latino spirituality lies in the incorporation of individuality and local elements, the artistic use of colors and materials, and the enjoyment and appreciation of the senses. Native American traditions continue to be an intrinsic quality in material religious culture in many Latin American and U.S. Latino communities. As important as indigenous elements are in the production of culture and the expression of religion, the transformation of the Americas led to the establishment of a unique form of Christianity.

After the conquest of Mexico by Cortés, religious compatibility with Christianity (especially Catholicism) and political adaptation (to Spanish laws and regulations) were critical concepts in the colonial project. Spanish missionaries sought to bring the gospel of Christ to American Indian subjects, while Spanish political authorities shared the religious responsibility to convert Indians to Spanish Catholicism.

Spanish bureaucrats and missionaries acquainted themselves with the diverse types of religious and linguistic groups in Mexico, their mythologies, oral traditions, and practices. In their effort to eradicate Aztec cosmogony, especially idols from the Nahua (a native people of Mexico) and rituals of human sacrifice and cannibalism, Spanish authorities used a plethora of strategies to achieve multicultural integration. Spanish political and religious authorities exerted a continuous and comprehensive influence over Mesoamerican cultures, seeking to change the landscape of mystical forces by introducing such concepts as monotheism, the Trinity, sin, and guilt.

The spiritual conquest of the Indian empires had historical antecedents in the Christian empires forged by Constantine, Theodosius, Justinian, and Charlemagne. In the words of the sixteenth-century Spanish chronicler Gerónimo de Mendieta, these were "very religious emperors whose empires prospered" and whom the Spanish monarchs were to emulate, gaining favor with God when they sought the conversion of all peoples of the world. Mendieta further stressed the point that God had had enough of the suffering of the Native Americans under the Aztecs and sent Cortés "like another Moses in Egypt" to save God's people. The "peregrination of the church," according to the Franciscan missionary in Mexico, Bernardino de Sahagún, was a historical process that began in Palestine with the birth of Christ and followed a westward path to Europe, New Spain, and Asia, in particular the Philippines, and then on to China and Japan.

Latino Political Development

The Spanish monarchy controlled the entire bureaucracy and all clerical institutions. It delegated religious authority to the bishops and the mendicant orders, establishing jurisdictional boundaries and educational programs. The Spanish Crown established schools for illegitimate orphaned mestizos, legitimate mestizo children, and Indians; Christian doctrine was fundamental to their education. The Crown also subsidized the foundation of schools for illegitimate and orphan girls to be educated and prepared for marriage. Young girls who were abandoned were likewise placed in institutions where they were groomed for marriage. King Charles issued a royal decree in 1535 allowing the children of Indian lords to learn about the faith, Castilian civic traditions, and the Spanish language. Charles followed up his decree with funds to establish a royal school where poor Spaniards, mestizos, and Indians were to study Latin. He further mandated that all royal towns had to establish hospitals for the indigent and the sick.

Part of the process of colonization was the introduction of democratic principles, in particular the practice of popular vote, local elections, and citizen rights. Indians designated their own executive officials, based on five methods of selection. One was by popular vote. Second was designation by tradition—that is, by powerful families and clans that exerted control by nepotism. The third process was that of patronage, or nomination by the emperor Moctezuma, which persisted as the cacique system of indigenous patronage. Similar to this was appointment or patronage on the part of the *encomendero* (Spanish lord). And the last method of executive selection was designation by an ecclesiastical official.

Latinos Move Northward

The conquest of Mexico was the beginning of a long process of Latino immigration into North America. The Latina and Latino collective memory in the United States began with the early sixteenth-century Spanish explorations. Fray Marcos de Niza journeyed to what is the modern Mexican state of Sonora and the U.S. state of Arizona. Juan Ponce de León brought Spaniards with him to colonize Florida, and Hernando de Soto explored the Mississippi River. Francisco Vásquez de Coronado found his way to the head of the Rio Grande, and Juan Rodriguez Cabrillo crossed the desert and arrived in California. Although none of these expeditions resulted in permanent settlements, the North American landscape took on an enduring association with the Spanish. Mountain ranges and rivers in the West and Southwest took Spanish names. Spaniards provided the language and scientific understanding of vegetation and wildlife.

The Spaniards hispanicized America, implementing systems of irrigation (*acequias*), water rights as communal property (not to be privatized), domesticated animals, and inheritance law. The last was especially important, ensuring that all legitimate children, male and female, were to obtain an equal portion of their parent's inheritance. Women had the additional benefit of receiving their share of the inheritance in the form of a dowry at the time of the marriage.

The Spanish also hispanicized parts of the western Pacific. In 1519, Ferdinand Magellan, a Portuguese working for the Spanish Crown, sought to connect Spain, the Americas, and the Far East. With this effort, the Spanish began a process that interconnected diverse and far-flung societies. With their occupation of the Philippines in 1564, the Spanish initiated global trade and mestizaje. Establishing the route from Acapulco to Manila, which took about three months to complete, Spain incorporated the

Philippines into the equation of Latina and Latino mestizaje. The other outpost that was slowly being developed was "las Floridas" (modern Florida) and the "Carolinas," especially through the efforts of Pedro Menéndez de Avilés in the 1560s.

The Spanish began to explore further, hoping to find commercial networks linked to the spice trade in the Far East. They began their trek north of Mexico City to the regions of Pusolana and Chichimeca. Francisco de Ibarra searched for indigenous cities in Durango, traveling as far north in 1580 as the region known today as the modern state of New Mexico. In 1595, the viceroy Luis de Velasco issued specific instructions to Juan de Oñate, the governor of New Mexico, to colonize the region. In 1630, in New Mexico, there were only about 250 Spaniards, 700 mestizos, and 50,000 Indians. By 1639, there were about fifty households in the royal town of Santa Fe. The Indians there were tax-exempt, whereas the Spaniards and mestizos paid tithes of wheat, maize, cattle, horses, mules, sheep, and goats. In 1812, the Latino population increased to 102 communities, with an additional twenty-six Indian pueblos served by Franciscan missions. The communities were self-subsistent, as they had no secure line of transportation or export commodity in great demand.

Another center of Spanish strategic position for trade and colonization was the California coast, first explored by Sebastián Vizcaíno. The first permanent settlement of Latinos in California was established in 1769 in San Diego under the leadership of Junípero Serra and Gaspar de Portolá. In 1784, the Franciscans began to establish a range of coastal missions, numbering about twenty-one by 1823, which began a process of religious and social integration. *Californios* established three autonomous town councils, in San José, Los Angeles, and Santa Cruz. The citizens of Los Angeles forged their town council in 1781, consisting of Spaniards, mestizos, *mulatas,* Indians, *coyotes, negros,* and *chinos.*

Texas also began to see the growth of Hispanic towns, populated by immigrants whose heritage goes back to the Iberian Peninsula, or Hispania. For example, immigrants from the Canary Islands had been arriving in Texas since 1731, and they formed a local council. By 1820 there were 2,500 Hispanics, most of them in San Antonio. In 1819, Spain and the United States negotiated a treaty that recognized Spain's jurisdiction of the Texan territory.

A statue of Franciscan friar Junípero Serra stands outside the San Fernando Mission in Southern California. The twenty-one missions he founded in Alta California were the first permanent Latino Hispanic settlements on the Pacific Coast. *(San Fernando Valley Collection. Urban Archives Center. Oviatt Library. California State University, Northridge)*

Spanish Mexicans were therefore the first Latinos in North America. When Mexico became independent from Spain in 1821, however, the doors were opened to foreigners—especially Anglo-Americans—for trade, bringing about another transformation, as Anglos and Latinos expanded interactions and forged new bonds. Anglo traders began to appear in major Hispanic centers, from Sante Fe to San Antonio, forming commercial partnerships. In California, ships from Boston and Britain began to arrive, and Californians could trade hides and tallow for manufactured goods.

In 1821, Moses Austin began the transformation of Texas as he brought with him 300 families from Louisiana. Within a generation or so, the Anglo-Americans began a propaganda campaign to justify their conquest. Senator John Randolph commented on the floor of the U.S. Senate that the Mexicans were inferior because they were a mixed breed with Negro blood. Journalists joined the campaign by writing disparagingly about the Mexicans, maintaining that the stain of Indian blood made them an inferior race. According to Texan historian Walter Prescott Webb, the "cruelty" of Mexicans "may be a heritage from the Spanish of the Inquisition; it may, and doubtless should, be attributed partly to the Indian blood."

In 1829, when Mexico's President Vicente Guerrero declared the emancipation of slaves, Anglo Texans took it as an affront and considered separating from Mexico. The Texas Revolution of 1836 began the process of the disenfranchisement of Latino communities. Seeking to acquire California, President James K. Polk declared that Mexico had invaded American soil, thus prompting the Mexican-American War of 1846, which resulted in the acquisition of Texas and New Mexico in addition to California. Invading Mexico City, Anglo soldiers forced the Mexican government to sign the Treaty of Guadalupe Hidalgo in 1848, which gave the United States the upper half of Mexico (the area encompassing all or parts of Arizona, California, Colorado, Nevada, New Mexico, Texas, Utah, and Wyoming).

Sam Houston was not alone in voicing the view that "Mexicans are no better than Indians, and I see no reason why we should not go on in the same course and take their land." Senator John C. Calhoun of South Carolina did not want the United States to take over all of Mexico because, as he declared on the Senate floor in 1848, "ours is the government of a white race," and "the greatest misfortunes of Spanish America are to be traced to the fatal error of placing these colored races on an equality with the white race." This statement reflected a deep fear of racial mixing and an unwillingness to incorporate brown Latinos/as and mestizas into the fold of U.S. laws and society.

Already meager in number, Latinos/as in the Spanish borderlands, such as California, constituted only about 15 percent after the Gold Rush of 1848. Thus, the Latino vote became inconsequential in elections in the new state of California. The California legislature passed laws prohibiting bullfights and other "Greaser" laws—including one that prohibited the translation of laws into Spanish, as required by the state constitution.

Besides racist justifications for the conquest of Mexican territories, leaders of the Anglo-American military empire claimed that Latino communities would be won over because they would be liberated from Mexican tyrants. The history of Anglo-American intolerance toward Mexicans and Latinos increased during the Texas Rebellion and the War of 1846–1848, and intensified when Anglo-Americans began to arrive in the hundreds to the newly conquered territories of California and Arizona, thereby "liberating" Latino communities.

Decline of Spain and the Spanish Identity

The disintegration of the Spanish imperial system began by the mid-eighteenth century. This decline facilitated the expansionist aims of the North American empire, as Spain and England continued a war of attrition that weakened both nations. The English easily defeated Spanish forces in the West Indies, leading England to fortify land bases in Lisbon and Havana. As England turned its attention to the War of American Independence, Spain temporarily expelled the British from the Gulf of Mexico and the shores of the Mississippi, but it was not able to sustain its military and naval apparatus.

In the meantime, the Spanish global system was no longer able to maintain its colonial empire. The bureaucracy had become more decentralized than ever, as local oligarchies undermined royal authority. While England emerged as a powerful imperial nation-state, the Spanish system could no longer afford the price of empire, nor were Spanish American subjects willing to foot the bills to sustain it. The Bour-

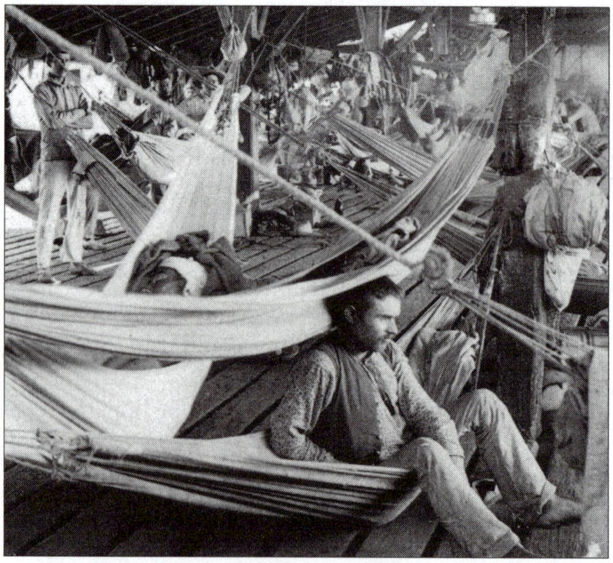

Spanish troops find respite at Cienfuegos, the nation's last camp in Cuba, during the Spanish-American War in 1898. Spain's humiliating defeat in that conflict cost the country its last overseas territories. *(Library of Congress)*

bon monarchy that governed the Spanish empire attempted to change the old system, imposing new mechanisms of centralization that antagonized the Spanish American locals. Revolts in Spanish America began to occur repeatedly by the 1760s, beginning in Guanajuato and Real del Monte in Mexico. The 1781 *comunero* revolt in Venezuela was one of many other Creole revolts that broke out in South America. These were followed by Indian rebellions that represented a widespread reaction to Bourbon reforms and innovations.

By the early nineteenth century, Spanish America was about to become Latin America, for Spain was losing its hold over the region's emerging nation-states. Local governments began to trade with North America and England, and with other Spanish-speaking jurisdictions. Free commerce and neutral shipping essentially muscled out Spain from its traditional monopolies.

A New, Latino Identity

The transformation of Spanish America to Latin America is critical to any discussion of U.S. Latino culture and history, as it accelerated the formation of a new identity, which in turn gave rise to modern Latino identity in the United States. From their status as Spanish citizens of autonomous municipalities, Latinos/as became subjects of coalescing nation-states, such as Mexico, Argentina, Venezuela, Colombia, and other republics. From 1793 to 1808, Spain and its colonial territories endured uninterrupted warfare, and these conflicts helped shape national identities. Beginning with the French Revolution in 1789 and followed by the Napoleonic orders for the military occupation of Spain in 1807, the transformation of Latin America was based on the imposition of French legal and political models, the Napoleonic Code, and the revolutionary *pronunciamientos,* or dictatorships. New regimes arose to fill the gap caused by the downfall of the Bourbon monarchy in Spain and the rise of revolutionary programs all over the Spanish-speaking world. The basic mechanism was the liberal revolutionary pronunciamiento, a "pronouncement," or intervention, by a military general who denounced parliamentary and constitutional institutions as decayed or corrupt.

The independent republics of Latin America were the result of different processes. Some of these constitutional dictatorships and juntas were the political forces that established national identities. Military leaders forged independent republics, liberating New Granada in 1819, Venezuela in 1821, and Ecuador in 1822. New Spain achieved its independence as Mexico in 1821, when Augustín de Iturbide was declared its emperor, much like Napoleon becoming emperor of the French republic. (Cuba and Puerto Rico would remain Spanish possessions until the U.S. invasion in 1898.) The general pattern of dictatorships was firmly established in the Americas: the formation of national identities based on the exercise of military power that configured new territorial boundaries.

Liberal revolutionaries forced upon their constituents a new way of understanding themselves, not as Latinos/as or Hispanics, but as Mexicans, Americans, Cubans, Colombians, and other nationalities. Ethnic rivalries could be subsumed into larger categories of nationhood and patriotic sentiment. Subsequent Spanish invasions in Latin America only antagonized the local populations.

While Spanish America was further fragmented by independence movements and pronunciamientos, an additional player affected Spanish-speaking communities in the Southwest and the West Indies: the United States. One of the most important traditions of the North American empire was expansionism, or the spirit of Manifest Destiny, in which the United States acquired territories claimed by other European states and newborn republics in Spanish America. The invasion of Mexico was imperialist (as its purpose was to acquire and control land and people) and based on a strategy of labor exploitation.

The United States had also achieved independence from England. President Thomas Jefferson had decided on a course of expansion and negotiated with Napoleon to enlarge U.S. territory through the Louisiana Purchase. In 1819, President James Monroe, who as minister to France had established strong ties with that nation, purchased Florida from Spain and strongly endorsed a protectionist foreign policy by which he warned European powers not to meddle in Latin America—a policy that came to be known as the Monroe Doctrine.

While Spain was seeking to hold on to its colonial territories in the Americas, King Ferdinand VII of Spain was ousted by a pronunciamiento. A year later, in 1820, Spain suffered a "constitutional" pronunciamiento, or military coup.

Regarding Latino identity, two historical factors played the essential formative roles: the decline of Spain and the rise of the North American empire. Spain had declined as a naval power, and its own colonial possessions had assumed full independence as separatist revolts sought support from Spain's enemies. The remnants of its colonial empire—Cuba, Puerto Rico, and the Philippines—were finally lost with the military victory of the United States over Spanish forces in 1898. Since the Cuban economy was based on the tobacco and sugar trade with the United States, Cubans wanted a partnership of free trade with their northern neighbors. In the spring of 1898, President William McKinley ordered his admirals to attack Spanish forces in the Philippines; by May 1, the Americans had destroyed the Spanish fleet in Manila, and by July the Americans had destroyed the Spanish squadron outside Santiago de Cuba. The fears of patriot José Martí, that Cuba would soon be subordinated to the United States, were about to be realized.

Regarding the Spanish-American War, Protestant and Anglo-American historians have justified the aggressiveness of the North Americans because they liberated people from Spanish rule, which in their perspective was despotic and corrupt. This ideology of liberation became a justification for incorporating Latino populations into the fold of U.S. society.

Aurelio Espinosa

Further Reading

Acuña, Rodolfo. *Occupied America: A History of Chicanos.* 6th ed. New York: Pearson Longman, 2007.

Brading, David A. *The First America: The Spanish Monarchy, Creole Patriots, and the Liberal State, 1492–1867.* New York: Cambridge University Press, 1991.

Burkhart, Louise M. *The Slippery Earth: Nahua-Christian Moral Dialogue in Sixteenth-Century Mexico.* Tucson: University of Arizona Press, 1989.

Burkholder, Mark A., and Lyman L. Johnson. *Colonial Latin America.* New York: Oxford University Press, 1998.

Elliott, John H. *Imperial Spain, 1469–1717.* New York: Penguin, 1963.

Gerhard, Peter H. *The North Frontier of New Spain.* Princeton, NJ: Princeton University Press, 1982.

Gibson, Charles. *The Aztecs Under Spanish Rule: A History of the Indians of the Valley of Mexico, 1519–1810.* Stanford, CA: Stanford University Press, 1964.

Jennings, Francis. *The Invasion of America: Indians, Colonialism, and the Cant of Conquest.* Chapel Hill: University of North Carolina Press, 1975.

Kamen, Henry. *Spain's Road to Empire: The Making of a World Power, 1492–1763.* New York: Allen Lane, 2002.

Lockhart, James, and Stuart B. Swartz. *Early Latin America: A History of Colonial Spanish America and Brazil.* New York: Cambridge University Press, 1983.

Pagden, Anthony. *Spanish Imperialism and the Political Imagination: Studies in European and Spanish-American Social and Political Theory, 1513–1830.* New Haven, CT: Yale University Press, 1990.

Weber, David J. *The Spanish Frontier in North America.* New Haven, CT: Yale University Press, 1992.

History: 1900–1965

Although Latinos/as entered the United States in the twentieth century under a variety of conditions from a number of home nations, they also shared many experiences and circumstances. Divided geographically by both their countries of origin and their places of residence in the United States, they shared a common language and many cultural elements.

Diverse Origins, Shared Experiences

Immigrants from Caribbean islands such as Cuba brought with them a variety of traditions and settled primarily on the East Coast, especially in Florida. Many came in search of economic advantage, while others fled the island for political reasons—both before the revolution of the 1890s and after the rise to power of Fidel Castro in 1959. Among Cubans more than other Latino groups, many immigrants were educated professionals and white-collar workers. Immigrants from Mexico and Central America settled heavily in the Southwest, taking jobs in agriculture, mining, and the railroads. These were typically unskilled and semiskilled laborers who, in their search for a supportive economic and cultural environment, moved into established communities where earlier immigrants from their native countries had settled. Living in such communities enabled them to speak their native language, Spanish, while adjusting to life and finding work in an alien land. Even among Latinos/as who were multigenerational U.S. citizens, such communities—which existed in many cities and towns—perpetuated customs like the celebration of *quinceañera* (the coming of age for girls at age fifteen), *Día de los Muertos* (Day of the Dead, November 1), and the making of traditional foods. To promote community life and protect individual members, they formed *mutualista*s, or mutual aid societies, that organized social events, engendered cultural identity, and battled for legal rights and civic entitlements as necessary. Meanwhile their traditions, customs, music, foods, and other cultural expressions gradually moved beyond local communities to influence American culture at large.

One common challenge faced by Latinos/as of diverse backgrounds was resistance and outright racism on the part of dominant Anglo society. Anglo stereotypes of Latinos/as as lazy, ignorant, and unclean became pervasive and were used as an excuse to deny them jobs, rights, and basic human respect. Throughout the Southwest, the property rights of Spanish-speaking peoples came under attack by newly arriving Anglos. In Northern California and Texas, where Latinos/as became a minority during the eighteenth century, Anglos ignored, altered, or passed laws to disenfranchise Spanish speakers and strip them of property. The institution of property taxes based on land area rather than on production discriminated against Latino ranchers. Existing laws requiring public documents to be published in both Spanish and English were revised so that only English was required.

Young Latinos/as, meanwhile, were either sent to poorly subsidized segregated schools or denied access to education entirely. In 1885, for example, a state law in California formally segregated Latinos/as in public schools. Thus, as Latinos/as lost land and political power, they also lost ground economically from generation to generation. Often the only employment opportunities for men were low-skill, low-wage jobs, while women were forced to take jobs outside the home as domestics or in light industry like canning. Puerto Ricans on the East Coast and Latinos/as in Texas (Tejanos) and California (*Californios*) were particularly hard hit because of the large Anglo majorities that challenged them for economic success, political power, and social mobility. Latinos/as in Arizona and New Mexico fared somewhat better because Anglos were not as numerous in these regions. In New Mexico, Latinos/as even gained a measure of political clout into the early twentieth century; Miguel Antonio Otero served as territorial governor of New Mexico from 1897 to 1906. Yet even in these regions, opposition on the part of Anglo settlers increasingly cost Latinos/as political and economic power. In general, Cuban Americans fared best among turn-of-the-century Latino immigrant groups because many arrived with cash, professional training, or marketable skills to establish independent practices or retail businesses. One prominent example was Vicente Martinez Ybor, a Spanish-born Cuban who fled to Florida and in 1885 launched the cigar-making industry in a company town that took his name, Ybor City. Ultimately, virtually all Latinos/as in the United States at the turn of the twentieth century faced some challenges to their basic rights, economic opportunities, and social standing.

A political cartoon from 1914 depicts U.S. President Woodrow Wilson carrying his "white man's burden" of Mexico. Events in that country and the anti-Mexican climate at home kept him from promoting Mexican self-determination and prompted armed intervention that April. *(Library of Congress)*

Immigration in the Early Twentieth Century

Latinos/as living in the United States at the start of the century were soon joined by new waves of immigrants from throughout Latin America. The expanding political, military, and economic influence of the United States combined with domestic turmoil in a number of Latin American nations all contributed to the heavy flow of immigrants from that region. Many sought temporary employment and intended to return home once their own circumstances or the situation in the homeland improved; others sought a permanent change in nationality. In either case, both newcomers and long-standing Latino residents faced the same kind of hostility, resistance, and oppression that had existed in previous decades. A literacy test enacted in 1917 and a strict numeric limit established in 1924 severely reduced the number of immigrants from Europe and other areas. Immigrants from Latin America, however, were exempt from the quota under Section 4c of the 1924 Immigration Act, thus ensuring landowners in the Southwest with a continued flow of cheap labor.

The Mexican Revolution of the 1910s, like the Cuban independence movement of the 1890s, was born in part out of the exile community in the United States. Francisco Madera, the leader of revolutionary forces against dictator Porfirio Díaz, lived in San Antonio, Texas, for a time and met with other revolutionaries there to organize their campaign to seize control of the Mexican government. It was in San Antonio that they wrote the historic Plan of San Luis Potosí, which demanded repeal of the fraudulent Mexican presidential election of 1910 and called on the Mexican citizenry to rise in armed rebellion. In the decade of turmoil that followed, an estimated 10 percent of the Mexican population fled north across the border. As against the 49,642 Mexicans who arrived in the United States from 1901 to 1910—a figure itself nearly twice the total of the previous seven decades combined—the figure skyrocketed to 219,004 for the period 1911–1920 and to 459,287 for the decade after that.

Many of the new arrivals settled in Texas and California to work in agriculture, although farm owners in the Midwest and Washington State also relied increasingly on Mexican migrant labor during planting and harvest times. By the 1920s, Mexican American laborers were also finding jobs in the steel and automobile industries of the Great Lakes region, establishing Latino communities in such cities as Chicago, Detroit, and Flint, Michigan. In an effort to protect the economic rights of Mexican nationals, President Venustiano Carranza in 1920 worked out a deal with the U.S. government whereby Mexican workers would receive a contract before traveling to jobs across the border.

Many of the new immigrants preferred to live in communities that allowed them to maintain their culture and language, establishing barrios—neighborhoods or districts in which Latino populations, businesses, and civic groups predominated—in cities across the United States. During this period, communities such as Boyle Heights (East Los Angeles) drew large numbers of Mexican immigrants, who mixed freely with established Latino families. Yet while a growing number of Mexican immigrants were settling in urban areas in search of better-paying industrial jobs, a majority continued to settle in smaller rural communities and work in menial agricultural jobs. Meanwhile, a small Latino middle class began to emerge in certain urban centers during the 1920s, gradually growing and spreading through the rest of the century.

Immigration from Central America also increased during the early decades of the twentieth century, jumping from 8,192 in the period 1901–1910 to 17,159 over the next ten years, before leveling off at 15,769 in 1921–1930. These émigrés often traveled north through Mexico and blended in with Mexican immigrants, finding jobs in many of the same fields as agricultural laborers.

Immigration from Caribbean states and islands likewise grew during this period. In the first decade of the twentieth century, 17,280 emigrated from the islands to the United States; approximately 40,000 more came in each of the next two decades. An estimated 100,000 Cubans arrived in the United States during the first few decades of the twentieth century, either seeking economic opportunity or fleeing political oppression. Puerto Ricans were not subject to U.S. immigration laws, as the island had become a territory of the United States after the Spanish-American War in 1898. Consequently, residents were allowed to move freely on the mainland as a result of the Jones-Shafroth Act—which granted them citizenship—in 1917. Many Puerto Ricans moved to East Coast cities during this time in search of employment in heavy industry and textiles while others found jobs as domestic laborers.

Contributions to American Culture and Society

In addition to their contributions to the economic development and cultural diversity of the United States, Latino/as continued making important inroads in politics and other fields. Ezequiel Cabeza De Baca was the first Latino governor of New Mexico, serving a few months in early 1917 before dying in office. Octaviano Ambrosio Larrazolo, the governor of New Mexico from 1919 to 1921, also became the first Latino U.S. senator in 1928 (succeeding Andrieus Jones, who died in office). Louisiana became the first state to send a Latino to the U.S. House of Representatives, electing Ladislas Lazaro in 1912. Lazaro was elected to a total of eight terms as a Democrat, serving from 1913 to his death in 1927.

Latinos/as contributed increasingly to the arts during this period as well, including the newly emerging field of cinema. Rita Hayworth (born Margarita Carmen Cansino) made numerous movies and was billed as the "Love Goddess" in the 1940s. Lupe Velez (born María Guadelupe Villalobos Vélez) achieved prominence as a comic foil in the 1930s. Anthony Quinn (born Antonio Rodolfo Oaxaca Quinn) established himself as a major character actor in the 1930s and 1940s, while Cesar Romero became renowned for his roles as the "Latin lover." Xavier Martínez was a prominent portrait and landscape artist in the early twentieth century, as well as a teacher at the California Academy of Arts and Crafts. Likewise, sculptor Enrique Alferez produced a number of works in the art deco style for the Works Progress Administration during the Great Depression.

Latinos served with distinction in the U.S. armed forces during both world wars. David Barkley earned a Medal of Honor—the nation's highest military distinction—for his actions in World War I; another thirteen Latinos received the award for gallantry in World War II. An estimated 250,000–500,000 Latinos served in the U.S. military during World War II. (The armed forces did not keep accurate records of Latinos at the time.) Soldiers of the largely Latino 200th and 515th antiaircraft artillery battalions served in the Philippines and were subjected to the infamous Bataan Death March there in 1942. Other units known to include large numbers of Latinos during World War II were the 141st Regiment of the 36th Infantry Division, the 65th Infantry Regiment, and the 158th Regimental Combat team.

Latino/as also contributed to the war effort through the Mexican Farm Labor Program, which was established in 1942 by an agreement between the U.S. and Mexican governments. Under the arrangement—commonly referred to as the Bracero Program—Mexico agreed to supply guest workers to help support U.S. agricultural production during the war. The program was expanded through another agreement to provide labor for American railroads. The program grew so rapidly that by 1945 Mexico was supplying approximately 125,000 guest laborers in the United States. The workers signed contracts before leaving Mexico and were paid for their labor, with a portion of the total withheld in a savings account and remunerated upon completion of the contract and return to Mexico. The flow of labor north across the border under the Bracero Program helped reinforce traditional customs among Latinos/as living in the United States already. Mexican labor for U.S. railroads was no longer needed after World War II, but the agricultural program continued until 1964.

Ongoing Oppression and Renewed Resistance

Despite their impressive accomplishments and increasing contributions to U.S. society at large, Latinos/as faced oppression throughout the nation. In many places they were effectively barred from serving on juries, voting, or holding office. Often they lived in substandard housing in segregated communities, attended segregated schools, and held menial jobs, all while being portrayed in the media as ignorant, lazy, or criminal. An unknown number were lynched or murdered by private citizens or even officials of state agencies such as the Texas Rangers. Lawyer, politician, and Mexican American advocate J.T. Canales challenged such actions in court during the 1910s and demanded investigations into Texas Ranger treatment of Latinos/as.

Some Latinos in Texas resorted to more violent means of action. Gregorio Cortez, a legendary figure among Tejanos, led law enforcement on a chase across South Texas in 1901 after killing three officers who tried to arrest him for a crime he claimed not to have committed. Cortez was eventually captured, jailed, and convicted in three different trials. A review of the evidence led to his pardon in 1913, after which he was hailed by Latinos/as in the region as a hero and defender of the rights of the oppressed. Still other Tejanos advocated breaking away from the United States to rejoin Mexico or form their own republic. During the Mexican Revolution, for example, radical Mexicans and Mexican Americans in South Texas signed a manifesto called the Plan of San Diego in 1915 that advocated an independent state consisting of what is now Texas, New Mexico, Arizona, Colorado, and California. Although no large-scale uprising materialized, numerous "bandit" raids in South Texas are attributed to Latinos motivated by the plan.

In California, school segregation was finally challenged during the 1931 Lemon Grove Incident. After the all-white local school board built a separate new school for Latinos/as, a number of students refused to attend. Their parents organized a boycott and sought legal aid in suing the school district. In what historians recognize as the first successful school desegregation case in America, the court ruled that Latinos/as were "white" and not subject to the same rules as segregated African Americans and Asians in the district.

Another organized reaction to the oppression suffered by Latinos/as was the creation of the League of United Latin American Citizens (LULAC) in 1929. LULAC was the outgrowth of a number of Latino self-help organizations, or mutualistas, across South Texas at the turn of the twentieth century. In 1927, members of three mutualistas—the San Antonio–based Knights of America, the Corpus Christi Council of the Order of the Sons of America, and the rapidly growing League of Latin American Citizens—met in Harlingen, Texas, to discuss a merger of their organizations to pursue economic, political, and legal rights for Latinos/as. By 1929, after months of debate over membership requirements and structure, LULAC was formed at a meeting in Corpus Christi.

Cofounded by J.T. Canales, and with Ben Garza, Jr., serving as the organization's first president, LULAC concentrated initially on eliminating discrimination in public facilities and institutions. In 1936, LULAC succeeded in convincing the U.S. Census Bureau to designate all Latinos/as of Mexican descent as "white" rather than "Mexican," which it regarded as demeaning. Nine years later, LULAC scored another major success in securing the desegregation of the Orange County School district in Southern California.

Despite such successes, the Great Depression brought new challenges to Latinos/as across the United States. As paid labor became scarce, Latinos/as, African Americans, and other minorities often lost jobs to whites willing to take work they had previously disdained. The U.S. government drastically curtailed immigration from Latin American states in an attempt to cut off the supply of cheap labor competing for jobs with Americans. From 1931 to 1940, only 22,319 immigrants came from Mexico, 5,861 from Central America, 7,803 from South America, and 15,502 from Caribbean islands. Earlier immigrants were rounded up and sent back to Mexico in a massive repatriation program from 1929 to 1937. During that period, some 500,000 Mexicans were sent south across the border, 60 percent of whom were natural-born or naturalized U.S. citizens.

World War II Era to 1950

The plight of the Latino community continued into World War II despite its many contributions to the war effort. The worst incidents occurred in Southern California, where Los Angeles police on August 2, 1942, found the body of José Díaz at the Sleepy Lagoon Reservoir. Díaz, who had been planning to join the military, had attended a party and became involved in a fight between rival Latino youth gangs. Local officials cast the incident as a riot on the part of Latino youth gangs, whose colorful clothing gave them the nickname "zoot suiters" or *pachucos.* Police arrested more than 600 Latino youths in the incident and eventually indicted twenty-two of them for murder. Some were beaten while in police custody, and the case was presented to the public in a way that made anyone wearing a zoot suit a target of vigilantes. Eighteen of the defendants were found guilty on charges of murder or assault, or both, but all convictions were reversed on appeal in 1944.

In the meantime, the hysteria over the incident helped set off the so-called Zoot Suit Riots of spring 1943. On May 31, a group of about fifty U.S. servicemen converged on East Los Angeles with the purpose of attacking young Latino men in response to the alleged stabbing of a sailor. Over the next several days, fights between pachucos and servicemen spread throughout the city. Local police generally turned a blind eye to the actions of the servicemen and arrested pachucos. The public at large, following newspaper coverage, sided with the servicemen, though minority groups in the city supported the pachucos. In the end, only nine servicemen were arrested as opposed to hundreds of pachucos. By June 9, 1943, the military was forced to intervene and stop the violence by ordering all troops to stay out of Los Angeles.

From 1941 to 1950, total U.S. immigration from Latin America increased across the board, rebounding from the low levels of the Depression as the

"Rosa the Riveter": Amid ongoing discrimination and sometimes violent social opposition during the World War II years, Latina workers—such as these Mexican American women at a California aircraft factory—contributed mightily to the war effort. *(Charles E. Steinheimer/Stringer/Time & Life Pictures/Getty Images)*

demand for workers grew again. Arrivals from Mexico leaped to 60,589 during the decade, not including guest workers in the Bracero Program. Immigration from Central America climbed to 21,665, with another 21,831 coming from South America and 43,275 coming from the Caribbean region.

Postwar Activism

The experience of World War II and growing anger at oppression led more Latinos/as to push for social change. In 1947, LULAC won the case of *Mendez v. Westminster School District* in federal appeals court, successfully challenging school segregation in California. In 1948, the organization had similar success in Texas with the case of *Delgado v. Bastrop ISD,* likewise in federal court. LULAC also worked with local communities on pilot training and job programs that were precursors of the federal Head Start and Job Corps programs. In 1947, the American GI Forum and its founder, Héctor P. García, intervened in the incident involving a decorated U.S. serviceman named Felix Z. Longoria, who was killed in action in the Pacific Theater but refused full burial services at his segregated hometown cemetery in Three Rivers, Texas, because he was Mexican American. The American GI Forum appealed the case to U.S. senator and future president Lyndon B. Johnson, who arranged to have Private Longoria buried at Arlington National Cemetery—the first Mexican American to be so honored.

In the wake of the Longoria incident, the American GI Forum went on to pursue broader rights and benefits for Latino veterans, including medical care at Veteran's Administration facilities. The organization expanded its interests even further in subsequent years, focusing on such issues as educational access and voting rights. In 1954, the American GI Forum and LULAC joined as defendants in the U.S. Supreme Court case of *Hernandez v. Texas.* Together they provided legal aid to the primary defendant, Pete Hernandez, a Mexican American farm laborer who had been convicted of murder by an all-white jury in Texas. The legal defense appealed the case on the grounds that barring minorities from juries—no Mexicans had served on a county jury in twenty-five years—violated the Fourteenth Amendment rights of minority defendants. The Supreme Court agreed with that argument.

While maintaining the guest worker program, the Eisenhower administration hoped to eliminate waves of immigrant laborers from Latin America who were arriving in the United States without proper documentation. By 1954, up to 1 million per year were entering the country. To round up and deport the masses of undocumented workers, the U.S. Immigration and Naturalization Service (INS) that year launched Operation Wetback. While the initial plan called for the deportation of up to 4 million illegal immigrants, the INS ultimately succeeding in removing only about 130,000. According to the government, another 1 million or so returned to Mexico by their own means.

Meanwhile, the Bracero guest worker program was revised and maintained through 1964. Laborers from poorer agricultural regions of Mexico signed contracts (written in English) with U.S. farmers and expected hefty increases in pay. Soon complaints were voiced about workers not receiving full remuneration even after their return to Mexico. There were also complaints about poor living conditions, harsh treatment by employers, and rampant discrimination by other Anglos. The reporting of such abuses, combined with mechanization of cotton and other agricultural production, led to the demise of the program in 1964.

In the following year, Congress passed the landmark Immigration and Nationality Act, marking the first substantial change in U.S. immigration laws since the 1920s. The legislation dramatically changed the face of the Latino community in the United States. Under the new law, non–Western Hemisphere nations were given a combined limit of 170,000 immigrants per year, with an annual maximum of 20,000 per nation. Nations of the Western Hemisphere were given an annual ceiling of 120,000, without national limitations. Immigrants from these nations would be received on a first-come, first-permitted-entry basis.

In the immediate post–World War II years, Latinos/as played an increasingly influential and prominent role in U.S. public life and culture. Individuals like Mexican American painter Manuel Gregorio Acosta and Mexican American photographer Edgar Domingo Evia y Joutard had a significant influence in the fine arts; Evia's work was at the heart of postwar popular culture, appearing in mass-circulation magazines and high-profile advertising campaigns for well-known consumer products. Desi Arnaz, a Cuban-born musician and nightclub owner, was a pioneer of the new medium of television as a star of the hit sitcom series *I Love Lucy* and established the Desilu entertainment production company with his wife, Lucille Ball. The Puerto Rican–born actress, singer, and dancer Rita Moreno starred in a number of prominent films and stage productions, most notably *West Side Story* (1961), for which she won an Academy Award for best supporting actress.

In the realm of national defense, Latinos served with distinction in the Korean War, with eight receiving Medals of Honor. In 1961, Democratic candidate Henry B. Gonzalez was elected to the U.S. Congress by the citizens of San Antonio, Texas, and surrounding communities and continued to serve until 1999. In 1965, Eligio "Kika" de la Garza, who represented South Texas until 1997, joined him on Capitol Hill. In the meantime, Latinos/as from virtually every nation of origin achieved increasing success and prominence in business, education, science, the media, and the arts.

Thus, by 1965, changes in immigration law, the end of the Bracero Program, growing interest in civil rights, and a population on the verge of explosion set the stage for major transformations in the Latino community during the final decades of the twentieth century.

Michael Faubion

Further Reading

Acuña, Rodolfo. *Occupied America: A History of Chicanos.* 6th ed. New York: Pearson Longman, 2007.

Allsup, Carl. *The American G.I. Forum: Origins and Evolution.* Austin, TX: University of Texas Center for Mexican American Studies, 1982.

Anton, Alex, and Roger Hernandez. *Cubans in America: A Vibrant History of a People in Exile.* New York: Kensington, 2003.

Balderrama, Francisco, and Raymond Rodríguez. *A Decade of Betrayal: Mexican Repatriation in the 1930s.* Albuquerque: University of New Mexico Press, 2006.

Barrera, Mario. *Race and Class in the Southwest: A Theory of Racial Inequality.* South Bend, IN: University of Notre Dame Press, 1979.

Camarillo, Albert. *Chicanos in a Changing Society: From Mexican Pueblos to American Barrios in Santa Barbara and Southern California.* Cambridge, MA: Harvard University Press, 1979.

García, Mario T. *Mexican Americans: Leadership, Ideology, and Identity.* New Haven, CT: Yale University Press, 1989.

Garcia, Richard. *The Rise of the Mexican Middle Class: San Antonio 1929–1941.* College Station: Texas A&M University Press, 1991.

Griswold del Castillo, Richard. *La Familia: Chicano Families in the Urban Southwest, 1848 to the Present.* South Bend, IN: University of Notre Dame Press, 1984.

Gutiérrez, David G. *Walls and Mirrors: Mexican Americans, Mexican Immigrants, and the Politics of Ethnicity.* Berkeley: University of California Press, 1995.

Harris, Charles, and Louis Saddler. *The Texas Rangers and the Mexican Revolution: The Bloodiest Decade, 1910–1920.* Albuquerque: University of New Mexico Press, 2007.

Mason, Mauricio. *The Zoot-Suit Riots: The Psychology of Symbolic Annihilation.* Austin: University of Texas Press, 1984.

Meier, Matt S. and Feliciano Rivera. *The Chicanos: A History of Mexican Americans.* New York: Hill and Wang, 1972.

Montejano, David. *Anglos and Mexicans in the Making of Texas, 1836–1986.* Austin: University of Texas Press, 1987.

Sanchez, George J. *Becoming Mexican American: Ethnicity, Culture, and Identity in Chicano Los Angeles, 1900–1945.* New York: Oxford University Press, 1995.

History: 1965–Present

Beginning with the social and cultural revolutions of the mid-1960s and continuing to the era of heightened global security in the first decade of the twenty-first century, Latino history in the United States is one of troubled times. During these four decades, Latinos/as continued to face xenophobia and racism based on insidious stereotypes, but they also made significant gains, with increased opportunities within the social, political, and economic realms of U.S. life.

Turbulent Journeys

The end of the Bracero Program—a contract labor initiative to bring agricultural and railroad workers from Mexico to the United States—set the stage in the mid-1960s for national attention to be focused on Latinos/as with regard to both labor rights and immigration. The federal program had begun in 1942, and had allowed skilled Mexican farmworkers to agree to temporarily live and work in the United States, helping to fill labor shortages during World War II. When the program ended in 1964, hundreds of thousands of workers were abruptly denied work in the United States. Facing unemployment back in Mexico, many former *braceros* took desperate measures, including illegally remaining in the United States, to provide for themselves and their families. Thus began a period of upheaval and historic transformation for the Latino community.

In 1965, the National Farm Workers Association (NFWA, predecessor of the United Farm Workers), under the direction of César Chávez, contributed to the upheaval by joining a strike among Filipino American grape pickers. Their union, the Agricultural Workers Organizing Committee (AWOC), led by Larry Itliong, had taken action in response to the discrepancy between the higher daily wages previously paid to federal bracero grape pickers and those currently paid to Filipino American pickers in the vineyards surrounding Delano, California. The AWOC had begun its strike on September 8, 1965, and the NFWA joined with them on September 16. Two thousand workers left the fields, and the strike lasted more than five years. Popularly known as *La Causa* (the cause), it became a powerful symbol of Latino identity and the quest for equality in the face of social and economic injustice. The United Farm Workers (UFW)—as the union was called after the merger with the AWOC—ultimately secured better wages for the grape pickers, safer working conditions, the right to unionize, and by 1970, health care, and a community center. Chávez and Dolores Huerta, the leaders of the UFW, were recognized for their nonviolent approach, which included boycotts, peaceful demonstrations, and hunger strikes. The UFW success was not merely the result of the sacrifices of its members and their commitment to nonviolence, but also involved the support of other groups throughout the nation, who played a significant role in the battle and brought national attention to the injustices faced by Latinos/as. For example, the UFW gained the support of national leaders such as Robert F. Kennedy and the Catholic Conference of Bishops. The taste of victory was bittersweet for the picketers, however, because—during the five-year period of the strike—about 95 percent of farmworkers sacrificed their homes, cars, and financial resources for the cause.

The 1960s also saw the beginning of rapidly rising rates of immigration from Latin America to the United States, especially Cuban immigration into south Florida. Many Cubans, especially those opposed to the socialist policies of Cuban leader Fidel Castro, began immigrating to the United States starting in 1959. In 1965, Castro allowed Cubans with relatives in the United States to leave the island, but only if their relatives would retrieve them by boat from the fishing village of Camarioca, Cuba. Crossing the Straits of Florida was dangerous, and the small

An audience of Mexican migrant workers in northern California attends an outdoor play about the effects of chemical pesticides. Since the 1960s, traveling theater groups have played a vital role in informing and entertaining migrant farmworkers. *(Kim Komenich/Time & Life Pictures/Getty Images)*

vessels could not safely accommodate the number of people wanting to leave the island. After several disasters at sea, the United States on December 1, 1965, initiated the "Cuban airlift" to safely extract islanders. Some 45,000 Cubans were removed in the first year of the airlift, and approximately 250,000—about 10 percent of the island population—immigrated before Castro called a halt to the program in April 1973.

Besides witnessing labor unrest and new patterns of immigration, the 1960s saw the establishment of critical new measures to protect the civil rights of minority groups in the United States. The Voting Rights Act of 1965 guaranteed the right to vote for minority citizens, particularly African Americans who were denied the vote in the South; activists seized upon this opportunity to ensure the inclusion of Latino voters in the Southwest. Their efforts finally succeeded in 1975, when Congress extended the provisions of the Voting Rights Act to include Latino citizens, after a lobbying campaign by the Mexican American Legal Defense and Education Fund (MALDEF). Separately, the Crusade for Justice was established in Denver, Colorado, in 1966, as a political activist and civil rights organization for Mexican Americans. The Crusade and its high-profile leader, Rodolfo "Corky" Gonzales, led frequent protests and rallies to draw attention to inequities and injustices plaguing the Latino community.

The Crusade for Justice set the agenda for a nationwide Latino youth movement paralleling other radical minority movements in the United States. The first Chicano Youth Liberation Conference, held in March 1969, published El Plan Espiritual de Aztlán, a document outlining the doctrine of Chicano unity and the goal of independence from Anglo domination. The Plan reached university campuses across the United States and led directly to the establishment later that year of the Movimiento Estudiantíl Chicano de Aztlán (MEChA), a formidable political student movement representing Latinos/as, particularly those of Mexican heritage.

Throughout the 1960s, Latinos/as fought to gain a political voice, but not without adversity. The Crusade for Justice garnered negative press for several incidents of street violence in Denver in the 1960s and 1970s, despite the absence of direct proof of the Crusade's involvement. In 1966, Puerto Ricans in Chicago instigated rioting on Division Street (popularly known as Paseo Boricua) in response to police violence against a young man after the Puerto Rican Day Parade. Chicago-area Latinos/as recognized that the riots reflected a larger problem—lack of community togetherness—and the incident resulted in the establishment of several grassroots organizations, including the Spanish Action Committee of Chicago. Similarly, in the Latino-dominant neighborhood of East Harlem in New York City, the Young Lords Party (YLP) was organized in 1969 in response to the city's lack of attention to proper trash removal services in that community. The YLP, formed by a group of Puerto Rican students involved in campus anti–Vietnam War protests, recognized the inhumanity of the city's neglect and took action by hauling the trash into the middle of Third Avenue, a major thoroughfare, and setting fire to it. Although the tactics were radical, the spirit of the YLP protest was community-based and compassionate: to highlight the basic rights of citizens to enjoy clean streets. Combined with the high media visibility of the UFW strike and rapid immigration, activism in the streets became a source of palpable antagonism between Latino community groups and what was called "the establishment."

The flourishing of Latino arts and culture accompanied the political and social turbulence of the late 1960s. El Teatro Campesino originated with the UFW in California at mid-decade, beginning with informal *actos* (plays)—in the field or on flatbed trucks—to stir workers to strike for better living conditions. Under the direction of Luis Valdez, El Teatro Campesino provided workers, many of whom could not read or write, with a vehicle of cultural identification. Meanwhile, in New York, several formal theater companies began serving the interests of Latinos, including the Puerto Rico Traveling Theater and IntAR, both established in 1967, and the Teatro Repertorio Español, in 1969. All three companies have supported Latino playwrights, actors, and audiences since their inceptions. In 1967, the Berkeley, California–based publishing house Editorial Quinto Sol founded the Chicano literary magazine *El Grito* (*The Scream*) and later published *El Espejo: The Mirror,* the first anthology of contemporary Latino literature in the United States. As the 1960s drew to a close, then, the groundwork had been laid for great strides in the political and cultural representation of Latinos/as in the coming decades.

Reaction, Reform, Recognition

The 1970s saw a distinct upsurge in racism directed at Latinos, in the wake of a rapid rise in immigration from Latin American countries. The Immigration and Nationality Act of 1965 had abolished long-standing national-origin quotas on immigration and limited the total number of visas for the Western Hemisphere to 120,000. Exempt from the new limits, however, were visas granted for family reunification, which led promptly to so-called "chain immigration" and a rush of new arrivals in the years that followed.

Sometimes the immigration was motivated by violence and unrest in the home country. Indeed, over the course of the 1970s, the rise of dictatorial governments in Argentina, Brazil, Chile, Peru, El Salvador, and Guatemala motivated waves of immigrants seeking political asylum. In Mexico, economic turmoil prompted desperate workers to seek a better life by crossing the border. Some Latin Americans entering the country were undocumented, and many sought work in the United States illegally: as many as 12 million in 1970, according to Immigration and Naturalization Service (INS) commissioner Leonard Chapman. Starting in 1977, more than 1 million undocumented workers were being deported annually. Many Latinos/as who remained, including citizens, resident aliens, and undocumented workers, faced racial discrimination in the workforce as well as increasing levels of racially motivated violence.

The escalation of labor unrest in central California is one example. After the success of the UFW in the Delano grape strike, the union was encouraged to pursue contracts with lettuce growers throughout the Salinas Valley agricultural region. To resist the power of the UFW and avoid the threat of strikes, however, about seventy corporations in Salinas Valley made sweetheart deals with the powerful Teamsters Union, in a contract that provided no job security and few benefits. In the summer of 1970, the UFW urged workers who did not agree with the conditions of those contracts to walk off the fields, and Chávez called for a national boycott of lettuce to put pressure on agribusiness. The situation in Salinas soon turned violent, as tensions escalated between the UFW and Teamsters. Adding to the chaos, Judge Gordon Campbell of Monterey County imprisoned Chávez for defying a court order and held him without bail. While in prison, Chávez received visits from Coretta Scott King, widow of the Reverend Martin Luther King, Jr., and Ethel Kennedy, widow of Robert Kennedy, former U.S. Attorney General. The involvement of these high-profile figures helped characterize the Salinas lettuce strike in the media as not just a labor matter but part of the larger civil rights issue in America.

The 1970s saw continued protest and violence in urban centers, too, as Chicano activist groups allied with other national movements. The Brown Berets, organized in 1967, comprised young Chicano men and women fighting the institutional oppression of Latinos/as in Los Angeles County. In March 1968, the group organized student walkouts in East Los Angeles to protest the poor quality of education offered in their community. Their radical politics and "direct action" approach allied them with the Black Panthers in the African American community. The Brown Berets also supported UFW labor struggles and took part in the Chicano Youth Liberation Conference.

The Brown Berets' highest-profile protest was the National Chicano Moratorium against the Vietnam War in Los Angeles. On August 29, 1970, the Berets led 30,000 Chicanos/as and their supporters to the streets in protest of the Vietnam War, marching along Whittier Boulevard in the East LA barrios. Specifically, the National Chicano Moratorium protested the higher percentage of Latino casualties in the Vietnam War relative to their percentage of the population. The Los Angeles Police Department (LAPD) used tear gas to break up the rally, and disorder inevitably ensued. A stray tear gas shell at a restaurant near the rally killed Rubén Salazar, a Chicano journalist who worked for the *Los Angeles Times.* Although his death was officially deemed an accident, Chicano protesters characterized it as murder and held up Salazar as a martyr to institutional violence against Latino people.

As is often the case in American history, the cycle of strong action and reaction was followed by reform. In direct consequence of the lettuce strike, Governor Jerry Brown led the state legislature in passing the California Agriculture Labor Relations Act, which took effect on August 28, 1975. The purpose of the law was to allow workers to decide for themselves, without retribution, whether they wanted union representation. When the elections began, the UFW won the majority of votes where it was on the ballot. In 1977, the Teamsters Union agreed to leave the lettuce fields, and the UFW-led lettuce boycott ended the following year.

Equal access to quality education was another Latino issue that activists brought to a head in the 1970s. In the case of *San Antonio Independent School District v. Rodríguez* (1973), the U.S. Supreme Court considered whether or not Texas had violated the Equal Protection Clause of the Fourteenth Amendment by not redistributing funds from wealthier school districts to economically disadvantaged ones—in other words, whether school financing based on local property taxes is constitutional. Although the court held that education is not a fundamental right protected by the U.S. Constitution and that local school financing is not subject to federal judicial scrutiny, the case brought national attention to the unequal system of school financing. The following year, in 1974, the U.S. Congress passed the Equal Education Opportunity Act to create a legal infrastructure for equality in public education. Specifically, the measure included provisions for bilingual education for Latino students and assistance for students who are Spanish-language dominant.

While immigration, labor unrest, and civil rights struggles seemed to dominate the media coverage of Latinos/as during the 1970s, the decade also saw tremendous growth in the Latino contributions to the arts. In 1970, the Centro Cultural de la Raza in San Diego, California, and Galería de la Raza in San Francisco were founded as spaces dedicated solely to the furtherance of Chicano and Mexican American arts.

Many Chicano arts collectives followed suit, such as Self Help Graphics and Art in East Lost Angeles, La Raza Galería Posada in Sacramento, California, and La Peña Cultural Center in Berkeley. In 1975, artist Peter Rodríguez established the Mexican Museum in San Francisco to encompass the traditional and contemporary arts of Chicanos/as.

Several Latinos/as in the 1970s garnered particular critical acclaim in art, music, and literature. The Cuban-born conceptual artist and feminist Ana Mendieta became world-renowned for a series of earthworks she called *siluetas,* begun in 1972. In these enigmatic works, Mendieta photographed or filmed her body's impression in mud, sand, and grass, or being burned in effigy. The Argentine American composer Mario Davidovsky won the Pulitzer Prize in 1971 for innovative scores, which he named *sincronismos* (synchronisms). These compositions coupled traditional orchestral live performance with electronic music recorded on tape. And the year 1972 also brought the publication of Rudolfo Anaya's celebrated novel *Bless Me, Ultima,* which, over the next two decades, became the widest-read work by any Chicano author in the United States.

Expanded Horizons

The efforts of activists and artists during the 1970s afforded significant visibility and new opportunities for Latinos/as in the 1980s. In the context of a general flourishing of the mass media, which brought a proliferation of entertainment, newspapers, and magazines to virtually every segment of the U.S. population, Latinos/as capitalized on the video and print media to represent themselves and construct a new public identity.

The film industry in earlier decades had tended to present Latino characters in stereotypical forms, but Latino-directed films in the 1980s attempted to reverse the tide. Luis Valdez, the founder and director of El Teatro Campesino in the 1960s, released a filmed version of his acclaimed stage play, *Zoot Suit,* in 1981. The commanding performance of Edward James Olmos as the play's mythical character El Pachuco received considerable attention from critics. While the film enjoyed primarily cult success, it paved the way for Valdez's blockbuster *La Bamba* (1987), starring Lou Diamond Phillips as Latino rock 'n' roll icon Ritchie Valens, and Olmos's Academy Award–nominated performance as inner-city math teacher Jaime Escalante in *Stand and Deliver* (1988). As depicted in such other major releases as *Born in East L.A.* (1987) and *The Milagro Beanfield War* (1988), the Chicano experience had unprecedented exposure in Hollywood during the late 1980s. *Stand and Deliver,* written and directed by Ramón Menéndez, was singular in its involvement of Latinos in all aspects of production.

The Ballad of Gregorio Cortez (1982), directed by Moctezuma Esparza, presented a TV film version of Américo Paredes's 1958 dissertation on the mistaken identity and killing of a Mexican American man in turn-of-the-century Texas. The work was especially notable for reversing the "bandido" stereotype of Mexicans in typical Hollywood Western fare. In 1984, filmmakers Paul Espinosa and Isaac Artenstein directed the influential documentary *Ballad of an Unsung Hero,* about Spanish-language radio pioneer Pedro J. González. Espinosa and Artenstein's work attempts to exonerate González of rape charges brought against him in 1934, demonstrating instead his setup by powerful Anglos opposed to his political message. Also in 1984, Gregory Nava released the highly acclaimed *El Norte,* a heart-wrenching drama about indigenous Guatemalan siblings who take enormous risks to flee political oppression in their mountain village and come to the United States. Nava presents an emotionally sympathetic view of immigration at a time of mounting political pressure to stem immigration from Latin America.

While more Latinos saw themselves on the silver screen in less stereotypical representations, the number of circulating publications for Latino audiences also increased dramatically in the 1980s. On April 22, 1980, the New York–based, Spanish-language daily newspaper *Noticias del Mundo* was launched. In September 1985, *Vista* (designating itself as "The Magazine for All Hispanics") and *Saludos Hispanos* began distribution as inserts in American newspapers serving areas with significant Latino populations. On November 21, 1987, the *Miami Herald* began circulating *El Nuevo Herald,* a Spanish-language daily newspaper serving the Latino population of south Florida. In April 1988, *Hispanic* magazine published its first issue,

The variety of Spanish-language magazines and other mass media testify to the rapid growth of the Latino population, its influence on the communications industry, and the mainstreaming of Latino culture. *(Tim Boyle/Getty Images)*

featuring Latina actress Raquel Welch on the cover. Fred Estrada, the publisher of *Hispanic* (and one of the original investors in *Vista*), believed that all Americans—not just Latinos/as—would be well served by more Latino entrepreneurs and successful, high-profile role models in the media.

Hispanic magazine filled a market niche for upwardly mobile Latinos/as, and wisely so. The economic viability of the Latino demographic underwent extreme expansion over the 1980s. Following the nationwide trend of aggressive business development, Latino-owned businesses in the United States actually exceeded the growth curve for non-Latino-owned businesses. In a two-year period beginning in 1980, the fifty-one largest Latino-owned companies in the country reported revenue increases of 47 percent. This was a giant leap, considering that the overall growth of the U.S. economy during the same time frame was considerably slower, about 17 percent.

While business prospects for Latino entrepreneurs seemed rosy during the 1980s, a further increase in immigration during the decade and persistent racism and xenophobia across the United States resulted in conflicting public opinion about the future of Latino life, culture, and community. Latinos/as represented 40 percent of the 6.3 million immigrants granted permanent residence in the United States during the 1980s. Most were of working age and arrived on U.S. soil seeking gainful employment. The Refugee Act of 1980, regarded by some as a humanitarian gesture on the part of the federal government, opened America's doors to any people unable or unwilling to return to their homeland because of persecution, especially those fleeing Communist countries. Although the Refugee Act set an important precedent for a system of asylum, it also served the agenda of U.S. policymakers and businesses seeking an advantage in the Cold War by depopulating countries with strong Communist parties and introducing a new domestic base of consumers for American goods. In response to the millions of refugees arriving from Southeast Asia, Africa, the Soviet Union, and Cuba, the INS began more aggressively detaining and deporting undocumented immigrants. Allegations of civil and human rights violations against refugees and undocumented immigrants were commonplace.

In the same year as the Refugee Act, the escalating influx of Cubans to the United States provoked government and media attention to the issue of immigration. Beginning on April 15 and ending on October 31, 1980, Fidel Castro granted exit visas to thousands of Cubans seeking to leave the country with the proviso that they arrange transportation to another country from the port of Mariel. Cuban Americans in the United States organized a fleet of boats to pick up the refugees and carry them the 90 miles (145 kilometers) to south Florida. Many of the vessels were barely seaworthy and could not accommodate the vast numbers of passengers seeking exile. Known as the Mariel Boatlift, the massive exodus from Cuba resulted in the resettlement of approximately 125,000 Cubans (colloquially known as *marielitos*) to the United States.

Mounting political and economic pressures from the new tide of immigration forced the U.S. government into action. In 1986, Congress passed the Immigration Reform and Control Act (IRCA), which promised amnesty to illegal aliens present in the United States since before January 1, 1982. Many Latinos/as were helped by the legislation, which made them legal residents. The legislation also appropriated increased budgetary funds for the surveillance and policing of the border (especially the U.S.-Mexico border), and imposed stiff penalties for employers of undocumented workers, who frequently operated beneath fair labor standards. Other provisions of IRCA protected formerly undocumented workers from discrimination based on their country of national origin.

Due to the positive effects of the new policies and laws, more Latinos/as sought representation in politics and the government. In 1980, Julián Nava became the first Chicano appointed as U.S. ambassador to Mexico. Before that appointment, by President Jimmy Carter, Nava had led community initiatives in his native Los Angeles, working for the school board during the embattled 1970s. Another prominent Mexican American, Lauro F. Cavazos of Texas, became the first Latino appointed to the presidential cabinet, named secretary of education by President Ronald Reagan in 1988 and serving two years. In 1989, Ileana Ros-Lehtinen was elected as a U.S. representative from Florida's Eighteenth District; born in Cuba in 1952, Ros-Lehtinen was the first Latina elected to Congress.

As the 1980s gave way to a new decade, Latinos/as looked toward expanded horizons, though not without complex challenges. The media recognized the upward mobility of a rapidly changing middle-class demographic, but not all Latinos/as in the United States had access to these channels of power. Some questioned the ability of the nation's resources to sustain the tidal force of Latino newcomers; in 1989, the INS announced that Latinos/as accounted for the majority of immigrants to the United States at 61.4 percent. Many were not economically mobile, lacked professional skills, and were based in urban areas without sufficient educational and social resources to advance their status.

Borders and Crossovers

The world watched as cataclysmic social and political events resulted in the breakup of the Soviet Union in the early 1990s. International borders were drawn and treaties negotiated between the newly independent republics. In the Americas, however, the North American Free Trade Agreement (NAFTA) proposed to dissolve the economic barriers between Canada, the United States, and Mexico by eliminating tariffs on goods exchanged between these countries over fifteen years. The agreement was signed into law in 1992 and went into effect on January 1, 1994.

NAFTA incorporated the opinions and support of Latino community leaders throughout its planning stages. In 1991, President Carlos Salinas of Mexico attended the annual dinner for MALDEF in Los Angeles, where he expressed the hope that Mexican Americans would ardently support NAFTA, thereby helping strengthen ties between the United States and Mexico. The assumption of common interest during the planning stages of NAFTA quickly turned into opposition, however, as critics voiced serious concerns. For example, NAFTA promised U.S. corporations a larger role in setting up *maquiladoras,* large factories on the Mexican side of the border. Labor rights activists argued that the deliberately low wages paid to workers in maquiladoras would result in the continued poverty and squalid lifestyle of many Mexicans in the borderlands region. At worst, the maquiladora trade would force greater numbers of workers north as desperate conditions necessitated the risk of illegal immigration.

Employment, both undocumented and legal, remained a salient issue for Latinos/as during the early 1990s. As ever, unemployment rates among Latinos/as remained higher than in the non-Latino population; in 1992, at the end of a nationwide economic recession, the unemployment rate for Latinos/as was an estimated 10 to 12 percent, while the national unemployment rate was 5.5 percent. Labor statistics did show overall increases in the employment of Latino workers from 1990 and 2000, but this was attributable largely to the expansion of poor-paying service sector jobs and the sheer growth of the Latino community. Many of those working at low-paying jobs were not officially counted or legally employed. The wages paid to many Latinos/as in the local service economies or sweatshop industries, often below the legal minimum, could not meet the rising cost of living, especially for families. Even among those legally employed, many workers were dissuaded from unionizing for fear of losing their jobs. The "greater employment" statistics themselves reflected the economic marginalization of poor Latinos/as and a widening disparity between the type of work performed by Latino and white workers. Latinos/as were overrepresented in entry-level, service sector, and manual labor jobs, whereas whites frequently found work in professional occupations. The persistent lack of quality schools in economically disadvantaged areas and the ongoing legislative challenges to bilingual education resulted in a lower level of educational attainment and a greater language barrier among U.S. Latinos/as, negatively affecting their employment opportunity.

In 1993, two events heightened the fear and resistance to foreigners in America: the terrorist bombing of the World Trade Center in New York City and the thousands of Haitian refugees who poured into boats headed for the United States. A xenophobic anti-immigration backlash became evident in public discourse and the political climate, contributing further to the discrimination against Latinos/as in the mid-1990s. For example, on November 8, 1994, California voters passed Proposition 187; it denied state-funded health care, education, and welfare benefits to those who could not verify their immigration status. Condemned from its inception for implicitly targeting Latinos/as, the measure was ultimately barred from taking effect by court order. In 1998, U.S. District Judge Mariana Pfaelzer ruled most of Proposition 187 unconstitutional, saying that it gave the state too much regulatory power over immigration.

The cultural border dividing Latinos/as from the "mainstream" began to blur in the late 1990s, and nowhere more conspicuously than in the music industry. Selena Quintanilla, known by her millions of fans simply as Selena, became famous for her exuberant and inspiring performance of Spanish-language Tejano music. A hybrid musical form, Tejano incorporates elements of country and western, pop, and Mexican-style *ranchera* music. Tragically, Selena was murdered on March 31, 1995, by the president of her fan club; some 10,000 mourners congregated for her funeral in Corpus Christi, Texas; and candlelight vigils were held in her remembrance across the country. Selena was a modern icon, symbolizing a new generation of Hispanic Americans who participated in mainstream U.S. culture while identifying fully with her Latino roots. At the same time, her popularity in the society at large had as much to do with her pop icon image—light skin, Caucasian features, and upfront sexuality—as it did her musical and cultural origins.

Nevertheless, because she was so beloved, the notoriety of Selena's murder catalyzed a larger crossover between Latino-dominant and mainstream audiences. In 1997, film director Gregory Nava (*El Norte,* 1984) released a motion-picture biography of Selena and her rise to stardom, titled *Selena.* The film starred Jennifer Lopez, a Latina actor, singer, and dancer, of New York–Puerto Rican descent, in the title role. With the colossal box office success of *Selena,* Lopez was catapulted into stardom. Artists like Lopez were instrumental in positioning the entertainment industry for the "Latin Boom." From 1999 into the twenty-first century, the industry vigorously promoted Latino artists to consumers—only this time, not just Latino consumers. Pop stars Ricky Martin, Christina Aguilera, Enrique Iglesias, and Marc Anthony joined Lopez in the spotlight and on the pop charts. Like Selena, these recording artists are lighter-skinned Latinos, and each relied on a strong component of sexuality to sell their music. Martin, a Puerto Rican recording artist, released his debut English-language album, *Ricky Martin,* in 1999. The record includes the English version of his 1998 Spanish track "Copa de la Vida," which catapulted Martin into international fame when it became the official song of that year's World Cup soccer tournament. It was the English-language track "Livin' la Vida Loca," however, with its lyrical allusions to sexual abandon that brought Martin mainstream recognition in the United States.

Some regard the Latino cultural crossover as a positive by-product of multiculturalism, contributing to the tolerance of cultural difference in American society. Others, like the Mexican-born performance artist Guillermo Gómez-Peña, object that the mainstream enjoyment of Latino entertainment infrequently reconciles "fun" with the political struggles experienced by many Latino groups. Gómez-Peña and other Chicano artists, such as Victor Ochoa, Lalo Alcaraz, Ruben Ortiz, and Steve Callis, used their artistic talents in the mid-1990s to question the true interpenetration of cultural exchange between Latinos and Anglos. Gómez-Peña's poignant and often humorous "ethno-cyborgs," such as those performed in *El Mexterminator* (1995), cobble together ethnic fears and stereotypes in characters such as Cyber-Vato and La Cultural Transvestite. The point of his provocative performances is to question why, in an age of purported political and economic integration, some cultural boundaries remain unassailable.

Looking Ahead

The terrorist attacks of September 11, 2001, have cast long shadows on the political, social, and cultural life of the United States—among other things, making the security of American borders a top policy priority. Suspicion of immigrants and foreigners became more pronounced among Anglo elites, constitutional rights once considered sacrosanct were subject to compromise in the name of "homeland security," and restrictions on immigration were tightened. The new era of law enforcement included provisions for secret surveillance, detention without notice or bond, and secret hearings on the comings and goings of foreigners in the United States. While the brunt of the new attitudes and policies was directed at Muslims and Arab Americans, it also fell on the millions of immigrant Latinos/as and their families. Latino rights and advocacy agencies, such as the National Council of La Raza (NCLR), monitor the fairness of national policies with an eye toward the civil rights of Latinos/as.

In 2001, "non-whites" represented a majority of residents in California, with Latinos/as comprising about a third of the state's population. During the course of the next few years, New Mexico and Texas joined California as majority-minority states in which Latinos/as are the dominant minority demographic. As of 2005, according to the U.S. Census Bureau, 42.7 million people in the United States identified themselves as "Latino" or "Hispanic," accounting for 14.4 percent of the total population. Some demographers project that the United States will be "majority-minority" by 2050, with a significant proportion of Latinos/as. The nature and extent of law and policy changes as a function of this shift remain to be determined, but long-standing social inequities would demand attention. The percentage of Latinos living below the poverty line remains significantly higher than the percentage of whites. Latino males are incarcerated at a rate more than twice that of whites, suggesting a disparity in access to legal resources. And the poorest Latinos/as continue to face inordinate difficulty in accessing the nation's health care system. The prospect of a majority-minority thus suggests a redistribution of resources to better serve the needs of an expanding demographic—a policy shift that recognizes the history of institutional injustice and persistent problems faced by the Latino community. For many in the community, the 2008 election of Barack Obama and his 2009 nomination of Sonia Sotomayor—the daughter of Puerto Rican immigrants who was raised in a Bronx, New York, housing project—as the first Latino/a to sit on the U.S. Supreme Court raised hopes for just such a shift and just such a recognition.

Michael Alvar de Baca

Further Reading

Acuña, Rodolfo. *Occupied America: A History of Chicanos.* 6th ed. New York: Pearson Longman, 2007.

Cantú, Norma, and Olga Nájera-Ramírez, eds. *Chicana Traditions: Continuity and Change.* Urbana: University of Illinois Press, 2002.

De Anda, Roberto M., ed. *Chicanas and Chicanos in Contemporary Society.* Lanham, MD: Rowman & Littlefield., 2004.

Flores, William V., and Rina Benmayor, eds. *Latino Cultural Citizenship: Claiming Identity, Space, and Rights.* Boston: Beacon, 1997.

Gann, L.H., and Peter J. Duignan. *The Hispanics in the United States: A History.* Boulder, CO: Westview, 1987.

Haney-López, Ian F. *Racism on Trial: The Chicano Fight for Justice.* Cambridge, MA: Harvard University Press, 2003.

Kanellos, Nicolás, and Bryan Ryan, eds. *Hispanic American Chronology.* New York: UXL, 1996.

Maciel, David R., and Isidro D. Ortiz, eds. *Chicanas/Chicanos at the Crossroads: Social, Economic, and Political Change.* Tucson: University of Arizona Press, 1996.

Maciel, David R., Isidro D. Ortiz, and María Herrera-Sobek, eds. *Chicano Renaissance: Contemporary Cultural Trends.* Tucson: University of Arizona Press, 2000.

Moore, Joan, and Harry Pachon. *Hispanics in the United States.* Englewood Cliffs, NJ: Prentice-Hall, 1985.

Morales, Rebecca, and Frank Bonilla, eds. *Latinos in a Changing U.S. Economy: Comparative Perspectives on Growing Inequality.* Newbury Park, CA: Sage, 1993.

Navarro, Armando. *Mexicano Experience in Occupied Aztlan: Struggles and Change.* Walnut Creek, CA: Altamira, 2005.

Vásquez, Francisco H., and Rodolfo Torres, eds. *Latino/a Thought: Culture, Politics and Society.* Lanham, MD: Rowman & Littlefield, 2003.

Villarreal, Roberto E., and Norma G. Hernandez, eds. *Latinos and Political Coalitions: Political Empowerment for the 1990s.* New York: Greenwood, 1991.

A–Z ENTRIES

A

Acculturation and Assimilation

Social scientists define assimilation or acculturation as the process by which immigrants—including Europeans, Latin Americans, Asians, and other minority groups—conform to rules, ideologies, and common practices of American society and culture. Public schools, churches, the government, and other social institutions are involved in acquainting new people with its values and norms and in motivating them to envision being part of the host society.

Since its origin, the United States has been challenged to integrate newcomers from different parts of the world, achieving different levels of success in acquainting these new people with its values and norms and in motivating them to envision being part of American society. The experiences of immigrants in the United States, particularly Latinos/as, are diverse because of (1) differences in the way they have been assimilated into mainstream American culture, (2) differing degrees of assimilation, and (3) diverse countries of origin. Thus, not all Latino immigrants assimilate in the same way or to the same degree.

Restrictive immigration policies that targeted Latino immigrants at the end of the nineteenth and beginning of the twentieth centuries seemed to ensure that they would have a difficult time gaining the acceptance of Americans and assimilating into U.S. culture. Furthermore, economic differences among Latino immigrants, as well as the immigrants' political significance to the United States, have played a part in their acceptance and integration. This is exemplified by the reception of Cubans from 1959 to the 1980s compared to the reception of Nicaraguans in the 1990s. Cubans received monetary as well as political and social support to settle in the United States, because they were seen as victims of a Communist country with which the United States had contentious relations. By contrast, Nicaraguans escaping their country's Communist government in 1990 requested political asylum but did not receive it. The American political culture in the latter year—after the demise of the Soviet Union—no longer deemed it important to welcome the Nicaraguans as political refugees.

Throughout the nation's history, Americans have viewed Latino immigrants as outsiders, perceiving them as having an adverse effect on the quality of American life and as causing financial burdens to society in welfare, health care, court, and jail costs. These and many other stereotypes, formed by media coverage, political discourse, and race relations, have shaped complex attitudes about Latino immigrants. Despite the obstacles they face in America, however, including learning a new language, earning a living, and navigating social systems, Latino immigrants generally bring with them a strong work ethic, and through social and economic contributions enhance the general productivity and culture of the United States.

Mexicans

Mexican immigrants in the American Southwest represent a unique immigrant population, as they were native to the region before it was annexed under the Treaty of Guadalupe Hidalgo (1848), which ended the Mexican-American War. The fact that Mexico and the United States share a national border has contributed to the steady flow of immigrants from the former country, making Mexicans and Mexican American immigrants both the oldest and the newest immigrants in the United States. While some Mexicans became citizens without moving from their homes (when the U.S. border was pushed south after 1848), others became immigrants by crossing the border. Thus, for historical and geographical reasons, Mexicans and their descendants have also been distinguished by their reluctance to assimilate.

The economic and social status of Mexican Americans in the United States today is directly correlated to the low level of acceptance accorded by American society through history and up to the present. For instance, government and education policies that have kept Mexican Americans poorly educated and undocumented have effectively transformed them into a low-wage labor force needed by American farmers. Other perceptions that have contributed to the generally low socioeconomic standing of Mexicans and Mexican Americans are: that they are exclusively suited for manual work; that they possess low intellectual abilities; that their cultural and family values are primitive; and that Mexican family relationships are archaic. Within this context, the perceived lack of effort to abandon their culture of origin and adopt American values (including American conceptions about work and the family) and behavior has typically been understood as a reluctance to accept American values, and thus as a failure to assimilate. In reality, difficulties in assimilating have been a function of resistance on the part of the cultural mainstream and a lack of social resources and institutions to facilitate the process.

Today, many Mexicans enter the United States based on family ties rather than job skills. They settle in highly concentrated ethnic communities in Los Angeles; San Antonio, Texas; Detroit; and Chicago, making it less necessary to learn English, which in turn makes it harder to assimilate in the broader culture. According to the 2000 U.S. Census, about 80 percent of non-Mexican immigrants are fluent in English, compared to 49 percent of Mexican immigrants. Those who settle in Mexican enclaves also tend to have lower wages and poorer educational attainment than their European or Asian immigrant counterparts. For example, the average annual wage income of non-Mexican working immigrants is $21,000 per year, compared to only $12,000 per year for Mexican working immigrants. Those with lower incomes tend to live in more concentrated areas because rents are less expensive and ethnic support systems stronger; generally, however, they are slower to acquire the skills necessary to sustain the incomes needed to live in more diverse neighborboods.

Cubans

Sociologists generally consider Cubans to be the most successful of the Latino immigrants in the United States, both economically and in terms of social and cultural assimilation. Unlike other Latino immigrant groups, Cubans share a very similar demographic profile with the non-Latino white population of the United States. The relatively privileged status of those who escaped Fidel Castro's Communist regime in the 1960s (most were wealthy professionals) prompted a warm welcome from both the U.S. government and ordinary citizens. The federal government opened a Cuban Refugee Center in Miami, Florida, and offered medical and financial aid to new arrivals. Cuban immigrants received bilingual education. In 1966, Congress passed the Cuban American Adjustment Act, which allowed any Cuban who had lived in the U.S. for a year to become a permanent resident—a privilege that has never been offered to any other immigrant group. In addition, the Miami area was already well known to Cubans, as Cuba was for many Americans; only 90 miles (145 kilometers) separate the island from the U.S. mainland. Many of the early refugees thus had a level of familiarity with American language and culture, which made them unique as political refugees. With that advantage, and the organized support of the government, the Cuban immigrants of the 1960s quickly succeeded economically and assimilated easily. While a desire to return home at some time in the future helped preserve their native culture and language, they became fully functional bicultural, bilingual citizens.

The next major group of Cuban immigrants received a very different welcome. In 1980, under international pressure, the Cuban government opened the port city of Mariel to any Cuban who wanted to leave for the United States. In the six months the port remained open, more than 125,000 Cubans made their way to U.S. shores. Known as *marielitos,* these new arrivals were much less affluent than their predecessors, were generally stigmatized as "undesirables," and had a much harder time assimilating into U.S. culture than the asylum seekers of the 1960s.

Puerto Ricans

Immigrants from Puerto Rico represent a special case, in that Puerto Rico is a commonwealth of the United States and the residents of the island have been U.S. citizens since 1917. As such, they are not legally restricted from visiting their homeland and can move freely throughout the fifty states. Technically, then, resettlement is considered internal migration and not immigration at all. In moving to the mainland, however, Puerto Ricans leave a homeland with its own distinct identity and culture, and the transition often involves many of the same cultural conflicts and emotional adjustments that other immigrants face. Travel between the mainland and the island contributes to the duality of Puerto Rican American culture, language, and identity.

Puerto Rican immigrants are heavily concentrated in New York and other urban areas of the Northeast, but new arrivals are settling throughout the country, with large numbers in the states of Connecticut, New Jersey, Florida, and Texas, and in the city of Chicago. Puerto Ricans are generally bilingual and bicultural in everyday life, but with poor education, high unemployment, low wages, and rampant discrimination preventing them from enjoying full assimilation in U.S. society. Many Puerto Ricans, not surprisingly, tend to idealize their island homeland and its culture, further slowing the assimilation process. To help reverse that vicious cycle, the Puerto Rican government has implemented programs to reach out to Puerto Rican communities in the United States in cultural affairs, civic participation, and aspects of daily life, recognizing that this is a population whose future is closely linked with the future of Puerto Rico, and vice versa.

Central and South Americans

During the 1980s, Latin America faced a series of economic problems as a result of the implementation of neoliberal economic policies. Additionally, political turmoil and U.S. intervention in Nicaragua, Guatemala, and El Salvador prompted a significant change in the flow of immigrants from Central America to the United States. The distribution of these Central American immigrants was different from previous Latino groups in that they did not confine themselves to already established Latino communities. In addition, many immigrants left children in their countries of origin and worked to send money home to support them. While similar to other Latino immigrants, the socioeconomic status of Central and South American immigrants has facilitated a varied process. Some have been able to purchase property in their home country, visit when money and documents made it possible, and remain in close contact with their relatives and native culture.

By comparison with twentieth-century European immigrants, for example, assimilation and acculturation for Latino immigrants seem both less likely and less relevant, since most do not come to the United States with the intention of breaking away from their past and their old country. Studies have shown that levels of acculturative stress among Central and South American immigrants are related to marital status, ineffective social support, negative expectations for the future, and, within families, a lack of agreement about the decision to migrate. Additionally, among the other factors accounting for these differences is the level of education of a large segment of these newcomers, who arrive to America with the hope of finding occupations that reflect their educational status.

Emerging Patterns

The diverse experiences of Latino immigrants in the United States have been distinct from the experiences of other immigrants. While defined by the heterogeneity and range of experiences with assimilation and acculturation, Latinos/as have faced unique social and political receptions, varied economic burdens, and different immigration legislation, all of which has impacted the process of assimilation into American institutions and culture. However, recent arrivals from South and Central America, as well as from other parts of the Latino Diaspora, have experienced assimilation in distinct ways given the predominance of polices of multiculturalism. Notwithstanding the promotion and acceptance of diversity, persistent obstacles in the form of economic barriers, persistent inequality, restrictive immigration policies, and societal prejudice remain in place for the acculturation and assimilation of Latino immigrants into dominant American institutions.

Sara Z. Poggio

See also: Cubans; Guatemalans; Mexicans; Nicaraguans; Puerto Ricans; Salvadorans.

Further Reading

Alba, Richard D., and Victor Nee. *Remaking the American Mainstream: Assimilation and Contemporary Immigration.* Cambridge, MA: Harvard University Press, 2003.

Gordon, Milton. *Assimilation in American Life: The Role of Race, Religion, and National Origins.* New York: Oxford University Press, 1964.

Hondagneu-Sotelo, Pierrette. *Gender and Contemporary U.S. Immigration: Contemporary Trends.* Berkeley: University of California Press, 2003.

Poggio, Sara. "Cuban Immigration to the United States." In *Encyclopedia of American Immigration,* ed. James Ciment. Armonk, NY: M.E. Sharpe, 2001.

Portes, Alejandro, and Robert L. Bach. *Latin Journey: Cuban and Mexican Immigrants in the United States.* Berkeley: University of California Press, 1985.

Acosta, Oscar (1935–?)

Oscar Zeta Acosta was a Chicano attorney, author, politician, and political activist who played an influential role in the Chicano Movement in California during the 1960s and 1970s. He published two significant novels of the movement—*The Autobiography of a Brown Buffalo* (1972) and *The Revolt of the Cockroach People* (1973)—both of which became literary staples of academic courses in Latino studies.

Acosta was born on April 8, 1935, in El Paso, Texas, and grew up in the San Joaquin Valley near Modesto, California. After graduating from Oakland Joint Union High School in 1952, he received a music scholarship to the University of Southern California. Instead of accepting it, he chose to join the U.S. Air Force, following in the military footsteps of his father, who had been drafted during World War II. While in the military, Acosta was stationed in Panama, and he became a Baptist missionary at a leper colony. Four years later, he was honorably discharged from the military. After leaving the military, Acosta began to fall into occasional spells of depression. He attempted suicide in New Orleans before beginning a ten-year psychiatric treatment in 1957.

Back in California, Acosta enrolled in Modesto Junior College and later in San Francisco State University, where he majored and obtained a degree in creative writing. After graduating from San Francisco Law School he passed the California bar exam in 1966, and the following year took a position as an antipoverty attorney for the East Oakland Legal Aid Society.

Acosta spent much of his time actively fighting the legal system, which led him to move to East Los Angeles and join the Chicano Movement working as an activist and lawyer for the next five years. He made his mark by exposing the Los Angeles County jury selection process for racist practices in the case of *Carlos Montez et al. v. the Superior Court of Los Angeles County* in 1966. In 1967, he represented the "Biltmore Six," who had been charged with arson for attempting to burn down the Biltmore Hotel during a speech by California governor Ronald Reagan.

On Christmas Eve 1969, Acosta participated in a protest and prayer vigil conducted by a Chicano group outside St. Basil's Roman Catholic Church. At the time, many Chicanos/as were unhappy with the Catholic Church as administered by the Diocese of Los Angeles; some believed that Catholic school tuition was too expensive for poor Chicano families and that there was not enough available financial aid. When Acosta and the others tried to enter the church while Cardinal James McIntyre celebrated the midnight mass, they were arrested and charged with rioting.

In 1970, Acosta ran for county sheriff of Los Angeles, campaigning on a promise to dissolve the sheriff's department. During the race, he was cited for contempt of court and spent two days in jail. Although he lost the race to the incumbent, he did obtain more votes than one candidate, Everett Holladay, the Monterey Park chief of police. Acosta gained popularity during this election because he backed the antiestablishment Chicano group *Católicos por La Raza.*

Acosta was well known for leading a wild life that included heavy drug use. He was arrested for amphetamine possession by the Los Angeles Police Department during the Biltmore Six trial. The celebrated "Gonzo" journalist and author Hunter S. Thompson, himself notorious for drug and alcohol abuse, featured his relationship with Acosta in his best-selling book *Fear and Loathing in Las Vegas* (1972). Thompson's book details their friendship and shared drug experiences as well as Acosta's involvement in the Chicano Movement. The publisher of the first edition opposed Thompson's decision to include any identifiable mention or images of Acosta anywhere in the book, but Thompson refused, and a picture of the two friends appears on the book's back cover. Thompson did agree to alter several parts of the text and to portray Acosta as a Samoan instead of a Chicano.

Acosta's ultimate fate is unknown. In the spring of 1974, he went to Mazatlán, Mexico, but then disappeared. He was last seen by his family on Thanksgiving Day 1973, although a few days before he disappeared he made a phone call to his son Marco. In 1996, a collection of his miscellaneous writings, *Oscar Acosta: The Uncollected Works,* was published.

Nicole Martone

See also: Blowouts; Chicano Movement; East L.A. Thirteen.

Further Reading

Guajardo, Paul. *Chicano Controversy: Oscar Acosta and Richard Rodriguez.* New York: Peter Lang, 2002.

Moore, Burton, and Andrea A. Cabello, eds. *Love and Riot: Oscar Zeta Acosta and the Great Mexican American Revolt.* Mountain View, CA: Floricanto, 2003.

Stavans, Ilan. *Bandido: The Death and Resurrection of Oscar "Zeta" Acosta.* Evanston, IL: Northwestern University Press, 2003.

Acuña, Rodolfo (1932–)

A groundbreaking educator, social activist, and author, Rodolfo Francis Acuña has been called the "godfather of Chicano studies" and is recognized as one of its most influential scholars. Born on May 18, 1932, in Boyle Heights, California, he, like many other Chicanos/as, was raised Mexican in the United States. Both of his parents were Mexican immigrants—his father a tailor, his mother legally blind, a condition that limited her education to elementary school. By Acuña's own account, their experiences helped to establish his concerns about the fate of Chicanos/as in the United States.

After volunteering for service during the Korean War, Acuña enrolled in college through the GI Bill. Working sixty hours a week and carrying eighteen units, he earned two bachelor's degrees (1957 and 1958) and a master's degree (1962) at California State University, Los Angeles. While earning his PhD in Latin American history at the University of Southern California (1968), he taught high school history and lectured at a local community college in Los Angeles. His experiences as a child, a teacher, and an activist all contributed to a strong working-class identity, establishing a foundation for his life's work and his efforts to motivate Chicano students to complete their college educations.

A historian by training, Acuña has spent much of his career defying academic convention, merging scholarship and activism in working to break down the boundaries between academia and the community. In addition to his many scholarly accomplishments, he has worked tirelessly—and successfully—on behalf of those who are less fortunate. His commitment to the empowerment of Chicanos/as in the United States has earned him a number of honors, including the Dr. Ernesto Galarza Award for Distinguished Community Activism and Scholarship. In 1989, Acuña was honored as a National Association of Chicana and Chicano Studies (NACC) scholar for his lifetime of achievement in the field.

Of his many books, the most influential and enduring is *Occupied America: A History of Chicanos* (1972). In it, Acuña sets forth the most comprehensive historical account of Chicanos/as in the United States to date. In several revised additions, it has appeared on the reading lists of most Chicano history courses in American high schools and universities. Some critics have argued that the work is too controversial for high school students, while others state that it is an honest account of social inequality that deserves to be studied. Both its controversy and its

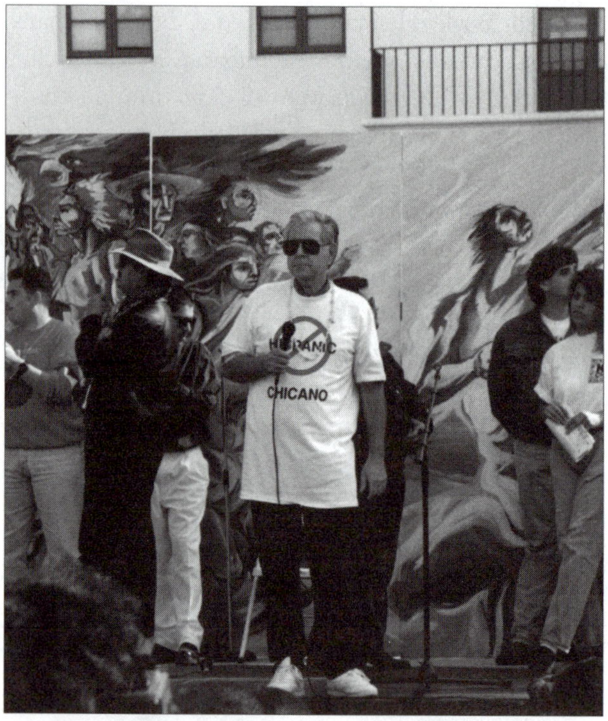

Chicano studies scholar Rodolfo Acuña (center, sunglasses) demonstrates against the University of California, Santa Barbara, in 1991 after he was denied a professorship. He sued the school for discrimination and won. *(Rodolfo F. Acuña Collection, 1816–2007. Urban Archives Center. Oviatt Library. California State University, Northridge)*

vitality lie in the fact that it presents Chicanos/as as the central focus of analysis rather than passive victims of circumstances.

Acuña was instrumental in establishing the Chicano studies department at California State University, Northridge (CSUN), which now offers both a Bachelor of Arts degree and a Master's degree in the field. The department is one of the largest of its kind, with twenty-two full-time teaching faculty. Acuña is noted for his unique methodological and theoretical approach to Chicano studies. The field, he has argued, is not merely about the struggles of Chicanos/as in the United States, but about the importance and possibility of enacting social change both in academia and in the community at large. Those who teach and study Chicano history and culture, he maintains, must devote their efforts to effecting changes in Chicano life. Chicano studies, according to Acuña, is a public trust: Those who teach it do so not for their own benefit, but to find ways to give something back to the community.

Although renowned for his academic accomplishments, Acuña has not escaped professional disappointment. In the 1980s, he was turned down for a position in Chicano studies at the University of California, Santa Barbara, despite his qualifications. With the help of the For Chicana/Chicano Studies Foundation, which has been influential in helping other Chicano studies professors with legal problems, he sued the university, alleging age and race discrimination. Although a jury ruled in Acuña's favor, the judge did not compel the university to hire him, but instead awarded him monetary damages.

Paul López

See also: Chicano Studies.

Further Reading

Acuña, Rodolfo. *A Community Under Siege: A Chronicle of Chicanos East of the Los Angeles River, 1945–1975.* Los Angeles: UCLA Chicano Studies Research Center, 1984.

———. *Anything but Mexican: Chicanos in Contemporary Los Angeles.* New York: Verso, 1996.

———. *Occupied America: A History of Chicanos.* 5th ed. New York: Pearson Longman, 2004.

———. *Sometimes There Is No Other Side: Chicanos and the Myth of Equality.* Notre Dame, IN: University of Notre Dame Press, 1998.

Afro-Latinos

The term "Afro-Latino" refers to people of African descent in both Latin America and the United States. In both areas, the use of the term is complicated by people's perception of themselves and their attitudes toward "race."

In Latin America, the distribution of Afro-Latinos reflects the history of African slavery throughout the region. Approximately 30 percent of all Latin Americans are of African ancestry, including 45 percent of Brazilians, 62 percent of Cubans, 84 percent of Dominicans, and 26 percent of Colombians. Afro-Latinos in Ecuador, Nicaragua, Peru, and Venezuela range from 5 to 10 percent of the national population.

Many Afro-descendants, however, do not identify themselves as such. A history of discrimination against darker-skinned Latin Americans has encouraged people to deny or downplay their African roots and regard lighter skin as more desirable. Also, Latin America has historically seen much more racial mixing than has the United States. This practice has resulted in a broader range of intermediary skin colors and physical features and the emergence of a variety of terms to describe people.

Because racial lines in Latin America are much more fluid than in the United States some have claimed that racial prejudice and discrimination are less severe. Despite the region's celebration of *mestizaje* (racial mixing), an examination of history and cultural practices demonstrates the privileging of "whiteness" in Latin America. During most of the twentieth century in Brazil, for instance, European immigration was encouraged to help "whiten" the population, and Brazilians spoke favorably of "improving the race" by marrying lighter-skinned partners. Throughout Latin America, Afro-descendants have remained poorer and less educated than their lighter-skinned counterparts.

Segregation laws are no longer in place in any Latin American countries, and the rights of Afro-descendants are recognized in most. Nevertheless, racial discrimination exists in institutions and social practices across the region, and antidiscrimination laws are often poorly enforced. Groups fighting to challenge the subordinate position of Afro-Latinos in Latin American countries have been able to bring national and international attention to their plight—and to achieve some material success in recent years. Colombia, for instance, now assigns seats in the House of Representatives to Afro-Colombian representatives, and Afro-Colombian history has been made a mandatory part of the school curriculum. Similarly, Brazil now mandates Afro-Brazilian history and has introduced affirmative action programs that include the use of quotas in the public university system. One outcome of the publicity and educational programs throughout the region has been a growing awareness and acknowledgment among Latin Americans of their African ancestry.

Because race is a cultural construct and not a biological reality, racial categories—and what are believed to be racially distinct groups—vary from one society to another. In Latin America, with its broad range of racial designations, a person of mixed African and European ancestry may be viewed as "white" or some intermediary term—such as *trigueño* (olive-skinned), *moreno* (brown-skinned), or mulatto (mixed)—depending on factors such as skin color, hair texture, social class, and occupation. In the United States however, with its binary black-white categories, that same person is typically considered "black."

This shift in perception is particularly troubling for darker-skinned Latinos/as who migrate to the United States and find themselves viewed as "black." In *Down These Mean Streets* (1967), the first widely read book on the Puerto Rican experience on the mainland, Piri Thomás describes his experience with this perception. After applying for a job and being been told there are no openings, he learns that a lighter-skinned Puerto Rican friend had been hired for the same position. Moreover, in Thomás's family, as in many Latino families, the range of variation in physical features also meant that his siblings—and mother—were not even considered of the same "race."

Given this history and experience, some Latinos/as in the United States are reluctant to be identified with "blackness." When asked their race in the 2000 U.S. Census, only 2.7 percent of "Hispanics"—or nearly 1 million—identified themselves as racially black, alone or in combination with some other race. Half of all U.S. Latinos/as indicated "white" on the census form, with Cubans being the most likely to do so (85 percent). Forty-seven percent of all Latinos/as, however, declared themselves to be "some other race" than black or white, typically writing in "Hispanic" or "Latino."

Latinos/as most likely to declare themselves black were Dominicans (12.7 percent) and Puerto Ricans (8.2 percent). New York City, with its large Puerto Rican and Dominican populations, had the highest share of Afro-Latinos (9.2 percent). Almost a quarter million Mexicans, migrating largely from Mexico's southern Costa Chica region since the 1980s, also checked off "black."

Self-declared Afro-Latinos differed demographically from those Latinos/as who checked off "white." They collectively had lower incomes and higher rates of poverty than other groups—despite having a higher level of education. They were also more likely to live in less integrated neighborhoods, and to be more segregated from whites than their "white" Latino counterparts.

Almost half of U.S. Afro-Latino children have a non-Latino black mother or father, pointing to the greater likelihood of crossing racial lines, particularly among Dominicans and Puerto Ricans. African-Americans and Afro-Caribbean populations share African cultural roots, which along with their close proximity in cities like New York have led to much cross-cultural sharing and syncretism. In fact, college courses often examine the shared African roots of New York's Puerto Ricans and Dominicans.

While Afro-Latinos struggle to straddle the main racial divide in the United States, they also represent, in important ways, both their Latin American past, with its racial intermingling, and perhaps a U.S. future in which racial lines may be less rigid.

Ellen Bigler

See also: Brazilians; Colombians; Cubans; Dominicans; Race; Thomás, Piri.

Further Reading

Flores, Juan. *From Bomba to Hip-Hop: Puerto Rican Culture and Latino Identity.* New York: Columbia University Press, 2000.

Thomás, Piri. *Down These Mean Streets.* 1967. New York: Vintage Books, 1997.

Afro-Mexicans

Afro-Mexicans (also widely referred to as *afro-mestizos*) are persons of Mexican descent with significant African ancestry. Intermarriage and amalgamation have occurred more extensively in Mexico than most other Latin American countries, producing a population that ranges in skin color from very light to very dark. A precise count of the Afro-Mexican population is difficult to determine, but most estimates place it at about 1 percent of the Mexican population, or about 10 million. Historically, Afro-Mexicans have been majorities in certain communities in Mexico; today, they are largely assimilated in the population of coastal states such as Guerrero, Oaxaca, Michoacán, Veracruz, Campeche, Quintana Roo, and Yucatán. In recent years, blacks who immigrated to Mexico from Caribbean countries such as Cuba or from various African nations as contract workers have added to the Afro-Mexican population.

History

During Spanish colonial rule in the sixteenth and seventeenth centuries, Mexico played a major role in the transatlantic slave trade. Between 1519 and 1650, approximately 120,000 African slaves were taken to Mexico, or about two-thirds of all slaves brought to Spain's colonies during this period. Roughly two-thirds of the slaves taken to Mexico were males, who comprised an important source of labor for the colonial Mexican economy. Male slaves were used primarily for mining, cattle ranching, and sugar plantation farming, although they performed a variety of other work as well. Female slaves served primarily as domestic servants. Historians estimate that, during the entire period of Spanish colonial rule (1519–1821), at least 200,000 African slaves were imported to Mexico.

Slaves in Mexico often experienced harsh and inhumane treatment at the hands of their masters, resulting in resistance on the part of slaves, including armed uprisings and rebellions. Between 1560 and 1580, there were several violent revolts among slaves who worked in mines or on sugar plantations, where the working conditions were the most brutal and dangerous. Some slaves managed to flee their owners, which led to the establishment of *palenques* (communities of runaway slaves) throughout the colony.

An additional form of slave resistance took root through exogamous marriages with Amerindians or Europeans. Marriages between African males and Indian females, and between Spanish males and African females, occurred with increasing frequency. The offspring of such unions were referred to as *zambos* and mulattos, respectively. According to Spanish law, children of slave mothers and free fathers were considered free upon birth and exempt from slavery. Although a child of a slave mother was technically born into slavery, the mere fact of having a free father enhanced one's chances of gaining freedom; this was particularly true after the Catholic Church pressured Spanish men to marry African women with whom they had engaged in sexual intercourse.

During the 1700s, colonial authorities sought to improve the defense of Mexico as fears of foreign attacks on the Spanish colonies intensified. Colonial law excused Indians from military service, but all other segments of the Mexican population (whites, mestizos, zambos, and mulattos) were required to serve if called upon. Large numbers of zambos and mulattos comprised militias in the areas surrounding Mexico City and the coastal regions of Eastern Mexico. Afromestizo soldiers played an important role in Mexico's struggle for independence against Spain, which was attained in 1821. An afromestizo general in the Mexican Revolution, Vicente Guerrero, went on to become the nation's second president.

Afro-Mexicans Today

Despite their prominence in Mexican history, afromestizos' presence in Mexican society and their contributions to it have remained largely unknown. The afromestizo heritage is generally overlooked in Mexican nationalist ideology, overshadowed by the indigenous and European elements of the nation's identity. Today the most prominent Afro-Mexican communities are found along the Pacific coast of southern Mexico in a region known as the Costa Chica. Advocacy groups in the Costa Chica, such as México Negro (Black Mexico), seek to raise afromestizo pride and increase understanding of the African influence in Mexico's history.

In recent decades there has been a sizable migration of afromestizos from the Costa Chica to California, Arizona, New Jersey, North Carolina, and New York City. The largest immigrant community is found in Winston-Salem, North Carolina, where Afro-Mexicans have found employment in construction, restaurants, and factories. Because of their physical appearance, immigrants from the Costa Chica are often mistaken for African Americans by white and black Americans, as well as other Mexicans.

Meanwhile, anthropologists and sociologists have begun to explore Mexico's African diaspora and culture in greater detail. Topics of interest include afromestizo identity, historical and contemporary relations between afromestizos and indigenous Mexicans, and the afromestizo influence on popular Mexican culture, such as music and dance.

Justin D. García

See also: Mexicans; Race.

Further Reading

Bennett, Herman L. *Africans in Colonial Mexico: Absolutism, Christianity, and Afro-Creole Consciousness, 1570–1640.* Bloomington: Indiana University Press, 2003.

Dzidzienyo, Anani, and Suzanne Oboler, eds. *Neither Enemies nor Friends: Latinos, Blacks, Afro-Latinos.* New York: Palgrave Macmillan, 2005.

AIDS/HIV

Acquired Immune Deficiency Syndrome (AIDS) has had a disproportionate impact on Latino communities as compared to its impact in other U.S. populations. Likewise, the diagnoses of the related human immunodeficiency virus (HIV) among Latinos/as have continued to rise in recent years while those among non-Latino whites have decreased. For Latino men in their mid-thirties to forties, AIDS represents one of the leading causes of death. And while advances in treatment have served many HIV carriers in the United States, Latinos/as have consistently suffered inordinately. At the same time, compared with other groups, Latinos/as have routinely experienced barriers to care. Consequently, activists have exerted pressure to address the specific needs of Latino communities through education and other resources, and Latino AIDS organizations have helped address the need for treatment and care within the community.

Facts and Figures

For the period 2001–2005, Latinos/as accounted for 19 percent of new HIV/AIDS diagnoses in the United States, while constituting only 14 percent of the total national population; non-Latino blacks accounted for 51 percent and non-Latino whites accounted for 29 percent. By the end of 2005, a total of more than

77,000 Latinos/as had died from the disease. According to the Centers for Disease Control (CDC), the proportion of new AIDS diagnoses among Latinos/as has also risen over the course of the epidemic, from 15 percent in 1985 to 20 percent in 2005. Moreover, HIV-positive Latinos/as are more likely than African Americans or whites to have their HIV infection turn into AIDS within a twelve-month period; as of 2004, Latinos/as represented 43 percent of the cases in which HIV-positive status became an AIDS diagnosis within one year's time. By the end of 2005, an estimated 78,054 Latinos/as were living with AIDS, or about one-fifth of all people in the United States with the diagnosis. Of the total number of pediatric AIDS cases in 2005, almost 20 percent were among Latino children.

While AIDS prevalence increased 20 percent among non-Latino whites between 2001 and 2005, it rose 31 percent among Latinos/as during the same period. In 2005, the rate of AIDS cases per 100,000 population among Latinos/as was 3.5 times that of whites (but only about one-third that of African Americans). Among U.S. cities, New York City accounts for approximately 7 percent of the U.S. Latino population but 25 percent of all Latino AIDS cases; of those cases, 35 percent are among Latinas. By virtually any measure, then, Latinos/as in the United States have been disproportionately affected by the HIV/AIDS epidemic, accounting for a greater—and growing—percentage of AIDS cases and deaths than their percentage of the national population.

Transmission

Among Latino men, HIV transmission patterns differ from those of non-Latino white men, although both groups are most likely to be infected through sex with other men. In the case of white men, 72 percent of AIDS cases from 2001 to 2005 resulted from sex with other men, compared to 50 percent in the case of Latino men. On the other hand, injection drug use and heterosexual sex represent a greater share of new AIDS diagnoses among Latino men (28 percent and 17 percent, respectively) than among non-Latino white men (12 percent and 6 percent). From 2001 to 2005, non-Latina white women were slightly more likely to have been infected by injection drug use than Latinas (38 percent for non-Latina white women and 26 percent for Latinas). And while heterosexual sex is the most common mode of transmission for both Latinas and non-Latina white women, Latinas are slightly more likely than non-Latina white women to have been infected through heterosexual sex (71 percent of AIDS diagnoses among Latinas from 2001 to 2005, and 59 percent of diagnoses among white women). Among men who have had sex with men (MSM), Latinos have been especially affected. In major U.S. cities, the percentage of Latino MSM ages 23 to 29 already infected with HIV was approximately 15 percent in 2005, compared to 9 percent of non-Latino white MSM.

Barriers to Care

While advances in treatment have benefited many HIV carriers in the United States, certain groups have consistently lagged behind. These include people of color, women, immigrants, and the poor. Within these groups, Latinos/as are said to face specific socioeconomic and cultural barriers that limit access to preventive services and therapies. Poverty and lack of health insurance, in particular, are common barriers for many Latinos/as. Compared with other U.S. populations, Latinos/as are poorer and disproportionately underinsured at all income levels. It is estimated that more than 80 percent of Latinas and 50 percent of Latino men with AIDS have household incomes of under $10,000. In turn, poverty affects the quality of available health care; this is especially true for those living outside urban centers, since poor Latinos/as who otherwise qualify for government assistance programs are restricted from accessing care from HIV specialists. Even in states with AIDS Drug Assistance Programs (ADAPS), which help people who do not qualify for Medicaid, there are long waiting lists that severely undermine access to care for those who might benefit from drug-related therapies. Many Latinos/as report postponing care, even when it is otherwise available, due to lack of transportation.

In addition, many Latinos/as experience barriers involving language, immigration status, and economic oppression. Many simply do not know where or how to access care, while others are excluded from the system and unsure of their rights. The Latino Commission on AIDS estimates that language barriers set many Latinos/as back at least a year from accessing combination therapies after protease inhibitors—a highly effective drug treatment—were first introduced to the market in the 1990s, citing lack of information available in Spanish. Even when money or language barriers are not a problem, there is a related obstacle to treatment in the form of suspicion of government-sponsored programs on the part of many Latinos/as. Thus, more often than African Americans or non-Latino whites, Latinos/as are more likely to self-treat with over-the-counter medications and less likely to obtain information from professional health-care providers, relying instead on familiar and traditional alternatives from their own communities. Homeopathic therapies are considered particularly risky, since little is known about their use in the treatment of AIDS.

Also relevant to health-care access for Latinos/as is the fact that Catholic tradition, predominant in Latino culture, makes the open discussion of sexuality difficult for many. Taboo topics commonly include homosexuality, extramarital sex, and the use of condoms. Due to a relative lack of discussion regarding these issues, and given their relevance to the spread of HIV/AIDS, family members may not know that they are at risk for HIV infection. Moreover, these factors often lead to a late diagnosis of HIV/AIDS. Latinos/as are frequently diagnosed only after becoming very ill and seeking emergency care. In terms of self-reporting, Latinos/as are more likely than whites to report ever having been tested for HIV (53 percent compared to 44 percent); these rates may be overestimates, however, because 22 percent of Latinos/as assumed that an HIV test was a routine part of a health exam. Because of the various barriers to health care among Latinos/as, treatment educators at the grassroots level are pressing for HIV education materials in Spanish and encouraging frank discussions of sexuality.

Latinas

Women in general, and Latinas specifically, defer treatment longer than men and are offered treatment much later in the course of the disease. Part of the explanation for this may lie in the fact that women have learned to accept a different health standard than men. That is, if they are able to wake up, care for their children, and go to work, then women generally consider themselves healthy. Even when Latinas are taking the latest available drugs, they are more likely to be taking them to sustain their families than for their own individual gain. Thus, activists have made the case that HIV education should consider treatment issues in a comprehensive way and develop family models with integrated services that address the specific needs of women.

Immigrants and Special Hurdles

Legally, social activists have long pushed for increased rights for immigrants with HIV. Among Latinos/as, at least 6 percent of those accessing health care for HIV/AIDS are immigrants. The United States maintains a ban prohibiting people with HIV from entering the country, except under special circumstances. Other policies that operate at the state level, such as the reporting of people who test positive for HIV and the mandatory testing of pregnant women, keep many immigrants from getting a test or seeking care for the disease. Many immigrants fear being deported, even though health-care providers are not legally obligated to report anyone to the Immigration and Naturalization Service.

For immigrants, documented or undocumented status can determine if, when, and how they may access care for HIV. Without the required documents, immigrants find it hard to qualify for public assistance programs. Under the Ryan White CARE Act (1990), access to assistance was expanded to include HIV-positive patients regardless of citizenship status. Federal AIDS Drug Assistance Programs, for example, help to pay for HIV medications and primary HIV care and do not require proof of citizenship. Still, activists argue that the ability to reach a service provider is restricted and encourage health care providers to care for undocumented migrants.

Activism and Education

Within Latino communities, there are several noteworthy national and regional organizations that focus on HIV/AIDS activism and education. The leading national organization is the Latino Commission on

AIDS, a nonprofit membership group dedicated to promoting health, research, treatment, and other services to Latino communities. Minority Health Care Communications, Inc. (MHCC) is a nonprofit national health organization that specializes in conferences, seminars, and workshops regarding HIV/AIDS and cancer in the African American and Latino communities. MHCC hosts an annual conference, the National Conference on Latinos and AIDS, which serves health professionals who provide care for Latinos/as; the conference is organized to update the knowledge and skills of health providers for patients with HIV/AIDS. Another significant annual event is National Latino AIDS Awareness Day (NLAAD), first held on October 15, 2003. NLAAD is recognized by national, regional, and local HIV/AIDS groups, state health organizations and faith-based organizations, as well as the National Institute of Allergy and Infectious Diseases (part of the National Institutes of Health). In connection with NLAAD, local Latino AIDS education providers organize diverse activities, including HIV testing fairs and candlelight vigils, to recognize the state of HIV/AIDS among Latinos/as.

Another notable national project is the Prevenir es Vivir (To Prevent is to Live) national poster campaign. Prevenir es Vivir aims to promote health education for Latinos/as regarding HIV/AIDS and targets traditionally hard-to-reach audiences by using posters, community art, public radio, and the Internet to provide access to lifesaving information regarding HIV/AIDS. The Prevenir es Vivir Web site offers health education and discussion concerning safe sexual practices and the prevention of HIV/AIDS.

Regional and local organizations of note include Latinos/as Contra SIDA, Inc. (Latinos/as Against AIDS), based in Hartford, Connecticut. Latinos/as Contra SIDA (LCS) is a nonprofit organization founded in 1986; its slogan is "¡Porque el SIDA nos afecta a todos!" ("Because AIDS affects us all!"). LCS has a strong history of advocating for culturally appropriate programs aimed at slowing the spread of HIV among Latinos/as, and it offers a comprehensive array of services to Latinos/as in the Hartford area.

Progreso Latino, located in Central Falls, Rhode Island, works to coordinate statewide participation in National Latino AIDS Awareness Day. Events organized by Progreso Latino both celebrate the lives of those who have died of AIDS and offer hope to those living with HIV/AIDS. Progreso Latino works in conjunction with NLAAD to produce radio programs and newspaper articles designed to broaden awareness of HIV/AIDS, specifically among Latinos/as.

In the greater Philadelphia area, Esperanza USA is geared primarily to Jewish and Latino communities and provides faith-based support for those living with HIV/AIDS. The organization disseminates HIV/AIDS information to Latino communities in the area and specifically addresses the misconception that HIV/AIDS is a white, gay disease; that misunderstanding has contributed to the high infection and mortality rates in communities of color.

Many other organizations and agencies in urban centers across the United States serve Latinos/as in the fight against HIV/AIDS. Among them are Project Inform in San Francisco; Bronx AIDS Services (BAS) and Queens Pride House (QPH) in New York City; and Mujeres Unidas Contra el SIDA (Women United Against AIDS) in San Antonio, Texas. Most organizations and agencies serving Latinos/as, like many other nonprofit groups, face severe budget constraints and other operational challenges. The largest national organization serving gay Latinos/as, LLEGÓ, formerly located in Washington, D.C., closed its office in August 2003 because of insufficient financial resources. Even more than "mainstream" HIV/AIDS-oriented service organizations, those serving communities of color often exist in a state of peril. All the same, the fact that a number of such organizations have been able to render services since the onset of the HIV/AIDS epidemic in the United States suggests an encouraging resilience in these groups.

Latino communities themselves are making important strides in the fight against HIV/AIDS. As the U.S. Latino population continues to grow, however, it remains to be seen whether government agencies and mainstream organizations will meet their responsibilities in the areas of Latino-specific education, equal access to treatment, and the benefits of quality and affordable health care.

Mary K. Bloodsworth-Lugo

See also: Gay and Lesbian Organizations; Health and Health Care; LLEGÓ.

Further Reading

Centers for Disease Control and Prevention. "HIV/AIDS among Hispanics/Latinos." http://www.cdc.gov/hiv/resources/factsheets/hispanic.htm.

———. "HIV/AIDS Among Hispanics—United States, 2001–2005." *MMWR: Morbidity and Mortality Weekly Report.* 56:40 (October 12, 2007): 1052–57.

Klevens, R.M., T. Diaz, P.L. Fleming, M.A. Mays, and R. Frey. "Trends in AIDS among Hispanics in the United States, 1991–1996." *American Journal of Public Health* 89:7 (1999): 1104–6.

Latino Commission on AIDS. http://latinoaids.org.

Marin, Barbara, and Gerardo Marin. "Effects of Acculturation on Knowledge of AIDS and HIV among Hispanics." *Hispanic Journal of Behavioral Sciences* 12:2 (1990): 110–21.

National Minority AIDS Council. http://www.nmac.org.

Prevenir es Vivir. http://www.contrasida.org.

Alamo, Battle of the

The Battle of the Alamo, a thirteen-day siege and military confrontation in the Texas Revolution, began on February 23, 1836, and ended on March 6, 1836, at a former Spanish mission known as San Antonio de Valero in the Mexican state of Coahuila y Texas. Defending Mexican territory against independence-seeking Texians (Anglo-American residents) and their Tejano (residents of Hispanic descent) allies, some 6,000 Mexican soldiers under the command of the nation's president, General Antonio López de Santa Anna, laid siege to the mission where the rebel forces had withdrawn. Mexican forces finally broke through and succeeded in killing virtually all the rebels while retaking the mission. Although the battle had little strategic value for either side, the events leading up to it, the battle itself, and the aftermath exposed the volatile race and class tensions between Mexicans, Tejanos, and Euro-Americans; affected diplomatic relations and policy between Mexico and the United States; and ultimately led to the Mexican-American War (1846–1847), in which Mexico lost half its territory.

U.S. Expansion and Border Disputes

U.S. interests in Spanish lands began as early as 1767, when Benjamin Franklin identified Mexico and Cuba as future sites of U.S. expansion. Filibustering expeditions, border disputes, and offers by the United States to buy Texas soon brought the countries into conflict. The Adams-Onís Treaty of 1819 was an attempt to resolve the border dispute between the United States and Spain by establishing the line between the two nations (along the Sabine River in Texas, north to the Rocky Mountains, and west from there to the Pacific Ocean) and transferring Spanish Florida to the United States; in exchange, the United States would renounce its claim on other parts of Texas and Spanish territory. Many North Americans, however, continued to claim Texas as part of the United States and argued that the Río Grande was the border. The dispute continued once Mexico freed itself from Spanish rule in 1821. Five years later, President John Quincy Adams offered to buy Texas for $1 million; in 1830, President Andrew Jackson offered $5 million.

Background

A civil war and the vastness and distance of Coahuila y Texas made it difficult for the Mexican government to protect and govern its northern land. Moreover, the increasing number of Euro-American immigrants who did not obey the guidelines set forth by the Mexican government created animosity between Mexicans and settlers, as the immigrants squatted illegally in the area. By the 1830s, Euro-American immigrants outnumbered Mexicans by ten to one.

In 1824, the Mexican Republic adopted its first constitution, regarded as a victory for the *federalistas* (federalists) who promoted states rights, Euro-American colonization, and economic growth. The constitution granted states the right to colonize their lands and instituted the *empresario* system (relying on contracted land agents) as the official colonization policy. The constitution also allowed Euro-American immigrants to settle the state of Coahuila y Texas as long as they became Roman Catholic, pledged their allegiance to the Mexican government, and obeyed Mexican law. Slavery was vaguely condemned, but individual states were allowed to implement their own policies concerning the institution. However, the quick turnover in Mexico's governing party created discontent with Mexican policy among Texians and their Tejano allies. In September 1829, Mexican

President Vicente Guerrero angered colonists by nullifying states' rights. He also freed all slaves, but Texas managed an exemption. Later in 1833, General Antonio López de Santa Anna came to power and overturned the Constitution of 1824, further angering Texians and increasing their desire for separation from Mexico.

In 1828, Manuel Mier y Téran, the head of Mexico's boundary commission, toured the Mexico-Texas frontier, assessing the threat from Native American and Euro-American populations in the area. He warned the Mexican government of a restless political atmosphere, and proposed that it take control of the situation by halting Euro-American colonization and flooding the area with Mexican and European settlers. He also proposed that Mexican troops be sent into the area and that commercial relations between Texas and Mexico be increased to disrupt the economic ties between Texas and the United States. The Mexican government implemented Mier y Téran's recommendations, adding a provision that no new slaves could be brought into the area. This policy, known as the Law of April 6, 1830, heightened tensions between Texians and Mexico.

Texas's wealthy slave-owning class and slave traders argued that the law violated their personal liberties. Since the onset of colonization, Euro-Americans had migrated with their slaves, consistently lobbying in Saltillo, the capital of Coahuila y Texas, and in Mexico City to protect slavery. Slave owners, using any means to protect their way of life, resorted to "freeing" their slaves and then forcing them to sign lifelong indentured servant contracts.

In October 1833, Mexican authorities arrested an American empresario, Stephen F. Austin, for sedition; he had written a note to the San Antonio municipal government urging it to declare Texas a separate state. Austin's ambitions in Texas began much earlier in 1821 when he inherited a land grant to settle 300 families in the area. Upon release from prison on July 13, 1835, Austin again stressed the need for a free Texas.

Fighting Begins

On October 2, 1835, Mexican forces marched into Texas and asked Texians in Gonzales to return a cannon that the Mexican government had given to the people years before. Texians draped the cannon with a banner that read "Come and Take It" and used the weapon to defend themselves. The Mexican troops withdrew without the cannon, but the skirmish officially brought the two sides into conflict.

The insurgents in Gonzales nominated Austin as commander of the Army of the People. Made up of both Texians and Tejanos, the army was determined to oust Mexican forces and create an independent Texas. After defeating Mexican forces near the Purísima Concepción mission, insurgents met on November 3 and declared an independent Texas, establishing a temporary government and an army. The insurgents also promised soldiers land in return for their service, elected War Party leader Henry Smith as governor, and appointed war hero and former governor of Tennessee Sam Houston as major general. Later that year, the Army of the People forced Mexican General Martín Perfecto de Cos and his troops to retreat out of San Antonio de Béxar and south of the Río Grande. It was clear to Santa Anna that Mexico could not control Texas as long as Euro-American colonists continued to settle in the area.

Siege and Battle

On February 16, 1836, Santa Anna crossed the Río Grande. He trekked toward San Antonio de Béxar not only to seek revenge for General Cos and his men, but also to reclaim Mexican land from political insurgents. Although the size of his Army of Operations caused alarm for the insurgents, many of his troops were ill prepared. Some had been forced into the army, which marched hundreds of miles from the interior of Mexico in harsh and unpredictable weather. Malnutrition and dehydration were not uncommon, and some men died of dysentery and other illnesses. Among the troops were Mayan Indians who did not understand their Spanish-speaking commanding officers. Escape attempts were common.

Santa Anna's military advisers recommended that he take the town of Goliad because it would give Mexican forces access to the coastline. But Santa Anna insisted on taking Béxar, at the center of Texas politics; capturing it, he maintained, would declare his intention of crushing insurgent resistance. On

February 23, the Mexican forces arrived in San Antonio de Béxar and immediately observed the insurgents' flag. In response, General Santa Anna raised a red flag bearing a skull and crossbones, indicating that he would have no mercy for insurgents and traitors who opposed the Mexican government. Those inside the Alamo responded with cannon blast.

The 150 men who took refuge in the Alamo were a divided lot: some believed they were fighting a war for independence against a tyrannical Mexican government; others believed that it was their destiny to save Texas from Mexicans; some, with no political inclinations, simply got caught in the fervor. Some believed they were like the American patriots who had fought against the British, while others fought to protect their economic and personal interests, whether land, slaves, or political gain. Volunteers like William Barret Travis had abandoned his pregnant wife and child, and was in Texas looking for a new meaning in his life. David Crockett, after losing his bid for a fourth term in Congress, went to Texas and fought in hopes of refreshing his celebrity and political career. Many Tejanos remained loyal to their Texian allies; the list of Tejano volunteers included Juan Abamillo, Juan Antonio Badillo, and José Esparza.

Mexican forces believed that defeating the men in the Alamo would be easy. The mission building was in no condition to withstand cannon fire, and the food and supplies in the garrison would run out soon enough. Travis pleaded to General Houston to send reinforcements, but he was skeptical of the wisdom of fighting that particular battle. On March 1, a small group of reinforcements arrived under the direction of Lieutenant George C. Kimball, but they were not enough to defeat the Mexican forces. Again, Travis pleaded to Houston and the Texas government to send help. Houston though, was delayed by a Texian convention at Washington-on-the-Brazos, where on March 2 they declared Texas's independence.

On March 6, Santa Anna launched a frontal assault on the Alamo and finally defeated the Alamo fighters. He ordered that all defenders of the Alamo be executed, sparing the lives of only a few women and children. The final list of casualties included more than 200 Alamo fighters and as many as 600 Mexican soldiers. Later that month, Mexican troops went on to defeat Texian forces near Goliad, where Santa Anna ordered that all prisoners be executed.

On April 21, 1836, at the Battle of San Jacinto, the Mexican Army was finally defeated and Santa Anna captured. In exchange for his release, the Mexican leader signed a peace treaty that ensured the independence of Texas.

Results of the Battle

After the battles of the Alamo and Goliad, the United States contributed massive aid and weapons to Texians so that they could engage in war with Mexico. Thousands of volunteers rallied under the war cries "Remember the Alamo!" and "Remember Goliad!" For Mexicans and their allies, the Battle of the Alamo symbolized U.S. aggression and expansion. For Texians and their allies, it symbolized a fight against Mexican cruelty and a tyrannical government. In any event, the battle brought to the fore the deep racial and class divisions between Tejanos and Euro-Americans and between Texians and Mexicans. Tejanos lost most of their lands and political influence in the area. A social hierarchy was created in which Mexicans, regardless of place of birth, were forced to occupy an inferior position in the United States. After the battle and to the present day, the national myth of the Alamo justifies the occupation of Mexico by ignoring Texian and U.S. aggression, exaggerates Mexican cruelty, and embellishes the deeds of the Alamo defenders.

Jennifer R. Mata

See also: Mexican-American War; Mexicans; Tejanos.

Further Reading

Davis, William C. *Lone Star Rising: The Revolutionary Birth of the Texas Republic.* New York: Free Press, 2004.

Hardin, Stephen. *The Alamo 1836: Santa Anna's Texas Campaign.* Westport, CT: Praeger, 2004.

Montejano, David. *Anglos and Mexicans in the Making of Texas, 1836–1986.* Austin: University of Texas Press, 1987.

Roberts, Randy, and James S. Olson. *A Line in the Sand: The Alamo in Blood and Memory.* New York: Touchstone, 2001.

Romero, Rolando J. "The Alamo, Slavery, and the Politics of Memory." In *Decolonial Voices: Chicana and Chicano Cultural Studies in the 21st Century,* ed. Arturo J. Aldama and Naomi H. Quiñonez. Bloomington: Indiana University Press, 2002.

Albizu Campos, Pedro (1891–1965)

Pedro Albizu Campos was an activist leader and influential spokesman for the cause of Puerto Rican independence. In 1930 he became president of the Puerto Rican Nationalist Party, which was later implicated in a number of violent acts against U.S. authorities—including an assassination attempt against President Harry S. Truman and an armed attack on the U.S. House of Representatives. As head of the party, Albizu Campos was charged with twelve counts of sedition and sentenced to a long prison term. Known as "el Maestro" (the Teacher), Albizu Campos was an inspirational speaker whose memory is beloved among many Puerto Ricans, even though his following was relatively small.

Puerto Rican nationalist Pedro Albizu Campos was jailed in 1950 (among other times) on charges of masterminding the November 1 assassination attempt against President Harry S. Truman at Blair House in Washington, D.C. *(George Silk/Stringer/Time & Life Pictures/Getty Images)*

Origins and Upbringing

Albizu Campos was born on September 12, 1891, in Tenerías Village, Ponce, Puerto Rico. He was the child of Alejandro Albizu and Juana Campos and the nephew of Juan Morel Campos, a famous composer of *danzas,* the classical music of Puerto Rico. In 1912, Pedro Albizu Campos was awarded a scholarship to study chemistry at the University of Vermont and a year later entered Harvard University, where he went on to earn a law degree. While at Harvard, he also studied English literature, philosophy, chemical engineering, and military science, and learned to speak fluently in English, French, German, Portuguese, Italian, Latin, and Greek. His studies were interrupted by the outbreak of World War I, however, and Albizu Campos entered the U.S. Army as a second lieutenant assigned to an African American regiment. This first sustained exposure to American racism helped mold his attitude toward the United States and its relations with what he consistently referred to as the motherland, Puerto Rico.

After the war, Albizu Campos returned to Harvard, where, having met the future Indian nationalist leader Subhas Chandra Bose and the Hindu poet Rabindranath Tagore, he became interested in the cause of Indian independence. Also during his years at Harvard, Albizu Campos helped establish several centers in Boston for Irish independence and, having met Eamon de Valera, helped draft the constitution for the Irish Free State. In 1922, he married the Peruvian scholar and scientist Laura Meneses. Upon obtaining his law degree, he declined a clerkship on the U.S. Supreme Court and a place in the U.S. diplomatic corps, choosing to return to Puerto Rico to take up the causes of the poor and disaffected.

Activism

In 1922, Albizu Campos joined the Puerto Rican Union Party (Pardito Union de Puerto Rico), which supported greater self-government for Puerto Rico but was divided between those that supported U.S. statehood and those that desired independence. When, in 1924, the Union Party merged with the Republican Party and decided not to pursue Puerto Rican independence, Albizu Campos ended his affiliation with the former and joined the Partido Nacionalista de Puerto Rico (Nationalist Party), which had formed in 1912 to liberate Puerto Rico. Albizu Campos became vice president of the party, traveling to different countries in Latin America seeking solidarity for the Puerto Rican independence movement. In 1930, he was elected president of the Nationalist Party and formed the first women's branch of the party, the Las Hijas de Libertad (Daughters of Freedom). Members of the Daughters of Freedom included the poet Julia de Burgos, the writer and educator Margot Arce de Vázquez, and Olga Viscal Garriga, who became a student leader and spokesperson of the Nationalist Party branch in Rio Piedras.

During his presidency, in 1932, Albizu Campos published a manuscript in which he accused the Rockefeller Institute for Medical Research of deliberately infecting several Puerto Rican citizens with cancer and causing the deaths of thirteen. Cornelius Rhoads, the chief pathologist who conducted the cancer experiments in San Juan, Puerto Rico for the New York–based institute, admitted to the charge, stating that "Porto Ricans [*sic*] are the dirtiest, laziest, most degenerate and thievish race of men ever to inhabit this sphere." The following year, Albizu Campos led a strike against the Puerto Rico Railway and Light and Power Company to oppose its alleged monopoly on the island. In 1934, he successfully represented oppressed sugarcane workers against the U.S. sugar industry in their fight for better working conditions.

In 1935, police under the command of Colonel E. Francis Riggs killed four nationalists at the University of Río Piedras. The following year, nationalists Hiram Rosado and Elias Beauchamp exacted revenge by killing Riggs. Rosado and Beauchamp were arrested and executed without a trial, causing Albizu Campos to publicly declare them martyrs and heroes. In the aftermath, the San Juan Federal Court ordered the arrest of Albizu Campos and several other nationalists for seditious conspiracy to overthrow the U.S. government in Puerto Rico. In 1937, after a trial dominated by North American jurors, Albizu Campos was found guilty and sentenced to ten years' imprisonment at a federal penitentiary in the United States.

In 1947 Albizu Campos returned to Puerto Rico where, according to the Federal Bureau of Investigation (FBI), he was believed to be preparing—along with other members of the Nationalist Party—for an armed struggle against the proposed plans to change Puerto Rico's political status to a commonwealth of the United States. He was jailed after a group of Puerto Rican nationalists stormed La Fortaleza—the mansion of Governor José Luis Muñoz Marín, founder of the Popular Democratic Party—on October 30, 1950. Two days later, nationalists attacked Blair House in Washington, D.C., where President Harry S. Truman had been in residence while the White House was under repair, in an attempt to assassinate him. Albizu Campos was charged with masterminding the attacks and sentenced to eighty years in prison.

In 1953, Governor Muñoz Marín pardoned Albizu Campos; however, the pardon was revoked the following year after a nationalist attack on the U.S. House of Representatives. On March 1, 1954, four Puerto Rican nationalists fired into the gallery of the Capitol Building in Washington, D.C., wounding five members of Congress in an effort to attract international attention to their cause. While in prison, Albizu Campos repeatedly charged that he was a target of human radiation experiments. U.S. officials and the mainland and island press dismissed the allegations as the ravings of a madman, although his attendants reported that burns on his skin were indeed consistent with radiation exposure. Albizu Campos's allegations were never proven, but in 1995 the U.S. Department of Energy disclosed that prisoners had been the subject of human radiation experiments without their consent from the 1950s through the 1970s.

By 1964, Albizu Campos was partially paralyzed from a stroke. With Albizu Campos's death imminent and under international pressure, Governor Muñoz Marín pardoned the leader a second time, and he was released from prison. Shortly thereafter, on April 21, 1965, Albizu Campos died in Hato Rey, Puerto Rico.

Victor Villanueva

See also: Nationalism; Puerto Ricans.

Further Reading

Ribes Tovar, Frederico. *Albizu Campos: Puerto Rican Revolutionary.* New York: Plus Ultra, 1971.

Wagenheim, Kal, and Olga Jiménez deWagenheim, eds. *The Puerto Ricans: A Documentary History.* Princeton, NJ: Markus Weiner, 2002.

Algarín, Miguel (1941–)

Miguel Algarín, a Puerto Rican professor of English, poet, writer, and editor, is most widely known as the founder of the Nuyorican (New York–Puerto Rican) Poets Café in New York City. An emeritus professor at Rutgers University, in New Jersey, where he taught Shakespeare, American literature, and creative writing for more than thirty years, he is also the recipient of three American Book Awards as well as the Larry Leon Hamlin Producer's Award at the 2001 National Black Theatre Festival.

Born on September 11, 1941, in Puerto Rico, Algarín came to the United States at age nine and received his elementary and high school education in New York City. His family's values centered on culture, literature, and storytelling, and this influenced his personal and professional pursuits. Graduating from the University of Wisconsin in 1963 with a Bachelor of Arts degree in Romance Languages, he went on to receive a Master of Arts in English Literature from Pennsylvania State University. At Rutgers, he received his doctorate and eventually became head of the Puerto Rican studies program. During the course of his education, he became especially interested in the works of William Shakespeare. His love of Shakespeare's stories about England inspired him to create a place where he, like Shakespeare, could tell stories of his roots. Thus was born the Nuyorican Poets Café.

In 1973, Algarín and his friends—poets, playwrights, and other writers—would gather in his apartment in New York City's East Village to share their writings. The sessions soon became so popular that his apartment could no longer accommodate all the people who attended, and in 1974 Algarín began looking for a more a suitable place to hold the gatherings. Algarín and his friend, the playwight Miguel Piñero (best known for the 1974 Tony Award–winning play *Short Eyes*) rented space in an Irish bar, the Sunshine Cafe, on East Sixth Street, in a heavily Latino neighborhood known as Loisaida.

Loisaida, the Spanglish term for the area on and around Avenue C on the Lower East Side, was home to a largely minority population (Dominicans, Puerto Ricans, and African Americans, among others), many of whom were no strangers to economic and social privation. It was in this atmosphere and for this community that Algarín established his new venue for the sharing of poetry and Puerto Rican culture, the Nuyorican Poets Café. The community of poets and playwrights who frequented the café became part of a growing movement to raise awareness about Puerto Rican culture in New York.

In 1980, Algarín purchased a building on East Third Street to expand the facility. The café became increasingly popular over the years, emerging as a widely respected arts organization and featuring not only poetry recitations, but also prose readings, theatrical performances, musical performances (including rap and hip-hop), and visual arts exhibits. Some of the more widely known Nuyorican poets include Victor Hernández Cruz and Tato Laviera. It has contributed significantly to the growing phenomenon of "slam" poetry (competitive events in which poets perform their pieces live and are judged by audience members picked at random). The only surviving original member of the café, Algarín has served as its president and the longtime radio host of its live broadcasts on WBAI.

In addition to being an academic, a founder of the Nuyorican Poet's Café, and an accomplished poet in his own right, Algarín has edited a number of published collections, including *Nuyorican Poetry: An Anthology of Puerto Rican Words and Feeling* (1975, with Piñero), *Action: The Nuyorican Cafe Theatre Festival* (1997), and *Aloud: Voices from the Nuyorican Poets Cafe* (1994). His original writings include *Mongo Affair* (1985), *Love Is Hard Work: Memorias de Loisaida* (1997), *Body Bee Calling from the Twenty-First Century* (1982), *Time Is Now* (1982), *Time's Now/Ya Es Tiempo* (1985), and *On Call* (1994). He also has written several plays produced in New York and has translated Pablo Neruda's *Song of Protest* (1994).

Nicole Martone

See also: Nuyorican Poets Café; Puerto Rican Literature.

Further Reading

Eleveld, Mark, ed. *The Spoken Word Revolution: Slam, Hip-Hop & the Poetry of a New Generation.* Naperville, IL: Sourcebooks MediaFusion, 2003.

Silén, Iván, ed. *Los paraguas amarillos/los poetas latinos en New York.* Binghamton, NY: Bilingual Review, 1983.

Alvarez, Julia (1950–)

Hailed by critics as one of the best of contemporary Latina writers, Julia Alvarez has appealed to Latino readers with themes of biculturalism and identity yet has succeeded in attracting a diverse mainstream audience as well. In addition to winning a devoted readership and major awards for her works of fiction, she has found success as a poet, nonfiction writer, and author of children's books.

Julia Alvarez was born in New York City on March 27, 1950. Three months later, her family returned to their native country, the Dominican Republic, where Alvarez lived until the age of ten, witnessing the country's repressive political and economic system. Actively involved in the Dominican political scene, her family supported a rebel group seeking to overthrow the dictator Rafael Trujillo. The political turmoil finally forced Alvarez's family to flee the Dominican Republic in 1960. They relocated to New York City, where her father worked as a doctor and her mother raised Julia and her sisters.

Alvarez's interest in writing took hold while she was in high school. She further developed her skills while attending Connecticut College, where she won the Benjamin T. Marshall Prize in poetry in both 1968 and 1969. After two years in Connecticut, she transferred to Middlebury College in Vermont, where she studied literature and writing, graduating summa cum laude in 1971.

Alvarez's poetry soon captured the attention of critics, and in 1974 she was named the winner of the American Academy of Poetry Prize. After obtaining her master's degree from Syracuse University the following year, Alvarez sought out a new experience and moved to Kentucky, where she served as writer-in-residence for the Kentucky Arts Commission's school poetry program until 1977. She then engaged in projects associated with the National Endowment for the Arts and taught English and creative writing at Phillips Andover Academy, a college preparatory school in Massachusetts, from 1979 to 1981.

Advancing her career as an English teacher, Alvarez successively joined the faculties of the University of Vermont (1981–1983), George Washington University (1984–1985), the University of Illinois (Urbana-Champaign) (1985–1988), and finally her alma mater, Middlebury College (1988–). At the same time, she brought together the experiences and observations of her own life in her first published collection of poetry, titled *Homecoming,* in 1984. The work features Alvarez's insights into such matters as work, personal relationships, household tasks, and the desire to marry—a hope that became a reality five years later, in 1989, when she married Bill Eichner.

In 1991, Alvarez garnered critical acclaim for her first published novel, *How the García Girls Lost Their Accents,* which was selected as an American Library Association Notable Book and won the prestigious PEN Oakland/Josephine Miles Award. This work recounts the stories of a Dominican family who migrate to the United States and chronicles their efforts to adapt to American culture. Critics also praised Alvarez's second novel, *In the Time of the Butterflies* (1994), which is a fictionalized account of the Mirabal sisters, rebel supporters who were assassinated in 1960 during the Trujillo regime. The work was chosen as a finalist for the National Book Critics Award. The next year, she returned to poetry with her second published collection, *The Other Side/El Otro Lado,* which focuses on her experiences and dual identity as a Dominican and an American.

In her third novel, *¡Yo!* (1997), Alvarez continues the story of one of the characters in *How the García Girls Lost Their Accent.* The nonfiction work *Something to Declare* (1998) further examines her experiences of adjusting to life in the United States while still balancing her Dominican identity. Like several of her fictional characters, Alvarez finds that maintaining a balance between one's cultural identity and life in a new home is a complicated and often difficult matter. *In the Name of Salomé* (2000) was cited by critics as a poignant story about a family living in the Dominican Republic.

Alvarez turned her attentions to children's literature in 2000, publishing *The Secret Footprints,* followed the next year by *How Tia Lola Came to Stay,* about the changes in a young boy after his aunt from the Dominican Republic moves in with the family. After two more children's books, *Before We Were Free* (2002) and *Finding Miracles* (2004), Alvarez returned to poetry in 2004 with the publication of *The Woman I Kept to Myself.*

She has also continued her prolific work with the novel *Saving the World* (2007). The text centers upon the lives of two courageous women. One is a Latin American novelist named Alma Huebner who lives in Vermont. When her husband Richard entreats her to work with him on an AIDS project in the Dominican Republic, she objects, insisting that she must stay in the States to work on her novel. As she writes, she becomes fascinated with her main character, Isabel Sendales y Gómez, a sixteenth-century Spanish rectoress who accompanies a group of orphan boys, live carriers of the smallpox virus, to the New World, in an attempt to eradicate the deadly disease. Isabel's valor encourages Alma to take risks in her life and to fight against injustice.

Whether describing life in the Dominican Republic or the life of Dominican immigrants in the United States, Julia Alvarez notes the significance of ethnic heritage and the process of cultural adaptation. Like the Puerto Rican writer Esmeralda Santiago and Cuban author Cristina Garcia, Alvarez adds to the tradition of Latina storytellers who have gained critical and popular acclaim with the sharing of their personal bicultural experience.

Dorsía Smith Silva

See also: Dominicans.

Further Reading

Henao, Eda B. *Colonial Subject's Search for Nation, Culture, and Identity in the Works of Julia Alvarez, Rosario Ferré, and Ana Lydia Vega.* Lewiston, NY: Edwin Mellen, 2003.

Mujcinovic, Fatima. *Postmodern Cross-Culturalism and Politicization in U.S. Latina Literature: From Ana Castillo to Julia Alvarez.* New York: Peter Lang, 2004.

Sirias, Silvio. *Julia Alvarez: A Critical Companion.* Westport, CT: Greenwood, 2001.

American GI Forum

In 1948, Army major and physician Héctor P. García observed medical personnel refusing to treat sick Mexican American veterans at the naval station at Corpus Christi, Texas. In response to this and other injustices, he founded the nation's first Latino veterans' advocacy group, the American GI Forum. Originally established to work on behalf of Mexican American veterans, the group later broadened its base to work for the civil rights of the broader Latino community. Today it is the nation's largest Latino veterans' organization in the United States.

Mexican American soldiers fought valiantly in World War II, winning more Medals of Honor than any other racial or ethnic group. But when nearly half a million Latino soldiers, most of them Mexican Americans, returned home following the end of the war, they found themselves still treated as second-class citizens. The discrimination, notably in Texas, included signs on restaurants and other establishments that said "No Dogs or Mexicans Allowed." Realtors discriminated against people of Mexican descent by using special codes to identify them and to prevent them from buying property. In addition, theaters, swimming pools, and other public places allowed entry to Mexican Americans only on certain days.

Mexican Americans who had served in the armed forces were often denied the benefits entitled to them as veterans. While Anglo veterans in Texas and elsewhere used the new federal GI Bill to gain educational, medical, housing, and other benefits, many Mexican Americans and other minorities had a different experience. These veterans found themselves ignored by the American Legion and other veterans' organizations when they sought help. In Texas, for instance, they found that compensation checks processed through the Veterans Administration were often six to eight months overdue. Likewise, applications for post-secondary education under the GI Bill were not processed in a timely fashion, preventing Mexican American veterans from attending school.

The GI Forum first came to national attention in 1949, when the organization fought on behalf of the family of a decorated Mexican American soldier, Felix Z. Longoria, who had been killed in combat. When his body was brought home, his widow was informed that he would have to be buried in the town's segregated "Mexican cemetery." The only funeral home in their town of Three Rivers, Texas, refused to allow its chapel to be used for Longoria's wake because he was of Mexican descent. The GI Forum took up the family's cause, publicizing the incident and bringing it to the attention of the national media, who turned the spotlight on the local, state, and federal institutions involved. García also sought help from U.S. Senator Lyndon B. Johnson (D-TX). Longoria finally was buried with full military honors at Arlington National Cemetery in Virginia.

By the end of 1949, more than 100 local chapters of the GI Forum had been established in twenty-three states, with total membership exceeding 20,000. Ladies' auxiliaries and junior forums ensured the involvement of entire veteran families and contributed to the success of the organization. By working to expand access to the GI Bill, the Forum made it possible for many Mexican American veterans to attend college. A number of those who did so would go on to become leaders of the Chicano community in the 1960s and 1970s.

The Forum also became active in using the courts to fight for Latino rights. It fought inequities in the educational system and took a leading role in publicizing police brutality cases in Texas during the early 1950s. The GI Forum organized voter registration drives throughout the Southwest and the first majority Mexican American electorate in the Rio Grande Valley. The Forum also initiated local "pay your poll tax" drives to bring Tejanos (Texans of Mexican descent) to the polls. Its efforts helped paved the way for the Twenty-Fourth Amendment to the U.S. Constitution, which abolished the poll tax in 1964. This in turn strengthened voter registration projects among impoverished Mexican Americans.

Family members of Private Felix Z. Longoria, who was killed in action during World War II, attend his funeral at Arlington National Cemetery. The American GI Forum lobbied for the honor after Longoria had been denied burial in his Texas hometown cemetery. *(AP Images/LBJ Presidential Library)*

In the mid-1960s, middle-class assimilationist-oriented organizations such as the GI Forum and the League of United Latin American Citizens (LULAC, formed in the 1920s) strongly supported President Lyndon B. Johnson and the federal government's War on Poverty programs. As the 1960s progressed, however, the Forum and LULAC soon found their leadership challenged by a new generation of Chicano leaders, who rejected assimilation and argued for cultural nationalism and more direct social action. As a result, the middle-class groups effectively lost control of the political and social agenda for Mexican Americans in the Southwest and elsewhere. In historical perspective, the GI Forum is remembered for having laid much of the foundation for postwar efforts to improve the condition of Mexican Americans throughout the United States.

Héctor García, the founder of the GI Forum, was appointed ambassador to the United Nations during the Johnson Administration in the mid-1960s and was awarded the Presidential Medal of Freedom by Ronald Reagan in 1984. He died in 1996. The Forum today continues to provide financial support, job training, and counseling for Latino veterans. Its Hispanic American Education Foundation has given over $5 million in scholarships to more than 20,000 students since 1978, helping to ensure that more Latinos/as continue their education beyond high school.

Ellen Bigler

See also: Education; García, Héctor P.; League of United Latin American Citizens; Mexicans; Military, Latinos in the; Tejanos; Vietnam War.

Further Reading

American GI Forum. http://www.agif.us.

Ramos, Henry A.J. *The American GI Forum: In Pursuit of the Dream, 1948–1983.* Houston, TX: Arte Público, 1998.

Americanization

See **Acculturation and Assimilation**

Anaya, Rudolfo Alfonso (1937–)

Known as the "godfather of Chicano literature in English," Rudolfo Alfonso Anaya was born in the village of Pastura, New Mexico, on October 30, 1937, to Rafaelita Mares and Martin Anaya. He spent his childhood in Santa Rosa, New Mexico, and the town and its surrounding area would form the setting for his first novel, *Bless Me, Ultima* (1972). The people and landscape of New Mexico's eastern plains (*llanos*) imbued Rudolfo with the mythical themes that permeate his work. His grandfather and uncles farmed the Puerto de Luna Valley, and the Pecos River was his playground. Raised in a house where Spanish was the primary language, Anaya grew up surrounded by storytellers, and oral tradition played an important part in nurturing his imagination. In 1952, when he was fifteen, his family moved to Albuquerque.

When he was a sophomore in high school, Anaya suffered a serious spinal injury in a swimming accident. Out of this difficult time he forged some of the central themes and questions addressed in his later writings. His first three novels, *Bless Me, Ultima, Heart of Aztlán* (1976), and *Tortuga* (1979), chronicle a semiautobiographical rite of passage.

After graduating from high school, Anaya attended the University of New Mexico and received a Bachelor of Arts in Education (1963) and a Master of Arts in English Literature (1969). He taught in Albuquerque public schools from 1963 to 1970. From 1974 to 1991 he taught creative writing at the University of New Mexico, becoming professor emeritus.

In 1983 Anaya became the founding editor of *Blue Mesa Review,* a creative writing journal at the University of New Mexico With his wife, Patricia, he established a national literary prize called the Premio Aztlán in 1993, an annual award given to the author of a work of fiction that explores Chicano culture. The award was reestablished in their honor by the University of New Mexico Libraries in 2004, and the Department of English created the Rudolfo Anaya Scholarship Fellowship Fund.

In 2002, Anaya was awarded the National Medal of Arts by President George W. Bush for his "exceptional contribution to contemporary American literature that has brought national recognition to the traditions of the Chicano people, and for his efforts to promote Hispanic writers." His long list of national and international awards also includes the Premio Quinto Sol for *Bless Me, Ultima.*

Anaya has also written eight children's books, two of which, *Farolitos of Christmas* (1987) and *My Land Sings* (1999), have won the Tomas Rivera Award. Other novels include *Alburquerque* (1992), *Zia Summer* (1995), *Rio Grande Fall* (1996), *Shaman Winter* (1999), and *Jemez Spring* (2005). In addition to his novels, he has produced short stories, poetry, works of nonfiction, and even an opera libretto, based on the story of Hernán Cortés and his mistress, La Malinche. At least three of Anaya's plays, *Angie, Los Matachines* (1992),

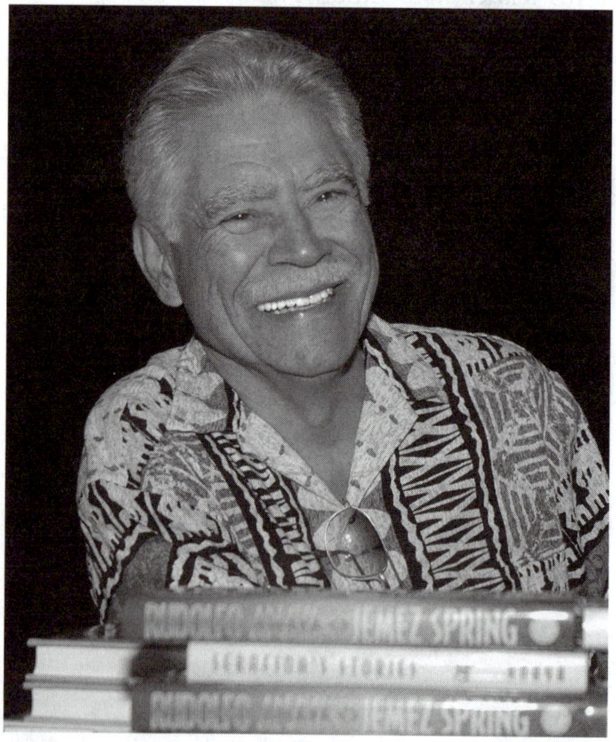

New Mexico native Rudolfo Alfonso Anaya has been an advocate as well as a leading practitioner of Chicano literature. His novels, stories, poems, and children's books evoke the myths, magic, and landscape of the Latino Southwest. *(Steve Snowden/Getty Images)*

and *Who Killed Don Jose* (1987), have been performed in Albuquerque, San Diego, Denver, and Santa Fe.

Anaya's works show a profound influence of the old storytellers, the myths of the Mexican American people, and the landscape and the cultural history of New Mexico. Through the magic of words and the evocation of landscape, he conveys aspects of the Chicano culture in the Southwest to a wider audience. Acting as a literary shaman (spiritual healer), he transports readers to a different place and time, while creating stories with universal themes. In 2004, Anaya donated his papers to the Center of Southwest Studies at the University of New Mexico Zimmerman Library.

Irma Flores-Manges

See also: Chicano/a.

Further Reading

Baeza, Abelardo. *Man of Aztlán: A Biography of Rudolfo Anaya.* Austin, TX: Eakin, 2001.

Dick, Bruce, and Silvio Sirias, eds. *Conversations with Rudolfo Anaya.* Jackson: University Press of Mississippi, 1998.

Gonzáles, César A., and Phyllis S. Morgan. *A Sense of Place: Rudolfo A. Anaya: An Annotated Bio-Bibliography.* Berkeley, CA: Ethnic Studies Library Publications, 2001.

Anzaldúa, Gloria (1942–2004)

The lesbian poet and author Gloria Anzaldúa stands as one of the most recognized contemporary Mexican American literary figures in the United States. Her numerous writings, which include poetry, fiction, children's books, memoirs, and literary and cultural criticism, are recognized as some of the most powerful examinations of the identity of Mexican American women and of life in the Texas-Mexico border region, or Borderlands. Foremost in her work are insights into the experience of the Chicana who faces everyday struggles over her mixed-blood heritage, or *mestizaje*, her sexuality, and her political awareness. Anzaldúa's books are listed as required reading in a variety of university programs, including literary studies, Latino studies, Chicano studies, feminist studies, and gay and lesbian studies.

Born Gloria Evangelina Anzaldúa on September 26, 1942, on a ranch in Jesus Maria of the Valley, in the Rio Grande Valley, Texas, she was the eldest child of sharecropper, field-worker parents Urbano and Amalia Anzaldúa. The family moved to Hargill, Texas, on the Mexican border, where the Anzaldúas worked in the fields. After her father's death, she took up regular work in the fields at age fourteen, alongside her siblings and mother. An inquisitive young woman, she developed a love for books and art and attended college, receiving a bachelor of arts degree in English and art from the University of Texas Pan American in Edinburg in 1969. She continued her education at the University of Texas at Austin, where she received master of arts degrees in English and education in 1973, then did additional graduate work at the University of California, Santa Cruz.

Her interest in education led her to teach high school English and to participate in bilingual preschool programs, special education, and educational programs for children of migrant worker families. Toward the end of the 1970s, she became a lecturer in feminist literature at San Francisco State University, and in the mid-1980s she taught creative writing at the University of California, Santa Cruz. During the late 1980s and early 1990s, she taught classes in Chicano studies, women's studies, and literature at various universities, including the University of Texas at Austin, Vermont College of Norwich University, Georgetown University, and Colorado University.

In 1981, Anzaldúa and coeditor Cherríe Moraga published the anthology *This Bridge Called My Back: Writings by Radical Women of Color,* a collection of essays, poems, and letters that introduced the perspectives and experiences of women of color, challenging the predominant middle-class white feminism of the time. The anthology includes several of Anzaldúa's essays in which she staked her claim as a writer and activist. In the essay "Speaking in Tongues: A Letter to 3rd World Women Writers," she argues for a new type of writing that mixes fact and theory in a more personal way to counter the often abstract writing of academia. Her second anthology, *Making Face, Making Soul/Haciendo Caras: Creative and Critical Perspectives by*

Women of Color (1990), continued the legacy of *This Bridge* by highlighting contributions by women of color and reemphasizing the need for a more inclusive feminist movement.

Anzaldúa's most celebrated contribution, however, is her 1987 book *Borderlands/La Frontera: The New Mestiza,* named one of the 38 Best Books of 1987 by the *Literary Journal* and one of the 100 Best Books of the Century by both *Hungry Mind Review* and the *Utne Reader.* In this work, Anzaldúa mixes poetry, autobiography, theory, cultural criticism, mythology, Spanish, English, and Spanglish to describe her experience as a mixed-raced lesbian living at the U.S.-Mexico border. One of the central concepts of the book is the "new mestiza," Anzaldúa's designation for the woman who stands at the border, carrying multiple histories and legacies, whose life is filled both by feelings of alienation and by possibilities for personal growth. Despite the many difficulties the new mestiza faces, she has the great strength and will to overcome the obstacles in her path as she travels between the Anglo and Mexican worlds.

While providing a powerful portrait of the new mestiza and her experience, Anzaldúa also underscores the significance of spirituality in the development of what she calls "mestiza consciousness"—the level of awareness needed to handle life's ambiguities and contradictions, and to understand higher alternatives to such dichotomies as queer/straight, subject/object, and male/female. Anzaldúa expresses this spirituality through allusion to the Virgen de Guadalupe (Our Lady of Guadalupe) and Aztec and Yoruba divinities.

Borderlands and Anzaldúa's other texts give readers insight into the author's struggle as a new mestiza caught in the Borderlands. These works allow the reader to empathize with Anzaldúa's anger, pain, confusion, strength, and determination, to think more about what it means to be caught between Anglo and Mexican cultures, and to question the cultural practices that undermine mestizo identity.

Anzaldúa received numerous honors and awards for her writing, including the Before Columbus Foundation American Book Award, the National Endowment for the Arts Fiction Award, the Lesbian Rights Award, the Sappho Award of Distinction, the Lamda Lesbian Small Book Press Award, and the American Studies Association Lifetime Achievement Award. She died of complications from diabetes on May 15, 2004.

Mariana Ortega

See also: Chicano Studies; Feminism; Mestizo/a; Mexicans.

Further Reading

Ikas, Karin Rosa. *Chicana Ways: Conversations with Ten Chicana Writers.* Reno: University of Nevada Press, 2002.

Keating, AnaLouise. *Women Reading Women Writing: Self-Invention in Paula Gunn Allen, Gloria Anzaldúa and Audre Lorde.* Philadelphia: Temple University Press, 1996.

Lugones, Maria. "On Borderlands/La Frontera: An Interpretive Essay." *Hypatia* 7 (1992): 31–37.

Ramos, Juanita. "Gloria E. Anzaldúa." In *Contemporary Lesbian Writers of the United States: A Bio-bibliographical Sourcebook,* ed. Sandra Pollack and Denise D. Knight. Westport, CT: Greenwood, 1993.

Yarbo-Bejarano, Yvonne. "Gloria Anzaldúa's Borderlands/La Frontera: Cultural Studies, 'Difference,' and the Non-Unitary Subject." *Cultural Critique* 28 (1994): 5–28.

Arenas, Reinaldo (1943–1990)

Reinaldo Arenas was a world-renowned Cuban-born writer who escaped to the United States during the Mariel Boatlift of the early 1980s. He was born on July 16, 1943, in Holguín in the province of Oriente. Arenas was born into poverty, with his father abandoning the family soon after Reinaldo's birth. During his youth, Arenas moved to Sierra Maestra, where he worked in a guava paste factory. As the nation's economy worsened under the dictatorship of Fulgencio Batista, Arena joined the revolution of Fidel Castro at age fifteen and fought against the Batista government for three years. With Castro's rise to power, Arenas was granted a scholarship to study agricultural accountancy. He later studied philosophy and literature at the Universidad de La Habana but never completed his degree.

In 1963, Arenas was offered a job at the Biblioteca Nacional José Martí. This position marked the beginning of Arenas's career as a writer, and in 1965, his first novel, *Celestino antes del alba* (*Celestino Before*

Dawn), won a First Mention Award at the Cirilo Villaverde National Competition. The National Union of Cuban Writers and Artists published *Celestino antes del alba* in 1967. It was his only novel to be published in Cuba.

By the mid-1960s, Arenas had abandoned the revolution, and his writings were censored and declared antirevolutionary by the Castro regime. No longer permitted to publish in Cuba, he began sending his manuscripts abroad. His novel *Hallucinations,* for instance, was smuggled out of Cuba to France, where it was published in 1968 and nominated for a prestigious Prix Medicis. In 1968, Arenas left the Biblioteca Nacional and became an editor for the Cuban Book Institute in Havana. From 1968 through 1974, he worked as a journalist and editor for *La Gaceta de Cuba,* a literary magazine also published in Havana.

In 1973, Arenas was falsely accused of sexual molestation after an incident on a beach and placed under arrest. Arenas escaped from prison and attempted to flee Cuba on an inner tube. However, he was caught and imprisoned again, this time for charges of "ideological deviation" and for publishing abroad without official consent. He was sent to El Morro Castle, which housed those convicted of serious offences. To survive in this environment, Arenas befriended the other inmates by helping them write letters to their wives and girlfriends. He was finally released from prison in 1976.

By the early 1980s, Arenas had left Cuba as part of the Mariel Boatlift. He arrived first in Miami and later settled in New York. He made a number of public appearances against the Castro regime and published extensively, but he grew increasingly critical of the Cuban emigrant community and the American gay community, both for squandering their freedom. "If exile—that is to say, freedom—teaches us anything," he declared, "it's that happiness does not lie in being happy but in being able to choose our misfortunes."

Although primarily a novelist, Arenas also wrote articles, short stories, and experimental theater pieces. His fictional works include *Before Night Falls: A Memoir* (1993); *Farewell to the Sea: A Novel of Cuba* (1986); *Singing from the Well* (a translation of *Celestino antes del alba,* 1990); and *The Doorman* (1991). Many of his short stories, such as those collected in *Mona and Other Tales* (2001), led to his association with the Latin American literary booms of the 1960s. Like the works of a number of his contemporaries, many of Arenas's writings experimented with magical realism—a literary effort to fuse reality and fantasy. Reflecting on his generation, Arenas stated in 1988, "We live on fury, indignation, rage, alienation, and the desperation of trying to hold on to a world that exists only in our hopes."

In 1987, Arenas was diagnosed with AIDS, and throughout his illness he struggled to complete the literary works that he considered important to his legacy. He dedicated his autobiography, *Before Night Falls* (1992), to his closest friend, Lazaro Gomez Carriles. The film version, released in 2000, was directed by Julian Schnabel.

Arenas's memoir was published posthumously, as he committed suicide by taking an overdose of drugs and alcohol on December 7, 1990, in New York City. Just before his death, he wrote a letter to the Miami Spanish newspaper, *Diario las Américas,* expressing regret that his health would not allow him to continue the struggle for Cuban independence. "I want to encourage the Cuban people out of the country as well as on the Island to continue fighting for freedom," he wrote.

Mary K. Bloodsworth-Lugo

See also: Cubans; Mariel Boatlift.

Further Reading

Cacheiro, Adolfo. *Reinaldo Arenas: Una Aprecición Política.* Lanham, MD: International, 2000.

Ocasio, Rafael. *Cuba's Political and Sexual Outlaw: Reinaldo Arenas.* Gainesville: University Press of Florida, 2003.

Zendegui, Ileana C. *The Postmodern Poetic Narrative of Cuban Writer Reinaldo Arenas (1943–1990).* Lewiston, NY: Edwin Mellen, 2004.

Argentines

As a group, Argentine Americans have particular characteristics and immigration histories that separate them from other Latinos/as. Compared to other well-established groups, such as Mexicans and Hondurans, the Argentine American community has a relatively recent history in the United States. According to U.S. Census reports, a total of 44,803 Argentines lived in the United States as of 1970; the figure increased to 92,563 by 1990. Thus, more than half of the Argentine American community either immigrated or was born during that twenty-year period. By 2000, there were 100,000 Latinos/as in the United States who called themselves Argentines.

Before the influx of the last three decades of the twentieth century, the vast majority of Argentine immigrants to the United States were highly educated professionals, especially doctors and scientists in search of greater economic and professional opportunities. This would change dramatically with the beginning of Argentina's Dirty War in 1976 and the overthrow of President Isabel Perón by the armed forces. The new military junta carried out a campaign of repression and "ideological war," entailing the imprisonment, torture, or murder of known or suspected political opponents. The turmoil ended in 1983 with a return to civilian democratic rule, but not before an estimated 15,000–30,000 Argentines, especially Jews, disappeared (and were presumed to be dead).

The period of domestic upheaval greatly increased Argentine emigration and altered the character of the Argentine community in the United States. The Falklands/Malvinas War in 1982, as well as the changing global economy, further contributed to the rise in Argentine immigration to the United States and the shifting demographics of the Argentine American community. Compared with their predecessors, the new arrivals represented a more heterogeneous group, including less educated people and those of more diverse class and professional status.

Argentine immigrants arriving between 1980 and 1990 did maintain the general settlement patterns of previous generations, living in New York City and other metropolitan areas. Through the 1980s, 23 percent of Argentine Americans lived in New York City, compared to 20 percent in the 1970s. In the years since, New York and Los Angeles have retained large enclaves of Argentine Americans, attracting new arrivals with already existing communities and extensive social and cultural networks. In New York especially, the presence of a sizable Italian American community (many Argentine Americans are ethnically Italian) has also been a draw for newcomers.

Community-based organizations have not only served as a cultural nexus and source of unity for the Argentine American community, but have also contributed directly to immigration in particular cities. For example, organizations like the Argentine American Chamber of Commerce, based in New York City, have long promoted economic cooperation between the United States and the Argentine community. Another key resource is the Argentine–North American Association for the Advancement of Science, Technology and Culture, based in New Jersey, which, through its research and public programs, promotes cooperative ventures between Argentine academics and professionals and their North American counterparts working in the fields of science, technology, and cultural exchange. Similarly, the Argentine Association of Los Angeles promotes cultural, economic, and social activities within the Argentine American community there. The Sociedad Sanmartiniana de Washington (San Martín Society of Washington, D.C.), by sponsoring cultural events such as Argentine Independence Day and San Martin's Birthday, serves as a cultural bridge between Argentine, Argentine American, and other communities.

Communal organizations are not the only source of unity and cultural cohesion for the Argentine American community. Others include restaurants, churches, shops, and the media. Argentine restaurants serve empanadas and *dulce de leche*, both traditional foods. These and other delicacies have been incorporated and assimilated into mainstream American cuisine. In both large and small cities, there are churches and specialty shops with heavy Argentine influences. Finally, the availability of the television station SVR, one of the most popular stations in Argentina, is broadcast to viewers in Miami, Florida.

Although Argentina is a heterogeneous nation with large numbers of Germans, Poles, Czechs, Danes, Japanese, Koreans, and Jews, 90 percent of Argentine immigrants to the United States are of either Italian or Spanish ancestry. Despite demographic changes in the last few decades, the Argentine American community continues to be defined by its upward mobility, high levels of educational attainment, and disproportionate number of professionals. Such energy and enthusiasm, as well as ethnic links between the Argentine community and European homelands, have contributed to heightened levels of assimilation and acculturation for Argentines in the United States. Likewise, these factors have helped Argentine Americans establish common political and cultural projects that attempt to link or define them in relationship to other Latinos/as.

David J. Leonard

See also: New York.

Further Reading

Lattes, Alfredo E., and Enrique Oteiza, eds. *The Dynamics of Argentine Migration, 1955–1984: Democracy and the Return of Expatriates.* Trans. David Lehmann and Alison Roberts. Geneva, Switzerland: United Nations Research Institute for Social Development, 1987.

Norden, Deborah. *The United States and Argentina: Changing Relations in a Changing World (Contemporary Inter-American Relations).* New York: Routledge, 2002.

Rodriguez, Julio. "Argentinean Americans." Countries and Their Cultures. http://www.everyculture.com.

Armed Forces

See **Military, Latinos in the**

ASPIRA

ASPIRA is a national nonprofit organization dedicated to the education and leadership development of Puerto Rican and other Latino youth. Its name is taken name from the Spanish verb *aspirar,* "to aspire."

In 1961, Antonia Pantoja and a group of other Puerto Rican educators and professionals established ASPIRA in New York City to specifically address the exceedingly high dropout rate and low educational attainment of Puerto Rican youth. They believed that by focusing on the education of young people, enhancing their leadership skills, and promoting cultural pride, the Puerto Rican community as a whole could lift itself from poverty. ASPIRA's goals and activities are grounded in the belief that Puerto Ricans and other Latinos/as have the collective potential to improve their community's economic, political, and social standing.

In 1972, this view propelled ASPIRA into national prominence and legal history, when, together with the Puerto Rican Legal Defense and Education Fund, it filed a class-action suit on behalf of New York City's non–English speaking children against the Board of Education. Their principal complaint focused on the school system's failure to provide adequate learning resources to Puerto Rican students of limited English proficiency. In 1974, the suit resulted in a consent decree, a judicial ruling that formalizes an agreement between parties. The decree guaranteed bilingual education to all children in New York City who need it.

Emphasizing awareness, analysis, and action on the part of students, ASPIRA focuses on three specific program areas: leadership, youth development and educational achievement, and parental engagement. Goals in each area are pursued through associate offices, school-based clubs, and a variety of programs.

Throughout the decades, ASPIRA has helped hundreds of thousands of youth by providing them with the tools they need to remain in school and contribute to the community. It achieves this primarily through the ASPIRA clubs, which seek to develop leadership qualities in middle school and high school students and to foster cultural and self-awareness, enhanced critical thinking, and a commitment to social action. The clubs also aim to help students learn to work together, improve their self-esteem, and gain a better understanding of their community. ASPIRA believes that fostering the overall development of Latino youth early in their academic career is key to ensuring their future academic success and positive personal growth. ASPIRA offers children as young as six a variety of youth development and educational achievement programs intended to enhance their creativity, logic, and deductive reasoning skills.

Another central component of ASPIRA is the APEX (ASPIRA Parents for Education Excellence) program, which encourages Latino parents to become involved and informed advocates for their children's education. Statistics show that, when parents are actively involved in education, their children are more likely to complete high school and pursue a college degree. Toward that end, ASPIRA offers parents a variety of professional development sessions and personal counseling designed to foster leadership skills and an understanding of educational policy, school budgets, and parental rights. A parallel organization to APEX is the Teachers, Organizations, and Parents for Students Program (TOPS), which brings together teachers, corporate volunteers, and parents to promote academic achievement in Latino youth.

On a broader scale, for twenty-five years ASPIRA's National Health Careers Program has worked to fulfill several objectives, including recruitment of high school and college students; entry of those students into allied health programs and professional schools; and dissemination of financial aid information to students. In addition, the ASPIRA Public Policy Leadership Program gives selected students a hands-on introduction to policymaking and government action. It provides ninety high school students with the opportunity to study public policy and work with local leaders in community service internships.

Of ASPIRA's over 250,000 alumni, more than 98 percent remained in school, while approximately 90 percent went on to college. Outside of New York, ASPIRA maintains associate offices in Florida, Illinois, New Jersey, Pennsylvania, and Puerto Rico. The ASPIRA Association, Inc. continues to advance its mission through research and advocacy activities at the national level. Together each component of ASPIRA has helped students become leaders who serve and educate the Latino community today.

Madeleine E. López

See also: Education; Puerto Ricans.

Further Reading

ASPIRA. http://www.aspira.org.

Pantoja, Antonia. *Memoir of a Visionary: Antonia Pantoja.* Houston, TX: Arte Publico, 2002.

Sánchez Korrol, Virginia E. *From Colonia to Community: The History of Puerto Ricans in New York City.* Berkeley: University of California Press, 1994.

Santiago Santiago, Isaura. *A Community's Struggle for Equal Educational Opportunity, Aspira versus Board of Education.* Princeton, NJ: Educational Testing Service, 1978.

Assimilation

See **Acculturation and Assimilation**

Aztlán

The concept of Aztlán, which originated with the Mexica (Aztec) people, alludes to a legendary lost homeland somewhere in the north of Mexico. According to myth, the place called Aztlán (literally, "place of the heron") was the geographic origin of the Mexica people. It is variously said to have been located in the northwestern region of present-day Mexico and in the American Southwest. Although the actual territory and boundaries have been disputed, the passionate belief in its existence has motivated Mexican people for hundreds of years and provided a source and symbol of cultural identity to the present day. Aztlán has inspired great migrations, dreams of conquest, and contemporary social movements. At the most fundamental level, Aztlán is a story and a concept that links a people to a geographic location—the ancestral home of millions of Chicanos/as throughout North America and the world—and to a heritage that remains relevant to Mexicans and Mexican Americans in the twenty-first century.

The Aztecs—who referred to themselves as the Mexica or Tenochca—began as a Náhuatl-speaking nomadic tribe, which settled in the central basin of Mexico during the thirteenth century and ultimately built a powerful empire. According to their own legends, the Aztecs originated in a place called Aztlán (also Azatlán), a name derived from the Náhuatl words *aztatl,* meaning "heron," and *tlan,* meaning "place of"; another possible derivation is the Náhuatl *tlanti,* literally meaning "tooth" and implying rootedness in one place. Most of what is known of Aztlán legend derives from Spanish colonial texts, or written accounts of what the Aztecs told the Spaniards. According to these sources, the sun and war god *Huitzilopochtli* (hummingbird wizard) commanded a southern migration around the year 1116 C.E. to find a new settlement. The journey would not end until around 1248 C.E., when the tribes settled near Lake Texcoco and later founded the city of Tenochtitlán. The Mexica encountered and intermarried with Toltec groups, of Mayan and Olmec descent. The Toltec referred to the settlers as *Chichimec,* meaning barbarian, in reference to their tradition of human sacrifice. During the period of empire building, Aztlán seemed to be forgotten.

According to colonial historian Fray Diego Durán, the legend of Aztlán was revived during the reign of Moctezuma Ilhuicamina before the Spanish conquest in the sixteenth century. Durán's texts note that Moctezuma ordered an expedition to return to the northern homeland to bring back the people left behind in the original migration. According to the texts, Aztlán was marked by a hill with a curved top. There, the expedition members found one of their goddesses and they were returned to a youthful state. The myth inspired a number of Spanish campaigns to explore the territory north of Tenochtitlán.

In 1969, Rodolfo "Corky" Gonzales, at the Chicano Youth Liberation Conference in Denver, introduced El Plan Espiritual de Aztlán (The Spiritual Plan of Aztlán), a declaration of political consciousness that sought to liberate Latinos/as from the perils of American racism and exploitation. Gonzales's plan revived the legend of Aztlán in the context of the struggle for civil rights, turning it into a symbol of power (ownership) and belonging. In his text, Gonzales invoked such phrases as "with our heart in our hands and our hands in the soil" to convey the importance of rolling up one's sleeves and working for basic human rights. The association with national roots and ancestral pride helped resuscitate the concept of Aztlán as a motivation and organizing principle for Chicanos/as to resist discrimination and effect change. At the same conference, the Chicano poet and activist Alurista reinforced the sense of mission and cultural identity with a poem about Aztlán that became the preamble for the Plan Espiritual. Other activists and organizations, such as Movimiento Estudiantíl Chicano de Aztlán (MEChA, or Chicano Student Movement of Aztlán), invoked the ancestral homeland—appropriated from the Mexican people after the Mexican-American War—as a political rallying cry and symbol of unity. The concept of Aztlán continued to galvanize a nationalist movement that emphasized cultural, spiritual, and political power, as well as the right of Mexicans living in the United States to preserve their cultural heritage. These tenets supported historical claims to a pre-Spanish nativity and elevated the politics of colonization and national marginalization. One year after the Denver conference, Chicano Park—the site of a mural featuring Aztlán as a symbol and the words "La Tierra Mia" (My Land), was dedicated to the city's Chicano community.

Aztlán remained synonymous with the Chicano civil rights movement through the 1960s, and the link has continued into the early twenty-first century. Conversely, groups hoping to curb illegal immigration have pointed to the concept of Aztlán—and the sense of identity associated with it—as evidence of Mexican resistance to assimilation and hostility toward the United States. The high percentage of Latino residents in the American Southwest, some anti-immigrants groups have argued, represents a threat by foreigners who hope to reclaim their ancestral homeland. Thus, to the present day, Aztlán remains a contentious cultural construct, an ancient symbol complicated by issues of race, nationality, political power, and competing social movements.

Jason Oliver Chang and Bernardo Aguilar-González

See also: Chicano Movement; Gonzales, Rodolfo "Corky"; La Raza; Movimiento Estudiantíl Chicano de Aztlán; Plan Espiritual de Aztlán, El.

Further Reading

Bierhorst, John. *History and Mythology of the Aztecs: The Codex Chimalpopoca.* Tucson: University of Arizona Press, 1992.

Gonzalez, Rodolfo. *The Spiritual Plan of Aztlán.* Chicano Youth Conference, Denver, 1969.

Guy, Donna, and Thomas Sheridan. *Contested Ground: Comparative Frontiers on the Northern and Southern Edges of the Spanish Empire.* Tucson: University of Arizona Press, 1998.

Spicer, Edwards. *Cycles of Conquest: The Impact of Spain, Mexico and the United States on Indians of the Southwest, 1533–1960.* Tucson: University of Arizona Press, 2003.

Vélez-Ibáñez, Carlos. *Cultural Bumping: Mexican Cultures of the Southwest United States.* Tucson: University of Arizona Press, 1996.

B

Baca, Judith F. (1946–)

Judith Baca is a Chicana muralist and community organizer in Los Angeles credited with helping bring public murals—the art of the streets and communities—to mainstream public awareness. Coupling the power of art with her convictions of social justice, she has conceived and facilitated hundreds of inner-city murals, including a monumental seven-year project called the *Great Wall of Los Angeles.* Baca's art crosses ethnic barriers in seeking to promote peace in local communities and, because it is painted on concrete walls and tiles rather than on canvas, challenges preconceived definitions of art.

Baca was born on September 20, 1946, in South Central Los Angeles. As a young child, she was raised in an all-female household that included her mother, grandmother, and two aunts. When Baca was six years old, her mother married, and the family moved 20 miles (32 kilometers) north to Pacoima in the San Fernando Valley. This move would prove influential on Baca's later life, as she was now required to speak primarily in English, a challenge for the second-generation Chicana. While she had excelled at her former school, she found the transition difficult and instead focused her energy on painting.

After earning a bachelor's degree in art from California State University at Northridge in 1969, Baca began teaching at her alma mater, Bishop Alemany High School, a Catholic school in Mission Hills, California. While there, she facilitated a mural project that united students from diverse backgrounds in the common endeavor of creating art. In 1970, however, Baca, along with ten nuns and seven other teachers, was fired for publicly protesting the Vietnam War.

Working for the city of Los Angeles on a special program that taught art in school and park settings, she formed Las Vistas Nuevas (New Views) and brought together members of four rival gangs to create murals in Hollenbeck Park in East Los Angeles. City officials were encouraged by her ability to work with otherwise "difficult" young people and engage them in industrious and imaginative activities. Her determination to transform negative attitudes into a creative impulse had a positive impact on the youths participating in the project—and became her life's work.

Inspired by the Mexican muralists Diego Rivera, David Alfaro Siqueiros, and José Clemente Orozco, Baca traveled to Mexico to learn the techniques and traditions of other Latino artists. In 1974, drawing on the techniques learned in Mexico and working in cooperation with the Los Angeles Department of Recreation and Parks, Baca launched the city's first citywide mural project. Comprising more than four hundred mural works in a cross-section of municipal communities, the project engaged more than a thousand Los Angeles youth in illustrating aspects of their lives in inner-city neighborhoods. In describing the program, Baca said, "We consciously avoided Western European aesthetics, instead privileging Chicano popular culture, religious iconography, Mexican calendars, tattoos, street writing, whatever could better and more accurately portray our direct life-experience."

In 1976, Baca began logistical planning and fundraising for the *Great Wall of Los Angeles,* a landmark mural that extends 2,750 feet (840 meters, or more than half a mile) along the Tujunga Wash drainage canal in LA's San Fernando Valley. Baca guided participants in depicting the multi-ethnic history of the city from Neolithic times through the late 1950s, including such events as the Dust Bowl migration and the Zoot Suit Riots. Hundreds of young artists worked on the *Great Wall of Los Angeles* over the course of seven summers and completed the project in 1984. The Tujunga Wash, said Baca, is "an excellent place to bring youth of varied ethnic backgrounds from all over the city to work on an alternate view of the history of the U.S., which included people of color who had been left out of American history books," said Baca.

Also in 1976, Baca cemented her commitment to public art by founding the Social and Public Art Resource Center (SPARC) in Venice, California. SPARC is a community center dedicated to producing, preserving, and conducting community-based public art projects and educational programs, with an emphasis on cultivating Latino artists. In 1980 she joined the faculty at the University of California, Irvine, as a fine arts professor. Since 1996, she has held academic appointments as vice chair of the César Chávez Center for Interdisciplinary Studies, which she cofounded at the University of California at Los Angeles.

In the 1990s, Baca undertook an ambitious and innovative new project, a traveling mural titled *World Wall: A Vision of the Future without Fear.* Consisting of eight 10-by-30-foot (3-by-9-meter) panels, arranged in a 100-foot (30-meter) semicircle, the work is dedicated to the themes of global interdependence, peace, and an end to racism. Artists around the world were asked to depict a moment of change in their nation's history that marked a transition to peace. Baca completed four of the panels: *Triumph of the Heart, Nonviolent Resistance, Balance,* and *Triumph of the Hands.* The other four panels have been completed by international artists: *Dialogue of Alternatives* by Finnish artists Juha Saaski, Sirkka-Liisa Lonka, and Aaro Matinlauri; *The End of the Twentieth Century* by Soviet artist Alexi Begov; *Israeli-Palestinian Relations* by artists Ahmed Bweerat (Palestinian), Suliman Monsour (Palestinian), and Adi Yekutieli (Israeli); and *Tlazolteotl: Fuerza Creadora de lo No Tejido* by Mexican artists Martha Ramirez Oropeza and Patricia Quijano Ferrer.

Baca has been integrally involved in other public-art projects including *Great Walls Unlimited: Neighborhood Pride* in Los Angeles, in which artists from diverse ethnic groups across the metropolitan area created more than 100 murals depicting themes of diversity; *La Memoria De Nuestra Tierra* (Our Land Has Memory, 1996), a 9-by-23-foot (2.7by-7.0-meter) work at the University of Southern California that depicts the role of land in the area's history; a ceramic-tile mural of the same name and theme in Colorado, created in collaboration by Chicano youth and the Southern Ute; and a tile mural on the Venice Boardwalk (2001) that depicts the history of that beach community. In 2002, Baca returned to the *Great Wall of Los Angeles* site with some of the original artists and their children to repair damages and recall stories in and about the work.

Rebecca Tolley-Stokes and Gina Misiroglu

See also: Los Angeles; Mural Art.

Further Reading

Pohl, Frances F. "The World Wall, a Vision of the Future without Fear: An Interview with Judith F. Baca." *Frontiers: A Journal of Women Studies,* ed. Cordelia Chavez Candelaria and Mary Romero. 11:1 (1990).

Telgen, Diane, and Jim Kamp, eds. *Latinas!: Women of Achievement.* Detroit, MI: Visible Ink, 1996.

Balseros

Balseros, or rafters, is a term applied to all Cubans who have migrated to the United States by means of small boats or rafts. Since the advent of the Fidel Castro regime in 1959, Cubans have been seeking refuge in the United States by any and all means, many escaping the island on makeshift sea vessels. Despite the long history of migration by raft or small boat, the term "balsero" is currently used almost exclusively to refer to Cubans who came to the United States during the 1990s.

No one knows exactly how many Cubans left Cuba by raft during the 1990s. The lack of reliable statistics is related at least in part to the high mortality rate among the rafters. The 32,385 refugees who were picked up by the U.S. Coast Guard represent only the fortunate; countless Cubans did not survive the 90-mile (145-kilometer) journey. Desperate to leave the island, many departed on rafts that were far from seaworthy, and drowned; others died from exposure or lack of food and water.

Cuba faced a severe financial crisis in the early 1990s, after the collapse of communism in Europe and the end of financial subsidies from the Soviet

Cuban raft refugees—or *balseros*—reached U.S. waters by the tens of thousands in the summer of 1994. The Castro regime had responded to protests against economic conditions by granting "dissidents" the freedom to leave. *(Doug Collier/AFP/Getty Images)*

Union. Economic support from Moscow had been substantial, and the collapse forced Cuba to become financially self-sufficient. Known as the "special period," the transition was far from easy, and the country fell into a severe recession. Economic conditions worsened in 1992, when the United States tightened its long-standing embargo against the island with the Cuban Democracy Act, or Torricelli Bill (after Senate sponsor Robert Torricelli [D-NJ]). Disillusioned by the revolution and unable to secure adequate food and other basic necessities, many Cubans chose to leave the island.

Unlike previous waves of Cuban refugees, the emigrants of the 1990s did not have the opportunity to leave by plane or other legal means. This exodus was largely an illegal one, not sanctioned or mediated by the U.S. or Cuban governments; thus, those seeking to leave the island had to make their way across the ocean to U.S. shores by whatever means they could. Piecing together rafts from scraps, found materials, and inner tubes obtained through Cuba's black market, Cubans began leaving the island in increasing numbers during the early part of the decade. The tensions in Cuba reached a climax during the summer of 1994, when ordinary citizens took to the streets of Havana to demand better economic conditions. In response to the protest, Castro granted all "dissidents" who wished to leave the island the freedom to do so. The U.S. administration, under President Bill Clinton, was less than thrilled by the unregulated influx of Cuban refugees and responded by intercepting more than 30,000 balseros off the coast of Florida. After being picked up by the Coast Guard, the balseros were taken to the U.S. naval base at Guantánamo Bay, Cuba.

The interception of Cuban refugees and their detention at Guantánamo Bay marked a dramatic change in U.S. policy toward Cuban refugees. Since the early 1960s, the United States had maintained an open-door policy, which assured that virtually all Cubans who arrived on U.S. shores would be granted asylum. This policy gave Cuban refugees preferential treatment over all other refugee groups. With the influx of refugees in the 1990s, Washington fundamentally altered this policy. The balseros who were taken to Guantánamo remained at the naval base for more than eight months, as Washington formulated a policy that served U.S. interests and would placate Castro. To de-escalate the standoff, the Clinton administration agreed to accept all Cubans detained at Guantánamo, tightened future visa allowances, and declared a new refugee policy that would allow the United States to turn back any Cuban rafters who failed to make landfall.

Cheris Brewer Current

See also: Brothers to the Rescue; Cuban Refugee Program; Cubans.

Further Reading

Fernández, Alfredo A. *Adrift: The Cuban Raft People.* Houston, TX: Arte Público, 2000.

Masud-Piloto, Felix Roberto. *From Welcomed Exiles to Illegal Immigrants: Cuban Migration to the U.S., 1959–1995.* Lanham, MD: Rowman & Littlefield, 1996.

Baseball

Baseball, America's traditional "national pastime," has arguably become more important in certain Latin American countries than in the United States, where professional football has exceeded baseball in fan interest, and basketball, golf, lacrosse, and other sports have continued to attract new participants. The Latino influence on baseball, meanwhile, has grown exponentially in the last half century as a result of both its local popularity and the increasing number of Latino players in Major League Baseball (MLB). Although the cost of developing and acquiring Latino talent has increased significantly in recent years, it is still materially less than that of drafting U.S. amateur players. Consequently, Latinos today account for about one-third of major-league players and an even larger share of the game's stars, who are now paid on a par with U.S.-born players. MLB takes advantage of the Latino influence to promote the diversity of the game and market it internationally.

Origins

Although baseball has long been characterized as the American national pastime, some scholars recently have argued that the game actually had its roots in the Caribbean as a derivative of *batos*, played by the now-extinct Ciboney Indians of Cuba, and a game played by Puerto Rico's Caguana people before the arrival of Columbus. Yet there is no firm evidence linking these activities with the development of the modern game, and historical records indicate that the United States introduced baseball to Latin America in the late nineteenth century. American sugar companies and U.S. Navy personnel began playing the game in Cuba in the aftermath of the Spanish-American War to reinforce American interests and culture. Corporate interests used the game to provide a release for local workers from the hardships of field and factory labor; Navy personnel used the game to create rapport with local communities. From Cuba, the game spread throughout the Caribbean, usually through similar means.

Cuban-born catcher Miguel Angel "Mike" González played with five different teams. In 1938, while playing with the St. Louis Cardinals, he became Major League Baseball's first Latino manager. *(Library of Congress)*

Cuba was the source of the first Latin baseball players in the American professional game. Esteban Enrique (Steve) Bellán, a light-skinned Cuban, played for the Troy (New York) Haymakers and New York Mutuals of the National Association from 1871 to 1873. The first Latino in the modern major leagues was Louis R. Castro, a Colombian who appeared briefly with the Philadelphia Athletics of the American League in 1902. The most outstanding Latino major leaguer of the pre-integration era was Cuban pitcher Adolfo (the "Pride of Havana") Luque, who compiled 194 wins in a twenty-year career and, in 1919, became the first Latino to appear in a World Series. Perhaps the best player never to don an MLB uniform in that era was Martín Dihigo, a Cuban who starred in the Negro Leagues as both a pitcher and an infielder in the 1920s and 1930s. Dihigo became the first Latino inducted in the Baseball Hall of Fame in 1977; he also is enshrined in the Cuban, Mexican, and Venezuelan halls. The first Latino to serve as a major league manager was Miguel Angel ("Mike") Gonzalez, who led the St. Louis Cardinals for a brief period in 1938.

Discovery and Exploitation

Hindered by MLB's long-standing color line, Latino participation was confined to a few light-skinned players until African American Jackie Robinson broke the major league racial barrier in 1947. During the previous decade, Clark Griffith, the owner of the

Washington Senators sought to reduce the team's operating expenses by signing Latino players. In 1934, Griffith dispatched "Papa Joe" Cambria to Cuba, where he signed more than 400 players over the next twenty-five years. Several of these players were instrumental in helping the Senators, perennial losers, finish second in 1943 and 1945, while many American-born major leaguers were serving in World War II. The combination of the war and the signing of Jackie Robinson to a minor-league contract in 1945 opened the door for players of color. Saturnino Orestes Arrieta Armas ("Minnie") Minoso became MLB's first black Latino when he joined the Cleveland Indians in 1949.

Branch Rickey, the general manager of the Brooklyn Dodgers who had signed Robinson, followed Griffith's strategy when he left the Dodgers to head the Pittsburgh Pirates in 1951. After securing the highly touted Puerto Rican prospect and future Hall of Fame member Roberto Clemente, Rickey designated a valued assistant, Howard Haak, to scout the Caribbean, primarily Puerto Rico, Panama, and the Dominican Republic. Haak worked the Caribbean circuit for almost fifty years, following Rickey's "quality out of quantity" policy of mass signings and securing young players for little or no compensation.

With Haak's broad geographic scouting effort and Fidel Castro's takeover of Cuba in 1959, Latin baseball resources shifted to other Caribbean countries, principally the Dominican Republic. In working arrangements with local baseball organizations, major-league teams opened "academies" to develop local talent, brought to them by *buscones* (scouts), who profited at the expense of the signee lured by the American dream. Characterized by historian Alan M. Klein as "the baseball counterpart of the colonial outpost," an academy operates like a foreign subsidiary of an American company, securing raw materials (athletes), refining (training) them, and shipping partial products (players) to the United States for finishing (in minor leagues) and marketing (fan consumption). According to a 1981 study, the player development cost for an academy graduate was markedly less, about 10 percent, than that of an American-born player. While that gap has narrowed significantly in recent years because of competition, tougher local agent negotiations, and upgraded academy practices, the Caribbean source remains cost-effective. At the start of the 2008 season, Latin-born players accounted for approximately 40 percent of combined major and minor league rosters.

With all the progress, however, the exploitive neocolonial approach still extends to such facets of the game as the production of baseballs. At the factory of the American sporting goods company that produces MLB balls in Costa Rica, for example, the average local worker is paid a piecework rate for each hand-sewn, 108-stitch ball, which sells in the United States for about thirty times the local labor cost. The factory imports the rubber core, cowhide cover, and stitching yarn from the United States, while taking advantage of cheap Costa Rican labor and benefiting from local government practices by hiring the labor in a free-trade (no tax) zone.

Resistance and Response

To offset the perception and fact of abuses in Latin America, Major League Baseball in 2000 set up a branch office in the Dominican Republic to monitor and control team activities, to improve relationships with Latin American governments and baseball organizations, and to promote the sport among the general population. The investment and participation on the part of American professional teams has not only produced more and better players, but it has helped engender a distinctive style of play—called *beisbol romántico*—in the Dominican Republic and throughout Latin America. Emphasizing speed and fundamentals, the flashier Latin style of "small ball" has begun to transform the traditional MLB model, based on power hitting.

Beisbol romántico prevails in Latin American competition, despite MLB influence on both the winter leagues, which include non-Latin as well as Latin professional players, and the summer leagues, which include local academy prospects. In 1949, selected Latin American countries began participating in a Caribbean World Series at the conclusion of their winter league play. Cuba withdrew after its fifth consecutive title in 1960, and the series was suspended for a decade. Since resuming in 1970, the Caribbean World Series has been played every year except one (1981), with the Dominicans taking over from the Cubans as the perennially dominant team. The Latin American summer leagues provide an inexpensive venue for young American players to prove their readiness for U.S. minor-league competition.

Although the adversarial Cuba-U.S. political relationship has prevented Cuba from being an official conduit to the American major leagues, several Cuban players have defected in order to sign and play with an MLB team. In 2002, for example, pitcher José Contreras, a star of the Cuban national team, slipped away during a tournament in Mexico and ended up signing with the New York Yankees. Other notable Cuban players who defected to sign lucrative contracts in the American major leagues have included the brothers Orlando ("El Duque") Hernandez and Livan Hernandez, both pitchers as well. Back in Cuba, meanwhile, baseball has continued to thrive, and the national team has been dominant in international competition. The Cubans won 152 straight games in tournament competition during the early 1990s, and have captured a majority of biennial International Baseball Federation World Cup titles and Olympic gold medals.

Beisbol in Baseball

Led by Dominican-born Alex Rodriguez, MLB's highest-paid player, virtually every major league team counts Latinos among its stars. Latino participation in All-Star Games is disproportionately high, as is the number of Latino players who win major individual honors (such as the Most Valuable Player award and Cy Young Award). In 2006, the National Baseball Hall of Fame and Museum in Cooperstown, New York, launched a five-year program called "*Beisbol!* Baseball!" which includes two traveling exhibits and a forum honoring Roberto Clemente, the first Latino Hall of Fame inductee.

As established teams increasingly reflect the Latinization of the game—the Los Angeles Angels of Anaheim and the New York Mets have led the way in recent years—Major League Baseball has considered adding a new team or relocating an existing franchise to a Latin American location such as San Juan, Puerto Rico, or Monterrey, Mexico. At the same time, it has expanded professional opportunities for Latinos off the field and sought to broaden the appeal of the game to the growing Latino marketplace across the U.S. mainland.

Robert F. Lewis, II

See also: Clemente, Roberto; Rodriguez, Alex; Sosa, Sammy; Valenzuela, Fernando.

Further Reading

Bjarkman, Peter C. *Baseball with a Latin Beat: A History of the Latin American Game.* Jefferson, NC: McFarland, 1994.

Burgos, Adrian, Jr. *Playing America's Game: Baseball, Latinos, and the Color Line.* Berkeley: University of California Press, 2007.

Klein, Alan M. *Sugarball: The American Game, the Dominican Dream.* New Haven, CT: Yale University Press, 1991.

Krich, John. *El Beisbol: Travels Through the Pan-American Pastime.* New York: Prentice Hall, 1989.

Ruck, Rob. *The Tropic of Baseball: Baseball in the Dominican Republic.* Westport, CT: Meckler, 1991.

Wendel, Tim. *The New Face of Baseball: The One-Hundred-Year Rise and Triumph of Latinos in America's Favorite Sport.* New York: HarperCollins, 2004.

Basketball

Although American basketball at all levels, especially the professional National Basketball Association (NBA), is most directly associated with the African American community and its particular history and culture, the sport has long been popular in Latino communities throughout the United States. The recent success of a number of Latino players at the college level and in the NBA has resulted in even greater interest in the game within the Latino community and has intensified efforts on the part of league organizers, the media, and equipment and clothing manufacturers to reach and court Latino consumers. At the same time, the game has become increasingly globalized via the media, leading to a growing popularity of basketball throughout Latin America and further enhancing the status of basketball as both a spectator sport among and a game played by Latinos/as.

Basketball was invented in Massachusetts in the 1890s and quickly became popular on the East Coast, and as long as the game has been played it has found a niche within the Latino community. While never as popular as baseball or soccer, the game has generated Latino involvement at virtually every level—from local parks and community recreation facilities to the Olympic Games, the National Collegiate Athletic Association (NCAA), and the NBA. The internationalization of the NBA since the 1990s has resulted in a major increase in the number of Latino NBA players, which in turn has contributed to growing Latino fan interest and has focused efforts on the part of the league to expand the fan based in the Latino community.

In the 2005–2006 season, there were a total of nineteen Latino players in the NBA, compared to only twelve the previous year. This represented a significant advance, not just because of the sheer numerical increase but because several Latino players achieved star status at the time. (As of the 2007–2008 season, the number of Latino players in the NBA remained unchanged, at seventeen.) Since the early 2000s, Emanuel "Manu" Ginobili (Argentina) has emerged as one of the NBA's most dynamic players, helping the San Antonio Spurs win multiple league championships and leading his country to a gold medal in the 2004 Olympics. His explosive, intense, even flashy style of play, moreover, challenged conventional stereotypes of Latino basketball players as timid outside shooters incapable of playing defense. While his Latino NBA brothers have not reached his level of stardom, Carlos Arroyo (Puerto Rico), Leandro Barbosa (Brazil), Francisco Garcia (Puerto Rico), Eduardo Najera (Mexico), Nene (Brazil), Andres Nocioni (Argentina), Anderson Varejao (Brazil), Charlie Villanueva (USA, Dominican), and others are formidable players who have made valued contributions to their respective teams.

Their contributions extend off the court as well, as they are ambassadors of the game in their native countries and hometowns. In particular, the successes and visibility of Ginobili, Nene, and Najera have contributed to the increased popularity of basketball in Argentina, Brazil, and Mexico. The NBA, which began telecasting its playoff finals in Spanish in 2002, is now regularly broadcast on stations throughout Latin America. That same year, the NBA reached agreement with Telemundo to televise NBA games, Women's National Basketball Association (WNBA) games, and other basketball-related programming on this, the largest Spanish-language station within the United States. Also, beginning in 2002, the NBA launched specific events geared toward the Latino community at its annual All-Star Weekend.

The success of Latino players has contributed to increased interest in the NBA among the Latino community, especially in cities with large Spanish-speaking populations. Ginoboli and Najera, both of whom play for teams in Texas, have been especially instrumental in bringing Latino fans to the NBA. Likewise, when Carlos Arroyo was traded to the Orlando Magic during the 2005–2006 season, ticket sales and overall interest in the team grew dramatically among Hispanics throughout Florida.

Already as of 2002, in fact, Latinos/as accounted for more than 13 percent of the league's fan base, with 64 percent of Latinos/as describing themselves as fans of the NBA game; given the increased number of successful Latino players and NBA efforts to better market itself to the Latino community, the number of fans is expected to rise incrementally in subsequent years. According to a 2006 ESPN Deportes Latino fan poll, a semiannual survey of U.S. Latino sports, Latinos/as are more likely than blacks, whites, or Asians to pay more than $50 for an NBA ticket.

Nor is the visibility of Latinos in basketball limited to the NBA, or even men's college basketball. Latinas have also become increasingly visible in women's collegiate basketball, with the likes of Levy Torres of Florida State, Milena Flores and Erica Gomez of the University of California, Los Angeles (UCLA), Rebecca Lobo of the University of Connecticut, and Cyndi Valentin of the University of Indiana helping to bring attention to the women's game. Lobo, one of the most heralded players to enter the WNBA in 1997, was also the first Latina player in that league.

While Latinos/as have not made significant inroads as coaches and in management, there have been Latino basketball referees. Tommy Nuñez became the first Latino/a to referee in the NBA, paving the way for others, including his son, Tommy Nuñez, Jr., and Luis Grillo.

Although soccer, boxing, and baseball continue to be the sports most associated with Latino communities inside and outside the United States, recent trends suggest that basketball may join their ranks in future decades.

David J. Leonard

Further Reading

Araton, Harvey. *Crashing the Borders: How Basketball Won the World and Lost Its Soul at Home.* New York: Free Press, 2005.

Boulais, Sue, and Barbara Mavis. *Tommy Nuñez: A Real-Life Reader Biography.* Hockessin, DE: Mitchell Lane, 1997.

Lobo, RuthAnn, and Rebecca Lobo. *The Home Team: Of Mothers, Daughters, and American Champions.* New York: Kodansha America, 1997.

Bay of Pigs Invasion

The Bay of Pigs invasion in April 1961 was an unsuccessful attempt by U.S.-trained and -armed Cuban exiles to land in southwest Cuba and overthrow the government of Fidel Castro. The overt interference in Cuban politics was part of a broader, ongoing effort on the part of the United States to support anti-Communist regimes in the Western Hemisphere during the mid-twentieth century. Despite substantial aid and training provided to the attack force by the U.S. government, the operation was a disastrous failure, an embarrassment for Washington, and a source of ongoing distrust, resentment, and anti-American rhetoric on the part of the Castro regime.

Plans to destabilize Cuba by means of an invasion had begun under the Eisenhower administration, when the Central Intelligence Agency (CIA) started recruiting Cuban exiles to serve as a military force. The CIA proceeded to train a Cuban exile force totaling 1,500 men, using bases in both Guatemala and the United States. The exile group adopted the name Brigade 2506 in recognition of the group's first pre-invasion casualty—trainee number 2506. When John F. Kennedy assumed the presidency in January 1961, he agreed to move forward with the attack. Word leaked to the Cuban intelligence service, the G-2, however, and once informed, Castro acted swiftly to arrest more than 100,000 Cubans suspected of being security threats or of potentially aiding in the invasion.

The assault began on the morning of April 15, 1961, with Operation Puma, a limited U.S. air attack intended to ensure Brigade 2506 complete air superiority over the island prior to the landing at the Bay of Pigs (Playa Girón). While the initial plan called for a major air attack, U.S. officials canceled the second wave of strikes because President Kennedy wanted the operation to look as if the Cuban exiles had planned it (and thereby absolve his administration of responsibility).

The ground invasion followed when 1,500 members of Brigade 2506 landed at the Bay of Pigs on the swampy southwest coast of Cuba. Despite the difficult landscape and the loss of surprise, Brigade 2506 succeeded in overwhelming the Cuban force awaiting them—but only briefly. The United States had assumed that an exile invasion, in isolation, would be enough to spur an anti-Castro revolution across the island. The assumption proved naïve, however, as anti-Castro sentiment was far from universal in Cuba and Castro's foreknowledge of the invasion allowed him to remove dissenters in the area. Thus, the invasion of Brigade 2506 was not enough to trigger the intended uprising. While support from both the Air Force and Marines was made ready, President Kennedy opted to avoid "direct" U.S. involvement.

Brigade 2506's early success at the Bay of Pigs was quickly squelched, and, by the time the fighting ceased on April 21, more than sixty exiles were dead

Cuban armed forces and militiamen celebrate their victory over U.S. mercenaries in the failed Bay of Pigs invasion in April 1961. *(Keystone/Hulton Archive/Getty Images)*

and more than 1,200 captured by Cuban forces. The captured members of Brigade 2506 were held by the Cuban regime for twenty months, released only when the United States paid $53 million in food and other nonmilitary supplies. Cuban losses from the invasion are unknown; estimates range from 2,000 to 5,000 individuals.

All told, the Bay of Pigs invasion and Cuba's public ransoming of Brigade 2506 was a Cold War catastrophe for the United States—both a military humiliation and a diplomatic embarrassment. The failure of the operation was blamed primarily on the CIA and not the performance of the Cuban exiles themselves. The invasion also accelerated the deterioration in Cuban-American relations, which only worsened the following October with the Cuban Missile Crisis—the confrontation between the United States and Soviet Union over the presence of Soviet missile bases on the island.

Cheris Brewer Current

See also: Castro, Fidel; Cubans.

Further Reading

García, María Cristina. *Havana USA: Cuban Exiles and Cuban Americans in South Florida, 1959–1994.* Berkeley: University of California Press, 1996.

Triay, Victor Andres. *Bay of Pigs: An Oral History of Brigade 2506.* Gainesville: University Press of Florida, 2001.

Bear Flag Revolt

The Bear Flag Revolt, which began in Sonoma, California, was an attempt by Euro-Americans to gain control of California in June 1846, when the region was still part of Mexico and the Spanish-speaking residents called themselves *Californios.* Later that year, when the U.S. Congress, spurred by President James Polk, declared war on Mexico, the Bear Flag Revolt became part of the larger fight to annex Northern Mexico, which included all or parts of the present-day states of Arizona, California, Colorado, Nevada, New Mexico, Texas, Utah, and Wyoming. The Bear Flag Revolt led to the creation of the short-lived California Republic, or Bear Flag Republic, and the capture and imprisonment of the local Mexican command.

Almost no Euro-Americans lived in California until the early 1840s, when settlers began arriving overland from Illinois, Missouri, and Kentucky into Northern Mexico. At the beginning of the revolt, Euro-American immigrants, squatters, and trappers seeking control of the territory stole horses en route to the residence of General José Castro, the military commander of California. They then proceeded to the Sonoma Valley where they placed General Mariano Guadalupe Vallejo, the regional leader, under arrest. The Euro-American squatters and trappers of Alta California called themselves "Bears." The Californios called them by the Spanish-language equivalent, "*Osos.*"

When the Osos arrived at the Vallejo residence in Sonoma, Robert Semple, a recent Euro-American immigrant to the area, tried to establish order and negotiated a treaty with Vallejo. According to the proposed treaty, the men of the Vallejo family would not take up arms during the insurrection and the Osos would leave them under house arrest. By the time the treaty was signed by Vallejo and Semple, the Osos outside were drunk and insisted that the Californios were their prisoners and should not be released.

The Osos robbed local residences of food and horses. Some of them then gathered their stolen goods, forced General Vallejo, his brother Salvador Vallejo, and his secretary Victor Prudón to mount horses, and headed toward Sacramento, where John Sutter, a Swiss immigrant, had built a fortified trading post. The prisoners were ultimately brought to Sutter's Fort, where they were fed coarse food, allowed no communication with friends or family, and subjected to insults and verbal abuse by guards. When Julio Carrillo, a brother-in-law of General Vallejo, attempted to visit him, the Osos imprisoned him as well.

The Osos who remained behind in Sonoma painted a bear on a piece of white cloth, along with a star (in honor of Texas, which had broken away from Mexico ten years before). They proclaimed themselves citizens of the California Republic and included the name on the flag. For the Mexican and indigenous people of the area, the Bear Flag Revolt resulted in a time of indiscriminate violence. While some Osos stayed in the town of Sonoma, others rode throughout the Napa and Sonoma Valleys stealing supplies and sexually assaulting native women.

The Bear Flag Republic, headed by President William B. Ide, lasted only twenty-five days. Army Captain John C. Frémont, who was leading a U.S. government expedition in the region, took over command of the combined Oso force and led them south to Monterey. As it turned out, the town had already been captured by U.S. naval forces under Commodore John D. Sloat, since the Mexican-American War had recently begun. The United States conquered the California territory by the opening months of 1847, and Mexico formally ceded it to the United States in the treaty that ended the Mexican-American War. A bear still strides across the official California state flag.

In the 1970s, Chicano scholars began to turn up nineteenth-century histories and to reexamine the myths of white settlement, including the heroism and bravery of the Bears/Osos. In the 1990s, an organization in Napa, California, calling itself the "Bear Flag Resistance Committee" began protesting Bear Flag commemorations. Today, the events of 1846 are widely contested: Although many Euro-Americans continue to celebrate it, indigenous peoples, Chicanas/os, and others mark the occasion by calling for a new understanding of their past.

Linda Heidenreich

See also: Mexican-American War.

Further Reading

Castañeda, Antonia. "Engendering the History of Alta California, 1769–1848." In *Contested Eden: California Before the Gold Rush,* ed. Ramón A. Gutiérrez and Richard J. Orsi. Berkeley: University of California Press, 1998.

Heidenreich, Linda. "The Colonial North: Histories of Women and Violence from Before the U.S. Invasion." *Aztlán* 30 (2005): 21–54.

Sánchez, Rosaura. *Telling Identities: The Californio Testimonios.* Minneapolis: University of Minnesota Press, 1995.

Bilingualism

In a broad sense, bilingualism can be defined as competence in two or more languages. More specifically, however, researchers and theorists tend to disagree as to the exact level of competence a person must have in order to be classified as bilingual. For comparative purposes, therefore, social scientists have established a distinction between bilingualism as an individual trait and bilingualism as a fundamental characteristic of a social group, community, region, or nation. The distinction is especially useful in considering Latinos/as in the United States today, for, according to research from the PEW Hispanic Center, 47 percent of all Latinos/as consider themselves Spanish-dominant, 28 percent regard themselves as bilingual, and 25 percent see themselves English-dominant.

Individual versus Societal Bilingualism

Discrepancies in the definition of bilingualism center primarily on the question of proficiency. Scholars who favor a narrow definition argue that only individuals who have a native-like command of two languages can be called bilinguals. Others take a broader view, subscribing to a definition that includes those who can communicate at some viable level, in at least some situations, in more than one language. Language proficiency, however, can also vary across four basic skills: reading, writing, speaking, and listening.

Among Latinos/as in the United States, there is wide variation among individuals in all four skills in both English and Spanish. Some speak Spanish at home with their families but switch to English when they need to read, write, or otherwise communicate outside the home. Others understand Spanish perfectly when they hear or read it, but have difficulty when they themselves are required to speak or write; such persons are said to have a receptive competence in Spanish. Conversely, those whose strengths are in speaking and writing are said to have a productive competence in that language.

Aside from receptive and productive competence, individual proficiency in speaking, listening, reading, and writing may also vary over time, generally as a function of changes in circumstances and surroundings. Finally, of course, there is virtually always a distinction in the relative competence of an

A Spanish-speaking elementary school teacher in Texas instructs her largely Latino class on Spanish pronunciation. Less than half of Latinos/as today say they are Spanish-dominant; about one quarter are bilingual and one quarter are English-dominant. *(Mario Villafuerte/Stringer/Getty Images)*

individual in one language versus another. Few people, if any, speak, listen, read, or write in two different languages with equally proficiency; one is more dominant than the other.

For sociologists, bilingualism is examined as a characteristic of a particular community or group of people, or as a means of comparing communities. Bilingual and multilingual speakers are generally found in concentrated groups, whether local communities or broader regions (for example, Dominicans in New York; Cubans in Miami; Mexicans in the Desert Southwest). Indeed, some whole countries are bilingual or multilingual, even if not all residents are. In Canada, for example, English and French are the two official languages. Most French-speaking Canadians are concentrated in the province of Québec, while English is the official and dominant language in the rest of the country. Relatively few Canadians are proficient in both English and French. Thus, while bilingualism can be understood at the individual or societal levels, the two levels are not necessarily connected.

Bilingualism among Latino Americans

According to the PEW Hispanic Center, bilingualism apparently plays a significant role in identity formation among Latin Americans. For instance, the majority of self-identified Spanish-dominant and bilingual Latinos/as (68 percent and 52 percent, respectively) identify by their country of origin, whereas the majority of English-dominant Latinos/as (51 percent) identify as American.

Bilingualism also plays a vital—and changing—role in education. The percentage of students in U.S. public schools who speak a language other than English is growing at a rapid rate. In 2000, this group comprised about 20 percent of the student population; of them, approximately 70 percent were Spanish speakers. The most popular country of origin among Spanish-speaking students in the United States was Mexico, followed by Puerto Rico, Cuba, the Dominican Republic, El Salvador, and other Central and South American nations.

Regardless of the country of origin, most Latinos/as in the United States are joined by a common language—Spanish—which is spoken in about four-fifths of Latino households. Many inhabitants of large, integrated communities of Spanish speakers are not recent immigrants, but they continue to use Spanish in many social contexts, resorting to English outside their own communities. Studies suggest that bilingualism in many Spanish-speaking communities is transitional only and tends to shift toward English dominance from generation to generation. This shift may be accelerated by the English-only movement (which advocates English as the official language of the United States).

Finally, bilingualism correlates with the way Latinos/as view different issues. For example, according to another study conducted by the PEW Hispanic Center, 65 percent of Spanish-dominant Latinos/as favor allowing all illegal immigrants to remain in the United States, whereas only 41 percent of English-dominant Latinos/as and 42 percent of bilingual Latinos/as thought the same. In a multitude of ways, fluency in more than one language—and immersion in more than one culture—profoundly influence a person's opinions and perspectives. This is especially relevant to the Latino experience, suggesting that factors other than country of origin and time in the United States affect the ways in which they view society and themselves.

Gisela Ernst-Slavit

See also: Education; Proposition 227 (1998).

Further Reading

Baker, Colin. *Foundations of Bilingual Education and Bilingualism.* 4th ed. Clevedon, UK: Multilingual Matters, 2006.

García, Eugene E. *Teaching and Learning in Two Languages: Bilingualism and Schooling in the United States.* New York: Teachers College Press, 2005.

Zentella, Ana C. *Growing Up Bilingual: Puerto Rican Students in New York.* Malden, MA: Blackwell, 1997.

Blair House Attack

In 1950, two Puerto Rican nationalists—those who supported the island's independence as represented by the Puerto Rican Nationalist Party—brought international recognition to their cause by attempting to assassinate U.S. President Harry S. Truman in Blair House, the official state guesthouse for the president of the United States, located on Pennsylvania Avenue in Washington, D.C. The attempt resulted in the murder of one White House police officer and the death of one of the nationalists.

On November 1, 1950, Puerto Rican nationalists Griselio Torresola and Oscar Collazo approached Blair House at 1651 Pennsylvania Avenue, where President Truman and his family were residing while the interior of the White House, a block away, was undergoing renovations. Collazo and Torresola planned to approach Blair House from opposite directions and shoot their way inside, but they were foiled in a gun battle at the front steps of the residence. Secret Service agents and White House police guarding the front door exchanged fire with the attackers, awakening President Truman from a nap upstairs. A guard saw him come to the window and motioned the president to take cover. Approximately thirty shots were fired in less than three minutes, killing Torresola instantly and wounding Collazo in the chest. Three White House policemen were injured, two of whom recovered from multiple wounds. The third, Leslie Coffelt, who had fired the bullet that killed Torresola, died later that day.

The assassination attempt came two days after Torresola and Collazo, who were living in New York City and participating in the local branch of the Nationalist Party, received news of the October 30 uprising of approximately 2,000 nationalists on the island of Puerto Rico—during which Torresola's sister had been wounded and his brother Elio arrested. In July of that year, President Truman had signed Public Act 600, which allowed island residents to draft their own constitution establishing the Commonwealth of Puerto Rico. This action, coupled with the reversal of Governor Luis Muñoz Marín, a long-time advocate of independence who now came out in favor of commonwealth status, angered the nationalists, who responded by attacking La Fortaleza, Muñoz Marin's home, and declaring the town of Jayuya Puerto Rico's sovereign capital. In addition, island nationalists regarded President Truman's 1946 appointment of Jesús T. Piñero, Puerto Rico's first native governor, as an explicit example of U.S. colonial hegemony. Collazo and Torresola believed that the assassination of President Truman would further the cause of Puerto Rican independence.

Convicted of murder, attempted assassination, and assault with the intent to kill, Collazo was sentenced to death. However, one week before his scheduled execution on August 1, 1952, Truman commuted his death sentence to life imprisonment. In September 1979, after twenty-nine years in federal prison, U.S. President Jimmy Carter pardoned the sixty-five-year-old Collazo. Following his release, Collazo returned to Puerto Rico and continued to participate in activities of the Puerto Rican independence movement until his death on February 21, 1994.

Today, Puerto Rican nationalists, statehood advocates, U.S. officials, and other people worldwide continue to differ ideologically on the political status of Puerto Rico. Even the attack on Blair House is also viewed from different ideological perspectives. In 1979, Cuban President Fidel Castro decorated Collazo and other nationalists for their courage against what he considered imperialist acts administered by the United States. Images honoring Collazo and Torresola can be found in a mural located at the Puerto Rican Cultural Center of Chicago, while a plaque outside Blair House commemorates police officer Leslie Coffelt and his defense of President Truman on November 1, 1950.

Brian Montes

See also: Albizu Campos, Pedro; Nationalism; Puerto Ricans.

Further Reading

Lidin, Harold J. *History of the Puerto Rican Independence Movement.* Buffalo, NY: Waterfront: 1982.

Lopez, Alfredo. *Doña Lichás Island: Modern Colonialism in Puerto Rico.* Boston: South End, 1987.

Trias Monge, Jose. *Puerto Rico: Trials of the Oldest Colony in the World.* New Haven, CT: Yale University Press, 1999.

Blowouts

Between 1968 and 1972, Chicano students from different social classes joined forces with parents, barrio youth, and other community members to participate in a number of events that came to be known as "blowouts," when thousands of students walked out of class to protest racism in and outside their schools. By virtue of such racism, they charged, school systems were failing to provide an equitable education to Chicano students. Beginning in Los Angeles under the leadership of Sal Castro, a teacher at Lincoln High School, the blowouts soon spread to urban centers throughout the Southwest and Midwest, especially Texas, Colorado, Arizona, and New Mexico, and then across the nation.

Chicano students blamed the schools and local boards of education for creating many of the oppressive conditions in which they found themselves. Many schools were still segregated and lacked Chicano teachers, counselors, and classes related to Mexican American culture and history. Classrooms were often overcrowded, and students suffered from high dropout rates. Anglo teachers, it was charged, were badly trained and lacked understanding of the communities in which they taught. The blowouts came after years of frustration from unsuccessful attempts at improving the educational system. For students, a walkout seemed like the only tool available for creating positive change.

Given the general conditions at many schools, students demanded dramatic changes in the educational experience. High on their list of demands were equal treatment of Latino students, an end to school discrimination, general improvement in the quality of instruction, the inclusion of Chicano history and cultural classes in school curricula, the hiring of Chicano teachers and counselors, and the dismissal of racist faculty and administration. They also demanded that they be allowed to speak Spanish on school grounds, that schools create programs to address the obstacles faced by migrant students, and that school facilities be repaired and maintained. An end to discriminatory college counseling was another demand, since guidance counselors discouraged Chicano students from applying to college and suggested that they try to join the armed forces or enroll in some type of vocational schooling.

The leaders of the walkouts came from college and university groups like the Texas-based Mexican American Youth Organization (MAYO) and from Chicano leaders like Sal Castro in Los Angeles and José Angel Gutiérrez in Texas. Gutiérrez, with the help of MAYO, organized middle school and high school students in Texas for a number of blowouts. Between 1968 and 1972, few walkouts in the state occurred without the involvement of Gutiérrez and MAYO.

The response by school officials was generally negative, and at times hostile. In most cases, they used political manipulation to avoid students' demands. They also resorted to disciplinary action—such as suspension, expulsion, or withholding of diplomas—against those involved in the protests. In some cases, school buildings were locked up to keep students from demonstrating. In others, school officials threatened to use physical force to keep students in class or called on police and other law enforcement authorities to break up the demonstrations. Reactions from the Anglo community were generally negative; most viewed the resistance as juvenile delinquency or a threat to political and economic power.

With the exception of the walkouts in Crystal City, Texas, and Los Angeles, most failed to change school policy or give the community greater control over the schools. This failure may be attributed to a combination of bad timing, lack of parental and community support, the response of law enforcement agencies, minimal student participation, lack of leadership, and insufficient support from Chicano organizations. Still, the blowouts were the first events in which Chicano youth played a direct role in educational protest. They also represented the first loud call for Chicano power and set the stage for future activism. The burgeoning political and cultural awareness among Chicano youth contributed to the formation of the Chicano Student Movement and the Chicano Movement in general.

Ultimately, the walkouts brought about some educational improvements, specifically in administration, the treatment of Spanish-speaking students, and school curricula. They led directly to the development of courses relating to Mexican American culture and history, resulted in the hiring of more Chicano teachers and counselors, and forced school officials to develop programs designed to address the special needs of Spanish-speaking students. Even college campuses were affected by the walkouts, as a number of institutions initiated Chicano studies programs and began active recruitment of Chicano students.

Walking out became more than a fight for educational rights, and sometimes it accomplished more than a shakeup of local schools. On occasion it resulted in political developments that went beyond the issues of school reform. In Texas, for example, blowouts led to the formation of La Raza Unida Party (LRUP), a Mexican American political organization that gained political ascendancy in South Texas.

Jesse J. Esparza

See also: Acosta, Oscar; Chicano Movement; Crystal City; Education; East L.A. 13; East Los Angeles; Gutiérrez, José Angel; Mexican American Youth Organization.

Further Reading

Acuña, Rodolfo. *Occupied America: A History of Chicanos.* 6th ed. New York: Pearson Longman, 2007.

Briegel, Kaye. "Chicano Student Militancy: The Los Angeles High School Strike of 1968." In *An Awakened Minority: The Mexican Americans*, ed. Manuel P. Servin. New York: Macmillan, 1974.

Gómez-Quiñones, Juan. *Mexican Students Por La Raza: The Chicano Student Movement in Southern California, 1967–1977.* Santa Barbara, CA: Editorial La Causa, 1978.

Rosales, F. Arturo. *Chicano! The History of the Mexican American Civil Rights Movement.* Houston, TX: Arte Público, 1996.

Bolivians

Bolivian Americans represent only a small segment of the U.S. Latino population (approximately 1 percent) and an even smaller part of the total U.S. population (approximately one-tenth of 1 percent). Like other Latino/as, however, Bolivians have made their presence felt in many areas of society, culture, and everyday life.

Before becoming an independent republic in 1825, Bolivia for three centuries had been part of the Spanish Empire's viceroyalty of Peru. Prior to the Spanish conquest, for several centuries it had been the quarter of the Inca Empire called the Kollasuyo. Bolivia today is a multi-ethnic, multicultural, multilingual society with a strong indigenous American Indian presence. Its principal social institutions and dominant culture, however, remain profoundly Spanish, even as power has shifted from the *mestizos* (people of mixed race) to the indigenous segments of the population. Traditional Spanish culture places an emphasis on education in the humanities and careers in the liberal professions (for example, lawyers, professors, and writers). Bolivians share this attitude and value education as a source of pride and social prestige.

Few Bolivians immigrated to the United States prior to World War II, though some Bolivians were among the miners in the California gold rush of 1849–1850. The early Bolivian immigrants arrived by boat via the Pacific Ocean, initiating a connection between Bolivia and California that has continued to the present day. During the nineteenth century and the first half of the twentieth century, a tiny elite of landed gentry and mine owners dominated Bolivia. While members of this class frequently traveled or studied abroad, they seldom emigrated permanently. Most Bolivians, however, were landless Indian peasants who provided the labor for farms and mines. They did not have the means or knowledge to emigrate in large numbers until the era of inexpensive international air travel in the last decades of the twentieth century. Sandwiched in between these two extremes was a small but growing mestizo urban middle class, with ascending expectations and ambitions. People of this group became the emigrants, and most Bolivian Americans trace their roots from them.

During the course of the twentieth century, there were four significant waves of Bolivian immigration to the United States, dominated by Jewish refugees, landed gentry, middle-class professionals, and laborers, respectively. In the 1930s, some 20,000 Jewish refugees, primarily from Germany, Austria, and Czechoslovakia, arrived in Bolivia, fleeing Nazi-occupied Europe. Following the end of World War II, many of these Jewish Bolivians emigrated to the United States or Israel. The next wave came to the United States following the Bolivian Revolution of 1952, when the landed gentry were dispossessed of their holdings and the government expropriated the nation's largest mines. The third wave, many times larger than the previous one, began following the passage of the U.S. Immigration and Nationality Act of 1965. According to the U.S. Census, whereas in 1960 there were 1,792 persons born in Bolivia residing in the United States, by 1980 the number had increased to 14,620. This number doubled again to 32,194 by 1990. This wave of immigrants was made up largely of university-educated, upwardly mobile professionals, typically medical doctors, engineers, and economists, who found better prospects for themselves and their children in the United States. (Bolivia was and remains the poorest country in South America, and perhaps the least stable politically.) The final wave of immigrants began arriving in the United States in the 1980s and was made up largely of unskilled laborers. According to the 2000 U.S. census, there were 52,913 U.S. citizens or permanent residents who were born in Bolivia. In addition, an estimated 100,000–150,000 U.S.-born citizens have at least one parent or grandparent who was born in Bolivia. Other estimates place the total number of Bolivian Americans as high as half a million.

Bolivian Americans are widely dispersed throughout the United States and are generally well assimilated into mainstream society. Because of their Spanish dialect and their Spanish-Indian mestizo racial makeup, Bolivian Americans are often mistaken for Mexican Americans. For these reasons, they do not stand out in American life as Bolivians per se. However, a number of Bolivian Americans have attained widespread recognition for their individual achievements. Among the better known are four Californians: actress Raquel Welch (neé Tejada) of San Diego, conductor and violinist Jaime Laredo of San Francisco, State Assemblyman Alberto Torrico of Fremont, and high school calculus teacher Jaime Escalante of Los Angeles.

Among first generation of Bolivian American immigrants, most have university degrees. Thus, a substantial number of Bolivians in the United States are professionals, with engineers and medical doctors predominating. The tradition of pursuing higher education and professional careers has been passed on to their children, who attend many of America's elite universities. Bolivian American women are known for their high level of enterprise and achievement in academic, professional, and civic pursuits. Today, a sprinkling of Bolivian Americans can be found as tenured faculty at American universities, lawyers in Wall Street law firms, executives of Fortune 500 corporations, attending physicians at leading teaching hospitals, civil servants in local, state, and federal government, schoolteachers, real estate brokers, law enforcement offices, and members of the armed forces. Recent decades have also brought a substantial number of Bolivians without university degrees who have contributed to the nation's economy by pursuing a wide range of occupations and trades.

The Bolivian American experience today has as much in common with the experience of non-Latino Asian immigrants such as Indians and Chinese as it does with the experience of other Latino immigrants such as Mexicans and Salvadorans. Like the Indians and Chinese who entered into the United States following passage of the Immigration and Nationality Act of 1965, most Bolivians are university-educated professionals who found it relatively easy to secure white-collar employment. Economic security afforded entry into middle- and upper-middle-class neighborhoods, access to good schools, and opportunities to pursue excellence in a wide cross-section of activities. On the other hand, the Bolivian experience also has much in common with that of other Latino immigrants, including racial and ethnic discrimination, and, for those without university degrees or professional training, lesser opportunities in the job market. On balance, the Bolivian American experience is an immigrant success story—resulting from the pull of the United States as a land of opportunity, the push of a politically unstable and economically stagnant Bolivia, and the "carpe diem" attitude of the Bolivian Americans themselves.

Nelly S. González

See also: Mestizo/a.

Further Reading

Einstein, Carol. "Jaime Laredo, Musician." In *Claims to Fame Book 2: Fourteen Short Biographies.* Cambridge, MA: Educators Publishing Service, 2000.

Gumucio, Reynaldo J. *My Life Story.* Springfield; MO: Springfield-Greene County Library, Ethnic Life Stories Project, 2003. http://thelibrary.org/lochist/els/toc.cfm.

Romero, Maritza. *Jaime Escalante: Inspiring Educator.* New York: PowerKids, 1997.

Boricua

Boricua is a slang term that Puerto Ricans use to identify themselves, as in the phrase *"Yo soy Boricua."* Unlike the official Spanish term, *"Puertorriqueño,"* the word "Boricua" directly references the pre-Columbian indigenous name of the island—Borinquen or Borikén. Though the words can almost be used interchangeably, Boricua is generally used in a more friendly tone than its more formal counterpart, and the etymology of the term "Boricua" has different political implications. Since it alludes to the indigenous inhabitants and culture of the island prior to the Spanish (and later the American) conquest, "Boricua" is often considered a term of pride, one that acknowledges, yet resists and deplores, the particular kind of colonial violence that has marked the long history of Western empires in Puerto Rico.

The Spanish colonial rule over Puerto Rico lasted from the sixteenth century until 1898 and was, by all accounts, brutal and vicious for those who were not colonizers. Though accounts differ, scholars generally agree that the native population of Puerto Rico, the Taínos and the Arawaks, were decimated within a few generations of Spanish colonization.

By the middle of the sixteenth century, the Dominican priest and Spanish colonist Bartolomé de las Casas had begun advocating the use of African labor as a way of saving the indigenous populations from extinction. Scholars also agree that the practice of fleeing to the mountains (*irse las montañas*) was an important survival strategy for the native population and later African slaves. Given the historical context of enslavement and genocide, popular use of the term "Boricua," which translates as "Brave Lord," and its association with the pre-Columbian world, represents a challenge to colonial labels.

In the mainland United States, Boricua also has another political connotation. Mainland Puerto Rican scholars have begun to use the term to signify people of Puerto Rican descent without making explicit reference to geographic location. The term "Puerto Rican," for instance can wed a person's identity to the island itself. Likewise, the term "Nuyorican" (usually used to refer to persons of Puerto Rican ancestry born or raised in New York City) localizes a person to that particular place, or at least to the mainland. On the other hand, the term "Boricua" denotes a specific ethnic identity that has been formulated through multiple histories of colonialism, and, in this sense, it is more appropriate than either of the other two terms. Also, for many years, Puerto Ricans have felt the need to make a cultural distinction between those on the island and those on the mainland. This concern relates to claims about authenticity and reflects the different experiences that mark the two groups. In this context of differentiation, Puerto Rican is a term that, for the most part, signifies those living on the island.

A number of labels have been used to denominate mainland Puerto Ricans, including Nuyorican and Neo-Rican. Of the two, Nuyorican has been the most widely used; Neo-Rican never really experienced widespread use. The problem for many mainland Puerto Ricans, however, is that large numbers of the population do not live in New York City, as the term implies. Rather, there have been long-standing Puerto Rican communities throughout the Northeast and the Rust Belt of the Upper Midwest since the beginning of mass migration in the 1940s. Indeed, cities like Philadelphia, Chicago, Paterson, New Jersey, and Buffalo, New York, all have sizable Puerto Rican populations that are not strictly encapsulated in the term "Nuyorican." For this reason, many scholars have begun to use the term "Boricua" to refer to people living in various locations within the Puerto Rican diaspora.

A parallel can be drawn with the term "Chicano," insofar as Boricua signifies resistance to colonization. Like Chicanos, Boricuas, whether born in the United States or on the island, are essentially a conquered population who are American citizens by birth. The use of Boricua, then, also signals an uncomfortable cultural negotiation between being a citizen of empire and a spoil of it. Insofar as Boricua inherently points to a history of conquest, it is also a cultural affirmation, as Boricua names a cultural distinction that cannot be assimilated into mainstream American culture, even as it is a part of it. Similarly, by insisting on the popular use of its own name, Boricua/Borinquen/Borikén also resists the earlier conquest by refusing complete assimilation into the Spanish colonial past.

Lorna Perez

See also: Chicano/a; Identity and Labels; Puerto Ricans.

Further Reading

Flores, Juan. *Divided Borders: Essays on Puerto Rican Identity.* Houston, TX: Arté Publico, 1993.

González, Lisa Sánchez. *Boricua Literature: A Literary History of the Puerto Rican Diaspora.* New York: New York University Press, 2001.

Santiago, Roberto, ed. *Boricuas: Influential Puerto Rican Writings—An Anthology.* New York: One World, 1995.

Boxing

For many Latinos living in the United States, the talent, determination, and strength displayed by successful boxers—along with the glory, fame, and money that some of them earn—represent an attractive way to build the personal confidence to succeed in American society at large. At the same time, boxing talent can be a route away from the difficulties associated with inner-city life. More important, for many Latinos today, boxing represents a means of asserting cultural identity and expressing cultural pride. Indeed, many fight in a way that represents what they believe to be their heritage. Thus, in several respects, boxing provides a glimpse into what it means to be a Latino. Latinos have become a dominant force in the North American boxing scene in recent decades, adding a new dimension to the conduct, flavor, and diversity of the sport, and joining the ranks of champions.

In the history of boxing, Latinos (including those from the Caribbean) have comprised a formidable list of world-class boxers: lightweights Roberto Durán, Julio César Chávez, and Erik Morales, junior lightweight Héctor "Macho" Camacho, light middleweight Oscar de la Hoya, and middleweight Félix "Tito" Trinidad are among the most notable. Latinos have become a dominant group in international boxing, with several nations—such as Mexico, Puerto Rico, and Cuba—particularly known for producing great fighters. The talent is evident in the United States as well, where cities such as Los Angeles have developed as Latino centers for boxing. Besides being reflected in the number of champions, the respect and admiration that Latino fighters have earned is visible in the amount of money they have earned through cable television royalties, fight purses, and endorsements.

With the success of high-profile champions, Latinos also came to regard boxing as a positive extracurricular activity for young adults and at-risk youth. As evidenced by statistics collected from Latino students in the mid-1990s, participation in organized athletics is correlated with better grades, lower dropout rates, and college attendance. This is particularly true of gyms in urban settings, where aspiring boxers develop self-confidence and a respect from peers that replaces the tendency to get in trouble. This has certainly been the case in places such as East Los Angeles, where boxers like Oscar de la Hoya have opened gyms in low-income areas long plagued by gang violence and drugs. By teaching young boxers about hard work and emphasizing how a commitment to sports and education can facilitate achievement, boxing has kept many Latino youth on the path to success.

Despite their popularity and success in the North American boxing scene, Latino fighters have not succeeded in professional sports without acknowledging their race, ethnicity, culture, and community. Often Latino boxers "perform their ethnicity" in the ring, by wrapping themselves in the flag of their country of origin, wearing shorts displaying their national colors, or making statements in Spanish. The displays of nationalism or ethnic pride have led to heightened rivalries with boxers of different backgrounds—such as African Americans, Italians, and Russians—as well as between Latinos themselves; perhaps no rivalry is greater than that between Puerto Rican and Mexican fighters.

National and ethnic identity has even come to be associated with different styles of fighting. The stereotypical view of Mexican boxers is that of a hardworking, nontechnical "fighter" or "brawler" who focuses less on craft or strategy and more on heavy punching. This style of boxing is physically punishing, as fighters are willing to take hard blows in pursuing their attacks. The style thus corresponds to the general stereotype of Mexican men as macho, self-sacrificing individuals who are willingly to sacrifice their safety and well-being for their families or personal goals. Yet Mexicans are far from alone in sustaining this stereotype. The great Panamanian champion Roberto Durán was regarded as the quintessentially "macho" Latin fighter (at least until his second bout with Sugar Ray Leonard, in 1980, when he quit in the eighth round).

Finally, while boxing remains a predominantly male sport, Latinas have entered the ring in recent years for many of the same reasons as men—pursuing the respect of the community, material advantage, self-esteem, and sheer love of the sport.

Grant Joseph Silva

See also: De La Hoya, Oscar; Nationalism.

Further Reading

Kawakami, Tim. *Golden Boy: The Fame, Money, and Mystery of Oscar de la Hoya.* Kansas City, MO: Andrews McMeel, 1999.

Melnick, Merrill J., and Donald Sabo. "Sport and Social Mobility Among African American and Hispanic Athletes." In *Ethnicity and Sport in North American History and Culture,* ed. George Eisen and David Wiggins. Westport, CT: Greenwood, 1994.

Rodriguez, Gregory. "Boxing and Masculinity." In *Latino/a Popular Culture,* ed. Michelle Habell-Pallan and Mary Romero. New York: New York University Press, 2002.

Bracero Program

The Bracero Program was a federal contract labor program that grew out of a series of bilateral agreements between the Mexican government and the U.S. government. Beginning in 1942 until the program's demise in 1964, approximately 4.6 million Mexican men signed contracts to come to the United States and work primarily in the agricultural fields and railroad maintenance yards. These workers, called *braceros*, were hired on a short-term basis, for periods usually lasting from six weeks to eighteen months; at the end of the contract they were transported back to Mexico. They accounted for about one-fifth of all migratory workers in the United States and constituted the backbone of the U.S. agricultural and railroad workforce during and after World War II.

With the advent of World War II and conscription into the armed forces, U.S. agricultural growers complained to the federal government about severe labor shortages created when workers left the fruit fields for the battlefields. On August 4, 1942, the Roosevelt administration responded by finalizing the first contract labor agreement, under which Mexican farm laborers could be imported into the United States. Washington persuaded the Mexican government, as a wartime ally and "good neighbor" to the south, to sign off on the agreement. In turn, the U.S. government promised to settle outstanding oil company claims after Mexico nationalized foreign-owned oilfields. U.S. officials also claimed that the program would contribute to Mexico's economic development and transform it from a "backward" country into a modern nation-state. Similarly, the Mexican government reasoned that braceros would eventually return home with more money and new skills and ideas, and would introduce modern technology into the nation's agricultural sector. The Mexican government thus agreed to the first contract, but only with certain guarantees: payment of the prevailing wage received by domestic workers, free transportation back to Mexico at the end of the contract, free housing and meals at reasonable prices, occupational insurances at employers' expense, and employment for at least three-fourths of the contract period.

Mexican workers arrive in California under the Bracero Program—a temporary contract labor initiative between the U.S. and Mexican governments—in 1942. The guest workers filled U.S. labor shortages from World War II to 1964. *(J.R. Eyerman/Stringer/Time & Life Pictures/Getty Images)*

While listed on paper, however, the contract stipulations were rarely put into practice. First, the wage guarantees under the terms of the contract were generally ignored. Bracero wages were arbitrarily determined by the employer, and, since braceros could not organize a union to bargain collectively, they were forced to accept what they were given or be deported back to Mexico. In fact, the Bracero Program produced downward pressure on local farm wages because growers hired undocumented workers alongside braceros. As for living conditions, five to seven braceros typically were housed in cramped, military-style barracks with hard beds, poor ventilation, lack of facilities for washing, and no privacy. Bracero workers often complained about the lack of recreation and isolation due to the remote locations of camps. Complaints about the food were commonplace. A daily diet consisted of bland and poorly prepared food that sent some braceros to hospital beds and others to their employer's office to demand their native diet of tortillas and beans.

The Mexican government offered little help in resolving the contractual discrepancies and improving the plight of the migrants. In order to be chosen as a bracero, Mexican men had to pay for their transportation in advance at the recruiting center, endure long lines and a grueling inspection, purchase the required permits, and pass a medical examination. Once they met all the requirements and passed all the tests, they were handed over to a U.S. employer for transportation to the work site. When braceros complained to the Mexican consul about their low wages, poor housing conditions, and employer abuses, they were promised an investigation of grievances, but this usually came to naught. To ensure that the men would return to Mexico at the termination of the contract, U.S. employers deducted 10 percent of their wages into a special savings account that was to be made accessible only upon retirement. But the braceros never received the money. Into the twenty-first century, former braceros and their families have intensified their efforts to collect unpaid retirement funds that mysteriously disappeared somewhere between U.S. and Mexican banks. More recently, a class action lawsuit against the Mexican government was settled giving each ex-bracero $3,500, but only if he worked between 1942 and 1946 and could provide documentation of bracero work.

When the wartime agreement expired at the end of 1947, the Bracero Program was extended annually until a new agreement was reached in 1951 and Congress passed Public Law 78, which made labor importation legal until 1964. Growers lobbied the U.S. government to extend the program not because of labor shortages but out of a desire to hire cheap, docile, and easily disposed laborers. Under the first postwar agreement, the U.S. government was no longer the primary labor contractor for the braceros; now farm owners themselves served as recruiters and contractors. Moreover, the migrant workers were no longer guaranteed a minimum wage and other labor protections. After 1951, at the insistence of the Mexican government, the U.S. government resumed direct control of contracting. And although braceros had no legal or political rights, they did manage in some instances to organize and demand higher wages, preparation of Mexican food, and more recreational facilities. If their demands were not met, their only recourse was to slow down or stop working altogether. Many simply left their jobs and broke the contracts.

One of the program's most outspoken critics was Ernesto Galarza, an activist scholar whose books *Strangers in Our Fields* (1956) and *Merchants of Labor* (1964) exposed the exploitation and abuse of braceros and called for the termination of the program. Growing public outcry against the program also increased after the airing of a 1960 CBS television documentary by the respected journalist Edward R. Murrow, *Harvest of Shame*, which depicted the poverty and despair of migrant workers. The contract labor program ended on December 31, 1964, but U.S. growers continued to hire Mexican workers as undocumented immigrants. The termination of the Bracero Program ultimately led to a significant increase in undocumented migrant workers (in part because of the social networks and employment relations established over the years), the relocation of manufacturing assembly plants known as *maquiladoras* to the U.S.-Mexico border, and the creation of a small-scale temporary worker visa program known as H-2A Certification.

In the early twenty-first century, more than four decades after the demise of the Bracero Program, U.S. employers and politicians, both Democrat and Republican, raised the prospect of a guest-worker program in some new form that would allow hundreds of thousands of Mexican workers into the country. The prospect was raised in the context of a major overhaul of federal immigration law that did not immediately come to pass. With all the arguments for and against such a program, and what form it should take, few could disagree that the dark side of the Bracero Program—poverty wages, employer abuses, lack of adequate government protection, and the absence of any enforcement or redress mechanism—must not be repeated.

José M. Alamillo

See also: Galarza, Ernesto; Mexicans; Migrant Workers; Operation Wetback; Repatriation.

Further Reading

Calavita, Kitty. *Inside the State: The Bracero Program, Immigration, and the I.N.S.* New York: Routledge, 1992.

Gonzalez, Gilbert G. *Guest Workers or Colonized Labor? Mexican Labor Migration to the United States.* Boulder, CO: Paradigm, 2007.

Brazilians

Brazil has long been a nation that receives immigrants, but a new trend emerged in the 1980s, as significant numbers of Brazilians began emigrating to developed countries, including the United States. Of an estimated 1.9 million Brazilians living abroad today, about 1 million are believed to live in the United States. The total according to the U.S. census figure is much lower, reflecting the difficulties of counting and the nature of the census questionnaire, which does not list "Brazilian" as a choice, and the reluctance of many Brazilian residents to answer census questions because of their undocumented status.

Almost 90 percent of Brazilians reside on the East Coast, with large communities in New York City (300,000), Miami (200,000), and Boston (150,000). Portuguese-speaking enclaves in the Northeast made initial settlement easier, though Portuguese and Brazilian immigrants did not necessarily develop a close affinity. Brazilians have also begun moving farther west; metropolitan Los Angeles, for example, claims to have 33,000 Brazilians.

Brazilian immigrants, called *brazucas*, have a specific profile. In the past brazucas have tended to be young, in their later twenties through forties, typically middle class, and well educated, with perhaps half having attended college. The profile has changed in recent years, however, as the establishment of communities and changes in immigration law have made it easier for working-class immigrants to succeed in America.

The Brazilian immigrant community remains relatively well off, a function of changes in both Brazil and the United States in the postwar period, especially the economic globalization of the latter part of the twentieth century. Brazilians have formed part of the new wave of transnational immigrants who maintain family, cultural, and legal connections in both their new homeland and their country of origin. This is aided by greatly improved and easier access to transportation and communication technologies. As a pull factor, immigration to a more developed country provides opportunities for the middle class to maintain their class position; as a push factor, economic crises at home (including rampant inflation) have forced many Brazilians to seek opportunities abroad.

In the United States, brazucas tend to take manual jobs (restaurant service, housecleaning, babysitting, shoe shining, and the like), which they would not necessarily take in Brazil. Although the compensation is modest by U.S. standards, it is still superior to the wages in Brazil for middle-class jobs. Most brazucas do not intend to remain permanently in the United States; their goal is usually to earn enough money to meet financial needs at home—make a down payment on a house, buy a car, or send their children to private school—and then leave. Working-class Brazilians in America also send money home to help support family members or repay the loans taken for the trip itself; as of 2004, Brazil ranked second to Mexico in terms of U.S. dollars received from abroad.

Regardless of purpose, entry into the United States—not easy to begin with—has become even more difficult since the national security initiatives following the terrorist attacks of September 11, 2001. The crackdown on undocumented immigrants has made it more difficult for Brazilians whose tourist visas have expired or who do not have a green card for employment to enter or remain in the country. As a result, an increasing number of Brazilians have entered the United States by crossing its borders, especially the one with Mexico, illegally.

As they have for decades, brazucas quickly discover that Americans often lump them together with other Latinos/as and harbor perceptions of Brazilian culture shaped by images of Carmen Miranda, *Carnaval*, and the Amazon wilderness. Few realize that Brazil has the largest non–Spanish speaking population in South America. Brazilians, with their long tradition of "racial" intermixture and more fluid notions of race, do not readily fit into the U.S. "racial" binary of black and white. With their strong sense of national identity and pride of culture, Brazilians reject even general classification as "Latino"—though there is a stronger willingness to interact and share identity with Hispanic communities in some locations than in others. In Miami, for example, where many Cubans enjoy high status, better-off Brazilians are more likely to embrace their *latinidade* (Latin roots) than elsewhere. Still, Brazilians anywhere in the United States publicly embrace symbols of their "brazilianness," from dancing the samba to celebrating *Carnaval.* U.S. access to TV Globo Internacional and a busy Brazilian press in the United States have helped maintain a strong national identity and close ties with the homeland.

Ellen Bigler

Further Reading

Beserra, Bernadete. *Brazilian Immigrants in the United States: Cultural Imperialism and Social Class.* New York: LFB Scholarly Publishing, 2003.

Margolis, Maxine. *An Invisible Minority: Brazilians in New York City.* Boston: Allyn and Bacon, 1998.

———. *Little Brazil: An Ethnography of Brazilian Immigrants in New York City.* Princeton, NJ: Princeton University Press, 1994.

Brothers to the Rescue

Brothers to the Rescue, Inc. (Hermanos al Rescate) is a nonprofit, anti-Castro, Cuban exile organization based in Miami, Florida. The organization was founded in 1991 by José Basulto, a veteran of the Bay of Pigs (on the side of the exiles), following the death of Gregorio Pérez Ricardo, a fifteen-year-old boy who succumbed to dehydration while fleeing Cuba on a raft. Since its inception, Brothers to the Rescue has carried out more than 2,400 aerial search missions and has rescued more than 4,200 rafters (*balseros*) trying to escape Cuba through the Florida Straits. Such attempts were especially common in the early 1990s. In 1994 alone, an estimated 50,000 or more Cubans attempted to reach the United States on homemade rafts.

Brothers to the Rescue relies on volunteer pilots. Their volunteers come from a number of countries, including Argentina, Peru, France, Jamaica, Nicaragua, Puerto Rico, Switzerland, the United States, and Venezuela. Its ranks also include Cubans who were once rafters themselves. The organization is supported by donations from various other groups as well as individuals.

When a raft is sighted, the Brothers to the Rescue pilots inform the U.S. Coast Guard, which then sends a helicopter or ship to pick up the rafters. The Brothers also airdrop food and water supplies to rafters in more remote areas so they can survive until help arrives. Other activities of the Brothers include delivery of supplies to a Cuban refugee camp in the Bahamas, humanitarian aid to families of Cuban political prisoners, and support of human rights for all Cubans. Considered a terrorist organization by the Cuban government, Brothers to the Rescue has continued to support internal opposition to the Castro regime, encouraging nonviolent rebellion.

In 1996, the Brothers sent unarmed civilian planes over Cuba to drop flyers containing the United Nations's Universal Declaration of Human Rights. Immediately the Cuban government accused the pilots of violating Cuban airspace and issued warnings to the planes. Brothers to the Rescue ignored the warnings and continued the flights. On February 24, 1996, the Cuban air force shot down two Brothers to the Rescue planes that had been flying close to the island. As a result, three U.S. citizens, Armando Alejandre, Carlos Costa, and Mario de la Peña, and a legal U.S. resident, Pablo Morales, were killed. One plane and its crew survived.

At the urging of Cuban Americans and other supporters, the U.S. government launched an investigation, concluding that the planes had been in international airspace. The Cuban government, claiming a violation of Cuban airspace, accused Washington of fabricating evidence about the planes' locations and being disinclined to enforce the existing international laws regarding violations of sovereignty. The incident resulted in the United States and Cuba confronting each other at the United Nations, and the UN Security Council passing a resolution at the end of the year that denounced Cuba for downing the planes.

Prior to this incident, many inside the United States predicted that President Bill Clinton was ready to relax the thirty-seven-year U.S. embargo on Cuba. In the wake of the plane incident, however, President Clinton condemned the Cuban government's aggressive behavior, ended all commercial flights to Cuba, restricted domestic travel of Cuban diplomats, and authorized compensation for the families of the victims of the downed planes. Furthermore, Republican members of Congress used the incident to pressure President Clinton to support stronger sanctions against Cuba. As a result of the Brothers to the Rescue incident and the turmoil that followed, President Clinton signed into law the Helms-Burton Act, which intensified the U.S. embargo, including the imposition of sanctions on companies that did business with Cuba.

The friction between the U.S. and Cuban governments continued. Under a new U.S. antiterrorism law, the families of the killed airmen won $187 million in damages after suing the Cuban government. In 2000, the U.S. government gave the families partial payment of $38 million seized from the frozen assets of Cuban telephone companies. The tragedy also left Brothers to the Rescue in turmoil, as the families of the victims excluded Basulto and the Brothers organization from the court settlement. Nevertheless, Brothers to the Rescue continues to play an active role in promoting nonviolent change in Cuba, as well as rescuing refugees fleeing the island.

C. Alison Newby

See also: Balseros; Bay of Pigs Invasion; Castro, Fidel; Cuban Refugee Program; Cubans.

Further Reading

Brothers to the Rescue. http://www.hermanos.org.

Gonzalez-Pando, Miguel. *The Cuban Americans.* Westport, CT: Greenwood, 1998.

Levine, Robert M. *Secret Missions to Cuba: Fidel Castro, Bernardo Benes, and Cuban Miami.* New York: Palgrave Macmillan, 2002.

Morley, Morris, and Chris McGillion. *Unfinished Business: America and Cuba after the Cold War, 1989–2001.* New York: Cambridge University Press, 2002.

Brown Berets

A group of radical Chicano activists who utilized direct action demonstrations and self-defense to protest discrimination against Mexican Americans in the American Southwest, the Brown Berets evolved from the Young Citizens for Community Action (YCCA). In 1966, several high school and college youths—including David Sánchez, Vickie Castro, Moctezuma Esparza, Ralph Ramírez, Rachel Ochoa, George Licón, and John Ortiz—organized the YCCA to oppose school segregation and support reform-minded politicians. At the same time, they began to focus on another major problem affecting area Chicanos/as: brutality on the part of the predominantly white Los Angeles Police Department (LAPD). After several demonstrations against police harassment, YCCA activists called for action beyond marches.

Chicano activist Carlos Montes, a founding member of the Brown Berets, addresses a crowd of protestors in Kansas City, Missouri, during the Poor Peoples' March on Washington in May 1968. *(AP Images/William Straeter)*

Early Activities

In January 1968, the YCCA, following in the footsteps of the Black Panther Party, transformed itself into a self-defense unit geared toward protecting community members from police brutality and other forms of state violence. Wearing khaki clothing and brown berets, the group emerged with a new agenda and a new name: the Brown Berets. The group also modeled its structural organization and the specific titles for its leadership after those of the Black Panther Party. The original Brown Berets were led by many of the original YCCA founders: Sánchez became the organization's first prime minister, while Ramírez was named the minister of discipline. New members Carlos Montes and Cruz Olmeda served as minister of information and chairman, respectively. The organization promoted Chicano cultural nationalism, demanded strict discipline, and emphasized masculinity as a desirable trait among its members; thus, a vast majority of the leadership was male.

The first test for the Brown Berets came in 1968 following student walkouts, commonly referred to as blowouts, at five East Los Angeles high schools. During that year, students began to protest in response to what they deemed years of harassment and abuse by school officials and administrators, which included punishment for speaking Spanish and the practice of expelling Latino youth if they received a failing grade. The students demanded Chicano teachers and counselors who would address Latino student needs. To publicize these issues, they began to walk out of their schools in March 1968, chanting "blowout" as they marched into the streets. The Brown Berets initially advised the students regarding tactics of civil disobedience and their civil rights. When LAPD officers attacked several protestors, the Brown Berets became the students' primary defenders. In addition to protecting the students, the Berets stood in for students when confronted by police.

In the months following the blowouts, sympathy and support for the Brown Berets increased after a grand jury indicted five of them for conspiracy to disrupt the operation of public schools, a charge that could have resulted in forty-five years in prison. The East Los Angeles community vigorously supported the Berets, and the plight of these militant activists became national news. Seizing on the groundswell of support and the increased militancy within the Chicano community, the Berets issued a ten-point program. This included: a call for unity among all people of Latin American descent, the right to bilingual education, the formation of a civilian review board made up of Chicanos/as to monitor police activity, the teaching of an accurate history of Mexican American people, the right to vote, and the right to trial by a jury of peers. Many of the demands were neither radical nor militant, but symbolic of Brown Beret efforts within the community. Indeed, most members did not identify themselves as revolutionaries. Unlike the Black Panthers, the Brown Berets refused to carry guns. Instead, they hoped to inspire community members to take a stance against police harassment and hoped to promote a "positive" vision of Mexican American culture.

Causes, Tactics, Competing Interests

Notwithstanding the reformist tendencies, some inside the Berets sought a more militant posture. These individuals took on a radical, pro-Marxist agenda and viewed the Brown Berets as a paramilitary force that could be used to protect the community from abusive police officers and other forms of violence. Sánchez disagreed with these sentiments and almost single-handedly kept the organization from adopting more militant tactics and ideologies. But others within the organization, including Olmeda, saw a problem with the disproportionate number of high school and college students who made up the Beret's membership. They hoped instead to align the group with older radicals, combat veterans, and even local gang members in an effort to maximize the Beret's potential as a revolutionary militia. The struggles between Sánchez and Olmeda compromised the effectiveness of the Berets and ultimately resulted in irreconcilable differences between the two men. Olmeda eventually left the organization and formed a rival group called La Junta.

Olmeda's departure cemented Sánchez's hold on the Brown Berets and ensured that the group still would advocate reformist tactics. However, the Berets continued to be portrayed by the media and local politicians as revolutionary, and this view was confirmed in early 1969 at the third annual Nuevas Vistas Conference held at the Los Angeles Biltmore Hotel, when the Brown Berets once again had trouble with the police. The conference was designed to open a dialogue between school administrators and the Mexican American community, but the keynote speaker was Governor Ronald Reagan, a political conservative whose presence almost guaranteed some form of protest. During Reagan's speech, protestors heckled him, eventually taking control of the stage and starting several small fires in the auditorium. It took a cadre of fifty LAPD officers and hotel security guards to end the protest. Although it was never determined how many Brown Berets were actually involved in the incident, the arrests of Carlos Montes and Ralph Ramírez generated widespread criticism. During the trial, testimony revealed that the Berets had been under police surveillance since shortly after the group's formation.

Despite the negative press and increased attention by law enforcement, the Brown Berets continued to serve the community through the end of the 1960s. Indeed, the group proved highly popular in the latter part of the decade. It expanded rapidly, opening chapters throughout the Southwest. David Sánchez claimed that the organization had more than 5,000 members. The group also expanded operations in the East Los Angeles Chicano community, opening a free medical clinic in late 1969 and drawing attention to such community issues as unemployment, inadequate housing, and poverty. The Brown Berets also became actively involved in the anti–Vietnam War movement, assisting students at the University of California at Los Angeles in forming the first National Chicano Moratorium Committee in 1969. Through the work of the Brown Berets, the Chicano Moratorium staged antiwar protests throughout the Southwest.

The succession of events damaged the unity of the Brown Berets, and the group foundered in the early 1970s. While they continued to defend Chicano activists, the Berets also engaged in less successful protests. For example, members participated in the Caravan of the Reconquest, a driving tour through California, Arizona, Colorado, New Mexico, and Texas to protest the "theft" of these lands from Mexico during the Mexican-American War. And in 1972, members of the group occupied Santa Catalina Island off the California coast in a symbolic protest mirroring the nineteen-month occupation of Alcatraz Island by the American Indian Movement beginning in 1969. But the borrowing of tactics from other groups further divided the Brown Berets leadership; many felt that Sánchez had acquired too much power and was not using it wisely. When the executive committee finally fired him in late 1972, it was too late to save the organization. The Berets continued to suffer from police harassment, and the Federal Bureau of Investigation had succeeded in infiltrating the group. The Brown Berets—a symbol of Chicano pride and inspiration to an emerging generation of Mexican Americans—finally dissolved in 1973.

Brian D. Behnken

See also: Blowouts; Chicano Movement; East Los Angeles; Nationalism; Vietnam War.

Further Reading

Acuña, Rudolfo. *Occupied America: A History of Chicanos.* 5th ed. New York: Pearson Longman, 2004.

Chávez, Ernesto. *"¡Mi Raza Primero!" (My People First): Nationalism, Identity, and Insurgency in the Chicano Movement in Los Angeles, 1966–1978.* Berkeley: University of California Press, 2002.

Haney-López, Ian F. *Racism on Trial: The Chicano Fight for Justice.* Cambridge, MA: Harvard University Press, 2003.

Rosales, F. Arturo. *Chicano! The History of the Mexican American Civil Rights Movement.* Houston, TX: Arte Público, 1996.

C

Carnalismo

The term *carnalismo* refers to emotional relationships between Latino men in parts of Mexico and the western United States. Mexican American—or Chicano—males have referred to each other as *carnal* or *carnales* since the great waves of Mexican immigration to the Southwest during the 1920s. Literally meaning "of the flesh" (*carne*), the term has been used to refer to brothers (or "brotherhood"), but also to the tight bonds formed between friends in *pachuco* and barrio culture.

Perhaps the most significant images of pachuco males in U.S. society are those of the Zoot Suit Riots of 1943 in Los Angeles, where U.S. military personnel and civilians attacked young men and teenagers dressed in zoot suits. The zoot suit, consisting of a long jacket and high-waisted pegged trousers, was seen as a sign of pomposity and arrogance, two characteristics that were not tolerated among people of color in the United States. In addition to their flamboyant clothes, pachucos spoke in the *caló* Spanish dialect. Caló is said to incorporate Romany (or Gypsy) words imported to Mexico by Spanish gypsies in the nineteenth century—although *carnal* (pronounced car-NALL) is believed to be Spanish in origin.

In the barrio, being a carnal means being willing to die for a comrade in arms during times of barrio warfare. Some scholars believe that historic conditions of racism and second-class status for Mexican Americans in the Southwest fostered extremely close friendships among males, macho in their attributes and usually using the caló dialect. In working-class and poor Latino communities where neighborhoods become islands of safety, carnalismo symbolizes bonds of love that are often masked as *machismo.*

Prison is one place where carnalismo takes the form of bonding. California Latino prison gang members refer to each other as *carnales* when speaking about official members. (This has a parallel in Italian American organized crime, in which Mafia members introduce one another as "a friend of ours.") More recently, Latina gang members in the western United States have called themselves *carnalas,* in a feminine version of traditional street bonding. They have even applied the name to all-female gangs, such as *Las Rojas Carnalas.*

During the Chicano Movement of the late 1960s and early 1970s, political activities aimed at social justice were dominated by men. At this time Chicano college students began referring to carnalismo—a political and social brotherhood of activists. A term rich in history, carnalismo has taken on different connotations with changing social, political, and geographic conditions. When describing the social bonds of poor and working-class men, it illustrates an aspect of Latino life that is ever changing and hard to define—one piece of the complex language and cultural experience of Latinos in the United States.

E. Mark Moreno

See also: Chicano/a; Chicano Movement; Machismo; Zoot Suit Riots.

Further Reading

Espinoza, Dionne. "'Revolutionary Sisters': Women's Solidarity and Collective Identification among Chicana Brown Berets in East Los Angeles, 1967–1970." *Aztlan* 25:1 (Spring, 2005): 17–58.

Limon, Jose E. "'Carne, Carnales, and the Carnivalesque: Bakhtinian 'Batos,' Disorder, and Narrative Discourses." *American Ethnologist* 16:3 (August 1989): 471–86.

Mazón, Mauricio. *The Zoot-Suit Riots: The Psychology of Symbolic Annihilatio.* Austin: University of Texas Press, 1984.

McWilliams, Carey. *North from Mexico: The Spanish-Speaking People of the United States.* Updated by Matt S. Meier. New York: Greenwood, 1990.

Castellanos, Rosario (1925–1974)

Rosario Castellanos was, after the seventeenth-century writer Sor Juana Inés de la Cruz, the first Mexican woman author whose work was widely recognized outside Mexico. Her writings—poems, novels, short stories, and essays—reflect a constant concern for the oppression under which Mexican women have lived since colonial times. Although she was a victim of such oppression herself, Castellanos emerged as a central figure of modern Mexican literature thanks to the originality and quality of her work.

Castellanos was born in Mexico City on May 25, 1925, to a well-to-do family of Chiapas, Mexico's southernmost state. She spent her childhood and youth in Comitán, then an isolated, provincial town in Chiapas with a strong indigenous presence and where her father had large landholdings. In 1941, Castellanos and her family moved to Mexico City, after the agrarian reform of President Lázaro Cárdenas partially affected their land possessions. Castellanos began writing poetry at the age of fifteen, and in 1950 she obtained a master's degree in philosophy at the Universidad Nacional Autónoma de México (UNAM). As a student, she was involved with the group of writers later referred to as the *generación de 1950.* This group, known for its break with symbolism, until then the dominant trend in Latin American letters, counted among its members Emilio Carballido and Jaime Sabines of Mexico, Ernesto Cardenal of Nicaragua, and Augusto Monterroso of Guatemala.

Castellanos's parents died in 1948, the same year in which she published her first volumes of poetry: *Apuntes de fe* (*Notes on Faith*) and *Trayectoria de polvo* (*Trajectory of Dust*). After graduate work in Madrid and a fellowship at the Centro Mexicano de Escritores, Castellanos directed a puppet theater group of the Instituto Nacional Indigenista in San Cristóbal de las Casas, Chiapas. Her experience with indigenous communities had a decisive impact on her work and inspired two of her best-known novels: *Balún-Canán* (1957) and *Oficio de tinieblas* (*Book of Lamentations*; 1962).

From 1960 to 1971 she served as professor and press secretary of the UNAM. While engaged as visiting professor at the University of Wisconsin–Madison, she was awarded both the Xavier Villaurrutia Prize and the Sor Juana Inés de la Cruz Prize. In 1971 Castellanos was appointed Mexico's ambassador to Israel. She died there on August 7, 1974, in an accidental electrocution at her Tel Aviv residence.

Contrary to the literary fashions of her time, whereby many Mexican writers looked down on native and national subjects, Castellanos denounced the inequality and injustice in Mexican society and pointed to the indigenous population as the people who have suffered most keenly. But Castellanos did not attempt to vindicate the Mexican *indios* and avoided casting them in a mythological light, as writers of the so-called *indigenista* movement had done. On the contrary, Castellanos regarded native peoples as "human beings, absolutely equal to whites, only placed in special and unfavorable circumstances," which "had atrophied their best qualities."

The poetry of Rosario Castellanos, influenced especially by the work of Chilean poet Gabriela Mistral and the Frenchman Saint-John Perse, is characterized by an intimate tone and the expression of suffering implicit in the human condition. Her images are removed from mere symbolism and express a concrete reality. Although much of her narrative writing has a distinctly poetic tone, her style became more sober and direct in her later works. According to Emmanuel Carballo, one of Mexico's foremost literary critics, the author reached her creative maturity with her book of short stories *Los convidados de agosto* (*August Guests*; 1964) "because she does away with any anthropological preoccupation (her characters are no longer Indians or Whites, they are human beings) and because her style rejects prose-poetry and follows the norms of narrative prose."

In her work, Castellanos manifested an abiding concern for the subordination of women to men in Mexico's patriarchal society. Although the author cannot be properly considered a "feminist," she is considered a precursor of Mexico's women's liberation movement for her powerful denunciation of the oppression of Mexican women. This was the main theme of *Mujer que sabe latín* (*A Woman Who Knows Latin*; 1973) and of many of her essays. "Nobody in this country," wrote the Mexican poet José Emilio Pacheco, "has been . . . so keenly aware of the meaning of the double condition as a woman and as a Mexican. Neither has anyone made such awareness the raw material of her work."

Alberto Hernández-Lemus and
Juan Carlos Hernández Lemus

See also: Indigenismo; Mexicans; Women.

Further Reading

Ahern, Maureen, ed. *A Rosario Castellanos Reader: An Anthology of Her Poetry, Short Fiction, Essays, and Drama.* Austin: University of Texas Press, 1988.

Castellanos, Rosario. *Cartas a Ricardo.* Mexico City, Mexico: Consejo Nacional para la Cultura y las Artes, 1994.

Franco, María Estela. *Rosario Castellanos: Semblanza psicoanalítica otro modo de ser humano y libre.* Mexico City, Mexico: Plaza y Janés, 1984.

O'Connell, Joanna. *Prospero's Daughter: The Prose of Rosario Castellanos.* Austin: University of Texas Press, 1995.

Castillo, Ana (1953–)

Using her works in poetry, fiction, and essay as a form of social protest, the Chicana writer Ana Castillo—also known as Ana Hernandez Del Castillo—has emerged as a leading force in contemporary Chicano and Latino studies, women's studies, and American literature. She has worked in both academia and the community to help to define an oppositional Chicana feminism that honors La Chicana while building connections to other Latino/a and women's issues, and one that challenges the boundaries of the mainstream by highlighting the power of marginalized voices.

Born in Chicago on June 15, 1953, Castillo began melding her talents as a writer and her activist impulses as a young college student in the 1970s. While attending Chicago City College and then Northeastern Illinois University, she participated in the organization of Latino artists into the Association of Latino Brotherhood of Artists, recognizing the potential of art in helping to build coalitions among Latinos/as in the United States. She received her bachelor's degree in art from Northeastern Illinois in 1975 and two years later self-published her first book of poetry, *Otro Canto,* which explicitly examined themes of oppression among Third World peoples. Castillo worked as writer in residence for the Illinois Arts Council from 1977 to 1979, and in the latter year she also earned a master's degree in Latin American and Caribbean Studies at the University of Chicago. In 1991, she received a PhD in American Studies from the University of Bremen in Germany.

Throughout her career, Castillo has rigorously balanced her life as a writer, teacher, and activist. In 1986, however, her work as a writer took center stage when, while teaching at various colleges and universities in California, she published *The Mixquiahuala Letters.* This landmark epistolary novel launched her into the forefront of the burgeoning Chicana feminist literary movement. Told in a series of letters, the story chronicles the journey through Mexico of two American women with different relationships to their Mexican ethnicity. Reflecting Castillo's belief in the need for coalitions between Latinas specifically, and between women more generally, *The Mixquiahuala Letters* earned her the Before Columbus Foundation's American Book Award in 1987. Indeed it marked only the beginning of her contributions to the field of oppositional Chicana feminism.

The long list of Castillo's seminal works in Chicana literature and women's studies attests to her devotion to her craft as a writer and her life as an activist and coalition builder. Her several books of poetry include *Women Are Not Roses* (1984), *My Father Was a Toltec* (1988), and *I Ask the Impossible* (2001). The last was completed while she was a dissertation fellow in the Chicano Studies Department at the University of California, Santa Barbara. Castillo's fictional works include the short story collection *Loverboys* (1997) and the novel *Peel My Love Like an Onion* (1999). Collective works include the Spanish-language translation of the groundbreaking feminist text *This Bridge Called My Back* (1981), which she translated with Cherríe Moraga in 1988; *The Sexuality of Latinas* (1991), coedited with both Norma Alarcón and Cherríe Moraga; and her own edited collection, *Goddess of the Americas/La Diosa de las Americas* (1996), which reimagines la Virgen de Guadalupe from varied perspectives, including feminist, indigenous, and erotic, in an effort to reclaim a specific Latina power within the Catholic religion.

Although the span and impact of Castillo's work are far-reaching, two in particular, along with *Mixquiahuala Letters,* underscore her commitment to the power and spirit of Latinas, as well as her place as a leading voice in Chicana feminism. Her 1993 novel *So Far From God* and her 1994 essay collection *Massacre of the Dreamers: Essays on Xicanisma* represent Castillo's most serious efforts to address the breadth of Chicana/Latina experience. Completed with the aid of a fellowship from the National Endowment for the Arts, *So Far From God* tells the story of Sofia and her four daughters, who live in New Mexico and confront the daily tribulations of modern life. Castillo tells their story in the style of magical realism, integrating aspects of magical fantasy and questions of faith into the traditional form of the novel. Sofia's youngest daughter dies and is resurrected as "La Loca," propelling the story forward in its ambitious quest to examine the ways in which the spiritual, the sensual, and the feminine combine to bring power and faith to the world. The novel earned Castillo the 1993 Carl Sandburg Literary Award in Fiction.

Massacre of the Dreamers: Essays on Xicanisma explores the trajectory of Chicana feminism and the directions the movement is headed. The idea of *xicanisma* is Castillo's own creation, giving name to a new kind of Chicana feminism that challenges the limitations of using binaries like black/white, masculine/feminine, or straight/gay to create identity. Although the essays cover varied topics, all deal in some way with the plight of brown women in both Latin America and the United States facing systems of patriarchy and oppression.

Castillo's efforts to blend activism with the creative arts have had a profound effect on the shape and direction of contemporary Chicana feminist politics, as well as the mainstream American market for Latina/o literature. While she continues to write, she also maintains a rigorous, international speaking schedule, raises a son, and teaches as a writer in residence in the English Department at De Paul University in Chicago.

Lisa Guerrero

See also: Chicano Studies; Feminism.

Further Reading

Alarcón, Norma. "The Sardonic Powers of the Erotic in the Work of Ana Castillo." In *Breaking Boundaries: Latina Writing and Critical Readings,* ed. Asuncíon Horno-Delgado, Eliana Ortega, Nina M. Scott, and Nancy Saporta Sternbach. Amherst: University of Massachusetts Press, 1989.

Dubrava, Patricia. "Ana Castillo: Impressions of a Xicana Dreamer: A Profile." *Bloomsbury Review* 15:6 (November–December 1995): 5, 13.

Spurgeon, Sara. *Ana Castillo.* Boise, ID: Boise State University, 2004.

Castro, Fidel (1926–)

Cuban revolutionary leader Fidel Castro rose to national power in 1959 after overthrowing the dictator Fulgencio Batista and became head of the first Communist nation in the Western Hemisphere. In February 2008, by which time he was the longest-ruling head of state in the world, Castro officially announced that he would be giving up his positions as president and commander in chief. (He had effectively ceded power to his brother Raúl in mid-2006 due to illness.) During his nearly half century in power, tens of thousands of Cubans were exiled or fled to the United States. His leadership was marked by close relations with the Soviet Union and tense relations with the United States, the latter characterized by such events as the 1961 Bay of Pigs invasion—a failed attempt by Cuban exiles, supported by the U.S. government, to topple the Castro regime; the 1962 Cuban Missile Crisis, a diplomatic showdown between the United States and the Soviet Union over the U.S. discovery of Soviet missile bases on Cuba; the 1980 Mariel Boatlift, in which more than 120,000 Cubans fled the island for the United States; and other incidents. Cuban Americans held strong opinions regarding Castro and his regime. While some supported his leadership, a majority regarded him as a self-aggrandizing dictator who stymied the nation's economic potential and abused the rights of the people. In the aftermath of Castro's regime, untold thousands of exiles hoped for the opportunity to return to Cuba.

Early Life and Education

Castro was born on August 13, 1926, in the small town of Birán in northeastern Cuba, some 400 miles (640 kilometers) from the politically charged streets of Havana. The son of wealthy sugar plantation owners Angel Castro and Lina Ruz González, he had six brothers and sisters. Moving from school to school because of poor behavior and academic difficulties, he had a challenging time making friends and accepting discipline from teachers and other school authority figures. In 1941, he entered Belén College, an exclusive Jesuit high school in Havana. Despite his tumultuous education experience, Castro excelled in athletics and developed an abiding interest in the lives of political leaders, especially those involved in the Cuban Independence Movement, such as José Martí, Antonio Maceo y Grajales, and Calixto García Iñiguez. In 1941, Castro sent a note to U.S. President Franklin Delano Roosevelt to congratulate him on his reelection and also to ask him for "ten American dollars"—an ironic request given his future relationship with the United States.

In 1946, Castro enrolled in the University of Havana law school, where he became politically active. The following year, he joined forces with fellow Cubans and Dominican exiles in an attempted yet aborted plot to overthrow dictator Rafael Trujillo in the Dominican Republic. After receiving his law degree in 1950, Castro became leader of the Cuban People's Party (Ortodoxo Party) in 1951. He ran for the national House of Representatives on the Ortodoxo ticket in 1952, but before the elections took place General Fulgencio Batista overthrew the government of President Carlos Prío Socarrás.

Revolution

The Batista regime was marked by widespread poverty and lack of social and economic opportunities for fully one-third of the Cuban population. The regime, which had the support of the United States, fell into a vicious circle whereby it alienated the common people through repressive policies, which only intensified the political opposition and elicited further repression. In 1952, Castro convened a small group of Ortodoxos with the goal of toppling Batista. The group, nicknamed *Fidelistas,* was made up primarily of working-class Cubans, including sugarcane workers and peasant farmers, along with students and labor organizers. Despite the risk of arrest and even death, Castro forged ahead with his plan to oust Batista and initiated a string of attacks against prominent military installations, including the Moncada Army Barracks in Santiago de Cuba. Castro's "Moncada Manifesto," read to the Fidelistas prior to their attacks on military facilities, reflected Castro's long-standing interest in Cuba's historical heroes, his desire to end the autocratic rule of the political machine, and his goal of achieving social, economic, and political justice for all Cubans.

On August 1, 1953, the civilian police arrested Castro in Santiago de Cuba. Drawing upon his exceptional oratorical skills, he defended himself at trial that September. Castro used the trial to point the finger of blame at the Batista government and called dozens of witnesses who had experienced torture or witnessed executions at the hands of the president and his army. Castro argued that his attacks were justified insofar as they were combating the cruelty of the Batista regime. Using the trial as a platform to spread his revolutionary message, he encouraged followers to resist foreign economic dominance and advocated equitable distribution of wealth among the Cuban people—ideas that resonated with many victims of poverty and social immobility. In October 1953, Castro was found guilty and sentenced to fifteen years in prison. While incarcerated, he spent much of his time instructing his fellow revolutionaries in history and political philosophy and composing speeches and other writings. After serving two years of his sentence, he was released as part of a general amnesty signed by Batista in 1955. Castro immediately returned to Havana to take up the cause of revolution.

During a brief period of exile in Mexico, Castro befriended a like-minded revolutionary named Ernesto "Che" Guevara, a young Argentine physician committed to spreading Marxism throughout

Latin American. Together, Guevara and Castro initiated the 1956 guerrilla invasion of Cuba—a surprise return that marked the true beginning of the revolution. Castro's guerrilla forces ousted Batista in late December 1958 and inaugurated Castro as commander in chief of the armed forces and prime minister of the Cuban government.

Regime

Castro immediately began filling government positions with revolutionaries and seizing private property to redistribute the nation's wealth. He nationalized whole industries to free them from U.S. control and from that of private interests on the island. He also collectivized much of the nation's agricultural land and sought to develop world-class health and education systems. Those who opposed the ideals of the revolutionary were imprisoned, exiled, or, at various times, simply allowed to leave.

As a result of Castro's radical socialist agenda and his strengthening ties with the Soviet Union, relations between the United States and Cuba deteriorated. The Bay of Pigs incident of April 1961 confirmed his distrust and deepened his hatred of the United States, aggravated even further by the Cuban Missile Crisis the following October. Washington imposed a strict embargo on trade with the island that remained in effect into the twenty-first century and severed diplomatic relations as well. Castro's rhetoric continued unabated, however, and he promoted the spread of the revolution by supporting communist rebels and guerrilla movements in a number of other countries, including Nicaragua, Ethiopia, and Granada.

With the collapse of the Soviet Union in the early 1990s, Castro's revolution suffered a major setback. Without support from the Soviets, who had subsidized much of Cuba's economy with inexpensive petroleum and a market for sugar, unemployment and inflation increased rapidly. In addition to entreating the United States to lift its trade embargo, Castro adopted a quasi-free market economy, encouraged foreign investment in Cuba, and created a tourist industry designed to attract foreign money into the country. Washington reiterated its refusal to negotiate on trade matters until the Communist regime disbanded.

After undergoing intestinal surgery in July 2006, Castro temporarily relinquished power to his brother Raúl, who had been serving as defense minister and had long been designated as Castro's successor should he become incapacitated or die. Fidel Castro effectively disappeared from public view in the months that followed, fueling rumors of dire illness or even death. Then in February 2008, days before his official term was to expire, the eighty-one-year-old leader announced that he would not "accept" a new term as president. The National Assembly promptly elected Raúl Castro as his successor, with other high-ranking government officials retaining leadership roles in the new regime. In the United States, the announcement was greeted with joy among disaffected exiles in Florida and elsewhere, who reiterated their long-held dream to return to a free, democratic Cuba; and by U.S. government officials, including President George W. Bush, who expressed hope that Castro's retirement would hasten the political transformation of the island republic. In the meantime, Washington made clear that the U.S. economic embargo would remain in effect.

Legacy

Castro's influence remains ever present among Cuban Americans—even younger generations who have never lived on the island but who have strong opinions about Castro, his regime, and his effect on life in Cuba. Later generations of Cuban Americans have even initiated a unique style of art and literature that focuses almost exclusively on the exile experience in the United States and their feelings about Castro and his government.

In short, Castro remains a highly controversial figure—by some accounts a beloved and benevolent leader who rescued Cubans from exploitation at the hands of the United States and provided them with health care, education, and other social services they otherwise would have been denied; and by other accounts, a ruthless dictator who prohibited dissenting political speech and limited the potential economic growth of the island nation. In either case, he forced tens of thousands of Cubans into exile, many settling in Miami and other parts of Florida and the East Coast of the United States. Whatever one's perspective, Fidel Castro was one of the most significant political figures in the modern history of the Western Hemisphere, and his legacy will have a profound and enduring impact on Cuba and its people.

Sarah Stohlman

See also: Bay of Pigs Invasion; Cuban Refugee Program; Cubans; Guevara, Ernesto "Che"; Mariel Boatlift.

Further Reading

Coltman, Leycester. *The Real Fidel Castro.* New Haven, CT: Yale University Press, 2003.

Leonard, Thomas M. *Fidel Castro: A Biography.* Westport, CT: Greenwood, 2004.

Quirk, Robert E. *Fidel Castro.* New York: W.W. Norton, 1993.

Skierka, Volker. *Fidel Castro: A Biography.* Trans. Patrick Camiller. Malden, MA: Polity, 2004.

Staten, Clifford L. *The History of Cuba.* Westport, CT: Greenwood, 2003.

Central American Resource Center

The Central American Resource Center is a nonprofit immigration and human rights organization founded in the 1980s, serving large metropolitan areas in the United States with sizable Central American populations. The center has major offices in New York, Los Angeles, and Houston, Texas, and works to protect the civil rights of immigrants, increase understanding between native-born and newcomer communities, and raise awareness of the interaction of human rights disasters and immigration.

Salvadoran archbishop Oscar Romero, a well-known critic of violence and injustice in El Salvador who was perceived by right-wing civilian and military circles in that country as a dangerous enemy, inspired work of the center. Denouncing human rights abuses in often outspoken terms, his sermons deeply irritated conservative factions, and on March 24, 1980, a professional assassin killed Romero. Following the model of Archbishop Romero, the Central American Resource Center works to raise awareness of human rights abuses in Central America.

The center is dedicated to the spirit of Emma Lazarus's poem, *The New Colossus* (1883), which appears on a brass plate on the base of the Statue of Liberty in New York Harbor. Lazarus's sonnet is considered a guiding light for a new generation of immigrants—many of which are of Central American origin—no less than for previous generations. The poem is best known for its closing lines:

> Give me your tired, your poor,
> Your huddled masses yearning to breathe free,
> The wretched refuse of your teeming shore.
> Send these, the homeless, tempest-tost to me—
> I lift my lamp beside the golden door.

The center, with the assistance of the American Immigration Lawyers Association, acts as a clearinghouse for local lawyers willing to work pro bono (without pay) to assist recent immigrants to navigate the U.S. immigration system. In certain cases, the lawyers represent clients referred by the center in court. The lawyers actively prosecute unscrupulous parties who promise immigrants green cards (which allow non-U.S. citizens to work) in exchange for large sums of money. In 1999, for example, the center brought to court Manuel Herrera—perhaps the most notorious person in the New York metropolitan area taking advantage of recent immigrants. A grand jury returned a sixteen-count indictment charging Herrera with a variety of felonies and misdemeanors. In September 1999, Herrera pled guilty to defrauding immigrants.

The center also keeps recent immigrants up-to-date on changes in U.S. immigration law, such as the Legal Immigration Family Equity Act (LIFE) of 2000, which allows Salvadorans and Guatemalans to apply for permanent resident status even if they were deported in the past and extends amnesty provisions for certain groups, and Section 245(i) of the U.S. Immigration Act, which permits undocumented family members of U.S. citizens and permanent residents to receive green cards.

In line with its mission to increase understanding between native-born and newcomer communities, the center sponsors a speaker's bureau to communicate with religious congregations, schools, and other organizations on immigration, refugee, or human rights issues. The bureau's presentations have included the likes of *Meet Your Neighbor, Rosa Gomez,*

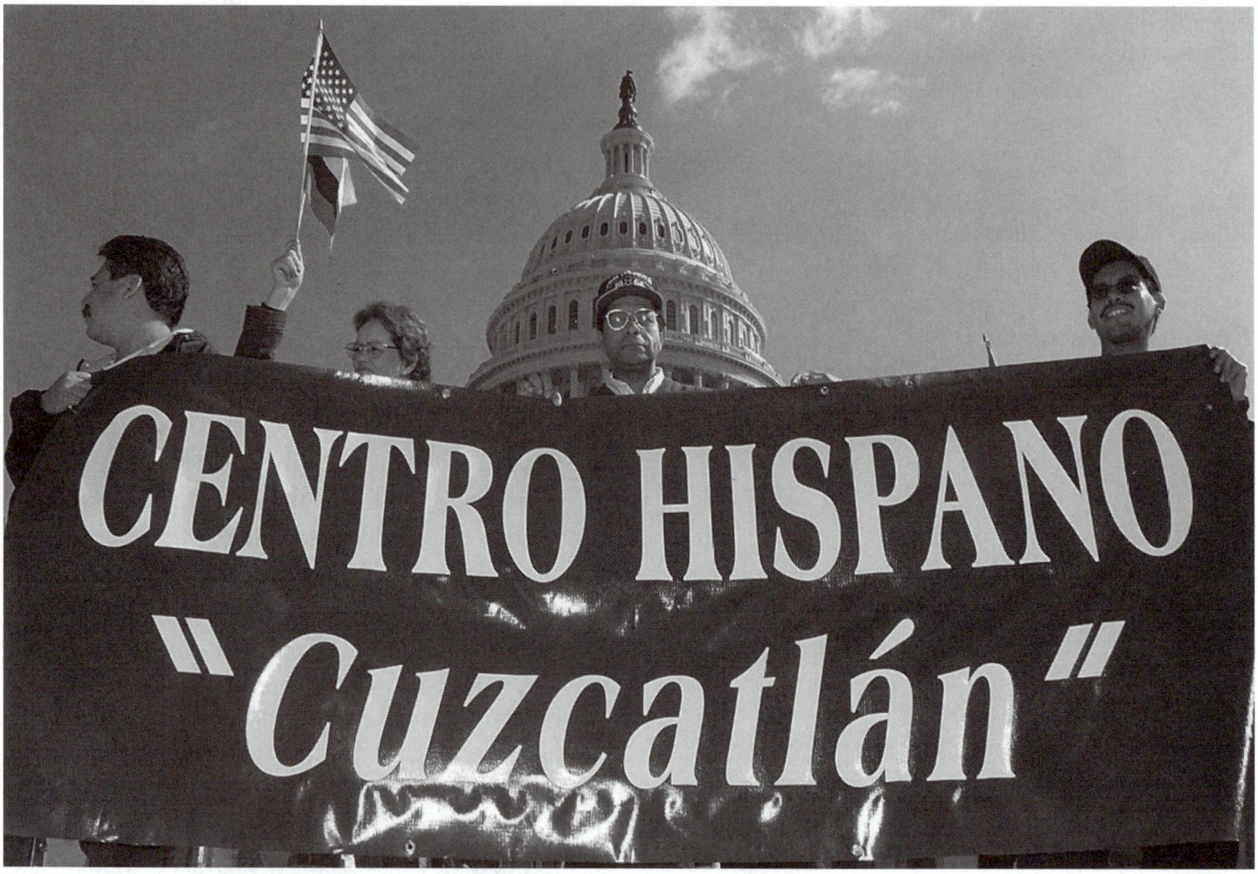

Members of the Central American Resource (formerly Refugee) Center rally on the steps of the U.S. Capitol in 1997 to support the Nicaraguan Adjustment and Central American Relief Act (NACARA), providing various immigrant benefits. The measure was passed. *(Tim Sloan/AFP/Getty Images)*

a play for middle school students about the migration of a woman from war-torn Central America to a city in the United States; *Today's Immigrants: Burden or Boon?,* which looks at the myths and realities of modern immigration; *Human Rights in Central America*; *Immigration Law for Teachers and Social Service Workers*; and *Immigration Updates for Central Americans.*

The center also monitors local nativist (anti-immigration) groups that could push for local anti-immigration legislation or restrictions on future immigration. In New York, for example, the Central American Resource Center of New York (CARECEN-N.Y.) kept a watchful eye on the Sachem Quality of Life Organization, a group based in Farmingville, Long Island, whose aim is deportation of Mexican day laborers.

Overall, since the early 1980s the Central American Resource Center has ably served the Central American immigrant community by providing information and legal assistance, promoting the cause of immigration through education and selected legal action, and raising awareness of human rights abuses in Central America.

Robert O. Kirkland

See also: Guatemalans; Salvadorans.

Further Reading

Aguayo, Sergio. *From the Shadows to Center Stage: Nongovernmental Organizations and Central American Refugee Assistance.* Washington, DC: Hemispheric Migration Project, 1991.

Castro, Max J., ed. *Free Markets, Open Societies, Closed Borders: Trends in International Migration and Immigration Policy in the Americas.* Coral Gables, FL: North-South Center, 1999.

Gutiérrez, Margo. *Sourcebook on Central American Refugee Policy.* Austin, TX: Central American Resource Center, 1985.

Chávez, César (1927–1993)

César Chávez was a Mexican American grassroots labor organizer who rose from an impoverished life as a California migrant farmworker to cofound and lead the National Farm Workers Association (NFWA)—later the United Farm Workers of America (UFW)—the first major agricultural union in the United States. Chávez dedicated his life to improving the working conditions and pay rates of exploited migrant workers through nonviolent forms of protest, such as strikes, boycotts, and periods of personal fasting. In 1965, he led the NFWA into a strike against grape growers in Delano, California. A nationwide boycott of grapes followed, successfully forcing union contracts with growers in California's Central Valley in 1970. His ongoing leadership for *La Causa* (the cause) throughout the 1970s and 1980s earned him heroic status among farmworkers and recognition as a strong national role model for Latinos/as in America.

Background

César Estrada Chávez was born on March 31, 1927, in the North Gila Valley of Arizona, in a small town near the Colorado River. He was the second of three children born to Mexican immigrant parents, Librado Chávez and Juana Estrada. In the 1920s and 1930s, Chávez's father was a relatively successful entrepreneur in the North Gila Valley. In addition to owning and operating the family farm, he also owned an automobile repair shop, a small grocery store, a post office, and a pool hall. Librado Chávez's success gave him considerable political influence in the community, and he spent many evenings encouraging fellow residents to increase their political power by voting as a bloc in local, state, and national elections. Assisting his father in these efforts helped instill in young César a belief that one has the power to enact political change by talking with individuals, listening to their concerns, and encouraging them to take advantage of their political opportunities—beliefs that no doubt influenced Chávez's later involvement with labor organizing on behalf of farmworkers.

Chávez's mother was a locally known *curandera* (faith healer), who utilized various herbs and other natural items to treat the illnesses and infirmities of many individuals living in the North Gila Valley. She was also an extremely pious woman who was devoted to the icons of Mexican Catholicism, including the Vírgen de Guadalupe and St. Eduvigis. From his mother, Chávez learned compassion and morality—traits that also informed his later work with poor farmworkers in California.

During the Great Depression, the Chávez family encountered serious financial hardship. The farm became unprofitable, and Librado Chávez was unable to pay his property taxes for many years. As a result, the land was seized by the state and sold to the local bank president. Forced to leave the North Gila Valley and look for work, the Chávezes moved to California where twelve-year-old César and his family became farmworkers.

The Chávez family first found work in the Oxnard area of California, a small, agricultural town located about 50 miles (80 kilometers) north of Los Angeles. Chávez, his parents, and his brother and sister worked nearly every day in the fields, picking walnuts and beans. Chávez realized that working as a migrant "farmworker" was very different from working on one's own farm—hard, backbreaking work, and a far cry from the relatively affluent lifestyle that Chávez remembered from the North Gila Valley. It was in the fields of central California, however, that Chávez learned firsthand about the power of unionizing. Strikes among farmworkers were relatively commonplace during this time, though they were rarely successful. Unfortunately, the 1930s and early 1940s were also marked by widespread poverty and lack of employment opportunities, and replacement workers, or scabs, were almost always willing to take the jobs of striking agricultural laborers. The power of farmworkers to make demands on growers was therefore greatly diminished.

After working in Oxnard for a few years, the family moved north to a small barrio in San Jose, California, called Sal Si Puedes, which in English means "get out while you can." This was an impoverished area inhabited primarily by struggling farmworkers and their families. During World War II, fearing what would happen if he were drafted into the armed services, Chávez decided to take his fate into his own hands and enlisted in the U.S. Navy. He was deployed for two years, during which he worked as a deckhand aboard ships in the Pacific campaign. His experience in the Navy proved humiliating and unpleasant, as he frequently encountered racism and was assigned to the least desirable and degrading jobs. Yet he returned from the Navy more self-confident and committed to ensuring that Mexican Americans receive the same rights as other Americans—a determination that framed his life's work on behalf of migrant farmworkers.

Fateful Encounters

In 1948, back in California, Chávez married his high-school sweetheart, Helen Fabela, the Mexican American daughter of two immigrant farmworkers. Soon after they were married, he and Helen moved back to Sal Si Puedes, where Chávez quickly found work picking apricots. It was there that he met one of the most influential figures in his life, Father Donald McDonnell, a Catholic priest who taught him some valuable lessons about community organizing. Father McDonnell helped him discover that while impoverished, Mexican American community had power in organization. Working alongside Father McDonnell, Chávez also learned about such influential historical figures as Mahatma Gandhi, whose philosophy of nonviolent resistance would have a profound effect on Chávez's work and the entire farmworker movement.

In 1952, Chávez befriended Fred Ross, another figure who would be an influence in his life. A committed community organizer who had learned of Chávez's efforts in Sal Si Puedes, Ross set about helping Chávez combat some of the problems faced by Mexican Americans in the impoverished barrio. Ross was a local organizer who worked with a fledgling, grassroots organization called the Community Service Organization (CSO), which had called upon politicians and other civic leaders in the state to combat the problems faced by poor Mexican Americans and take on such issues as pollution, police brutality, and other social and economic ills. Ross trained Chávez in grassroots organizing and got him a job with the CSO; Chávez took advantage of the opportunity and used his platform to inform outsiders about the plight of migrant farmworkers.

During his involvement with the CSO, Chávez met powerful community organizers such as Saul Alinsky, who furthered his practical education in effective organizing techniques and strategies. Chávez remained with the CSO for ten years, resigning his position in 1961 when organization members voted against a plan to unionize California's farmworkers. Believing that such a union was not only possible but essential, Chávez began his crusade to establish a powerful labor organization on behalf of farmworkers.

Organizing

After resigning his position with the CSO, Chávez embarked upon one of the longest and most difficult journeys of his life: the effort to unionize the hundreds of thousands of farmworkers spread throughout California's Central Valley. On September 30, 1962, Chávez and cofounder Dolores Huerta called the first meeting of the National Farm Workers Association in Fresno, where the movement's early leaders discussed how they would accomplish this ambitious goal. Drawing upon the organizational knowledge he gained during his time with the CSO, Chávez and his colleagues traveled from town to town, holding in-house meetings, then larger gatherings of farmworkers, and finally encouraging farmworkers to take an open stand against the injustices they experienced in the fields.

On September 16, 1965, the NFWA launched its first major strike, against grape growers in Delano. Following in the footsteps of Filipino workers who had been on strike for about a month, Chávez and the members of the NFWA refused to pick grapes for Delano-area growers and launched a massive campaign to educate potential scabs—many of them Mexican immigrants—on the importance of their cause. At the same time, the NFWA initiated a boycott against such companies as the Schenley Vineyards Corporation, S&W Fine Foods, DiGiorgio Corporation, and TreeSweet Corporation. After nearly seven months of striking, the NFWA staged a massive march from Delano to Sacramento to protest the unjust working conditions of California's grape growers. The march garnered national attention for the farmworkers' cause, which resulted in the first-ever worker's contract for farmworkers.

Capitalizing on the success of their first strike and boycott, Chávez and the members of the NFWA—which in August 1966 merged with its largely Filipino counterpart, the Agricultural Workers Organizing Committee, to form the United Farm Workers Organizing Committee (UFWOC)—initiated a strike against a powerful table grape grower, Giumarra Vineyards Corporation (GVC). Chávez and the UFWOC encouraged Americans across the country to boycott all table grapes until Giumarra agreed to negotiate a fair labor contract. This effort also proved successful, and a worker's contract was signed by the GVC and UFWOC in late 1967.

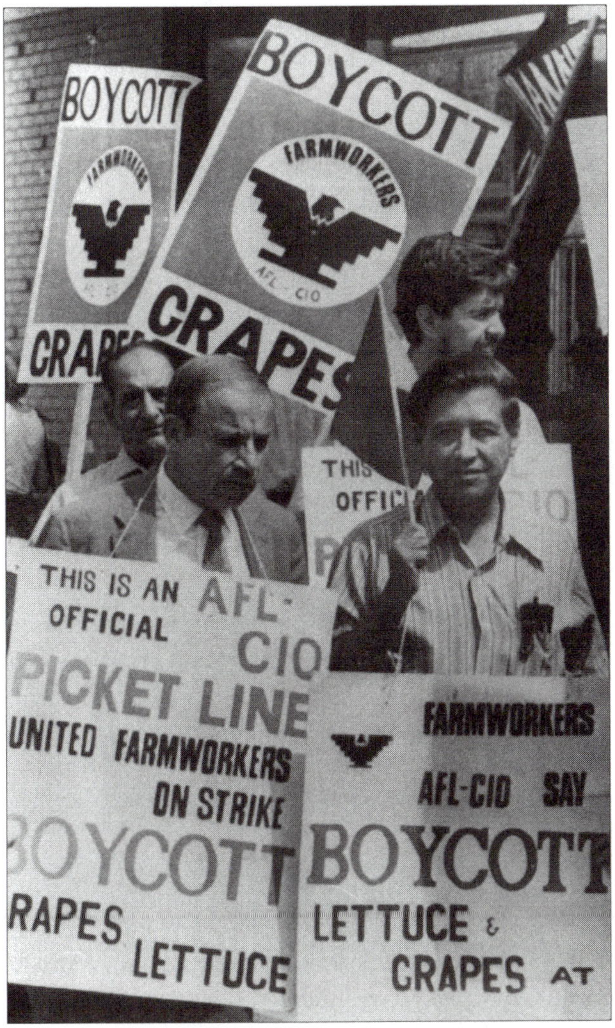

United Farm Workers leader César Chávez (right) pickets a New Jersey supermarket with local union officials and rank and file during the nationwide boycott of nonunion lettuce in the early 1970s. *(AP Images)*

After the successful campaigns against powerful farm owners, Chávez and the UFWOC launched additional campaigns against farm owners throughout California on issues such as the use of pesticides, wage scales, and a variety of labor practices. Debates between farm owners and members of the UFWOC were often tense, and violent responses on both sides were not uncommon. In 1968, following the tactics of resistance pioneered by Gandhi, Chávez embarked on a monthlong fast to protest violence, to raise awareness of the plight of farmworkers, and to encourage followers to support his nonviolent approach to social change. The fast brought Chávez further national media attention and led to his growing recognition as one of the most significant leaders of the civil rights movement of the 1960s and 1970s. In the 1980s, Chávez continued his work on behalf of farmworkers, leading a four-year boycott of California-grown table grapes and undertaking a thirty-six-day fast in 1988 to protest the rampant use of pesticides by grape growers.

Legacy

Since his death from natural causes on April 3, 1993, Chávez has continued to occupy a vital position in the collective memory of Mexican Americans and the entire nation. He is regarded as a peaceful revolutionary who overcame insurmountable odds to improve the living conditions and economic prospects for some of the poorest members of American society. In 1994, President Bill Clinton honored Chávez with the Presidential Medal of Freedom, the nation's highest civilian award. His birthday is commemorated as a state holiday in California. Even now, in the twenty-first century, images of Chávez are prominently displayed at protest marches for immigrants' rights and other demonstrations on behalf of social justice. His legacy is an important one not only for the Mexican American community, but also for other racial and ethnic groups in the United States and across the world that seek to triumph over poverty and racial oppression.

Sarah Stohlman

See also: Community Service Organization; Grape Strikes and Boycotts; Huerta, Dolores; Migrant Workers; United Farm Workers of America.

Further Reading

Bruns, Roger. *Cesar Chavez: A Biography.* Westport, CT: Greenwood, 2005.

Chávez, César. *The Words of César Chávez.* Ed. Richard J. Jensen and John C. Hammerback. College Station: Texas A&M University Press, 2002.

Dalton, Frederick John. *The Moral Vision of César Chávez.* Maryknoll, NY: Orbis, 2003.

del Castillo, Griswold, and Richard A. Garcia. *César Chávez: A Triumph of the Spirit.* Norman: University of Oklahoma Press, 1995.

LaBotz, Dan. *César Chávez and la Causa.* New York: Pearson/Longman, 2006.

Matthiessen, Peter. *Sal Si Puedes (Escape if You Can): Cesar Chavez and the New American Revolution.* Berkeley: University of California Press, 2000.

Ross, Fred. *Conquering Goliath: César Chávez at the Beginning.* Keene, CA: United Farm Workers, distributed by El Taller Grafico, 1989.

Chávez Ravine

A section of municipal Los Angeles, Chávez Ravine is separated from the nearby downtown area by low hills and the city's Chinatown. Since 1962 it has been the site of Dodger Stadium, home of the Los Angeles Dodgers baseball team. For several generations before that, however, Chávez Ravine was a low-income residential neighborhood, populated mostly by Mexican Americans. In the early 1950s, the city expropriated the land and told residents that new, low-income housing would be built for them. By the end of the decade, however, they had been forced to leave, and the land was used to entice the Brooklyn Dodgers to move to Los Angeles.

Originally populated by Tongva Indians, the land became part of a cattle ranch under Spanish rule. In the nineteenth century, the ravine was named for Julian Chávez, a judge and city councilman who owned the property. During the 1920s and 1930s, downtown redevelopment forced many Mexican American families away from central Los Angeles and into Chávez Ravine, crowding its 315 acres of slopes and dirt roads. Three close-knit neighborhoods developed there: La Loma, Bishop, and Palo Verde. The hills of Elysian Park formed its northern edge, with freeways bordering it on the south and east.

Recognized as a slum as early as the 1910s, Chávez Ravine was filled with 1,145 dwellings—including a number of shacks and tents—by 1949. A third of the homes had no toilets, and half were considered substandard. At the same time, however, city planners and designers consistently described the area as "charming." In spite of poverty and poor sanitation facilities, residents loved their neighborhoods and took a great deal of civic pride in them. Outdoor religious festivals, impromptu concerts, school events, and verdant gardens gave Chávez Ravine a unique vitality missing from many planned suburbs.

The Housing Act of 1949, also called the Taft-Ellender-Wagner Act, gave U.S. cities money to build public housing, and Los Angeles qualified for $110 million. Within a year, the city council voted to use the money to rebuild "blighted" neighborhoods, starting with Chávez Ravine. Architects Richard Neutra and Robert Alexander were hired to design new homes.

The residents of Chávez Ravine were informed of the plans in July 1950, in a letter from the Housing Authority. Stunned by the news that their homes would be assessed and bought by the government, most residents moved, believing they had no choice. Some sold their homes; absentee landlords who had sold their properties forced others out. All were promised that they would be the first to occupy the new development, to be called Elysian Park Heights.

Between 1949 and 1951, the political climate changed. The public housing came to be viewed as a socialist project, and the city council voted to cancel it. The California Supreme Court ruled that the city must, because of its contract, build the project, and the U.S. Supreme Court concurred. In spite of the legal rulings, a special election was held in Los Angeles, and the citizens voted against the housing project.

Many of the homes and schools in Chávez Ravine had already been demolished; some were set ablaze as a training exercise for the Los Angeles Fire Department. In 1953, Norris Poulson took office as the new mayor of Los Angeles, having been elected in part because of his antihousing project stance. Poulson promptly canceled plans for Elysian Park Heights and arranged for the city to buy the vacated properties in Chávez Ravine. The city agreed that the land would be used only for public projects and paid $1,279,000 for it.

Rumors soon began circulating that the Brooklyn Dodgers baseball team might move west, and in 1957 the city of Los Angeles struck a deal with team owner Walter O'Malley. O'Malley would trade a nine-acre minor league stadium that he owned for the area known as Chávez Ravine. Los Angeles also contracted to invest $2 million in roads and improvements in the ravine, funded by taxpayers. Many argued that the arrangement violated the terms of the city's acquisition of the ravine. O'Malley then promised to provide a public recreation area. Another special election was held, and voters approved the deal by a small majority. The recreation area was never built.

The city's contract with the Dodgers was upheld by the state Supreme Court. Twenty families who remained in Chávez Ravine were forced to move during the course of 1958 and 1959; the eviction of the last family, the Arechigas, was broadcast on the local news. Poignant scenes of Los Angeles County sheriff deputies lifting an aged grandmother who refused to leave her rocking chair shocked many and became a symbol of the decade-long "Battle of Chávez Ravine." Dodger Stadium, with seating for 56,000, opened in April 1962.

Vickey Kalambakal

See also: Los Angeles.

Further Reading

Hines, Thomas. "Housing, Baseball, and Creeping Socialism: The Battle of Chávez Ravine, Los Angeles, 1949–1959." *Journal of Urban History* 8:2 (February 1982): 123–43.

Normark, Don. *Chávez Ravine, 1949: A Los Angeles Story.* San Francisco: Chronicle, 1999.

Chicago

Chicago and the surrounding metropolitan area have long been home to a large and diverse Latino population. Although the American Southwest is generally associated with Mexican Americans, Miami with Cubans, and New York City with Puerto Ricans, each of these groups, along with others from Central and South America, have historically settled in Chicago in sizable numbers. These communities have taken a central place in the economic, political, and cultural life of the metropolitan area.

Lured by prospects of employment on the railroad, more than 600,000 Mexicans settled in Chicago in the early part of the twentieth century. By World War II, with the prospect of defense jobs and the development of the Bracero Program—a contract labor program between the United States and Mexico that brought low-wage workers to America—Chicago took in tens of thousands more Mexicans.

Although Latinos/as have resided in Chicago and other areas of Illinois since before the 1920s, the city's Latino community experienced especially rapid growth during the 1990s. In the last decade of the twentieth century, the number of Latinos/as living in Illinois grew by 69 percent, to comprise 12 percent of Illinois's total population. By contrast, the state's population of other racial and ethnic groups grew by a combined 3 percent during the same period. By the beginning of the twenty-first century, Illinois was home to the fifth-largest Latino community in the United States: 27 percent of Chicago residents, or 1.6 million people.

U.S. Census data show the rapid growth of Chicago's various Latino communities over the course of the twentieth century:

Latino Populations in Chicago

	1900	1910	1930	1950	1960	1970	1980	1990
Mexican	102	252	19,362	24,335	44,686	89,097	254,656	352,560
Puerto Rican	N/A	N/A	N/A	255	32,371	78,963	113,888	119,866
Cuban	N/A	N/A	N/A	N/A	2,500	14,177	11,948	10,044

Source: U.S. Census.

Most of the growth in the state's Latino population has occurred in the Chicago area, where 92 percent now reside. Nevertheless, Cook County (including Chicago) recorded the slowest growth in Latino population over the course of the century, with 54 percent. The most rapid growth took place in McHenry County, with 223 percent.

Although Chicago's Latino community is immensely diverse, it is defined by its ethnic enclaves. Thus, Mexicans are located in the following communities: South Lawndale (80 percent), Lower West Side (83 percent), Brighton Park (34 percent), East Side (35 percent), New City (35 percent), West Town (32 percent), Logan Square (26 percent), Gage Park (33 percent), Chicago Lawn (23 percent), and Hermosa (24 percent). Pilsen has been the traditional port of entry for Mexican immigrants since the mid-twentieth century. Farther southwest is Little Village or *La Villita,* Chicago's largest Mexican American neighborhood, where shops, restaurants, and street festivals abound. Puerto Ricans are prominent in Hermosa (37 percent), Humbolt Park (24 percent), West Town (25 percent), and Logan Square (31 percent). Cubans constitute a much smaller minority, 1–3 percent in Rogers Park, Edgewater, Albany Park, Lincoln Square, and Logan Square.

A major recent trend in Latino immigration is to settle directly in suburban areas without living, and assimilating, in Chicago first. Thus, the number of Latinos/as in the suburban Chicago area more than doubled from 1990 (291,053) to 2000 (651,473). The trend has prompted efforts to restrict the number of Latinos/as in certain communities. Some towns, like Cicero, have tried to do so by restricting the number of residents in a single house, but most of these efforts have failed because they violate federal law. In 2002, for example, the city of Elgin agreed to a settlement following a federal investigation into claims that municipal housing inspectors were applying tougher standards when inspecting Latino homes.

The history of Latinos/as in Chicago is equally defined by exceptionalism, or the uniqueness of experience there, and the common experiences of Latinos/as throughout the United States. For example, the city has been highly successful in absorbing Mexican migrants, resulting in lower rates of poverty (25 percent), especially in comparison to other parts of the United States (31 percent). Likewise, Mexicans, despite popular opinion, have long contributed to the financial stability of Chicago, with businesses in Mexican neighborhoods contributing more to the city's coffers through taxes than any other area in the city, with the exception of the elite shops on Michigan Avenue. In contrast, the Puerto Rican community has the highest rate of poverty, 38 percent, among the city's Latinos/as.

Despite the rapid growth of the Latino population, very few vote (or are able to vote), helping to account for the lack of Latino impact on policy decisions. Less than 52 percent of Latinos/as were eligible to vote in 2000, compared to 67 percent of whites and 74 percent of African Americans. Of the Latinos/as who were registered, fewer than 30 percent actually voted, compared to 56 percent of registered whites and 67 percent of registered African Americans.

A number of prominent Latinos/as have emerged in Chicago government since the late twentieth century. Irene Hernandez, a Democrat representing the city's 4th Ward (North Side), became a member of the Cook County Board in 1974. Since then, a succession of Latinos/as have been elected as city aldermen, state representatives, and suburban mayors and councilmen. Redistricting after the 1980 census created the first Latino state legislative district, as a result of which Joseph Berrios, a 31st Ward precinct captain, won a seat in the state house in 1982. The first Latino representative from the state of Illinois, Luis Gutiérrez (D), has served in the U.S. House of Representatives since 1993.

New institutional resources dedicated to Chicago Latinos/as include the Center for Metropolitan Chicago Initiatives (CMCI) of the Institute for Latino Studies at the University of Notre Dame. The CMCI conducts policy-relevant research regarding the city's Latino community, highlighting such problems as school segregation, gender inequality, labor shortages, and youth issues. Estimating the Latino economy in metropolitan Chicago at $20 billion in 2003, the institute has demonstrated how Latino businesses have revived decaying neighborhoods and bolstered the city's overall financial stability. The city's International Latino Cultural Center develops and promotes awareness of Latino culture through a variety of cultural events, including comedy, dance, music, poetry, theater, and visual arts exhibitions, among them the annual Chicago Latino Film Festival.

Frank A. Salamone

See also: Bracero Program; Mexicans.

Further Reading

Eastwood, Carolyn. *Near West Side Stories: Struggles for Community in Chicago's Maxwell Street Neighborhood.* Chicago: Lake Claremont, 2002.

Ganz, Cherly W., ed. *Pots of Promise: Mexicans and Pottery at Hull-House, 1920–40 (Latinos in Chicago and the Midwest).* Champaign: University of Illinois Press, 2005.

Padilla, Felix M. *Latino Ethnic Consciousness: The Case of Mexican Americans and Puerto Ricans in Chicago.* South Bend, IN: University of Notre Dame Press, 1985.

Chicanisma

Chicanisma (or *xicanisma*) refers to a form of feminist critical consciousness that bears essential connections to the Chicano Movement (*El Movimiento*) of the 1960s and 1970s. Yet the meaning and significance of chicanisma transcend the conditions of its genesis and the initial political aims of El Movimiento. To understand the contours of chicanisma, one needs to be familiar with its context.

Origins

Starting in the late 1950s, many people of Mexican ancestry living in the American Southwest began to undergo a transformation of political sensibility and self-identity. Community activists and students increasingly rejected theories that blamed Mexican Americans for their own poverty and marginal status. At the same time, they questioned their elders' strategies of assimilation and participation in mainstream politics as a solution for the discrimination they faced. Taking inspiration from the civil rights and black power movements (the liberation struggles taking place within the black community), they forged new ways to fight for social justice, self-determination, and a more positive cultural and social identity. The extent to which they succeeded politically is a topic of continued debate, although the cultural impact of their efforts is undeniable.

Part of the strategy was to invoke the term "Chicano," adapting its meaning to the new sensibility. Although the origins of the term are obscure, it was often used as a derogatory label for poor immigrant workers from Mexico, particularly those with obvious indigenous ancestry. Thus, applying the "Chicano" label to themselves without shame was meant to signify the movement's focus on the rights of the poor and working-class members of the community and its positive revaluation of *mestizo* (mixed race) and indigenous heritages. In this respect, the Chicano Movement bears similarities to *mestizaje* movements in Mexico. But the term "Chicano" locates these social struggles in a specific geographic and historic space, the U.S.-Mexico borderlands. As such, "Chicano" represents an attempt to forge a new form of American identity (as distinct from Mexican political nationalism) that rejects Anglo definitions of American-ness and affirms links with global struggles against U.S. imperialism. Chicanismo thus reflects a particular political awareness, a coming-to-consciousness, and a reaffirmation of identity connected with the aims of the Chicano Movement.

Chicanisma signifies the particular coming-to-consciousness of women within that movement, particularly those women who contend that the well-being of the community depends as much on dismantling sexism within it as it does on battling outside oppressions.

Women were involved in the Chicano Movement since the beginning, just as they have always worked actively on behalf of their families and communities. Indeed, women were responsible for most of the day-to-day operation of early activist organizations both within communities and on college campuses. Yet, as in other arenas of life, those in Movimiento organizations often struggled against sexism and attempts to restrict their roles to traditional activities of nurturing children and serving men. The struggle was particularly acute for young college women, who were already expanding traditional roles by pursuing higher education. A common response to Chicanas' questions regarding equality, family roles, child care, reproductive choice, sexuality, and *machismo* was that such concerns threatened to undermine Chicano culture and El Movimiento. Chicanas who questioned or complained about sexism were often accused of selling out to Anglo culture. At the same time, Chicanas struggled against Anglo feminists. They found that Anglo feminists' tools of analysis, while helpful in some respects, did not give due attention to the ways race and class differences affected women's lives. As such, Chicanas discerned that Anglo feminists' political tactics were often naïve and exclusionary. In response to contemporary Anglo feminists' calls for loyalty to women *against* men, Chicanas insisted on their loyalty to Chicano men and to the overall goals of the Chicano Movement. Faced with these challenges on several fronts, Chicanas responded with an explosion of historical research, artistic and literary creation, and theoretical formulation.

Notable Figures and Core Concepts

Out of this response, a stance of chicanisma was forged with several defining features. Some of their writing focuses on community organizing and education, like that of Mirta Vidal and Francisca Flores, or scholarship and theory, like that of Ana Nieto-Gomez, Marta (or Martha) Cotera, Mary Helen Ponce, and Gloria Anzaldúa. Yet their work often crosses boundaries. Ana Castillo and Cherríe Moraga are poets, playwrights, and nonfiction essayists, while Helena María Viramontes is a novelist and professor. Many combine literary forms or work in several genres. Estela Portillo-Trambley, Denise Chávez, Sandra Cisneros, Pat Mora, Lorna Dee Cervantes, Bernice Zamora, and Lucha Corpi are poets and novelists; Gloria Velázquez and Demetria Martinez work as journalists in addition to writing novels and poetry. Jamie Lujan is an actress as well as a writer, while Olga Angelina García Echeverría and Elba Rosario Sánchez have produced recordings of their poetry and books. Chicanisma has been portrayed by such visual artists as Patricia Rodriguez and the Mujeres Muralistas, Patssi Valdez, Amalia Mesa-Bains, Carmen Lomas Garza, Santa Barraza, Linda Vallejo, Ester Hernandez, Delilah Montoya, Kathy Vargas, and Alma Lopez. Collectively, their work, whatever its genre, demonstrates chicanisma's strong historical connection to the Chicano Movement and the women's movement of the 1960s and 1970s. These artists exhibit a strong loyalty to their culture. However, while Chicanas have remained firmly attached to a specific history, home, and place, and their work has involved themes grounded in daily life and people's material situations, chicanisma quickly evolved beyond the cultural nationalism characteristic of early Chicano vision. Indeed, Chicana theorists such as Gloria Anzaldúa and Ana Castillo have argued that narrow, nationalistic understandings of what it means to be Chicana/o are counterproductive. While this critique of narrow nationalism stems from the 1970s, Castillo's coining of the term "xicanisma" in the 1990s was meant to amplify the point that Chicanas' insights are rooted in their lives but offered to women—and men—of all backgrounds.

Other central themes arise from Chicanas' struggles along multiple fronts—gender, sexuality, class, race, and nationality—and their movements between such diverse social contexts as the barrio and the university. The experience of being perceived in radically different ways depending upon social context, and of not fitting into the prevailing U.S. racial categories, has afforded Chicanas unique insight into the ways that concepts and systems of classification are changeable and arbitrary, yet have great power to shape reality. Chicanisma in its theoretical articulations thus insists on race and class analysis and has made sophisticated contributions to such projects. Chicanisma continues the project of reviving suppressed indigenous and, more recently, African heritages, but goes beyond earlier rhetoric in criticizing narrow understandings of race and authentic identity. The result is a model of self-identity and understanding that admits ambiguity and challenges dualistic systems of dividing the world (for instance, black-white, male-female, straight-gay), yet remains committed to specific history, anticolonialism, and racial justice.

The lingering traumas of double conquest, first by the Spanish, then by the United States, have caused Chicanas both great suffering and great opportunity for insight into the dynamics of colonization. Chicanisma confronts all of this head-on; one hallmark of chicanisma literary, analytical, and artistic works is their emotional intensity. At the same time, a recurring theme of chicanisma culture is that clashes between geographic, linguistic, social, and psychological systems result not only in grief but also in unexpected possibilities for connection, creativity, and growth. Thus, for example, the theme of borders and their multiple, contradictory effects is an important feature of chicanisma, as is anticolonialism in all aspects—military, social, economic, and psychological. Similarly, chicanisma emphasizes interdependence and the strength that can result from connection to others, even as Chicana writers and thinkers have explored the myriad ways that family and community structures upholding sexism, homophobia, and sexual violence wreak havoc in people's lives.

As such, chicanisma denotes a willingness to raise difficult questions about deep-seated social practices and cultural icons. For example, two of the most famous voices of the movement, Gloria Anzaldúa and Cherríe Moraga, discuss lesbianism and homophobia within the Chicano community, while Ana Castillo searches for the roots of machismo not only in Spanish and Moorish cultures but in Mesoamerican worldviews as well. Chicana writers and artists have reflected on such figures as Our Lady of Guadalupe and Malintzin Tenépal/La Malinche. Their reflections thus entail both criticism of the ways these images have been used to set impossible standards for female behavior or to promote distrust of Mexican women, and recognition of both figures as heroines.

Finally, chicanisma takes seriously the religious dimension of Chicano culture, with its myriad roots. Roman Catholicism has been a central defining feature of the culture, but the Church has been the target of considerable criticism by Chicanas who oppose its views about sexuality and the role of women, which they deem harmful and unjust. Meanwhile, Judaic, Muslim, African, and indigenous worldviews have also played important parts in the expression of chicanisma, as Chicanas have produced penetrating reflections on these multiple elements, and on the significance of female elders and other spiritual teachers outside the Catholic Church hierarchy. Whether their individual spiritual responses involve a rejection of Catholicism and a hearkening back to indigenous deities and practices (as was the case with Gloria Anzaldúa) or they choose to remain ambivalently associated with Catholicism (as is the case with Demetria Martínez), Chicanas have stressed the importance of spirituality for the survival and creative renewal of individuals and cultures, and have made it a major theme in work expressing chicanisma over the last three decades or more.

Agnes B. Curry

See also: Chicano/a; Chicano Movement; Cisneros, Sandra; Feminism; Moraga, Cherríe.

Further Reading

Anzaldúa, Gloria. *Borderlands/La Frontera: The New Mestiza.* 1987. San Francisco: Aunt Lute, 2007.

Arrendondo, Gabriela F., Aída Hurtado, Norma Klahn, and Olga Nájera Ramírez, eds. *Chicana Feminisms: A Critical Reader.* Durham, NC: Duke University Press, 2003.

Castillo, Ana. *Massacre of the Dreamers: Essays on Xicanisma.* Albuquerque: University of New Mexico Press, 1994.

García, Alma M., ed. *Chicana Feminist Thought: The Basic Historical Writings.* New York: Routledge, 1997.

Garcia, Ignacio M. *Chicanismo: The Forging of a Militant Ethos among Mexican Americans.* Tuscon: University of Arizona Press, 1997.

Martínez, Demetria. *Confessions of a Berlitz-Tape Chicana.* Norman: University of Oklahoma Press, 2005.

Ruíz, Vicki L. *From Out of the Shadows: Mexican Women in Twentieth-Century America.* New York: Oxford University Press, 2008.

Torres, Edén E. *Chicana without Apology: Chicana sin vergüenza.* New York and London: Routledge, 2003.

Chicanismo

Chicanismo can be defined as a collective consciousness of self-determination among Chicanos/as as a united people, accompanied by a spirit of active resistance against all forms of oppression. It is the expression of cultural nationalism from a people whose identity comes from both Spanish and indigenous roots, who are aware of a shared history of struggle, and who maintain a deep sense of pride in their cultural heritage. It is an awareness and sense of unity among all Chicanos/as across religious, gender, economic, generational, and sexual orientation differences.

The concept of chicanismo evolved out of the Chicano civil rights movement of the 1960s and 1970s, also known as the Chicano Movement, *El Movimiento*, or *La Causa.* Although the construct has taken on new meanings and associations since that time, it was utilized in the Chicano Movement as a guiding ideology and expression of pride in cultural identity. From the beginning and over the course of time, chicanismo has carried different meanings and points of emphasis among different groups. As first used among young Chicano activists, the movement emphasized an ideology of Chicano nationalism; to others within and outside the Chicano Movement, the term emphasized a sense of cultural pride. Nevertheless, while different segments of the Chicano community had different perspectives and understandings, the construct itself did have some unifying aspects.

The spirit of chicanismo both acknowledges and supersedes the regional differences among Chicanos/as across the United States (in Tejanos, *Californios,* Hispanos, and others). Since the Chicano Movement included different groups of activists in different regions with some distinct struggles, the developing sense of chicanismo in the 1970s was increasingly invoked as a uniting ideology behind the separate efforts within the movement. Through the lens of chicanismo, local struggles were viewed as the shared pursuit of an underlying goal—promoting social justice and cultural pride for Chicanos/as. Among the campaigns that came to be associated with the Chicano Movement were the struggle for labor unity and economic rights by the United Farm Workers of America, the demand for educational reform in public schools (including organized walkouts in East Los Angeles), and the creation of community and political empowerment groups (such as Crusade for Justice, La Raza Unida). Thus, chicanismo was the underlying spirit of the Chicano Movement and the cause of Chicano nationalism.

Another important aspect of chicanismo is its strong connection with the culture's indigenous roots and particularly, during the Chicano Movement, with Aztec myths and mythology. In the context of modern cultural history, several events have been instrumental in defining and evolving the concept: publication of the epic poem *Yo Soy Joaquín* (*I Am Joaquín*), the first Chicano Youth Liberation Conference, and El Plan de Santa Barbara.

Yo Soy Joaquín

The beginnings of chicanismo are closely connected, in time and perspective, with the epic poem *I Am Joaquín* by Chicano civil rights activist Rodolfo "Corky" Gonzales in 1967. In terms of forging a sense of chicanismo, the presentation of the poem in a first person narrative was important in building a collective identity. The use of one name, Joaquín, was meant to be representative of the entire Chicano people, past, present, and future. The poem highlighted an important aspect of chicanismo, that of a shared history, and helped build a distinctive cultural identity by claiming that past events and historical figures (including Cortés, Cuauhtémoc, Zapata, Juarez, and others) have come together in the present and have resulted in the creation of a distinctive people—Chicanos. Thus, *I Am Joaquín* put forth the notion of a cultural consciousness rooted in both Spanish and indigenous cultures, emphasizing that Chicanos/as originated from both the conquered (indigenous) and the conquerors (Spaniards). A call for all Chicanos/as to claim this heritage as their own, the poem constructed a framework of historical lineage that until then was not often expressed or taught to Chicanos/as, while not ignoring another key aspect of chicanismo—a shared sense of struggle against oppression and injustice.

Chicano Youth Liberation Conference

The Chicano Youth Liberation Conference, held in Denver, Colorado, in March 1969, was another significant event within the Chicano Movement and a progressive step in the growing sense of chicanismo. The conference more clearly began to define a plan of Chicano self-determination built on a foundation of nationalist sentiment and cultural affirmation. For many of the participants, it was a chance to interact with Chicanos/as from different regions in the United States, contributing in a concrete fashion to the growing sense of "a people" within the movement. It was at this conference that Aztlán became a major symbol of the Chicano Movement and of chicanismo. Although the myth of Aztlán did not originate at the conference, a poem presented there by Alurista (the pen name of Alberto Baltazar Urista Heredia), in which Chicanos/as were connected to this mythical homeland, helped crystallize a growing sense of chicanismo. Aztlán came to represent the Chicano homeland, both historically and symbolically. Historically and geographically, Aztlán was located in an area of Mexico that was annexed by the United States after the Mexican War in 1848. Thus, Chicanos/as had historical legacy with lands that were once part of Mexico. Symbolically, the idea of Aztlán as a place of origin also meant that all Chicanos/as had a common heritage, symbolizing their shared roots and cultural unity. Thus, chicanismo included a reawakening of long, historic ties to the American Southwest.

The idea of Aztlán was so powerful that it became the foundation of El Plan Espiritual de Aztlán, a manifesto written and adopted at the Denver conference. El Plan Espiritual de Aztlán was one of the first coherent outlines of the goals of the Chicano Movement. It identified nationalism as the common denominator that unified all Chicanos/as, regardless of religious, political, or class affiliations. Of the plan's seven organizational goals, "unity" was the first and most important. In addition, defending Chicano cultural values, especially those that emphasize humanism and the collective good, was also considered crucial. Reflecting the more politically militant leanings of the emerging Chicano Movement, the plan ended with a call for the creation of an independent Chicano political party. In the aftermath of the Denver meeting and the issuance of El Plan, the idea of chicanismo became more solidified within and outside the movement.

El Plan de Santa Barbara

A month after the Denver Conference, in April 1969, the Chicano Coordinating Council on Higher Education met at the University of California at Santa Barbara to form a unified approach to reform Chicano higher education. The conference resulted in El Plan de Santa Barbara, a detailed blueprint for improving access to and quality of education for Chicanos/as. The plan contributed to the evolving ideology of chicanismo in several ways, including two aspects that are particularly noteworthy. First, it was here that the word "chicanismo" was used for the first time in a major document of the Chicano Movement. Second, it represented the first attempt to clearly define chicanismo. In El Plan de Santa Barbara, chicanismo is explicitly invoked as a foundation for the commitment to improve conditions for Chicanos/as in American society.

The plan also highlighted one of the essential aspects of chicanismo, which began to emerge with *I Am Joaquín*—that an individual's identity is rooted in the identity of his or her community. While chicanismo is associated with both a cultural and political consciousness, it is also said to encompass all Chicanos/as. Chicano nationalism is viewed as the vehicle for ultimate cultural liberation. At the same time, chicanismo is also related to the broader concept of *La Raza* (literally, "the race," referring to all people of Latin America who share the legacy of Spanish colonialism), thus expanding the ties to an international scope. This last aspect would become increasingly important, as some Chicano activists identified with the struggles and increasing oppression of indigenous and poor peoples of Mexico and Central America in the 1970s, 1980s, and 1990s, especially as the United States saw more arrivals from these countries.

Post–Civil Rights Era

By the mid- to late 1970s, chicanismo continued to be connected to an inclusion of indigenous roots and symbols but also emphasized the awareness and consciousness of a common struggle for civil and human rights of oppressed peoples everywhere. A significant shift in the ideology of chicanismo begun during the movement began to flourish in the mid-1970s and into the 1980s and 1990s. The shift was a challenge offered by Chicanas that the movement and the concept of chicanismo carried with it an inherent degree of sexism and patriarchy. Thus, Chicana feminism evolved almost directly from the ideology of chicanismo and the Chicano Movement. The leadership and structure of the latter, like those of other civil rights movements, were often patriarchal. While many women did a significant portion of the organizing, they were often still expected to function within strict gender roles (cook and clean after meetings, carry out secretarial duties, and the like).

Although chicanismo was meant to refer to all Chicanos/as, Chicana feminist writers, artists, and scholars of the 1980s and 1990s such as Gloria Anzaldúa, Marta Cotera, and Elizabeth Martinez noted the contributions of Chicanas in the movement and gave attention to the female experience in the Chicano community. However, while Chicana feminism represented a strong critique of past and existing sexism, Chicana feminists do not necessarily distance themselves from the idea of chicanismo. In fact, some state that the inclusion of Chicana feminism strengthens and fulfills the true ideals of chicanismo.

Although chicanismo continues to evolve, it is rooted in the many ideals and ideologies that emerged throughout the evolving Chicano Movement. On an individual level, it represents feelings of cultural pride and connection to all Chicanos/as. For many, it also embodies a willingness to work toward justice for Chicanos/as at various levels in society with varying levels of militancy depending on the individual. From a collective standpoint, it is the recognition of Chicanos/as as a distinct people with a shared history. Historically, it was the guiding ideology of the Chicano Movement.

Manuel X. Zamarripa

See also: Aztlán; Chicano/a; Chicano Movement; Gonzales, Rodolfo "Corky"; La Raza; La Raza Unida Party; Plan de Santa Barbara, El; Plan Espiritual de Aztlán, El; *Yo Soy Joaquín.*

Further Reading

Burciaga, José Antonio. *Drink Cultura: Chicanismo.* Santa Barbara, CA: Capra, 1993.

García, Alma M., ed. *Chicana Feminist Thought: The Basic Historical Writings.* New York: Routledge, 1997.

García, Ignacio M. *Chicanismo: The Forging of a Militant Ethos among Mexican Americans.* Tucson: University of Arizona Press, 1997.

Gonzales, Rodolfo. *Message to Aztlán: Selected Writings of Rodolfo "Corky" Gonzales.* Ed. Antonio Esquibel. Houston, TX: Arte Público, 2001.

MacDonald, Victoria-María. *Latino Education in the United States: A Narrated History from 1513–2000.* New York: Palgrave MacMillan, 2004.

Chicano/a

The term "Chicano/a," defined in simplest terms, refers to people of Mexican ancestry living in the United States; it is used most often used in reference to those born and raised on U.S. soil. In the fullest sense, however, the terms "Chicano" (male) or "Chicana" (female) carry profound political and social implications and have changed in meaning over the course of the past two centuries. Indeed, intense debates continue over the terms' precise definition, whether or not they should be used at all, and, if so, in what context. The experience of Chicanos/as as both a conquered and an immigrant people shapes outside understandings and misunderstandings, as well as responses—to the word as well as to the people—in mainstream American society. As distinct from the terms "Hispanic" and "Latino," which include all Spanish-speaking peoples and all peoples of Latin American ancestry (such as Puerto Ricans, Cubans, Dominicans, Hondurans, for instance), Chicano and Chicana refer specifically to Mexicans. They therefore stand for a unique historical experience and sociocultural legacy, as Chicanos/as can be seen as both a conquered and an immigrant people.

The term "Chicano" has also been identified, erroneously, as a derivative of the English word "chicanery," connoting trickery or deception. This mistake no doubt has been based on the stereotype of people of Mexican heritage as sneaky and thieving. Not surprisingly, then, the terms "Chicano" and "Chicana" did not become popular self-identifiers in the Mexican American community until the Chicano civil rights movement of the 1960s.

For the first century after the Treaty of Guadalupe Hidalgo, signed in 1848 at the end of the Mexican War, the majority of Mexican Americans—reflecting the spirit of assimilation—gave up their national designation and identified as Hispanic. Over time, however, some began to argue that "Hispanic" neither captured the indigenous roots nor embraced the distinctive culture and history of the Mexican American people. Still, it was not until the Chicano Movement in the 1960s and 1970s, which emphasized cultural pride and confrontation with American racism, that "Chicano" emerged as a common identifier.

In the 1970s, with the heavy influx of Spanish speakers from far-flung nations in Central and South America under federal immigration legislation, the term "Hispanic" gained broad acceptance in mainstream America. The administration of President Richard M. Nixon in particular adopted the term, which could include Latinos/as of diverse national backgrounds, including more wealthy and conservative Cuban Americans. Government agencies and committees were redesignated as Hispanic, while advertisers and consumer goods manufacturers adopted the term because it allowed them to target Chicanos,

Geraldine Gonzales, wife of the late Chicano leader Rodolfo "Corky" Gonzales, spreads his ashes during a tribute at the 2006 Chicano Park Heritage Festival. The festival is a celebration of ethnic culture held annually in San Diego, California. *(Sandy Huffaker/Stringer/Getty Images)*

Puerto Ricans, Cubans, and other Latinos all at once. Even some Mexican Americans preferred the term "Hispanic," which they said emphasized unity rather than division among those of Latin American ancestry. Still other Mexican Americans preferred its more middle-class, professional, assimilationist connotation to the more confrontational stance of Chicanos and Chicanas. Such were the sometimes-divisive political and ideological implications of the term.

The award-winning author and professor Carlos Muñoz, Jr., himself a leader of the Chicano Movement in the 1960s, argues in his book *Youth, Identity, and Power* (1989) that calling all Mexican Americans "Chicano" is problematic in that the origins of the term are lost. "The political and ideological significance attached to the term by the founders of the Chicano movement has been largely lost or modified to fit contemporary struggles," he writes. The late Chicano journalist Rubén Salazar offered a simpler definition. As he wrote in a *Los Angeles Times* article in February 1970, "a Chicano is a Mexican-American with a non-Anglo image of himself." Thus, according to Salazar and others, identifying oneself as a Chicano/a is not simply recognition of heritage, ethnicity, or nationality, but a sense of self and belief in what it means to be Mexican American. In any event, for both Martinez and Salazar, to identify oneself as Chicano/a is a political decision connected to communal and cultural histories.

By the mid-1980s—the "decade of the Hispanic," as it came to be known—a *Los Angeles Times* poll showed that about one quarter of Chicanos/as preferred the designation "Mexican," one quarter preferred the term "Mexican American," 18 percent preferred "Latino," and 14 percent preferred "Hispanic." The issue was complicated by the 2000 U.S. Census, which for the first time allowed Latinos/as to classify their ethnicity as Hispanic/Latino and to choose from multiple racial/national backgrounds. Debates thus ensued regarding the appropriate box(es) to check for Chicanos/as, indicating that the issue of terminology—if not identity—was far from resolved.

Susan Marie Green

See also: Chicanisma; Chicano Movement; Identity and Labels; La Raza; Salazar, Rubén.

Further Reading

Anaya, Rudolfo, and Francisco Lomeli. *Aztlán: Essays on the Chicano Homeland.* Albuquerque: University of New Mexico Press, 1991.

García, Ignacio. *Chicanismo: The Forging of a Militant Ethos among Mexican Americans.* Tucson: University of Arizona Press, 1997.

Gómez-Quiñones, Juan. *Chicano Politics: Reality and Promise 1940–1990.* Albuquerque: University of New Mexico Press, 1990.

Gutierrez, David G. *Walls and Mirrors: Mexican Americans, Mexican Immigrants, and the Politics of Ethnicity.* Berkeley: University of California Press, 1995.

Muñoz, Carlos, Jr. *Youth, Identity, Power: The Chicano Movement.* New York: Verso, 1989.

Chicano Art

Most Chicano art, at least since the latter part of the twentieth century, has derived directly from the experiences of growing up Chicano in an Anglo society. For many Chicano artists, these experiences include a combination of racism, segregation, and the denial of basic human rights. Gaining inspiration from the Chicano Movement in the 1960s and 1970s—a period of Mexican American civil rights activity—Chicano artists, through various media and forms of expression, used art to showcase their proud and rich history and also to demand their rightful economic and political place in the United States. Furthermore, they used art to articulate their feelings about racism and the civil rights struggle. Of great importance also was their need to locate their native cultural roots.

Chicano art is also rooted in deep traditions of culture, history, and identity. For example, some artists of the 1970s searched for their identity through cultural nationalism, a sense of communal patriotism that stressed feelings of pride and loyalty to historical Mexican culture. Because the goal of the Chicano Movement was to promote self-rule, self-appreciation, and basic human rights, it was not surprising that Chicano art also tended to emphasize similar themes—as it continues to do today. Although most Chicano art calls attention to social injustice and human rights abuse, what separates it from Latino or Mexican American art is the depiction of the experiences of a people who are politically, ideologically, and culturally distinct.

For the most part, Latino artists have emphasized the Spanish component in their art, while Mexican Americans have embraced their Mexican background. Chicanos/as, on the other hand, embrace an indigenous background—that is, they embrace that part of their background that connects them to the pre-Columbian Indians of Mesoamerica. While Latino and Mexican American artists have created works that reflect their particular identities and backgrounds, they do not consciously try to identify their works with a specific view of society. Chicanos/as, however, have done precisely that: they have consciously tried to make the connections between their historical legacies and their current social conditions.

Chicano artists have used paintings, murals, and sculpture as powerful vehicles to communicate the social injustices and other experiences of the community. During the 1960s, pioneering organizations, such as the Mexican American Liberation Art Front (MALAF), a group founded in San Francisco, helped up-and-coming Chicano artists and promoted works of art that represented the goals and ideals of the Chicano Movement.

Appearing in urban centers throughout the country, street murals employed strong Indian motifs, glorified Chicano history, romanticized barrio lifestyles, and focused on various Mexican themes. Common to most murals produced during the 1960s and 1970s were depictions of pyramids, Olmec colossal heads, the Aztec calendar stone, Toltec figures, references to *La Virgen de Guadalupe* (the Virgin of Guadalupe), phrases such as *Viva La Raza* (long live the people), and acts of violence against Chicanos/as by police and other law enforcement authorities. Artists such as Peter Rodriguez of San Francisco and Melesio Casas of San Antonio, Texas, took their inspiration from Mexican muralists Diego Rivera, Jose Clemente Orozco, and David Siqueiros, who pioneered the rebirth of art in Latin America. Some of the best-known Chicano murals can be found in San Diego's Balboa Park, referred to by many as Chicano Park.

Sculptures also proved to be instrumental in the advancement of a Chicano art movement. Known as one of the pioneers of the sculpture movement, Luis Jimenez used fiberglass and neon lights to create images of the American West and Southwest.

Chicano art has effectively spread the message of the Brown Power movement and provided Chicanos/as with an opportunity to speak out against repression, victimization, discrimination, racism, classism, and sexism. Furthermore, it highlights the artists' perception of the historical, cultural, and ethnic heritage of the Indio-Spanish-Mexican people of the Southwest.

Jesse J. Esparza

See also: Chicano/a; Chicano Movement; Gonzalez, Jose-Luis; Mural Art.

Further Reading

Cockcroft, Eva, John Weber, and James Cockcroft. *Toward a People's Art: The Contemporary Mural Movement.* New York: E.P. Dutton, 1977.

Kanellos, Nicolás, and Claudio Esteva-Fabregat, eds. *Handbook of Hispanic Cultures in the United States: Literature and Art.* Houston, TX: Arte Público, 1993.

Quirarte, Jacinto. *Mexican American Artists.* Austin: University of Texas Press, 1973.

Chicano Moratorium

See **National Chicano Moratorium**

Chicano Movement

The Chicano Movement was a period of heightened political activism and cultural creativity in the Mexican American community that intensified in the second half of the 1960s and continued into the early 1970s. The collective struggle of Mexican Americans to improve their lives and claim their civil rights was not new. What was new was the widespread involvement of working-class Mexican American youth and the strength of the cultural nationalism that helped unite diverse segments of the Mexican American population.

Roots

The United States acquired parts of what was then northern Mexico in 1848, through the Treaty of Guadalupe Hidalgo, which ended the Mexican-American War. While the treaty guaranteed rights for resident Mexicans in the area, those who stayed on lost much of their land and their rights to the Anglos who poured into the area in the following years. Mexicans were considered an inferior "race" and routinely faced economic, social, and political discrimination at the hands of the dominant Anglo population.

Statistics suggest that the pattern continued well into the twentieth century. In 1960, for example, per capita income in the Southwest was $968 for persons with Spanish surnames while $2,047 for Anglos. Nearly 30 percent of Latinos lived in substandard housing, versus only 7.5 percent of Anglos. The median number of years in school for Spanish-speaking persons over the age of fourteen in Texas was 8.1, compared to 12.0 for Anglos—to say nothing of the comparative quality of the schools. Reflecting the racism experienced by Chicanos, "No Mexicans Allowed" signs were common in Texas.

The Movement Flourishes

The early to mid-1960s was a period of increased activism in Mexican American communities. *Viva Kennedy* clubs were formed to garner support for John F. Kennedy's presidential bid; the Twenty-Fourth Amendment to the U.S. Constitution abolished the poll tax in 1964; and in Crystal City, Texas, working-class Mexican Americans took control of the city council from Anglos in 1963. The tactics and successes of the black civil rights movement inspired minority communities across the nation. The federal government's War on Poverty, though largely unsuccessful in meeting its objectives, legitimized the grievances and demands of the poor. Even events on the international scene, including the Cuban Revolution in 1959 and anticolonial struggles in several African and Asian countries, inspired resistance to the status quo at home.

The Chicano Movement, or *El Movimiento*, can be seen as a series of smaller movements that cross-fertilized and energized one another. By the mid-1960s, as African American communities exploded in protest, Mexican American activism was taking off in several directions, led by activists working in very different areas and utilizing diverse tactics. At Texas A&I University (now Texas A&M University–Kingsville) in 1964, students formed the precursor to the Mexican American Youth Organization (MAYO). Led by José Angel Gutiérrez and others, they focused on issues such as admissions, discrimination, segregated dorms, and housing quality. California youth, perhaps because of their different historical and social experiences, came to activism slightly later. Reies López Tijerina, working in New

Vietnam War protestors raise their fists during a National Chicano Moratorium Committee march in Los Angeles in 1970. The spirit of youth activism, along with cultural identity and pride, were at the heart of the Chicano Movement. *(David Fenton/Hulton Archive/Getty Images)*

Mexico, organized people around the issue of land grant titles, arguing that violation of the terms and conditions of the Treaty of Guadalupe Hidalgo had wrongfully stripped Mexicans of their communal lands. Initially utilizing political pressure to further his claims, Tijerina led mass demonstrations that included the occupation of national forestland. César Chávez, organizing farmworkers in California, utilized nonviolent tactics and made particularly effective use of a nationwide boycott of produce to press growers for union recognition. In Denver, Colorado, Rodolfo "Corky" Gonzales organized the more militant Crusade for Justice in 1966, a community-based organization that had great appeal to urban youth frustrated by the slow pace of change.

The Chicano Movement was an era in which the arts—dance, murals, theater, literature, and music—flourished and were used to promote pride of heritage, unity, and social critique. Community-based educational programs immersed Chicanos/as in culture and the arts. Rodolfo "Corky" Gonzales's epic poem *Yo Soy Joaquín* (*I Am Joaquín*) was read and analyzed repeatedly across "Aztlán" (the U.S. Southwest). The poem spoke eloquently to the loss of identity Chicanos experienced in a society dominated by Anglos where negative stereotypes, racism, and economic oppression shaped their lives, offering little hope of acceptance into society at large. The poem captured their anguish as it celebrated their mestizo history, pride, and determination as a people:

> I am Joaquín,
> Lost in a world of confusion,
> Caught up in a whirl of a gringo society,
> Confused by the rules, Scorned by
> attitudes . . .
> I am Cuauhtémoc. . . . The Maya Prince. . . .
> the sword and flame of Cortez. . . .
> In a country that has wiped out
> All my history, stifled all my pride. . . .
> I look at myself and see part of me who rejects
> my father and my mother
> and dissolves into the melting pot to disappear
> in shame. . . .
> La Raza! . . .
> Chicano!
> Or whatever I call myself. . . .
> I am the masses of my people and I refuse to
> be absorbed.
> I am Joaquín. . . .
> I SHALL ENDURE!

The Chicano Movement questioned and rejected the elusive goal of assimilation and challenged the Eurocentrism of academic texts and institutions. Activists began using the word "Chicano," originally a negative term directed at poor Mexican Americans, to define themselves and assert a new positive identity. Like African Americans who rejected the term "Negro" and turned the meaning of black on its head to become a badge of pride, so Mexican Americans—*La Raza*—redefined themselves as Chicanos and celebrated "brown pride." This cultural nationalism, with its celebration of Chicanos/as as a distinct people with a shared history and a common identity, was given further impetus by the claim of Chicano leaders that Chicanos/as were not "foreigners" in the Southwest but descendants of the original inhabitants of Aztlán. Aztec Indian legend held that their ancestors' homeland, Aztlán, was located northwest of the capital of Tenochtitlán (now Mexico City). Thus, descended from the Aztecs, Mexican Americans were recognized as the original—and rightful—inhabitants of the region; Anglos were the foreigners. The myth served to unify Chicanos/as and promote pride in their Indian heritage.

The later 1960s saw an increasing radicalization of urban Chicano youth and a greater willingness to confront directly the institutions that oppressed them. Students took to the streets to protest educational conditions in their high schools and universities. In 1967, Mexican American college students in the Los Angeles region met to discuss their role in promoting social change. High school students in Los Angeles, influenced by the Black Power movement, organized to focus on education equality and later police brutality. An estimated 10,000 to 15,000 Chicano high school students in East Los Angeles, assisted by college groups and the Brown Berets, walked out of class in 1968 to protest school conditions. Their demands included community control of the schools, bilingual education, more Chicano teachers, smaller classes, more resources, and the teaching of Chicano history. University students, too, marched to demand the admission of more Chicano students, the hiring of Chicano professors, and the creation of Chicano studies programs.

Momentum continued to build. The First Chicano Youth Liberation Conference, led by "Corky" Gonzales, was held in Denver in 1969. Participants formulated El Plan Espiritual de Aztlán, which provided an ideological framework and political program for the broader Chicano Movement. Gonzales later helped found La Raza Unida. Chicano students in the Southwest and beyond marched to protest high dropout rates, poor facilities, racism, cultural bias, and tracking practices that left them unprepared for college. Demonstrations became more confrontational as police repression and frustrations on both sides increased, with police targeting the Brown Berets in particular. Investigations revealing the role of police infiltrators in instigating conflict and violence in Chicano (and other) organizations and demonstrations further polarized militant youth.

U.S. military participation in Vietnam also moved Chicano youth to the left, as Chicano servicemen were dying at a disproportionate rate. At the Second Annual Chicano Youth Conference, plans were drawn up for hundreds of local moratoria to be held, with a national gathering in East Los Angeles. The National Chicano Moratorium, held on August 29, 1970, drew an estimated 20,000 to 30,000 participants and ended peacefully in a park. A minor incident, however, led to the massive deployment of police, which spiraled into a major confrontation and ultimately the death of celebrated journalist Rubén Salazar. A second Chicano moratorium, in January 1971, also ended in violence. Public sentiment against demonstrations took much of the momentum out of the movement. Internal struggles over political ideology, police repression, and infiltration by law enforcement agencies further weakened it.

Legacy

Perhaps the most significant impact of the Chicano Movement on Mexican Americans was on their self-image, instilling pride and a sense of a common racial identity. The movement was also attended by a renaissance in Chicano culture and the arts, as well as the widespread establishment of Chicano studies programs. Chicanas, responding to the male domination of the movement, built a body of Chicana feminist research, theory, and literature. And the Chicano Movement helped make way for greater Chicano participation and involvement in mainstream politics. What remained largely unchanged was the inferior quality of education available to Chicano youth, a circumstance that has left many Chicanos/as on the lower rungs of the social and economic ladder.

Ellen Bigler

See also: Acosta, Oscar; Aztlán; Blowouts; Brown Berets; Chávez, César; Chicanisma; Chicano Art; Chicano Studies; Gonzales, Rodolfo "Corky"; Gutiérrez, José Angel; La Raza; Mestizo/a; Mexican American Youth Organization; Mexicans; National Chicano Moratorium; Nationalism; Plan Espiritual de Aztlán, El; Tijerina, Reies López; *Yo Soy Joaquín.*

Further Reading

Acuña, Rudolfo. *Occupied America: A History of Chicanos.* 6th ed. New York: Pearson Longman, 2007.

Haney-López, Ian F. *Racism on Trial: The Chicano Fight for Justice.* Cambridge, MA: Harvard University Press, 2003.

Martinez, Elizabeth, ed. *Five Hundred Years of Chicano History in Pictures.* Rev. ed. Albuquerque, NM: Southwest Organizing Project, 1991.

Muñoz, Carlos, Jr. *Youth, Identity, Power: The Chicano Movement.* New York: Verso, 1989.

Rosales, F. Arturo. *Chicano! The History of the Mexican American Civil Rights Movement.* Houston, TX: Arte Público, 1996.

Chicano Studies

Born out of the social turbulence of the 1960s, the academic field of Chicano studies emerged as part of that decade's civil rights struggle in America. Among the participants in the civil rights and antiwar struggles were Chicano college and university student activists. In addition to being concerned with the number of causalities resulting from the Vietnam War, and with persistent inequality and violence, Chicano students also sought affirmation of their cultural identity and experiences in American society at large. On campus, Chicanos/as were critical of curricular emphasis on assimilation, the promulgation of racist stereotypes, and the teaching of biased history. Chicano student activists thus began demanding courses that would reflect their cultural values, engender pride in their heritage, and correct the historical record. Indeed, they called upon colleges and universities to institute course programs and academic departments called Chicano studies.

One of major steps toward the development of Chicano studies programs was El Plan de Santa Barbara. In April 1969, at the campus of the University of California, Santa Barbara, Chicano students from twenty-nine campuses across the state met to formulate a "master plan." Within the plan was a set of guidelines to be used to recruit Chicano professors, students, and administrators at various California universities. Among many items covered within El Plan de Santa Barbara was the desire among Chicano activists to have courses offered in Chicano studies. Although the conference was a success, the future direction for Chicano studies remained unclear, as the plan provided far more rhetoric concerning Chicano nationalism than specific curricular, disciplinary, or methodological stipulations.

Course Offerings

Following waves of protests and struggle, the first Chicano studies courses—Politics of the Southwest and Mexican American History, both taught by graduate students—were offered in 1968 at California State University, Los Angeles. Shortly thereafter, campuses throughout the University of California (UC) and California State University systems would begin offering Chicano studies courses. Among the schools that offered courses were University of California, Los Angeles (UCLA), UC Berkeley, UC Santa Barbara, San Fernando Valley State College (later changed to California State University, Northridge), and San Francisco State University.

The emergence of Chicano studies programs, particularly in California, was based on two factors. One was the growing population of Mexican Americans. Although small in number by comparison to African Americans, Mexican Americans represented a growing segment of the minority population. They were especially prevalent in California, a primary destination for many native Mexicans. Secondly, the Chicano student movement, popularly known as the Chicano Movement, was beginning to emerge in the state. Students in the movement were demanding the creation of programs or departments that would offer Chicano studies courses. In short, the students of the Chicano Movement made California school administrators aware of their desire for courses that would advance their knowledge and appreciation of cultural heritage. Their demands were met after a number of protests and walkouts by Chicano high school and university students in the state. Among the most notable were the 1968 Los Angeles "blowouts."

Since the inception of the field, offerings in Chicano studies have ranged from introductory courses to advanced undergraduate and graduate courses. Most introductory courses focus on the historical growth and development of the Chicano community. Other introductory courses spotlight Chicano culture, including literature, the arts, and Indian heritage. Advanced courses in Chicano studies have grown over the decades to include such topics as Mexican immigration, U.S-Mexico relations, border studies, the Chicano family, and other subjects in history, the social sciences, and the humanities. Study of Náhuatl (the indigenous language of Mexico) or the Mesoamerica period in Mexican history is especially sought after among Chicano students. Internships offer students the opportunity to learn and work in community groups and to expand their practical skills beyond the classroom.

As the Chicano Movement grew and began to attract more academically trained scholars, an increasing number were Chicanas. They soon sensed their second-class status. Current scholarship regards the lack of female voices, leadership roles, or other contributions as a distinct weakness of the early Chicano Movement. So, too—in Chicano studies—was the absence of courses on gender identity and Chicana issues. Feminist issues, or the lack thereof, as addressed by the Chicano Movement, attracted the attention of working-class Chicanas who had secured admission to the university. As a critical mass of Chicana scholars began to form, so too did the desire for courses that addressed their struggle as working-class women. The first courses offered by Chicana feminists focused on critical theory and gender.

Resistance

From its inception, Chicano studies has taken a different educational approach from more traditional disciplines. As a result, Chicano studies has experienced resistance from academic institutions, who see it as not academically rigorous enough. Another major component has always been a desired link between the academy and the Chicano community. In short, Chicano studies would not only serve to educate Chicanos/as about their cultural heritage, but also promote knowledge about securing social change within Chicano communities. Dating back to El Plan de Santa Barbara, it was clear that Chicano studies was not merely a discipline for learning about Chicano history and culture, but would advocate social change. Chicano historian and a founder of Chicano studies Rodolfo (Rudy) Acuña explains that the discipline of Chicano studies is a public trust; those who teach Chicano studies do so on behalf of the Chicano community.

Other issues currently facing Chicano studies departments and programs include cutbacks in course offerings; insufficient funding by academic administrations to keep programs or departments from closing completely; loss of academic autonomy; and uncertainty about who gets hired for teaching positions.

The Future

In 2005, University of California, Santa Barbara inaugurated the first PhD program in Chicano studies. In 2006, Michigan State University offered the first Chicano studies PhD program in the Midwest. After many years of struggling to secure graduate programs offering doctoral degrees, Chicano studies is moving toward critical acceptance as a legitimate field of study. Other graduate programs in Chicano studies are planned for UCLA, the University of Arizona, and the University of Texas at Austin. The coming few decades are likely to see increased interest in establishing graduate programs at colleges and universities throughout the Southwest and Midwest. The future development of Chicano studies will remain in the hands of young Chicana and Chicano scholars who are trained in the field, while the continued struggle of Chicano activists will ensure that Chicano studies is offered at college and universities throughout the nation.

Paul López

See also: Acuña, Rodolfo; Anzaldúa, Gloria; Blowouts; Chicano/a; Chicano Movement; Education; Movimiento Estudiantíl Chicano de Aztlán; Plan de Santa Barbara, El; Samora, Julian.

Further Reading

Acuña, Rodolfo. *Occupied America: A History of Chicanos in the United States.* 6th ed. New York: Pearson Longman, 2007.

———. *Sometimes There Is No Other Side: Chicanos and the Myth of Equality.* Notre Dame, IN: University of Notre Dame Press, 1998.

Contreras, Raoul. "Chicano Studies: A Political Strategy of the Chicano Movement." In *Mapping Strategies: NACCS and the Challenge of Multiple Oppressions,* ed. Maria Antonia Beltran-Vocal, Manuel de Jesus Hernandez-Gutierrez, and Sylvia Fuentes. NACCS Proceedings, Chicago, 1996.

García, Alma. "Chicano Studies and 'La Chicana' Courses: Curriculum Options and Reforms." In *Community Empowerment and Chicano Scholarship,* ed. Mary Romero and Cordelia Candelaria. NACCS Proceedings, Los Angeles, 1992.

Chileans

The Chilean American population in the United States is relatively small compared to that of other Latino subgroups. According to the 2000 U.S. Census, there were 68,849 Chilean Americans living in the United States, representing barely 0.15 percent of the Latino population. Most have settled in urban areas of California, New York, and Florida, with the largest number in California. Chileans have immigrated to the United States in response to specific economic and political factors at home and to promises both real and mythical of a new life.

The first significant wave of Chilean immigrants arrived in the United States during the California Gold Rush in 1849. Chilean merchant ships that had docked in San Francisco the previous year returned home with fabulous strike-it-rich stories and rumors of enormous gold nuggets for the taking. Within months, ship after ship set sail for California loaded with Chilean prospectors seeking their fortunes. Many settled in mining towns that had sprouted up in the California foothills; the Chilean presence was pervasive. To the present day, evidence of the Chilean prospectors in Northern California exists in place names like Chili Gulch and Chileno Valley. Those less prepared to rough it in the mining camps found jobs in the burgeoning town of San Francisco. They took work as bricklayers, bakers, and importers, or bought property and began commercial interests. In San Francisco, most settled in a section of town known as *Chilecito,* or Little Chile. The 1852 state census lists 5,511 Chileans in California, though the actual number was probably significantly higher, as the census did not account for those living aboard ships and those who avoided enumeration for fear of discrimination.

Because Chile lies on the Pacific coast of the South American continent, Chilean ships could reach the port of San Francisco almost a year before ships from the Eastern United States, which had to travel around Cape Horn. American citizens on their way to strike it rich in California were told that foreigners had already arrived there and were extracting all the wealth. Such reports aroused anger and resentment against foreigners, in particular Chinese, Mexicans, and Chileans. The California legislature passed laws to protect American prospectors, including the Foreign Miner's Tax (1852), while many Americans took matters into their own hands by threatening, lynching, and rioting against Asian and Latin American newcomers. It was during the 1850s, in reaction to such treatment, that the mythical figure of Joaquín Murrieta, a notorious California bandit, emerged as a symbol of Latino resistance to Anglo-American racism and discrimination. Murrieta, originally said to be a Mexican miner but later identified as Chilean, was mythologized as a kind of Robin Hood figure who avenged economic and racial injustices against Latinos/as.

In the century after the California Gold Rush, Chilean immigration to the United States was sporadic. Children of wealthy families would come to attend college or graduate school, and professionals would come to pursue careers, but these were relatively few in number. During the 1960s, however, with Chile's economic performance among the poorest in South America and inflation running rampant, waves of Chileans left the country for the United States seeking economic opportunities. They tended to be less educated and had fewer professional skills than those who had immigrated during the previous century.

An even larger wave of immigration occurred beginning in 1973, when democratically elected president Salvador Allende was overthrown in a military coup (supported by the U.S. government) that brought the repressive General Augusto Pinochet to power. Hundreds of thousands of Chileans fled to other Latin American countries, Europe, Canada, and the United States. They believed they were leaving the country only temporarily, but Pinochet prohibited any exiles and expatriates from returning for fifteen years. While eventually many did return, others remained in their adopted countries of exile, including the United States.

In general, Chilean Americans have found economic stability in the United States. Their median household income has been higher than that of the overall Latino population and even slightly higher than that of the average U.S. household. Part of the reason for this is that Chilean Americans have made education a priority. Approximately 31 percent of adults over the age of twenty-five hold a bachelor's degree or higher, compared to about 10 percent for Latino Americans overall and 24 percent for the entire U.S. population.

According to the 2000 U.S. Census, a relatively high number of Chilean Americans—55,410, or about 80 percent—are foreign born. First-generation immigrants have maintained close ties with their cultural traditions; indeed more than 58,000 were found to speak Spanish in the home. While second- and third-generation Chilean Americans have become more integrated into U.S. culture, they have also maintained connections to their heritage. Community members have founded Chilean cultural centers and social clubs to foster pride in Chilean heritage and support among family and friends. Such groups sponsor heritage days, folk dance performances, concerts of traditional music, and other cultural events.

At the same time, Chilean Americans have made important contributions to mainstream American culture, particularly in the arts. Isabel Allende, niece of deposed president Salvador Allende, is a best-selling author whose novels of "magical realism"—some written in Spanish, some in English—have won widespread critical acclaim. The Chilean novelist, playwright, essayist, and journalist Ariel Dorfman teaches at Duke University, while the late Fernando Alegría, a Stanford professor, wrote more than two dozen books of poetry, fiction, and criticism as well as a history of Latin America. Marjorie Agosín, a journalist, poet, and professor at Wellesley College, has published several books of poetry and a memoir and is a passionate advocate for women's rights. The émigré artist Roberto Matta, who settled in the United States in 1948, became one of Chile's best-known painters and sculptors as part of the surrealist movement.

Molly Metherd

Further Reading

Burson, Phyllis J. "Chilean Americans." Countries and Their Cultures. http://www.everyculture.com.

Lopez, Carlos U. *Chilenos in California: A Study of the 1850, 1852, and 1860 Censuses.* San Francisco: R and E Research Associates, 1973.

Lorca de Tagle, Lillian. *Honorable Exiles: A Chilean Woman in the Twentieth Century.* Austin: University of Texas Press, 2000.

Monaghan, Jay. *Chile, Peru, and the California Gold Rush of 1849.* Berkeley: University of California Press, 1973.

Cholos

The word *cholo* is used among people of ethnic Mexican background in the western United States to refer to a Mexican American gang member (a "banger"). More specifically, it refers to a barrio style of dress, walking, and language adopted by young people in Los Angeles during the Chicano Movement for civic and political empowerment in the late 1960s. The cholo style eventually spread to Latino barrios from Texas and California to the Pacific Northwest. In its classic (or Hollywood form), the cholo uniform consists of khaki work pants, plaid flannel or wool shirt buttoned at the top, and tank shirt, among other articles. Largely through the popular *Low Rider* magazine, which featured pictures of young people in cholo attire, the style became a cultural identifier for alienated young Mexican Americans, especially in the Southwest.

The phenomenon took hold across areas populated by Mexican Americans during the mid-1970s, as the Chicano Movement lost much of its active grassroots support. Latinos/as were still underrepresented in politics and the professions, and police brutality was still a threat faced by barrio young people. In the last decades of the twentieth century the term was applied almost exclusively to gang members, but in recent years Mexican Americans or Chicanos/as not involved in gangs began to use it.

The term itself is of obscure Latin American origin. Peruvians historically have used the term to describe *mestizos*, or those of mixed Indian-Spanish origin, while people in Bolivia have used it to describe Indians or peasants in a derogatory manner. During the 1920s, between 500,000 and 2 million Mexican immigrants entered the United States, creating a large new minority group facing unique problems. Eventually, Mexican Americans in California who had become more established as permanent residents or citizens referred to newer, poorer arrivals from Mexico as *cholos.* By the early 1940s, with the popularity of the zoot suit, or "drapes," and the *pachuco* street dialect among Mexican American young people in Los Angeles, girls began calling themselves *cholitas* and adopted their own defiant urban style, including short skirts and high pompadour hairdos.

The Zoot Suit Riots in the summer of 1943 fostered further barrio defiance against police brutality and second-class status. Scores of boys who identified themselves as pachucos were humiliated when American servicemen stationed in Los Angeles, urged on by civilians, tore off their clothes and left them on the streets. It would be the younger generation, sons and daughters of the riot victims, who would call themselves cholos more than two decades later. They would adopt the slang dialect of their pachuco predecessors—known as *caló*—and create a barrio culture of their own.

During the late 1960s, in Los Angeles, the Chicano Movement caught the imagination of many young people in the barrios, including the *batos locos* (crazy guys), whose energy focused on street rallies and marches rather than gang fights. Film footage and photos of these activities show young men and teens wearing buttoned-up plaid shirts and tapered work pants, an early cholo look. By 1977 and the creation of *Low Rider* magazine in San Jose, California, the "L.A" look swept Latino communities in the western United States. The cholo uniform, often augmented with Stacy Addams brand shoes for young men and Asian-style "Mary Jane" slippers for women, became common. Other features of the style were hairnets for men, who often slicked back their hair and wore low-slung bandannas around their heads. Women, like their forebears, wore high pompadours on top, but with the hair on the bottom allowed to grow long. The youths also adopted a cholo stance, with feet apart and legs close together.

But there were negative aspects to the cholo phenomenon. Although Hollywood exploited it with films like *Boulevard Nights* (1979), barrios across the United States began to witness the formation of street gangs made up of cholas and cholos. The uniform demonstrated the economic and social hopelessness of some aspects of barrio life. Many young people adopted the dress as a way to drop out of the American system—and in many cases into prison. This process has been referred to as *choloization*. Today, *cholismo* among young people continues to demonstrate the alienation of barrio youth. In California and other states, cholas and cholos have grouped themselves into gang factions known as *Norteños* and *Sureños*, often with tragic results. In its way, cholismo carries on a tradition started by the original pachucos who migrated out of Texas in the 1920s and into California. It is a culture created by historical, racial, and ethnic injustice that now refuses to die among young people without hope.

E. Mark Moreno

See also: Chicano Movement; Gangs; Zoot Suit Riots.

Further Reading

Haney-López, Ian F. *Racism on Trial: The Chicano Fight for Justice.* Cambridge, MA: Harvard University Press, 2003.

Rodríguez, Luis J. *Always Running: La Vida Loca, Gang Days in L.A.* New York: Simon and Schuster, 2005.

Vigil, James Diego. *Barrio Gangs: Street Life and Identity in Southern California.* Austin: University of Texas Press, 1988.

Cinco de Mayo

Not Mexican Independence Day or Mexico's "Fourth of July," as it is often misunderstood in mainstream American culture, Cinco de Mayo—the fifth of May—commemorates the Battle of Puebla on May 5, 1862, when 4,000 ill-equipped Mexican soldiers defeated an army of 8,000 French troops. This unexpected victory greatly boosted Mexican national spirits, even though Mexico came under French occupation one year later. After Mexico reestablished its independence in 1867, Cinco de Mayo became a relatively minor holiday in Mexico, mostly celebrated in Puebla and Mexico City. In the United States, however, the holiday grew in popularity from a Mexican nationalist celebration to a highly commercialized pan-Latino event.

When news of the 1862 battle reached Spanish-language newspapers in the United States, members of the Mexican expatriate community began organizing fund-raising events to collect and send money to Mexican troops. In subsequent years, Mexican social clubs organized events on May 5 to support the Mexican struggle against French occupation. In a show of patriotism and support, the Los Angeles Spanish-language press printed their front pages in red, white, and green.

By the early decades of the twentieth century, Cinco de Mayo had become a popular patriotic celebration in Mexican American communities, bringing together neighbors and compatriots to attend patriotic speeches, musical performances, dances, queen of community contests, and other festive activities. In the context of limited economic opportunities and a racially restricted environment, Cinco de Mayo offered a social space for Mexican immigrants to reminisce about the homeland and build a sense of community in an alienating environment.

Costumed performers portray ancient Aztec culture in a Cinco de Mayo celebration in Glendale, California. The Fifth of May holiday has grown from a Mexican patriotic event to a pan-Latino community celebration. *(David McNew/Getty Images)*

The organizational force behind Cinco de Mayo observances was patriotic committees, made up of representatives from mutual-aid societies, fraternal lodges, voluntary associations, and sport and recreational clubs. An official from the Mexican consulate office typically played a visible role in Cinco de Mayo celebrations by delivering speeches, crowning the queen, and reminding audiences of the historical significance of the Battle of Puebla.

By the 1930s and 1940s, Cinco de Mayo celebrations in America evolved from primarily Mexican nationalist events into bicultural celebrations. A new group of second-generation Mexican Americans, born or raised in the United States, identified less with Mexican nationalism and associated more with certain aspects of American culture. The new leaders, some of whom were returning World War II veterans, transformed Cinco de Mayo celebrations to include Mexican and American flags, the singing of both national anthems, and the inclusion of popular American dance styles and musical genres. The presence of city officials also helped to foster better intercultural relations between the Mexican and Anglo communities.

Beginning in the 1960s and 1970s, a new group of Mexican Americans, who called themselves Chicano/as organized Cinco de Mayo celebrations on high school and college campuses. Inspired by the civil rights movement and having endured a loss of culture and identity, Chicano/as used Cinco de Mayo to reclaim a cultural nationalist identity and to make connections between the French colonization of Mexico and the Anglo-American conquest of the Southwest. Chicano/a activists also pointed out that General Ignacio Zaragoza, the Mexican commander at the Battle of Puebla, was a *Tejano* (Texan of Mexican ancestry), thus linking the struggle for self-determination north of the U.S.-Mexico border. With passage of the 1968 Bilingual Education Act, public schools in the United States began to integrate Cinco de Mayo into bilingual programs and a multicultural curriculum.

In 1980, the U.S. Census Bureau introduced a new term, *Hispanic*, to categorize all Latino subgroups. As immigrant groups from throughout Latin America increasingly populated U.S. cities, Cinco de Mayo celebrations underwent major changes. In San Francisco, for example, organizers transformed Cinco de Mayo into the Latin American Fiesta to reflect the Bay Area's diverse Hispanic communities; salsa music thus shared the stage with traditional Mexican mariachi sounds. Other Cinco de Mayo fiestas were organized under themes of *Latina América* and *La Raza* to highlight the visions of the Latin American revolutionaries who sought to unite the Latin American countries against U.S. imperialism.

In light of the rapid growth of the Latino population, U.S. advertisers have sought to tap into this market through Cinco de Mayo celebrations. The value of goods purchased by U.S. Latinos from 1986 to 1996 reached over $223 billion. According to a 2003 report by the Selig Center for Economic Growth at the University of Georgia, the Hispanic buying power was expected to increase from 5.2 percent in 1990 to 9.6 percent in 2008.

During the 1980s, the U.S. beer industry in particular began to use Cinco de Mayo to promote sales of their products by spending millions on Spanish-language advertising and sponsoring drinking events. For example, at the entrance to one supermarket in a Mexican neighborhood stood an eight-foot stack of twelve-packs under the slogan "Cinco to Drinko." One liquor store ad went so far to claim that Tecate beer was "a pure Mexican vitamin." A television commercial for Corona beer featured a man wandering into a pub in Ireland only to find a "wild" Cinco de Mayo celebration under way. A José Cuervo tequila ad appealed to the cultural memory of Mexican American consumers by using the tagline "Si Se Puede" ("Yes, we can," made famous by the labor leader César Chávez during the farmworkers movement) alongside "Si Se Party, Si Se Cuervo."

In response to the commercialization of Cinco de Mayo, Latino activists have waged battles against the alcohol industry and staged their own alcohol-free celebrations. In 1997 a coalition of health, substance-abuse prevention, and community activists met in Oakland, California, and formed an organization called Latinos and Latinas for Health Justice (LLHJ) to liberate Cinco de Mayo from the clutches of the alcohol industry. LLHJ launched a statewide campaign called Cinco de Mayo con Orgullo (Cinco de Mayo with Pride) to promote alcohol-free, family-oriented celebrations and to educate the public of the health problems caused by alcohol and tobacco abuse. By 2003, the Cinco de Mayo con Orgullo campaign had been organized in twenty-four California cities and twelve counties in Arizona and continued to promote alcohol-free celebrations in other states.

In 1998 the U.S. Postal Service issued the first Cinco de Mayo stamp, and in 2001 President George W. Bush held the first-ever Cinco de Mayo commemoration at the White House. These two examples revealed the extent to which Cinco de Mayo has entered the American mainstream, becoming as popular in many areas as such other national or ethnic holidays as St. Patrick's Day. The rapid increase in the Latino population has certainly contributed to the widening popularity of the event, but the multibillion-dollar alcohol industry and others have also fueled the growth of Cinco de Mayo and contributed to negative images of Latino culture and history. The onslaught of commercials, racist stereotypes, and all-you-can-drink happy-hour promotions prompted the comedian Paul Rodríguez to jokingly ask *Los Angeles Times* readers, "Aren't You Just Sicko de Mayo?"

The commercialization of Cinco de Mayo has not been without resistance from community activists, who have waged campaigns against the alcohol industry and other corporate interests said to promote negative stereotypes and alcohol abuse in the Latino community. Latinos and Latinas for Health Justice, Latinos Por La Paz, and other student and community organizations represent a new social movement aimed at reclaiming Cinco de Mayo as a symbol of anti-imperialist struggle and self-determination of *La Raza.*

José M. Alamillo

See also: Chicano/a; Mexicans; Tejanos.

Further Reading

Alamillo, José M. "More Than a Fiesta: Ethnic Identity, Cultural Politics and Cinco de Mayo Festivals in Corona, California, 1930–1950." *Aztlán* 28 (Fall 2003): 57–85.

Cabello-Argandona, Robert, ed. *Cinco de Mayo: A Symbol of Mexican National Resistance.* Encino, CA: Floricanto, 1991.

Carlson, Alvar. "America's Growing Observance of Cinco de Mayo." *Journal of American Culture* 21 (Summer 1998): 7–16.

Sommers, Laurie Kay. "Symbol and Style in Cinco de Mayo." *Journal of American Folklore* 98 (1985): 476–82.

Circular Migration

Circular migration, also known as "revolving door" migration, is the process whereby an individual repeatedly enters and exits a destination country, with the border functioning as a metaphorical revolving door. While some have argued that this pattern often leads to permanent settlement, others contend that most circular migrants stay in the United States only temporarily and eventually return to their countries of origin. Recent studies indicate that a large proportion of people engaged in circular migration are not seeking to settle in a new country. Their goal, rather, is to work abroad temporarily and then return to their native land. Failing to find economic opportunities at home, migrants have identified temporary migration as a means of securing capital and then returning home to spend it.

The concept of circular migration stands in contrast to the more widespread understanding of migration as permanent settlement, which explained the arrival of large numbers of European immigrants in the late nineteenth and early twentieth centuries and still explains migration patterns from some parts of the world today. Immigration research and immigration policy in the United States are predicated on the assumption that every worker from abroad wants to settle there. According to the popular myth of immigration, migrants move to a receiving country, settle there permanently, and are assimilated into a new culture. Yet this story represents a shrinking proportion of all migration. In reality, an increasing number of those who enter the United States are, instead, engaging in a pattern of circular migration. This is particularly true for Latin American immigrants, given their geographic proximity to the U.S. border. In fact, Latin American immigration to the United States historically has been composed of workers who move there temporarily in order to take advantage of economic opportunities rather than to settle.

Historical Antecedents

Mexican immigration to the United States between 1848 and 1917 can be described, by and large, as circular migration. Some Mexican laborers entered the United States to work for a few years before returning to Mexico, moving north again only if driven by economic necessity. Others would follow seasonal work patterns, arriving in the United States in the spring and working through the fall but returning to their families in Mexico for the winter. This pattern held even during the Mexican Revolution (1910–1920), when many migrants crossed the border as family units to escape the economic and military turmoil that gripped their homeland. Few among those arriving during this period intended to make the United States their permanent home, as evidenced by the tiny percentage that sought to legalize their status as permanent residents.

The shift from circular to permanent migration among Mexican nationals entering the United States came about as a result of federal immigration laws. Legislation such as the Immigration Reform Act of 1917 required those entering the country to pass both a literacy test and a health exam, and to pay a fee. While migrant workers do not always desire to settle in destination countries, highly restrictive policies and barriers to entry often push them into settlement.

Puerto Ricans, who have been U.S. citizens since 1917 and therefore are not subject to immigration laws, have also consistently engaged in patterns of circular migration. Physical proximity and relatively affordable transportation have encouraged many Puerto Ricans to migrate back and forth between the island and the mainland, spending substantial periods of residence in both places. These Puerto Rican migration flows have fluctuated systematically according to employment conditions in the United States and Puerto Rico. When the economy on the island was booming, the flow of people from the mainland back to Puerto Rico intensified. Likewise, when the island's employment opportunities were shrinking—as was the case in the 1950s following enactment of the Industrial Incentives Act of 1947, also known as Operation Bootstrap—Puerto Rican migration to the United States intensified.

Globalization and Circular Migration

In the twenty-first century, circular immigration is on the rise once again. This is particularly true for Mexican immigrants entering the United States. Surveys by the Public Policy Institute of California suggest that a substantial number of Mexican immigrants entering the United States are engaging in circular migration. Other research indicates that 50 percent of immigrants from western Mexico return to their home country after two years. In other words, only half of Mexican immigrants actually settle permanently in the United States. After ten years, nearly 70 percent of the original sample had returned. While the reasons underlying each individual's decision to remain or return vary, the resurgence of circular migration can be seen as the result of globalization.

The forces of globalization have substantially increased nonpermanent, circular migration between nations, which is taking place today on an unprecedented scale. Modern advances in transportation and communication technologies have greatly reduced the time and distance between origin and destination countries. This means that migrants are able to maintain closer and more intimate linkages with their birthplaces than ever before. Cheaper international phone calls, the advent of e-mail and fax, and the ease and affordability of international travel have not only made it possible for migrants to interact in real time with their home country on a regular basis, but also to visit home more frequently for holidays and in case of emergency. The pressure to bring entire families to the destination is not as great as in the past, and the likelihood of return migration has increased. Migrants who practice circular migration often do so to obtain the best of both worlds. They work in high-paying, high-cost locations so that they may return to low-income, low-cost origins. While they are away, they can maintain ties with their country of origin by keeping their family there, remaining citizens of that country, and making frequent visits.

The American anthropologist Roger Rouse has studied the effects of globalization on migration patterns between the rural town of Aguililla, in the Mexican state of Michoacán, and Redwood City, an urban area on the northern edge of California's Silicon Valley. By the early 1980s, he found, almost every family in Aguililla had members who were or had been abroad, and the local economy depended heavily on the influx of dollars. Indeed many of the area's small farming operations were being sustained by migrant remittances. Migrants from Aguililla, meanwhile, had established a substantial outpost in Redwood City, where they found work principally in the service sector. Those arriving in the United States call upon social networks created in Aguililla to secure jobs and housing, but few Aguilillans abandon their *municipio* forever. Most remain in the United States briefly, usually long enough to raise capital to send home. Those who stay longer keep in close touch with family back home and eventually return.

Legislating Circular Migration

The concept of circular migration is not only transforming how academics study immigration, it also offers a potential solution to contemporary immigration debates. Official sponsorship of circular migration patterns is not new. At various points in time, the U.S. government has actively participated in promoting circular migration in order to meet domestic labor demands. In 1940, for example, after President Franklin Delano Roosevelt signed the Selective Service Act, concern over potential labor shortages led to the passage of the Emergency Farm Labor Program, which remained in effect from 1942 to 1962. Also known as the Bracero Program, this bilateral agreement between the United States and Mexico issued temporary visas to Mexican agricultural workers and helped meet a U.S. labor shortage.

More recently, faced with the challenges posed by undocumented immigration, President George W. Bush proposed the creation of a controversial new temporary worker program. On January 7, 2004, the White House unveiled a program that would offer temporary legal status to employed undocumented workers already in the United States as well as to those in foreign countries who have been offered jobs in the United States. Under the proposed terms, participants would be issued a three-year renewable visa with the understanding that they would eventually be required to return to their home countries. In theory such a program would simultaneously satisfy the demand for labor on the part of American businesses and the desire of foreign workers, particularly those from developing nations, to access U.S. labor markets. In 2005, Senators John McCain (R-AZ) and Edward M. Kennedy (D-MA) introduced a similar measure in Congress: the Secure America and Orderly Immigration Act of 2005. This bill was designed to promote migration agreements between the United States and foreign countries to control migration flows and to encourage the eventual return migration of foreign nationals entering the United States under such agreements. The proposed legislation addressed the U.S. dependence on foreign labor, as well as the issues associated with illegal immigration, by promoting and formalizing circular migration. The measure never came to a vote in the Senate, but some of its concepts were incorporated into the Comprehensive Immigration Reform Act of 2007. This bill, although backed by President Bush and many congressional leaders, failed in a Senate procedural vote, effectively killing it.

Patricia Kim-Rajal

See also: Bracero Program; Mexicans; Puerto Ricans.

Further Reading

Acevedo, Gregory. "Neither Here Nor There: Puerto Rican Circular Migration." *Journal of Immigrant and Refugee Services* 2:1/2 (2004): 69–85.

Daniels, Roger. *American Immigration: A Student Companion.* New York: Oxford University Press, 2001.

García y Griego, Manuel. "The Importation of Mexican Contract Laborers to the United States, 1942–1962." In *Between Two Worlds: Mexican Immigrants in the United States,* ed. David G. Gutiérrez. Wilmington, DE: Scholarly Resources, 1996.

Reyes, Belinda I. *The Dynamics of Immigration: Return Migration to Western Mexico.* San Francisco: Public Policy Institute of California, 1997.

Sánchez, George J. *Becoming Mexican American: Ethnicity, Culture and Identity in Chicano Los Angeles, 1900–1945.* New York: Oxford University Press, 1995.

Sassen, Saskia. "U.S Immigration Policy toward Mexico in a Global Economy." In *Between Two Worlds: Mexican Immigrants in the United States,* ed. David G. Gutiérrez. Wilmington, DE: Scholarly Resources, 1996.

Cisneros, Henry (1947–)

An exemplar of diversity in modern American politics and the increasing visibility of Latino leaders, Henry Cisneros was the first Latino mayor of a major U.S. city (San Antonio, Texas) and later served as U.S. secretary of housing and urban development under President Bill Clinton. Having committed his life's work to empowering the poor and people of color in the United States, he left government in December 1996 amid accusations of wrongdoing.

Born on June 11, 1947, in San Antonio, Henry Gabriel Cisneros completed his primary education in that city and went on to receive both his bachelor's and master's degrees (1968 and 1970) in urban and regional planning from Texas A&M University. He later earned a PhD (1976) in public administration from George Washington University.

Choosing a career in public service rather than academia because of his desire to give back to his community, Cisneros turned to politics. In 1975, he was elected to San Antonio's city council and was reelected twice. As a council member, he emphasized economic development and cooperation among the city's various communities. As a moderate Democrat, he won the 1981 citywide election to become San Antonio's first Mexican American mayor since the 1840s. During his eight years in office, Cisneros dramatically improved the economy of the city, attracting major companies in the biomedical and high-tech industries, increasing tourism, and enhancing the city's infrastructure. His ample success and popularity in San Antonio, along with his personal charisma, soon made Cisneros a high-profile national figure. In 1984, Democratic Party leaders interviewed him as a potential candidate for vice president.

After leaving the San Antonio mayor's office in 1989, he became chairman of the Cisneros Asset

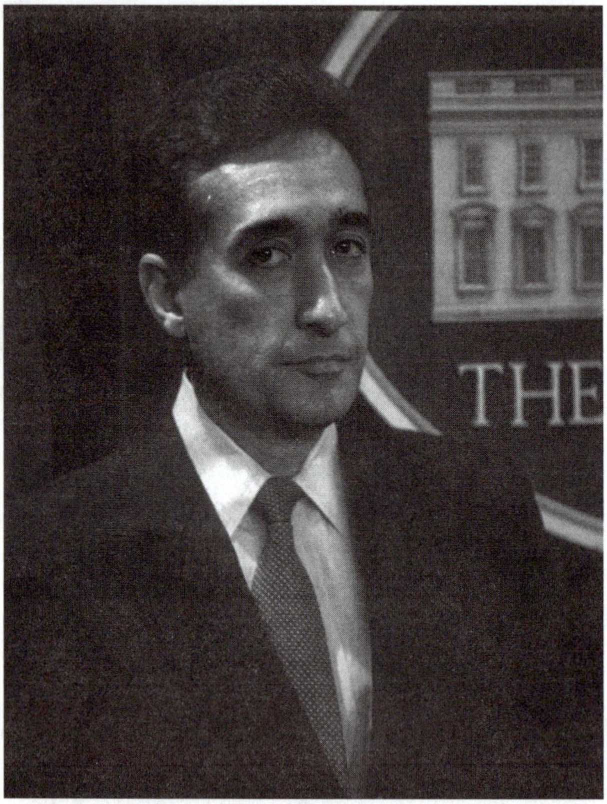

Henry Cisneros was the first Latino mayor of a large U.S. city (San Antonio, Texas), and he served in the cabinet of President Bill Clinton. Leaving public office amid controversy, Cisneros became president of Univision, the Spanish-language television network, in 1997. *(Dirck Halstead/Time & Life Pictures/Getty Images)*

Management Company, which worked with nonprofit organizations across the country, while serving as deputy chairman of the Federal Reserve Bank of Dallas and on the board of the Rockefeller Foundation.

On January 22, 1993, Bill Clinton appointed Cisneros as secretary of housing and urban development (HUD), making him the first Latino/a to hold this cabinet-level position. During his four-year tenure, he successfully reformed the public housing system and resisted efforts to substantially reduce or eliminate the department. With a legacy of mismanagement at HUD and staunch Republican opposition, Cisneros faced ample difficulty as secretary. Under his leadership, howevever, HUD had particular success battling homelessness, even turning the HUD building into a temporary shelter during cold nights. Cisneros's leadership was also visible in efforts to clean up public housing; within eighteen months of his taking office, nearly 240,000 dilapidated housing projects throughout the nation were torn down, with many tenants moving into more desirable and safer facilities.

Cisneros resigned under a cloud of personal and political scandal, accused of lying to the Federal Bureau of Investigation (FBI) regarding payments made to a woman with whom he was said to be having an affair. In March 1995, U.S. Attorney General Janet Reno appointed an independent counsel, David Barrett, to investigate possible perjury committed by Cisneros during his background check when appointed to the cabinet. Fearing negative publicity and embarrassment for himself and his family, Cisneros had lied about the amount of money he had paid to the woman. In December 1997, Cisneros was indicted on eighteen counts of conspiracy, giving false statements, and obstruction of justice. In September 1999, Cisneros negotiated a plea agreement in which he admitted making false statements to the FBI, a misdemeanor for which he was fined $10,000. In January 2001, he was pardoned by President Clinton.

After retiring from political office, Cisneros remained active in public affairs, serving as president of Univision, the nation's largest Spanish-language television network, based in Los Angeles. As the head of Univision from 1997 to 2000, Cisneros oversaw significant growth in the network, attracting corporate sponsorship and increasing viewership. During this period, Cisneros also served as a board member for Latino Public Broadcasting and the American Democracy Institute. In August 2000, he formed American City Vista, a joint venture with KB Home to build reasonably priced residences in downtown areas of major cities. American City Vista later became CityView, with Henry Cisneros as its chairman.

Anita Damjanovic and David J. Leonard

See also: Politics; Univision.

Further Reading

Bredeson, Carmen. *Henry Cisneros: Building a Better America.* Berkeley Heights, NJ: Enslow, 1995.

Cisneros, Henry, ed. *Interwoven Destinies: Cities and the Nation.* New York: W.W. Norton, 1993.

Wolff, Nelson, and Henry Cisneros. *Mayor: An Inside View of San Antonio Politics, 1981–1995.* San Antonio, TX: *San Antonio Express News*, 1997.

Cisneros, Sandra (1954–)

One of several contemporary authors responsible for popularizing Latino literature in the American mainstream, Sandra Cisneros is a poet, short story writer, and novelist whose works focus on the themes of poverty, isolation, cultural identity, and gender role in the daily lives of Latinos/as. In her writings, Cisneros seeks to disrupt readers' prejudices by artistically dispelling stereotypes related especially to Latina women. In an interview for the online journal *Las Mujeres*, she said, "I'm trying to write the stories that haven't been written. I feel like a cartographer; I'm determined to fill a literary void."

Born in Chicago on December 20, 1954, Sandra Cisneros is the only daughter in a family of seven children. Her loneliness as a child was heightened by her family's frequent moves between Mexico and the United States, prompted by her father's homesickness for his own country. This chaotic home life made it hard for her to form lasting friendships, but did offer opportunities for her to observe diverse people and places, which served as the basis for the creative writing she was beginning to do in secret.

Her Mexican-American mother and Mexican father emphasized the importance of education as a means of escaping poverty. This lesson resonated with Cisneros, a hardworking student scared to share her writings at school for fear that her teachers and peers would not be interested in her experiences. In the tenth grade, she was encouraged by a teacher to read her material to her classmates and to work on the school's literary magazine; she would eventually become the magazine's editor.

After high school, Cisneros studied English at Loyola University of Chicago, receiving her BA in 1976. After college, yearning to become a writer, she entered the Masters of Fine Arts program at the Iowa Writer's Workshop at the University of Iowa, where she would find some of the most important inspirations of her career. Finding herself among classmates from more privileged backgrounds than her own, Cisneros felt anxious about her ability to compete and alienated by her ethnic identity. From this experience, she realized that her experiences as a Latina were both unique and as important as those being described by her classmates. She channeled this realization into her first book, a semiautobiographical work of fiction titled *The House on Mango Street.* With the help of a grant from the National Endowment for the Arts (NEA), the first of two she would receive, Arte Público Press published *The House on Mango Street* in 1984, six years after she completed her graduate degree.

The House on Mango Street, which won the Before Columbus Foundation's American Book Award in 1985, introduced the female character-type that guides the reader through many of Cisneros's works. Drawing on her experiences with brothers trying to force her into traditional female roles, she concentrates her writing on heroines who struggle for the freedom to identify themselves on their own terms. *House* comprises a series of short scenes narrated by Esperanza Cordero, Cisneros's literary twin, a Mexican American girl in Chicago who desires a life outside the poverty, shame, and loneliness of Mango Street and finds it by becoming a writer. Although she succeeds in leaving Mango Street, Esperanza holds onto the knowledge that she will never be far away from it. As another character says to Esperanza, "You will always be Mango Street. You can't erase what you know. You can't forget who you are."

In 1980 she published the book of poetry *Bad Boys*, followed in 1985 by *The Rodrigo Poems.* In 1987, Third Woman Press published *My Wicked, Wicked Ways*, another collection of poetry and one of Cisneros's best-known works. The sixty poems read like a short story, showcasing Cisneros's ability to mix genres (poetry and prose). The success of that work enabled Cisneros to sign what is considered the first Chicana contract with a major publishing house, Random House, followed by the publication of a collection of short stories titled *Woman Hollering Creek* (1991). In 1994, she published both a poetry collection, *Loose Woman*, and a children's book, *Hair/Pelitos* with Alfred A. Knopf, another top publishing house. In 1995, she was awarded the prestigious MacArthur Foundation Fellowship, with a grant of $225,000. And in 1998, she was included in the *Norton Anthology of American Literature*, another notable first among Chicana writers.

Beginning with *The House on Mango Street,* Cisneros has helped shape the national debate over multiculturalism and the literary canon, making clear the need for ethnic voices in understanding American culture. *House* has become a mainstay on course syllabi in high schools and universities across the country and, along with her other works, has helped bring both critical and scholarly attention to the works by other Chicana writers, including Helena María Viramontes, Ana Castillo, and Cherríe Moraga.

Sandra Cisneros has also taught at the Latino Youth Alternative High School in Chicago; the Guadalupe Cultural Arts Center in San Antonio, Texas; the University of California, Berkeley; the University of Michigan; and the University of New Mexico. Throughout her career, she has returned repeatedly to her own communities, honoring her belief that it is the connection between art, politics, and the power of everyday life that makes people who they are and gives them something worth saying.

Lisa Guerrero

See also: Chicanisma; Chicano/a.

Further Reading

Brackett, Virginia. *A Home in the Heart: The Story of Sandra Cisneros.* Greensboro, NC: Morgan Reynolds, 2005.
Mirriam-Goldberg, Caryn. *Sandra Cisneros: Latina Writer and Activist.* Berkeley Heights, NJ: Enslow, 1998.
Saldívar-Hull, Sonia. *Feminism on the Border.* Berkeley: University of California Press, 2000.

Clemente, Roberto (1934–1972)

The professional baseball player Roberto Clemente, born on August 18, 1934, in Barrio San Anthon in Carolina, Puerto Rico, was among the first great Latino players in the major leagues and one of the most beloved public figures in modern Latin American history. After eighteen seasons as a right fielder for the Pittsburgh Pirates, in which he excelled in all facets of the game, Clemente died at age thirty-eight while on a relief mission for earthquake victims in Nicaragua. Aside from his dazzling play, he is remembered for being the first Latino player to be elected to the Baseball Hall of Fame, a role model who paved the way for future generations of Latinos/as in American professional sports, and a humanitarian off the field.

Puerto Rican–born Roberto Clemente is one of the most revered figures in modern Latino history—for his all-around excellence as a major league baseball player and for his humanitarian efforts. He died on a hurricane relief mission to Nicaragua in 1972. *(Diamond Images/Getty Images)*

An outstanding all-around athlete, Clemente excelled as a youth in track and field events such as the javelin and sprint races, but soon found that baseball was his true love. At age eighteen, he attended a tryout by the Brooklyn Dodgers, who promptly signed him to a contract and placed him on their AAA minor-league team, the Montreal Royals in the International League. The Dodgers did not protect their rights to his contract, however, and the Pirates made him their first pick in the 1954 draft.

Installed as Pirates' right fielder the following spring, Clemente almost single-handedly led a resurgence of the team, which had been mired in last place in the National League. Known for his all-around skill and exciting style of play, Clemente spent his entire career with Pittsburgh, helping bring the city World Series championships in 1960 and 1971. He was named the National League's Most Valuable Player (MVP) in 1966 and won the league batting title four times (1961, 1964, 1965, 1966). In the field, where he was known for his powerful throwing arm, he was a twelve-time winner of the Golden Glove.

Clemente compiled a lifetime batting average of .317, hitting .311 or higher in thirteen seasons. He played in a total of 2,433 games, compiling exactly 3,000 career hits, 240 home runs, 1,305 runs batted in, and 1,416 runs scored. In his two World Series, he had at least one hit in every game he played and was named MVP in 1971. In addition, Clemente is regarded as one of the greatest right fielders in major league history. Few base runners challenged his throws, many fewer successfully. He belongs to an elite group of players who have a .300 or better lifetime batting average and won at least ten Golden Gloves.

Still near the top of his game, Clemente died tragically in a plane crash on December 31, 1972. Proud of being Latino and regarding himself as an ambassador of his people, he had volunteered to direct a relief mission for victims of a Nicaraguan earthquake. While on their way to deliver food and supplies, Clemente and four others were killed when their small plane went down off the coast of his native Puerto Rico. Clemente was survived by his widow and three young boys. He had insisted that each of his children be born in Puerto Rico as a sign of loyalty to his people and his Latino pride.

Already a hero in his native island, Clemente was elevated to the status of legend throughout the Spanish-speaking world, including many communities in the United States. For the first time, the Baseball Writers' Association of America set aside the standard five-year waiting period for election to the Baseball Hall of Fame. Clemente was formally inducted on August 8, 1973, becoming the first Latino to be so honored. At the induction ceremony, Commissioner Bowie Kuhn announced the creation of the Roberto Clemente Award to be given to a player who most embodied the spirit of Clemente in terms of sportsmanship and community service. In his native Puerto Rico, the stadium in San Juan was renamed Coliseo Roberto Clemente. His hometown named a major thoroughfare after him as well as a sports complex, the Ciudad Deportiva Roberto Clemente. In the United States, schools and parks in New York City and elsewhere were named for him. Pittsburgh dedicated the Sixth Street Bridge in his honor. Making the traditional—but rare—gesture of respect for a star, the Pirates retired his number (21) in 1973. The team's new stadium, opened in 2000, contains additional tributes: the left field wall stands 21 feet high, and a statue of the right fielder stands at the park's outfield entrance. In 2002, Clemente was posthumously awarded the Presidential Medal of Freedom, one of the highest honors available to U.S. civilians.

Frank A. Salamone

See also: Baseball.

Further Reading

Healy, Nick. *Roberto Clemente: Baseball Legend.* Mankato, MN: Capstone, 2006.

Markuson, Bruce. *Roberto Clemente: The Great One.* Champaign, IL: Sports, 1998.

Walker, Paul Robert. *Pride of Puerto Rico: The Life of Roberto Clemente:* San Diego, CA: Harcourt Brace Jovanovich, 1991.

Cofer, Judith Ortiz (1952–)

Widely known for her poetry, fiction, short stories and essays, Judith Ortiz Cofer uses literature as a vehicle for exploring and documenting the ethnic integration of Latino migrants into American society. Having personally suffered the experience of migrating to a foreign land, she uses her remembrances to express the bewildering sensation of finding oneself in a strange environment with the need to assimilate to a culture that is not one's own. Following her father's instructions not to reveal her background and avoid Puerto Rican neighbors in New Jersey, she found assimilation to be particularly difficult and lonely. Intending to set an example for future generations, she has used her literary works not only as an outlet to release her emotions, but also as proof of a migrant's ordeal.

Born Judith Ortiz in the Puerto Rican town of Hormigueros on February 24, 1952, she moved with her family to Paterson, New Jersey, at the age of two, when her father was assigned to the Brooklyn Navy Yard in New York. Every six months, however, when her father went to sea, she traveled to Puerto Rico. The constant moving played an important role in shaping her character and identity. As a teenager growing up in such different worlds, she experienced a dual life, influenced by bicultural and bilingual experiences. Her prime concern during adolescence was to reconcile the conflicting moral values of the two cultures. Yet each time she returned to her homeland, she felt like a stranger who had assimilated so much to mainland life that she had become a *gringa*.

Seeing education as a way to overcome social and linguistic barriers, she concentrated on earning a degree and becoming a writer or an educator. With this in mind, while attending high school in New Jersey, she spent most of her time at the library, where she expected to find the tools to gain power and independence. While she was still in high school, Ortiz's family moved to Augusta, Georgia, in order to be closer to their relatives after her father retired from the military. The only Puerto Rican in her school, she was able to detach herself from racial and cultural prejudices, and she excelled academically, winning a scholarship to attend college. In 1971, she married Charles Cofer. She graduated from Augusta College in 1974 with a BA in English and from Florida Atlantic University with an MA degree in English in 1977, just one year after her father died in a car accident. In the following years, she became a bilingual teacher of Spanish and English, and also a lecturer at poetry workshops at Sweet Briar College in Virginia, Westchester University in Pennsylvania, and the Guadalupe Cultural Arts Center in San Antonio, Texas.

Although her teaching career was a source of satisfaction, her passion for literature compelled her to write regularly. Already by 1987, she had published three books of poems—*Peregrina* (*Pilgrim*; 1986), *Reaching for the Mainland* (1987), and *Terms of Survival* (1987). In these collections, she describes the processes of change and transformation suffered by thousands of Puerto Rican migrants who leave their birthplace to make a living in the United States. *The Line of the Sun* (1989), her first novel, chronicles a kind of Puerto Rican rite of passage and includes autobiographical references to the U.S. Navy and Paterson. In the novel, the narrator—a girl who moves from Puerto Rico to New Jersey—is forced to find a balance between the American and Latino aspects of her identity. *The Line of the Sun* was nominated for a Pulitzer Prize in 1990, but it was also the precursor to her masterpiece, *Silent Dancing: A Partial Remembrance of a Puerto Rican Childhood* (1990), in which Ortiz Cofer uses her personal experiences to describe the complexity of growing up in two societies that are in many ways contradictory. In the memoir, organized around twelve stories, she re-creates the atmosphere of Paterson's Puerto Rican barrio and explores with humanity and humor the unsuccessful struggle of Puerto Rican teenagers to transcend their ancestral roots.

Ortiz Cofer's other works include a collection of essays, short fiction, and poetry titled *The Latin Deli: Prose and Poetry* (1993), which pays homage to the many Puerto Rican and Latina women who have been deprived of freedom and forced to adjust to life on the mainland by protective and often oppressive male relatives. This sense of seclusion is shared by the teen protagonists of her next series of twelve short stories, published under the title *An Island Like You: Stories of the Barrio* (1995), in which Ortiz Cofer analyzes adolescents' diverse responses to racial and cultural stereotypes and to their parents' trapped lives. This rebellious attitude in particular marks María Elena's passage from innocent adolescence to womanhood in *The Year of Our Revolution: New and Selected Stories and Poems* (1998), in which the author follows the teenager's attainment of independence by removing her mother's religious artifacts from her bedroom wall and adopting poetry and rock music as her spiritual guides.

In *Woman in Front of the Sun: On Becoming a Writer* (2000), also based on personal experience, Ortiz Cofer confesses her love of language and describes her path to becoming a writer. In this collection of essays, interwoven with poems and folklore, she explains how her close relationship with a Roman Catholic nun helped her discover the magic of words and story writing. Ortiz Cofer's passion for reading is fictionalized in her novel *The Meaning of Consuelo* (2003), which chronicles the childhood and young adulthood of Consuelo, a bookish girl who has to look after her sister Milagros, suffering from schizophrenia, while her parents fight over her father's infidelity.

Ortiz Cofer's many literary honors include the Anisfield Wolf Book Award for *The Latin Deli*, a PEN/Martha Albrand Special Citation for *Silent Dancing*, and an Américas Award for Children's and Young Adult Literature for *The Meaning of Consuelo.* She has also won fellowships from the National Endowment for the Arts, the Witter Bynner Foundation for Poetry, and the Bread Loaf Writers' Conference. She continues to pursue her teaching career as Franklin Professor of English and Creative Writing at the University of Georgia.

Jorge Abril Sánchez

See also: Puerto Rican Literature.

Further Reading

Day, Frances Ann. *Latina and Latino Voices in Literature for Children and Teenagers.* Portsmouth, NH: Heinemann, 1997.

Dick, Bruce. *A Poet's Truth: Conversations with Latino/Latina Poets.* Tucson: University of Arizona Press, 2003.

Hernández, Carmen Dolores. *Puerto Rican Voices in English: Interviews with Writers.* Westport, CT: Praeger, 1997.

Kevane, Bridget A. *Latino Literature in America.* Westport, CT: Greenwood, 2003.

Telgen, Diane, and Jim Kamp, eds. *Latinas! Women of Achievement.* Detroit: Visible Ink, 1996.

Colombians

In 2000, according to the U.S. Census, there were 470,684 Colombians living in the United States; they represented 0.17 percent of the national population and just over 1 percent of the Hispanic/Latino population. Colombian immigrants are mostly of Spanish descent, concentrated in California, Florida, New Jersey, and New York. Today, most Colombians arrive with tourist visas and quickly apply for asylum. Colombians have been immigrating to the United States in significant numbers since the 1960s, with sharp increases during the 1980s and 1990s. The history of Colombian immigration to the United States is unlike that of many other Latinos/as in that most did not flee their homeland to escape political persecution or come in hopes of finding work as farmers or laborers, but rather arrived as middle-class professionals in search of a higher standard of living no longer available in Colombia.

To understand the reasons for Colombian immigration to the United States, it is necessary first to understand a period of bloody civil war in Colombia known as *La Violencia* (literally, The Violence). A political struggle between Conservatives and Liberals turned explosive with the assassination of Liberal Party leader Jorge Eliecer Gaitán in 1948. His supporters became so enraged at the murder that they rioted in the capital city of Bogotá, leaving an estimated 2,000 people dead. The conflict escalated until 1957, when the two sides reached an agreement to share political power. In the meantime, however, the nine years of La Violencia had left an estimated 180,000 to 200,000 people dead. The economy and general character of the country were so transformed by this conflict that even college graduates and trained professionals could not find work. Disaffected youth were recruited for emerging paramilitary groups such as the M-19 and FARC (Revolutionary Armed Forces of Colombia), and violence became a socially accepted form of conflict resolution.

In the aftermath of the civil war during the early 1960s, an abundance of educated, mostly white professionals arrived legally in the United States, where they found well-paying, white-collar jobs and quickly secured legal residency status. Initially, Colombian émigrés populated middle-class suburbs such as Jackson Heights in Queens, part of New York City, attractive because of its proximity to employment in nearby Manhattan. Working-class Colombians likewise filled the nearby neighborhoods of Corona, Elmhurst, and Flushing, while smaller enclaves emerged in Los Angeles, Washington D.C., San Francisco, and Houston, Texas.

It was not uncommon during the 1960s and 1970s to find many Colombians employed as journeymen printers, typesetters, nurses, laboratory technicians, and bilingual office personnel. That is not to say that all Colombian émigrés were as successful initially in securing well-paying jobs. Those who entered the country illegally resorted to factory work—especially women—and were often the recipients of low pay and sexual harassment from their bosses, and lived constantly in fear of deportation.

By the end of the 1970s, smuggling Colombians into the United States by way of the Bahamas and South Florida became a lucrative business, commanding fees as high as $6,000 per person. Like other undocumented immigrants, many Colombians legalized their status by marrying U.S. citizens through professional marriage brokers. Wealthy Colombians were especially attracted to South Florida because of the climate, economy, and cultural tolerance established by Cuban exile communities.

In the 1980s, as drug cartels, insurgent groups, and the government waged war against each other in Colombia for control of the drug trade, bombings, executions, and kidnappings became increasingly commonplace. The escalation of violence led to a new class of Colombian immigrant to the United States: traffickers and hired gunmen hiding in the diaspora communities of New York and Miami. In this way, turf wars between the notorious Medellín and Cali drug cartels spilled over to the United States, as both sought to control the growing cocaine market. The new influx of migrants and violence created tension with earlier generations of Colombians already established in America; many middle-class Colombians felt that the newcomers were diminishing the quality of community life with drugs, violence, and corruption of civic organizations, while giving Colombians a bad reputation.

Like other immigrant groups, meanwhile, Colombians were affected by the rising cost of living, overcrowding, and rising crime in the cities where they had settled. Thus, in the 1990s, many began moving to the suburbs. Communities in coastal Connecticut and New York witnessed heavy influxes of Colombians that quickly filled service-sector jobs undesired by the local populations.

Colombians also faced the nativism increasingly directed at Latino and Asian immigrants during the economic recession of the 1980s and 1990s. As guerrilla violence in Colombia spiraled out of control, undocumented migration from Colombia increased and large new enclaves of undocumented Colombians sprouted up in California.

The population of Colombian Americans in 2000, an estimated 580,000 including illegal immigrants, represented an increase of 66 percent from 1990. Colombian émigrés to the United States had created civic associations as early as the 1960s, when *Colombianos en el Exterior* (Colombians Abroad) was established to provide a link between Colombians residing abroad—especially in the United States—and those residing in the homeland. The organization finally broke apart, however, according to the same Conservative and Liberal divisions that ravaged Colombia during La Violencia. Other groups sought to promote cultural integration through the Día de la Raza parade, a celebration that brings together Hispanics under their common Spanish, African, and Indian ancestries.

Colombians in the United States continue to make significant contributions to the economy and general character of their enclaves. In South Florida, the Colombian business class has strengthened the local economy as investors, members of the international business community, and other professionals engaged in import-export trade, real estate, and small businesses. The thriving Colombian diaspora in the United States has come at a price for the Colombian nation, however, as the political elite acknowledges the drain of capital and brainpower as the educated and employable leave the country.

Juan Declet

Further Reading

Antonio, Angel-Junguito. *A Cry of Innocence: In Defense of Colombians.* Plantation, FL: Distinctive, 1993.

Collier, Michael W., Eduardo A. Gamarra, et al. *The Colombian Diaspora in South Florida: A Report of the Colombian Studies Institute's Colombian Diaspora Project.* Working Paper Series, 2003.

González, Juan. *Harvest of Empire: A History of Latinos in America.* New York: Viking, 2000.

Sturner, Pamela. "Colombian Americans." Countries and Their Cultures. http://www.everyculture.com.

Colonialism

See **Conquest of the Americas**

Communist Party

Communist parties are organizations that promote a sociopolitical philosophy based on the interpretation of Marxism put forth by Vladimir Lenin and the Russian Bolsheviks. Communist parties began to emerge throughout the world in the early twentieth century, following the creation of the Communist International (Comintern). Communists believe that socialism will replace capitalistic institutions in order to achieve Communist ideals. According to party platforms, true Communist societies are free of labor exploitation, social inequity, poverty, unemployment, racism, and sexism. Communist party members believe that true communism is achieved through the extension and continuation of democracy. Party platforms call for an end to powerful corporations and private ownership of wealth. Although Communist parties in the world today may or may not formally include the term "communist" in their name, most share the desire to curb capitalistic exploitation.

Latinos in the CPUSA

The Communist Party of the United States of America (CPUSA), founded in 1919 and headquartered in New York City, advocates sociopolitical reform of U.S. domestic policies concerning Latin American immigrants and workers. Immigrant labor reform has historically topped the priority lists of Communist parties in North America. As a result, many Latino workers have looked to the CPUSA for guidance and organizational structure.

Progressive Mexicans in the United States began to seek the CPUSA's help in organizing strikes among Mexican workers during the 1920s and 1930s. In 1928, CPUSA formed the Trade Union Unity League (TUUL), with a mostly Mexican American membership, to launch a revolutionary movement outside the American Federation of Labor (AFL). The TUUL, in turn, formed the Cannery and Agricultural Workers Industrial Union (CAWIU) hoping to unite the Mexican workforce on a single platform. Mexicans, who represented a significant majority of the agricultural and cannery workforce, became the backbone of the new union. Between 1928 and 1930, strikes led by the CAWIU were staged in California and several Southwestern states. Mexican workers also formed CPUSA cells in several California towns. By 1933, over two dozen Mexicans belonged to the Young Communist League (YCL) in Tulare, California, and by 1934 there were fifteen members of the Mexican Communist party cell in Brawley, California. Most Mexican CPUSA members worked in the cotton fields. The CPUSA and the CAWIU were responsible for a series of labor strikes headed by Mexican immigrants throughout the 1930s and 1940s.

The CPUSA continues to fight for immigrant workers' rights. On January 22, 2004, the party's Political Action Commission called for a coalition of marginalized citizens, including Latinos/as, to take a stance against the administration of President George W. Bush in the *People's Weekly World,* a Communist newspaper. Then on January 31, the commission held a conference in New York City with the theme, "Build Unity to Take Back Our Country in 2004! Defeat Bush and the Ultra Right!" Latino mobilization groups attended the event and participated in roundtable discussions on worker and immigrant rights.

CPUSA and Latin American Communist Parties

Always sympathetic to Latin America and its social inequities, the CPUSA supports Communist organizations throughout Latin America. Orthodox Communist parties (those directly linked to the Comintern) are found in every Latin American republic today. These parties were created for two common reasons: to defend and serve the interests of the former Soviet Union, and to gain power within their country by establishing a proletariat dictatorship necessary for realization of their creed. Throughout the Cold War of the 1950s and 1960s, the U.S. government was directly and vehemently at odds with both American Communist parties and Latin American Communist parties. On January 1, 1959, Marxist forces under Fidel Castro overthrew the government of Fulgencio Batista in Cuba. The Communist regime proceeded to nationalize the sugar industry and sign trade agreements with the Soviet Union, and in 1960 the government seized U.S. assets on the island. More broadly, the Cuban revolution had a ripple effect throughout Latin America, and thereafter the United States participated in a number of interventions to stop the spread of communism.

U.S. interventionist actions in Latin America angered the CPUSA. On September 11, 1973, leftist President Salvador Allende of Chile was overthrown by a military coup led by General Augusto Pinochet.

Washington supported the coup as a step toward eliminating the Communist threat in Latin America. Immediately following the fascist uprising, the Political Committee of the CPUSA declared that it was the solemn duty of U.S. citizens to "protest and express solidarity with the people of Chile in every possible form." Thereafter the CPUSA actively participated in developing the Chile Solidarity Movement into a nationwide force for human rights and democracy, while advocating an end to the Pinochet dictatorship.

Communist organizations and activities declined—and even disappeared in many places—after the fall of the Soviet Union in 1991. Throughout the twentieth century, however, Communist parties in the United States and throughout Latin America were involved in a wide range of foreign and domestic activities that profoundly affected the course of history and culture.

Stefanie Tacata

See also: Castro, Fidel.

Further Reading

Bart, Philip, ed. *Highlights of a Fighting History: 60 Years of the Communist Party, USA.* New York: International Publishers, 1979.

Guerin-Gonzales, Camille. *Mexican Workers and American Dreams: Immigration, Repatriation, and California Farm Labor, 1900–1939.* New Brunswick, NJ: Rutgers University Press, 1994.

Weber, Devra. *Dark Sweat, White Gold: California Farm Workers, Cotton, and thDe New Deal.* Berkeley: University of California Press, 1994.

Community Service Organization

The Community Service Organization (CSO) was a nonpolitical, nonpartisan organization based primarily in California from 1949 to the late 1970s and dedicated to improving community relations in and the general welfare of the Mexican American community. Having no citizenship or language restrictions, the CSO established the goals of making community members aware of their civic responsibilities and rights for achieving liberation. In doing so, the organization encouraged political participation, the learning of English, acquiring citizenship, and voter registration.

Founded in Los Angeles in 1947 by Fred Ross—who later joined with César Chávez in organizing the Delano grape strike and became leader of the United Farm Workers Organizing Committee—the CSO was initially set up to support the candidacy of Mexican American Edward Roybal for a seat on the Los Angeles city council. After successfully campaigning for Roybal, the CSO in 1949 turned its focus to larger community-based issues, such as civil rights and citizenship. Inspired by the ideas of social activist Saul Alinsky, the founder of a Chicago-based community organization called Industrial Areas Foundation (IAF), the CSO adopted a philosophy of nonviolence as a method of organizing. Part of the CSO's objective was to use the power of the ballot to promote social action programs and to improve relations between all ethno-racial, national, and religious-based community groups. It also had a broader goal of integrating Latinos/as into American society and culture. Its membership ranged from the young to the elderly, from recent immigrants to longtime residents and citizens, and from working-class people to professionals.

By the 1950s, the CSO began focusing its efforts on solving the problems of the Mexican American community. In addition to successfully pursuing civil rights violations cases, it also conducted several citizenship, English-language, and get-out-the-vote programs. From Los Angeles, the CSO spread to San Jose and then to other cities within the state. Soon thereafter it emerged in major urban centers outside California, especially in Arizona.

During the 1960s, however, the CSO suffered a decline in membership, partly because the IAF withdrew some of its financial and personal support and partly because of the popularity of Chicano nationalism and waning support for legalistic, assimilation-based projects. Its shrinking membership was also attributed to increased competition from other, more activist and radical Chicano-based organizations that captured the spirit of confrontation, identity-based politics, and aggressive politics of the late 1960s. As nationalist and confrontational politics lost its hold

Among the programs offered by the Community Service Organization (CSO) in Los Angeles was a buyers' club, which offered discounted items to low-income families. The CSO worked at the grassroots level to support and empower Mexican Americans. *(Community Service Organization Papers. Urban Archives Center. Oviatt Library. California State University, Northridge)*

on the Chicano Movement, the CSO recaptured its prominence with the Chicano community. Focusing on community empowerment with the development of consumer complaint centers and buyers' clubs within Mexican-American communities throughout the United States, the CSO saw resurgence in its membership and reestablished its prominence within the broader community. By the end of the 1970s, it had about thirty chapters in California and Arizona.

The historic legacy of CSO is significant given its role as a training ground for the prominent leaders, including César Chávez, Dolores Huerta, a co-organizer of the United Farm Workers, and others, who made up the backbone of the Chicano civil rights struggle. Serving as an important space for organizing and teaching the necessary skills for community-based action, the CSO represents the history of behind-the-scenes organizing within the Chicano movement.

Jesse J. Esparza

See also: Chávez, César; Corona, Bert; Roybal, Edward R.

Further Reading

Meier, Matt S., and Feliciano Rivera. *Dictionary of Mexican American History.* Westport, CT: Greenwood, 1981.

Ross, Fred W., Sr. *Community Organization in Mexican American Communities.* Los Angeles: American Council on Race Relations, 1947.

Congressional Hispanic Caucus

In December 1976, five Latino members in the U.S. House of Representatives formed the Congressional Hispanic Caucus (CHC) to monitor legislative, executive, and judicial actions affecting the national Latino community. The founding members were Edward R. Roybal (D-CA), Herman Badillo (D-NY), Eligio "Kika" de la Garza (D-TX), and Baltasar Corrada del Río (I-PR). From its founding, the purpose of the caucus has been to serve as a forum for Latino members of Congress to develop legislative agendas based on issues of interest to their community. Over the years, caucus members formed fourteen task forces to specialize in specific areas such as health, education, and civil rights.

From the outset, another important goal of the caucus has been to raise Latinos/as' political awareness and participation. Founding members saw this as a key component to achieving equal representation in all levels of government. In 1978, Roybal, de la Garza, and Corrada formed a nonprofit educational institute called the Congressional Hispanic Caucus, Inc. Three years later, in October 1981, the House Administration Committee required all fundraising efforts to be conducted on nongovernment premises, forcing the nonprofit organization to move off Capitol Hill. The organization also changed its name to the Congressional Hispanic Caucus Institute, Inc.

The caucus was formed as a result of a particular history involving Latinos/as in U.S. politics. Latinos/as have served in the U.S. Congress since the early 1820s. The first elected member was Joseph Marion Hernandez, a delegate of the Spanish territory of Florida from 1822 to 1823. Since then, dozens of Latinos/as have been elected, but most since the 1960s. The increase was a direct result of the growth in U.S. Latino population, the emergence of Latino grassroots organizations, and the increasing participation of Latino voters. The Twenty-fourth Amendment to the U.S. Constitution (ratified 1964) and the Voting Rights Act of 1965 helped facilitate this participation by outlawing poll taxes and the requirement that voters take literacy tests, respectively. The latter measure also provided for federal registration of voters in areas that had less than 50 percent of eligible registered voters, enabling minorities in underrepresented areas to go to the polls.

Today, the CHC comprises all Latino Democrats in the House of Representatives. In March 2003, five Republican Latino members officially broke ties with the CHC and formed their own caucus, the Congressional Hispanic Conference. The Republicans contended that the CHC had grown unduly partisan, summarily rejecting Republican views. In the years since, however, the two organizations have come together from time to time to work on issues such as access to higher education for Latinos/as.

Ruben Espejel

See also: Politics; Roybal, Edward R.

Further Reading

Gutiérrez, David G. *Walls and Mirrors: Mexican Americans, Mexican Immigrants, and the Politics of Ethnicity.* Berkeley: University of California Press, 1995.

Hero, Rodney. *Latinos and the U.S. Political System: Two-Tiered Pluralism.* Philadelphia: Temple University Press, 1992.

Conquest of the Americas

The European conquest of lands and indigenous peoples in the Western Hemisphere began in 1492 with arrival of Christopher Columbus from Spain. He was soon followed by other adventurers—known as conquistadors—who landed on the islands of the Caribbean and the shores of North, South, and Central America over the course of the next half century and more. They came in search of gold and other commodities, sponsored by the Spanish Crown, which hoped to enhance its status through the acquisition of colonies. The conquistadors enslaved and brutalized the native peoples, who they often referred to as subhuman. In addition to this abuse, the conquerors brought European diseases such as smallpox and measles; it is estimated that these diseases wiped out as much as 90 percent of the pre-1492 population.

When Christopher Columbus returned from his first voyage in 1493, two countries—Spain and Portugal—both laid claim to non-Christian lands "discovered" outside Europe. Under the Treaty of Tordesillas in 1494, Spain was granted all territories west of a north-south meridian in the Atlantic Ocean; Portugal would lay claim to all lands discovered to the east of it (eventually including Brazil). Knowing nothing of the size of the American continents, the Spanish felt cheated. The millions of native peoples already living in the so-called New World were yet unknown at the time of the Treaty of Tordesillas. Their fate was never considered.

Spain encouraged young noblemen and merchants to venture to the new lands, hoping to profit from their efforts in trade and colonization. Current scholarship stresses the disastrous consequences of Spanish attitudes on indigenous communities. In 1492, Spain concluded a war of liberation against the Moorish (Muslim) invaders who had occupied parts of their country for 800 years, and expelled all Jews as well as Moors. In addition, the Spanish Inquisition had been established a decade earlier to cleanse the country of Protestant heretics and Jewish and Islamic converts to Catholicism whose loyalty was in doubt. Thus, some historians have suggested, the conquistadors who crossed the Atlantic in search of riches brought with them cultural values that promoted warfare, religious rigidity, and intolerance. The writings of many of these explorers, a majority of whom came from the noble class in Spain, show that they considered the native peoples of the New World ignorant, savage, and faithless.

On his second voyage in 1493, Columbus brought seventeen ships to Hispaniola (present-day Haiti and the Dominican Republic). His initial contact with the local Taíno tribe was friendly at first but became contentious in 1495, when he captured and enslaved 1,600 men, women, and children, sending 500 of the healthiest to Spain. The Taíno, like other native tribes, were subjected to systematic violence and enslavement over the succeeding decades, as they were forced to mine gold, construct buildings, and provide food for the Spanish. Records and letters report rapes, torture, attacks by Spanish dogs, dismemberment, and mass suicides. Untold numbers died in an outbreak of influenza in 1493; smallpox followed in 1507. Thousands more were killed in organized uprisings, as the spears used by Taíno rebels were no match for the swords and guns used by the Spanish. In less than twenty-five years, from 1492 to 1516, the native population dwindled from at least 1.5 million to an estimated 12,000. By 1555, the Taíno of Hispaniola had all but disappeared.

Nicolás de Ovando became the Spanish governor of Hispaniola in 1502. The Taíno were in revolt when he arrived, and he took strong measures to control the native population. Ovando persuaded the *cacique* (chieftain) Anacaona to invite all her nobles to a feast, at which time the Spanish trapped and burned them alive; Anacaona was subsequently garroted. The Dominican priest Bartolomé de las Casas, who accompanied Ovando's expedition, documented the murder and dismemberment of thousands of men, women, and children on a neighboring island. As governor, Ovando was also responsible for introducing the *encomienda* system of slavery, in which the Spanish crown rewarded loyal colonists and soldiers with deeds giving them native men and women to use as laborers. In spite of his atrocities, Ovando's governorship was considered a success and he returned to Spain in 1509 as a wealthy man.

The lands now known as Cuba, Puerto Rico, the Yucatán Peninsula of Central America, and Panama all experienced the brutal tactics of Spanish colonialists. Spanish explorers and settlers also advanced to the southern coast of what is now the United States. Juan Ponce de León, who had conquered Puerto Rico in 1509, explored coastal Florida, where he was fatally wounded in a battle with the Calusa tribe in 1521. Other explorers mapped Florida's coastline and searched for gold. By the 1520s, Spain's economic and geographic interest shifted from Florida to Mexico and Central America. Upon heading south, however, the explorers left behind diseases like influenza that swept northward and ravaged native populations.

Along with contagious diseases, the reports of Spanish cruelty spread quickly among far-flung native tribes. Indigenous groups fought enslavement any way they could but died in such large numbers that, by 1513, the Spanish governors were importing slaves from Africa to perform work previously done by natives. Father De las Casas wrote a firsthand account of the cruelty he witnessed on Hispaniola and Cuba and began a lifelong career of advocacy for the Indians. In European courts, the Dominican priest pled for fair treatment and an end to slavery, but he had limited success.

Aztec and Incan Empires

During the first half of the sixteenth century, two other Spanish conquistadors—Hernán Cortés and Francisco Pizarro—succeeded in vanquishing sophisticated and complex native societies that had ruled large empires for centuries. Although the Spanish were vastly outnumbered, their steel weapons and armor enabled them to be conquerors rather than conquered. Cortés, who had heard tales of great wealth in the New World, borrowed heavily to fund an expedition and landed his force of 800 men (including 500 soldiers) along the gulf coast of Mexico in 1519. The Aztec, or Mexica, Empire centered in faraway Tenochtitlán (now Mexico City) was controlled by the Totonac Indians, who met Cortés when he arrived at their shores. Moctezuma, the Aztec emperor, had been warned about Cortés but believed he was a returning god and planned no resistance to the Spanish force. Cortés, on his way to Tenochtitlán, formed alliances with the Tlaxcalans and other neighboring tribes, which together hoped to shatter the power of the Aztecs. By the time Cortés faced Moctezuma in 1519, he had 6,000 armed allies.

Moctezuma greeted Cortés peacefully and showered him in gold, only to be taken hostage without a battle. The Aztecs finally succeeded in driving the Spanish and their allies from the city, albeit briefly, but they were outraged that Moctezuma had not put up a fight. The Aztec ruler died of unknown causes, perhaps at the hands of his own people. Cortés returned to Tenochtitlán in 1521 with a force of up to thirty times larger than his original party and laid siege to the island city for eighty days. Smallpox raged through the population, leaving corpses piled in the streets, and the lack of food and water finally forced the emperor, Cuauhtémoc, to surrender. Tenochtitlán was burned to the ground and Cuauhtémoc tortured. Historians estimate that 25 million people lived in the land now called Mexico before the Spanish invasion; by 1540, only 6 million were left, and the number continued to decline for many years thereafter.

In South America, the vast Inca Empire—covering what is now Peru, Ecuador, Bolivia, and part of Chile—was ruled in the early sixteenth century by a succession of emperors: Huayna Capac, his son Huáscar, and another son named Atahualpa. A smallpox epidemic weakened the empire, killing Huayna Capac and setting off a civil war in 1632 that put Atahualpa on the throne. Meanwhile, during previous expeditions in the Caribbean and Central America, conquistador Francisco Pizarro had heard tales of the gold-rich land called Birú (Peru). After eight years of preparation, exploration, and appeals to the Spanish Crown for a claim, Pizarro, with 168 men and 27 horses, landed on the Pacific coast and met Atahualpa at Cajamarca in November 1532. Atahualpa led an army of 80,000; Pizarro hid his men and asked for a parley. The Incan ruler approached Pizarro with great ceremony, carried on a litter by eighty lords. At a signal, Spanish soldiers rushed out of hiding and took Atahualpa prisoner. The Incans, who had never seen horses, swords, or guns, died in large numbers. Pizarro demanded a huge ransom for Atahualpa and, upon receiving it, promptly had the emperor killed. The ransom was returned to Spain, where it fueled a desire for more exploration and colonization.

Other Aspects

The boundaries of New Spain (Mexico) extended south to Costa Rica and north to California (which was thought to be an island), Arizona, New Mexico, and southern Texas. As with Florida, however, Spain paid little attention to its North American territories, possibly because no gold or silver was found there during Spain's rule. Other explorers—such as Hernando de Soto in the Southeast; Vasco Núñez de Balboa, who crossed the isthmus of Panama; and Juan Bautista de Anza, who explored the Southwest in the 1770s—were as daring and cruel as the early conquistadors, and their tales remain grimly fascinating. Nevertheless, most of Spain's activity in the north was that of missionaries seeking conversions.

In Mexico, South America, and the Caribbean islands, the Spanish goal was to establish colonies, mines, and plantations that could be exploited with cheap slave labor to supply goods and riches to the mother country. Silver was discovered in Mexico in 1545, providing the most valuable export of New Spain. Rather than improve the Spanish economy, however, gold contributed to inflation and Spain gradually lost its powerful position in the Americas.

A secondary goal was the conversion of native peoples to Roman Catholicism. Priests accompanied all the expeditions to the New World, and the necessity of conversion was preached to the peoples they encountered—in European languages. Decimated by disease and warfare, enslaved native peoples were given a new god in place of traditional spirits and idols. The resulting religions were often syncretic blends of old and new: Catholic saints, for example, replaced a pantheon of minor gods but received the sacrifices and prayers of the displaced spirits.

The smallpox epidemic that began in 1518 spread from the Caribbean islands to Mayan, Aztec, and Incan lands. This was followed in 1531 by an outbreak of measles, a disease just as deadly, that traveled north through Mexico and into North America. De Soto's party, seeking gold north of Florida in 1539–1541, brought diseases that spread rapidly among natives and ultimately killed up to 75 percent of the tribes in the Southeast. Bubonic plague struck in the 1540s.

An exception to the ruthlessness of the conquistador is Álvar Núñez Cabeza de Vaca, who sailed to Florida in 1527 under Pánfilo Narváez, who had helped conquer Cuba. Shipwrecked and starving, most of the sailors of the expedition died, including Narváez. Cabeza de Vaca, however, survived eight years in North America, traveling through Florida, west to Texas, and then southwest as far as California, encountering many tribal people, before making his way to Mexico City. He left an extensive written record of his travels and, like De las Casas, urged fair treatment of the Indians.

In 1542, Spain passed the so-called *Leyes Nuevas* (New Laws) to discourage the encomienda system and indigenous slave labor in the American colonies. The measures were only sporadically enforced, however, and three years later, after revolts by landowners, the encomienda system was restored. In succeeding decades, wars in Europe led to a decline in Spanish power that was reflected in its American colonies by the turn of the seventeenth century. Still, it would be another 200 years—in the first decades of the nineteenth century—before the lands conquered by Spain in the Western Hemisphere began achieving independence.

Vickey Kalambakal

See also: Día de la Raza.

Further Reading

Restall, Matthew. *Seven Myths of the Spanish Conquest.* New York: Oxford University Press, 2003.

Schwartz, Stuart B. *Victors and Vanquished: Spanish and Nahua Views of the Conquest of Mexico.* Boston: Bedford/St. Martin's, 2000.

Wood, Michael. *Conquistadors.* Berkeley: University of California Press, 2000.

Consumerism

The growth of consumerism in the United States has had important consequences in the everyday lives of Latinos/as, much as it has for all U.S. residents. Social scientists studying consumerism have shown how purchasing power and the use of commodities can help create, change, or reinforce social identities.

Modern marketing practices began in the period after World War I. Fundamental to this new "science" was the idea that markets could be segmented, or seen as distinct, separate groups of consumers. It has not been until relatively recently that Latinos/as living in the United States have begun to be regarded as a commercially viable market. One important consequence of the recent marketing appeals to the Latino community has been a reinforcement of what it means to be Latino/a, for both Latinos/as and non-Latinos/as alike.

Development of the Latino Marketplace

Although major U.S. corporations have heavily courted Latinos/as in recent years, this was not always the case. Before the 1970s, marketing to Latinos/as did not occur at the national level, instead taking place only on a relatively small scale in particular cities, such as Los Angeles, Miami, New York, and San Antonio, Texas. Like most representations of Latinos/as in U.S. popular culture at that time, Latinos/as were generally either depicted in demeaning and stereotypical ways or not present at all. Early ads sometimes depicted Latinos as thieves, such as the snack-food mascot Frito Bandito and the smelly banditos in deodorant commercials during the 1960s. Also from this era came Juan Valdez, the fictional character associated with a Colombian coffee brand who served as a one-dimensional depiction of a Colombian peasant happy simply to bring freshly brewed coffee to Anglo consumers.

In the 1960s and 1970s, however, a number of forces began to take shape that would lead to the realization that Latinos/as constituted a viable market segment. First, Spanish-language television began to make headway. In the late 1960s, Emilio Azcárraga, a Mexican television entrepreneur, bought several television stations in San Antonio and Los Angeles, and began broadcasting Spanish-language television from Latin America to Spanish-speaking audiences in the United States. Most programming of this era came from Mexico and Venezuela, which continue to be important exporters of media content to Spanish-language outlets today. During the 1970s, Azcárraga's network of stations (known as Spanish International Network, or SIN) was able to penetrate media markets in most major U.S. metropolitan areas. In 1976, his stations became the first network connected by satellite, and by 1982 SIN could claim to reach 90 percent of all U.S. Latino households. The development of a national Spanish-language television network allowed advertisers to target Latinos/as on a national basis instead of trying to reach them separately in different metropolitan areas.

A second factor was the growing body of knowledge about Latinos/as as a distinct market. In the 1960s and 1970s, most advertising professionals specializing in what they termed the "Hispanic" market were Cuban and Puerto Rican immigrants living in New York. These early advertising professionals were largely from upper middle-class backgrounds in their home countries, trying to carve a niche for themselves in the U.S. advertising industry. During this formative period, it was assumed that marketing professionals who were themselves Latino/a would be able to understand all other Latino/as in general. Because of this, and the fact that corporate clients generally did not fund market research into Latino preferences, most of the early knowledge about Latinos/as as consumers was based on the mere assumptions of Latino marketing professionals. The "typical" Latino/a consumer was seen as a "family oriented, Catholic, traditional, conservative, and immigrant Spanish-speaking individual." Some have argued that these early characterizations have endured to the present era, regardless of whether or not they ever were accurate. Beyond that, say other critics, even thinking in terms of a "typical" Latino/a erases significant cultural differences between subgroups.

The Twenty-First Century

In contrast to their limited focus on Latinos/as during the 1960s through the 1980s, corporate decision-makers, advertising agencies, and media companies in the 1990s began to recognize the Latino market segment as a significant consumer block in the United States. Corporations have invested heavily in attempts to understand and appeal to these consumers. By 2005, over eighty major U.S. advertising agencies focused exclusively on marketing to Latinos/as, with their corporate clients jockeying for an edge.

The reaching out to Latinos/as on the part of U.S. corporations in the early twenty-first century was an inevitable consequence of the growing presence of Latinos/as in American society, in terms of both population and purchasing power. By 2005, Latinos/as had become the largest minority group in the United States and represented an estimated $700 billion in annual consumer spending. Additionally, Latinos/as came to represent a more sizable portion of media consumers. In 2005, Nielsen Media Research increased its estimate of the number of Latino households with television sets to 11.2 million. Because the Nielsen ratings are the U.S. entertainment industry's standard for knowing how many people watch which programs, the expanding Latino audience is more heavily courted by advertisers and exerts a greater influence on programming than ever before.

A second notable demographic fact recognized by marketing firms in recent years is the age of U.S.-born Latinos/as. The population of Latinos/as during this period has been much younger than the U.S. population as a whole. As of 2005, 34 percent of Latinos/as were under the age of 18, compared with 25 percent of the U.S. population as a whole. This fact has led to a shift in marketing toward second- and third-generation Latino immigrants. Whether these viewers would prefer Spanish- or English-language programming is yet uncertain, and the separate networks have taken different approaches. Univision continues to broadcast entirely in Spanish; Telemundo, on the other hand, offers bilingual programming; and Sí TV, a cable channel that debuted in the early 2000s, plans to offer only English-language content.

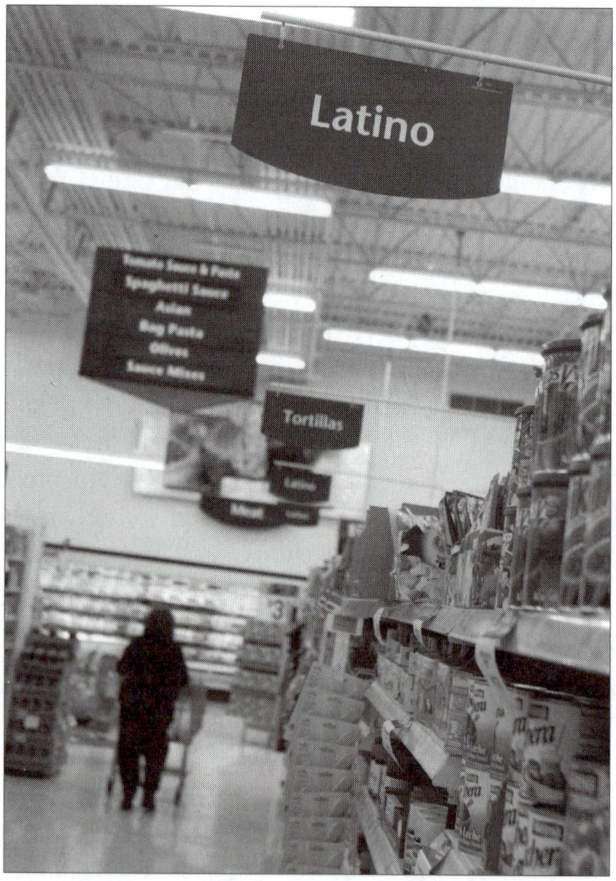

Reflecting the emergence of the Latino consumer market even outside major cities and the Southwest, the Wal-Mart store in Bentonville, Arkansas, maintains a special Latino foods section. Consumer spending by Latinos/as approaches $1 trillion per year. *(Gilles Mingasson/Getty Images)*

By the early years of the twenty-first century, advertisers saw the increasing importance of appealing to bilingual audiences on English-language television. One practice that emerged was for television advertisers to give a nod to Spanish-speaking audiences by having an ad spoken in English while the background song played in Spanish. This fit with the advertising industry's assessment that a significant portion of Latinos/as in the United States was bicultural (that is, were consumers of both English- and Spanish-language media content).

Steve Zafirau

See also: Cinco de Mayo; Popular Culture; Television; Univision.

Further Reading

Dávila, Arlene. *Latinos, Inc.: The Marketing and Making of a People.* Berkeley: University of California Press, 2001.

García Canclini, Néstor. *Consumers and Citizens: Globalization and Multicultural Conflicts.* Minneapolis: University of Minnesota Press, 2001.

Corona, Bert (1918–2001)

Bert Corona, a Latino civil rights activist, labor organizer, and educator, dedicated his long working life to defending the rights and dignity of undocumented immigrant workers in California and throughout the United States. He was associated with a number of major Latino organizations and unions, including La Hermandad Mexicana Nacional, or Mexican National Brotherhood, a national nonprofit organization whose Los Angeles chapter Corona founded in the 1960s. Originally established in San Diego in 1951, La Hermandad functioned as a contemporary *mutualista* (mutual aid society), organizing and assisting undocumented workers when even progressive labor unions like the United Farm Workers (UFW) did not offer assistance. As its longtime director, Corona helped make La Hermandad a major provider of services for immigrant workers, with three offices in the Los Angeles basin and a peak membership of more than 30,000. Although changes in immigration policy and federal funding compromised the organization's effectiveness by the 1990s, Corona—then known as "El Viejo" (the old man)—remained a stalwart in the movement to protect undocumented workers and Latino immigrants in general throughout his remaining years.

He was born Humberto Noé "Bert" Corona on May 29, 1918, in El Paso, Texas, the child of Mexican immigrants. Like many others who migrated in the early part of the twentieth century, Corona's parents, Noé Corona and Margarita Escápite Salayandia, came to the United States to escape the violence and destruction that resulted from the Mexican Revolution. They settled first in El Paso, a gateway and distribution city for many Mexican immigrants. Unlike other Mexican families who left during the revolution, however, the Coronas migrated back to Mexico at the conclusion of the fighting in the early 1920s. Noé Corona served under the famous Mexican revolutionary of the north, Pancho Villa, who stood as best man at Noé and Margarita's wedding. Because of his close ties to Villa, however, the elder Corona was assassinated in Chihuahua in 1924. Humberto's mother promptly returned to El Paso with her children and mother. The mistreatment of Mexican immigrants in local elementary schools led her to send Humberto to a private school in Albuquerque, New Mexico, after which he returned to El Paso to attend the local segregated high school for Mexicans.

After graduating from high school in 1934 and working odd jobs for two years, Corona moved to Los Angeles to attend the University of Southern California on a basketball scholarship. Exposed to life in the barrios, the plight of Latinos/as in the city, and the fledgling labor movement, he remained in school but devoted his energies to working as an organizer and recruiter for the Congress of Industrial Organizations (CIO). In 1938, while working for the CIO, he also joined with labor organizer Luisa Moreno to form the League of Spanish-Speaking People and contributed his efforts as well to the Mexican American Movement (MAM) and the Asociación Nacional Mexico-Americana (ANMA). In 1941, he was elected chapter president of the CIO (Local 1–26), serving in that capacity until enlisting into the U.S. Army in 1943.

In the meantime, Corona became increasingly active in politics as well, working within the system to empower Latinos/as politically and economically. In

Legendary labor organizer and civil rights activist Bert Corona—referred to since the Chicano Movement as *El Viejo* (the old man)—walks to his office in downtown Los Angeles in 1999. The son of Mexican immigrants, he began organizing migrant workers in the 1930s. *(AP Images/ Ventura County Star/Dave LaBelle)*

the 1938 Los Angeles city council election, he worked on the campaign of Latino candidate Eduardo Quevedo. Despite the failure of that campaign, Corona continued to see the road to betterment for Latino Americans through access to political office. He continued campaigning on behalf of Latino civic leaders and supported another important politician running for city council in 1949—Edward Roybal, who went on to serve in the U.S. House of Representatives.

In the early 1950s, Corona helped establish chapters of Saul Alinsky's Community Service Organization—which was dedicated to training Mexican Americans to organize in their communities—at which time he met the young Chicano farm labor organizer César Chávez. Unlike Chávez and the UFW, which at one time supported U.S. Immigration and Naturalization Service (INS) deportations of undocumented workers, Corona and La Hermandad believed that organizing the undocumented was a necessary component of unionizing agricultural labor. In addition, having witnessed several waves of nativism during the twentieth century—such as the Mexican Repatriation of 1931–1934, during which an estimated 2 million Mexicans and Mexican Americans, approximately half of whom had been born in the United States, were deported to Mexico, and Operation Wetback, the 1954 INS project to remove more than 1 million illegal immigrants from the southwestern United States—Corona believed that defense of the Mexican immigrant would be an ongoing role for organizers. "An organizer demonstrates compassion to those he organizes," said Corona. "The organizer works with, not for, the working class. He builds an organization and develops leadership so that one day he can move on to the next fight."

Corona was a founding member of the Mexican American Political Association (MAPA) in California in 1959, an organization whose mission was to support and promote Mexican American candidates in the Democratic Party, becoming MAPA president by the early 1960s. The fledgling organization helped set up Viva Kennedy Clubs that, for the first time in U.S. history, united large numbers of Mexican Americans in support of a presidential campaign. In addition to supporting the election of John F. Kennedy as president, organizers worked to register voters within the Latino community.

Although he never completed his college degree at the University of Southern California, Corona devoted much of his time to educating others on the benefits of social activism and the keys to effective community organizing. He served as a lecturer at Stanford University and taught throughout the California State University campuses at San Diego, Fullerton, Northridge, and Los Angeles.

Bert Corona died in Hollywood from complications of kidney failure on January 15, 2001, at the age of eighty-two. He was the subject of a 1994 biography, *Memories of Chicano History: The Life and Narrative of Bert Corona,* by Mario T. García, who donated the tapes of his interviews from 1980 to 1991 to the California Ethnic and Multicultural Archives at the University of California at Santa Barbara, where they remain available to the general public.

Susan Marie Green

See also: Community Service Organization; Mexican American Political Association; Viva Kennedy Clubs.

Further Reading

García, Mario T. *Memories of Chicano History: The Life and Narrative of Bert Corona.* Berkeley: University of California Press, 1994.

Ramos, George. "Bert Corona; Labor Activist Backed Rights for Undocumented Workers." *Los Angeles Times,* January 17, 2001.

Corridos

The *corrido* is a popular ballad of Mexico, often performed to waltz and polka rhythms, that recounts heroes and deeds of epic dimensions. Its basic structure is that of paired eight-syllable (octosyllabic) lines, which form a quatrain, although some corridos do not conform to this pattern. The most conventional corridos also lack a chorus, something that distinguishes them from another of Mexico's traditional folk songs, the *rancheras*—again, however, there are exceptions to this rule.

Scholars have generally concluded that the corrido's immediate ancestor is the Spanish *romance* of the Middle Ages, which was taken to America by the first explorers. However, the many similarities between these artistic forms—especially their octosyllabic nature—have not prevented some scholars from denying the relationship. For them, the origins of the corrido are to be found in native lyrical forms (indigenous poetry)—although an early influence of the romance on the corrido is also seen as likely. At the same time, however, the development of this artistic form in Mexico over the past 500 years has made its form, style, and themes quite different from—and often richer than—those of its Spanish counterpart. The classification of the corrido on the basis of subject matter, by historian Vicente Mendoza, demonstrates the thematic richness of this popular art form; the topics are as diverse as "history, revolutions, politics, shootings, heroes, bandits, prisons, kidnappings, persecutions, evil deeds, assassinations, fatalities, accidents, disasters, crimes, horses, cities"—often with a large comical component.

In its most essential and primitive form, the corrido is an anonymous composition produced by a witness (or many witnesses) to events that—often because of their heroic nature—are deemed worthy of preserving in words and music. It is composed soon after the events it recounts and is therefore sung in the first or third person—a further sign of its popular character. Corridos may also have more than one author. In this case, each person composes a different stanza, but all take part in singing the composition. This process is in keeping with the anonymity of the earlier corridos—as opposed to those professionally written in the last decades of the twentieth century—and also explains the name of this song form. The term "corrido" refers to the fact that all notes in the octosyllabic stanzas are sung without interruption, as well as to the connection of stanzas in a sequence that are sung one after another.

The development of the corrido has been the subject of much discussion, especially when it comes to its earliest manifestations. It is generally agreed that its earliest examples took shape in the nineteenth century. The growth in popularity of the corrido during the first years of the twentieth century went hand in hand with the Mexican Revolution, which brought compositions hailing the deeds of Mexico's war heroes. It is precisely because the corrido achieved its reputation during the Revolution that most of these ballads report the activities of (usually outlawed) male protagonists. The classic corpus of corridos includes such works as *Corrido de Heraclio Bernal, Corrido de Juan Sin Tierra, Corrido de Benjamín Argumedo, Corrido de la traición a Cuco, Corrido de Emiliano Zapata, Corrido de Pancho Villa,* and *Corrido de Gregorio Cortez,* of which many different versions are extant today. The multiple versions provide excellent examples of how the corrido is able to transform, adapt, and bring its themes up to date so as to perpetuate itself over time.

By the middle of the twentieth century, however, the prevailing subject matter of corridos switched from the revolutionary heroes to the Mexican workers who left their country in search of a better life. The new "heroes" were the millions of migrant workers who crossed the border (often unlawfully) between Mexico and the United States and challenged the oppression they encountered in capitalist, Anglo North America. In its most essential form, however, the theme of the corrido remained the same, for these ballads—as the Spanish romance before them—had always been composed in the context of border conflict and could therefore be categorized as frontier literature.

The last decades of the twentieth century saw the appearance of the so-called *narco-corridos,* a highly controversial form that focused on drug dealers and illegal border crossings. In recent years, this popular art form has begun to lose its anonymity, with writers and musicians recording at professional studios and targeting specific audiences. Professor Ángel Salas, Manuel Sánchez, José Ramírez Mendoza, and Paulino Vargas, who scored a number of hits with groups like *Los tigres del norte,* are some of the most notable corrido composers of the late twentieth century.

David Arbesú

See also: Migrant Workers; Music.

Further Reading

Custodio, Álvaro. *El corrido popular mexicano: su historia, sus temas, sus intérpretes.* Madrid: Júcar, 1975.

Mendoza, Vicente T. *El corrido mexicano.* Mexico City, Mexico: Fondo de Cultura Económica, 1954.

Nicolopulos, James. "Reversing Polarities: Corridos, Fronteras, Technology, and Counter-discourses." In *Reflexiones 1998: New Directions in Mexican American Studies,* ed. Yolanda C. Austin Padilla. Austin: Center for Mexican American Studies, University of Texas, 1998.

Costa Ricans

Until the end of the twentieth century, the Costa Rican community in America was regarded as one that differed significantly from other Latino immigrant groups in composition and cultural experience. First and foremost, the relative number of Costa Ricans immigrating to the United States was generally much smaller than that of other groups from Mesoamerica. Secondly, due to their small numbers, the Costa Ricans who did enter the United States and secure legal resident status or full citizenship tended to integrate more smoothly into the mainstream of U.S. society or into other Latino communities. There were few significant Costa Rican enclaves per se. While a fair number of young Costa Ricans have traditionally returned home after completing a college education or job training program, and a significant portion of older immigrants return to their homeland to retire, Costa Ricans in America have, over time, established themselves culturally, economically, and politically.

Unlike many other Latino groups, Costa Ricans generally have not sought to come to the United States to escape war, economic hardship, or political oppression. At least until recently, few were forced to immigrate illegally, instead arriving through the prescribed legal channels of the Immigration and Naturalization Service (INS). A large percentage of Costa Ricans immigrated because they had married an American, to pursue higher education, or because they had been offered a job. As such, Costa Rican immigration to the United States was consistently low. From 1931 to 1990, only 57,661 took up residence in the United States.

Inside Costa Rica, meanwhile, structural changes brought about by the economic crisis of the 1980s and a shift to neoliberal economic policies in the 1990s were affecting the social fabric of the nation; domestic social indicators have steadily worsened in the years since. Wealth has been increasingly concentrated in the upper stratum, and the middle class has steadily shrunk. Nevertheless, Costa Ricans generally enjoy a higher standard of living than people in other Central American countries, a situation that has attracted foreign labor and put even greater strain on the economy. Indeed, Costa Rica took on one of the highest immigrant loads relative to its population in the Western Hemisphere. Urban job markets such as professional services became especially saturated.

As a consequence, immigration to the United States and other countries has increased significantly in recent years. According to the Statistical Information System on Migrations in Central America, Costa Rica saw a net emigration of approximately 190,000 nationals between 2000 and 2005. Costa Rica's largest newspaper, *La Nación,* has estimated that the total number of legal immigrants in the United States is about 70,000. According to unofficial sources, the true number of Costa Rican immigrants—included the undocumented—is as high as 220,000, or nearly 6 percent of Costa Rica's total population. According to the 2000 U.S. Census, 45 percent of all legal immigrants from Costa Rica entered the United States between 1990 and 2000 and remain noncitizens. U.S. immigration statistics also indicate that the number of deportable aliens from Costa Rica—most of whom entered without a visa—has increased six-fold (to 1,321 per year). The new influx of Costa Rican immigrants in the twenty-first century also includes two "new" demographic groups: professionals who cannot find work due to the reshaping of the labor market and people from rural areas seeking social and economic mobility; a large percentage of the latter group come from southern regions of Costa Rica and enter the United States through the southwestern frontier.

The changing causes and circumstances of immigration have directly affected the Costa Rican experience in America. Unlike other Latino immigrant groups, Costa Ricans traditionally eschewed distinct ethnic/national enclaves and integrated into existing communities—both those inhabited by a majority of European Americans and those of other Latino groups. Nevertheless, many Costa Ricans, especially those of older generations, actively retained native customs and cultural practices. Prominent among these have been the solemn observance of Semana Santa (Holy Week) and the celebration of Rosario del Niño, during which families prepare a nativity scene for display at Christmas and then pray to it until February. Traditional Costa Rican cuisine, music, and dance can be found in certain communities.

While high levels of assimilation and acculturation have long defined, the experience of Costa Rican immigrants, that trend has been changing in recent times. Distinct national communities, social networks, and cultural institutions have become increasingly evident.

According to the 2000 U.S. Census, Costa Ricans were clustered in the New York City–Long Island (New York)–Pennsylvania region (18 percent) and the Miami–Fort Lauderdale–Orlando–Tampa region of Florida (17 percent), followed by the Los Angeles–Long Beach–Santa Ana region of Southern California (7 percent). Whereas evidence of distinct Costa Rican culture was scarce as recently as the mid-1990s, the increase in immigration, establishment of national/ethnic communities, and trends in identity formation have raised its visibility. In Anaheim, California, and Trenton, New Jersey, for example, it is commonplace to find Costa Rican products, restaurants, and cultural networks in immigrant neighborhoods.

Costa Ricans maintain their own *pulperias* (small stores), read their own publications, and listen to their own radio programs; they can even enjoy broadcasts of soccer games from the homeland. The incorporation of Costa Rican programming into DirecTV's direct-broadcast satellite service and the easy access to Costa Rican media by means of the Internet strengthen national ties and cultural unity. Today, homesick Costa Ricans can even order their favorite sauces from specialty Web sites that also enable them to send remittances home. More traditional ties, such as the Catholic Church and affiliated community groups, also reinforce connections between Costa Ricans and their homeland, regardless of levels of assimilation.

Bernardo Aguilar-González, Jason Oliver Chang, and David J. Leonard

Further Reading

Biesanz, Martin, et al. *The Ticos: Culture and Social Change in Costa Rica.* Boulder, CO: Lynne Rienner, 1998.

Hall, Charles, et al. "A Brief Historical and Visual Introduction to Costa Rica in Quantifying Sustainable Development." In *Quantifying Sustainable Development: The Future of Tropical Economies,* ed. Charles Hall. San Diego, CA: Academic Press, 2000.

Novas, Himilce. *Everything you Need to Know About Latino History.* New York: Plume, 2008.

Coyotes

Border coyotes are smugglers who specialize in leading illegal aliens across the Mexican border into the United States, usually for a fee. Indeed, a large majority of the undocumented Mexican migrants who come to the United States cross the border for the first time with the help of a paid guide known as a coyote or *pollero* (chicken gatherer).

Although coyotes have conducted their trade for a number of decades, their activities became especially noteworthy after 1964. That year the United States and Mexico ended the Bracero Program, which had brought thousands of Mexican agricultural workers across the border to help fill U.S. labor shortages since 1942. Termination of the program left Mexican workers with little possibility of entering the United States legally.

In recent years especially, coyotes have become a virtual necessity for illegal immigrants to get past heightened U.S. border security. In an earlier time, migrants tended to depend on social ties to help them locate a guide, most likely a friend or relative, to lead them across the border. In recent years, however, the majority have to rely on the services of a paid coyote, who will charge anywhere from $150 to $1,500 for his services. Although many migrants are willing to pay whatever they can, the fees have increased as routes across the border have become more remote and more dangerous. Whereas coyotes in the past could lead their clients across the border at various frontier towns and cities, they have been forced increasingly to follow routes across the treacherous Rio Grande or stretches of desert. Once inside the United States, trailers and other modes of ground transportation, sometimes dangerous, are used to carry migrants away from crossing points. Death by suffocation, overheating, and starvation has been widely reported.

The governments of both Mexico and the United States have repeatedly blamed coyotes for the violence and death suffered by migrants. Yet millions of illegal immigrants have entered the country under the safety and guidance of hired guides. Indeed, coyotes are widely regarded in the migrant community as heroic figures to be thanked for helping them start a new life in *El Norte* (The North).

Observers of life along the U.S.-Mexico border have identified three basic types of coyotes: local agents, local and border smugglers, and border-only smuggling businesses, each with a menu of prices and services. A local coyote might work with one or two helpers, mostly family members. These help him organize groups of five or six migrants, taking them to and across the border, and transporting them to their final destination—often where the coyote himself is headed. A local and border coyote is someone who operates in town with, at best, a handful of helpers. This person generally guides migrants across the border but does not transport them to their final destinations. Instead, he contacts someone on the other side of the border to arrange for transportation. Coyote businesses, finally, operate on a larger scale and smuggle migrants into the United States on a full-time, full-service basis. These businesses actively recruit migrants and employ guides to lead the migrants across the border and deliver them to their final destinations.

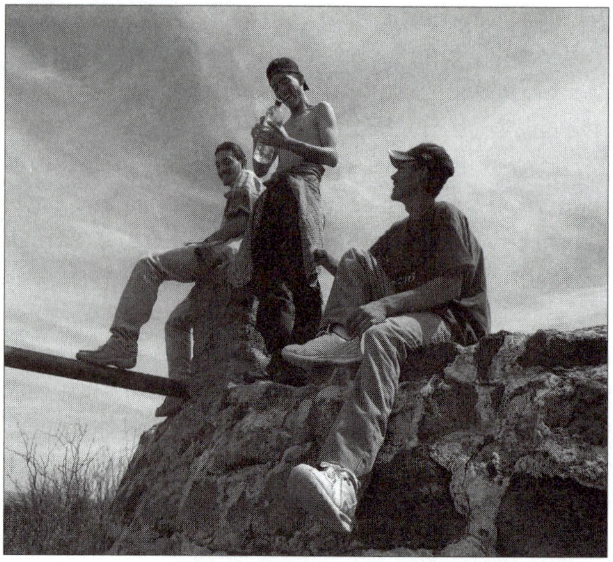

A group of coyotes, individuals who smuggle illegal aliens into the United States from Mexico, await dark before leading a crossing into Arizona. Charging hundreds or thousands of dollars, coyotes are now considered essential for Mexicans seeking illegal entry. *(Scott Olson/Getty Images)*

The method of payment for a coyote's services depends on a variety of factors. Migrants might be asked to pay the fee up front or upon arrival. Sometimes the coyote will allow migrants to pay off the debt in labor. The terms of payment depend on the amount of money the migrant possesses, his or her relationship with the coyote, and the kind of labor he or she may be able to provide. The price of a coyote's service also varies depending on a number of factors—how far the migrant is transported, the provision of food, water, and a place to sleep, and the distance covered and how long it takes to lead the migrant to his or her destination.

Anita Damjanovic

See also: Bracero Program; Illegal Immigration; Migrant Workers.

Further Reading

Conover, Ted. *Coyotes: A Journey through the Secret World of America's Illegal Aliens.* New York: Random House, 1987.

López Castro, Gustavo. "Coyotes and Alien Smuggling." *Migration between Mexico and the United States: Binational Study* 3 (1998): 965–74.

Spener, David. "This Coyote's Life." *NACLA Report on the Americas* 33:3 (November/December 1999): 22–23.

Cruz, Celia (1925–2003)

Often cited as the most influential woman in the history of Cuban music, Celia de la Caridad Cruz Alfonso—better known as Celia Cruz—was born on October 21, 1925, in Havana. In her autobiography, *Celia: My Life* (published posthumously in 2004), Cruz describes her childhood in Santo Suárez, a poor neighborhood of Havana, and explains how friends and family predicted her life as an entertainer. It is unlikely, however, that anyone prophesized the success of the woman who became known as the "Queen of Salsa" or "Queen of Latin Music."

As a teenager, Cruz began competing in talent shows and won first prize in an amateur radio contest. From 1947 to 1950, she studied voice, piano, and theory at the Conservatory of Music in Havana. Her professional breakthrough came in 1950, when she was hired as lead singer for the famous Cuban band La Sonora Matancera. As an unknown performer and because she had replaced La Sonora Matancera's previous singer, Cruz struggled to gain audience acceptance, but soon she won their hearts and became famous with her signature shout "*¡Azucar!*" (sugar). Cruz remained with the band for fifteen years, much of it spent on international tour.

In 1960, in the aftermath of the Cuban revolution, Cruz moved to the United States. The following year, she married Pedro Knight, the lead trumpeter in La Sonora Matancera. With Fidel Castro in control of the island, the couple decided not to return to their homeland and instead became citizens of the United States, launching a career there. While Celia's career was blossoming, Pedro's career was fading and eventually he became her manager.

In 1966, Celia began performing with drummer and bandleader Tito Puente, one of the luminaries of Latin music in the United States. The collaboration produced eight albums for Tito Records, a label widely credited with introducing salsa music to mainstream American audiences. Celia later signed with Vaya records, which elevated her to true star status. Her big breakthrough came in 1974, when she recorded the album *Celia and Johnny,* a duet with Johnny Pacheco, a co-owner of Vaya's sister label Fania.

During the 1980s, Cruz toured frequently throughout Latin America, performing multiple concerts and television shows at every stop, singing with both younger artists and those of her own era. In 1991, she recorded a song titled "Mi Tierra" (My Land) with Cuban pop star Martika, about a young Cuban American woman who yearns for her homeland. The song became an instant hit in many Latin American countries and won Cruz a legion of younger fans. Later that year, she recorded an anniversary album called *La Sonora Matancera.*

Cruz's health fell into precipitous decline in early 2003, and on July 16 she succumbed to a cancerous brain tumor at her home in Fort Lee, New Jersey. Her body was brought to Miami and New York, where her legions of fans—especially in the large Cuban communities in those two cities—paid their final respects.

Celia Cruz, known as the "Queen of Salsa" across Latin America and the best-known female figure in modern Cuban music, spent much of her career on the U.S. circuit. A flamboyant performer, she won five Grammy awards and achieved superstar status. *(David Corio/Michael Ochs Archives/Getty Images)*

Although she was known as the Queen of Salsa in Latin America, her career reached its peak in the United States with her appearance in the 1992 film *The Mambo Kings*, starring Andy García and Antonio Banderas. Singing only in Spanish, Cruz won a total of five Grammy awards over her career. The last came in February 2004 for best salsa album of the previous year, *Regalo del Alma,* released posthumously. In 1994 she was awarded the National Medal of Arts, the highest official honor for an American entertainer. A street in Miami is named in her honor, and her orange, red, and white polka-dot dress and shoes are in the permanent collection of the Smithsonian Institution in Washington, D.C. Aside from her many recordings and sheer vocal talent, Cruz will be remembered for her outrageous costumes, wild wigs, vibrant stage persona, and trademark shout, "*¡Azucar!*"

Anita Damjanovic

See also: Cubans; Music; Puente, Tito.

Further Reading

Cruz, Celia, with Ana Cristina Reymundo. *Celia: My Life.* New York: Rayo, 2004.

Roberts, John Storm. *The Latin Tinge: The Impact of Latin American Music on the United States.* 2nd ed. New York: Oxford University Press, 1999.

Rodríguez-Duarte, Alexis. *Presenting Celia Cruz.* New York: Clarkson Potter, 2004.

Crystal City, Texas

Crystal City, a small town in southwest Texas (population 7,190 in the 2000 U.S. Census), has been home to a majority Latino population since its founding in 1910. The close proximity of the town to the Texas-Mexico border and employment opportunities in the surrounding farmlands contributed to the immigration of both Mexican migrant workers and Mexican Americans. The town is known primarily for two notable historical events: the internment of people of Japanese origin and those of German descent during World War II and the electoral successes of Mexican American political groups during the 1960s and 1970s.

Founded by land developers Carl Groos and Edward Buckingham, Crystal City was established in hopes of attracting wealthy Texans to the region's crystal-clear artesian springs. When the town was incorporated, however, most of the territory was sold as farmland. Crystal City lies in the heart of Texas's Winter Garden region, so named because the crops grow only during the winter months. The farming of crops like spinach made Crystal City an important stop on the migrant labor trail. Latino farmworkers contributed to the economic development of the city throughout the twentieth century.

Because of its remote location and small population in the 1940s, Crystal City was chosen as one of several sites for the relocation of Japanese and German families during World War II. Covering 300 acres, the town's camp had more than 150 living units and nearly 700 other buildings, including several schools, a college, and recreational facilities. Although only a few Mexican Americans were employed at the camp, when it closed in 1947 the buildings were converted into low-income housing for Crystal City's Latino poor.

Crystal City was also the site of several Mexican American political victories in 1963 and 1970. In 1961, Juan Cornejo and Andrew Dickens organized a political machine to challenge the Anglo families who had controlled municipal politics for decades. Anglo political control of the city purposefully excluded Mexican American citizens, who were subjected to Jim Crow segregation in neighborhoods, schools, and frequently at the ballot box. Cornejo, Dickens, and volunteers from the Teamsters Union formed the Citizens Committee for Better Government (CCBG) as an alternative political party to the Anglo-controlled Democrats and to challenge the local establishment. These events caught the attention of the newly formed Political Association of Spanish-Speaking Organizations (PASO), which brought much-needed organizational and financial support to the CCBG. The unified efforts of the Citizens Committee, PASO, and the Teamsters Union proved a boon to Dickens and Cornejo's efforts, and the CCBG chose five Latino candidates to run for the city council in 1963. *Los Cinco Candidatos*, as they were called, included Cornejo, Manuel Maldonado, Reynaldo Mendoza, Antonio Cárdenas, and Mario Hernández. At first, Anglos downplayed the campaign of Los Cinco, but on Election Day they convinced employers to double the wages of Latinos as a way of keeping them from the polls. The effort failed. Los Cinco beat all five white incumbents, replacing the Anglo government with the city's first Mexican American government. Cornejo became the city's new mayor.

Los Cinco found governing more difficult than winning the election. Anglo employers cut the wages or fired several of Los Cinco, who were also harassed by Texas Rangers. The rangers were notorious in Texas Latino communities for their heavy-handed administration of the law. Mayor Cornejo experienced ranger harassment firsthand when Captain Alfred Allee threw him against a wall and banged his head into the sheetrock. Anglo politicians eventually reorganized, united with upper-class Mexican Americans, and formed the Citizens Association Serving All Americans (CASAA) "for the express purpose of kicking Mayor Juan Cornejo and his councilmen out of office and keeping any more such political groups from taking over civic affairs." CASAA swept to victory in 1965, and its leaders initiated a series of public reforms that improved conditions in poor Mexican American neighborhoods, indicating that coalition politics could indeed serve all citizens.

The victory for CASAA did not put an end to the hopes of radical Latino politicians. For example, José Angel Gutiérrez, a Crystal City native who had assisted in the campaign of Los Cinco, helped form La Raza Unida Party (LRUP) in 1970 to recapture the city government. Gutiérrez ran for a seat on the school board, as did local businessmen Mike Pérez and Arturo Gonzáles. LRUP also fielded two candidates for the city council and a host of others for offices in surrounding counties. CASAA could not muster viable alternatives to the LRUP slate. Voters elected all RUP municipal candidates and a handful of those outside the city. The LRUP's success prompted new campaigns in the region as well as several unsuccessful attempts to elect state legislators and a Chicano governor. But internal dissension, the arrest of LRUP gubernatorial candidate Ramsey Muñiz for drug possession, and the reorganization of opposition groups like CASAA ensured the decline of the party. The LRUP had difficulty duplicating its Crystal City successes outside the Winter Garden area, and those elected in the 1970 Crystal City balloting, like their predecessors, were voted out of office in the ensuing years.

The victories in 1963 and 1970 initiated a process of coalition building that resulted in more unified Anglo-Latino governments. Crystal City continues to enjoy successful coalition politics today. It remains an agricultural hub with a population consisting mainly of Mexicans and Mexican Americans.

Brian D. Behnken

See also: Blowouts; Gutiérrez, José Angel; La Raza Unida Party; Mexican American Youth Organization; Peña, Albert A., Jr.

Further Reading

Montejano, David. *Anglos and Mexicans in the Making of Texas, 1836–1986.* Austin: University of Texas Press, 1987.

Navarro, Armando. *The Cristal Experiment: A Chicano Struggle for Community Control.* Madison: University of Wisconsin Press, 1998.

Rosales, F. Arturo. *Chicano! The History of the Mexican American Civil Rights Movement.* Houston, TX: Arte Público, 1996.

Shockley, John Staples. *Chicano Revolt in a Texas Town.* Notre Dame, IN: University of Notre Dame Press, 1974.

Cuban Adjustment Acts (1966, 1996)

The Adjustment Acts of 1966 and 1996 are part of the ever-developing U.S. immigration policy toward Cuban refugees, which continues to grant them preferential treatment over other Latino immigrants. While separated by thirty years, the two legislative measures allowed the U.S. government to construct an immigration policy that accords special treatment to those fleeing the Castro regime.

1966 Legislation

In 1966, the U.S. Congress passed the first legislative measure addressing the issue of Cuban refugee status. Up to this point, all Cubans refugees were officially "parolees." Technically, in order for them to lose this status and become naturalized U.S. citizens, they would have to exit the country and reenter under a permanent visa. To avoid this technicality, and in acknowledgement of the nontemporary nature of the Cuban refugee presence, Congress passed the Cuban Adjustment Act of 1966, which allowed all Cubans who entered the United States after January 1959 to apply for permanent residency.

The legislation was necessitated by the U.S. government's ad hoc approach to Cuban immigration, effectively granting asylum to all Cubans who arrived on U.S. shores whether or not they had secured a visa. Throughout the 1960s and 1970s, Cubans immigrated on regular visas, on extended visitors visas, or as refugee parolees. The various options had created a range of official statuses, with single families maintaining several immigration classifications among their members. The Cuban Adjustment Act of 1966 granted a sort of universal status to all Cubans who were classified as refugees or visa overstays.

In addition to regularizing the refugee's immigration status, the law's provisions allowed many refugees to initiate the citizenship process. The Adjustment Act of 1966 also allowed Cubans to count up to thirty months of their stay in the United States toward the five years required for citizenship, thereby allowing refugees to obtain citizenship much sooner than regular immigrants. Additionally, by regularizing the refugees' immigration status, the 1966 legislation allowed many Cubans to access jobs that carried residency or citizenship requirements. Among these were professional positions in public schools, state hospitals, and other local, state, and federal institutions. Half or more of the states required nurses, dentists, architects, doctors, teachers, and veterinarians to either prove citizenship or declare the intent to become a citizen.

1996 Legislation

Like its 1966 predecessor, the Adjustment Act of 1996 provided alterations in federal immigration policy specifically to offer Cuban refugees greater opportunity to obtain legal status. Specifically, the 1996 legislation was a response to the influx of *balseros* (rafters) in the early 1990s and to the Illegal Immigrant Reform and Immigrant Responsibility Act of 1996 (IIRIRA). The IIRIRA was written as an attempt to limit the number of undocumented immigrants in the United States. While written in broad terms, IIRIRA was specifically concerned about the U.S.-Mexico border and provided for security "improvements" along the Southwest frontier. In order to limit the number of immigrants who could enter the nation illegally and later apply for legal status, the IIRIRA required that immigrants must cross the border at an official port of entry (airport, seaport, or border checkpoint). Because a large number of Cuban refugees had arrived by way of boat, landing in a myriad of unsanctioned locations along the Florida coast, their ability to gain legal status was placed in jeopardy by the IIRIRA. In response, the Cuban Adjustment Act of 1996 provided that all Cubans who arrive in the United States and are granted parole status may apply for permanent legal status after they have lived in the country for one year.

Cheris Brewer Current

See also: Balseros; Castro, Fidel; Cuban Refugee Program; Cubans.

Further Reading

Pedraza-Bailey, Silvia. *Political and Economic Migrants in America: Cubans and Mexicans.* Austin: University of Texas Press, 1985.

U.S. Citizenship and Immigration Services. http://www.uscis.gov.

Cuban American National Foundation

The Florida-based Cuban American National Foundation (CANF) was established in 1981 as a Cuban exile association and developed into a conservative political powerhouse during the 1980s and 1990s. While CANF bills itself as a nonprofit organization dedicated to advancing freedom and capitalism in Cuba—claiming to be the largest Cuban exile organization in the United States, with thousands of members across the country—its primary function is as a political lobby on U.S.-Cuban foreign policy.

Founded by Raul Masvidal, Carlos Salmon, and longtime director Jorge Más Canosa, CANF has been the leading Cuban-American lobby in Washington, D.C., for more than two decades. It supported the expulsion of Fidel Castro and his government from Cuba, calling for the establishment of "a pluralistic, market-based democracy in Cuba—one fostering economic prosperity with social justice—grounded in the rule of law, and constitutionally guaranteed protection for fundamental human rights as well as the social, political, and economic rights of the Cuban people." More broadly, "CANF seeks to engage, support, and empower the Cuban people in ways that do not aid or legitimize the Castro regime." CANF's position continues unchanged with the ascension of Castro's brother Raul to the presidency of Cuba.

During the 1980s, CANF deftly positioned itself as "the voice" of the Cuban community in America and leveraged the U.S. government to maintain a hard-line stance toward Castro's Cuba. The CANF and other hard-liners mandated that all contact with Cuba should be avoided, as trading, traveling to, or negotiating with Castro all represented legitimizations of the revolution. Thus, CANF's position included the continuation of the U.S. embargo against Cuba and a condemnation of any "dialogue." While Cuban Americans and Cubans did not (and do not) universally support CANF's vision, this vocal and savvy organization was able to extend the United States's isolationist Cold War policies for Cuba long after the end of the Cold War.

CANF's strength during the 1980s and 1990s was directly attributed to its chairman, Jorge Más Canosa, who headed the organization from its inception until his death in 1997. Más Canosa is credited with forging the political alliances needed to influence the Reagan, Bush, and Clinton administrations' foreign policy on Cuba. Additionally, Más Canosa used his political clout as head of CANF to lobby the United States to establish anti-Castro, pro-democracy radio and television stations—Radio Martí and TV Martí—that originate in the United States and broadcast to Cuba. Más Canosa's role in CANF cannot be underestimated, and the decline of the organization's political might is directly tied to Más Canosa's death.

In an effort to inspire anti-Castro sentiment within the Cuban community, CANF has also provided financial support to nonviolent protests and pro-democracy campaigns on the island. In addition, however, it has been alleged that CANF is connected to various terrorist acts against Cuban businesses, civilians, and government institutions. The controversial anti-Castro terrorist Luis Posada Carriles, for example, claimed in 1998 that CANF funded or had knowledge of his bombing campaign on the island the previous year. Indeed, Más Canosa had issued a statement in 1997 supporting attacks against the Castro regime. "We do not think of these as terrorist actions," he stated. And according to a former director of the CANF executive board, José Antonio Llama, CANF had established its own paramilitary group as early as June 1992. Notwithstanding these accusations, CANF has long denied accusations regarding any support of violence or acts of terrorism.

CANF has also been at least partly responsible for the political influence of Cuban Americans in South Florida. CANF board member Xavier Suarez, the mayor of Miami from 1985 to 1993, actively supported Más Canosa's various attacks on the city officials and media who did not agree with CANF's agenda. Its local political influence in South Florida is considered especially significant given Florida's importance in national politics. In addition to its presence in Florida and Washington, D.C., CANF also maintains chapters in Los Angeles, New York, Puerto Rico, New Jersey, Texas, and New Orleans.

Although CANF has been a prominent voice in the often-heated debates regarding Cuban-American relations and U.S. foreign policy toward Cuba for more than two decades, and while it has acted as a bridge between the Cuban people and exiles living in the United States, the organization is not without its detractors. Some have taken issue with its unbounded eagerness to dominate Cuban-American politics and influence U.S. policy. Other critics argue that CANF's range of activities to undermine the Castro regime stretches beyond legal bounds.

Since 2007, Jorge Más Santo, Más Canosa's son, who has been credited with advancing an increasingly moderate platform, has chaired the foundation.

Cheris Brewer Current and Stefanie Tacata

See also: Castro, Fidel; Cubans; Politics.

Further Reading

Bardach, Ann Louise. *Cuba Confidential: Love and Vengeance in Miami and Havana.* New York: Random House, 2002.

Cuban American National Foundation. http://www.canf.org.
Haney, Patrick J., and Walter Vanderbush. "The Role of Ethnic Interest Groups in U.S. Foreign Policy: The Case of the Cuban American Foundation." *International Studies Quarterly* 43:2 (June 1999): 341–61.
Torres, María de los Angeles. *In the Land of Mirrors: Cuban Exile Politics in the United States.* Ann Arbor: University of Michigan Press, 1999.

Cuban Refugee Center

The Cuban Refugee Center (CRC), also known as *El Refugio* and the Freedom Tower, was a program that processed and assisted nearly a half-million incoming refugees from 1961 to 1974. The services and sense of community offered at the CRC made the facility a sanctuary and place of respite for displaced Cubans. Although the services have moved to other facilities, the Freedom Tower building continues to be an important part of Miami's physical and cultural landscape for the Cuban American community.

Opened in 1961 and funded by the U.S. government, the center served as the administrative hub of the Cuban refugee relief effort. In light of the political tensions with the Castro regime and in the aftermath of the Bay of Pigs invasion and Cuban Missile Crisis, the U.S. government held that the most effective policy with respect to Cuban refugees was one of acceptance and assistance. Upon arriving on U.S. shores, Cubans were encouraged to register at the CRC, as all forms of assistance—from student loans to job referrals—depended on a personal record. Even those Cuban refugees who did not enter the country by way of Miami would still have to travel to the CRC to register.

The number and types of services provided through the CRC were extensive, addressing both

The Cuban Refugee Center in Miami provided job referrals, financial support, medical assistance, and other essential services to new arrivals beginning in the 1960s. The Freedom Tower where it was housed still stands as a memorial to Cuban immigration. *(Michael Rougier/Stringer/Time & Life Pictures/Getty Images)*

immediate and long-term needs. Thus, emergency medical, financial, and material assistance was often accompanied by classes in English and vocational or professional certification. Most incoming refugees arrived at the center in a state of destitution and relied on the program to provide for their immediate needs as they searched for housing, jobs, and self-sufficiency. Staff social workers interviewed refugees upon registration and required them to disclose their dependants, place of residence, and employment status. Based on these criteria, staff calculated a monthly financial benefit, a maximum of $60 a month for single persons and $100 for families.

To augment substandard paychecks, indigent refugees could receive additional material assistance in the form of food and medical care. Those who qualified for welfare payments could supplement their checks with a surplus commodity allowance. Florida's Welfare Department administered this program, and the Cuban Refugee Program (CRP) funded it; in all, 60 percent of refugees received food from the CRP.

By registering with CRC, refugees were also eligible for medical assistance. Refugees underwent physical examinations and a chest X-ray to rule out communicable diseases and determine what other medical services might be needed. Those deemed eligible for need-based medical insurance could access a clinic in the CRC itself. Area hospitals could be accessed upon referral from the CRC clinic or in emergency situations.

The Cuban Refugee Center—sometimes referred to as "Miami's Ellis Island"—was closed in 1974 due to a slowdown in incoming refugees, and the refugee program was moved to a smaller location. When the Freedom Tower was slated to be sold that year, the Cuban exile community in Miami mounted a concerted effort to purchase it. Although foiled in their efforts to raise the necessary funds, the refugee community maintained an emotional if not a financial interest in the building. In 1997, Cuban businessman and chairman of the Cuban American National Foundation Jorge Más Canosa bought the Freedom Tower and made plans to turn it into a museum of the Cuban exile experience. The need for large-scale restoration and Más Canosa's death that same year put a stop to the plans. His son, who inherited the Freedom Tower, later sold the building to a real estate developer. The developers donated the Freedom Tower, which had been added to the U.S. National Register of Historic Places on September 10, 1979, to Miami-Dade College. The Freedom Tower, while currently being used as an art museum, remains a monument to Cuban immigration. On October 6, 2008, its future was preserved, having been named a U.S. National Historic Landmark.

Cheris Brewer Current

See also: Castro, Fidel; Cuban Refugee Program; Cubans.

Further Reading

García, María Cristina. *Havana USA: Cuban Exiles and Cuban Americans in South Florida, 1959–1994.* Berkeley: University of California Press, 1996.

Levine, Robert M., and Asis Moises. *Cuban Miami.* New Brunswick, NJ: Rutgers University Press, 2000.

Cuban Refugee Program

The Cuban Refugee Program (CRP) was created in 1961 to provide material assistance to Cuban refugees fleeing Castro's revolution. Housed in the Cuban Refugee Center in downtown Miami and funded by the U.S. government, the ambitious program set out to ameliorate the economic and social effects of displacement by offering a broad range of social services, effectively providing for the immediate needs of refugees while ensuring an individual's long-term economic viability. The location and function of the CRP were widely known, due in part to a number of English and Spanish media outlets. Refugees were encouraged to come forward and take advantage of the available services.

Providing individuals and families with a means of survival was the program's initial function. The restrictions of the Castro regime on what refugees could take with them became increasingly stringent, and luggage eventually was limited to a change or two of clothing. The lack of material resources and in many cases inadequate social or familial contacts necessitated further aid from the U.S. government. Refugees who desired assistance were registered, interviewed, given medical checkups, and provided an identification card and number that acted as proof of registration and a means of organizing the relief effort. By 1963, over 75 percent of incoming Cuban refugees had registered at the CRP.

The CRP had a relatively progressive agenda, with a staff that included past refugees, veterans of previous refugee assistance programs, and government workers employed by the Department of Health, Education, and Welfare. The CRP funded and dispensed financial assistance checks, food, medical care, and education and retraining with federal monies. The services provided by the center fell into three general categories—emergency assistance, education, and resettlement.

At the beginning of the Cuban Refugee Center's operation, more than 40 percent of refugees lacked sufficient food, clothing, or medical attention. After 1961, most incoming refugees arrived at the center in a state of destitution and relied on the program to provide for their immediate needs as they searched for housing and jobs. The cap on financial support was $60 per month for an individual and $100 per month for a family unit.

The CRP did not limit its assistance to basic needs, however, offering a broad range of services to help Cuban refugees attain self-sufficiency. Educational opportunities were offered at all levels, with children free to attend public schools, college students eligible for low-interest or interest-free loans, and vocational, language, or recertification classes provided for adult refugees.

The sheer number of immigrants that settled in Miami created a unique socioeconomic situation, in which immigrants competed with each other to find housing and jobs. The CRP therefore attempted to resettle Cuban refugees in other parts of the United States as well. To encourage resettlement, the government offered access to the same need-based services available in Miami and promised free transportation back to Cuba when political circumstances allowed. Altogether, the CRP resettled almost 300,000 Cuban refugees across the United States, with large concentrations in New York, New Jersey, California, Illinois, and Puerto Rico.

When the Cuban Refugee Program began to be phased out in 1978, it had provided refugees with the longest-enduring refugee assistance program in U.S. history. The CRP is noteworthy as well for having preceded and eclipsed the expansion of national welfare services through the War on Poverty and social service programs like Medicaid and Aid to Dependant Families. Finally, the total amount of funding that went into the Cuban Refugee Program, $1.4 billion, was startling in its generosity, effectiveness, and breadth of disbursement, providing some type of service to some 70 percent of all adult Cuban refugees.

Cheris Brewer Current

See also: Castro, Fidel; Cuban Adjustment Acts (1966, 1996); Cubans.

Further Reading

Pedraza-Bailey, Silvia. *Political and Economic Migrants in America: Cubans and Mexicans.* Austin: University of Texas Press, 1985.

Cubans

At 3.7 percent of the aggregate population, Cubans currently constitute the third-largest Latino group in the United States (after Mexicans and Puerto Ricans). Drawn to U.S. shores both as economic immigrants and as political refugees, many Cuban Americans can trace their community origins to the early nineteenth century. Regardless of the push factors, lax U.S. immigration and refugee policies compared with those for other groups have provided Cubans with preferential immigration status and facilitated their settlement.

Nineteenth- and Twentieth-Century Immigration

As former colonies, the United States and Cuba had long maintained closer economic ties with each other than with their respective mother countries. The economic relationship compelled many Cubans to consider the United States an attractive alternative whenever political or economic strife hit the

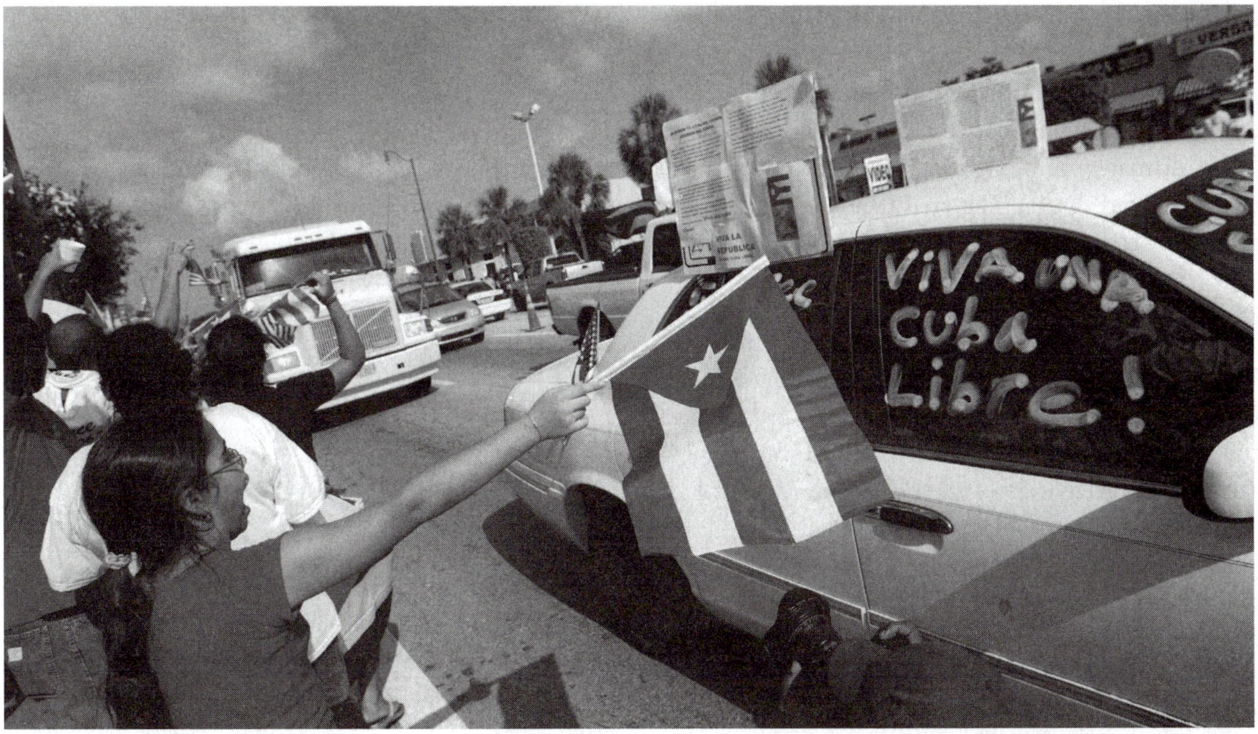

Cuban Americans in the Little Havana section of Miami celebrate Fidel Castro's relinquishment of power following his surgery in 2006. Many in the refugee community harbor a decades-long desire to return to their homeland. *(Roberto Schmidt/AFP/Getty Images)*

island. Cubans pulled by the promise of jobs, business opportunities, or political freedom began migrating to the United States in the nineteenth century, settling largely in cities—Tampa and Key West, Florida; New Orleans, Louisiana; Philadelphia; and New York. Thus, it was in New York and not Havana where the Cuban revolutionary philosopher José Martí wrote his poetry and essays, and garnered support for the Cuban independence movement. Nor did Cuba's independence in 1902 halt northward migration; on the contrary, more than 100,000 Cubans immigrated during the first fifty years of the twentieth century. Inexpensive sea passage, combined with lax immigration regulations and the prospect of employment, prompted large numbers of Cuban emigrants to enter the United States.

1960s and 1970s

As in the case of many political upheavals, the resignation of Fulgencio Batista and ascendancy of Fidel Castro on January 1, 1959, produced a heavy outmigration from the island. Immediately wary of Castro's political leanings, the U.S. government did nothing to halt the flow of refugees. Dedicated to assisting anyone fleeing Communist countries, it provided an unlimited number of visas to Cubans; by the spring of 1961 more than 125,000 Cubans had reached U.S. shores. The flow of Cubans did not slow until the Cuban Missile Crisis in 1962 brought a halt to flights between the U.S. mainland and the island.

This travel ban between the United States and Cuba was lifted at the end of 1965, when Castro announced that the Cuban seaport of Camarioca would be opened for any Cubans who wished to leave. A total of 3,000 refugees left the island in the following month. The boatlift was cause for concern on the part of U.S. authorities, as it put those in the boats—many of which were small, old, or otherwise inadequate—at risk and made it difficult for immigration authorities to control the entry of the newcomers. To manage the process, the two governments reached an informal agreement that allowed for a more methodical exit process. The United States, for its part, offered the refugees access to a program called Freedom Flight. All Cubans cleared by the two governments would be provided air transportation funded by the U.S. government. The flights ran twice daily from 1965 to 1973, ultimately bringing more than 250,000 Cubans to the United States. The arrival of Cuban refugees essentially ceased with the end of the program.

Marielitos

In response to the economic trials on the island, many Cubans took advantage of a new opportunity to leave the island in 1980. The chance to leave was precipitated by an occupation of the Peruvian Embassy that August, in which more than 10,000 Cubans seeking political asylum took refuge in the embassy compound. The incident focused international attention on their grievances and finally forced Castro to loosen his regime's emigration policies. The port of Mariel was opened to all Cubans who wished to leave, though no transportation was provided. Fishing boats piloted by Cuban exiles soon began arriving from Florida, and, over the next six months, nearly 125,000 Cubans, who became known as *marielitos,* made their way to U.S. shores.

To secure the upper hand in the exchange, Castro insisted that foreign boats had to pick up individuals released from Cuban prisons and hospitals before relatives and other "normal" refugees could be taken in. Only about 6 percent of all Mariel refugees had a diagnosed mental disorder or violent criminal background, but the arrival of such "undesirables" was not well received in the U.S. media and the entire migration was a source of controversy in American society at large.

Balseros

The halt in immigration that followed Mariel was once again interrupted during the early 1990s. In response to the worsening economic situation produced by the fall of the Soviet Union in 1991—the Communist regime in Moscow had provided significant economic and military support to Cuba for decades—many Cubans became desperate to leave the island. Accordingly, Castro announced in the summer of 1994 that all those who wished to leave the island could do so without interference by the coast guard.

This time, however, the United States did not openly welcome the wave of Cuban refugees, and no boatlift was organized. Instead Cubans took to the sea in fishing boats, rowboats, and rafts made of almost anything that would float. There are no reliable estimates of the number of Cubans who left in the so-called *balseros* exodus—the shoddy vessels meant that many did not survive the 90-mile (150-kilometer) journey—but a total of 32,000 were fortunate enough to be picked up by the U.S. Coast Guard. Unlike earlier refugees, however, the balseros were not granted immediate asylum. Upon being picked up at sea, they were taken to the U.S. military base at Guantánamo Bay (Cuba), where they were held for a number of months before being allowed into the United States. In the aftermath of the balsero exodus, U.S. policy regarding Cuban refugees underwent a fundamental change. In the past all Cuban refugees who reached international waters were granted entry into the United States; after 1994, only those who reached dry land were granted asylum.

Cheris Brewer Current

See also: Balseros; Castro, Fidel; Cuban Adjustment Acts (1966, 1996); Cuban American National Foundation; Cuban Refugee Center; Cuban Refugee Program; González, Elián; Mariel Boatlift; Marielitos; Miami.

Further Reading

Masud-Piloto, Felix Roberto. *From Welcomed Exiles to Illegal Immigrants: Cuban Migration to the U.S., 1959–1995.* Lanham, MD: Rowman & Littlefield, 1996.

Olson, James S., and Judith E. Olson. *Cuban Americans: From Trauma to Triumph.* London: Prentice Hall International, 1995.

Culture Clash

Established in 1984, Culture Clash is a comedy troupe devoted to portraying the complexities of Latino life in the United States. The California-based group has dedicated itself to the themes of its first book, *Life, Death, and Revolutionary Comedy* (1998), which captures its flair for dramatic absurdity. The three performers/writers that make up Culture Clash—Richard Montoya, Ric Salinas, and Herbert

Siguenza—draw on stereotypes, pop culture, and current events to poke fun at everyday life and comment on contemporary politics. Highlights of the group's history include the premiere of its play *A Bowl of Beings* on PBS's *Great Performances* series (1992); the coproduction, with director Lourdes Perez, of the comic film *Columbus on Trial* (1992); and the development and airing of thirty episodes of *Culture Clash* (1994), the first Latino-themed variety show, for Fox Television. More recently, the trio has focused on location-specific performances, using interviews to develop portraits of American life across the nation. Culture Clash has become a staple of American theater, not only proving the widespread appeal of Latino comedy but finding critical and popular success in the mainstream culture as well.

Culture Clash began performing at the Galería de la Raza in San Francisco, California, on May 5, 1984, as part of a Cinco de Mayo celebration organized by gallery curator René Yañez. The original troupe, known as "Comedy Fiesta," included comediennes Monica Palacios and Marga Gómez, and scholar/artist José Antonio Burciaga. The early performances, under the direction of Yañez, relied on sketch and stand-up comedy and drew widely from vaudeville, activist theater, Mexican *carpa* (tent) theater, and performance art. Shortly after the departure of Palacios and Gómez in 1986, the group adopted the name Culture Clash to pay homage to the British music invasion of the 1980s and as a reference to the cultural borders shaping life in the Americas. Burciaga retired in 1988, and Culture Clash officially became the trio of Montoya, Salinas, and Siguenza.

All three performers came to Culture Clash with a background in theater and the arts and a keen awareness of biculturalism. Montoya grew up in Sacramento, California, with a strong Chicano identity as the son of poet/artist José Montoya and the nephew of activist printmaker Malaquías Montoya. Salinas was born in El Salvador and raised in San Francisco, and Siguenza was born in San Francisco, but raised in both El Salvador and the United States. Both Salinas and Siguenza had prior experience with other Latino theater companies in San Francisco: the former at Teatro Latino and the latter at Teatro Gusto.

Though comedy is always center stage in their performances, Culture Clash is also driven by political concerns. In 1988 in San Francisco, the three produced Culture Clash's first narrative play, *The Mission*, in which the actors, playing themselves, staged a kidnapping of singer Julio Iglesias in order to demand time on national television. The play mocked the limited opportunities for Latinos/as in Hollywood, partly drawing on firsthand experience. Through their plays, Culture Clash has grappled with a wide spectrum of other social issues, including AIDS, gang violence, drugs, border politics, and gentrification. Their work also has sought to challenge the social injustices associated with racism, homophobia, and sexism, perpetuated from within and outside the Latino community.

In 1991, the members of Culture Clash moved to Los Angeles in order to be closer to the movie and television industries. Although producing a show with Fox Television in 1994 proved difficult because of creative differences, the experience helped them expand their geographic and cultural scope. Their most recent work includes three plays that grapple with the experiences of Cubans and Haitians in Miami, in *Radio Mambo: Culture Clash Invades Miami* (1995); Puerto Rican poets in New York, in *Nuyorican Stories* (1999); and life in Washington, D.C., after the terrorist attacks of September 11, 2001, in *Anthems: Culture Clash in the District* (2002). The troupe's new community-based repertoire, largely reliant on oral histories, is more reflective in tone than earlier skits, though still laced with humor. *Water and Power*, written by Culture Clash member Richard Montoya and starring all three members of the group, premiered at the Mark Taper Forum in Los Angeles in 2006. The play, which continued the group's tradition of biting comedy and social commentary, explores the corruption and power struggles within multicultural Los Angeles.

The work of Culture Clash reflects a wide array of influences, inspired by the vaudevillian antics of the Marx Brothers and Cantinflas (Mario Moreno Reyes), the dark stand-up humor of Lenny Bruce and Richard Pryor, and the political theater of Bertolt Brecht and Anna Deavere Smith. In 1998, Culture Clash staged a contemporary version of the classic Greek comedy *The Birds* by Aristophanes, using the ancient text to comment on current political events. By bringing to bear diverse influences and extending beyond Latino-themed material—though the latter remains essential to its work—the group has been rewarded with invitations to perform at a number of prestigious venues, including Lincoln Center in New York City and Kennedy Center in Washington, D.C.

The success of Culture Clash has advanced the position of Latinos as writers, performers, and producers in American entertainment. Although its independent streak may keep it ever on the fringe of mainstream culture, the group has established a loyal following of fans who eagerly await each new production. In their work and in their lives, Culture Clash has crossed multiple cultural borders, constantly challenging audience expectations and inspiring a new generation of performers and writers.

Cary Cordova

See also: Film; Television.

Further Reading

Culture Clash. *Culture Clash: Life, Death and Revolutionary Comedy.* New York: Theatre Communications Group, 1998.

———. *Culture Clash in AmeriCCa: Four Plays.* New York: Theatre Communications Group, 2003.

D

De La Hoya, Oscar (1973–)

Oscar De La Hoya is a Mexican American boxer who rose to superstardom during the 1990s and won professional world championships in six different weight divisions. His athletic talent, charisma, good looks, and mainstream popularity earned him the nickname "The Golden Boy." Although De La Hoya was certainly not the first Mexican American fighter to gain prominence, he is arguably the most popular American fighter of Mexican descent in the history of the sport. Despite later disappointments in the ring, he remains one of the biggest stars in boxing.

Early Life

De La Hoya was born in East Los Angeles, California, on February 4, 1973, the second son of Cecilia and Joel De La Hoya, Sr. With an older brother and younger sister, he grew up in a blue-collar section of Los Angeles, a neighborhood bordered by an area notorious for crime, drugs, and gangs.

Boxing had played a part in the lives of the De La Hoya family for several generations. Oscar's grandfather, Vicente De La Hoya, had been an amateur boxer in Mexico during the 1940s, and his father took up prizefighting after migrating to the United States from Mexico as a teenager but quit the sport after thirteen professional fights. De La Hoya's father encouraged his son to take up boxing, hoping to steer the boy away from gangs and drugs. At age six, Oscar began training regularly at a local gym.

As a teenager, De La Hoya produced one of the most impressive amateur boxing records of all time, registering 223 wins (153 by knockout) and only 5 losses. He won the 1990 Goodwill Games championship in the featherweight division and captured the Lightweight gold medal at the 1992 Summer Olympics in Barcelona, Spain, as he had promised his mother he would before she died of cancer in 1990. De La Hoya was the only U.S. fighter to win a gold medal in boxing that year.

Professional Career

De La Hoya made his professional debut on November 23, 1992, when he scored a first-round knockout over Lamar Williams. After a string of ten more victories, De La Hoya captured his first professional title in the Junior Lightweight division by scoring a technical knockout over Jimmi Bredahl in March 1994.

Despite his emergence as one of the brightest young stars in boxing, many Mexican and Mexican American fans seemed reluctant to embrace De La Hoya early in his professional career because many of his victories were against popular Mexican and Chicano fighters. During his first three years as a professional, De La Hoya decisively defeated Jorge "Maromero" Paez in 1994; Rafael Ruelas, Genaro "Chicanito" Hernández, and Jesse James Leija in 1995; and Julio César Chávez in 1996—which earned him the wrath of many Latino fight fans. His one-sided defeat of the revered Chávez, nicknamed "El Gran Campeón Mexicano" (The Great Mexican Champion), on June 7, 1996, was particularly devastating to the Mexican public. Chávez had never been knocked out or had a technical knockout in 100 professional fights and was regarded by many boxing experts as the greatest fighter in Mexico's history. De La Hoya finished off Chávez with a fourth-round technical knockout.

After his win over Chávez, De La Hoya was regarded as one of the three best pound-for-pound fighters in the world, along with Pernell Whitaker and Roy Jones, Jr. In April 1997, De La Hoya won a controversial decision over Whitaker, the welterweight champion, in a fight that is most remembered for

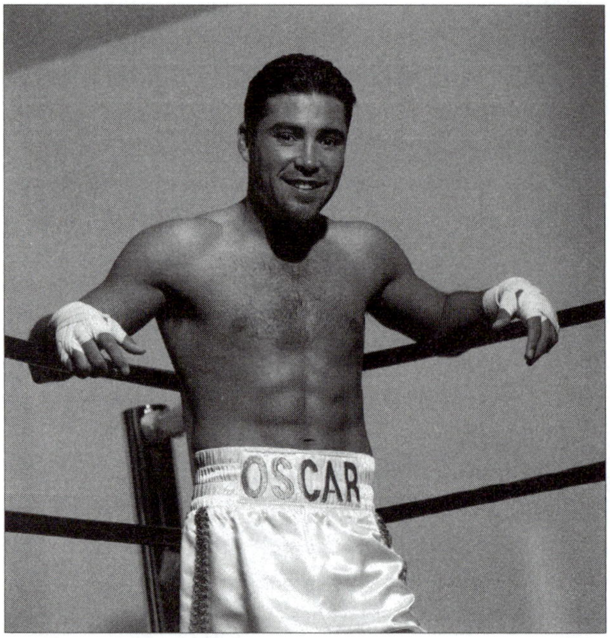

Growing up in East Los Angeles, Oscar De La Hoya avoided crime and drugs by taking up boxing. Perhaps the most popular Mexican American fighter in the history of the sport, the "Golden Boy" has won dozens of title belts in multiple weight classes. *(Jeff Katz/Getty Images)*

the allegedly racist comments made by television announcer Larry Merchant before the fight. As De La Hoya entered the ring to a recording of a mariachi band, Merchant expressed his distaste for the Mexican music. Merchant issued an apology to De La Hoya and boxing fans the following week.

Setbacks

By 1999, Felix "Tito" Trinidad, a slugger from Puerto Rico with one-punch knockout power in either hand, had established himself as De La Hoya's leading challenger. The two met on September 18, 1999, in a bout dubbed the "Fight of the Millennium." Both men were undefeated, and their ethnic backgrounds rekindled memories of the great Mexican–Puerto Rican boxing rivalries of the past. After dominating the first half of the fight with his jab and superior craftsmanship, De La Hoya became passive in the later rounds and eventually lost a twelve-round decision, along with his World Boxing Council (WBC) welterweight title, to Trinidad.

Another twelve-round loss, against "Sugar" Shane Moseley, in June 2000 led some to speculate that De La Hoya's best days as a fighter were over. Many pointed out that his usual tenacity and killer instinct had been absent in the Trinidad and Moseley fights. However, De La Hoya bounced back to capture both the WBC and World Boxing Association super welterweight championships by beating Javier Castillejo and Fernando Vargas, respectively, in June 2001 and September 2002. De La Hoya secured a rematch with Moseley in September 2003 but lost in a split decision by the judges on the twelfth round. Nine months later, he struggled to a twelve-round decision over middleweight champion Felix Sturm.

In September 2004, De La Hoya challenged Bernard "The Executioner" Hopkins for the undisputed middleweight championship of the world. He looked sharp in the first few rounds, but Hopkins's superior power proved to make the difference. In the ninth round, Hopkins landed a crushing body blow that sent De La Hoya to the canvas. For the first time in his career De La Hoya had been knocked out.

In and Out of the Ring

De La Hoya always hinted that he wished to retire from boxing at a young age, but he was still fighting well into his thirties. In June 2006, after defeating the Nicaraguan super welterweight Ricardo Mayorga for the WBC crown, he announced that he would not fight again that year—but that he was not retiring either. In the meantime, he had branched out into business as early as 2001, when he launched Golden Boy Promotions, becoming the first Mexican American to establish a professional boxing promotion firm. According to its mission statement, Golden Boy Promotions strives to "recruit, develop, and retain the best and bravest young fighters." That same year, De La Hoya married the Puerto Rican singer Millie Corretjer.

Justin D. García

See also: Boxing.

Further Reading

Quinn, Rob. *Oscar De La Hoya.* Philadelphia: Chelsea House, 2001.

Torres, John Albert. *Sports Great Oscar De La Hoya.* Springfield, NJ: Enslow, 1999.

Del Rio Independent School District v. Salvatierra (1930)

Del Rio Independent School District v. Salvatierra was the first U.S. court case to challenge the segregation of Mexican American public school students. In 1930, with the help of lawyers from the League of United Latin American Citizens (LULAC), several parents in Del Rio, Texas, filed suit against the school district, charging that Mexican American students were being denied the privileges granted to other white students (Mexican Americans being regarded by Texas law as white).

In February 1930, the Del Rio school board was set to vote on the proposed expansion of several elementary schools. Their plans included the addition of five rooms to the existing two-room school building for Mexican American students. In March, Jesús Salvatierra and several other parents filed a lawsuit against the school district, seeking an injunction to end the racial segregation of white and Mexican American students. The parents argued that the school district's policies were designed to "completely segregate" Mexican American students from white students in the same grade.

According to the 1876 state constitution, school districts in Texas could maintain separate schools for white and "colored" students. Although "colored" students were considered to be those of African descent, the school district maintained separate school facilities for Anglo, African American, and Mexican American students. According to the plaintiffs, segregating Mexican American students from other white students was illegal, since Mexican Americans were white under state law.

The school district argued that Mexican American students had been segregated because of their special educational needs and not because of their race. Specifically, it was argued, the Mexican American students were much less proficient in English than their Anglo classmates. In addition, many Mexican American students were said to start class late in the school year because they were from migrant working families and typically missed several weeks or months of school. Thus, in the eyes of the school district, the educational interests of Mexican American students were best served by placing them in separate schools in which they could learn from teachers who were trained to teach English language and citizenship skills. The practice of segregation was said to offer a "fair opportunity" to all students because it enabled the district to meet the particular educational needs of all its students.

The Texas District Court of Val Verde County ruled that the school district had illegally segregated Mexican American students on the basis of race. Since Mexican Americans were considered white under Texas law, the court found, Mexican American students should not be segregated from other white students. The court issued an injunction that prohibited the school district from continuing to segregate Mexican American students.

The school district appealed the decision to the Texas Court of Civil Appeals in San Antonio. The appellate judges agreed in part with the decision of the lower court, finding that no school district in the state had the authority to segregate Mexican American students "merely or solely" because they were Mexican American. However, the appellate court found that the school district did not deny Mexican American students educational privileges accorded to white students, accepting the argument that it segregated them on the grounds of unique educational needs. Accordingly, the appellate court lifted the injunction against the Del Rio Independent School District and allowed it to continue sending Mexican American to separate schools. The parents and their lawyers appealed their case to the U.S. Supreme Court. The case was dismissed in 1931 due to lack of jurisdiction, the high court determining that the case was not its to decide.

Despite the adverse ruling, the *Del Rio* case was a landmark step in the fight against the segregation of Mexican American students on the basis of race. That struggle was eventually won in the 1946 California case *Mendez v. Westminster School District of*

Orange County, upheld by a federal appeals court the following year.

Billie Gastic

See also: Education; League of United Latin American Citizens; *Mendez v. Westminster School District* (1946).

Further Reading

Alvarez, Robert R., Jr. "The Lemon Grove Incident: The Nation's First Successful Desegregation Court Case." *Journal of San Diego History* 32:2 (1986): 116–35.

Ferg-Cadima, James A. "Black, White and Brown: Latino School Desegregation Efforts in the Pre- and Post-*Brown v. Board of Education* Era." Report of the Mexican American Legal Defense and Education Fund (MALDEF), May 2004.

Valencia, Richard R. "The Mexican American Struggle for Equal Educational Opportunity in *Mendez v. Westminster:* Helping to Pave the Way for *Brown v. Board of Education.*" *Teachers College Record* 107:3 (March 2005): 389–423.

Día de la Raza

Día de la Raza (Day of the Race) is observed on October 12 in Latin America to commemorate—if not always celebrate—the arrival of Christopher Columbus in the Americas. Columbus Day, its counterpart in the United States, is observed on the second Monday of October.

On October 12, 1892, as the Spanish empire was celebrating the fourth centennial of the discovery, a royal decree was signed in the Franciscan Monastery of La Rábida, in Andalusia, Spain (under the regency of Marie Christine of Habsburg), expressing the intention to commemorate, either as a national holiday or as an anniversary, the day on which Columbus's ships reached the West Indies. Formal agreement from the Spanish Crown on the establishment of the holiday came shortly thereafter.

On October 4, 1917, Argentine president Hipólito Irigoyen issued a decree declaring October 12 a national holiday called the "Day of the Race." In the decree, he called on all American nations, including the United States, to mark the occasion. Día de la Raza was instituted to unite the people and countries that shared any of three main characteristics: language, ethnicity, or religion. Venezuela began celebrating the holiday in 1921, Chile in 1923, and Mexico in 1928.

In 1918, the Mexican philosopher Antonio Caso seized upon October 12 as an opportunity to praise *"la Raza,"* a term he coined to celebrate the *mestizo* race—the rich mixture of Spanish and indigenous bloodlines that characterizes much of the population of Latin America. The term "La Raza," has since been adopted by Latinos/as throughout the Americas.

The commemoration of Columbus's landing has been attended by increasing controversy and disputation over the course of recent decades, reflected in part by the variety of new designations for the event: *Día de las Culturas* (Day of the Cultures) in Costa Rica, Discovery Day in the Bahamas, and, as of 2002, *Día de la Resistencia Indígena* (Day of Indigenous Resistance) in Venezuela. Many argue that the day should not be celebrated but lamented for the devastation and suffering unleashed upon the land and its peoples. The best and true purpose of the holiday, it is said, is to call attention to the ongoing plight of indigenous populations throughout the Americas. In 1992, the United Nations Development Programme marked the quincentennial of Columbus's landing with the creation of the Latin American Indigenous People's Fund (Fondo indígenas) in cooperation with all the governments in the region, as well as those of Spain and Portugal.

All in all, Día de la Raza celebrates the evolution of a proud Latino identity while acknowledging its bittersweet history and inherent contradictions. Although the indigenous populations fought one another at various times and fought together against common enemies at other times, they forged strong alliances and enduring cultural bonds. Celebrating Día de la Raza, therefore, far from celebrating Columbus the man, means celebrating the cultural plurality and richness of the world he "discovered." Whether the event itself is regarded as a blessing or a curse, October 12 marks an opportunity for people everywhere to consider its impact on the course of history.

Anita Damjanovic

See also: Conquest of the Americas; La Raza.

Further Reading

O'Gorman, Edmundo. *The Invention of America: An Inquiry Into the Historical Nature of the New World and the Meaning of Its History.* Bloomington: Indiana University Press, 1961.

Todorov, Tzvetan. *The Conquest of America: The Question of the Other.* Trans. Richard Howard. New York: Harper & Row, 1984.

Washburn, E. Wilcomb. "The Age of Discovery." *American Historical Association Publication* 63 (1966): 1–26.

Día de los Muertos

In the early 1500s, when the Spanish conquistadors first arrived in the territory now known as Mexico, they witnessed a cultural practice among native peoples that, from their perspective, mocked death. The ritual, practiced at the end of July and beginning of August by the Purepecha, Nahua, Totonac, and Otomí peoples was, in fact, a celebration of the dead and a way to pay homage to ancestors. In pre-Hispanic societies, death was viewed not as the end of life but as a continuation of it, a passage from one state of existence to another. Thus, it was believed, the souls of the deceased return each year to visit relatives, feast on favorite foods, and be merry.

Today, more than 500 years later, Mexicans and Mexican Americans still observe the ritual known as *El Día de los Muertos,* or The Day of the Dead, in much the same way as their ancestors. One marked difference is that El Día de los Muertos is now observed in November, a result of the efforts of the Christian conquistadors to disrupt what they perceived as a barbaric ritual by aligning the celebration of the dead more closely with Christian beliefs. Thus, the Spaniards moved the date of observance to coincide with All Saints' Day (November 1) and All Souls' Day (November 2), respectively. The festivities were divided into separate commemorations of children and adults. November 1 thus became a day of remembrance for those who died as infants or children, referred to as *angelitos,* or little angels. Those who died as adults came to be honored on November 2.

In their homes, Mexicans and Mexican Americans honor dead family members by constructing altars and adorning them with *ofrendas,* or offerings. The adornments may consist of bread, flowers, symbolical decorations, and foods prepared especially for the occasion. Traditional fare includes *pan de muertos* (bread of the dead); *calaveritas de azucar* (sugar skulls), featuring the names of people on the forehead; and foods the deceased particularly liked. The offerings vary according to regional practice, but some elements are universal—colorful decorations, foods prepared for cemetery reunions, and offerings laid out on altars to commemorate the dead.

Another common element is a ceremony called *iluminación* (illumination), which typically begins in the afternoon and continues long into the night. People visit the cemetery where their loved ones are buried, decorate the gravesites with flowers, candles, and other ofrendas, sit on picnic blankets, and eat the favorite foods of their loved ones. The flowers and candles placed on the graves are said to guide the spirits of the deceased back to their living friends and relatives.

While the Day of the Dead is an age-old religious ritual, it is also a significant source of revenue for businesses that sell products related to the festivities. These include candles and votive lights, fresh seasonal flowers, baked goods, and all manner of skeletons, skulls, and coffins, including edible items made of sugar or chocolate. For outside observers, the Day of the Dead as celebrated today represents a

El Día de los Muertos (The Day of the Dead) is a centuries-old Mexican holiday, now celebrated in early November, that honors deceased family members and friends. Here, a reveler communes with the dead at a California cemetery. *(Gabriel Bouys/AFP/Getty Images)*

colorful and fascinating mix of indigenous and Roman Catholic rituals.

Anita Damjanovic

See also: Conquest of the Americas; Hispanic Heritage Month; Mexicans.

Further Reading

Salvador, R.J. "What Do Mexicans Celebrate on the Day of the Dead?" In *Death and Bereavement Around the World, Volume 2: Death and Bereavement in the Americas,* ed. John D. Morgan and Pittu Laungani. Amityville, NY: Baywood, 2003.

Toor, Frances. *A Treasury of Mexican Folkways.* New York: Crown, 1947.

Dominican Day Parade

An annual event, usually occurring on the second Sunday in August, New York City's Dominican Day Parade is an important cultural event for the local Dominican community as well as Dominicans throughout the United States. Established in 1982, the parade has become one of the largest in New York, with more than 500,000 people lining the streets to witness the event. The parade originates at Thirty-sixth Street and Sixth Avenue, traveling up Sixth Avenue to Sixty-second Street.

The Dominican Day Parade was organized to commemorate the anniversary of the beginning of the national war for restoration of Dominican Independence on August 16, 1863. Yet the importance of the parade transcends history, celebrating Dominican pride and cultural identity in America and the continued connection to the island. As a tribute to their country's fight for independence and their own pride in culture, community, and national identity, participants don traditional Dominican clothing and carry their country's flag. The red, white, and blue colors of the Dominican Republic are seen everywhere: in clothes, face paint, and the flags draped over the shoulders of many revelers. Those in attendance enjoy watching the costumed dancers—many of whom do the national dance, the merengue—and ethnically decorated floats, listening to Dominican music, and eating traditional island food.

Predominantly a celebration of Dominican American pride and culture, the parade also attracts participants and spectators from other Latino communities in New York City and surrounding areas. The increasing popularity and size of the parade is due largely to the increased immigration of Latinos/as, particularly Dominicans—the fastest-growing and second-largest Latino group in the New York metropolitan area.

And while it is primarily a cultural event, the New York Dominican Day Parade is increasingly a place of consumer capitalism. The occasion provides local businesses an ideal venue to showcase their products. Many larger companies have also chosen to participate in the parade, taking advantage of the public relations benefits associated with cultural enrichment, facilitating brand and product awareness, and building consumer loyalty in the Dominican and broader Latino communities. Likewise, many politicians also appear at the parade in order to show their respect to and support for the Dominican (and Latino) community, and through their presence possibly to gain support from their constituents in the next elections. Especially conspicuous at the event are the many charitable organizations that come to promote their services to the community. Typical visitors and participants are health clinics and shelters. Among those who marched in the 2008 parade, for instance, was Kathryn Soman, director of communications and external affairs for Health Plus, a not-for-profit managed care organization, who served as the International Madrina (godmother) for the parade. Above all, however, the day and all the festivities associated with it are a celebration of a unique culture and an occasion for Dominicans to demonstrate their patriotism and their ethnic pride.

Anita Damjanovic

See also: Dominicans; New York.

Further Reading

Egbert, Bill. "Wave of Pride on 6th." *New York Daily News,* August 13, 2007.

Phillips, Anna. "Thousands Brave Rain for Dominican Day Parade." *The Sun,* August 11, 2008.

Portlock, Sarah. "Dominicans Celebrate 25th Parade." *The Sun,* August 13, 2007.

Rosario, Frank. "Dominicans Go Grande." *New York Post,* August 11, 2008.

Dominicans

Dominicans constitute the fourth largest Latino nationality in the United States, after Mexicans, Puerto Ricans, and Cubans. At the turn of the twenty-first century, the Dominican Republic was one of the largest sources of immigration to the United States. The largest Dominican communities are found in the Northeast, particularly New York City.

According to the 2000 U.S. Census, approximately 765,000 Dominicans and Dominican Americans resided in the United States at the start of the twenty-first century. Estimates are unreliable, however, since undocumented immigrants comprise a relatively large segment of the Dominican community. At least one source put the figure as high as 938,000 in the same year. Whatever the actual population, the Dominican community in America has grown especially rapidly in the last half century. Between 1961 and 1986 alone, more than 400,000 Dominicans immigrated legally to the U.S. mainland, while another 44,000 migrated to Puerto Rico; an untold number of others settled in both places illegally.

Early Migration

Relatively few Dominicans migrated to the United States before the 1960s. From 1930 to 1961 dictator Rafael Trujillo ruled the Dominican Republic and sought to limit emigration from the Caribbean nation by issuing few passports. Following Trujillo's assassination in Santo Domingo on May 30, 1961, the island republic entered a period of political instability, as Trujillo had not designated a successor. In December 1962, Dominicans elected Juan Bosch as their new president. Bosch promoted left-wing policies and sought to improve relations with President Fidel Castro of Cuba. This move concerned right-wing opposition in the Dominican Republic as well as the American government, and in September 1963 Bosch was overthrown in a military coup. Civil war erupted in 1965 when Bosch's supporters launched an uprising to reinstate him as the head of government. President Lyndon Johnson sent U.S. Marines to the Dominican Republic that same year to ensure that a second Communist government would not take hold in the Caribbean.

Joaquin Balaguer, one of Trujillo's associates, assumed power in 1966. However, persecution and violence against Bosch's supporters continued well into the mid-1970s, and several thousand Dominicans were killed, tortured, or imprisoned. Most Dominican emigration in the 1960s and 1970s was thus politically motivated, as thousands sought refuge in Puerto Rico or the mainland United States. Unlike Cubans fleeing Castro, however, Dominican refugees were not officially recognized by the U.S. government and were not granted political asylum.

From the 1980s and to the present day, Dominican migration has been fueled primarily by economic, rather than political, factors. As the nation's economy entered a recession and unemployment rose, large numbers of Dominicans migrated to the United States, attracted by the prospects of higher wages and opportunities for work. Dominican migration has been described as a *cadena* (chain) network that systematically links one migrant to another. A common trend is for one Dominican to make a solo voyage to the United States, find employment and a place to live, and then sponsor a relative to follow. Most Dominican immigrants have entered the United States through the family reunification provisions of federal immigration law.

Settlement in New York

For several decades, the New York metropolitan area has served as the primary destination for Dominican immigrants; fully two-thirds of all Dominican Americans live in or around New York City. In the early days of migration, Dominicans concentrated in the Lower East Side of Manhattan. As more, wealthier Dominicans sought refuge in the United States during the 1960s and 1970s, they began settling in middle-class communities of Queens and Long Island. Today, the largest Dominican enclave is located in Washington Heights, on the Upper West Side of Manhattan. An estimated one-third of all New York Dominicans reside in Washington Heights, affectionately known by Dominicans as *Quisqueya Heights.*

Historically, many Dominican immigrants found work in New York's manufacturing sector, especially the garment industry. Deindustrialization since the 1980s has led to a decline in manufacturing jobs in the city, and most Dominican immigrants are now employed in service occupations in the secondary labor market (as janitors or restaurant workers, for example). Nevertheless, a sizable professional middle class and self-employed class have emerged. Dominicans own a large majority of the bodegas (Latino grocery stores) in New York and run numerous taxi operations on the outer edges of the city. Dominican students account for more than half of the enrollment at Hostos Community College in the Bronx and large enrollments at other colleges of the City University of New York.

As Dominicans have migrated, settled, and become an integral part of life in New York City, they have encountered competition and conflict with various established ethnic and religious groups. Puerto Rican residents have accused Dominican newcomers of undercutting wages, usurping jobs, and taking over the bodega trade. In the 1970s, tensions with Jewish residents increased as Dominicans sought greater involvement in local school boards and educational policies. African Americans at times have accused Dominican business owners of overcharging customers. At the same time, Dominicans—whose ancestry includes European, African, and Amerindian elements—face a rigid racial dichotomy new to their experience and identity whereby they are identified as simply "black" by mainstream American society.

Transnationalism

Dominicans have one of the highest degrees of transnationalism of any contemporary immigrant group in America, meaning that they participate in the social, cultural, political, and economic life of their homeland as well as the United States. Dominicans working in the United States send large portions of their wages to relatives back home; indeed, such remittances constitute the second-largest sector of the Dominican national economy after tourism. Dominicans living abroad who make return trips to their homeland represent about 20 percent of all tourists to the Dominican Republic. Every major political party in the Dominican Republic maintains an office in New York City, and Dominican politicians make frequent campaign trips to the city. Transnationalism between the Dominican Republic and the United States is further enhanced by dual citizenship. The Dominican constitution confers citizenship to children of Dominican parents who are born outside the country. With the growing number of Dominicans living in the United States, and as modern communications technologies connect more and more individuals in the two countries, transnationalism ensures all the more that immigrants from the island will continue to Dominicanize the United States and Americanize the Dominican Republic.

Justin D. García

See also: Alvarez, Julia; Dominican Day Parade.

Further Reading

Buffington, Sean T. "Dominican Americans." Countries and Their Cultures. http://www.everyculture.com.

González, Juan. *Harvest of Empire: A History of Latinos in America.* New York: Viking, 2000.

Guarnizo, Luis E. "Los Dominicanyorks: The Making of a Binational Society." In *Challenging Fronteras: Structuring Latina and Latino Lives in the U.S.* New York: Routledge, 1997.

Pessar, Patricia R. *A Visa for a Dream: Dominicans in the United States.* Boston: Allyn and Bacon, 1995.

E

East L.A. Thirteen

In March 1968, Chicano students in East Los Angeles organized a massive high school walkout—or "blowout"—to protest inadequate and unequal educational facilities. Prior to the walkout, students and activists had voiced their frustration about the educational system, citing rundown school buildings, the lack of books and other materials, the absence of bilingual education, high dropout rates, and classroom overcrowding. They demanded an end to systems of tracking (whereby students were placed into either college-bound classes, vocational training classes, or remedial classes) and called for the hiring of Chicano teachers and administrators. After repeated requests had gone unheeded, more than 10,000 students walked out of classes at twenty high schools throughout Los Angeles.

The students' demands were initially ignored, and community leaders were blamed for prompting the walkout. Thus, in the wake of the demonstrations, thirteen community leaders and college students—but not a single high school student—were indicted by a grand jury: Sal Castro, Moctezuma Esparza, Henry Gómez, Fred López, Carlos Montes, Carlos Muñoz, Jr., Cruz Olmeda, Ralph Ramírez, Joe Razo, Eliezer Risco, David Sánchez, Patricio Sánchez, and Richard Vigil. The community activists, who had been involved in a variety of local organizations and political struggles, were already well known among law enforcement authorities. The defendants were accused of instigating the student protesters, a situation that served to undermine the organizational role of the high school leaders. In reality, the young students were inspired but not controlled by the older activists. The aftermath of the demonstration also brought a severe backlash against community organizations from authorities, who raided the offices of *La Raza* (the Chicano newspaper) and the Brown Berets (a Chicano nationalist youth organization).

While the charges against the thirteen defendants included a variety of misdemeanors, ranging from disturbing the peace to trespassing on school grounds, each was also charged with the felony of conspiracy. The latter charge, which carried a sentence of up to forty-five years in prison, was often used against groups that engaged in organized protests and acts of civil disobedience during the 1950s and 1960s. Facing significant jail time, the activists inspired a wave of protest from the Chicano community, which began to call them the East L.A. Thirteen. Their lawyer and local supporters held street marches, gave public speeches, and used other tactics, in and out of the courtroom, to call attention to their cause.

The case of the East L.A. Thirteen came to be associated with a subsequent incident in 1968 and another set of Latino defendants—the Biltmore Six, accused of arson and conspiracy at the Biltmore Hotel in Los Angeles during a speech by Governor Ronald Reagan. Three of the East L.A. Thirteen, Moctezuma Esparza, Carlos Montes, and Ralph Ramírez, were also indicted in the latter case. Lawyer Oscar Acosta, whose style and tactics in the courtroom reflected the antiestablishment views of his clients, defended both groups of defendants. Arguing that the proceedings were discriminatory because of the racial composition of the jury, Acosta succeeded in obtaining a mistrial for his clients in the first Biltmore Six trial and an acquittal in the second trial. To support his defense in both cases and to further the political interests of the Chicano community in general, Acosta established the Chicano Legal Defense Fund, which was backed by prominent figures in the Chicano community.

With the support of the American Civil Liberties Union, the case of the East L.A. Thirteen was dismissed later in 1968 on constitutional grounds that the defendants' First Amendment rights of free speech and free association had been breached. In the years that followed, members of the original East L.A. Thirteen have continued to play an important role in the Chicano community as leaders, educators, activists, and artists. Esparza, for example, went on to become a successful film producer. His credits include *The Milagro Bean Field War* (1988), *Selena* (1997), and *Walkout* (2006), an HBO television movie based on the East Los Angeles student strike and its aftermath. The story of the East L.A. Thirteen itself continues to inspire Chicano youth and community activists to challenge inadequate schools, overzealous agents of the criminal justice system, and other manifestations of racism and discrimination in communities throughout the United States.

Sarah Hentges

See also: Acosta, Oscar; Blowouts; Brown Berets; East Los Angeles; Education.

Further Reading

Haney-López, Ian F. *Racism on Trial: The Chicano Fight for Justice.* Cambridge, MA: Harvard University Press, 2003.

Vigil, Ernesto B. *The Crusade for Justice: Chicano Militancy and the Government's War on Dissent.* Madison: University of Wisconsin Press, 1999.

East Los Angeles

Located a few miles outside of downtown Los Angeles, East Los Angeles (also known as "East Los" or "East LA") is a community nestled among the hills on the east side of the Los Angeles River. One of the largest and oldest Latin American communities in the United States, East Los Angeles is a place of great importance for Latinos/as in light of the civil rights campaigns, social injustices, and level of cultural awareness associated with the area. As summarized by the Chicano studies scholar and historian Rodolfo F. Acuña: "[s]ocial scientists have identified East Los Angeles with the Sleepy Lagoon case, the Pachuco Riots, the East L.A. school walkouts, and the 1970 Chicano Moratorium. East Los Angeles is where the Chicano journalist Rubén Salazar was killed, where lowriders cruised Whittier Boulevard."

East Los Angeles is a community that represents change in Latino identity—a Mexican community in the midst of a major U.S. metropolis. East Los Angeles is a model city for many Latinos/as in the United States, as it is deeply connected to its Mexican roots yet aware of its own place in American life and history.

The history of Mexicans in East Los Angeles is closely intertwined with that of greater Los Angeles itself. Mexicans have resided in the area from the very origins of the city, and, since the early twentieth century, Mexican immigrants and Mexican Americans have made up a majority of the population of East Los Angeles. Indeed, many immigrant groups traditionally have found East Los Angeles a welcoming area. Although their presence is not as prominent as it once was, many Japanese, African, Russian, and Jewish Americans at one time or another called this area home in significant numbers; other Latin American immigrants, such as Salvadorians and Guatemalans, now reside in the area as well.

East Los Angeles evolved into a dynamic urban setting with the rise of Los Angeles itself as a metropolitan center in the late nineteenth and early twentieth centuries. The development of a large-scale interurban railroad—the Southern Pacific Railroad in the mid-1870s—made East Los Angeles and surrounding neighborhoods, such as Boyle Heights, Commerce, and City Terrace, convenient places to live, given the easy access to other parts of town and the low cost of living. With better transportation, moreover, immigrants could provide a strong and steady workforce for the several industrial areas of the city.

At the same time, however, racism and economic prejudice were integral parts of the history of East Los Angeles, at least insofar as Mexicans and members of the other minority groups were concerned. For example, working-class Mexicans residing in the areas now known as Lincoln Park and Plaza de la Raza (previously referred to as "little Mexico" and "Sonoratown") were forbidden from living in, or even entering, the richer white neighborhoods of Los Angeles. These conditions, along with urban sprawl resulting from the development of the downtown area, contributed to the formation of modern-day East Los Angeles.

In the second half of the twentieth century, East Los Angeles became increasingly beset by many of the problems associated with inner-city life in modern America. Chronic poverty and unemployment, gang violence, drug trafficking, police abuse, and racism in many forms contributed to a dangerous and declining quality of life. The gang problem was especially intractable, making East Los Angeles notorious in the media and public consciousness. The many murals and paintings that adorn street-corner walls and the graffiti, or *placas,* designating which gangs lay claim to the area exemplify the culture of territorial violence.

For many Latinos/as, "East Los" has also been a place of triumph and celebration. Such organizations as the East Los Angeles Community Union and others have fought for economic self-determination and the rights of Latino/as living in the area. In this spirit, East Los Angeles is a place of hope, cultural identity, and historical resonance whose reputation as a strong Latino community contributes vitally to the diversity of greater Los Angeles and the entire United States.

Grant Joseph Silva

The overwhelmingly Latino community of East Los Angeles has been an epicenter of Chicano history, culture, economic difficulty, social injustice, and protest in the post–World War II era. *(Hector Mata/AFP/Getty Images)*

See also: Blowouts; Chicano Movement; Gangs; Los Angeles; Mexicans; Sleepy Lagoon Case.

Further Reading

Acuña, Rodolfo. *A Community Under Siege: A Chronicle of Chicanos East of the Los Angeles River (1945–1975).* Los Angeles: Chicano Studies Research Center, University of California at Los Angeles, 1984.

Chavez, John R. *Eastside Landmark: A History of the East Los Angeles Community Union, 1968–1993.* Stanford, CA: Stanford University Press, 1998.

Rodríguez, Luis J. *Always Running: La Vida Loca, Gang Days in L.A.* New York: Simon and Schuster, 2005.

Romo, Ricardo. *East Los Angeles: History of a Barrio.* Austin: University of Texas Press, 1983.

Ecuadorians

According to the U.S. Census Bureau, there were a total of 436,409 Ecuadorian Americans—immigrants from Ecuador or their descendants—residing legally in the United States as of 2005, representing about 1 percent of the Latino population and 0.15 percent of the total U.S. population. In addition, there were believed to be an equal number of undocumented Ecuadorian Americans. Of those not born in the United States, approximately 67 percent were not citizens, which in many cases reflected their desire to return to their home country.

The Ecuadorian population in the United States grew tremendously during the 1960s, boosted especially by two events at mid-decade. In 1965, the U.S. Immigration and Nationality Act instituted a national quota system that made it easier for Latin Americans to immigrate, precisely at a time when commercial air travel made long-distance international travel affordable for many ordinary people. Second, Ecuador's Land Reform, Idle Lands, and Settlement Act of 1964 redistributed agricultural land from absentee landlords to the peasants who farmed it; by choice or necessity, many peasants sold the land and relocated to cities or foreign countries—especially Venezuela and the United States.

Persistent economic, social, and political turmoil in succeeding decades resulted in an increasing flow of Ecuadorian immigrants. An economic crash in

1999 triggered a sharp spike in migration to the United States and western Europe. The following year, after the Ecuadorian currency (the *sucre*) went into hyperinflation and the U.S. dollar was adopted as the national currency, more than 10 percent of the Ecuadorian population reportedly left the country—most for the United States. In the typical immigration pattern, most initial immigrants have been middle-aged men whose wives or partners eventually join them, leaving behind children who are cared for by family members; the children usually do not come until the parents are financially established, by whatever means.

Ecuadorian immigrants come to the United States for a variety of reasons and under different terms, but most often for the prospect of economic improvement. The most common pull factor is a relative or prospective employer who offers a place to live, often with the promise of employment. Some arrive on a tourist visa and overstay their visit; others come with false passports. The number of Ecuadorian students attending universities in the United States has also increased in recent years; although a college education is likely to improve one's job prospects—which in turn might help obtain a work visa—most students opt to return to Ecuador. Second-generation Ecuadorians who complete a college education generally enjoy better job prospects than their parents.

The largest Ecuadorian community in the United States is located in New York City, numbering an estimated 114,900. Others are found in major metropolitan areas of Illinois, California, Florida, and Puerto Rico. Ecuadorian Americans generally work in the unskilled service sectors, such as domestic jobs, maintenance, restaurants, and construction. The average household income reported for Ecuadorian Americans in the year 2005 was $46,992. In recent years, more immigrants from the Ecuadorian middle class have been leaving the homeland for the United States, most of them settling among friends and relatives in New York and Miami. Upper-class Ecuadorians can easily move between Ecuador and the United States, since visas are granted on the basis of economic status and professional standing.

Urban areas with large Ecuadorian American populations generally have a wide variety of social and cultural organizations. Activities include events that commemorate national civic celebrations, leagues for soccer and *ecuavoley* (a modification of volleyball with three players per team), and tournaments of a national card game known as *cuarenta* (forty). In New York City, the Ecuador Sporting Club in Queens has welcomed Ecuadorian Americans since the late 1950s. The number of Ecuadorian organizations in the United States proliferated with the rise in immigration beginning in the 1960s. By the late seventies, the growing number of Ecuadorian Americans who attended college founded additional organizations to spread the national culture. In 1986, Casa de la Cultura Ecuatoriana "Benjamín Carrión," the central institution for the promotion of cultural development in Ecuador, formally recognized Casa de la Cultura Ecuatoriana Núcleo Internacional de Nueva York as an institution to spread the Ecuadorian culture through art exhibitions, literature, conferences, concerts, seminars, workshops, and dance presentations in New York.

In 1996, the group Ecuatorianos Residentes en el Exterior (Ecuadorian Residents Overseas) was granted approval for dual nationality by the homeland government; ten years later, Ecuadorians living in foreign countries were granted the right to vote in national elections. These developments reflected the desire of many Ecuadorian immigrants, including Ecuadorian Americans, to remain connected to their roots. Most who live overseas await economic, social, and political improvements in Ecuador that will allow them to return to their families, friends, and familiar way of life. In the meantime, Ecuadorian Americans work to make a living for their families and send remittances home, while struggling to raise awareness of their contributions to the economy and diversity of the Latino population in the United States.

Karina R. Vega-Villa

See also: New York.

Further Reading

Cho, Sang-Wook, and Julián Díaz. "Trade Liberalization in Latin America and Europe: The Migration Initiatives Appeal 2007." International Organization for Migration, Switzerland, 2007.

Hanratty, Dennis, ed. *Ecuador: A Country Study.* 3rd ed. Washington, DC: Federal Research Division, Library of Congress, 1991.
Pew Hispanic Center. http://www.pewhispanic.org.
Pineo, Ronn. *Ecuador and the United States: Useful Strangers.* Athens: University of Georgia Press, 2008.
Striffler, Steve. *In the Shadows of State and Capital: The United Fruit Company, Popular Struggle, and Agrarian Restructuring in Ecuador, 1900–1995.* Durham, NC: Duke University Press, 2002.

Education

The roots of Latino education in the United States reach back to the Spanish conquest and colonization of North America and the Caribbean. U.S. military victories in the nineteenth century (the Mexican War and Spanish-American War) also played a significant role in shaping this history. While the educational pursuits of Latinos/as in America through the centuries have been marked by the struggle to overcome barriers, there have also been important achievements and significant advancement.

Colonial Missions

With the Spanish conquest during the sixteenth century, native peoples and later *mestizos* (individuals of mixed Spanish and indigenous ancestry) in Latin America became subject to an educational system that had as one of its main purposes the promotion of Spanish culture, which was regarded as inherently superior to native cultures. The primary form of education for the indigenous in Latin America took place in Catholic missions that extended into present-day California, New Mexico, Florida, and Texas. Spanish priests were guided primarily by a belief that non-Christians were uncivilized, and conceived it their duty to convert the natives and instill Christian virtues. Although not all natives became part of the missions, those who did were often cajoled or forced by the Spanish military to remain in the settlements. In addition to Christian faith and practice, the missionaries also taught Native Americans to read and write in Spanish. Most of the missions became secularized after the independence of Mexico in 1821.

Education and Assimilation

Upon the conclusion of the Mexican War in 1848, northern Mexico was annexed by the United States under the Treaty of Guadalupe Hidalgo, resulting in the incorporation of many former Mexican citizens. Mexican Americans in the region would now be educated in parochial schools built in the years immediately following the war. Public schools offered instruction on Mexican culture, and Spanish was often spoken. However, with the influx of settlers from the East and a growing Anglo population—which took greater control of local school policies—the influence of Mexican Americans on education gradually waned. For example, public officials began eliminating classes on Mexican history and culture from the school curriculum. Thus, while the spread of public education enabled more Mexican Americans to take advantage of free public schooling by the 1870s, the opportunity came with a certain cost. Throughout the Southwest, Mexican American children were forced to attend segregated schools, commonly referred to as "Mexican schools." New Mexico began segregating schools for Mexican American children in 1872, and Texas enforced school segregation by the 1880s. Moreover, between 1870 and 1890, municipalities throughout the Southwest passed English-language laws that restricted or even prohibited the use of the Spanish language in public schools.

Upon the conclusion of the Spanish-American War in 1898, when Puerto Rico was ceded to the United States, learning English was identified as a primary means of facilitating the Americanization process and became a focus of public education on the island. In 1899, the Code of School Laws required that all teachers in Puerto Rican schools speak English. Shortly thereafter, however, U.S. General John Eaton was dispatched to supervise education in Puerto Rico, and he called for a somewhat different approach. Although learning English was still regarded as a high priority, Eaton supported the continued use of, and respect for, the Spanish language.

During the first half of the twentieth century, therefore, no consistent, integrated approach toward education was ever implemented on the island. One result was that Puerto Ricans who moved from the island to the U.S. mainland had difficulty in school because of their limited command of English. The problem became especially acute after 1917, when the Jones Act granted full U.S. citizenship to Puerto Ricans. Many migrated to New York City, Chicago, and other urban areas in the Northeast and Midwest; by 1968, there were an estimated 300,000 Puerto Rican students in New York City schools. Cultural and language biases in intelligence testing often incorrectly labeled many of these students as cognitively deficient. Many were tracked into classes for students with "low IQs."

One organization that questioned the use of intelligence testing among Puerto Rican students in the 1930s was Madres Y Padres Por Niños Hispanos (Mothers and Fathers in Support of Hispanic Children). Among the first academic critics of cultural bias in the construction and use of intelligence testing was the Mexican American activist and educator George I. Sánchez. In 1932, Sánchez questioned the then accepted idea that Spanish-speaking children were somehow genetically and culturally inferior to white students based on the results of IQ tests of the time. Sánchez's research and activism regarding Latino education helped lay the foundation for future bilingual programs such as Project Head Start in the 1960s.

Segregation

In the course of one decade, the 1930s, the number of school-age children in the Mexican American population doubled. As of 1930, Texas was the state with the smallest percentage of Mexican American residents attending public schools (50 percent); New Mexico had the highest (74 percent). Throughout the Southwest, however, the segregation of Mexican American students into substandard and inferior schools represented the norm.

In 1931, Mexican American parents in California waged the first successful lawsuit against school segregation in the United States, *Alvarez v. Lemon Grove,* after the community created a separate elementary school for Mexican students. In San Diego County Superior Court, Judge Claude Chambers ruled in favor of the parents, who had filed a petition asking the court to force the school board to reinstate the children into their original (integrated) school. "The exclusion was clearly an attempt at racial segregation by separating and segregating all the children of Mexican parentage . . . from the children of American, European and Japanese parentage," argued the parents in their legal petition. Accordingly, they maintained, the school board had "no legal right or power to exclude . . . [the Mexican children] from receiving instruction upon an equal basis." Judge Chambers affirmed this view, ordering the school board to reinstate the children at the main school: "To separate all the Mexicans in one group can only be done by infringing the laws of the State of California," he ruled. "I believe that this separation denies the Mexican children the presence of the American children, which is so necessary to learn the English language." The efforts of the school board, the resistance of the parents, and the court's ruling foreshadowed struggles in American education over the next several decades.

In 1947, in the case of *Mendez v. Westminster School District,* judges in the U.S. Court of Appeals for the Ninth Circuit ruled that the practice of segregating Mexican and American students under California law—which provided for the segregation of the "children of Chinese, Japanese or Mongolian parentage" but not "the segregation of school children because of their Mexican blood"—was unconstitutional. This challenge to the principle of "separate but equal" in education served as an important precedent for *Brown v. Board of Education,* the 1954 U.S. Supreme Court ruling that would declare school segregation to be unconstitutional.

Bilingual Education

Notwithstanding the generally inferior educational opportunities available to Mexican American youth, Mexican-only schools, which emphasized bilingual education, offered significant opportunities for Mexican American students in the early and mid-twentieth century. In fact, bilingual education had long been a part of Latino education in America. In 1887, for example, Olives Villanueva Aoy opened a bilingual private school for Mexican American students in El Paso, Texas; by the early 1900s, the school had the best attendance rate in the city. In 1909, the state legislature of New Mexico established a school specifically to educate Spanish-speakers and prepare them to be public school teachers. What distinguished these schools from the "Mexican Schools" was not only the inclusion of Spanish-language instruction, but also a higher quality of instruction, more resources, and better facilities. In 1957, the League of United Latin American Citizens opened a preschool for Spanish-dominant Latino children in Ganado, Texas, called the Little School of the 400. The preschoolers were taught 400 words of basic English based on the premise that this would allow them to successfully complete first grade once they entered public school. The following summer, LULAC initiated this project in several other Texas cities, including Sugar Land, Aldine, Rosenberg, Edna, and Fort Stockton. In 1959, the state legislature passed Texas House Bill 51—officially titled the Preschool Instructional Classes for Non-English Speaking Children and based on the Little School of the 400. By the following year, the program employed 614 teachers with more than 15,000 students in attendance. Students who attended these voluntary programs showed higher first-grade completion rates than those students who did not attend. Based on the concept of early educational intervention, the project became a model for the federal Head Start program initiated by the Johnson administration in 1965.

Meanwhile, African Americans and Puerto Ricans were fighting for full school integration in New York City schools beginning in the 1950s. In 1966, plans were made for the city's first fully integrated school in Harlem, but the plan was ultimately cut. In response, Puerto Ricans in the Ocean Hill–Brownsville section of Brooklyn established one of the first bilingual programs that was not federally subsidized, relying on community funding. In another effort to institute bilingual education in New York, Puerto Ricans in the Two Bridges section of lower Manhattan fought for community control of public schools in the early 1970s. Although they were initially successful in that campaign and instituted bilingual education, they were ultimately unable to compete with better-funded campaigns of the teachers' union. In 1972, the Puerto Rican Legal Defense and Education Fund and ASPIRA, founded by Antonia Pantoja in 1961 as an education advocacy organization for Puerto Rican students, sued the New York City Board of Education, alleging that Puerto Rican students were being denied equal educational opportunities based on the requirement of English language proficiency. The suit proved successful, and bilingual education in New York City became a legal mandate. In Texas, however—despite passage of the federal Bilingual Education Act of 1968—bilingual education would not be mandated until 1981, after twelve years of legislative struggles.

Student Walkouts

From the late 1960s to the mid-1970s, Chicano and Puerto Rican students pushed for a variety of much-needed educational reforms. The temporary wooden classroom buildings widely used for educating Mexican American children had been identified as "firetraps," to which teachers were often sent as punishment or for training before they began teaching at "regular" ("white") schools. In the late 1960s, Latino students in California and Texas began confronting local administrators about the conditions of their schools and the various forms of discrimination they experienced. They were being disproportionately tracked into vocational programs with limited opportunities to enroll in college preparatory courses. The vast majority of schools also had explicit rules against speaking Spanish, and many Latino students were assigned janitorial duties as a form of discipline.

Of the many high school walkouts—which participants referred to as "blowouts"—those in East Los Angeles and Crystal City, Texas, were particularly significant. In spirit and even in organization, the walkouts were also related to the Chicano Movement then under way and the spirit of cultural pride and militancy it engendered. In East Los Angeles, Mexican American students at several high schools began organized efforts to gain educational improvements, conducting student surveys and preparing a list of demands to present to the board of education. In early 1968, just before they were to present their demands, the administration at Wilson High School canceled a student stage performance, which prompted Mexican American students to declare a spontaneous walkout on March 1. Three other East Los Angeles high schools—Garfield, Roosevelt, and Lincoln—joined the walkout, and by mid-March some 15,000 students were boycotting East Los Angeles schools. Although the blowouts were generally peaceful, school authorities requested the presence of police, who began treating the protestors with force. Supportive parents and other adults in the community formed the Educational Issues Coordinating Committee to assist the students in presenting their demands to the board of education. There were thirty-six demands in all, including the rehabilitation of school buildings that were not earthquake-proof, the addition of courses that focused on Mexican American history and culture, the end of the "No Spanish" rule, more college preparatory courses for Mexican Americans, and an increase in the hiring of Mexican American teachers, administrators, and staff. The school board ultimately agreed to some of these demands.

In the fall of 1969, students in the small town of Crystal City, Texas, likewise staged a successful and historic walkout. Although Mexican Americans accounted for more than 80 percent of the student population, school officials had allowed only one Mexican American cheerleader on the high school squad. When school officials turned a deaf ear to Chicano protests, the students staged a walkout. Several of the protesters received threats of violence from Anglo community members, and student organizers sent representatives to Washington, D.C., to request assistance from the Justice Department. They returned to Crystal City with two federal mediators. Students demanded the right to speak Spanish, more Mexican American teachers and staff, and a more rigorous curriculum to prepare for college. They also demanded that teachers, administration, and staff learn about Mexican traditions and culture and refrain from calling Mexican American students racist names. As in East Los Angeles, the Crystal City walkouts brought increased public attention to the issue of Latino education and led to significant reforms in staffing, curriculum, and culture at public schools in the American Southwest.

Latino students did not resort to school walkouts of this magnitude again until 1994, when Proposition 187 was presented to California voters as a statewide ballot initiative. Among other things, Proposition 187 called for the denial of educational services to undocumented immigrants and their children or anyone "reasonably suspected" of being an "illegal alien." Less than a week before the November 1994 vote, approximately 10,000 middle and high school students (primarily Latino) walked out of thirty-two California schools to protest the state initiative—which passed easily but was later overturned by a federal court.

Attainment Levels

Latinos/as in the United States have historically completed fewer years of formal education than the general population, and their struggle for equal and quality education persists today. In 1940, the median number of years of schooling for Mexican American adults in California was 7.5, compared to 10.5 years for whites. In 1975, according to the U.S. Census Bureau, there was a 26.6 percent difference in high-school completion rates between whites and Latinos/as nationwide. The gap remained about the same for the next decade and a half, indeed climbing slightly to 27.5 percent in 1989. According to President George H.W. Bush's National Education Goals Report in 1991, high-school completion rates between 1975 and 1990 rose 12 percent for African American students and 2 percent for white students, while decreasing 3 percent for Latino students. The trend has continued into the first decade of the twenty-first century, with Latinos/as recording the second-highest dropout rate (after Native Americans) of any ethnic or national group. Latino students, moreover, have also continued to live in areas of concentrated poverty, attending overcrowded and segregated schools with few or no Latino or bilingual teachers (3 percent of public school teachers in 1988). These conditions have been directly related to educational attainment, or lack thereof. In the 1990s, Latino students at every age were enrolled below grade level compared to white or African American students; 22 percent of those six to eight years old were enrolled below grade level, rising to 48 percent among those aged fifteen to sixteen.

These conditions have continued in the following decade. Among the three largest Latino subgroups in the United States—Cuban Americans, Mexican Americans, and Puerto Ricans—the U.S. Census Bureau reported that, as of 2004, Cuban Americans enjoyed the highest high-school graduation rate (70 percent), followed by Puerto Ricans (60 percent), and Mexican Americans (50 percent). As a group, however,

27 percent of Latino adults in the United States have less than a ninth-grade education (versus 4 percent for the white population), 43 percent have less than a high-school education, and 57 percent have graduated from high school (versus 85 percent for whites).

Higher Education

Between 1980 and 1990, Latino enrollment in higher education grew by 60.7 percent, to approximately 758,000 students—5.5 percent of total U.S. college enrollment, compared to 3 percent in 1980. The increase continued in the 1990s, with Latino enrollment in higher education reaching 1.3 million before decade's end.

Still, in the early 2000s, 70.4 percent of all Latinos/as over the age of twenty-five had never attended college, 13 percent had attended "some" college but not completed a degree, and 8.3 percent held a bachelor's degree, while 3.1 percent had completed an advanced degree (versus 18.2 percent and 9.5 percent, respectively, for whites). The Development, Relief, and Education for Alien Minors Act, which was originally proposed in 2001, sought to make higher education more accessible to Latino immigrants by granting legal residency to undocumented students who were raised in the United States, allowing them to apply to college or to serve in the U.S. military.

An Ongoing Struggle

Although Latinos/as now constitute the largest ethnic minority group in the United States and the majority of the student population in many large school districts in the country, the struggle for educational equality is ongoing. Continued de facto segregation, a decline in support for bilingual education, and increasing immigration are among the factors that continue to impact Latino education in America. Even after the *Brown v. Board of Education* (1954) decision declared segregation unconstitutional, between 1968 and 1986 the percentage of Latinos/as who attended schools that were predominantly nonwhite increased from 54.8 percent to 71.5 percent. In Texas, as recently as the 1993–94 school year, 64 percent of all Latino students attended schools in which 70 percent or more of the students were minorities. In comparison, 49 percent of all African American students and only 7 percent of white students attended such schools. Nationally, by the mid-1990s, Latinos/as were the most segregated group of students after Native Americans; 73 percent attended classes with predominantly nonwhite students. Latinos/as in California and Texas were more segregated than African Americans in Mississippi or Alabama. The trend continues to the present day.

Manuel X. Zamarripa

See also: Bilingualism; Blowouts; Crystal City, Texas; *Del Rio Independent School District v. Salvatierra* (1930); League of United Latin American Citizens; *Mendez v. Westminster School District* (1946); Proposition 187 (1994); Proposition 227 (1998); Spanish Language; Tracking.

Further Reading

Cockcroft, James D. *Latinos in the Struggle for Equal Education.* New York: Franklin Watts, 1995.
Jiménez, Carlos M. *The Mexican American Heritage.* Berkeley, CA: TQS, 2004.
MacDonald, Victoria-María. *Latino Education in the United States: A Narrated History from 1513–2000.* New York: Palgrave MacMillan, 2004.
Meier, Matt S., and Feliciano Ribera. *Mexican Americans, American Mexicans: From Conquistadors to Chicanos.* New York: Hill and Wang, 1993.
Muñoz, Carlos, Jr. *Youth, Identity, Power: The Chicano Movement.* New York: Verso, 1989
Nieto, Sonia, ed. *Puerto Rican Students in U.S. Schools.* Mahwah, NJ: Lawrence Erlbaum, 2000.
San Miguel, Guadalupe, Jr. *"Let All of Them Take Heed": Mexican Americans and the Campaign for Educational Equality in Texas, 1910–1981.* Austin: University of Texas Press, 1987.

Escalante, Jaime (1930–)

Jaime Escalante is a Bolivian-born educator whose signature term *ganas* ("desire") epitomized his beliefs as a teacher and educational reformer at Garfield High School in Los Angeles. Escalante was born in La Paz, Bolivia, on December 31, 1930. The son of educators, he displayed a passion for numbers and mathematics beginning in early elementary school. He was much affected by his mother's use of hands-on

Bolivian immigrant Jaime Escalante, the subject of the film *Stand and Deliver* (1988), taught mathematics to inner-city students at Los Angeles's Garfield High School from 1974 to 1991. Under his guidance, students labeled "remedial" came to excel in calculus. *(AP Images)*

materials to explain mathematical concepts. He would utilize this method in his own career as a teacher.

Escalante began his career teaching mathematics and science in La Paz. Twelve years later, in 1964, he moved with his family—his wife Fabiola and son Jaimito—to the United States. After furthering his studies in mathematics and science at the University of Puerto Rico, he settled in Pasadena, California, took night courses in English proficiency, then earned his associate's degree in engineering, and finally a bachelor's degree in mathematics and electronics in 1973.

This enabled him to secure a teaching position at Garfield High School in Los Angeles, the site of his famous accomplishments and the primary setting of the film *Stand and Deliver* (1988). The film, in which Escalante is portrayed by Edward James Olmos, chronicles Escalante's success at leading students labeled "remedial" to achieve top grades in advanced-placement calculus courses. As portrayed in the movie, Escalante spent years building the school's mathematics program, raising the instructional level of his courses year by year. Student enrollment in his classes increased accordingly. Escalante also helped to recruit and work with teachers at Garfield and surrounding middle schools, training them in his instructional methods.

Escalante never accepted the term "gifted" as it applies to students. Instead, he believed that, with *ganas* and quality instruction, all students can succeed. Throughout his career at Garfield High School, he worked primarily with students from low-income, Spanish-speaking neighborhoods. His service extended beyond classroom instruction. Escalante was a positive influence on both students and teachers across the country, showing them how an accessible, knowledgeable, and caring teacher can affect students.

Escalante's teaching career at Garfield, from 1974 to 1991, was not without struggle. He battled repeatedly with school administrators and colleagues and was finally forced to leave the school. In his absence, Garfield's advanced-placement mathematics program suffered significant declines in enrollment and success.

Shortly thereafter, Escalante began working for the Sacramento School District, eventually moving on to several other professional development projects. He received funding from the National Science Foundation and other agencies to support his professional development initiatives. While devoting much of his life to the success of Latinos/as in mathematics, Escalante has also taken stands against bilingual education and in support of California Proposition 227 in 1998, the "English only" law for public schools. In retirement from teaching, Escalante has remained focused on enhancing educational opportunities for Latino youth, lecturing at schools and universities and to Latino groups. Among his many professional awards and honors is the U.S. Presidential Medal for Excellence in Education, awarded in 1988.

David Slavit and Gisela Ernst-Slavit

See also: Education; Proposition 227 (1998).

Further Reading

Byers, Ann. *Jaime Escalante: Sensational Teacher.* Springfield, NJ: Enslow, 1996.
Romero, Maritza. *Jaime Escalante: Inspiring Educator.* New York: PowerKids, 1997.

Estefan, Gloria (1957–)

Known as the "Queen of Latin Pop," Gloria Estefan emerged during the mid-1980s as one of America's most successful pop singers and songwriters. Her stardom helped pave the way for a new generation of Latino artists who revolutionized the music industry in the 1990s with sensual moves, catchy lyrics, and what came to be regarded as a Latin beat. With her band, Miami Sound Machine, Estefan internationalized ballads and dances rooted in the rhythms of her native Cuba and, after decades of earning praise from fans and critics alike, became one of the biggest crossover stars of the last quarter of the twentieth century.

Early Life

Born Gloria María Milagrosa Fajardo in Havana on September 1, 1957, to Guadalupe López and José Fajardo, the future entertainer suffered the political turmoil of her mother country. Her father's position as a bodyguard in the employ of Cuba's President Fulgencio Batista forced the family to flee the island on the eve of the 1959 coup d'état led by Fidel Castro. The family migrated to Miami, Florida, and for the next two years, they lived in a Cuban ghetto near the Orange Bowl, awaiting the failure of the Cuban Revolution. The Castro regime remained firmly in control, however, and José Fajardo was arrested and sentenced to prison in Cuba after taking part in the unsuccessful attempt to topple Castro in the U.S.-led Bay of Pigs invasion in 1961.

Giving up hope of returning to Cuba, Guadalupe began teaching at a local school. Young Gloria took care of her younger sister, Rebecca, and her father, who, after being released from prison in 1963, was diagnosed with multiple sclerosis. In an attempt to bring some relief to José, Gloria would play the guitar and sing to him. She also found comfort in her music and often played for hours, mastering the techniques that would later establish her as a great performer.

Launching a Career

In 1975, Estefan enrolled in the University of Miami on a partial scholarship to pursue a degree in psychology. That same year, her passion for music prompted her to audition, along with her cousin, Merci Murciano, for a local Cuban-American band called the Miami Latin Boys. She needed to perform only a few songs to impress the group's leader and keyboardist, her future husband, Emilio Estefan. Estefan invited Gloria and Merci to join the band. The Miami Latin Boys became the Miami Sound Machine, a change that transformed its music as well into a fusion of American pop and disco with Cuban salsa rhythms.

After four albums for CBS Records with little recognition outside Latin America, the Miami Sound Machine decided to broaden its horizons and target Europe and the United States. As a result, in 1984 Estefan and her band signed with Epic Records and released their first album in English, *Eyes of Innocence,* including the international hit "Dr. Beat." The album topped dance charts around the world. The band's unexpected success created great expectations in the industry, which were exceeded with the 1985 release of *Primitive Love,* their second album in English. It included such hits as "Bad Boy," "Words Get in the Way," and "Conga." Given Estefan's popularity and ability to steal the limelight, the band was renamed Gloria Estefan & Miami Sound Machine in 1987. Its album of the following year, *Let It Loose,* included three Top Ten hits ("Rhythm Is Gonna Get You," "Can't Stay Away from You," and "1–2–3") and earned them their first number one single ("Anything for You") and an American Music Award for Best Pop Duo/Group.

Gloria Estefan, seen here in 1987 with the Miami Sound Machine, brought the ballads and dance music of her native Cuba to an international audience. Estefan, cited as the most successful crossover Latin musician in history, recorded a number of albums in Spanish. *(Sherry Rayn Barnett/Michael Ochs Archives/Getty Images)*

Going Solo

Despite the camaraderie among the members of the group, Gloria felt the need to pursue a solo career, and in 1989 she released *Cuts Both Ways,* which returned her to the top of the charts with hit singles such as "Don't Want to Lose You," "Here We Are," "Get on Your Feet," and "Oye Mi Canto" (Listen to My Song). Estefan's meteoric rise to stardom brought her money, awards, and fame but also meant life on the road. And one tour almost ended everything. On March 20, 1990, outside Scranton, Pennsylvania, while Estefan was sleeping on board her tour bus with her husband and their first baby, a speeding trailer collided with the bus. The Latin star suffered a broken and dislocated vertebra that required extensive back surgery and physical therapy. Her convalescence kept Estefan off the road and out of the studio for more than a year, but in 1991 she returned to the fore with the release of her album *Into the Light.* The album topped the charts again, with "Live for Loving You," "Can't Forget You," and the number one hit "Coming Out of the Dark." Her successful return was confirmed in 1992 with the release of her *Greatest Hits* album, which netted Estefan a star on the Hollywood Walk of Fame.

Having made it to the top, Estefan returned to her musical roots with her next album, *Mi Tierra* (My Land), in 1993. Her first record in Spanish in almost ten years, it earned her a Grammy Award—the first of five she would receive—for Best Tropical Latin Album and a World Music Award for Best-Selling Latin Performer in 1994. Estefan's success continued with *Christmas Through Your Eyes* (1993), a holiday album; *Hold Me, Thrill Me, Kiss Me* (1994), a collection of cover tunes; and *Abriendo Puertas* (Opening Doors, 1995), her second Latin album, for which she received another Grammy Award for Best Tropical Latin Album. *Destiny* (1996) included the hit single "Reach," which was selected as the official theme of the 1996 Summer

Olympics in Atlanta. In 1998, she recorded *Gloria!* This album was followed by *Alma Caribeña* (Caribbean Soul, 2000), which earned her a Grammy Award for Best Traditional Tropical Latin Album and a Latin Grammy Award for Best Music Video for "No Me Dejes de Querer" ("Don't Stop Loving Me"), and *Greatest Hits II: 1993–2000* (2001). In 2003, with the release of *Unwrapped,* Estefan announced the end of her promotional tours.

After a thirty-year professional career and almost 50 million records sold, Gloria Estefan is the most successful crossover Latin musician in history. Her life, spent overcoming hardships and achieving her dreams, has served as an inspiration for younger generations of Latinos/as. Estefan remains staunch in her opposition to the Castro regime and is one of the most beloved members of the Cuban exile community.

Jorge Abril Sánchez

See also: Castro, Fidel; Cubans; Music; Popular Culture.

Further Reading

DeStefano, Anthony M. *Gloria Estefan: The Pop Superstar from Tragedy to Triumph.* New York: Signet, 1997.

Dirks, Christopher. *The Gloria Estefan Scrapbook: A Celebration in Words and Pictures.* New York: Citadel, 1999.

González, Fernando. *Gloria Estefan: Cuban-American Singing Star.* Boston: Houghton Mifflin, 2003.

Stefoff, Rebecca. *Gloria Estefan.* New York: Chelsea House, 1991.

F

Family and Community

Family and community have played a crucial role in the development of a Latino identity in the United States. As primary social units, family and community give Latinos/as the necessary tools—including a sense of identity and purpose—to operate within mainstream U.S. culture.

Family

Although a family is conventionally defined as a group of persons connected by blood, affinity, or law, it is difficult to reduce the Latino family to so simple a definition. A host of characteristics makes the Latino family unique and distinctive, different from many others in the modern United States.

The Latino family may be made up of members who are Mexican American (including Chicano or Tejano), Mexican, Puerto Rican, Cuban, Costa Rican, Dominican, Honduran, Guatemalan, or any other people who come from, or whose ancestors come from, Latin America. Despite the cultural diversity and its influences on the family unit, there are commonalities that most Latino families share. It is these underlying characteristics that best define the Latino family.

Latino families are typified by close-knit relationships among the members, including those of the extended family, such as aunts, uncles, and even second cousins. Nonblood relatives such as *padrinos* (godfathers) and *madrinas* (godmothers) also may be considered part of the extended family. The large family unit serves as a source of support for all members in times of need. Often, family members take an active role in the care of children and other personal matters, including the resolution of marital problems. Latinos/as are more likely to utilize and depend on their extensive family network because of their strong sense of loyalty and trust in one another.

Although other ethnic groups are also family oriented in vital ways, the concept of *familismo* is characteristic of the Latino family in particular. The term refers to the strong familial bond common among Latinos/as and reflects their deep commitment to family life. It is based on the belief that the needs of the individual are secondary to the greater good of the family. Familismo is instilled in most Latinos/as during childhood.

A foundational aspect of the modern-day Latino family is deeply rooted in traditional gender roles. In the most traditional Latino families, a family member's gender determines the responsibilities and roles to which he or she is assigned. Typically, the male is considered the head of the household; he is the primary breadwinner and decision-maker for the family. The woman, on the other hand, fulfills the role of homemaker and family caregiver.

Another key factor in the conduct of traditional family life is the concept of *machismo,* which has no simple definition in English. Machismo refers to masculinity and behaviors similar to an alpha male of a group. For Latinos, the term is often used more as an adjective (Americanized as "macho") to describe the superior role that males play in the familial structure and the widely held belief that women can be treated as subordinates. Traditionally, Latino boys are taught to behave and act "like a man." This includes the suppression of intimate or passionate feelings, open affection, and other emotions regarded as feminine. At the same time, machismo implies that a Latino male is strong and able to protect the family.

Much like machismo, the experiences of traditional Latinas are typically described by the term *marianismo.* This word has evolved from the strong influence of Christianity on Latino life, in particular the deep reverence for Jesus's mother, the Virgin Mary. Traditionally, Latina women have emulated the submissive role of women in biblical times. The Latina is considered the opposite of the male macho figure, bringing balance to the family unit. She is generally thought of as obedient, moral, venerable, and possessing strong traditional values. According to custom, her primary goal in life is to serve her spouse and children and to make every effort to ensure their daily well-being. The woman is recognized as the person who holds the entire family together and manages the household. Children revere their female elders and are often disciplined by the father if they show a lack of respect to the mother.

A strong sense of respect toward women and elders is another characteristic that defines the Latino family. Children are taught to respect and obey their parents, women, and elders. Even as adults, men and women are expected to show the same respect and reverence to their parents as they did when they were younger. (Despite these expectations, many Latino males do not give their own spouse the same respect that is owed to their mother.)

In response to the ever-increasing integration of Latinos/as into mainstream American society, the structure of the Latino family in the United States has undergone significant changes. A trend has emerged whereby the male and female play equal roles in maintaining the household. Older generations tend to stick to the traditional ways of life, while younger Latinos and Latinas have become open to new ideas. As newer generations of Latino families emerge, the traditional gender roles are becoming more relaxed. Women have broken out of the mold and are now pursuing their own careers, while men are beginning to share more of the household responsibilities. Although traditional macho husbands and submissive wives are less frequent occurrences in the modern Latino family in the United States, the notion of male dominance and the separation of perceived responsibilities are so deeply instilled in the Latino way of life that, to some degree, they play a part in even the most modern of Latino families.

Community

The Latino community in the United States is highly diverse and the fastest-growing minority group in the country. Over the years, the presence of Latinos/as in the United States has developed into a strong, influential, relatively unified voice that no longer goes unheard.

People with origins from a wide variety of Latin American regions make up the Latino community in the United States. The three most dominant countries of origin are Mexico, Puerto Rico, and Cuba. Mexico accounts for the largest number of Latinos/as in the United States, due in part to the long border between the two countries and the long history that unites them. Latinos/as from Central and South America as well as from the Dominican Republic make up a smaller yet significant number of the people in communities across the nation.

In 2000, according to the U.S. Census Bureau, approximately 35 million people—or about 12.5 percent of the nation's population—were of Hispanic or Latino origin. The distribution of Latinos/as throughout the United States is widespread, but there are distinct concentrations throughout the country. The highest percentage of Latinos/as is in the Southwest (specifically Texas, New Mexico, Arizona, and California); however, recent trends suggest that although states along the U.S.-Mexico border have the highest concentration of Latinos/as, states that are farther away are slowly beginning to see an increase in their Latino populations. New York City, Chicago, and Miami have become three of the most popular destination cities for Latino immigrants. In recent decades, Alabama, Georgia, and the Carolinas experienced a gain of 200 percent or more in their Latino populations. The term "browning" has been coined to reflect the increase in Latino population in traditionally non-Latino states.

The U.S.-Mexico border region, stretching approximately 2,000 miles (3,200 kilometers) from the southern tip of Texas to California, is the site of particularly strong Latino communities. Four U.S. states—Arizona, California, New Mexico, and Texas—share the border with Mexico, and this close proximity to Mexico has allowed the Latino communities in this area to establish deeper roots because of their long-standing presence in the region.

The migration habits of Latino immigrants and Latinos/as already present in the United States have changed continuously over the years. Although typically found in community clusters, Latinos/as also live in regions of the country that traditionally do not have a Latino presence, including parts of the Northwest (Idaho, Washington, and Oregon) and the Midwest (Indiana, Ohio, Michigan, and Minnesota). Latinos/as in predominantly non-Latino neighborhoods are faced with the reality that their way of life is very different from that of their neighbors. As a result, they have been forced to make self-defining choices about their own culture. They may deny their culture completely and embrace absolutely the American lifestyle; integrate certain aspects of their Latino heritage with certain aspects of the American culture; or completely reject the American way of life and continue solely with their traditional lifestyle.

Despite the acculturation and assimilation processes that the Latino community experienced in the early part of the twentieth century, the rapidly increasing Latino population in recent decades has meant that certain aspects of Latino lifestyle are being introduced to and accepted as part of the American way of life. For example, on August 3, 1999, in the southwest Texas border town of El Cenizo, a city ordinance was passed making Spanish the "predominant language." Located 25 miles (40 kilometers) from the Mexican border town of Nuevo Laredo and about 15 miles (24 kilometers) south of Laredo, Texas, El Cenizo is a community with a Latino population of 7,000, making Latinos/as the majority in the town. Of that population, a large percentage are Mexican immigrants who speak only Spanish. The Predominant Language Ordinance required that all city functions, meetings, and notices be conducted and posted in Spanish. For residents, the measure affirmed their cultural identity and made a statement about the preferred terms of acculturation.

María Pabón López

See also: Machismo; Marianismo; Poverty, Culture of; Women.

Further Reading

González, Ray, ed. *Muy Macho, Latino Men Confront Their Manhood.* New York: Anchor, 1996.

López, María P. "The Phoenix Rises from El Cenizo: A Community Creates and Affirms a Latino/a Border Cultural Citizenship Through Its Language and Safe Haven Ordinances." *Denver University Law Review* 78 (2001): 1017–48.

Zambrana, Ruth E., ed. *Understanding Latino Families: Scholarship, Policy, and Practice.* Thousand Oaks, CA: Sage, 1995.

Farah Strike

In May 1972, some 4,000 workers walked out of the Farah Manufacturing Company in the cities of San Antonio and El Paso, Texas. The strikers, predominantly Mexican American women, walked out to protest what they regarded as exploitative working conditions in the men's pant manufacturing plants of Farah. They demanded maternity leave, higher wages, a safe working environment, an end to sexual harassment, and the right to be represented by a union. National and religious leaders from across the nation supported the strikers and publicly campaigned for their cause. Manufacturing companies and industrialists watched the strike closely. They knew that if the Farah strikers succeeded in their demands, labor relations in the Southwest and Texas would be forever changed. The strike finally came to an end in February 1974, when the company agreed to recognize the Amalgamated Clothing Workers of America (ACWA) as the bargaining unit for the strikers. Although the employees gained some of their key demands, their success was short-lived. Soon thereafter, Farah closed down a number of its plants and moved production south of the border as well as overseas. The real success of the strike was the sense of empowerment that many of the women gained.

Plant Conditions

In the 1920s, Lebanese immigrants Mansour and Hana Farah hired fifteen Mexican women and opened their first sewing factory on San Francisco Street in El Paso. Mansour Farah, who had learned shirt manufacturing and design in New York City, established a number of manufacturing facilities with his wife in the succeeding decades, including seven in El Paso, San Antonio, and Victoria, Texas, and one in

Albuquerque, New Mexico. With keen business savvy and a sense for changing market trends, they went into the men's pants business and founded the Farah Manufacturing Company. By the 1970s, when their son, William "Willie" Farah, became president, the company had more than 9,000 employees; Mexican American women comprised 85 percent of the payroll. Willie Farah, an outspoken antilabor employer, publicly dismissed unionization efforts as Communist activity and claimed that his factories were the cleanest and safest in the state of Texas.

Generations of women who worked at the plants knew otherwise. They were expected to sew on 3,000 belts a day and face a cut in pay if they did not meet their quota. Further, it was alleged, factory bosses, mostly white males, routinely singled out pretty women, giving them special favors if they dated these men. Bosses also forbade women to speak in Spanish and often made racist, sexist, and condescending remarks to them. Older women were subjected to especially aggressive treatment by the bosses and were typically fired or "forced out" of the factories rather than given the chance to retire. Poor ventilation in the factories caused asthma and other sicknesses with inordinate frequency; workers who suffered symptoms were often administered an aspirin by the factory nurse and told to go back to work. Because the company did not offer maternity leave and employees could not afford to lose any workdays, women sometimes gave birth in the company clinic. All in all, the women felt that they were being treated like machines rather than human beings.

The Strike

In 1969, Farah workers from a plant in El Paso contacted the ACWA and asked the union to represent them. Thus began a campaign inside the factory walls to recruit employees. Aware that the workers were unionizing, Willie Farah immediately took steps to thwart their efforts. His tactics included firing union organizers and spying on his workers. The antiunion campaign did not stop the women from organizing, however, but only led them to be more strategic and secretive about their efforts. They hid union cards in their personal belongings and recruited members while on break and during trips to the bathroom. They also held union meetings in their homes and organized their own fund-raisers. Women who were fired from the plants took their organizing activities into the communities, recruiting high school and community members to help in the crusade.

On May 3, 1972, union organizers from a plant in San Antonio were fired when they arrived late to work on Monday morning, having spent the weekend in El Paso at a pro-union rally. As soon as word spread about the firings, more than 500 fellow workers at the company's San Antonio plants walked off their jobs in solidarity. The strike had begun. In less than a week, thousands of workers had joined in, demanding the right to be recognized by a union, an end to unsafe working conditions, an end to racist and sexist tactics, and paid maternity leave.

To assist local efforts, the ACWA organized a national boycott of Farah products. They publicized the company's violent tactics against the strikers and personally attacked Willie Farah in the press. Nor were the attacks hard to substantiate, as Farah hired guard dogs to patrol his plants, installed security cameras and microphones around his factories, and allowed guards to attack and harass the strikers. The strikers and their sympathizers many times found their tires slashed or were frightened by random gunshots.

The ACWA may have succeeded in publicizing the strike and the sources of worker disgruntlement, but it failed to recognize many of the needs of the women. The strikers often complained about sexism and racism within the union itself and were angered by the fact that the male leadership usually ignored their requests. As the strike continued, their disillusionment grew. The union channeled funds to the national boycott rather than provide the funds needed to recruit more workers or provide educational opportunities for them. As the coffers began to dwindle, union leaders also stopped encouraging women to walk off the job. In response, the women took matters into their own hands. In El Paso, a group of strikers formed Unidad Para Siempre, which started its own Farah Distress Fund and began to circulate its own leaflets.

Culmination

In February 1974, the ACWA went into negotiation with the company and the strike was suspended. The negotiations failed to meet the strikers' expectations, but they did secure some changes. Among the gains were a starting rate and general pay increase for all workers; a formula to ensure that wage increases would coincide with federal minimums; time-and-a-half pay for overtime and double time for Saturday and holiday work; and, most important, hospital and disability insurance, including maternity leave. The detested piecework quota system remained in place.

The success of the strike was short-lived. In 1975, the company's plants in San Antonio were permanently closed; by 1992, only one plant remained open in El Paso. The success and personal empowerment of the women strikers outlived the Farah Manufacturing Company. Many expressed the view that going on strike helped them to speak out against injustice in their personal and public lives, motivated them to teach their children about social justice, and gave them a new sense of self by fighting for their own rights and the rights of their fellow workers.

Jennifer R. Mata

See also: Unions, Industrial and Trade; Women.

Further Reading

Coyle, Laurie, Gail Hershatter, and Emily Honig. *Women at Farah: An Unfinished Story.* Oakland, CA: Coyle, Hershatter, and Honig, 1979.

"Farah: The Strike That Has Everything." *The Texas Observer,* December 1972.

Honig, Emily. "Women at Farah Revisited: Political Mobilization and Its Aftermath Among Chicana Workers in El Paso, Texas, 1972–1992." *Feminist Studies* 22:2 (1996): 425–52.

Ledesma, Irene. "Confronting Class: Comment on Honig." *Journal of Women's History* (Spring 1997): 158–63.

Ruíz, Vicki L. *From Out of the Shadows: Mexican Women in Twentieth-Century America.* New York: Oxford University Press, 2008.

Farmingville, New York

Farmingville, New York, is a suburban hamlet located in Suffolk County on the eastern half of Long Island. Farmingville had a population of 16,500 at the turn of the twenty-first century, according to U.S. Census Bureau statistics, and is a solidly middle-class community with an average family income of over $70,000. Farmingville's residents are overwhelmingly white, with African Americans, Asians, and Latinos/as comprising less than 20 percent of the population. The town is largely of Italian, Irish, and German ancestry. Among Latinos/as in Farmingville, the two largest communities are Mexicans and Puerto Ricans. In the early 2000s, the town became the subject of unwelcome national attention over a series of hate crimes against members of the growing Latino community.

During the 1990s, Farmingville experienced a heavy influx of Mexican and Central American immigrants, both legal and illegal. This reflected a national trend, as immigrants from Latin America began bypassing traditional destinations in the United States, such as Southern California and Texas, and started to settle in new, dispersed areas throughout the United States. While urban areas like Los Angeles and Chicago continued to attract Latino immigrants, there was also a 70 percent increase in the population of Latinos/as living in suburban communities. The growth was accounted for not only by the choice of new settlement destinations by immigrants but also by the relocation of Latinos/as who had settled previously in urban centers but had moved to the suburbs due to the high cost of urban living or, conversely, their own upward mobility. A number of cities and towns experienced what demographers call hypergrowth (an increase of 300 percent or more) of the Latino population.

The movement into new areas produced demographic changes that came as a surprise to many longtime residents and was often met with strong resistance. The backlash was further fueled by the fact that many of the immigrants were undocumented yet took advantage of public services. As a result, by the early 2000s, grassroots immigration control organizations had become common in several states, and proposals to increase immigration enforcement and crack down on undocumented immigrants were introduced at the local, state, and federal levels.

In Farmingville, as the number of Mexican and Central American residents increased steadily through the late 1990s, many migrants sought employment as day laborers. Assembling in the morning at busy

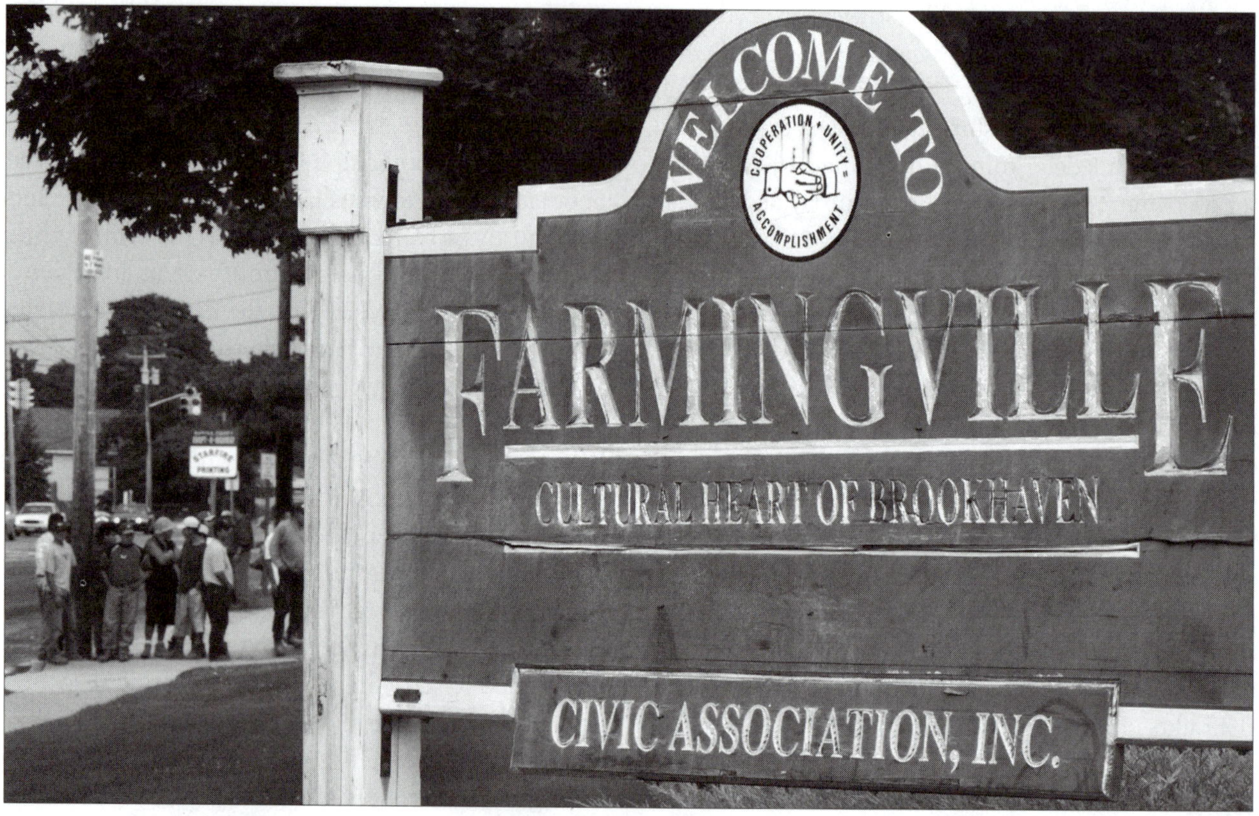

Undocumented day laborers line up for work behind the welcome sign in Farmingville, New York. The middle-class town became a focus of attention after residents complained that the influx of Latino laborers hurt property values and a spate of hate crimes followed. *(Spencer Platt/Getty Images)*

intersections in the hope of securing work, some were hired every day for manual labor jobs as gardeners, landscapers, and construction workers. Reaction to the congregation of day laborers in the town was mixed on the part of non-Latino Farmingville residents, yet often vehemently negative. Some local employers and public officials viewed their presence as a sign that the town's economy was growing and needed a larger pool of workers. Many others looked upon the day laborers as illegal intruders who undercut wages, brought a "foreign" language and culture to the town, increased crime, besmirched the image of the town, and caused a decline in property values. Amid the controversy surrounding day laborers, an immigration control advocacy group called the Sachem Quality of Life Organization was formed in 1998 and successfully lobbied for the defeat of a legislative proposal that would have constructed a designated hiring center for day laborers and employers.

Farmingville gained nationwide notoriety in early 2000 over a series of racially motivated hate crimes against Mexican residents. In September 2000, two local white men posing as contractors lured two Mexican day laborers into an abandoned warehouse, where the two victims were stabbed and beaten. The two perpetrators were tried, convicted, and sentenced to twenty-five-year prison terms for attempted murder and hate crimes. In July 2003, a group of five teenagers launched a bottle rocket at the home of a Mexican family in Farmingville, set it on fire, and left the family homeless. Four of the teenagers were subsequently arrested and charged with hate crimes and arson. Tensions within the community continued to escalate in succeeding years. In June 2005, four people were arrested for racially motivated verbal insults against Latinos/as, and three men in a neighboring town beat a sixty-one-year-old Ecuadorian man after asking him if he had a green card. That same month, town and county officials began cracking down on overcrowded houses and apartments—occupied predominantly by Latinos/as—for alleged health and safety violations. Six houses were shut down, resulting in more than 100 evictions.

Farmingville continues to experience an influx of immigrants from Latin America, many of whom still seek employment as day laborers. The town has become an unofficial national case study of a community in transition due to immigration and of relations between old-stock residents and Spanish-speaking newcomers.

Justin D. García

Further Reading

Chavez, Leo R. *Shadowed Lives: Undocumented Immigrants in American Society.* 2nd ed. Orlando, FL: Harcourt Brace, 1998.

Perea, Juan F., ed. *Immigrants Out! The New Nativism and Anti-Immigrant Impulse in the United States.* New York: New York University Press, 1997.

Feminism

The Latino community has a long tradition of strong women leaders. In the late nineteenth and early twentieth centuries, Lola Rodríguez de Tío was an active and influential participant in the Puerto Rican independence movement. In 1931, Emma Tenayuca led a strike against the pecan industry in San Antonio, Texas, to unionize shellers. More recently, women like Dolores Huerta, one of the founders of the United Farm Workers (UFW), and Norma Cantú, who served as assistant secretary for civil rights under President Bill Clinton, have continued to exemplify Latinas' commitment to social justice. Nevertheless, Latinas today remain subject to widespread discrimination and are relegated to subordinate status in their own communities as well as in mainstream American culture. Because of the combination of gender, class, racial, and ethnic discrimination they face in U.S. society, the majority of Latinas have less access to education and earn less money for comparable work than men in their own ethnic group or than Anglo-American women.

Contemporary Latina feminism seeks to address these inequalities and to expose and deconstruct the sexist and racist mythologies that have been used to justify and perpetuate this situation. Latina feminists challenge the various forms of discrimination to which Latinas and other women of color are subjected, while simultaneously addressing the specific material conditions that most directly affect their everyday lives. Among the core concerns of Latina feminists are employment and labor issues, poverty, education, health, child care, and reproductive rights.

Historical Antecedents: The Puerto Rican Experience

After the U.S. invasion and occupation of Puerto Rico in 1898, a number of U.S. companies began operating on the island. Many of the new factories they built relied primarily on female labor, giving rise to a new phenomenon: Puerto Rican women who worked outside the home. A number of these workers became active in the organized labor movement and developed a working-class feminist consciousness as they fought for universal suffrage and better working conditions. Among them were Luisa Capetillo and Franca de Armiño. Capetillo is believed to be the first Puerto Rican woman to have worn pants in public. She also worked as a labor organizer and advocated equal rights for women in such books as *Mi opinión sobre las libertades, derechos y deberes de la mujer (My Opinion About Women's Freedom, Rights, and Duties)*, published in 1911. Armiño (believed to be a pseudonym) was a poet, playwright, and essayist who led the Asociación Feminista Popular (Popular Feminist Association), a group that tried to improve both the working conditions and the political participation of working-class Puerto Rican women during the 1920s.

Meanwhile, a number of educated upper-middle-class women began echoing the calls of working-class *puertorriqueñas* for universal suffrage. Organizations like the Puerto Rican Feminine League (1917) and the Puerto Rican Association of Women Suffragists (1925) demanded that women be given the right to vote. The writings and activities of suffragists like Mercedes Solá, Ana Roqué, and Isabel Andreu de Aguilar were instrumental in bringing about the passage of a 1929 bill in the Puerto Rican Senate that granted literate women the right to vote. In 1932 women in Puerto Rico participated for the first time in legislative elections. Universal suffrage, which extended the vote to all women, was approved by the Puerto Rican legislature in 1936.

Puerto Rico's colonial relationship with the United States and the rapid industrialization that followed facilitated the development of a feminist movement on the island. The preference for female workers in many of the labor-intensive, U.S-owned industries that relocated to the island between 1905 and 1975 gave Puerto Rican women access to economic independence and allowed them to challenge traditional patriarchal family structures. The influx and dominance of U.S. popular culture, along with the U.S. government's heavy-handed attempts to "civilize" Puerto Ricans by denigrating native cultures, also helped to create a space from which Puerto Rican women could challenge certain aspects of gender discrimination.

El Movimiento and the Birth of Chicana Feminism

Mexican American women were also active in labor and civil rights organizations during the first half of the twentieth century, though gender was rarely addressed as a separate issue. In the late 1960s, however, a movement began to develop that focused on the specific problems facing Chicanas as women. Chicana feminism emerged as a result of experiences in the Chicano Movement, whose organizations tended to follow a trend toward exclusively male leadership. The movement's philosophies of chicanismo and *carnalismo* (brotherhood) led many Chicanos (and some Chicanas) to believe that Chicano cultural preservation required that men set the agenda and play strong public roles, while women worked to support them behind the scenes. Many Chicanas were not satisfied with this role and began challenging their second-class status within the larger Chicano social protest movement.

Chicana feminists aired their grievances in newsletters, pamphlets, and newspapers. In 1971, the first issue of the feminist newspaper *Las Hijas de Cuauhtemoc* (Daughters of Cuauhtemoc) was published by a collective of the same name formed by student activists at California State University, Long Beach. In its editorials, Anna Nieto Gomez called for an elimination of sexism in Chicano families, communities, and the Chicano Movement. Similarly, Bernice Rincón demanded that Chicanas be given greater access to key leadership positions. Enriqueta Longeaux y Vasquez, who published *El Grito del Norte* in New Mexico, asked Chicanas to challenge sexist practices within their communities. Mirta Vidal, a longtime activist for the rights of all Chicanos/as, pointed out that maintaining the cultural heritage of *La Raza* was being used as an excuse to keep women "barefoot, pregnant, and in the kitchen." Chicana feminists used these publications to address some of the key issues facing Chicanas, including the woman's role in the traditional Mexican family, lack of access to higher education, lack of reproductive freedom, and experiences with sexism and discrimination.

Chicana feminists also organized meetings that simultaneously addressed their concerns and allowed them to come together to create networks of like-minded individuals. From 1970 to 1977, no fewer than thirty-six conferences, workshops, seminars, and meetings were held at the local and national levels. Among these, the *Conferencia de Mujeres por la Raza* (Conference of Women for la Raza) was notable as the first Chicana national conference. Held in Texas at the Houston YWCA from May 28 to 30, 1971, it was attended by 600 women from local and regional organizations. Conference resolutions called for an end to the exclusion of female leadership in the Chicano Movement and for the creation of a commission to direct the organizing of women within the community. Most notably, participants unequivocally embraced *feminismo* (feminism) when they asserted that women were oppressed both as women and as part of *La Raza.*

Latina Feminism Today

By the 1980s, a small number of Chicana activists had entered U.S. colleges and universities and started to produce research studies on Latinas. Their scholarship challenged many of the assumptions inherent in both ethnic studies and women's studies by emphasizing the interconnectedness of race, class, gender, and sexuality. Chicana feminist theory is notable for its commitment to social change. Latina scholars have formed Mujeres Activas en Letras y Cambio

Social (MALCS, Women Active in Letters and Social Change) to affirm their continuing dedication to the unification of their academic life with their community activism. MALCS hosts a summer research institute, publishes a newsletter and scholarly journal, and was instrumental in establishing a permanent research center at the University of California, Davis, to develop Chicanas/Latinas as scholars.

Latina feminists have also focused on the persistence of exclusionary practices within mainstream feminist movements. They have joined other women of color in criticizing white middle-class feminists' limited attention to differences among women on the basis of race, ethnicity, class, and sexual orientation. Latina feminists are critical of any analysis that treats race or ethnicity as a secondary source of oppression. Instead, they call for a reformulation of feminist theory and practice in order to establish a more inclusive framework for analyzing the experiences of all women.

Many Latina feminists also question the heterosexism of Chicano/Latino culture and its deleterious effects on lesbians. Latina lesbians struggle against the sources of oppression facing other Latinas, but, in addition, they also contend with homophobia within their own communities and in society at large. The writings of Cherríe Moraga and Gloria Anzaldúa, among others, address the impact of this triple oppression on the psyches and lives of Latina lesbians.

Latina feminists are also creating common cause with women of color in the United States and in the rest of the Americas. Their goal is to form domestic and international alliances between Latina feminists and other women of color around women's issues. In the United States, organizations like the Women of Color Resource Center are working to create political agendas to span ethnic and cultural differences among Latina, Asian American, Native American, and African American feminists. Transnational alliances between Latinas in the United States and women in Latin America are being forged through a number of channels, including scholarly conferences, political mobilizations along the U.S.-Mexico border, and the growth of cultural and political alliances between Latinas living on the mainland and those residing in Puerto Rico.

Patricia Kim-Rajal

See also: Anzaldúa, Gloria; Chicanisma; Huerta, Dolores; La Raza; Moraga, Cherríe; Mujeres Activas en Letras y Cambio Social; Pérez, Emma; Rodríguez de Tío, Lola; Tenayuca, Emma; Women.

Further Reading

Acosta-Belén, Edna, ed. *The Puerto Rican Woman: Perspectives on Culture, History, and Society.* Westport, CT: Praeger, 1986.

Anzaldúa, Gloria. *Borderlands/La Frontera: The New Mestiza.* 1987. San Francisco: Aunt Lute, 2007.

Arredondo, Gabriela F., et al. *Chicana Feminisms: A Critical Reader.* Durham, NC: Duke University Press, 2003.

Blea, Irene I. *U.S. Chicanas and Latinas Within a Global Context: Women of Color at the Fourth World Women's Conference.* Westport, CT: Praeger, 1997.

García, Alma M., ed. *Chicana Feminist Thought: The Basic Historical Writings.* New York: Routledge, 1997.

Moraga, Cherríe. *Loving in the War Years: Lo Que Nunca Paso por sus Labios.* Cambridge, MA: South End, 2000.

Ferrer, José (1912–1992)

As an actor, director, and producer in Hollywood and on Broadway, the Puerto Rican–born José Ferrer has been recognized as a Renaissance man of American entertainment. A versatile stage and screen actor never typecast in Latino roles, Ferrer gained immense popularity during the 1950s and 1960s. He won an Academy Award for Best Actor—the first ever by a Latino—for his title role in the 1950 film *Cyrano de Bergerac.* One of the first actors to cross over into directing, Ferrer directed seven films and thirteen Broadway productions. In addition, he was the first actor to receive a U.S. National Medal of Arts, in 1985 from President Ronald Reagan, and the first Latino to join the Directors Guild, in 1956. His accomplishments in Hollywood over a period of more than forty years made him a major inspiration to subsequent generations of Puerto Ricans and Latinos/as aspiring to success in the film industry.

He was born José Vicente Ferrer de Otero y Cintrón on January 8, 1912, in the Santurce province of Puerto Rico. The son of Spanish-born U.S. citizens—his father was an attorney and his mother's family owned sugarcane land—Ferrer spent his childhood in Puerto Rico before moving with his family to New

York City in 1918. After attending public schools, he entered Princeton University, in New Jersey, where he studied architecture and music composition and from which he received his bachelor's degree in 1933. It was in college that Ferrer discovered his passion for performing, developing his artistic talents as a member of the university's thespian club, the Princeton Triangle Club. At the urging of his parents, he went on to study Romance languages at Columbia University, in New York City, from 1933 to 1934.

Ferrer made his professional debut on a showboat in Long Island, New York, in 1934, and followed this closely with his Broadway debut in 1935 as the Second Policeman in *A Slight Case of Murder.* The same year, Ferrer joined Joshua Logan's stock theater company in Suffern, New York, as assistant stage manager. His first major role on Broadway came in 1940, when he played the lead, part of it in drag, in *Charley's Aunt.* The success of the play established Ferrer as a rising star and laid the groundwork for his portrayal of Iago in Shakespeare's *Othello* in 1943, opposite Paul Robeson; *Othello* became the longest-running production of a Shakespeare play ever staged in the United States. Ferrer began his career as a stage director in 1941, debuting with Marcel Pagnon's *Topaz.*

The end of World War II brought new opportunities, as he produced his first Broadway play, *Strange Fruit,* in late 1945; this was followed the next year by his first Hollywood role, as narrator of a short film called *Bolivia.* It would be nearly three years, however, before Ferrer made his first actual film appearance, in *Joan of Arc* (1948). The film was well received, and Ferrer was nominated for an Academy Award for his role of Dauphin, playing alongside Ingrid Bergman.

Ferrer's big break came in 1950 when he gained international fame for his acclaimed performance in *Cyrano,* a role he had previously played on stage. Critics celebrated his rich, full voice and refined manner. In addition to the Academy Award (1951), he won a Golden Globe Award for his performance. His reputation now secure, Ferrer went on to play a number of notable film roles, including the Parisian painter Henri de Toulouse-Lautrec in *Moulin Rouge* (1952), for which he was nominated for another Academy Award; Mister Davison in *Miss Sadie Thompson* (1953); Navy lawyer Barney Greenwald in *The Caine Mutiny* (1954); Alfred Dreyfus, the Jewish army officer unjustly accused of treason and sentenced to life imprisonment, in *I Accuse!* (1958), a film he also directed; and a Turkish governor in *Lawrence of Arabia* (1962).

Ferrer also continued to excel in the theater, winning a Tony Award for Outstanding Director in 1952 for his direction of three plays—*Stalag 17, The Fourposter,* and *The Shrike.* He also played the lead of a victimized husband in *The Shrike,* earning another Tony for Outstanding Actor. He produced all three plays, which ran for a rarely achieved 1,265 performances.

Ferrer's work as a film director includes *The Great Man* (1956), a *Citizen Kane*–style look at the private life of a beloved radio and television personality who dies suddenly. Ferrer also starred in the lead, as a writer who attempts to break into the big time by preparing a eulogistic broadcast of the deceased celebrity—with mixed results. For his efforts, the Directors Guild of America nominated Ferrer for a Best Director Award in 1957. Other directing credits include *The High Cost of Loving* (1958), *Return to Peyton Place* (1961), and *State Fair* (1962). After that last project, Ferrer left directing and concentrated exclusively on stage and screen character acting, including a number of television cameos. Further contributing to his reputation as a Renaissance man, Ferrer also recorded several musical albums with his wife, singer Rosemary Clooney.

Ferrer remained active in the entertainment world until late in his life. His last stage performances came in 1990, and he was planning a return to Broadway before his death from colon cancer on January 26, 1992, at his home in Coral Gables, Florida.

Anita Damjanovic

See also: Film.

Further Reading

Berg, Charles Ramírez. *Latino Images in Film: Stereotypes, Subversion, and Resistance.* Austin: University of Texas Press, 2002.

Reyes, Luis, and Peter Rubie. *Hispanics in Hollywood: A Celebration of 100 Years in Film and Television.* Hollywood, CA: Lone Eagle, 2000.

Film

Although Latin Americans have played a highly visible role in U.S. cinema since the silent film era, it was not until the late 1960s that a body of work that could be classified as "Latino" per se—reflecting a U.S.-based rather than a Latin American reality—began to take shape. Yet while these and later efforts clearly reflected the Latino experience in America, it became evident early on that, despite some common story lines, themes, and styles, Latino filmmakers are not guided by a single audience, cinematic mode, aesthetic principle, or political motivation. The diversity of film and video productions reflects the cultural and ethnic diversity of Latinos/as and Latino communities.

Early Period

Among the elements that Latino filmmakers have had in common is an effort to correct the distorted portrayals of Latinos/as so pervasive in mainstream films by producing works that affirm and portray ethnic and national identities. Among the stereotypes they have countered in standard Hollywood fare are portrayals of Latinos/as as bandits, buffoons, and sexually charged vamps and seducers. In addition to identity-affirming characters, early Latino productions of the 1960s were characterized by links to the struggle for civil rights and the burgeoning Chicano Movement. Latino filmmakers thus aspired to create an "oppositional cinema" that documented social resistance movements, reclaimed Latino history, and exposed the conditions in which Latinos/as subsisted as a result of American institutions. The less-costly documentary was the predominant genre used by early Latino filmmakers, many of whom began their careers in public television. However, the general aspiration was to make feature-length films, the marker of success in the film industry.

Among the most notable films of the early period include *I Am Joaquín* (directed by Luis Valdez, 1969), a short regarded as the first Chicano film and based on an epic poem of the same name by Rodolfo "Corky" Gonzales; *Yo Soy Chicano* (Jesús Salvador Treviño, 1972), the first nationally broadcast documentary about Mexican Americans and their place in U.S. society; *After the Earthquake/Después del Terremoto* (Lourdes Portillo and Nina Serrano, 1979), a documentary about a Nicaraguan woman who migrated to San Francisco after the 1976 earthquake in her home country; *Chicana* (Sylvia Morales, 1979), a short film that traces the history of Chicanas in the United States; *El Súper* (León Ichaso and Orlando Jiménez Leal, 1979), a feature-length comedy about a Cuban exile family in New York; and *La Operación* (Ana María García, 1982), a documentary about a 1970s government program to sterilize Puerto Rican women. The variety of topics and genres reflects the diversity of views and experiences in different Latino communities.

1980s to the Present

By the early 1980s, Latino filmmakers had gained a small place in noncommercial film circuits and even directed a few studio releases, such as *Zoot Suit* (Luis Valdez, 1981), a musical about the Sleepy Lagoon murder trial in 1940s East Los Angeles, and *El Norte* (Gregory Nava, 1983), a melodrama about a Guatemalan brother and sister who migrate illegally to Los Angeles by way of Mexico. The late 1980s were also watershed years for Latino cinema thanks to the success of such mainstream releases as *La Bamba* (Luis Valdez, 1987), a biography of 1950s Chicano rock-and-roll star Ritchie Valens; *Born in East L.A.* (Cheech Marin, 1987), a border-themed comedy; *Stand and Deliver* (Ramón Menéndez, 1988), a biographical film on the experiences of Jaime Escalante as an East Los Angeles high school mathematics teacher; and *The Milagro Beanfield War* (Robert Redford, 1988), about a proposed development project in a rural New Mexico community. The decade also brought a growing roster of Latino actors working in Hollywood, including Puerto Rican Raul Juliá, Brazilian Sonia Braga, Cuban-born Venezuelan María Conchita Alonso, Cuban American Andy García, and Panamanian Rubén Blades. The Mexican American actor Edward James Olmos, a ubiquitous presence in early Chicano films who received an Oscar nomination for *Stand and Deliver,* became a prototype to many of the socially committed Latino movie stars.

The mainstreaming of Latino directors, actors, and films meant an expansion of the original definition of

Latino cinema as being solely "for and about" Latinos/as. Nevertheless, the access accorded to Latinos/as in Hollywood was typically limited and short-lived. Studios continued to choose non-Latinos/as to play the leads and to direct films like *The Perez Family* (Mira Nair, 1992), about the 1980s Mariel Boatlift from Cuba to Florida, and *The House of the Spirits* (Bille August, 1993), based on the best-selling novel by Chilean Isabel Allende. For some Latino actors and filmmakers, this raised the question of whether even to seek participation in a system that consistently excluded and misrepresented them.

Outside Hollywood, experimental Latino film and video makers worked in hybrid forms that combined different media, such as photography, original graphics, and written text, and challenged the representational strategies of mainstream-oriented Latino productions. Among the most notable experimental Latino filmmakers are Willie Varela, who began making independent movies in the early 1970s, and Henry Gamboa, co-founder of Asco (1972–1987), an East Los Angeles conceptual performance group. Short films like *Border Brujo* (Isaac Artenstein, 1993) and *Carmelita Tropicana* (Ela Troyano, 1994), which showcase the work of performance artists Guillermo Gómez-Peña and Alina Troyano, respectively, and documentaries like *AIDS in the Barrio: Eso No Me Pasa a Mí* (Peter Biella and Frances Negrón-Muntaner, 1990) deal with subject matter generally absent from mainstream Latino films, such as gay and lesbian identities. Another important development during this period was the growing number of Latino film scholars writing about Latino film and video productions, including such groundbreaking anthologies as Gary Keller's *Chicano Cinema* (1985), Chon Noriega's *Chicanos and Film* (1992), and Ana López and Chon Noriega's *The Ethnic Eye* (1996).

In the early 1990s, Mexican American director Robert Rodríguez emerged as a sensation among independent filmmakers when his *El mariachi* (1992), a feature-length film shot in two weeks on a $7,000 budget, was distributed by Columbia Pictures. By mid-decade, there was also a new group of glamorous Latino actors that rose to fame in Hollywood, among them Spain's Antonio Banderas, Mexico's Salma Hayek, and New York–born Puerto Rican Jennifer Lopez. The celebration of family values in films like *My Family/Mi familia* (Gregory Nava, 1995), the multigenerational Mexican American saga, became a common way for Latino filmmakers to appeal to mainstream U.S. audiences. Even Robert Rodríguez, who gained fame directing violent movies, had his biggest commercial success with *Spy Kids* (2001), a family-oriented film. However, lesser-known films such as *Star Maps* (Miguel Arteta, 1997) have questioned the mythical representation of families in Latino cinema.

The development of new media technologies has brought new types of Latino film and video productions in the twenty-first century, as reflected in such works as *Sin City* (Robert Rodríguez and Frank Miller, 2005), adapted from a graphic novel and shot in digital video, and *Carlita's Secret* (George Cotayo, 2004), one of a number of urban thrillers produced straight-for-DVD. Despite the differences in genres, styles, and themes, Latino filmmakers in the 2000s have continued to emphasize urban dramas that focus on intergenerational family conflict, including the critically acclaimed dramas *Washington Heights* (Alfredo de Villa, 2002), about a Dominican father and son living in New York City, and *Raising Victor Vargas* (Peter Sollett, 2002), a coming-of-age story about a boy of Dominican descent set in New York's Lower East Side.

Roberto Carlos Ortiz

See also: Chicano Movement; Popular Culture; Valdez, Luis; *Yo Soy Joaquín.*

Further Reading

Keller, Gary, ed. *Chicano Cinema: Research, Reviews, and Resources.* Binghamton, NY: Bilingual Review Press, 1985.

López, Ana M., and Chon A. Noriega, eds. *The Ethnic Eye: Latino Media Arts.* Minneapolis: University of Minnesota Press, 1996.

Noriega, Chon A., ed. *Chicanos and Film: Representation and Resistance.* Minneapolis: University of Minnesota Press, 1992.

Flores Magón, Ricardo (1874–1922)

Ricardo Flores Magón was a Mexican anarchist, liberationist, writer, journalist, and editor. He was influential in the ideologies leading to the Mexican Revolution of 1910 and active in the struggle against dictator Porfirio Díaz. Flores Magón was widely known as editor of the newspaper *Regeneración,* an instrument used in support of revolutionary activity against Díaz.

Flores Magón was born on September 16 (Mexican Independence Day), 1874, in San Antonio Eloxochitlán, Oaxaca, Mexico. His mother was Margarita Magón, a *mestiza,* and his father was D. Teodoro Flores, an Amerindian combatant of the Mexican-American War (1846–1848).

In 1893, Flores Magón began law school at Escuela Nacional de Jurisprudencia, only to drop out three years later. He founded *Regeneración* with his brother, Jesús, on August 7, 1900. In 1901, he became a leader in the liberal movement seeking to remove Díaz from power. Flores Magón represented a group known as the *intelectuals,* a group of elite liberals—politicians, writers, journalists, poets, and lawyers—who had risen above their working-class origins. In 1904, to avoid persecution from Mexican officials, he and his brother Enrique went into self-imposed exile in the United States, continuing to publish *Regeneración* from Missouri. During the early years of his exile, he became familiar with, and influenced by, the Russian-born anarchist Emma Goldman. He continued the struggle against Díaz from St. Louis and then from Los Angeles, in spite of his imprisonment by U.S. authorities for seditious behavior. In 1905, Flores Magón founded the Partido Liberal Mexicano (PLM), which supported the Mexican Revolution and organized unsuccessful uprisings against Díaz in 1906 and 1908. Flores Magón's articles in *Regeneración* supported the revolutionary uprisings and resulted in multiple imprisonments in the United States, the last one occurring during World War I.

Flores Magón explored the ideas of many anarchists, among them the works of Russian anarchist Mikhail Bakunin and French socialist and journalist Pierre-Joseph Proudhon, known for his essay "What Is Property?" His contemporary influences included Elisee Reclus, whose anarchist beliefs were based on natural laws and the idea that obeying them would create social liberation; the anarchist Charles Malato; Italian socialist Errico Malatesta; and Anselmo Lorenzo, considered "the grandfather of anarchism." Above all he admired the Russian geographer and philosopher Pyotr (Peter) Kropotkin, a supporter of communism whose book *The Conquest of Bread* (1892) Flores Magón considered the bible of anarchism. The book served as a handbook for communes in Baja California during the Magonista Revolt, an organized uprising that contributed to Díaz's resignation in 1911. Flores Magón in turn influenced revolutionaries of his time, including Emiliano Zapata in Mexico whose slogan *Tierra y libertad* (land and freedom) was the title of one of Flores Magón's articles.

In 1918, Flores Magón was arrested in the United States for espionage, having published articles opposing World War I. Sentenced to twenty years in prison, he was incarcerated at the U.S. Penitentiary in Fort Leavenworth, Kansas, where he died on November 22, 1922. His remains were eventually moved to the Rotonda de los Hombres Ilustres (Rotunda of Illustrious Men) in Mexico City. His major writings include *Semilla libertaria* (Libertarian Seed, 1923), *Tierra y Libertad, drama revolucionario en cuatro actos* (Land and Liberty: Revolutionary Drama in Four Acts, 1924), *Vida Nueva* (New Life, 1924), and *Epistolario revolucionario* (Revolutionary Poetry, 1925).

Nicole Martone

See also: Mexicans.

Further Reading

Albro, Ward S. *Always a Rebel: Ricardo Flores Magón and the Revolution.* Forth Worth: Texas Christian University Press, 1992.

Langham, Thomas C. *Border Trials: Ricardo Flores Magón and the Mexican Liberals.* El Paso, TX: Western Press, 1981.

MacLachlan, Colin M. *Anarchism and the Mexican Revolution: The Political Trials of Ricardo Flores Magón in the United States.* Berkeley: University of California Press, 1991.

Foods and Beverages

Among the most prominent food trends in the United States over recent decades has been the great rise in popularity of Latino cuisine. In fact, according to *Restaurants and Institutions* magazine's 2005 Menu Census, Mexican is the most popular ethnic food in the United States, found on 50 percent of restaurant menus. In addition, the combination of Mexican and Texan food, known as "Tex-Mex," is represented in 31 percent of menus. Nevertheless, with the increased immigration from Latin American nations other than Mexico, the trend has become even more diverse and eclectic, broadening to include Caribbean, Central American, and South American fare, as well as a new fusion style called "Nuevo Latino" or "New Latin" cuisine. At the same time, while Latin American foods have been influencing palates in the United States, imported convenience foods from the United States have reshaped the traditional diet in Latin American countries.

Tex-Mex Cuisine

Tex-Mex was introduced in the United States during the first half of the twentieth century. Many first- and second-generation Mexican immigrants had moved to Texas and began opening restaurants featuring food from their homeland. To adapt their restaurants to the local palate, they also tended to include traditional Texan dishes such as chili on their menus. This beans-and-ground-beef stew was particularly popular during the Depression Era because it provided an inexpensive, but hearty, meal. Yet in addition to serving this dish by the bowl, many of these early Mexican establishments began treating it as a sauce, ladling this *chili con carne* (chili pepper with meat) mixture over enchiladas (corn tortillas stuffed with meat, vegetables, or cheese) and tamales (a cornmeal dough called *masa* filled with meat and wrapped in a corn husk).

Another important adaptation to the local palate was the use of yellow American cheese in these dishes. In 1928, the Kraft Corporation introduced Velveeta cheese, which quickly gained popularity because of its mild flavor, because it melted well, and because it was less expensive than traditional cheeses. These qualities made it an ideal filling and topping for enchiladas. Thus was born the creamy Tex-Mex *chili con queso* (chili pepper with cheese) sauce, which would also later be used with the classic Tex-Mex creation, the nacho chip, created during World War II. Traditional nachos consist of crispy deep-fried corn chips topped with melted yellow cheese and sliced jalapeño peppers.

Perhaps the most dramatic dish in Tex-Mex cuisine—at least as served in restaurants—is the *fajita,* usually served on a sizzling platter or skillet accompanied by warm flour tortillas. This meal is a derivation of the traditional *carne asada* (grilled meat) dish, except that the cut of meat used for fajitas is from the *faja* or skirt steak section of the steer. Consequently, fajitas are traditionally prepared with marinated strips of beef, accompanied by grilled onions and bell peppers, and topped with such condiments as sour cream, guacamole, and tomato salsa. Fajitas first gained popularity when they were introduced as *tacos al carbon* (grilled tacos) in Houston during the 1970s. Currently, fajitas are also made with grilled chicken, pork, or shrimp.

Nuevo Latino Cuisine

"Nuevo Latino" cuisine has become popular in the United States largely because of its inclusiveness. Not only does the style include dishes inspired by Latin American ingredients and flavors, but it also features food from Spain, such as the trendy *tapas,* or appetizer-style dishes currently served in many restaurants and bars. Indeed, the lack of reference to any specific country suggests universality or shared food culture among Latinos/as. Many restaurants claiming to specialize in cuisine from a particular Latin American country may actually serve various dishes from other Latin American or Spanish regions.

Since the Latino population is currently the largest growing ethnic group in the United States, Latino foods are no longer limited to the "ethnic" aisle in grocery stores or to small eateries in immigrant neighborhoods. While generally upscale, Nuevo Latino cuisine has become part of the American mainstream. Some traditional Latin American foods and beverages that have gained prominence in the United States include:

Arepas: From Colombia and Venezuela, corn cakes served crispy on the outside and soft on the inside, often filled or topped with cheese or meat, much like a sandwich.

Caipirinha: From Brazil, a cocktail made from cachaça, a Brazilian sugarcane liquor mixed with lime juice.

Ceviche: Mainly a Caribbean dish, with variations found along the coastlines of Latin America, consisting of raw seafood marinated in lime juice.

Chimichurri: From Argentina, a sauce similar to pesto but made with parsley instead of basil, which is spread over grilled meat, particularly at *churrasquerías* (barbeque-style steakhouse restaurants).

Chipotle: From Mexico, a smoked and dried pepper.

Dulce de leche: From Argentina, a sweet caramel topping made from sugar and milk.

Empañada: Found throughout Latin America
...over served either baked or
...d with meat, vegetables, or

...from Spain and popular in
...drink made from ground

...cocktail traditionally made
...int leaves, and lime juice.
...n edible seed prepared and
...similar to rice.
...nish): A Mexican tomato-
...r dipping tortilla chips and
...ls; in recent years, salsa has
...as the most popular condi-
... States.

Spectra Energy
Stewart Title Company
Sysco Corporation
The Boeing Company
The Greensheet
Waste Management
Whole Foods
Williams

LENIENT = not AS strict OR SEVERE, tolerant etc.

...Latin cuisine "new" is the
...dients are combined with
...and cultures in the United
...orgia peach and a spicy ha-
...mbined to make a special
...d with Indian curry sauce,
or a tamale may be stuffed with duck and Chinese plum sauce; the possibilities are endless. Essentially, Nuevo Latino cuisine is Latino food reinvented for a generation that has more exposure to different cultures than any preceding it. Much in the same way that the diffusion of indigenous Latin American foods such as corn, chiles, potatoes, tomatoes, chocolate, and vanilla revolutionized eating habits throughout the "Old World" in the sixteenth century, so the concentration of Latin cultures in the contemporary United States has created a "New World" cuisine that reflects the effects of cultural blending in the twenty-first century.

The Changing Latino Diet

While cuisine in the United States has been influenced by Latin America's fresh, bold flavors, diets in Latin America likewise have been affected by U.S. convenience foods, often to their own detriment. During the late 1990s, for example, Central Americans suffered from the crash in the international coffee market and the damaging effects of Hurricane Mitch in 1998. Economic conditions worsened for many in the region. Forced to look for employment wherever they can find it, many workers have had to settle for jobs that pay less than $2 a day. Given this meager income, many poor families began replacing the traditional Central American diet of beans and rice with cheaper but less nutritional convenience foods such as instant soups. In fact, while the number of undernourished people in Latin America as a whole has been steadily decreasing, the number has actually been increasing in Central America. According to the United Nations Food and Agricultural Organization, 29 percent of the Nicaraguan population, 26 percent of the Panamanian population, and 25 percent of the Guatemalan population are undernourished, compared to an average of 10 percent for Latin America as a whole.

At the same time that certain populations are underfed, there has also been a rise in obesity in Latin America, particularly in urban areas. While about two thirds of Latin Americans lived in rural areas less than a century ago, more than three-quarters now live in cities. Thus, while poor rural families in the past were able to provide food for their families from local crops, now many of these families must survive on inexpensive convenience foods, such as hamburgers and other fried foods that are readily available from street vendors. In a study at Argentina's Institute of Higher Social Studies at General San Martín National University in Buenos Aires, researchers found out that the gap between the rich and poor in Latin America has grown significantly since the 1960s. During that decade, according to the study, people at all income levels had similar diets. Although those with lower incomes tended to consume cheaper cuts of meat, fewer dairy products, and a smaller variety of fruits and vegetables than their wealthier counterparts, their diet was still varied and balanced, with very similar nutritional value. In the late 1990s, however, observers found that Latin Americans with lower incomes tended to consume foods that served to satisfy hunger but were high in fats and sugars. In fact, nutritionists at the University of São Paulo found that soft drink consumption in Brazil increased by 400 percent in a period of thirty years. The increased consumption of high-calorie, low-nutrition food items and sugary soft drinks has greatly contributed to the increase of diabetes and obesity. According to a study by the Pan American Health Organization, approximately one third of the population in the 1990s was either overweight or obese in ten Latin American countries. In the United States, over 60 percent of Latinos/as are considered obese, with roughly 2 million suffering from diabetes. Food choices are thus crucial in terms of the health of Latinos/as inside the United States and beyond

Even though convenience foods tend to be less expensive than fresh produce, lower-income families in Latin American still end up spending an average of 67 percent of their total budget on food; this represents a significant increase from the 1970s, when the average was 45 percent. Thus, poorer Latin Americans are spending more money on food but getting less nutrition out of their diet. This trend particularly affects lower-income women, who tend to be overweight or obese yet give birth to underweight, malnourished children, creating a new generation that is at risk for health problems later in life.

Moreover, the shift from rural to urban living has led to a more sedentary lifestyle. According to a study by the British medical journal *Lancet,* more than half of Latin Americans residing in cities earn a living in the informal economic sector, for example, selling food items on the street. This means that they spend most of their day sitting or standing in stalls, often surrounded by unhealthy food choices. In addition, workers who have more traditional jobs, such as those in offices in major cities (Mexico City, Lima, and others), may spend much of their time simply commuting to work via buses and trains only to arrive at a job where they spend much of the day seated. Neither the street vendor nor the office worker has the time or the opportunity for exercise.

In response to the spread of unhealthy lifestyles, some Latin American countries have introduced programs to help promote better food choices and increase physical activity. In Chile, for example, where it is estimated that 9 million people will be obese by the year 2010, politicians such as Congressman Fulvio Rossi have launched a campaign against *comida chatarra* (junk food); under his plan, such foods would receive an additional tax and there would be increased time devoted to physical exercise in schools. Similarly, in the United States the Latino Nutrition Coalition was formed in 2005 in an effort to improve Latino eating habits, while maintaining the rich culture and traditions associated with Latino communities. The coalition describes its mission as "devoted to addressing and transforming the current dietary trends in Latinos in the United States, thereby reducing the negative health effects among this population. Our mission is to provide the Latino community, and those that serve them, with easy-to-understand nutrition, cooking, shopping, and health information." The Latino Nutrition Coalition has also developed a bilingual "Latino food pyramid," Camino Mágico—or Magic Road—which is available at Latino markets throughout the United States.

Annalisa V. Burke

See also: Tex-Mex.

Further Reading

Fraser, Barbara. "Latin America's Urbanisation is Boosting Obesity." *The Lancet* 365 (June 11, 2005): 1995–96.

Hearn, Kelly. "Globesity en Español: Latin America Fights the Battle of the Bulge" *In These Times* (March 2006): 8.

Latino Nutrition Coalition. http://www.latinonutrition.org.

Meitus, Marty. "Pan-Latin in Every Pot: A Feast of Recipes for a Trend in the Making." *Rocky Mountain News,* January 15, 2003, 3D.

Replogie, Jill. "Hunger on the Rise in Central America." *The Lancet* 363 (June 19, 2004): 2056–57.

Sharpe, Patricia. "Tex-Mex 101." *Texas Monthly* (August 2003): 58.

"2005 Menu Census: Regional/Ethnic." *Restaurants and Institutions* (September 1, 2005): 62.

Foraker Act (1900)

The Foraker Act, also known as the Organic Act, was signed by President William McKinley in April 1900, ending the U.S. military occupation of Puerto Rico and establishing the first generation of U.S. civilian rule on the island. Two years earlier, the Treaty of Paris had concluded the Spanish-American War and awarded Puerto Rico (among other territories) to the United States. Although the treaty stipulated the end of Spanish citizenship for native-born Puerto Ricans, it did not detail the specific relationship of the United States to its newly acquired possession, instead giving Congress the explicit power to determine and define the citizenship status of Puerto Ricans. Accordingly, the inhabitants of Puerto Rico essentially found themselves in the position of being without citizenship, citizenship being the designation of belonging to a nation-state, and Puerto Ricans were colonial subjects belonging to neither Spain nor the United States.

From September 1898 to April 1900, Puerto Rico was under the military rule of the U.S. War Department. In addition, for the first years of colonial rule government offices and positions were appointed and overseen by the United States. Under the Foraker Act, a form of government was established following the model of the three-branch U.S. system. Democratic participation was limited, however, as the president of the United States appointed the majority of government positions, including the head of the executive branch (the governor), the cabinet (which also served as the upper house of the legislature), and the chief and associate justices of the supreme court. The Foraker Act also established the Federal District Court for Puerto Rico, essentially subjecting the Puerto Rican judiciary to review by the U.S. Supreme Court. Under this system, only the lower house of the Puerto Rican legislature was democratically elected by the Puerto Rican people.

Furthermore, while the first democratic election in Puerto Rico under Foraker was held on November 6, 1900, the application of democracy was in fact narrow. The combined effects of limited suffrage (women were not allowed to vote), as well as political resistance to the new regime (the Federal Party boycotted the first election), resulted in a fairly small voter turnout—and for the smallest sector of the government. The mixing of appointed government and elected government led to tensions that ultimately enabled the island's elite to further their own political agendas. The governors of Puerto Rico under the Foraker Act—Charles Herbert Allen (1900–1901), William Henry Hunt (1901–1904), Beekman Winthrop (1904–1907), Regis Henry Prost (1907–1909), George Radcliff Colton (1909–1913), and Arthur Yager (1913–1921)—were appointed as a result of political favoritism on the part of the president, not because of their political qualifications or interest. Consequently, many of them were indifferent, if not hostile, to the needs and concerns of the Puerto Rican people. Instead, their first responsibility was furthering U.S. economic, military, and political interests.

In addition to establishing a civil-colonial government on the island and making Puerto Ricans subject to U.S. federal law, the Foraker Act granted broad powers to U.S. officials charged with administering the island. Aggressive programs of Americanization were put in place, including the official imposition of English as the primary language. By 1901, instruction in Puerto Rican public schools was conducted solely in English, and Puerto Rican teachers were required to pass English proficiency exams and were encouraged, as were students, to study in the United States. Not surprisingly, the Foraker Act was widely unpopular across the island. The limited sovereignty of the Puerto Rican people in their own affairs, the Americanization imposed on the island's inhabitants, and the question of citizenship status led to widespread political disaffection.

Lorna Perez

See also: Muñoz Rivera, Luis; Puerto Ricans; Spanish-American War.

Further Reading

Grosfoguel, Ramón. *Colonial Subjects: Puerto Ricans in a Global Perspective.* Berkeley: University of California Press, 2003.

Kaplan, Amy. "The Anarchy of Empire." In *Convergences: Inventories of the Present,* ed. Edward W. Said. Cambridge, MA: Harvard University Press, 2002.

Malavet, Pedro A. *America's Colony: The Political and Cultural Conflict Between the United States and Puerto Rico.* New York: New York University Press, 2004.

Foreign Miners' Tax (1850)

Part of a larger body of anti-Latino legislation, the Foreign Miners' Tax of 1850 was an attempt by the California state legislature to drive away Mexicans and South Americans working in the state's gold mines and to discourage Latino immigration in general during the middle part of the nineteenth century. While the law remained in effect for only one year, its passage spurred increased anti-immigrant violence throughout California, forcing many Latinos/as to leave the mines and, in some cases, the country.

In 1848, following the end of the Mexican-American War and the discovery of gold in California, immigrants from Europe, Mexico, South America, and Asia journeyed to the United States in the hope of finding gold and then returning to their homelands to establish better lives for themselves and their families. Among Mexicans, the largest number of immigrants came from Sonora (estimated by researchers to have been well over 10,000). Anglo-American miners felt that the U.S. victory in the Mexican-American War gave them a special claim to the land and gold in California. They were especially resentful of the Sonorans, who were skilled miners and had arrived in the region better equipped than the non-Latino miners.

The Foreign Miners' Tax reflected a wide-scale backlash against Latinos/as throughout the nation. This resentment was especially pronounced in the California mining region. Although particular white animosity was directed toward Sonorans, Euro-Americans tended to lump all Latinos/as—Mexicans, *Californios*, Peruvians, and Chileans—together under the label "greaser." While there were significantly fewer Peruvians and Chileans in the mines than Sonorans, all Spanish speakers became targets of racism. Anglo-Americans commonly threatened Latinos/as with violence, extorted money from them for "protection," and, not infrequently, lynched them. From 1848 to 1879, according to recent studies, one out of every 3,650 ethnic Mexicans living in the Southwest was lynched at the hands of Euro-Americans.

Despite its generic name, the Foreign Miners' Tax specifically targeted Latinos/as. In the legislation that enacted the tax, Latinos/as were referred to as "culprits of Mexico and South America." The measure imposed a fee of $20 per month on all noncitizen miners and, while challenged, was later upheld by state appeals courts. Passage of the tax also brought an increase in anti-Latino violence, and Euro-American and other non-Latino immigrant miners simply evicted Latinos/as from many of the better mines. In some areas, Latinos/as were able to stay only if they were employed by Euro-Americans and/or shared their earnings with them.

Faced with the heavy tax and increased violence, Latinos/as left the mines in large numbers. Thousands moved to large cities, such as Los Angeles, where they were eventually absorbed into established Latino communities. Others, especially Sonorans, returned home with stories of successful mining but also of discrimination and unchecked violence. A few stayed in the mining districts and fought back, becoming folk heroes in the process. Mexicans throughout California wrote songs, or *corridos,* that celebrated the lives of those who resisted; some of the songs are still sung today.

The exodus of Latinos/as from the mines resulted in an economic depression in several California mining towns, including Stockton. Without the revenue from foreign miners, who had spent a large portion of their incomes in local businesses, small merchants in these towns had difficulty keeping their doors open. In 1851, one year after passage of the tax, merchants from these towns successfully pressured the state legislature to repeal the measure. But it was too late. Because of the widespread violence, most Latino miners had no desire to return to California. While some Sonorans continued to work the mines, their numbers never equaled what they had been before the tax.

The Foreign Miners' Tax stands as an example of the discrimination Latinos/as faced during the California Gold Rush. Even though California had been part of Mexico until 1848—or perhaps *because* it had been part of Mexico—many Euro-Americans exhibited a strong animosity toward Latinos/as. The skills and success of Sonoran miners only increased the animosity. Whether natives of California or immigrants from Mexico, Chile, or Peru, Latinos/as were kept down by adverse legislation, routine discrimination, and sometimes deadly violence.

Linda Heidenreich

See also: Mexican-American War.

Further Reading

Carrigan, William D., and Clive Webb. "The Lynching of Persons of Mexican Origin or Descent in the United States, 1848 to 1928." *Journal of Social History* 37 (2003): 411–38.

Heizer, Robert F., and Alan F. Almquist. *The Other Californians: Prejudice and Discrimination Under Spain, Mexico, and the United States to 1920.* Berkeley: University of California Press, 1971.

Standart, Sister Mary Colette. "The Sonoran Migration to California, 1848–1856: A Study in Prejudice." In *Between Two Worlds: Mexican Immigrants in the United States,* ed. David G. Gutiérrez. Wilmington, DE: Jaguar, 1996.

Fuerzas Armadas de Liberación Nacional (FALN)

The Fuerzas Armadas de Liberación Nacional (FALN), loosely translated as the Armed Forces for National Liberation, was a clandestine Puerto Rican *independentista* (pro-independence) group that began to make its presence known within the United States in 1974.

Since the United States took control of Puerto Rico in 1898, strong factions in both Puerto Rico and the United States have called for the complete independence of the island. Independence has been pursued by means inside and outside of the political process and has ranged from acts of civil disobedience to violence. The push for independence resulted in the formation of the Puerto Rican Nationalist Party in 1922, the Ponce Massacre in 1937, and the 1954 attack on the U.S. Congress by four Puerto Rican Nationalists.

During the 1960s, peaceful political groups such as the Puerto Rican Independence Party (PIP) and the Movement for Independence (MPI) appeared on the political scene. However, groups such as the Independent Armed Revolutionary Movement (MIRA) resorted to violent forms of resistance. The FALN is a direct descendent of MIRA and was a proponent of the latter's aggressive practices.

Founded by Puerto Rican pro-independence advocate and revolutionary Filiberto Ojeda Ríos in 1967, MIRA was one of the first "modern" Puerto Rican independentista organizations dedicated to achieving its ends through any means necessary, especially through the use of violence. In the late 1960s, MIRA gained a reputation as a terrorist organization, and the group received training, arms, and ammunition from Cuba. In 1969 and the early 1970s, MIRA coordinated a bombing campaign on American businesses in New York City. MIRA—along with another independentista group, Armed Commandos for Liberation (CAL)—was infiltrated by the Federal Bureau of Investigation (FBI) in 1973, which resulted in twenty of its members being accused of conspiracy to overthrow the U.S. government. The group subsequently lost its support from the powerful Puerto Rican Socialist Party (PSP) and was eventually dissolved.

The exact origins of the FALN are unknown, but it is believed that in 1974, former MIRA leader Ojeda Ríos, now considered the *padrino* (godfather) of Puerto Rican independentistas, regrouped in New York City with some of the remaining members of MIRA and CAL to form the FALN.

Doctrine and Ideology

FALN's ideology was grounded in the pursuit of Puerto Rico's complete independence from the United States and the release of Puerto Rican political prisoners. A number of pro-independence activists from the 1950s and 1960s were held in American prisons. The FALN hoped to call domestic and international attention to their situation by committing violent acts against the U.S. government and corporate organizations, and eventually obtain the prisoners' release.

The FALN considered Puerto Rico's relationship to the United States as that of a colony and compared Puerto Rico's situation to that of other countries that were once considered colonies of European states. Using Algeria's struggle for independence from the French as an example, the FALN launched dual attacks against American control of Puerto Rico not only on the island but also in the United States. The organization considered the struggle a war for independence and believed revolutionary violence to be an effective method to achieve their goals.

Activities and Operations

The FALN waged its campaign against the United States by detonating bombs in and around military and government buildings, financial institutions, and corporate headquarters in Chicago, New York, and Washington, D.C. Between 1974 and 1983, FALN was responsible for more than 100 bombings or incendiary attacks, close to twenty attempted bombings or bomb threats, and a total of five deaths and eighty-three injuries.

The majority of the FALN-engineered bombings destroyed property without causing human casualties, but there were several notable exceptions. On January 24, 1975, in reprisal for a right-wing bombing in Puerto Rico in which two independentistas were killed, the FALN bombed the historic Fraunces Tavern in New York City, killing four people and injuring more than fifty. In another incident in August 1977, a bomb planted in an umbrella at Mobil Oil corporate offices in New York City killed one company employee and injured five other people. A violent attack also took place on March 15, 1980, when armed members of the FALN raided the Democratic presidential campaign headquarters of Jimmy Carter and Walter Mondale in Chicago and the Republican headquarters of George H.W. Bush's presidential campaign in New York City. In both locations, campaign workers were tied up and the offices vandalized.

Arrests and Trial

The FALN operatives were hard to track down, despite the fact that some members were on the FBI's most wanted list for many years. However, on April 5, 1980, eleven members of the FALN were arrested at Northwestern University in Chicago for conspiracy to commit robbery, bomb-making, and sedition. They were also charged with firearms and explosives violations. At their trial, all eleven declared themselves political prisoners and refused to take part in the proceedings, requesting that the international community grant them a military tribunal. The group consisted of FALN members Elizam Escobar, Ricardo Jiménez, Adolfo Matos, Dylcia Pagán, Alicia Rodríguez, Ida Luz Rodríguez, Alberto Rodríguez, Luis Rosa, Freddie Mendez, Alejandrina Torres, and Carmen Valentín. The group's requests were denied, and they were tried in Chicago and found guilty of all charges in February 1981. They were convicted on a variety of charges, ranging from bomb-making and conspiracy to armed robbery, and given sentences ranging from thirty-five to ninety years.

A second group of FALN members was tried in Chicago in 1985. The three members were Edwin Cortés, Alberto Rodríguez, and Alejandrina Torres. These last arrests marked the end of bombing activity in the United States, and the FALN remained out of the political spotlight until 1999.

Clemency and Controversy

In August 1999, in a controversial decision, President Bill Clinton granted clemency to sixteen FALN members who had been imprisoned since the 1980s. None of these members had been connected to violence that resulted in human injury or death. The move was criticized by a number of groups that regarded the FALN as a terrorist organization but praised by Puerto Rican and U.S. activist groups that regarded the original sentences of the FALN members as unfair and politically motivated. The debate continues to the present day. All sixteen FALN members who were released from prison denounced the use of violence according to the terms of their release, but most have claimed that they will continue to participate in the struggle for the independence of Puerto Rico.

Timothy P. Gaster

See also: Puerto Ricans.

Further Reading

Fernández, Ronald. *Prisoners of Colonialism: The Struggle for Justice in Puerto Rico.* Monroe, ME: Common Courage, 1994.

Torres, Andrés, and José E. Velázquez. *The Puerto Rican Movement: Voices from the Diaspora.* Philadelphia: Temple University Press, 1998.

G

Galarza, Ernesto (1905–1984)

One of the earliest Chicano scholars and advocates for farmworker rights in the mid-twentieth century, Ernesto Galarza wrote numerous books and hundreds of articles, reports, government testimonies, and literary pieces on Latin America, agriculture, and Mexican American labor in the United States. He was recognized for his work with a nomination for the Nobel Prize in Literature in 1976.

According to Galarza's memoir, *Barrio Boy* (1971), he was born on November 15, 1905, in western Mexico. His family lived in a small adobe house in the village of Jalcocotán, Nayarit, in the mountains near Puerto Vallarta. Like many families, Galarza's was displaced by the violence and destruction of the Mexican Revolution, which broke out in 1910. After trying unsuccessfully to relocate inside Mexico, he, along with his now divorced mother and two uncles, migrated to the United States. They ultimately settled in Sacramento, California, where Galarza went to school and worked in the fields to help support the family. These early experiences shaped his interest in, and understanding of, Latino immigration and labor.

With the encouragement and support of his teachers, Galarza successfully negotiated the segregated, English-only local public school system. He graduated from high school and earned a scholarship to Occidental College, where he received a bachelor's degree in 1927. He later attended Stanford University, where he earned his master's degree in 1929, and Columbia University in New York, where he took his doctorate in economics in 1947. Early in his career however, instead of pursuing a strictly academic path, he focused his energy on education, as he and his wife, Mae Taylor, ran a progressive school in Queens, New York. In 1936, Galarza joined the Pan American Union (later the Organization of American States). Because of his expertise in Latin American issues, he was made head of the Division of Labor and Social Information, and authored several articles on the region.

Galarza resigned his position at the Pan American Union in 1947 (he had resigned before but returned after he was encouraged to rejoin the organization) partly as a protest against what he alleged were unfair U.S. policies in Latin America, but also to work on immigrant labor and agricultural issues in the United States. In 1947, he took a position as director of research for the National Farm Labor Union (NFLU) and later the Agricultural Workers Organizing Committee (AWOC). There he focused his attention on organizing migrant farmworkers in California and elsewhere, despite bitter opposition from growers. He led influential strikes against the DiGiorgio Corporation, tomato and cantaloupe growers in California, and sugarcane and strawberry growers in Louisiana. During the 1950s, Galarza testified frequently at Congressional hearings concerning the status of Mexican and Mexican American workers. In 1964, he was appointed chief counsel for labor on the U.S. Congressional committee investigating a bus accident in Chualar, California, in which thirty-two Mexican laborers were killed.

By the late 1960s, Galarza also began focusing on securing urban Mexican American rights through several barrio-based organizations, particularly near his home in San Jose, California. He served as a consultant to such nonprofit groups as the Ford Foundation on Mexican American Affairs and was a guest lecturer at the University of Notre Dame, the University of California, Santa Cruz, and elsewhere. At the time of his death, on June 22, 1984, he was living and working in San Jose, dedicating himself to improving public education for Mexican Americans.

Galarza's many books include *Merchants of Labor: The Mexican Bracero Story* (1964); *Mexican Americans in the Southwest* (1966), with Julian Samora and Herman Gallegos; the Spanish-language poetry and photography collection *Zoo Risa* (1968); *Spiders in the House and Workers in the Field* (1970); the autobiographical *Barrio Boy* (1971); *Farm Workers and Agri-Business in California, 1947–1960* (1977); and the poetry collection *Kodachromes in Rhyme* (1982). By far his most popular book remains *Barrio Boy,* which offers a stirring narrative of immigration and assimilation, detailing both the physical relocation to a new country and the ideological and cultural changes associated with becoming Mexican American. Many consider his most influential work to be *Merchants of Labor,* in which he exposed the exploitation of Mexican contract workers in California agriculture and helped bring an end to the Bracero Program in 1964.

Susan Marie Green

See also: Bracero Program; Education; Migrant Workers.

Further Reading

Acuña, Rodolfo. *Occupied America: A History of Chicanos.* 5th ed. New York: Pearson Longman, 2004.

Galarza, Ernesto. *Barrio Boy.* South Bend, IN: University of Notre Dame Press, 1971.

Gamio, Manuel (1883–1960)

A preeminent figure in the fields of Mexican and Chicano studies, Manuel Gamio was a trailblazing archaeologist in Mexico and head of the Mexican Department of Anthropology from 1917 to 1924. He began the professional exploration of the city of Teotihuacán in 1918 and worked in the highlands of Guatemala researching the Mayan people. His fieldwork on the lives of Mexican immigrants in the United States, along with that of Paul Taylor, remains a foundation for contemporary Mexican immigration scholarship today.

Manuel Martínez Gamio was born in Mexico City on March 2, 1883, to wealthy landowners who had holdings in Oaxaca, Vera Cruz, and Puebla, and in the Dominican Republic. He graduated from the National Preparatory School in 1903 and obtained a bachelor's degree from New York City's Columbia University in 1906. He also obtained his master's degree from Columbia, studying under Franz Boas, one of the pioneers of modern anthropology and often referred to as the "father of American anthropology." Gamio received his doctorate from Columbia in 1922.

Although his scholarship consists of more than 130 publications, Gamio is best known among U.S. scholars for his work on Mexican immigration. His two most acclaimed books, *Mexican Immigration to the United States* (1930) and *The Life Story of the Mexican Immigrant* (1931), were published by the University of Chicago and funded by the Social Science Research Council. Both are cited in every prominent text on Chicano history. Gamio's scholarship remains both influential and relevant in contemporary circles, as his analysis of the Mexican American experience and the controversies associated with Mexican immigration remain true and accurate today.

The data for *Mexican Immigration to the United States,* chronicling the heavy influx during the 1920s—when Mexico was plagued by widespread violence and the U.S. economy was hungry for readily available, inexpensive labor—was compiled from records of the national Mexican post office, which provided the names, origins, and U.S. locations of migrant workers. Gamio determined that Mexican immigrants to the United States sent home between $8 million and $14 million annually through postal money orders during this decade. Today, total remittances to Mexico exceed $5 billion annually.

The Life Story of the Mexican Immigrant, consisting of seventy interviews collected between 1926 and 1927, provides insight into the attitudes, concerns, and aspirations of Mexican immigrants struggling to fulfill an elusive American Dream. Gamio perceived that immigrant workers feared the loss of cultural heritage among their children and were simultaneously angry and saddened by the treatment they experienced at the hands of Mexican American bosses and Anglo employers. As is still true today, most were confident that they would return to Mexico after making enough money, but they ended up staying because of marriage, children, grandchildren, and better-paying jobs.

Gamio's contributions to Chicano historiography might never have occurred, if not for his conflict with Mexico's President Plutarco Elías Calles and his followers in 1925. Based on his work in the Teotihuacán region, Gamio set up several developmental programs, including a training program promoting indigenous education and home building, which he sought to implement on a national scale. However, a dispute with the Mexican president over the purpose, scope, and size of the project forced Gamio to resign his position as inspector general of archaeological monuments with the Ministry of Public Education. Determined to continue his work, he then used his personal and professional connections in the United States to start a different anthropological project, a study of Mexican migration, funded by the Social Science Research Council. His contacts included Secretary of Agriculture Henry Wallace and American Federation of Labor leader Samuel Gompers, both heavily involved in the U.S. debates over Mexican immigration. Gamio also received assistance from a former colleague at the University of Chicago, a graduate student also working on Mexican migration as part of a larger project on immigration to the United States. The student, Robert Redfield, would later convince Gamio to publish a series of interviews as the foundation for *The Life Story of the Mexican Immigrant.*

In the mid-1930s, Gamio returned to Mexico and began serving in a number of significant academic and political positions, which put him at the forefront of indigenous anthropological education. Among these positions were director of the Department of Rural Population, adviser to the minister of Public Education, and, from 1942 until his death in 1960, director of the Mexican National Indigenous Institute. The works of Manuel Gamio remain indispensable sources of information and methodology in his fields of research.

Jaime R. Aguila

Further Reading

Gamio, Manuel. *Mexican Immigration to the United States.* New York: Arno, 1969.

———. *The Life Story of the Mexican Immigrant: Autobiographic Documents.* New York: Dover, 1971.

Walsh, Casey. "Eugenic Acculturation: Manuel Gamio, Migration Studies, and the Anthropology of Development in Mexico, 1910–1940." *Journal of Latin American Studies* 31:5 (2004): 118–45.

Gangs

Ethnic street gangs in American society have flourished in neighborhoods of poor immigrants since the early nineteenth century. They have taken root where economic and social deprivation have led young people to seek refuge among others who find themselves in similar circumstances. Poor and working-class Latinos/as provide a case in point. Latino gangs first formed during an early period of discrimination against Mexican Americans and have evolved during more recent discrimination against Puerto Ricans and Central American immigrants. All in all, for more than eighty years, Latino gangs have sought to create alternate cultures to mainstream Anglo-American society.

The Mexican Revolution of 1910, combined with a shortage of labor in the United States, prompted hundreds of thousands of Mexicans to flee the country for the American Southwest. During this period of turmoil and instability, the first manifestations of Latino gangs—known as the *pachuco* culture—emerged. Young men of El Paso, Texas, spawned these first gangs. They spoke a slang dialect known as *Caló,* and tattooed themselves on their hands or faces with the "luminous cross," symbolizing *la vida loca*—"the crazy life" of violence and illegal activities.

These young men—and women—often engaged in activities such as bootlegging along the borderlands during the 1920s. Several migrated to Los Angeles and influenced a younger generation of "Zoot Suiters"— known for wearing long coats and baggy pants pegged at the bottom—at the time of the Zoot Suit Riots in 1943. The subsequent generations became the *cholos* of the 1970s and "gang-bangers" of the 1990s. Salvadoran immigrants, who have formed modern groups such as the 18th Street gang and Mara Salvatrucha, also adopted gang culture. In the Midwest and on the East Coast, the Almighty Latin King and Queen Nation, made up primarily of Puerto Ricans, constitutes a culture in its own right,

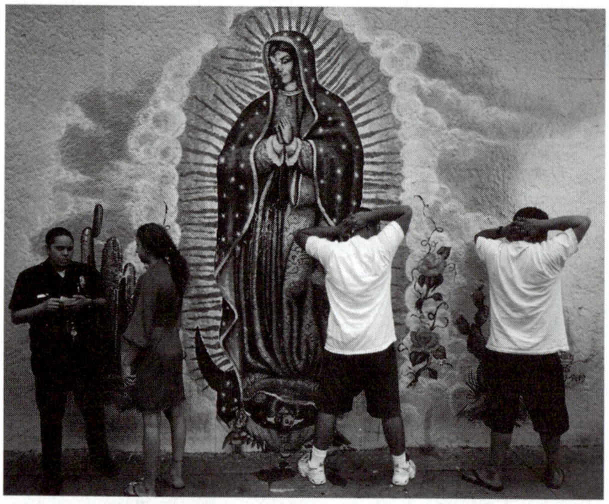

Police interview suspects after a gang shooting in the Boyle Heights neighborhood of East Los Angeles a community marred by gang violence for decades. *(Gilles Mingasson/Getty Images)*

with hundreds of members in Chicago, New York, and other cities. In short, everywhere in the United States where men and women of Latin American descent have faced job discrimination, school segregation, and social isolation since the early twentieth century, gangs have provided an outlet for disaffected youth.

California

During the late 1960s and early 1970s, the cholos of Los Angeles organized new gangs, usually based on both ethnicity and territory or turf. In addition to adopting the Caló language, these youths designed a specific dress code: plaid shirts buttoned at the top and khaki work pants, along with Stacy Adams leather shoes or "wino" slippers. Like their pachuco forebears, they also sported cross-shaped tattoos on their hands. They claimed allegiance to their neighborhoods, fought street battles for turf, and admired older gangsters from the Mexican Mafia prison gang. During the 1970s, cholo culture spread to the Southwest, northern California, and such remote locations as the Yakima Valley in Washington State.

By the early 1990s, gang factions in California became divided into *Sureños* (Southerners), who adopted the color blue and the number 13, and *Norteños* (Northerners), who adopted the color red and the number 14, as gang symbols. Sureños claimed geographic allegiance to southern California; their enemies, the Norteños, were loyal to northern California. The role model of the Northerners was the *Nuestra Familia* (Our Family) prison gang. Although the southern gang members of Los Angeles and other cities fought each other, migration by gang members to the north has for years caused bloodshed between the two groups in cities like Fresno, San Jose, and Salinas. The rivalry has spread to the Pacific Northwest, where gang violence has erupted in places like Portland, Oregon and the Yakima Valley. Those who survive the battles in California often look forward to membership in prison gangs, which have been increasingly weakened by crackdowns on the part of law enforcement.

The 18th Street gang (symbolized by XVIII, or 18) was created between 1960 and 1966 by immigrants in Los Angeles who had been shunned by Mexican American gang members centered on Clanton Street in what is now the Rampart section. By the early 1990s, the 18th Street gang spread from southern California to several U.S. states. It broke down racial barriers by admitting members of all races. In Los Angeles—where youths of Salvadoran descent featured prominently—the gang became so organized as to charge "taxes" on illegal activities like prostitution and drug dealing. In 1994, according to local gang investigators, at least thirty people were murdered in Los Angeles County for failure to pay their 18th Street taxes. As the gang peaked in the mid-1990s, there were an estimated 30,000 members across the United States. It was to be dwarfed in size and scope, however, by another massive gang of immigrants from El Salvador, now international in scope: Mara Salvatrucha, or MS-13 (Sureño).

This gang also was founded in Los Angeles in the 1980s, likewise in the city's Rampart area. It was the product of an immigration wave entailing tens of thousands who fled the conditions of El Salvador's twelve-year civil war (1980–1992), in which upwards of 100,000 people were killed or tortured. The children who grew up during this war, along with others who had been members of rebel factions or "death squads," formed MS-13 as protection against more established gangs, like their blood rivals, 18th Street. In the 1990s, the U.S. government deported hundreds of gang members—all immigrants who had been convicted of crimes—back to Central America. As a result, groups of MS-13 members sprouted up in El Salvador, Honduras, and Guatemala. They flourished in El Salvador's prison system, becoming more organized and gaining a reputation for extreme violence. In the United States, Mara Salvatrucha now has members on both the West and East Coasts, including 5,000 in the Washington, D.C., area and an estimated 50,000 worldwide. The gang is heavily involved in auto theft, immigrant smuggling, and drug trafficking. Members have also been responsible for murdering federal U.S. agents. In 2005, more than 700 MS-13 members were deported to Central America, though members claim to be able to reenter the United States at will.

Chicago and New York

By the 1970s, the Latin Kings became a powerful force on the streets of Chicago, especially in the South Chicago and Humboldt Park areas, which have large Puerto Rican and Mexican American populations. Like the California gangs, the Latin Kings, which include both Mexican and Puerto Rican factions, battled other ethnic gangs (especially African Americans) over street turf and adopted a unique style and set of symbols. The factions differ slightly with regard to the Kings symbol, but not with the colors, which are black and gold. For Puerto Ricans, the predominant symbol is a three-pointed crown, for Mexicans, a five-pointed crown—both crossed with pitchforks. By the 1980s, the gang had spread through the East Coast via prison systems, starting in Connecticut. Two inmates there wrote the *King Manifesto,* a document specifying rules and regulations for the gang. The document was adopted by a New York State branch, which started at the Rikers Island penitentiary as the Almighty Latin King and Queen Nation. It quickly spread throughout the state, claiming hundreds of members inside and outside prison walls, especially in New York City. The Latin Kings were among the latest of the ethnic gangs prominent in the city's history, starting with the Irish gangs of the Five Points area in the nineteenth century. Males and females in the city's public schools were sought for recruitment, turning the gang into one of the fastest growing in New York during the 1990s.

In the late 1990s, however, federal investigations resulted in hundreds of arrests of Latin Kings. Like its California Latino counterparts, however, the gang remained active, with loosely linked branches in several other cities. It also remains a powerful influence among young Puerto Ricans and Chicanos/as caught up in the economic and social hopelessness of the inner cities of the Midwest and East Coast.

E. Mark Moreno

See also: Chicago; Cholos; Los Angeles; New York; Prison Gangs; Zoot Suit Riots.

Further Reading

Irwin, John. *Prisons in Turmoil.* Boston: Little, Brown, 1980.

McWilliams, Carey. *North From Mexico: The Spanish-Speaking People of the United States.* New edition updated by Matt S. Meier. New York: Greenwood, 1990.

Moore, Joan. *Homeboys: Gangs, Drugs, and Prison in the Barrios of Los Angeles.* Philadelphia: Temple University Press, 1978.

Morales, Gabriel C. *Varrio Warfare: Violence in the Latino Community.* Seattle, WA: Tecolote, 2000.

National Alliance of Gang Investigators Associations. http://www.nagia.org.

Sanchez, Reymundo. *My Bloody Life: The Making of a Latin King.* Chicago: Chicago Review Press, 2000.

Garcia, Cristina (1958–)

Cristina Garcia is the first Cuban America woman to publish a novel written in English and to gain widespread national and international attention for her work. The author of four novels and the editor of two major literary anthologies, Garcia often explores the sensibility of Cuban Americans whose culture and loyalties swing between Cuba and the United States.

Born in Havana, Cuba, on July 4, 1958, she left Cuba with her parents in 1960 after the Cuban Revolution and settled in New York. She received a Bachelor of Arts degree in political science from

Barnard College in 1979 and a graduate degree in Latin American studies from the Paul H. Nitze School of Advanced International Studies at The Johns Hopkins University in 1981. Garcia worked as a journalist at a number of newspapers and in 1983 began to write for *Time* magazine. At *Time*, she held several positions, including correspondent and bureau chief in Miami, until 1990 when she retired from journalism to dedicate herself full time to fiction writing.

The first of Garcia's novels, *Dreaming in Cuban* (1992), was nominated for a National Book Award. Praised for its lyrical quality and humor, the novel examines the lives of one family, the del Pinos, who have been torn apart by the Cuban Revolution. One branch of the family, including the matriarch, Celia, her daughter Felicia, and Felicia's three children, remain in Cuba, loyal to the revolution and to President Fidel Castro. Another branch, including Celia's daughter Lourdes, her son-in-law, Rufino, and her granddaughter, Pilar, flees the revolution and lives in exile in New York. Lourdes has embraced her life in the United States and is vehemently anti-Castro. The narrative alternates between Celia and Felicia, both of whom are in Cuba, and Lourdes and her daughter, Pilar, in the United States; it also includes Celia's unsent love letters to an unnamed Spaniard. The multiple narrative perspectives reveal differing versions of family stories and expose the toll of exile on individuals and families.

Garcia's second novel, *The Aguero Sisters* (1997), takes up many of the same themes as *Dreaming in Cuban,* but focuses on the general history of the island rather than the revolution. The story moves between three generations of Cuban women: Blanca, her two daughters, Constancia and Reina, and their daughters. Constancia Aguero is a conservative businesswoman who lives in a condominium in Miami, drives a pink Cadillac, and runs her own cosmetics company, called *Cuerpo de Cuba,* which markets skin care products to wealthy Cuban exiles. Her half-sister, Reina, is a sensuous, earthy, master electrician living a restless life in Cuba. When Reina is struck by lightning, she flees Cuba for Miami and the sisters become reacquainted. Together they try to piece together family divisions and secrets. Like *Dreaming in Cuban*, the novel includes multiple settings and points of view, explores the fragmented lives of Cuban exiles, and offers a feminist view of Cuban and Cuban American history.

Garcia's third novel, *Monkey Hunting* (2003), is another family saga about emigration, albeit much wider in scope. Spanning two centuries and five generations, it includes characters that move between China, Africa, Cuba, and the United States. The novel begins in 1857, with Chen Pan leaving a life of poverty in China in the hope of finding riches on the mysterious island of Cuba. Chen falls in love with Lucrecia, a mulatto slave. The novel then traces the lives of these characters, their children, and their grandchildren. It explores how individuals who live between cultures construct their identities and how notions of home and place shift dramatically within the history of a family.

A Handbook to Luck (2007), Garcia's fourth novel, is written for a young-adult audience. Like her other works, it moves between parallel narratives of characters in exile. In this case, however, the movement is not solely between Cuba and the United States. Enrique Florit and his magician father Fernando have left Cuba to live in Las Vegas; Marta Claros has escaped family troubles and the brutal military police in El Salvador; and Leila Rezvani has come to Las Vegas from Tehran, Iran. The novel weaves together episodes of exile and violence as the characters search for a future somewhere between choice and destiny.

Garcia has also edited two literary anthologies: *Cubanismo! A Vintage Book of Contemporary Cuban Literature* (2003) and *Bordering Fires: The Vintage Book of Contemporary Mexican and Chicana and Chicano Literature* (2006). Both collections introduce and juxtapose U.S. Latino and Latin American writing for audiences reading in English and in Spanish.

Molly Metherd

Further Reading

Kandiyoti, Dalia. "Consuming Nostalgia: Nostalgia and the Marketplace in Cristina Garcia and Ana Menendez." *Melus: The Journal of the Society for the Study of the Multi-Ethnic Literature of the United States* 31 (Spring 2006): 81–97.

Socolovsky, Maya. "Unnatural Violences: Counter-Memory and Preservation in Cristina Garcia's *Dreaming in Cuban* and *The Aguero Sisters.*" *Lit: Literature Interpretation Theory* 11:2 (August 2000): 143–67.

García, Héctor P. (1914–1996)

The Mexican American physician and World War II veteran Héctor Pérez García was one of America's first modern-day civil rights leaders, fighting on behalf of Mexican Americans for half a century. Whether on behalf of World War II veterans or the disenfranchised in the barrios of Texas, García pressed for equality for the Mexican American community, especially in such areas as improved housing, education, jobs, and health care. The sacrifice of more than 750,000 Mexican American men and women during World War II and the countless others who had served on battlefields in previous American wars entitled them, in his view, to full citizenship rights. To this end, in 1948 he established the American GI Forum, which still boasts chapters in more than thirty states.

Formative Years

García was born in Llera, Tamaulipas, Mexico, on January 17, 1914. At the age of four, he moved with his family to Mercedes, Texas, in the Rio Grande Valley along the U.S.-Mexico border. His parents, José and Faustina, both former teachers, supplemented their children's public school education with homeschooling. Although the family struggled financially, the focus on education was never compromised. After school, Héctor and his siblings went to his uncle's dry-goods store, where they worked and received instruction in Mexican and world history and literature, math and science, music, art, Latin, and Greek. Héctor's father encouraged all his children to become physicians, both for the respect of the community and to overcome the limited employment opportunities available to Mexican Americans. Six of the seven García children, two of them women, became medical doctors.

García was one of the first Mexican Americans to graduate as valedictorian of his Mercedes public high school class. He went on to study zoology at the University of Texas at Austin, receiving his bachelor's degree in 1936. He pursued a medical degree from the University of Texas Medical Branch at Galveston, which only admitted one Mexican American student each year, and graduated in 1940. Upon receiving his medical degree, he began his internship at Creighton University's St. Joseph Hospital in Omaha, Nebraska.

The outbreak of World War II put García's plans for a medical practice on hold. From 1942 to 1946, he served as an officer in the infantry before becoming a U.S. Army Medical Corps physician. He attained the rank of major and was awarded the Bronze Star Medal and six battle stars.

During his years of service, García learned German, Italian, and Arabic, while exploring the cultures of the countries he visited. Although he emerged with enhanced pride from having fought for his country, he held strong opinions about his tour of duty: "These three long weary years of suffering and pain and hardships and heartaches have taught me how to be tolerant and how to be patient. I have seen poverty and have seen cruelty and I want to place myself above both of them. I do not seek to fight unless it's completely right."

GI Forum and Fight for Civil Rights

In 1946, García began practicing medicine in Corpus Christi, Texas. Because his office was located near the Veterans Administration (VA) building, he contracted with the VA to provide services to Mexican American veterans, many of whom were being denied treatment at the nearby naval air station hospital or denied financial assistance for medical expenses, disability pay, and education as specified by the GI Bill of Rights. Witnessing these socioeconomic and political injustices, García held town meetings to discuss veterans' concerns and to promote self-help. At times he even drove through town with a loudspeaker, advocating for the cause and pressuring the city to provide adequate services. Out of these efforts the GI Forum was born on March 26, 1948, at a meeting in a local elementary school with more than 700 in attendance. The fledgling organization, dedicated to addressing problems of discrimination and inequities faced by Latino veterans, elected García as its chairman.

The following year, one scandalous incident catapulted García and the American GI Forum into the national spotlight. The body of U.S. Army Private Felix Longoria, a Mexican American who had been killed in the Philippines in 1945 and posthumously awarded the Purple Heart, was returned to his hometown of Three Rivers, Texas. When the Anglo funeral parlor director refused the widowed Beatriz Longoria's request to hold a wake and bury her husband, she contacted García for help. After confirming her story, García contacted then State Senator Lyndon B. Johnson. An account in *The New York Times* called the incident to the attention of the entire country, and Senator Johnson arranged for the burial of Private Longoria in Arlington National Cemetery outside Washington, D.C. The soldier was duly honored, but the injustice in Three Rivers was never redressed.

In the aftermath of the Longoria incident, García traveled the country to organize new GI Forums. He also began to broaden his focus beyond veterans' issues, addressing the wider array of social inequalities facing Mexican Americans in his Corpus Christi community and beyond—segregated education, job discrimination, poll taxes, and lack of adequate housing and health care. His charismatic leadership attracted other Mexican Americans to the GI Forum and its cause, expanding the organization to a national presence. It soon became the leading civil rights organization in the United States.

The GI Forum helped achieve a number of notable legal victories, including a landmark U.S. Supreme Court ruling in *Hernandez v. State of Texas* (1954). The legal appeal began after an all-Anglo jury convicted Pete Hernandez, a Mexican farmworker, of murder in state criminal court. American GI Forum attorney Gus García, with the help of the League of United Latin American Citizens, appealed the verdict to the Supreme Court on grounds that Hernandez had not been granted a fair trial—no juror was Mexican American, hence, he was not judged by a jury of his peers. The high court justices agreed, declaring that members of racial minorities such as Mexican Americans are entitled to "equal protection of the laws" under the Fourteenth Amendment to the Constitution. In the 1950s, the GI Forum also fought for the elimination of the Bracero Program, a federal guest-labor program initiated during World War II, under which Mexican migrants were hired for low wages to work in the agricultural fields of California and the Southwest.

An admirer stands before a portrait of Héctor P. García, founder of the Mexican American veterans group American GI Forum, at a commemoration shortly after García's death in 1996. *(AP Images/Corpus Christi Caller-Times, David Adame)*

Political Activity and Later Life

García became increasingly involved in national politics, and was appointed in 1954 to the Advisory Council of the Democratic National Committee. In 1960, after Senator John F. Kennedy won the Democratic nomination for president, García served as national chairman of the Viva Kennedy Clubs, established to promote Kennedy's candidacy, support his proposals for civil rights, school desegregation, and equal opportunity; in the course of doing so, the clubs also enhanced the political influence of the Latino community. With Kennedy in the White House, García was named to the diplomatic delegation that signed a mutual defense treaty between the United States and the Federation of the West Indies in 1961. At the same time, García also played a key role in

establishing the Political Association of Spanish-Speaking Organizations (PASO), a national association that called for passage of social and economic measures for the advancement of Mexican Americans, including a minimum wage for migrant workers; welfare for elderly, widowed, and orphaned Mexican Americans; and federal aid to Latino education. García served as PASO's first president from 1960 to 1964.

In 1967, President Lyndon Johnson made one of the first major appointments of a Mexican American to the high ranks of government, naming García as an alternate U.S. ambassador to the United Nations, with a special mandate to improve relations with Latin American nations. The following year, Johnson appointed him as the first Mexican American to serve on the U.S. Commission on Civil Rights. On March 26, 1984, García was awarded the Presidential Medal of Freedom, the nation's highest civilian award, by President Ronald Reagan. On August 7, 1998, García was posthumously awarded Mexico's highest civilian award, the Aguila Azteca (Aztec Eagle).

Undistracted by accolades, García continued his fight on behalf of Mexican Americans. In 1987, he lobbied against the effort to make English the official language of the United States. In 1988, he traveled to the *colonias,* areas along the U.S. and Mexican borders inhabited by poverty-stricken workers, to advocate for increased medical and sanitary services. After a heart attack and an extended battle with cancer, Dr. Héctor Pérez García died on July 26, 1996.

Rita D. Hernandez

See also: American GI Forum; Health and Health Care; Military, Latinos in the; Viva Kennedy Clubs.

Further Reading

Carroll, Patrick J. *Felix Longoria's Wake: Bereavement, Racism and the Rise of Mexican American Activism.* Austin: University of Texas Press, 2003.

García, Ignacio M. *Héctor P. García: In Relentless Pursuit of Justice.* Houston, TX: Arte Público, 2002.

Ramos, Henry A.J. *The American GI Forum: In Pursuit of the Dream, 1948–1983.* Houston, TX: Arte Público, 2002.

Rivas-Rodriguez, Maggie, ed. *Mexican Americans & World War II.* Austin: University of Texas Press, 2005.

Gay and Lesbian Organizations

Organizations in the United States that advocate for Latino lesbian, gay, bisexual, and transgender (LGBT) persons operate at the national, regional, and local levels. The only national nonprofit organization specifically dedicated to LGBT Latinos/as, called LLEGÓ, closed in 2004. Its closure left the burden of advocacy on national mainstream LGBT-centered organizations, which offer some Latino resources, and to local and regional Latino LGBT organizations, which serve local communities while pressing for change nationally.

National Latino LGBT Organizations

While not specifically oriented toward Latinos/as, Immigration Equality—founded in 1994 as the Lesbian and Gay Immigration Rights Task Force—is nonetheless important to the community. As its name suggests, this national organization provides a vehicle for activism, services, and information (in English and Spanish) on immigration equality, and serves as an advocate for LGBT and HIV-positive individuals under U.S. immigration law. Immigration Equality defines its mission as, "Advocating for equal immigration rights for the lesbian, gay, bisexual, transgender, and HIV-positive community." Given the frequent intersection between the Latino and immigrant communities, this New York City-based organization—with chapters throughout the United States—provides a specific point of connection for many LGBT or HIV-positive Latinos/as and their partners.

The only nonprofit national civil rights group specifically dedicated to LGBT Latinos/as, LLEGÓ, closed its office at the end of August 2004. Headquartered in Washington, D.C., LLEGÓ provided information regarding HIV prevention and resources for LGBT Latinos/as. The organization sponsored LGBT-oriented events and worked in coalition with other local and national groups. The closing of the LLEGÓ office did not signal the absence of a need for the organization and its services to the Latino community; rather, it exemplified the financial burden faced by many nonprofit groups, especially those serving minority communities.

National Mainstream LGBT Organizations with Latino Resources

The Gay and Lesbian Alliance Against Defamation (GLAAD) was established in New York in 1985 specifically to oppose inflammatory press coverage of the AIDS epidemic. Soon thereafter, it opened offices in Los Angeles, and it has expanded its mission to promote fair representation in the media and to oppose discrimination based on sexual preference or gender identity. The organization operates a Web site, GLAAD.org *en español,* a Spanish-language network that includes Guía Informativa Sobre las Comunidades Latina/o (Information Guide About Latina/o Communities), Programa de Medios de Comunicación Para Gente de Color (Program of Media Communication for People of Color), Comunidad LGBT Latina/o (LGBT Latina/o Community), and La Comunidad LGBT en América Latina (The LGBT Community in Latin America).

Another advocacy group, the Human Rights Campaign (HRC), also maintains a Web site, but does not offer clear links for LGBT Latinos/as or information in Spanish. However, HRC does provide information about "coming out" in communities of color and addresses Latinos/as as one such community. This information includes an account of challenges faced by LGBT Latinos/as in the areas of family, religion, language, and society. The site also contains a resource guide for LGBT Latinos/as.

Highlighting connections between sexual identity and race-based forms of discrimination, Parents and Friends of Lesbians and Gays (PFLAG) offers the Families of Color Network (FOCN). FOCN originated in 1999 with the purpose of "creating awareness within PFLAG chapters of cultural differences within the LGBT community." Families of Color Network strives to build coalitions with local and national communities of color. Families of Color Network-Latino (FOCN-Latino) is a subdivision of FOCN and provides specific resources for Latino communities in addition to support, education, and advocacy.

Local and Regional Latino LGBT Organizations

The Austin, Texas, Latino lesbian and gay organization allgo defines itself as "a queer people of color organization," with a vision statement that reads as follows: "ALLGO envisions a just and equitable society that celebrates and nurtures vibrant people of color queer cultures." The body was founded by a group of Latino activists in 1995 as Austin's Latino/a Lesbian, Gay, Bisexual and Transgender Organization. Keeping with its vision, allgo works to create a network of queer people of color activists, groups, and allies and is considered the longest-standing queer people of color organization in the United States. Its programming has received national acclaim for employing a holistic model comprised of health, the arts, and community organizing.

A number of organizations serve the New York City metropolitan area. Among them is the Gay and Lesbian Dominican Empowerment Organization (GALDE), which supports Dominican LGBT communities in New York City and the Dominican Republic. GALDE's aim is to increase the political visibility of the Dominican LGBT community and to provide HIV/health awareness, educational services, and cultural activities. In pursuit of these aims, the organization provides a safe space in which education and empowerment are fostered, and advocates for the political, social, and educational rights of the Dominican LGBT community. Latinos y Latinas de Ambiente/NY (LLANY), founded in 1993, is a community-based organization that advocates for the socio-cultural needs and concerns of the Latino LGBT communities in the metropolitan area.

The Lesbian, Gay, Bisexual & Transgender Community Center, in New York City as well, was established in 1983 and has become the largest LGBT service organization on the East Coast of the United States and the second-largest LGBT community center in the world. More than 300 groups meet at the LGBT Community Center, which has promoted the development of numerous grassroots organizations. The LGBT Community Center provides social service, public policy, education, and cultural/recreational programs.

Mano a Mano, a network of New York City-based Latino LGBT organizations and activists was created in 1997 with the objectives of sharing information, addressing issues involving the New York Latino LGBT community, and assisting in the development of LGBT Latino organizations in the city. An offshoot of the organization, the Mano a Mano Email Network connects Latino lesbian, gay, bisexual and transgender communities in New York City to events, jobs, health resources, and news at the local, statewide, national, and international levels. The e-mail list also provides a forum for the discussion of Latino LGBT issues. Finally, the Venezuelan and American Lesbian Gay Organization (VALGO) is a nonprofit organization dedicated to helping the Venezuelan and Latin American communities of New York City to identify services and share networks. VALGO itself offers immigration services, social services, and recreational activities.

Latina-Specific Organizations

Amigas Latinas was founded in 1995 as a support and advocacy group for Latina lesbian, bisexual, and questioning women in the Chicago area; it remains the only group of its kind in greater Chicago. The organization's program includes monthly topical discussions, workshops, and educational training. It holds support groups in English and Spanish and participates in public events in both the Latino and LGBT communities. A central aim of Amigas Latinas is to give voice and visibility to the experiences of Latina lesbian, bisexual, and questioning women.

Las Buenas Amigas was founded in 1986 by a group of Latina lesbian friends to address a lack of unity among Latina lesbians in New York City. Some of the founding participants were members of Soul Sisters, an African American lesbian organization that included Latinas. Las Buenas Amigas provides a "family" and social network for new immigrants in the United States, offering a variety of educational, social, political, and recreational resources.

Latino-Specific Organizations

Asociación Gay Unida Impactando Latinos/Latinas a Superarse (AGUILAS) was created in 1991 by a group of Latino gay men in San Francisco; in English, the name of the organization translates as Association of United Gays Impacting Latinos/Latinas Toward Self-Empowerment. AGUILAS's mission is to foster knowledge and pride in gay and bisexual Latinos in the areas of language, culture, and history. AGUILAS aims to create a culturally sensitive space with programs that promote health, community building, and positive self-identity.

The Association of Latino Men for Action (ALMA) provides support, advocacy, and leadership opportunities for gay, bisexual, and questioning Latinos in Chicago. The organization uses cultural programming to foster a group identity through the experiences of Latino gay, bisexual, and questioning men. ALMA provides a voice on social and political issues locally and nationally.

Latino Gay Men of New York (LGMNY) is a nonprofit, community-based organization that promotes community building, positive self-image, and visibility and voice for gay, bisexual, transgender, and questioning Latinos in New York City. The group was founded in 1991, meets once a month at the LGBT Community Center in Greenwich Village, and is a member of Mano a Mano.

Mary K. Bloodsworth-Lugo

See also: AIDS/HIV; Lesbianas Unidas; LLEGÓ.

Further Reading

Carballo-Dieguez, Alex. "Hispanic Culture, Gay Male Culture, and AIDS: Counseling Implications." *Journal of Counseling and Development* 68:1 (1989): 26–30.

Marsiglia, Flavio Francisco. "Homosexuality and Latinos/as: Towards an Integration of Identities." *Journal of Gay & Lesbian Social Services* 8:3 (1998): 113–25.

Romo-Carmona, Mariana. "Lesbian Latinas: Organizational Efforts to End Oppression." *Lesbians of Color: Social and Human Services* 3:2 (1995): 85–94.

Gonzales, Rodolfo "Corky" (1928–2005)

Rodolfo "Corky" Gonzales is widely regarded as one of the most influential Chicano civil rights activists of the 1960s. A former prize fighter, businessman, and official of the Colorado Democratic

Party, he became one of the central leaders of the Mexican American civil rights movement and a leading advocate of Chicano nationalism and economic, political, social, and cultural self-sufficiency. Born on June 18, 1928, in the Mexican neighborhood of Denver, Colorado, to poor migrant farmers, Gonzales often worked beside his family in the fields. While in high school, he became interested in boxing and, like many poor immigrants before him, used it to as a way out of poverty. Having won sixty-five of his seventy-five bouts and a Golden Gloves championship, he became the third-ranked contender for the world featherweight title. By 1953, however, he left the ring to run a neighborhood bar and work as a bail bondsman.

Increasingly active in local politics, Gonzales became district captain of the Denver Democratic Party by 1959 and coordinator of the Colorado Viva Kennedy campaign during the presidential race the following year. He also served as chairman of the local antipoverty program, an experience that would greatly influence the direction of his life and career. In 1966, after a Denver newspaper accused him of discriminatory practices in the antipoverty program, Gonzales was forced to resign all of his political positions. Already frustrated with traditional politics, he abandoned his affiliation with the Democratic Party and concentrated his efforts on the problems of Colorado's Mexican Americans. In 1968, he organized the Crusade for Justice, an urban civil rights organization that promoted Chicano self-determination and cultural nationalism. He also purchased an old school and a church building, converting them into a Crusade school, theater, gymnasium, nursery, and cultural center to serve the community. The same year, with fellow activist and community leader Reies López Tijerina, he introduced the Plan del Barrio, a blueprint for improving education, providing better housing, increasing Chicano-owned businesses, and returning lost or stolen Spanish and Mexican land grants to their rightful owners.

As spokesperson of the Crusade for Justice, Gonzales was extremely active on a number of fronts, including organizing and supporting the Chicano school walkouts, protesting against police brutality, and demonstrating against the Vietnam War. But perhaps his most important contribution to the Chicano Movement was organizing the series of Chicano Youth Liberation conferences, the first of which was held in Denver over five days in March 1969. It was at this conference that Corky introduced El Plan Espiritual de Aztlán, a manifesto of Chicano self-determination and ethnic nationalism. The Plan de Aztlán was also designed to provide direction for Chicano youth in their effort to secure cultural and economic liberation, and called for the creation of a Chicano-based political party. The following year, Gonzales founded the Colorado chapter of La Raza Unida Party (LRUP), dedicated to the empowerment of the Chicano community. At the LRUP's 1972 national convention, held in El Paso, Texas, Gonzales lost his bid for the party's chairmanship to the founder of the Texas-based party, José Angel Gutiérrez. Gonzales returned home and continued his activities in support of Chicano civil rights.

Despite his many accomplishments as a civil rights leader, "Corky" Gonzales is perhaps best known for his 1967 epic poem, *Yo Soy Joaquín* (*I Am Joaquín*), which inspired Chicanos/as throughout the country to demand their civil rights and contributed vitally to the development of ethnic identity and pride among Chicano youth. As the momentum of the Chicano Movement waned in the latter part of 1970s, Gonzales's leadership began to decline as well. Although he remained head of the Crusade for Justice, the organization was now largely limited to Colorado. He continued to speak out for civil rights during the 1990s, but medical problems prevented him from becoming as involved as he would have liked. All in all, his life's work had an enduring impact on the development of Chicano self-identity, especially among youth, and his contributions as a community organizer, youth leader, political activist, and civil rights defender helped to create a new spirit of Chicano unity. Rodolfo "Corky" Gonzales died on April 12, 2005.

Jesse J. Esparza

See also: Aztlán; Chicano Movement; La Raza Unida Party; Movimiento Estudiantíl Chicano de Aztlán; Plan Espiritual de Aztlán, El; Viva Kennedy Clubs; *Yo Soy Joaquín.*

Further Reading

Gonzales, Rodolfo. *Message to Aztlán: Selected Writings of Rodolfo "Corky" Gonzales.* Ed. Antonio Esquibel. Houston, TX: Arte Público, 2001.

Marín, Christine. *A Spokesman of the Mexican American Movement: Rodolfo "Corky" Gonzales and the Fight for Chicano Liberation, 1966–1972.* San Francisco: R and E Research Associates, 1977.

Vásquez, Francisco H. *Latino/a Thought: Culture, Politics, and Society.* Lanham, MD: Rowman & Littlefield, 2003.

González, Elián (1993–)

Elián González Brotons, born in Cárdenas, Cuba, on December 6, 1993, was the young protagonist in a protracted immigration and custody dispute between the United States and Cuba from late 1999 to mid-2000. On Thanksgiving Day, November 22, 1999, the six-year-old Elián embarked in a small aluminum boat with his mother, his stepfather, and eleven other people to escape the Fidel Castro regime, only to become shipwrecked a few miles off the coast of Florida three days later. Only Elián and two adults, Arianne Horta and Nivaldo Fernández, were able to survive, clutching the three inner tubes they had taken on board to use as life jackets. The boy was lying unconscious on one of the tubes when he was rescued by fishermen and turned over to the U.S. Coast Guard. He was taken to Joe DiMaggio Children's Hospital in south Florida; both his mother and stepfather had died at sea.

The legal complications of Elián's case stemmed mainly from the 1994 migration agreement between the United States and Cuba, commonly referred to as the "dry feet/wet feet" policy. This law allows those Cuban refugees who make it to U.S. soil to remain in the country, but requires those intercepted at sea to be deported back to Cuba. Although the latter circumstance applied to Elián, the case was complicated by the facts that he was not of legal age, that his mother was now dead, and that his father knew nothing of his attempt to reach the United States. Elián's parents, Elizabeth Brotons and Juan Miguel González Quintana had separated in 1997, and Elizabeth had taken the child out of Cuba without his father's consent. He thus became the object of a political and public relations tug of war between Miami's Cuban-exile community and the Cuban government.

Since Elián had no legal representation in the United States, he was taken to his granduncle (on his father's side), Lázaro González, who lived in Miami. Elián's father promptly petitioned that the boy be returned home, igniting a diplomatic dispute between the United States and Cuba, all while attracting great media attention. Lázaro's request that Elián remain in Miami became a rallying cry to the U.S. Cuban exiles opposing Castro's regime—especially the Cuban American National Foundation. On the other hand, Juan Miguel's demands were backed by the Castro regime, making Elián yet another icon of the Cuban revolution.

On January 5, 2000, the U.S. Immigration and Naturalization Service (INS) ruled that Elián's father was the only person authorized to represent the child and act on his behalf. This decision, supported by President Bill Clinton and Attorney General Janet Reno, was a hard blow to the Cuban community in Miami, as it required the boy's return to Cuba no later than January 14. Elián's relatives in Miami appealed the decision in federal court, and seven days

Members of Miami's Cuban American community react to the U.S. Supreme Court decision in June 2000 not to hear the case of young Cuban refugee Elián González. The ruling ended the custody battle, and the boy was returned to his father in Cuba. *(Roberto Schmidt/AFP/Getty Images)*

later his grandmothers, Raquel and Mariela, traveled to the United States to take him back to Cuba. Although they were allowed to visit with him briefly, they were not permitted to take him away and returned to the island alone. Juan Miguel traveled to Washington, D.C., on April 6, but was not allowed to see his son until April 22. It was on that day, following an order from Attorney General Reno, that federal agents took Elián by force.

The U.S. Supreme Court sided with the Clinton administration, ruling that under U.S. law Elián should return to Cuba to be with his father. The anti-Castro community in Miami was overwrought, as Elián left the country from Dulles International Airport in northern Virginia on June 28, 2000, with his father, stepmother, stepbrother, and cousin. Thus ended a controversy that had stirred the passion of the Cuban exile community in America and exacerbated the already uneasy relationship between Castro and the U.S. government. In Miami, Elián continued to be referred to by the exile community as *Eliancito* or *el balserito,* echoing the refugee experience of so many Cubans who made the passage across the Straits of Florida in small boats or rafts. For Cubans in Cuba, the boy became a living icon of the Revolution, returned to his homeland by the imperialist United States; for anti-Castro Cubans in the United States, he became a symbol of all those who fail to escape the island's regime.

David Arbesú

See also: Balseros; Castro, Fidel; Cubans.

Further Reading

Bardach, Ann Louise. *Cuba Confidential: Love and Vengeance in Miami and Havana.* New York: Random House, 2002.

Dillman, David L. "The Paradox of Discretion and the Case of Elian Gonzalez." *Public Organization Review* 2:2 (June 2002): 165–85.

Martínez, María del Carmen. "Mothers Mild and Monstrous: Familial Metaphors and the Elián González Case." *Southern Quarterly: A Journal of the Arts in the South* 42:1 (2003): 22–38.

McLaren, Peter, and Jill Pinkney-Pastrana. "Cuba, Yanquización, and the Cult of Elián Gonzalez: A View from the 'Enlightened' States." *International Journal of Qualitative Studies in Education* 14:2 (March 2001): 201–19.

Gonzalez, Henry Barbosa (1916–2000)

A prominent Texas political figure and advocate for racial and social justice, Henry Barbosa Gonzalez served on the San Antonio City Council, in the Texas State Senate, and for nineteen terms in the U.S. House of Representatives (1961–1999). A liberal Democrat, but widely regarded as a maverick, he distinguished himself as a champion of civil rights, workers' rights, and women's rights.

Henry B., as his constituents knew him, was born in San Antonio, Texas, on May 3, 1916. Six years earlier, at the outbreak of the Mexican Revolution, his parents had fled Mexico to escape the violence there and traveled to Texas in search of a better life. Although he grew up in a happy, middle-class family, many of his neighbors and friends were poor, and this gave Gonzalez a lifelong understanding of the hardships of poverty.

Upon completing high school, Gonzalez enrolled at the University of Texas, but experiences with racial discrimination prompted him to return to San Antonio. He enrolled at San Antonio College, ultimately graduating in 1935 with a bachelor's degree. In 1940, he earned a law degree from St. Mary's University. During World War II, Gonzalez worked as a cable and radio censor for naval intelligence, after which he returned to San Antonio and accepted a position as a juvenile probation officer. His work with poverty-stricken Latino families convinced Gonzalez that he needed to run for elected office.

Gonzalez's entrance into politics began in 1950 with an unsuccessful run for the Texas House of Representatives. His campaign literature had emphasized that he was "backed by no special interest or pressure group," which appealed to local residents accustomed to San Antonio's business-dominated political machine. Many of Gonzalez's speeches also hinted at his growing social and racial awareness. He decried "discrimination that worked against proper progress of neglected people," and referred to Mexican Americans as *la raza,* indicating his political militancy. Although he lost the election, the campaign and his rhetoric propelled Gonzalez into the political limelight. In 1953 he ran for the San Antonio City Council and won easily. As a councilman, he opposed Mayor Jack White's plans to burn books at the city library; the mayor had deemed the books "communist." Gonzalez was also vocal in his opposition to a city housing plan that discriminated against African Americans and Mexican Americans. After winning reelection in 1955, he introduced motions to desegregate all city facilities, and the legislation passed easily.

With bigger objectives in mind, Gonzalez ran for the Texas State Senate in 1956 and easily defeated his Republican rival, Jesse Oppenheimer. His victory was noteworthy for at least two reasons: he was a political liberal within the Democratic Party, which at the time in Texas was relatively conservative; and he was the first person of Mexican descent elected to that office in more than 100 years.

In 1957, the Texas state legislature began debating several pieces of Jim Crow legislation in hopes of circumventing the U.S. Supreme Court's school desegregation decision in *Brown v. Board of Education* (1954). Barely six months into his term, Gonzalez, along with Abraham "Chick" Kazen, Jr., announced plans to stage a filibuster against any legislation attempting to enforce Jim Crow. When the first measure—a pupil placement bill that would have allowed local school officials to decide whom they would admit to their schools—came up for debate, Kazen filibustered for fifteen hours; then Gonzalez took over and spoke for twenty-four hours. Neither man had the political clout to defeat the bill, which eventually passed, but they filibustered against other bills that came to the Senate floor in 1957. Many legislators found Gonzalez's words inspiring. The Senate had "sown to the wind and reaped a whirlwind!" he warned. "The assault on the inner dignity of man, which our society protects, has been made. We all know in our hearts and minds that it is wrong."

These events set the stage for a Gonzalez gubernatorial run in 1958 against incumbent Governor Price Daniel, a pro-segregation governor in the mold of Orval Faubus (the Arkansas governor who stood against integration in 1957) and George Wallace (the segregationist Alabama governor). On a shoestring budget, Gonzalez ran a grassroots campaign to unseat Daniel and his support of racism in Texas. He traversed the state in his station wagon, often giving speeches standing on the tailgate of his car, and attending *tamaladas,* BBQs, and banquets in his honor. Almost all of the state's black and Latino newspapers endorsed the senator's campaign, but Gonzalez was a long shot and Governor Daniel was easily elected to a second term.

Once again, Gonzalez responded to election defeat by aiming higher and addressing larger issues. In 1961, he ran as a Democrat in a special election for the U.S. congressional seat based in San Antonio and won. As a member of Congress, the first piece of legislation he introduced was a resolution calling for the abolition of the poll tax, which helped advance passage of the Twenty-Fourth Amendment to the Constitution in August 1962 (and ratification in January 1964). After winning a full term in 1962, Gonzalez was reelected to Congress seventeen more times.

He vigorously supported the Civil Rights Act of 1964, the Voting Rights Act of 1965, and many of President Lyndon B. Johnson's Great Society programs. In 1976, he helped open new Congressional investigations into the assassinations of President John F. Kennedy (Gonzalez was in the motorcade when Kennedy was assassinated) and Martin Luther King, Jr. Gonzalez became chairman of the House Select Committee on Assassinations, a position that allowed him to continue the investigations of the murders of Kennedy and King. He later served as chairman of the Subcommittee on Housing and Community Development, where he fought against President Ronald Reagan's attempts to cut funds to housing programs for the poor.

As an activist politician, Gonzalez was in many ways ahead of his time. At the same time, he remained disconnected from the radical movements of the late 1960s. Some Chicano leaders regarded Gonzalez as a *Tío Tomás* (Uncle Tom), denouncing him as a sell-out who cared little for the working-class Latino poor. Likewise, Gonzalez was disturbed when, in 1970, Mexican American youths in Texas founded a new political party, La Raza Unida Party (LRUP), in opposition to the Democratic Party. When LRUP leader José Angel Gutiérrez argued that Chicanos/as should "eliminate the gringo," Gonzalez was incensed.

He used his political clout to pressure groups like the Ford Foundation to cut funding to radical Chicano groups like the Mexican American Youth Organization. Gonzalez also criticized LRUP election victories in south Texas as racist and fleeting. He viewed the LRUP and similar Chicano organizations as practicing "racism in reverse" by advocating a "hate the gringo" mentality. For Gonzalez, Chicano racism was no different from the legislative racism he had filibustered against in 1957.

Gonzalez served in the U.S. Congress for thirty-seven years before retiring because of health reasons in 1998. When he decided not to seek reelection, his son Charlie Gonzalez ran in his place and was elected to the seat; a position he still held as of 2008. Henry B. Gonzalez died in San Antonio of a heart attack on November 28, 2000.

Brian D. Behnken

See also: Politics.

Further Reading

Flynn, Jean. *Henry B. Gonzalez: Rebel with a Cause.* Austin, TX: Eakin, 2004.

Rodriguez, Eugene, Jr. *Henry B. Gonzalez: A Political Profile.* New York: Arno, 1976.

Sloane, Todd A. *Gonzalez of Texas: A Congressman for the People.* Evanston, IL: John Gordon Burke, 1996.

Gonzalez, Jose-Luis (1940–)

The painter, sculptor, art restorer, and administrator, Jose-Luis "Joe" Gonzalez, born in East Los Angeles in 1940, was one of the pioneers of the Chicano mural movement in the 1960s. Living and working in Los Angeles, he contributed greatly to the city's reputation as the "mural capital of the world" by creating, directing, and restoring some of the city's most prominent works. With his brother and a colleague, Gonzalez founded a studio and gallery in East Los Angeles that has provided vital support to Chicano art and artists.

Despite the presence of significant numbers of Mexicans in the United States, Chicano art did not have an important place in the art world until the 1960s. Its roots lay in the Chicano Movement, an alliance of disenfranchised farmers, workers, and students, many of whom used art as a means of expressing their political ideologies and forging alliances. In this time of instability and political upheaval, Chicano artists, who tended to use similar images and icons, developed a bicultural vocabulary that fused the artistic styles, techniques, and images found among artists in both the United States and Mexico. The Mexican heritage of Chicano artists was evident in the use of pre-Columbian design elements, brilliant color, expressionist forms, and a predominantly figurative approach. The new Chicano art was characterized by the use of public canvasses and art forms such as outdoor and indoor murals, posters, and screen prints. Joe Gonzalez played a prominent role in this movement and he was mostly closely associated its work.

By the 1980s, a distinct trend toward institutionalization became apparent in the Chicano art world, as many practitioners abandoned public venues for commercialized art exhibited in galleries and museums. Gonzalez, however, resisted the path of commercialization and remained committed to public art. In the aftermath of the Los Angeles (Sylmar) earthquake of 1971, the Archdiocese of Los Angeles selected Gonzalez to facilitate the restoration of the art collection at San Fernando Mission, a community landmark and Latino cultural monument. He also led the effort to restore a mural of Fletcher Martin, a renowned Los Angeles watercolorist and muralist heavily influenced by the work of David Alfaro Siqueiros. This particular mural, titled *Mail Transportation,* is located at the San Pedro Post Office and elucidates the fluidity between indigenous and U.S. cultures by depicting the myriad of ways in which people have communicated or transported "mail."

Reflecting his commitment to the Chicano community and cultivating a group of artists dedicated to speaking to and from the Chicano community, Jose-Luis Gonzalez, along with his brother Juan, and Juan's high school friend David Botello, founded Goez Art Studio and Gallery in East Los Angeles in 1969. One of the first Chicano galleries anywhere, the Goez Art Studio and Gallery has trained and promoted the work of many Chicano artists since its creation.

Even as he dedicated much of his time and energy to the restoration of existing public art and the cultivation of the community art scene, Gonzalez pursued his own artistic vision. Indeed, the rebirth of the East Los Angeles Chicano art scene can be traced to 1963, when Gonzalez began painting murals on building façades throughout the area. His efforts reflected a belief that art could help revitalize the alienated and impoverished Latino community, while inspiring its residents. In a work titled *A History of Our Struggle,* for example, Gonzalez, joined by Joel Suro Olivares, Robert Arenivar, David Botello, and Juan Gonzalez, documented the history of violence, capitalism, colonization, and resistance on the side of a building on First Street. Similarly, with *La Vida Breve de Alfonso Fulano,* Gonzalez joined forces with these same artists to produce a mural that told the story of Maravilla, one the earliest Latino settlements in East Los Angeles. In wake of his successes and notoriety as both an artist and a teacher, Gonzalez was commissioned in 1975 to lead a group of Chicano muralists to design a 300-square-foot (28--square-meter) mural displayed at the American Folklife Festival in Washington, D.C.

Joe Gonzalez regarded his murals as attempts to start a dialogue with the public, to promote cultural diversity, and to celebrate Latino history and culture in particular. Thus, even persons without knowledge of Chicano art, or art in general, are able to recognize and appreciate his murals as a form of public culture that brings compelling images and an inspirational message to otherwise dull, empty building walls.

Anita Damjanovic and David J. Leonard

See also: Chicano Art; East Los Angeles; Mural Art.

Further Reading

Arreola, Daniel D. "Mexican American Exterior Murals." *Geographical Review* 74:4 (October 1984): 409–24.

de Alba, Alicia Gaspar. *Chicano Art Inside/Outside the Master's House: Cultural Politics and the CARA Exhibition.* Austin: University of Texas Press, 1998.

Pérez, Laura. *Chicana Art: The Politics of Spiritual and Aesthetic Altarities (Objects/Histories).* Durham, NC: Duke University Press, 2007.

Graffiti

As hip-hop culture emerged in the early 1970s as an outlet for Latinos/as and blacks confined to America's ghettos, graffiti—along with rap music, break dancing, and deejaying—emerged as one of its major elements. In response to growing levels of cultural and economic alienation, graffiti—images or lettering scratched, scrawled, painted, or otherwise marked on public property—serves as a means of expressing hopes, dreams, frustrations, and group identity for a generation of young people. At the same time, their appearance has prompted significant levels of outrage and backlash from community leaders, who have argued that such behavior contributes to ethnic and racial stereotypes while defacing public property. An outlet for otherwise subordinate voices in society, graffiti are traditionally found on building walls, subway cars, subway stations, and train cars. Public officials in large cities such as New York, Los Angeles, and Chicago have long complained about the financial and moral costs of this illegal behavior. Nevertheless, graffiti artists continue to express their identity and cultural pride through this long-standing public art form.

The word "graffiti" comes from the Greek *graphein,* which means, "to write." This evolved into the Latin and Italian word *graffito* (plural *graffiti,* or scratchings). A highly stylized form of visual art, graffiti have played a key role in the production and dissemination of hip-hop culture. Graffiti began as a means of marking territory by gang members and of making political statements by community activist groups. Graffiti culture quickly became the center of a thriving social scene, as young men and women began to form crews that "tagged" together. (Often used as a synonym for graffiti, "tagging" refers specifically to a style of graffiti writing.) Graffiti artists or taggers have used a variety of implements and media to leave their mark. Initially the most common tools were pens, magic markers, and chalk. Eventually these gave way to spray paint as the primary graffiti medium. In an effort to produce more colorful and intricate designs and produce larger canvasses, artists often change the caps of the aerosol can, sometimes even adding different types of tips.

Regarded by some as vandalism, graffiti has gained recognition as an underground art form and creative expression of hip-hop culture. "Tags" are also used by gang members to mark turf and by community activists to make political statements. *(David McNew/Getty Images)*

Graffiti as an underground art movement began when Latino and black artists in New York City, Los Angeles, Philadelphia, and other urban centers began writing their names, or the names of their gangs, on city walls and public transportation facilities. As the wave of hip-hop culture gained momentum, so did the youth culture's interest in graffiti, causing residents of metropolitan areas across the country to recognize what the officials regarded as pervasive acts of vandalism. By 1969, Latino graffiti artists in Los Angeles developed a distinctive West Coast *cholo* style graffiti, reflecting the Chicano and Mexican American culture of East Los Angeles Among Latino gangs, graffiti were more commonly referred to as *placas* (plaques, or symbols of territorial street boundaries) or tagging. Gang members used graffiti to seek respect, as tags were regarded by Latino youths as declarations of strength and pride. To mainstream society they were manifestations of the societal ills that plagued city neighborhoods across the country. The prominent East Los Angeles painter Charles "Chaz" Bojorquez, whose aesthetic inspiration came from the Chicano Movement and cholo culture of the 1950s and 1960s, has used his art to express personal and cultural identity, define borders and territories, and recount conflicts.

In 1971, *The New York Times* published an article on TAKI 183, a graffiti artist from the Washington Heights section of upper Manhattan whose tag around the city sparked public concern. TAKI (the artist's nickname) 183 (the numbers in his street address) is widely regarded as the first graffiti artist to gain public recognition. Other artists include JULIO 204, FRANK 207, and JOE 136. By 1972, graffiti became a hot political issue in New York City, as residents called for anti-graffiti days on which city workers scrubbed walls, fences, subway cars, subway stations, and public buildings. Deemed "youthful vandals," graffiti artists came under widespread attack. That year, the General Welfare Committee submitted an anti-graffiti bill to the New York City Council that barred young adults from purchasing markers and spray paint. The measure, passed unanimously, made it illegal to sell spray paint to anyone under the age of eighteen. To the present day, the anti-graffiti efforts established in 1972 continue to be pursued—with not much effect. City officials continue to scrub trains, only to find them covered in graffiti the next day. Police continue to apprehend taggers, but many go unpunished by the courts.

Artist, organizer, and graffiti artist Hugo Martinez established the United Graffiti Artists (UGA) in 1972 to promote graffiti art and artists in galleries and other formal institutions. As a visual expression of hip-hop identity and street culture, graffiti art peaked in the latter part of the 1970s, when aesthetic forms and styles were largely established and the heaviest tagging took place. Still, graffiti art continues to represent an urban vernacular and social gesture that promotes the ongoing development of Latino and black culture in the twenty-first century.

Kristal T. Moore

See also: Gangs; Hip-Hop; Mural Art.

Further Reading

Castlesman, Craig. "The Politics of Graffiti." In *That's the Joint: The Hip-Hop Studies Reader,* ed. Mark A. Neal and Murray Furman. New York: Routledge, 2004.

Cesearetti, Gusmano. *Street Writers: A Guided Tour of Chicano Graffiti.* Los Angeles: Acrobat, 1975.

Jankins, Chaka. "As the Sun Sets, We Rise: The Life and Times of a Graffiti Artist." *Public Art Review* 6:2 (Spring–Summer 1995): 33–35.

Rivera, Raquel. *New York Ricans from the Hip Hop Zone.* New York: Palgrave Macmillan, 2003.

Romotsky, Jerry. *Los Angeles Barrio Calligraphy.* Los Angeles: Dawson's Book Shop, 1976.

Grape Strikes and Boycotts

The grape strikes and boycotts were a series of events that took place in the 1960s mostly in California, as a result of the politicization of the agricultural labor force. The actions led to the formation of the United Farm Workers Union, brought dramatically improved working conditions, and won fairer wages for thousands of migrant farmworkers.

The success of this labor movement stood in contrast to the situation earlier in the twentieth century. Several attempts to organize farmworkers had failed, in large part because organizers tried to use techniques that—while successful with factory workers and skilled artisans—proved to be inadequate to reach workers constantly on the move due to the seasonal nature of farm labor.

Additionally, farm owners had used government initiatives such as the Bracero Program (1942–1964) to replace workers who had been fired because they raised their voices or attempted to organize. At the same time, the growers had consistently and blatantly ignored state and federal labor laws. For example, they paid grape pickers an average of $0.90 per hour and an additional $0.10 per basket, well below the federal minimum wage, while confining them to abhorrent living conditions. They provided no portable toilets in the fields and forced workers to pay $2 a day or more to live in metal shacks that were infested with mosquitoes and lacked heating, plumbing, or cooking facilities. Child labor was common, and workers were often injured or died as a result of preventable accidents. Given these conditions, the average life expectancy for farmworkers was only forty-nine years.

Birth of the Movement

In the early 1960s, the tide began to change in the favor of agricultural workers. From 1962 to 1965, a small group of organizers, including César Chávez, traveled throughout California's agricultural valleys, inviting workers to meetings where they could voice their concerns about their working situation. As a result of previous negative experiences with unions (some unions did not even allow Mexicans to be members) and strikes that had provided no relief, the organizers identified themselves as members of the National Farm Workers Association (NFWA) rather than of a union per se. The process of organizing workers was slow and difficult at first but ultimately gained momentum.

On September 8, 1965, in the midst of NFWA's organizing campaign, about seventy members of the Agricultural Workers Organizing Committee (AWOC), a predominantly Filipino farmworker organization, went on strike against the Giumarra Vineyards Corporation in Delano, California, seeking higher pay and union recognition.

On September 16, one week after the AWOC walkout, the NFWA voted to join the strike and help coordinate it, marking the beginning of the statewide job action against grape growers. The joint leadership included César Chávez, Dolores Huerta, and Gilbert Padilla of the NFWA, and Larry Itliong, Andy Imutan, and Philip Veracruz of the AWOC. Leaders of both organizations understood that a successful labor campaign required broad support from the community and the development of powerful coalitions. In the interest of both, they agreed, it was important to portray the struggle as one not merely for higher wages and a union contract but for basic human dignity and justice. Thus, the movement came to be known as *La Causa* (The Cause).

Influence and Support

By the 1960s, at least two-thirds of farmworkers in California were of Mexican descent. On the strength of his determination and his support in the ever-expanding NFWA membership, Chávez, a Chicano himself, soon emerged as the acknowledged leader of the strike. In 1966, the NFWA and AWOC merged, forming the United Farm Workers Organizing Committee (UFWOC), and elected Chávez as its president. Shortly thereafter, Chávez led a 340-mile (545-kilometer) pilgrimage from Delano to the state capitol in Sacramento. Farmworkers and supporters carried banners that read *"Viva La Causa"* ("Long Live the Cause") and *"Huelga!"* ("Strike!"), calling on the government to pass laws that would force growers to recognize the farmworkers as a union and allow them to negotiate collective bargaining agreements.

Under Chávez's leadership, the farmworkers also sought to garner support from organized labor. The UFWOC began courting the support of progressive unions such as the International Longshore and Warehouse Union, United Automobile Workers, Aerospace and Agricultural Implement Workers of America, and the American Federation of State, County and Municipal Employees. After the backing of these organizations was secured, the UFWOC began seeking support from the national umbrella organization, the American Federation of Labor & Congress of Industrial Organizations (AFL-CIO). These and countless smaller labor organizations were early and lasting supporters that donated time and services throughout the campaign.

In addition to reaching out to the mainstream labor movement, UFWOC organizers appealed to Christian organizations, both Protestant and Catholic; radical student activists, including the Brown Berets and the Students for a Democratic Society (SDS); and other civil rights organizations. Strongly influenced by the teachings of Mohandas Gandhi and Martin Luther King, Jr., Chávez also found inspiration in the philosophical and tactical advantages of nonviolence and coalition building.

Chávez and the UFWOC relied on demonstrations, prayer sessions, marches, fasts, and the time-honored organizing tool of labor, *la huelga*—the strike. In time, he realized that work stoppages had limited potential in a small town like Delano, where growers often found support from the community and many of the farmworkers themselves. In 1967, therefore, Chávez launched a consumer boycott to further threaten profits of Giumarra Vineyards. The success of a consumer boycott depended on winning the hearts and minds of the community at large and grape consumers in particular. Following an attempt by Giumarra to disguise its shipments with the labels of other grape growers, the UFWOC began a national boycott of all table grapes.

On February 15, 1968, to broaden support, Chávez began a personal fast at his headquarters in Delano, adding new life to the movement. Farmworkers by the thousands came to Delano every day for a month to visit with him at evening Mass and to show their support. Chávez's fast lasted until March 11, when presidential candidate Robert F. Kennedy came to help celebrate the occasion. Weeks later, the UFWOC endorsed Kennedy's bid for the presidency, helping him to win the California primary that June. Kennedy was assassinated on the very night of his victory, but not before helping the UFWOC establish its place in national politics.

At the height of the boycott in 1968, more than 14 million Americans refused to purchase table grapes. Pressure from the American public became so great that growers could no longer afford to deny workers their rights. In 1969, Giumarra and other growers signed the first contracts with the UFWOC, ending the most abhorrent labor practices. The victory assured farmworker protection from poisonous pesticides and eliminated unfair hiring practices. The contracts also brought an immediate increase in wages, improved living conditions, and enhanced the quality of life for most farmworkers. Finally, contracts resulted in the creation of a health plan, providing for the construction of health clinics specifically for farmworkers.

Other workers around the country were inspired by what was happening in California and began calling upon Chávez for assistance. Organizers were promptly dispatched to South Texas, Arizona, Colorado, Washington State, and other locations. The victory in Delano, however, proved short-lived. Lettuce growers in Salinas brought in the Teamsters Union to prevent the UFWOC from organizing its farmworkers. The Teamsters, who had been expelled from the AFL-CIO in 1959 because of corruption charges, were more interested in maintaining the status quo and preventing farmworkers from striking than in establishing fair labor practices. In fact, the Teamsters were the only union in the post-World War II era to support the Bracero Program and the Republican Party. Contracts signed with the Teamsters were seen by other unions as "sweetheart deals" that failed to protect the rights of workers.

In 1972, the UFWOC was voted into the AFL-CIO and changed its name to the United Farm Workers Union (UFW). The following year, with the original grape contracts about to expire, the UFW returned to Delano for a new round of negotiations. This time, however, the growers circumvented the UFW and approached the Teamsters for new labor contracts. This sparked a bitter fight between the two unions over the direction of the movement. In the fall, the UFW held a series of strikes throughout the San Joaquin Valley with the support of the AFL-CIO. The Teamsters responded by sending biker crews from Los Angeles to intimidate the farmworkers. Over the course of the strikes, thousands of farmworkers were arrested and two were killed. In the aftermath of the deaths, the UFW called off the strikes and sought other methods to regain their lost contracts.

The UFW found an influential ally in California's Governor Jerry Brown. Under his leadership, the state legislature passed the California Agricultural Labor Relations Act (ALRA) of 1975, which guaranteed the rights of farmworkers to organize and select their union representation. It also required growers to bargain in good faith with the farmworkers' union of choice. The UFW won almost half of its subsequent 406 union elections, forcing the Teamsters to leave California's fields.

The success of the UWF in its battle with the wine industry was not achieved without resistance either. Growers used the elections of 1975–1980 to their advantage, backing government officials who helped delay negotiations for years. After the election of Republican Governor George Deukmejian in 1982, the agency responsible for enforcing the ALRA became less sympathetic to farmworkers. The UFW saw a gradual decline in membership and national power over the course of the subsequent decade, and the death of Chávez in April 1993 marked the unofficial end of an era that inspired a new generation of labor activists.

Nonetheless, the UFW continues to work in the spirit of César Chávez against abuses by grape growers. Recent victories for the UFW include a 2005 contract with winemaking giant Gallo, of Sonoma. The UFW also continues to fight for farmworkers' rights, mobilizing around four heat-related deaths on Giumarra Vineyards fields in July 2005.

Ruben Espejel

See also: Chávez, César; Huerta, Dolores; Migrant Workers; United Farm Workers of America.

Further Reading

De Ruiz, Dana Catherine, and Richard Larios. *La Causa: The Migrant Farmworker's Story.* Austin, TX: Raintree Steck-Vaughn, 1993.

Dunne, John Gregory. *Delano: The Story of the California Grape Strike.* New York: Farrar, Straus & Giroux, 1967.

London, Joan, and Henry Anderson. *So Shall Ye Reap: The Story of César Chávez and the Farm Workers' Movement.* New York: Thomas Crowell, 1970.

Ross, Fred. *Conquering Goliath: César Chávez at the Beginning.* Keene, CA: United Farm Workers: Distributed by El Taller Grafico, 1989.
Wells, Miriam J. *Strawberry Fields: Politics, Class, and Work in California Agriculture.* Ithaca, NY: Cornell University Press, 1996.

"Greaser Act" (1855)

After the end of the Mexican-American War in 1848, Euro-Americans were eager to solidify their power in the region they had just taken from Mexico. The lands acquired by the United States were vast and included all or part of present-day Arizona, California, Colorado, Nevada, New Mexico, Texas, Utah, and Wyoming. After the discovery of gold in California early that same year, the urge to establish and maintain Anglo rule in the area intensified, and Euro-Americans used both legal and extralegal means to displace the Mexicanos who still owned most of the land and held most of the public offices in the region. One strategy was to pass laws that discriminated against Mexicanos, as well as Chicanos/as who were born in the U.S. following the invasion. Some of these laws were directly and specifically aimed at Chicano and Mexicano communities and culture. In California, one the most overtly racist of these laws was the so-called "Greaser Act," which both criminalized everyday behavior and wrote racist language into the law of California.

Passed by the California legislature in 1855, the Vagrancy Act came to be called the Greaser Act because the text actually contained the word "Greaser." Section Two of the measure stated that "all persons who are commonly known as 'Greasers' or the issue of Spanish or Indian Blood . . ." and who were found loitering in public could be arrested. Designed to "protect honest people from the excesses of vagabonds," the law dehumanized Chicanos/as by depicting them as inferior to Euro-Americans—effectively incorporating racist stereotypes into state law. In addition, the law authorized local militias to keep the Mexican community at bay by terrorizing its members; allowed Anglos to confiscate Mexican property; and even allowed Anglos to lynch "recalcitrant individuals" with impunity. While Anglos were allowed to socialize in public places, the 1855 legislation stipulated that Chicanos/as could be arrested for doing so. If found guilty of vagrancy, they could be taken from their families and communities, jailed, and put into forced labor.

The Greaser Act and other racial laws of the time are part of a broader history of anti-immigrant and anti-Catholic agitation. Throughout the nineteenth century, Euro-Americans had used arguments of racial and cultural purity, temperance crusades, and Sabbath laws to consolidate power and attack other ethnic and cultural groups. According to the dominant nationalist ideology of the time—Manifest Destiny—white Protestants were destined to rule the continent because they were culturally superior. In California, many laws of the period were also tied to the anti-Catholic Hispanophobia of newly arrived Anglo Protestants from the East and Midwest. Anglo Protestants felt they were superior to Chicano Catholics and feared being corrupted by a different culture. Thus, the 1850s also saw California's first wide-scale passage and enforcement of Blue Laws, based on white Protestant religion and culture. The state enacted a law against bull, bear, and cock fights, as well as circuses and other "noisy amusements." The penalty for holding such events was a fine ranging from $10 to $500, though law enforcement authorities and the courts—both predominantly Anglo and Protestant—decided when to make arrests and how much to fine perpetrators on a case-by-case basis. Not surprisingly, the laws were enforced unequally throughout much of the nineteenth century.

The Vagrancy Act of 1855 was amended just one year after it was passed to eliminate the word "Greaser" from the text of the law, yet it still was disproportionately used against Mexicanos. Despite the passage and enforcement of discriminatory legislation, many Mexicanos remained in the state. As subsequent generations of Mexicanos migrated north, Euro-Americans lumped *Californios,* Mexicanos who lived in what would become the state of California, together with the newcomers, often under the racial category "greaser."

Linda Heidenreich

See also: Mexican-American War; Race.

Further Reading

Almaguer, Tomás. *Racial Fault Lines: The Historical Origins of White Supremacy in California.* Berkeley: University of California Press, 1994.

Camarillo, Albert. *Chicanos in a Changing Society: From Mexican Pueblos to American Barrios in Santa Barbara and Southern California, 1848–1930.* Cambridge, MA: Harvard University Press, 1979.

Heizer, Robert F., and Alan F. Almquist. *The Other Californians: Prejudice and Discrimination Under Spain, Mexico, and the United States to 1920.* Berkeley: University of California Press, 1971.

Gringo

Gringo/a is a Spanish term for a non-Latino person, especially a North American or U.S. citizen. The word "American," used to refer to citizens of the United States, is not favored in Latin America because its inhabitants also consider themselves American. In most Spanish-speaking countries "gringo" refers to a "foreigner" in a non-derogatory sense. It is conventionally used in reference to people of European descent who speak a non-Romance language such as English. In contemporary Latin American usage, the word refers specifically to citizens of the United States. In Argentina it refers to white, blond Europeans or Italians; in Spain it refers to any foreigners, especially those who speak English.

Depending on tone and context, "gringo" can be used pejoratively both in the United States and in Mexico. According to the *Oxford English Dictionary,* it is a "contemptuous name" for an Anglo-American or European foreigner in Latin America. The negative connotation of "gringo" stems, in part, from international conflicts between the United States and Latin America, such as the Mexican-American War (1846–1848) and the U.S. Marine landing in Veracruz, Mexico (1914). In fact, the first English record of the word appears in John Woodhouse Audubon's *Western Journal* (1849), chronicling his travels through the U.S. Southwest and Mexico. In one entry he wrote, "We were hooted and shouted at as we passed through, and called 'Gringos.'" In the twentieth century, Western films such as *Adios Gringo* (1965) helped popularize the negative use of the word. Interestingly, while most English dictionaries define gringo as a "disparaging" or "derogatory" name, Spanish dictionaries define it as a simple adjective with no negative connotation.

While the exact origins of the "gringo" are unknown, the word did exist in Spanish prior to the Mexican-American War. One of the first written records of the word appeared in the 1786 *Diccionario Castellano con las Voces de Ciencias y Artes,* compiled by Esteban de Terreros y Pando. According to this dictionary, "gringo" was a term used in Malaga, Spain, to describe foreigners who spoke Spanish with an accent. Most likely then, "gringo" is a modification of *griego,* the Spanish word for "Greek." Griego can mean "Greek, Grecian" as an adjective; "Greek, Greek language" as a noun; and "unintelligible language" or "one who speaks gibberish." Losing its explicitly Greek reference, "gringo" thus became analogous to the English phrase "it's Greek to me" or the Spanish phrase "*hablar en griego,*" meaning that something is unintelligible.

There are several additional theories about the derivation of the word in Latin America and the United States. Most of these—though widely discredited by etymologists—attribute the origins of the word to a contraction of "green go." According to one story, U.S. soldiers sung a Scottish folk tune by Robert Burns, "Green Grow the Rushes Oh," while invading the borderland during the Mexican-American War. Similar versions of the story cite other songs, such as "Green Grow the Lilacs" and "Green Grow the Grass." Contracting "Green Grow" into "gringo," local Mexicans were said to have used the term to refer to the invading soldiers.

Another common theory attributes the term to the supposedly green-colored uniforms worn by U.S. soldiers during the Mexican-American War. According to this account, Mexicans would shout or write on buildings "green go" or "greens go home" as a way of protesting the presence of U.S. armed forces. In both of these cases, some form of "green go" was contracted into the word "gringo." This theory is also implausible, however, because U.S. soldiers in the Mexican-American War did not wear green but various blue-colored uniforms.

The persistence of such explanations, however spurious, illustrates the way the meaning of a word can shift over time and location. Although the word "gringo" existed in the Spanish language almost 100 years before the Mexican-American War, the contemporary connection between the word and that conflict demonstrates how the meaning changed from referring to a foreigner with an accent in Spain to a non-Latino U.S. citizen.

Lena McQuade

See also: Mexican-American War.

Further Reading

Bender, Steven W. *Greasers and Gringos: Latinos, Law, and the American Imagination.* New York: New York University Press, 2003.

Malavet, Pedro A. "The Accidental Crit II: Culture and the Looking Glass of Exile." *Denver Law Review* 78 (2001): 767–71.

Grito, El

El Grito de Dolores (The Cry of Dolores) was the battle cry and symbolic beginning of the Mexican War of Independence from Spain in 1810. Mexicans and Mexican Americans throughout North America celebrate the event on September 16. The highlight of the fiesta is a reenactment of El Grito with public recitations and the ringing of church bells, often followed by fireworks and cries of "Viva Mexico!"

The historical event commemorated by the celebration was a fiery speech by Father Miguel Hidalgo y Costilla, a parish priest of the village of Dolores, in the state of Guanajuato, on the night of September 15–16, 1810. Father Hidalgo had gathered his congregation of native peoples and *criollos* (persons of Spanish heritage born in Mexico), ordered the church bells rung, and called for an armed revolt against the Spanish colonial government. "Long live our Lady of Guadalupe!" he declared, "Death to bad government! Death to the *gapuchines* (Spaniards)! Mexicanos, Viva Mexico!" His invocation of the Virgin of Guadalupe, the patron saint of Mexico and symbol of Amerindian faith, achieved mythic status in national lore and ensured a place of prominence for that image in Mexican politics and as an icon for society's underdogs.

The incident had been precipitated by the arrest of Don Ignacio Allende, an advocate of independence from Spain who, with his wife Doña Josefa Ortíz de Domínguez and Father Hidalgo had been members of a subversive literary club in Dolores. The arrest prompted Father Hidalgo to ring the church bell, summoning his parishioners and to deliver his historic cry for independence. He was joined in the rebellion by Allende, who had been freed, and the priest José María Morelos, among others who marched from Dolores to San Miguel de Allende and finally to Mexico City, carrying a banner of the Virgin of Guadalupe and picking up supporters along the way. All three of the Dolores rebels, along with some 15,000 other Mexicans, were killed before the war ended in 1821, when Mexico gained its independence.

The events of September 1810 are commemorated annually in Mexico and Mexican American communities throughout the United States. In Mexico City, the day includes traditional celebrations that date back to the original observances held in the late nineteenth century. Every year at 11 P.M. on September 15, the president of Mexico rings the actual bell from Father Hidalgo's church, now preserved at the National Palace on the Zócalo, or main square, in Mexico City, and repeats a variation of Hidalgo's historic cry. On the following day, a military parade starts in the Zócalo and proceeds through the city to the Paseo de la Reforma, one of the main downtown thoroughfares.

The celebration has a somewhat different flavor in the United States. Chicago marks the occasion with the annual 18th Street Mexican Independence Day Parade, an elaborate and colorful celebration of the country's culture featuring about 150 decorated floats, mariachi bands, Mexican food stalls, and other attractions. An estimated half a million spectators attend the festivities. The city of San Antonio, Texas, meanwhile, established a special municipal body—known as the 16 de Septiembre Commission—to promote public understanding of the meaning and significance of Mexican Independence Day. The celebration there lasts the entire month of September and includes a number of parades, festivals and other special events. The core event is the commemoration of El Grito on the night of September 15. In Los Angeles, El Grito is celebrated with an annual reenactment at City Hall that marks the beginning of Hispanic Heritage Month in the United States.

In recent years, towns such as Columbus, New Mexico, (located near the U.S.-Mexico border) mark Mexican Independence Day with celebrations that feature special symbols of common culture. The celebration is held at Pancho Villa State Park and, under a memorandum of understanding between the governors of New Mexico and Chihuahua, Mexico, those who attend are encouraged to cross the border and celebrate with residents of Palomas, Mexico, where carnival and food booths are featured in the village plaza.

In many locations, the celebration of El Grito is intertwined with the celebration of Central American Independence, commemorated on September 15. Thus it is not uncommon to see a mixture of cultural and national elements from a number of Mesoamerican immigrant groups.

Bernardo Aguilar-González

See also: Cinco de Mayo; Hispanic Heritage Month; Mexicans.

Further Reading

Archer, Christon, ed. *The Birth of Modern Mexico, 1780–1824.* Lanham, MD: Rowman & Littlefield, 2007.

Beezley, William, and David Lorey, eds. *Viva Mexico! Viva la Independencia! Celebrations of September 16.* Lanham, MD: Rowman & Littlefield, 2000.

Jiménez, Carlos M. *The Mexican American Heritage.* Berkeley, CA: TQS, 2004.

Meyer, Michael, William Sherman, and Susan Deeds. *The Course of Mexican History.* New York: Oxford University Press, 2007.

Novas, Himilce. *Everything You Need to Know About Latino History.* New York: Plume, 2008.

Guadalupe Hidalgo, Treaty of

See **Treaty of Guadalupe Hidalgo (1848)**

Guagua Aérea

Guagua aérea (air bus) was the term used by Puerto Ricans for the airplanes that took them from their island homeland to New York City during the great migration wave of the late 1940s and 1950s. In 1983, the term became the title of an influential essay by Puerto Rican writer Luis Rafael Sánchez, who used a trip aboard a guagua aérea as a metaphor of national identity. From that point on, the air bus became a common metaphor for the persistent migratory flow between Puerto Rico and the mainland United States.

From the early part of the twentieth century to the 1960s, the number of Puerto Ricans living in the United States increased from a little more than 2,000 to over 1 million. Since they had been granted U.S. citizenship by the Jones Act in 1917 and because the island was relatively close to the mainland (about 1,250 miles, or 2,000 kilometers, from Florida), Puerto Ricans could move back and forth with ease and frequency, creating a pattern of circular migration. This cycle made the air bus a particularly apt metaphor for the constant flow of Puerto Rican migrants into and out of the United States. As trips between San Juan and New York became commonplace on airline schedules, Puerto Ricans nicknamed the planes guaguas aéreas, inexpensive connections were called *vuelos kikirikí* ("cock-a-doodle-doo flights"), and crossing the Atlantic Ocean was referred to as *brincar el charco* (jumping the puddle).

Originally delivered as a lecture at Rutgers University, Luis Rafael Sánchez's essay "La guagua aérea" was first published in 1983 in the Sunday edition of *El nuevo día* (The New Day), one of Puerto Rico's leading newspapers. The essay opens with the image of a blonde flight attendant horrified at the sight of the Puerto Rican passengers taking a red-eye flight to New York City. Her horror anticipates a kidnapper or terrorist attack, but instead she sees a group of crabs in the middle of the corridor. Sánchez then describes several Puerto Rican idiosyncrasies using slang and popular sayings that create a vivid picture of Puerto Rican society while simultaneously providing critical commentary on social conditions and Puerto Rican experiences. The essay is full of pop culture references, including the astrologer Walter Mercado and pop-music group Menudo. Such local icons coexist with references to Hollywood star Kim Novak and U.S. men's magazines like *Playboy* and *Penthouse.* Laughter is pervasive throughout the flight, but the all-American crew does not get the humor or relate to the cultural allusions. Another recurring element is the telling of migration stories by the passengers. According to Sánchez, popular humor and personal anecdotes are creative ways in which Puerto Ricans have resisted prejudice and personal hardships.

"La guagua aérea" became one of the most influential essays of its time on the Puerto Rican national identity. It was interpreted as a rebuke of Antonio S. Pedreira's *Insularismo* (*Insularism,* 1934) and René Marques's "El puertorriqueno dócil" ("The Docile Puerto Rican," 1960), two influential studies that offered a negative assessment of the effects on Puerto Ricans of their dependent relationship to the United States. These analyses had already been challenged by José Luis González's 1980 essay "El país de los cuatro pisos" ("The Four-Storied Country"), which uses the metaphor of a four-storied building with an Afro-Antillean foundation to describe Puerto Rican culture. Those essays defined being Puerto Rican as being from the island. However, at the end of "La guagua aérea," Sánchez included a brief exchange between the narrator and the woman sitting next to him. They both identify themselves as Puerto Rican, but whereas he comes from a town on the island, she is from New York.

In 1994, "La guagua aérea" became the centerpiece of Luis Rafael Sánchez's first published collection of essays, which expanded on the metaphor of flight to discuss topics ranging from Puerto Rican popular culture to canonical Latin American authors. Sánchez's essay was also the basis for a popular 1995 Puerto Rican film. Directed by Luis Molina Casanova, *La guagua aérea* pieces together the flight between New York and Puerto Rico, using three of Sánchez's short stories as the basis of the narrative. However, whereas Sánchez's essays are critical commentaries concerning Puerto Rican identity, Molina Casanova's film is a nostalgic and humorous look at Puerto Rican history. The film spawned a 2005 sequel, *El sueño del regreso* (The Dream of Returning), in which five Puerto Rican families from New York return to the island for Christmas.

Roberto Carlos Ortiz

See also: Puerto Rican Literature; Puerto Ricans.

Further Reading

Sánchez, Luis Rafael. "The Airbus." Trans. Diana Vélez. *Village Voice* 29:5 (January 31, 1984): 39–43.

Sandoval-Sanchez, Alberto. "Puerto Rican Identity Up in the Air: Air Migration, Cultural Representations and *Me Cruzando el Charco.*" In *Puerto Rican Jam: Rethinking Colonialism and Nationalism,* ed. Ramón Grosfoguel and Frances Negrón-Muntaner. Minneapolis: University of Minnesota Press, 1997.

Guatemalans

The presence of about 400,000 Guatemalan immigrants in the United States has contributed to the Latino community's ethnic and linguistic diversity. Unlike the *mestizo,* Spanish-speaking Latino majority, many Guatemalan immigrants are indigenous people whose first language is a Maya dialect.

Guatemalans began migrating to the United States in appreciable numbers during the 1970s, largely in search of economic opportunity. During the next decades, levels of immigration escalated and the motivation changed from economic to political, as indigenous Guatemalans fled government oppression. The Guatemalan state had historically acted on behalf of the Hispanic minority, or *ladinos,* and—until peace accords were reached in 1996—-used its power to ensure their control over the indigenous Maya majority. It generally did this by promoting the concentration of landholding and compelling small subsistence farmers to become wage laborers on large plantations. This process engendered popular resistance and, in turn, official repression. The military presidencies of generals Romeo Lucas Garcia (1976–1980) and Efraín Ríos Montt (1982–1983), in particular, were characterized by a vicious campaign of state-sponsored violence against the Maya in the northwestern highlands. The government accused them of harboring supporters of the revolutionary Ejército Guerrillero de los

Pobres (EGP) and targeted them for elimination. By the army's own count, it destroyed some 440 villages and killed 150,000 Maya villagers. The surviving men and boys were forced into counterinsurgency civil patrols, and entire villages were relocated close to army bases, where the inhabitants could be closely supervised. Many—about a quarter million—opted to flee either to large cities in Guatemala or to neighboring, or more distant, countries. By 1986 at least 100,000 entered the United States illegally, and sizable Maya communities sprung up in Los Angeles; Houston, Texas; and the smaller agricultural hub of Indiantown, Florida.

The Maya who sought refuge in the United States were initially at a disadvantage because of the intersection of U.S. foreign and immigration policy. Specifically, Washington supported and often armed conservative anti-Communist Central American governments like Guatemala's military regimes. Accordingly, the Immigration and Naturalization Service (INS) was unwilling to grant political asylum to those who fled from an allied country. In 1984, for instance, only three out of 761 petitions from Guatemalan applicants were accepted. Guatemalan activists, however, succeeded in publicizing their plight and the United States' complicity in it through organizations like CORN-Maya in Florida and Ixim in Los Angeles. This public information campaign, in turn, contributed to the so-called Sanctuary Movement: Hundreds of churches and universities across the nation declared that they would offer protection to refugees in violation of laws against harboring undocumented immigrants. The alliance between Maya refugees and American peace activists led to a federal class-action lawsuit in 1985, *American Baptist Churches v. Thornburgh,* which challenged the low asylum rate for Guatemalans and Salvadorans. The INS settled in 1990 and agreed to reopen the case of every Central American applicant whose request had been denied (about 150,000) and guarantee that future requests would be processed without consideration of nationality. A tide of Guatemalan applications poured in, and applicants were given temporary work permits renewable until a distant asylum hearing. This favorable situation lasted until the late 1990s, when the signing of a peace agreement between the government and revolutionary forces in Guatemala removed the cause for asylum, although widespread poverty continued to fuel emigration.

The Maya who moved to the United States over the years have built homogeneous, cohesive communities of migrants from the same township who generally choose to work in the same sector. In Houston, for example, most Guatemalan immigrants are Maya from San Cristóbal Totonicapán employed in the maintenance crews of a local supermarket chain. In Indiantown and Los Angeles, most come from San Miguel Acatán and work in local nurseries or on golf courses and in the garment industry, respectively. The Maya of Morganton, North Carolina, instead, are from the village of Aguacatán and have found employment in a local poultry processing plant. Homogeneity in settlement has enabled these transplanted Maya communities to reproduce their culture of origin. In Indiantown, for example, the patron saint of San Miguel Acatán is celebrated annually in a three-day ceremony that brings together thousands of San Miguel Maya from all over Florida and nearby states. Additionally, immigrants have been sending remittances to Guatemala, enabling Maya to stage lavish celebrations of local festivities and fostering a revival of Maya culture in its own homeland.

Overall, migrants have created a network of social relations both within their new communities in the United States and between the community of settlement and that of origin. The process of cultural continuity, however, has been accompanied by cultural change. Ties have been forged with other North American indigenous people, and the idea of pan-Indianism has entered the Maya worldview. At the same time, the experience of migration has eased the historical factionalism among speakers of different Maya languages, and a new pan-Maya identity has slowly been forming. Meanwhile, new organizations like the Guatemalan Unity Information Agency (GUIA) of Los Angeles have addressed the needs of the youngest members in the community, those born in the United States, who risk losing their culture of origin and have at times been lured by the most negative aspects of American urban culture. Programs to teach specific Maya languages or marimba music have thus sprung up in all major centers of Maya settlement.

Although most Guatemalans came to the United States with no transferable skills, they have fared very well in their new home thanks to "social capital," the ethos of solidarity and mutual support in their community. Still, many remain undocumented and the majority are employed in low wage jobs. The question for the future is whether they will succeed in terms of social mobility as well as cultural preservation.

Paola Gemme

Further Reading

Burns, Allan F. *Maya in Exile: Guatemalans in Florida.* Philadelphia: Temple University Press, 1993.

Fink, Leon. *The Maya of Morganton: Work and Community in the Nuevo New South.* Chapel Hill: University of North Carolina Press, 2003.

Hamilton, Nora, and Norma Stoltz Chincilla. *Seeking Community in a Global City: Guatemalans and Salvadorans in Los Angeles.* Philadelphia: Temple University Press, 2001.

Loucky, James, and Marilyn M. Moors, eds. *The Maya Diaspora: Guatemalan Roots, New American Lives.* Philadelphia: Temple University Press, 2000.

Guevara, Ernesto "Che" (1928–1967)

Ernesto Guevara, known worldwide by the nickname "Che," was an Argentine Marxist revolutionary who became a key adviser to the rebel leader Fidel Castro during the Cuban Revolution of the 1950s. Che was executed in 1967 after an aborted attempt to start a similar revolution in Bolivia and became an international martyr for revolutionary politics and populist power. His image has been widely invoked by leftist organizations—including Latino groups in America—as a symbol of the struggle for justice and liberation from oppression. In addition, the iconic image of Che—in his signature beard, beret, and fatigues—has found a place on album covers, T-shirts, stickers, and other promotional items for revolutionary minded musical artists. For many, Guevara remains a powerful reminder of the "power of the people": a belief that oppression of the poor can and should be challenged by the downtrodden classes.

He was born Ernesto Guevara de la Serna on June 14, 1928, in Rosario, Argentina—the third largest city in the country. Born into a privileged, upper-class family, he was the first son of Ernesto Guevara Lynch and Celia de la Serna y Llosa. Guevara was a twelfth-generation Argentine, and many of his relatives and ancestors were prominent political leaders. His great grandfather served as governor of the Río de la Plata region during the eighteenth century, and his grandmother was an inspiration for Guevara's liberal politics. Both his mother and his father were also politically inclined: his father was an active supporter of the resistance during the Spanish Civil War and anti-Nazi campaigns throughout World War II, and an outspoken dissenter against Juan Perón's dictatorship within Argentina. His mother, also progressively minded, had been arrested for her political activism. Both of his parents remained supportive of their son throughout his life, even supporting his political ideals and efforts to enact revolution among the impoverished and oppressed of Latin America.

When he was twelve years old, the family moved to the town of Córdoba, where Guevara first encountered people who lacked the privileges that he had been afforded. The family lived in a house located near an impoverished shantytown, where Guevara frequently interacted with the poor children. He also devoted much of his youth to studying and learning; he was an above-average student who had a commitment to learning about different people and places and philosophical ideas. He displayed a particular aptitude for science and math, which led him, at the age of seventeen, to study medicine at the University of Buenos Aires.

During his time at the university, Guevara became increasingly interested in the peoples of Latin America and how they lived. In the early 1950s, Guevara and his friend Alberto Granados embarked on a motorcycle journey through South America. It was during the 8,000-mile (13,000-kilometer) trip that Guevara first took note of the injustices of poverty and developed his fledgling Marxist identity—one that advocated justice for all people, regardless of their socioeconomic position. The journey is notably chronicled in Guevara's collection of diary entries, published as *The Motorcycle*

Diaries: Notes on a Latin American Journey (film version, 2004).

Guevara's early involvement in revolutionary politics began soon after the motorcycle trip. When he returned to Buenos Aires, he quickly completed his medical degree and then moved to La Paz, Bolivia, where he began meeting with other political progressives, such as Ricardo Rojo—an exiled Argentine who was an active opponent of Perón's dictatorship. Rojo later became known for his book *My Friend Che* (1968), which documented his relationship with Guevara. In La Paz, Guevara joined with other radically-minded individuals in fighting for the rights of the indigenous people of Bolivia—many of whom had had their lands robbed by unjust laws and oppression at the hands of the Spanish colonial government.

In 1954, Guevara and Rojo traveled through Central America to Guatemala and then to Mexico City, meeting with political radicals along the way. In Mexico, Guevara encountered the man who was to have the most significant impact on his political involvement: Fidel Castro. They formed an immediate bond. Both were committed to international politics, and both believed in the possibility of a people's revolution. Castro convinced Guevara that Cuba was primed for just such a revolution, and Guevara worked alongside him to prepare for it.

More than four decades after his death, Argentine revolutionary Che Guevara remains an icon and inspiration to young political protestors—especially Latinos—such as those at this rally for U.S. immigration reform. *(Jensen Walker/Stringer/Getty Images)*

In 1956, Castro, Guevara (nicknamed "Che" by his Cuban associates), and eighty-two other guerrilla fighters set sail aboard a ship named *Granma* from Mexico, prepared to launch their attack against the repressive Cuban government. After landing on the island, the young revolutionaries declared war against the Cuban government, all the while impressing impoverished Cubans with their populist message and humane style of warfare. Camped in the mountains outside Havana, Guevara and Castro gathered followers among the peasants and laboring class of Cuba, ultimately launching one of the most successful citizen-based revolutions in history. Following the defeat of the Fulgencio Batista regime on January 1, 1959, Guevara, Castro, and the others worked to develop a government that was based on the socialist principles they espoused and that maintained the rights of all people regardless of their position in the socioeconomic system.

After holding several high-level positions in the new government, Guevara left Cuba in 1965 to spread the revolution, carrying his socialist revolutionary vision to other countries in Latin America and Africa. In 1967, on a mission to Bolivia to train guerrillas, he was captured by a Bolivian Special Forces unit (assisted by an agent of the U.S. Central Intelligence Agency) and brought to the village of La Higuera, where he was executed on October 9, 1967.

Sarah Stohlman

See also: Castro, Fidel.

Further Reading

Castañeda, Jorge G. *Compañero: The Life and Death of Che Guevara.* New York: Alfred A. Knopf, 1997.

Guevara, Ernesto "Che." *The Motorcycle Diaries.* Trans. Alexandra Keeble. New York: HarperPerennial, 2004.

Kellner, Douglas. *Ernesto "Che" Guevara.* New York and Philadelphia: Chelsea House, 1989.

Rojo, Ricardo. *My Friend Che.* New York: Dial, 1968.

Simons, Geoff. *Cuba: From Conquistador to Castro.* New York: St. Martin's, 1996.

Gutiérrez, José Angel (1944–)

A student activist, a county judge, an attorney, and one of the founders of La Raza Unida Party, (LRUP), José Angel Gutiérrez was born in Crystal City, Texas, on October 25, 1944. He excelled in school as a boy and went to earn a bachelor's degree from Texas A&I in Kingsville (now Texas A&M–Kingsville) in 1966, a master's degree from St. Mary's University in San Antonio in 1968, a doctorate from the University of Texas at Austin in 1976, and a law degree from the University of Houston in 1988.

Gutiérrez became politically active in the 1960s, when he helped found the Mexican American Youth Organization (MAYO) and LRUP. He was elected president of the Crystal City school district (1970–1973) and also served two terms as a Zavala County judge, from 1974 to 1978. In 1994, he created the Center for Mexican American Studies at the University of Texas, Arlington. He is the author of numerous published works, including *A Chicano Manual on How to Handle Gringos* (2003) and the autobiographical *The Making of a Chicano Militant* (1999).

Gutiérrez is best remembered for his involvement in the creation of LRUP. Following the successful campaign of five Mexican American political candidates who ran for city council in Crystal City in 1963, Gutiérrez began organizing a Chicano political party. He had worked with the Political Association of Spanish-Speaking Organizations (PASO) during the campaign, helping the politicians gain their subsequent victories and witnessing the great potential of community involvement in local politics. Additionally, for Gutiérrez, the experience illuminated the power of grassroots organizing. These experiences pushed him to organize the Mexican American Youth Organization while attending college. MAYO focused on issues of segregation, inferior schooling, and harassment of Latinos/as at the hands of police officers. The organization proved extremely militant, engaging in school walkouts, marches, and even violence. It encouraged students to boycott classes in places like Crystal City and San Antonio, for example, and in Houston it seized a church building to use as a community outreach center. MAYO promoted the ideology of *chicanismo,* which reflected the burgeoning militancy and sense of cultural nationalism that would define the Chicano Movement.

In the aftermath of his experiences during the Crystal City election, working with MAYO, and observing opportunities for transformation through collective political action, Gutiérrez turned his attention to the formation of La Raza Unida Party in 1970, the first Chicano political organization in the United States. One of LRUP's first targets for political action was the city election in Crystal City. Gutiérrez ran for a seat on the school board, as did local Latino businessmen Mike Pérez and Arturo Gonzáles. LRUP also fielded Ventura Gonzáles and Pablo Puente for two city council seats in Crystal City, and a host of other candidates for elections in surrounding counties. The party proved immensely successful in its first electoral effort, with all of its Crystal City candidates and several of those outside the city winning office.

In 1970, Gutiérrez became the school district president in Crystal City and quickly initiated plans to overhaul the system by hiring Chicano teachers and counselors. He helped implement a bilingual and bicultural education program in the district, worked to improve school facilities, and ended the practice of punishing students for minor infractions like dress style and use of Spanish language. The changes continued over several years, as Gutiérrez initiated Mexican American studies courses, expanded bilingual education, formed a grievance committee, and eased dress code regulations. He also joined forces with members of the municipal council to expand the number of Mexican Americans employed by the city.

The successes of La Raza Unida Party in Crystal City prompted the development of campaigns throughout southwest Texas as well as several unsuccessful attempts to elect Chicano state legislators and a Chicano governor. Gutiérrez worked hard to mobilize resources, assisting the party's expansion into California and Colorado. The height of La Raza Unida Party came with the Texas gubernatorial races of Ramsey Muñiz in 1972 and 1974, after which political infighting and Muñiz's arrests for drug possession helped doom the party. Disunity among Chicano leaders began in late 1972, when Gutiérrez called a meeting to discuss the development of a national La Raza Unida Party. This led to the founding of the Congreso de Aztlán, which would administer the national LRUP. Gutiérrez hoped that the Congreso would serve as the organizational arm of LRUP, but Rudolfo "Corky" Gonzales, founder of the Crusade for Justice in Denver and an important Chicano leader, viewed it as an entity designed to unify LRUP with his own Crusade for Justice. He also saw himself as the natural leader of the Congreso, and hence LRUP. But Gutiérrez, Muñiz, and others viewed the organizations as dissimilar. They also saw LRUP as their party. The disagreements between Gonzales and Gutiérrez nearly led to a fistfight on one occasion, which itself divided LRUP's leadership and damaged the party.

Despite the problems with La Raza Unida Party, Gutiérrez served three years on the Crystal City school board. In 1974, he ran for the office of county judge in Zavala County and was elected with ease. He proceeded to fire most of the Anglos on the board and replace them with Chicanos/as. He initiated a community outreach program and implemented reforms in community service agencies to provide for poor Mexican Americans living in the county. Gutiérrez and his fellow Chicano officeholders implemented a variety of government measures that sought to empower Chicanos/as, but the Anglo establishment thwarted their efforts. Gutiérrez was ultimately forced out of office in 1982.

After withdrawing from Texas politics, he left the state altogether, living in Oregon for the next five years. He ultimately returned to Texas to pursue a law degree and eventually opened a law practice in Dallas. By 1990, Gutiérrez again became a judge. At about the same time, he approached the administration of the University of Texas at Arlington (UTA) about forming a Mexican American studies program. The result of his efforts was the formation of UTA's Center for Mexican American Studies, one of the most vibrant ethnic studies programs in the Southwest. Gutiérrez served as the first director of the program, a position he held from its founding in 1994 until 1996. Ever a political radical, Gutiérrez has modified many of his militant ideas in favor of a more pragmatic approach to political organizing. Conservatives continue to lambaste him for a "kill the gringo" statement he made in the 1960s, but he is generally remembered with admiration and respect for his activities in the 1960s and 1970s. Gutiérrez continues to teach and write, while serving as associate professor in UTA's Political Science Department.

Brian D. Behnken

See also: Blowouts; Chicano Movement; Crystal City, Texas; Gonzalez, Rodolfo "Corky"; La Raza Unida Party; Mexican American Youth Organization.

Further Reading

Gutiérrez, José Angel. *The Making of a Chicano Militant: Lessons from Cristal.* Madison: University of Wisconsin Press, 1998.

Navarro, Armando. *The Cristal Experiment: A Chicano Struggle for Community Control.* Madison: University of Wisconsin Press, 1998.

Rosales, F. Arturo. *Chicano! The History of the Mexican American Civil Rights Movement.* Houston, TX: Arte Público, 1996.

H

Health and Health Care

With Latinos/as emerging in increasing numbers as a major segment of the U.S. population, the challenges of addressing their health through the existing health care system have become ever more apparent and difficult for policy makers and health-care providers to overcome. Despite representing the largest racial and ethnic minority in the United States, Latinos/as have faced disproportionate health challenges, including limited access to care and the burden of chronic and infectious diseases.

Limited Access

According to a 2000 report by the University of California, Los Angles (UCLA) and the Kaiser Family Foundation, Latinos/as have the highest uninsured rates of all ethnic groups in the United States. About four out of ten non-elderly Latinos/as have no form of health insurance. Latinos/as of every national origin have significantly higher uninsured rates than whites do, with Mexican Americans and Central and South Americans having the highest. The four states with the highest concentration of Latino residents—California, Florida, New York, and Texas—account for 73 percent of all uninsured Latinos/as. The report states that approximately 40 percent of Latinos/as living in California and Texas and more than one-third of Latinos/as living in Florida and New York are uninsured.

Education is an important correlate of health insurance coverage. According to the UCLA/Kaiser report, only about one in three Latino families whose primary wage earner has less than a high school education receive job-based insurance, leaving nearly half uninsured. Even among Latinos/as who are college graduates, 17 percent are uninsured, compared to only 7 percent of whites.

Although the majority of medically uninsured Latinos/as belong to working-class families, the low rate of coverage is largely driven by a lack of employer-based benefit plans. Only 43 percent of Latinos/as receive coverage through their employer, compared to 73 percent of non-Latino workers. Lower wage earners are the least likely to have insurance, and they either do not qualify for or cannot afford insurance premiums. Latinos/as are also more likely to work for employers who do not offer insurance. Latinos/as who are not U.S. citizens are even more likely to work in industries (such as agriculture, mining, service, and domestic employment) that offer little or no health coverage. The Latino subgroups least likely to have job-based coverage are Mexicans and Central and South Americans. Puerto Ricans have equally low rates of insurance coverage, but they are more likely to receive coverage by the federally funded Medicaid program because they are U.S. citizens. Cubans generally belong to higher tax brackets and therefore have higher rates of private insurance, primarily from employers (54 percent) but also purchased separately (11 percent). Because many Cubans are higher wage earners than other Latinos/as, more become ineligible for Medicaid, leaving 21 percent uninsured.

State and federal governments jointly finance Medicaid. It is subject to broad federal guidelines, yet states design and administer their individual programs, determining the benefits covered, program eligibility, rates of payment for providers, and the administrative procedures for the program. Established by legislation in 1965, Medicaid is the largest health insurer in the United States in terms of eligible recipients. According to *Health Issues in the Latino Community* (2001), Medicaid covers more than 41.3 million people and about four in ten

Latinos/as. The program emphasizes coverage for pregnant women and poor single parents with children, providing a safety net for 28 percent of Latino children.

Immigration and Health Care

Many of the disparities in access to health insurance in the United States have been institutionalized and perpetuated by a growing wave of anti-immigrant sentiment and legislation. In California, the debate over whether undocumented immigrants should receive health care intensified during the 1990s and resulted in the passage of Proposition 187 in 1994. This initiative was designed to restrict undocumented immigrants from government-funded health and social services, including public education. Proposition 187 also gave authority to all law enforcement agents to investigate detained persons suspected of violating immigration laws and to report them to the former U.S. Immigration and Naturalization Service. Although the constitutionality of Proposition 187 was immediately challenged in the courts and the measure was soon overturned, the anti-immigration sentiment and broader ramifications reverberated around the country and set the stage for dramatic federal policy changes in 1996.

The Personal Responsibility and Work Opportunity Reconciliation Act of 1996 legislated changes in the Temporary Assistance to Needy Families (TANF) program that restricted immigrant access to federal work support programs such as Medicaid and Food Stamps. Under the new TANF program, legal residents who entered the country after 1996 are generally not eligible for Medicaid and are restricted from receiving most federal public benefits for their first five years of residence. Those who are eligible may be reluctant to apply for Medicaid because they fear (incorrectly) that it will jeopardize future citizenship or that they will be required to repay Medicaid costs. The lack of knowledge, as well as the complex process of applying for Medicaid, has resulted in a dramatic decline in the number of Latinos/as enrolled in the program. The barriers to regular health care and other programs have forced low-income legal and undocumented immigrants either to avoid using health-care services or to use costly emergency rooms as their main source of medical care.

An alternative path to health care for low-income Latino children is the State Children's Health Insurance Program (SCHIP). Established in 1997, SCHIP provides health insurance to uninsured children in families with incomes above Medicaid's standards. TANF children ineligible for Medicaid due to income are likely to qualify for SCHIP if they meet other eligibility rules. Though the program's initial intent was to reduce the disparity in insurance coverage among low-income children, states have struggled to promote it, with differing degrees of success. Each state defines the group of children who may enroll in SCHIP based on factors such as geography, age, income and resources, residency, disability status, access to other health insurance, and duration of SCHIP eligibility. Yet Latino children are still more likely to be uninsured than whites or African Americans at all levels of income, especially the lowest end.

Disparities in Care for the Insured

Acquiring health insurance does decrease—but not eliminate—disparities in health access for Latinos/as. According to the 2000 UCLA/Kaiser report, about 12 percent of privately insured Latino men in fair or poor health are likely not to have seen a doctor in the past year, compared to 19 percent for white men. In general, Latinos/as are the least likely among all racial and ethnic groups to have a regular health provider when in need of health care (12 percent of Latino children versus 4 percent of white children, and 26 percent of Latino adults versus 15 percent of white adults). Differences also persist in physician care among women and children with comparable health coverage.

Although Spanish is the primary language of about 11 percent of adults in the United States, the nation's health-care system has been criticized for failing to communicate effectively with this population. Medical forms, including those required to qualify for Medicaid and SCHIP are rarely translated. Relatively few Latino physicians or professional translators are available to explain medical terminology. Federally funded health facilities are legally obligated to ensure language access to the communities they serve, yet the lack of necessary resources remains pervasive.

Mortality Rates and Health Issues

According to *Health Issues in the Latino Community,* the top ten leading causes of death for all Americans are heart disease, cancer, stroke, chronic lower respiratory disease, unintentional injuries (accidents), influenza and pneumonia, diabetes, suicide, kidney disease, and chronic liver disease. Although Latinos/as face similar rates of death due to heart disease and cancer, when age is taken into consideration, Latinos/as have higher mortality rates from diabetes, homicide, chronic liver disease, and HIV infection than the general population. (In 2000, the median age was twenty-six for Latinos/as and thirty-five for the population as a whole. More than one-third of the Latino population was younger than eighteen, compared to only one-fourth for the overall population.) During the 1990s, Latinos/as experienced a decline in mortality for all leading causes of death except diabetes. In general, Latinos/as have lower mortality rates than whites, but higher mortality rates than whites in the 25–44 age category. Among persons aged 45–74, mortality rates were 24 percent for Mexican Americans, 26 percent for Puerto Ricans, 16 percent for Cuban Americans, and 12 percent for whites.

Diabetes

Diabetes is one of the most serious health challenges facing Latinos/as in the United States. Diabetes is the sixth leading cause of death for all Latinos/as and the fourth leading cause for Latino women and elderly. Latinos/as are at higher risk of developing and dying from diabetes, and twice as likely as other populations to experience complications such as heart disease, high blood pressure, blindness, kidney disease, amputations, and nerve damage. Diabetes also has an earlier onset in Latino populations. Among Puerto Ricans and Mexican Americans, the age of onset is generally 30–50 years old, yet 10 percent of all Mexican Americans have diabetes as early as age twenty.

HIV/AIDS

Latinos/as in the United States are disproportionately affected by HIV/AIDS as well, accounting for a greater percentage among those who are infected and die from the disease than their representation in the overall population. Although Latinos/as represent approximately 14 percent of the total U.S. population, they account for about 19 percent or more of all AIDS cases. In fact, the proportion of new AIDS diagnoses among Latinos/as has grown over the course of the epidemic, rising from 15 percent in 1985.

According to the 2001 edition of *Health Issues in the Latino Community,* HIV transmission among Latino men who have sex with other men is estimated to occur in about 50 percent of cases, compared to 72 percent of white men. Intravenous drug use accounts for an estimated 28 percent of transmissions for Latino men, compared to 12 percent for white men. Heterosexual sex accounts for 17 percent of transmissions among Latino men, compared to 6 percent for white men.

Latinas, meanwhile, are more likely to be infected by heterosexual transmission than white women—71 percent and 59 percent, respectively. But Latinas are less likely than white women to be infected through intravenous drug use.

Latina Reproductive Health

According to the Center for American Progress in 2004, Latinas fare far worse than other ethnic groups in the area of reproductive health. During the 1960s and 1970s, thousands of Latinas suffered from forced sterilization. These women were sterilized in public hospitals following childbirth without their knowledge or informed consent. Other Latinas were sterilized during this time as a condition to receiving probation or welfare benefits. Although forced sterilization has since been largely eliminated, current laws limiting the amount of people in a family who are eligible for benefits raise similar reproductive control concerns for the growing Latina welfare population.

According to *Health Issues in the Latino Community,* the rate of maternal mortality rates among Latinas is 1.7 times higher than for white women, and the Latina teen pregnancy rate is more than twice that of white women. More than 25 percent of Latinas do not receive prenatal care during their first trimester. Latinas also contract chlamydia 3.5 times more than white women, and cervical cancer incidence among Mexican American and Puerto Rican women is two to three times higher than for white women.

Mental Health

The rate of mental disorders among Latinos/as is similar to those of the white population. However, adult Mexican immigrants and Puerto Ricans living in Puerto Rico have lower rates of depression than Mexicans and Puerto Ricans living in the continental United States. Latino youth experience proportionately more depression, drug use, and anxiety than do white youth. In 1997, Latino adolescents reported more suicidal attempts proportionally than white or black students, yet their actual suicide rate was 6 percent compared to 13 percent for white adolescents.

Only an estimated one in eleven Latinos/as with mental disorders is believed to contact mental health specialists, while fewer than one in five contact general health practitioners. Among immigrant Latinos/as with mental disorders, fewer than one in twenty contact mental health specialists, while fewer than one in ten contact general health practitioners.

Substance Abuse

Latinos/as have proportionally similar rates of alcohol and drug use to those of whites, albeit with notable gender differences. Latinas have unusually low rates of alcohol and drug use, while Latino men have relatively high rates. Latino subgroups also vary in their rates of alcohol and illegal drug dependence, and in their needs for substance abuse treatment. Compared to the general U.S. population, Mexicans and Puerto Ricans have high rates of heavy alcohol use and dependence, illicit drug use, and the need for drug abuse treatment. Latino adolescents have the highest levels of drinking, followed by whites. Latino men are twice as likely to die from cirrhosis, an often-fatal liver disease usually caused by long-term heavy drinking, and have also been found to consume alcohol in higher amounts per drinking session than whites, which may account for the disparity. In addition, Latino men experience higher rates of the serious and infectious liver disease, hepatitis C, which raises the risk of liver damage in heavy drinkers.

Environmental Hazards

Although pollution poses health risks for everyone, a large percentage of Latinos/as live and work in areas of heightened danger from air pollution, unsafe drinking water, pesticides, and lead and mercury contamination. An estimated 91 percent of Latinos/as live in metropolitan areas where the high concentrations of air pollution put them at risk for higher rates of asthma, lung cancer, allergies, and chronic bronchitis. Pregnant women are at particularly high risk of pregnancy complications, and there is a high risk of premature birth, low birth weight, and cardiac birth defects for babies.

One and a half million Latinos/as live in substandard housing along the U.S.-Mexico border, where there is a lack of drinkable water, and sewage contributes to waterborne diseases such as cholera, hepatitis, and giardiasis. Latinos/as in urban areas such as Albuquerque, New Mexico; Fresno, California; and San Francisco, which have poor drinking water distribution systems and significant levels of contamination, are also at risk of contracting water-based diseases. More than one-third of Latinos/as live in Western states where arsenic, industrial chemicals, and fertilizer residues contaminate local drinking water supplies. Farmworkers, 88 percent of whom are Latinos/as, are at increased risk of developing lymphoma, prostate cancer, and childhood cancers due to regular exposure to pesticides.

Latino children are also twice as likely as white children to be at risk of lead poisoning, primarily through dust produced by lead-based paint. Other sources are lead-glazed pottery and lead-containing candy brought into the United States from Mexico and other countries.

The harmful effects of mercury also pose a health threat to Latinos/as, who are exposed primarily by eating mercury-contaminated fish but also by certain cosmetics products, religious ceremonies, and folk remedies. The lack of Spanish-language signs and educational materials around local fisheries further aggravates the problem.

Once mercury accumulates in the body, it remains there for many months. Exposure to mercury is especially dangerous to children and women of reproductive age. In pregnant women, mercury can affect the brain of the developing child. Children seven years of age and under are at especially high risk of developing neurological and behavioral problems and learning disabilities due to exposure to mercury. Overall, Latino children have higher levels of mercury in their bodies compared to white children.

Ruben Espejel

See also: AIDS/HIV; Proposition 187 (1994).

Further Reading

Aguirre-Molina, Marilyn, Carlos W. Molina, and Ruth Enid Zambrana. *Health Issues in the Latino Community.* San Francisco: Jossey-Bass, 2001.

Brown, E. Richard, Victoria D. Ojeda, Roberta Wyn, and Rebecka Levan. *Racial and Ethnic Disparities in Access to Health Insurance and Health Care.* Los Angeles: UCLA Center for Health Policy Research and Kaiser Family Foundation, 2000.

Hooton, Angela. *Demanding Reproductive Justice for Latinas.* Washington, DC: Center for American Progress, 2004. http://www.americanprogress.org/issues/2004/b48006.html.

Kaiser Commission on Medicaid and the Uninsured. *Immigrants and Health Coverage: A Primer.* Washington, DC, 2004.

Hijuelos, Oscar (1951–)

Oscar Hijuelos is a critically acclaimed novelist best known for *The Mambo Kings Play Songs of Love* (1989), for which he became the first Hispanic to win the Pulitzer Prize for fiction. Born in New York City on August 24, 1951, Hijuelos is the son of Cuban immigrants. The Cuban American cultural heritage and immigrant experience form the central themes of his work, their exploration his chief contribution to American letters.

Hijuelos received both his BA (1975) and MA (1976) in English and writing from the City College of New York. After completing his degrees, he worked as an advertising media traffic manager until 1984. During this period, however, he devoted much of his free time to writing fiction. He completed several short stories, some of which were included in the *Best of Pushcart Press III* anthology of 1978.

Five years later, in 1983, Hijuelos published his first novel, *Our House in the Last World.* The novel tells the story of Hector Santino, a Cuban American in New York City born to immigrant parents, who learns to appreciate and honor his Cuban heritage. The novel is highly autobiographical, informed by Hijuelos's own feelings about his Cuban background. *Our House* was widely praised for its warm and celebratory depiction of the family's experiences in America, as well as for its departure from the writings of other Cuban writers who tended to focus on the political struggles of Cuba and life in exile. It also earned Hijuelos a fellowship from the National Endowment for the Arts in 1985.

In 1989, Hijuelos would cement his place in the pantheon of American fiction with his second novel, *The Mambo Kings Play Songs of Love.* Weaving themes of loss, memory, and desire, *Mambo Kings* tells the story of two brothers, Cesar and Nestor Castillo, who leave Havana for New York City in the early 1950s. They are laborers by day, but by night they become stars in the lush world of dance halls, where their orchestra plays the sensual music that earns them the title of "Mambo Kings." In 1989, in addition to winning the Pulitzer Prize, *Mambo Kings* was nominated for a National Book Critics Circle

In 1990, Cuban American novelist Oscar Hijuelos (right, with Spanish actor Antonio Banderas) was the first Latino writer to win a Pulitzer Prize for Fiction, for *The Mambo Kings Play Songs of Love. (AP Images/Stephen J. Boitano)*

Award and the National Book Award from the National Book Foundation. It was released as the movie *The Mambo Kings* in 1992, starring Antonio Banderas.

Hijuelos followed the great success of his second novel with *The Fourteen Sisters of Emilio Montez O'Brien* (1993), which tells the story of the only son of the Montez O'Brien family as told by the eldest daughter, Margarita. Within her narration of Emilio's story, the lives, loves, and tragedies of the entire Montez O'Brien family unfold, highlighting themes of femininity, family, sex, pleasure, love, and earthly happiness.

His fourth novel, *Mr. Ives' Christmas* (1995), is a bittersweet parable of loss and redemption. Despite his modest beginnings as an adopted orphan, Mr. Ives is introduced at the start of the novel as the epitome of the American Dream in the 1950s. He is a husband, a father, and successful career man, but his happiness is shattered when his son is killed at Christmas. In recounting Mr. Ives's journey through grief, Hijuelos tells a love story that examines how we recognize love and how we find peace.

Hijuelos followed up *Mr. Ives' Christmas* with the *Empress of the Splendid Season* (1999), a fictional examination of the costs and gains of assimilation. *Empress* tells the story of Lydia España, a once prosperous Cuban emigrée who now lives in New York working as a cleaning woman. Vividly depicting the desires and disappointments of American life, Hijuelos juxtaposes Lydia's life to the secret lives of her clients that she discovers while she "cleans up" their worlds.

A Simple Habana Melody (2002) is a novel that centers on a song, "Rosas Puras," and its writer, Israel Levis. The story takes place in post-World War II Havana. Israel has returned to his childhood home after witnessing the horrors of the war, including internment in a Nazi concentration camp; the return prompts him to consider his relationship to his most popular song, "Rosas," and the ways in which memories are shaped and loss is experienced. Like all of his novels, *Habana Melody* reflects Hijuelos's love for the rhythms and cadences of Latin music, which was inspired by his uncle, Pedro Tellerina, a member of the famous Xavier Cugat Orchestra in the early part of the twentieth century.

Oscar Hijuelos continues to live and write in New York; he has taught creative writing at several colleges and universities.

Lisa Guerrero

See also: Cubans.

Further Reading

Ryan, Bryan, ed. *Hispanic Writers: A Selection of Sketches from Contemporary Authors.* Detroit: Gale Research, 1991.

Shirley, Paula W. "Reading Desi Arnaz in *The Mambo Kings Play Songs of Love.*" *MELUS* 20:3 (Autumn 1995): 69–78.

Socolovsky, Maya. "The Homelessness of Immigrant American Ghosts: The Hauntings and Photographic Narrative in Oscar Hijuelos's *The Fourteen Sisters of Emilio Montez O'Brien.*" *PMLA* 117:2 (March 2002): 252–64.

Hip-Hop

A youth culture comprising rap music, break dancing, graffiti, deejaying, performance art, and a distinctive style in clothing and hair, hip-hop emerged in the heavily African American and Latino community of the Bronx, New York, in the early 1970s. Hip-hop—a term often used synonymously with "rap,"—marked a turning point from rhythm and blues (R&B), disco, funk, and soul music, and came to dominate youth culture in the barrios, ghettoes, and even suburbs across the country. Rapping, or MC'ing, is a vocal style in which the performer rhythmically recites rhymed lyrics, often extemporaneously, over a backbeat provided by a live band, drum machine, or makeshift percussion set. In break dancing, graffiti, and its other expressions, hip-hop embodied the free spirit and rhythmic intensity of young minorities in New York and other cities. Rappers, DJs (record spinners), "b-boys" and "b-girls" (dancers), "graf writers" (graffiti painters), and others who carried forth the hip-hop attitude and style were originally blacks and Latinos/as growing up amid the poverty, gang violence, and social chaos of the inner city. Musicians, dancers, and DJs alike would compete against each other for street credibility as an alternative to violence.

The social conditions and economic prospects facing young people in inner-city America during the 1960s and 1970s were generally appalling, nowhere more conspicuously than New York City. Among African American and Latino youth, particularly Puerto Ricans, hip-hop emerged as a means of expressing outrage against injustice, celebrating cultural identity, and finding a creative outlet. It is said that hip-hop was born in a South Bronx disco club frequented by Puerto Ricans and African Americans. There, Dr. Jive, Joko, and Hollywood scat-rapped over a beat on turntables played by DJ Lovebug Starski. Other legendary DJ artists of the early days include Afrika Bambaataa, Grandmaster Flash, and Kool DJ Herc (all African Caribbean), Kurtis Blow, Eddie Cheeba, Charlie Chase (Puerto Rican), and Disco Wiz (born Luis Cedeño; Puerto Rican-Cuban).

1970s to 1990s

Latinos/as have played an integral role in hip-hop music, dance, art, and style from their inception. In addition to DJs, Puerto Ricans and other Latinos/as from New York City rose to prominence as rappers (among the earliest of whom was Whipper Whip); break-dancers (including members of such groups, or "crews," as Rock Steady Crew and the New York City Breakers); and largely anonymous but prominently displayed graffiti artists. Some historians of hip-hop have argued that the corporate media designated African Americans as the face of hip-hop and marketing it to the masses as the "new" black art form; others have suggested that efforts to label hip-hop as exclusively a black art form was an attempt on the part of white society to divide the people of the ghettos or barrios. In any event, during the early years of commercialism, the ethnic identity of hip-hop artists was unknown to many consumers because the primary medium was audio recording rather than video. In reality, Latinos/as were active participants in all aspects of commercial as well as street hip-hop culture from the outset. In 1972, Hugo Martinez created United Graffiti Artists, a coalition of the best subway artists who displayed their artwork in galleries throughout New York City. DJ Disco Wiz and DJ Charlie Chase of the Cold Crush Brothers made names for themselves as the best hip-hop spinners of the time. In 1977, Joseph Torres and Richard "Crazy Legs" Colón were among the founders of the break dancing group Rock Steady Crew, and by 1981, The

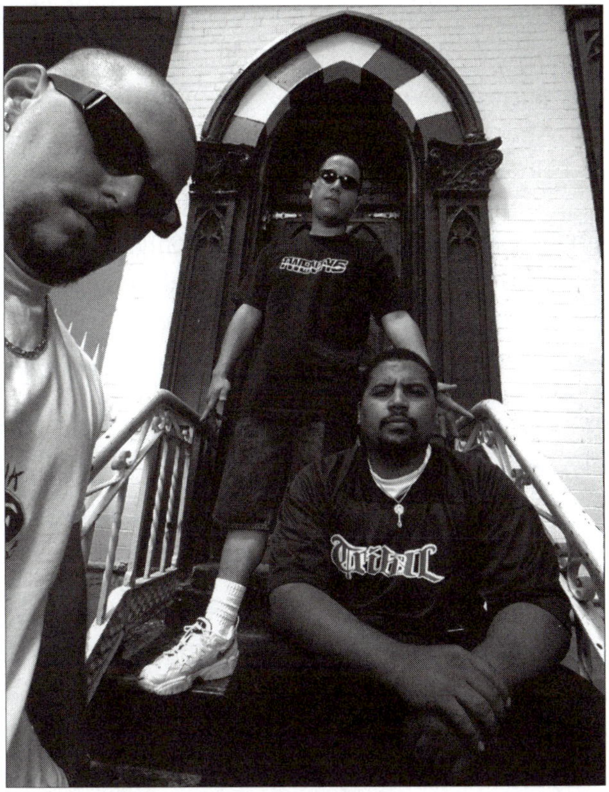

The Delinquent Habits, a Chicano rap group, is one of many musical acts, DJs, and break-dancers who have contributed to the heavily Latino character of hip-hop culture since its origin in the early 1970s. *(Bob Berg/Getty Images)*

Mean Machine was producing hip-hop records in Spanglish, a vernacular language mixing both Spanish and English words.

Charlie Chase, born Carlos Mandes in the barrio of New York City in the 1950s, started out in Latin bands playing salsa and merengue with the likes of such influential older musicians as Johnny Ventura, Johnny Pacheco, and the great Tito Puente. Influenced by such traditional Latin American genres as bomba, boogaloo, plena, mambo, and merengue—which rely heavily on syncopated rhythms and percussion, with improvisational call-and-response in the African tradition—Charlie Chase emerged as New York's number one Puerto Rican hip-hop DJ with the Cold Crush Brothers. Working hard to establish and maintain a Latino presence in hip-hop, he helped pave the way for such younger artists as Tony Touch, Fat Joe, Big Pun, and the Terror Squad, all of whom infused Latin rhythms over hip-hop beats in their music. The Cold Crush Brothers—whose original members also included rapper Whipper Whip, Tony

Tone, Easy A.D., Mr. Tee, and Dot-A-Rock—became known as "the Rolling Stones of hip-hop" for the energy of their live performances and growing popularity. After touring the boroughs of New York City and Boston, they became the first hip-hop group to sign with a major record label, CBS, in the early 1980s and were featured in the 1982 documentary film *Wild Style,* which proved seminal in spreading hip-hop culture. The Cold Crush Brothers toured Europe and Japan the following year, becoming the first hip-hop crew to forge an international following. Grandmaster Caz (formerly Grandmaster Casanova Fly), who had made rhyming integral to deejaying (prior to this time rapping was limited to DJs playing music with the MC simply talking as a way to move from one record to the next) when he teamed up with his old friend Disco Wiz and then Whipper Whip in the late 1970s, joined Chase in the Cold Crush Brothers in 1980 and was integral in the success of the group and the spread of hip-hop.

Although hip-hop culture gained increasing popularity among Puerto Rican youth in the barrios of New York City, it also resonated among Puerto Ricans in the homeland. After arriving on the island, rap music provided a nexus for young people, who found in hip-hop a source of cultural identity. Vico C, Ruben DJ, Lisa M, and other rappers during the early 1980s did not merely import or imitate North American styles but established cultural affinity by bringing a distinctive Latin identity to their music. Bearing lyrical and rhythmic similarities to the rap music of New York, hip-hop on Puerto Rico nevertheless adopted themes that reflected the daily life and cultural realities of the island. Young hip-hop artists fused merengue, reggae, and other Spanish and Caribbean musical traditions, with Spanish and English lyrics in a hip-hop beat.

Going Mainstream

Hip-hop in Puerto Rico in turn would impact the spread of the music and culture throughout the United States. By the early 1980s, hip-hop had broken the language barrier with such young performers as Mellow Man Ace (born in Cuba and raised in Los Angeles), Kid Frost (a Chicano from East Los Angeles), Gerardo (an Ecuadorian rapper and singer), and El General (a Panamanian also known as the "father of reggaeton"). Mellow Man Ace's single "Mentirosa" (1990) was the first Latino rap recording to go gold and the first hit record in Spanglish. El General helped establish the popular Spanish-language reggae rap in the Caribbean and Latin America. And Gerardo made his mark as a rapper with the hit single "Rico Suave" (1991).

Kid Frost's debut album, *Hispanic Causing Panic* (1990), became a rap anthem of *La Raza.* (The name of the movement was the title of the album's featured hit single.) Frost went on to assemble the rap supergroup Latin Alliance, which brought together Chicano and Puerto Rican artists, unified their musical styles, and established a political and cultural bridge between the East and West coasts. The group's only album, *Latin Alliance,* appeared in 1991, followed by Kid Frost's own second release, *East Side Story,* the following year. Other Latino hip-hop hits of the early 1990s included "On a Sunday Afternoon" by Lighter Shade of Brown (1994), "Mexican Power" by Proper Dos (1992), "Tres Delinquentes" by Delinquent Habits (1996), "Tequila" by A.L.T. and the Lost Civilization (1992), "Lowrider" by Latin Alliance (1991), and "Back to the Hotel" by N2DEEP (1992). In 1993, "Flow Joe" by Fat Joe reached the top spot on the Billboard rap rankings, followed by other hits from the Beatnuts, Cuban Link, DJ Angie Martinez, Noreaga, and Cypress Hill. Big Pun became the first to go platinum and double-platinum with his 1997 debut album *Capital Punishment.*

The nineties paved the way for new trends among Latino hop-hop artists, not least of which was the emergence of reggaeton. A Panamanian and Puerto Rican fusion of Jamaican reggae, hip-hop, Dominican merenrap (a fusion of merengue and rap)—combined with classic bomba and plena—reggaeton is a unique sound with diverse Latino and Caribbean roots. The most popular new genre on the New York youth scene by the early 1990s, "Spanish reggae," as it was called, was already spreading rapidly throughout the Caribbean, Central America, and South America. Aside from El General, pioneering artists included the Jamaican Shabba Ranks, Mellow Man Ace, DJ Playero, and DJ Nelson, among others. Later stars, in the early 2000s, included Daddy Yankee, Don Omar, Luny Tunes, and Tego Calderón.

Hip-hop as an art form has transformed the scope of an entire generation's cultural consciousness. From music and dancing to clothing, hair, and language, hip-hop has become ingrained in the fabric of American youth lifestyle. Moreover, as DJ Tony Touch has remarked, "there's always been a Latino presence in hip-hop, particularly in b-boy and graffiti." Once regarded as a local fad, American hip-hop has taken root throughout the world and found new expressions in diverse social milieus. Defined and redefined continuously in its brief history, hip-hop nevertheless has retained its roots in the Brown and Black Power movements of the 1960s–1970s and in the culture of the minority urban community as it has evolved ever since.

Kristal T. Moore

See also: Graffiti; Music.

Further Reading

Flores, Juan. *From Bomba to Hip-Hop: Puerto Rican Culture and Latino Identity.* New York: Columbia University Press, 2000.

George, Nelson. *Hip Hop America.* New York: Viking, 1998.

Keyes, Cheryl L. *Rap Music and Street Consciousness.* Urbana: University of Illinois Press, 2002.

Rivera, Raquel. *New York Ricans from the Hip Hop Zone.* New York: Palgrave Macmillan, 2003.

Rose, Tricia. *Black Noise: Rap Music and Black Culture in Contemporary America.* Lebanon, NH: University Press of New England, 1994.

Hispanic Heritage Month

Hispanic Heritage Week, now celebrated as National Hispanic Heritage Month, was initiated in September 1968, when the U.S. Senate and the House of Representatives passed a joint resolution authorizing President Lyndon Johnson to declare a weeklong celebration of Hispanic culture and tradition beginning on September 15. President Ronald Reagan and another act of Congress in August 1988 expanded the observance to thirty-one days—from September 15 to October 15. The beginning and end dates of Hispanic Heritage Month were chosen to encompass several independence days, or *Fiestas Patrias,* in Latin America: for Costa Rica, El Salvador, Guatemala, Honduras, and Nicaragua on September 15; for Mexico on September 16 (*El Grito*); for Chile on September 18 (*El Dieciocho*); and for Belize on September 21. The period also encompasses October 12, commemorating the arrival of Christopher Columbus in 1492 and the multicultural, multi-ethnic society that ensued. This date is variously celebrated in the United States as Columbus Day, Hispanic Heritage Day, or Fiestas de las Americas. In Latino communities and much of Latin America, the holiday is referred to as *Día de la Raza* (Day of the Race); in Puerto Rico and Panama as *Día del Descubrimiento de America* (Day of the Discovery of America); in Costa Rica as *Día de las Culturas* (Day of the Cultures); in Venezuela as *Día de la Resistencia Indígena* (Day of Indigenous Resistance); and in Spain as *Día Nacional* (National Day).

"Hispanic" is a term of convenience widely adopted in the 1970s (including by the federal government) that ties together a diverse group of peoples who are united in language, strong family ties, religious beliefs, and a shared legacy of Spanish colonialism; the term "Latino" is now widely preferred in what was previously referred to as the Hispanic community. The impetus for establishing Hispanic Heritage Week was the growing demand for recognition by various Latino organizations of the importance of their ethnic heritage and their contributions to life and culture in the United States. The express purpose was to celebrate the contributions and achievements of the diverse cultures that make up the Latino community.

Hispanic Heritage Week, and later Hispanic Heritage Month, has been introduced each year by a presidential proclamation in which the chief executive calls on Americans of all cultures to recognize and celebrate the history, culture, and innumerable contributions of Hispanic people in the United States. The sense and spirit of the holiday were well articulated by the proclamation of President Bill Clinton in 1999:

> During National Hispanic Heritage Month, we reflect on the history of a people who were part of this land long before the birth of the United States. Hispanics were among the earliest European settlers in the New World, and Hispanics

as a people—like their many cultures—share a rich history and great diversity. Hispanic Americans have roots in Europe, Africa, and South and Central America and close cultural ties to Mexico, the Caribbean, Central America, South America, and Spain. This diversity has brought variety and richness to the mosaic that is America and has strengthened our national character with invaluable perspective, experiences, and values.

Through the years, Hispanic Americans have played an integral role in our nation's success in science, the arts, business, government, and every other field of endeavor, and their talent, creativity, and achievements continue to energize our national life. For example, Hispanic Americans serve as NASA astronauts, including Dr. Ellen Ochoa, the first Hispanic woman in space. Mario Molina of the Massachusetts Institute of Technology shared a Nobel Prize in chemistry for research that raised awareness of the threat that chlorofluorocarbons pose to the earth's protective ozone layer. Cuban-American writer Oscar Hijuelos earned a Pulitzer Prize for fiction.

The achievements of today's Hispanic Americans build upon a long tradition of contributions by Hispanics in many varied fields. Before Dr. Ochoa and other Hispanic Americans began to explore the frontiers of space, Hernando de Soto and Francisco Vasquez de Coronado ventured into the vast uncharted land of the New World. A thousand years before Mario Molina calculated the effects of human actions on the atmosphere, Mayan priests accurately predicted solar and lunar eclipses. And before Oscar Hijuelos described a Cuban family's emigration to 1940s America, Miguel de Cervantes Saavedra gave us the classic adventures of Don Quixote and Sancho Panza.

National Hispanic Heritage Month is celebrated in many different ways. School children of all heritages learn about Hispanic culture, history, arts, and the contributions of Latinos to the United States. Many universities have week- or month- long celebrations encompassing a wide range of activities, from art exhibits and poetry readings to festivals honoring the diverse nations and people of Latin America. Cities with large Spanish-speaking populations generally sponsor their own events, hosted by local businesses, government, civic groups, community organizations, or individuals. The mayors of some cities make their own formal proclamations, like that of the president. And because the fiesta tends to continue past its set dates, many add *El Día de los Muertos* (The Day of the Dead) celebrations to the mix in early November. This tends to occur in areas with high Mexican and/or Mexican American populations, though some other Hispanic countries also observe a form of this celebration.

RuthAnne Tarletz de Molina

See also: Día de la Raza; Día de los Muertos.

Further Reading

Gonzalez, Juan. *Harvest of Empire: A History of Latinos in America.* New York: Viking, 2000.

Kanellos, Nicolás. *Hispanic First: 500 Years of Extraordinary Achievement.* Stamford, CT: Gale Research, 1997.

Hondurans

The Honduran community in the United States has a long history, dating essentially to the late nineteenth century. By the turn of the twentieth century, according to the U.S. Census Bureau, there were a total of 217,569 Hondurans living in the continental United States, accounting for .6 percent of the nation's Latino population. Since the late 1970s, the Honduran American community has grown rapidly with the relatively heavy influx of immigrants seeking more lucrative service-sector jobs and responding to reports from friends and family recounting positive experiences. Even more important than these pull factors, however, has been the push of political instability and economic hardship in the home country. Thus, by 2006, the official Honduran population had reached 490,317, according to the U.S. Census Bureau. The participation and contributions of Hondurans in American society, while not widely recognized, have grown commensurately with the increase in population.

Beginning in the late nineteenth century, Hondurans began visiting and immigrating to various American cities. New Orleans was an especially popular destination, following trade routes established by the Standard Fruit and Steamship Company. The result was a large and thriving Honduran American community in that city. Emigration from Honduras increased throughout the twentieth century. After the 1970s, driven by political instability, persistent poverty, a significant HIV/AIDS epidemic, and foreign trade, Hondurans fled their homeland for the promise of a better life in the United States. During the 1980s, Honduras became embroiled in the U.S.-supported Nicaragua Contra war against the Sandinista government, with rebel forces trained and stationed in Honduras. The resulting instability and fear of armed conflict between the neighboring states—and U.S. passage of the Immigration Reform and Control Act of 1986 (which granted amnesty to undocumented immigrants who arrived before 1982, many of whom had relatives in Honduras who hoped to follow)—propelled Honduran immigration to the United States to new heights.

Yet another important contributor to Honduran immigration was the devastation wrought by Hurricane Mitch in October 1998, which led to massive flooding and mudslides, killing an estimated 6,500 Hondurans and leaving an equal number missing. As many as 1.5 million people were left homeless, with many more losing their livelihoods because of damage in the agricultural sector. While Honduran Americans would play a vital role in providing aid to family members and friends in the homeland, conditions in Honduras caused a spike in immigration to the United States. In search of service-sector and agricultural employment, thousands of new immigrants, many of them illegal, joined previous generations in major cities such as New York City, Los Angeles, and Miami.

Unlike other Latino groups, few Hondurans succeeded in landing agricultural jobs. A much larger percentage found employment in the burgeoning domestic service industry, including restaurant, hotel, janitorial, retail, housekeeping, and laundry work. According to U.S. Census Bureau data, 33.7 percent of Honduran immigrants found employment in the service industry between 1980 and 1990, a 13 percent jump from those who arrived the previous decade. More than 25 percent of those who arrived between 1980 and 1990 took jobs as operators, fabricators, and laborers, an almost 10 percent increase from the decade before. Of those who entered the United States during the administration of President Ronald Reagan (1981–1989), almost 15 percent worked as professionals and managers, a jump from 5 percent ten years before. The trend toward higher-paying, more prestigious jobs continued through the 1990s, although anti-immigrant sentiment, persistent levels of poverty, and limited educational opportunities—particularly for Honduran boys, who are often expected to leave school at the age of sixteen to begin work—have remained obstacles to success.

Like the U.S. Latino population in general, the Honduran American community is extremely diverse, including those who ethnically identify as Mayan, black, African, mixed, Spanish, Palestinian, Chinese, and Caribbean (Carib). Yet they, like the Latino community as a whole, have been historically homogenized by mainstream American society, which blurs not only the differences within the community but also those between Hondurans and other Latino groups. Nativism, prejudice, and cultural stereotypes that lump Honduran immigrants with other Latinos/as because of their shared native language (Spanish), cuisine (rice and beans), religion (Catholicism), types of community formation (urban), and place of work (service sector), have made the Honduran American community virtually indistinguishable and largely unknown to most Americans despite its rich and complex history.

Regardless of these obstacles, Honduran Americans have gained prominence in a number of local communities. In Latino neighborhoods throughout the Northeast—places like Jackson Heights, Queens (New York City), and the Lower East Side of Manhattan—Honduran Americans have established storefront churches, retail businesses, community groups, and cultural organizations. In these communities as well as in New Orleans (at least before Hurricane Katrina devastated the area in 2005), Honduran American cuisine flourished, with dishes like tamales, a corn-based pie stuffed with capers, livers, and chicken; and *machuca,* a fried-fish coconut stew that includes plantains among its ingredients. Likewise, Honduran music is heard in Honduran enclaves throughout the United States. Garifuna music, a mix of Caribbean, West African, and indigenous genres, has found a growing audience as well.

Reflective of their relatively small population and their short time in the United States, Honduran Americans have remained all but absent from national politics, national service organizations, and the labor movement. However, the Honduran American community has distinguished itself in military service; a reported 13.7 percent of all Honduran Americans over the age of sixteen are veterans of the U.S. armed forces. While partly a function of poverty and limited educational opportunities available to Honduran American boys, such extensive military service also characterizes the assimilation and acculturation of the community.

The experiences of Honduran Americans overlap in many ways with those of other Latino groups, in terms of immigration patterns, experience with prejudice, limited job and education opportunities, and persistent poverty. At the same time, however, Hondurans' distinctive cultural attributes, patterns of acculturation and assimilation, communal formation, and diversity of experience in the United States demonstrate the distinctiveness of their experience.

David J. Leonard

See also: AIDS/HIV; Immigration Reform and Control Act of 1986.

Further Reading

González, Nancie. "Garifuna Settlement in New York: A New Frontier." *International Migration Review* 13:2 (1979): 255–63.

Maxwell, William. "Honduran Americans." Countries and Their Cultures. http://www.everyculture.com.

Norsworthy, Kent, with Tom Barry. *Inside Honduras.* Albuquerque, NM: Inter-Hemispheric Education Resource Center, 1993.

Housing and Living Conditions

According to the U.S. Census, Latinos/as constitute the largest ethnic group in the United States, with approximately 36.3 million people in 2000. Latinos/as from a variety of regions in Mexico, Central America, South America, and the Caribbean, and influenced by Jewish, Catholic, Spanish, African, indigenous, and Asian traditions have continued to arrive in the United States seeking opportunities to work and improve their lives. This is a long-standing and ongoing trend.

Latinos/as with diverse skills and educational backgrounds have come to the United States in search of better jobs and a better life for themselves and their children. They generally live in close proximity to each other, forming ethnic enclaves or barrios. Among these are the *colonias mexicanas* in San Antonio; El Barrio in New York; Humboldt Park, Pilsen, and La Villita in Chicago; Huntington Park and East LA in Los Angeles; and Little Havana in Miami. Life in these communities is vibrant and colorful, with stunning murals, the rich smells of Latino cuisine, and the distinctive music of a particular tradition. Recent arrivals, long-term, or native-born Latino residents live in barrios that provide a comfortable place for the families to speak Spanish—places that offer access to the cultural institutions, businesses, social services, and other resources necessary for daily life in the United States.

Life in the Barrios

Between the late 1880s and the 1920s, large numbers of Latino immigrants moved to urban neighborhoods. In the 1920s and 1930s, many Latinos/as, especially Mexicans and Puerto Ricans, settled in the Midwest, where they could find work in the automobile factories, steel mills, and packing plants. Life in the urban barrios was in many ways similar to that in their home villages, as families were able to find products, food, and services that reminded them of home and that were not available in other parts of the city. Though the barrios offered relatively inexpensive rental spaces, Latinos/as tended to live in substandard housing with families occupying basements and rented rooms. The neighborhoods consisted of rundown property that nobody else wanted. This housing stock lacked adequate sanitation and proper heat during the winter, while landlords often failed to make much-needed repairs.

As cities industrialized, urban planners did not take into account the growing population and increasing housing demands. Then, with deindustrialization, life in el barrio became difficult as many Latinos/as faced obstacles finding jobs and adequate and affordable housing. Some families resorted to living in substandard housing in inner cities. Often, more than one family would live in an overcrowded smaller home or apartment. This practice of doubling up prevented family members from becoming homeless.

To live in substandard neighborhoods meant that Latinos/as were distanced and marginalized from the larger city. Segregation and isolation magnified the problems of the community. The neighborhoods became increasingly run down and unsafe, with rising rates of crime, unemployment, and poverty. These adverse conditions placed strain and pressure on families, especially youth. Despite the poor conditions, the barrio was a familiar place where Latinos/as could preserve their customs and unique cultural flair. The barrio gave them a sense of security and identity not offered elsewhere.

Public Housing and Rental Markets

The U.S. government established housing policies such as the Housing Act of 1949 to address the needs of the poor. While public housing provided many low-income families a place to live, it did not solve the social problems in the barrio. Instead, public housing exacerbated the problems facing poor people. Residents in public housing were isolated and eventually neglected by government authorities. The government failed to facilitate racial integration, and the severe housing problems continued due to persistent inequality. Some positive changes and infrastructure improvements were introduced in certain communities by paving roads and improving utilities and sewer systems. However, the nature of public housing eroded the fabric of the community and the internal dynamics of the barrio.

Latino families who sought public housing had difficulty securing access to it. Eligible Latinos/as were largely underrepresented in housing provided by the government. Some families did not qualify for welfare, other public benefits, or housing subsidies because of their immigration status or because they did not meet residency requirements. Others were simply not interested in government assistance. In addition, although some Latinos/as managed to live in public housing, it was not attractive to many Latinos/as because it discouraged the sense of familiarity and community that existed in the barrios.

Home Ownership

Federal housing policy has promoted both home ownership and suburbanization. The suburbanization process along with highway construction encouraged by the government after World War II led to further isolation in the barrio. In the mid-1940s the GI Bill allowed veterans returning from World War II to purchase homes at a low cost. Many Latinos/as who served in the armed forces benefited from the program. Middle-class families, including many Latinos/as, who could afford to left the cities and moved to the suburbs, purchasing new, larger homes.

While many Latino veterans also had access to education and job training as a result of the GI Bill, this did not allow them access to better jobs that could facilitate entry to suburbia. Many Latino families in the United States fell under the official poverty line, making it harder for them to bear the rising costs of housing, property taxes, and education, and to face other priority issues in most large cities. Even those who had improved their socioeconomic status had difficulty moving out of the barrio. Some Latinos/as became members of the middle class as a result of owning businesses in the barrio, which enabled them to purchase better homes in adjacent neighborhoods and towns.

Discrimination

Latinos/as have tended to live in neighborhoods previously occupied by other (mostly European) immigrants, with deteriorating infrastructures and poor-quality housing. Discrimination in employment as well as housing remains a constant obstacle to improving conditions or buying a home. Despite laws prohibiting discrimination in housing—whether in renting a property, applying for a mortgage, or buying into a community of choice—the problem is still widespread for Latinos/as. Families may be steered to areas that the real estate industry designates as acceptable to that ethnic group, but not to other neighborhoods. Latinos/as are also victims of predatory lending and other abuses in the banking and real estate industries. Although the Fair Housing Act of 1968 protects individuals and families against housing discrimination on the basis of race, ethnicity, national origin, religion, familial status, sex, and disability, many state and local governments continue to selectively enforce housing codes and ordinances that target only Latino families but not other racial or ethnic groups. In the 1990s, the U.S. Department of Justice filed lawsuits against seven municipalities in various parts of the country for violating the fair housing rights of Latinos/as.

Latino Housing Today

The lack of affordable housing is perhaps the most pressing issue facing Latino families in many neighborhoods in the twenty-first century. Although many have been able to realize the American Dream of becoming home owners, the costs associated with housing are increasingly high. Gentrification—the process by which affordable but physically deteriorating neighborhoods undergo physical renovation, rapidly inflating property values, and an influx of wealthier residents—urban revitalization, and condominium conversion continue apace in cities across the United States. One consequence of such transformations is the pricing out of long-term poor residents and the pushing out of low-income residents. Many are Latinos/as, who are displaced from their communities and cultural roots by rising housing costs and property taxes.

At the same time, an increasing numbers of Latinos/as have been able to pull together the resources to buy a home. Fair-housing advocates work hard to ensure that Latino families and other minorities have access to better housing. Community-based organizations funded by the U.S. Department of Housing, local government, and private institutions assist Latino/as through educational campaigns to increase home ownership, rental programs, and the development of new properties for low-income households. Fair-housing advocates also monitor housing practices in the banking and real estate industries to ensure best practices and to protect and educate Latinos/as about their rights as home owners or tenants. Yet, while many Latinos/as have succeeded in moving to the suburbs and buying a home of their own, many return to the barrios to retain their sense of culture and community. The barrio remains a place of Latino pride, the preservation of culture and identity, and the closest place to home in America.

Madeline Troche-Rodríguez

See also: Poverty.

Further Reading

Bratt, Rachel G., et al. *Critical Perspectives on Housing.* Philadelphia: Temple University Press, 1986.

Gonzales, Manuel G. *Mexicanos: A History of Mexicans in the United States.* Bloomington: Indiana University Press, 1999.

Hoobler, Dorothy. *The Mexican American Family Album.* New York: Oxford University Press, 1994.

Suárez-Orozco, Marcelo M., and Mariel M. Páez, eds. *Latinos: Remaking America.* Berkeley: University of California Press, 2002.

Huerta, Dolores (1930–)

Dolores Fernández Huerta, the Mexican American labor organizer and cofounder (with César Chávez) of the United Farm Workers (UFW), was born into a working-class family in Dawson, New Mexico, on April 10, 1930. Both of her parents were committed to workers' rights. Her father, Juan Fernández, had been a miner who also worked the sugar beet circuit to supplement the family income. He was active in the local union and eventually elected to the New Mexico state legislature. Huerta's mother, Alicia Fernández, worked two jobs, as a cannery worker and waitress, and saved enough money to buy her own restaurant. Later, when she purchased a hotel, she sometimes allowed farmworker families to stay free of rent.

Dolores's parents divorced when she was just five, and she moved with her mother to Stockton in northern California's San Joaquin Valley, where she attended public schools and was active in the Girl Scouts and Catholic youth organizations. In high school, she was an excellent student and excelled in composition. One of her teachers, however, did not believe that a young Chicana could produce the quality of essays she turned in, accused her of plagiarism, and refused to award her the grade she had earned. This was one of several events that would set the young Dolores Huerta on the path of Chicana activism.

Huerta's experiences teaching farmworker children and working with the Community Service Organization (CSO) were other turning points in her life. After graduating from college with a teaching certificate, Huerta began her career as an elementary school teacher in Stockton. Seeing the poverty in which so many of her students lived, however, Huerta realized that much work needed to be done outside the classroom and left her teaching position after only a few months.

In 1955, she met Fred Ross, the founder of the CSO, and helped establish a Stockton chapter. Huerta worked for the CSO from 1955 to 1962, registering voters, fighting police harassment, and seeking health care for the poor. By the time she resigned her position, she had successfully lobbied state legislators for, among other things, an old-age pension, the right to register voters door-to-door, and bilingual driver's license exams. Her lobbying experience would prove to be an important asset after the founding of the UFW.

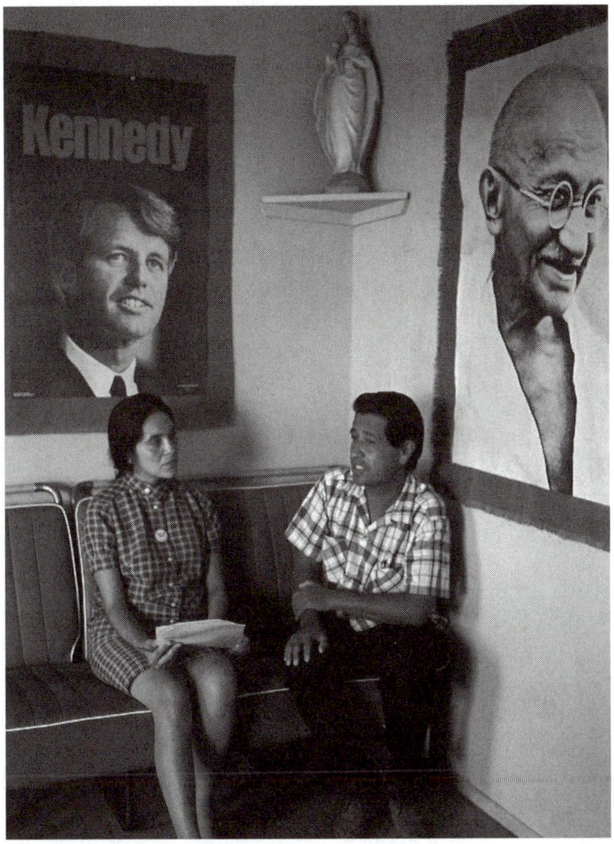

Pioneering Mexican American labor leader Dolores Huerta confers with César Chávez, her cofounder of the United Farm Workers, during its historic grape strike in 1968. Huerta was the union's chief contract negotiator. *(Arthur Schatz/Time & Life Pictures/Getty Images)*

In 1962, César Chávez, a fellow organizer in the CSO, requested human and economic resources to begin organizing farmworkers. When the CSO rejected his request, Huerta and Chávez resigned and together founded the National Farm Workers Association (NFWA). The organization was catapulted into national attention in 1965, when Filipino workers belonging to the Agricultural Worker's Organizing Committee asked the NFWA to join them in their grape boycott. The two organizations joined together to form the UFW and prevailed in the boycott. Chávez was elected its first president, and Huerta, along with Gilbert Padilla, its first vice presidents.

Throughout the 1960s, Huerta served as the union's primary contract negotiator. In the 1970s, after negotiating several contracts guaranteeing minimum wages, bathrooms, and health benefits, she successfully lobbied the state legislature and the governor of California to pass and sign the Agricultural Labor Relations Act (1975). For the first time in U.S. history, there was state legislation guaranteeing the right of farmworkers to engage in collective bargaining.

By the 1980s, Huerta had begun to focus much of her energy on pesticide control. Growers continued to use highly toxic pesticides in the fields, often without protecting the workers. In 1988, while demonstrating against pesticide abuse and the policies of Republican presidential candidate George H.W. Bush, Huerta was hospitalized with broken ribs and a ruptured spleen after police began clubbing the protestors. She had come a long way from her days at the CSO, when she was a registered Republican (although it is important to note that by the time she left the organization, she was no longer a Republican).

Indeed, Huerta's efforts on behalf of farmworkers and others often came at a high price. Her children—eleven in all—grew up without advantage, and she often faced violent opposition. However, her efforts were highly successful, bringing gains in worker rights and protections over the course of four decades. Several of her children have followed in her footsteps as activists. Now in her seventies, she continued to organize, educate, and protest for labor interests.

Linda Heidenreich

See also: Chávez, César; Grape Strikes and Boycotts; Migrant Workers; United Farm Workers of America.

Further Reading

Chávez, Alicia. "Dolores Huerta and the United Farm Workers." In *Latina Legacies: Identity, Biography, and Community,* ed. Vicki L. Ruíz and Virginia E. Sánchez Korrol. New York: Oxford University Press, 2005.

Murcia, Rebecca Thatcher. *Dolores Huerta.* Bear, DE: Mitchell Lane, 2003.

United Farm Workers: http://www.ufw.org.

Worth, Richard. *Dolores Huerta.* New York: Chelsea House, 2007.

I

Identity and Labels

With more than 37 million people, Latinos constitute the largest non-white ethnic group in the United States, comprising 13 percent of the population. A number of different ethnic identity labels have been applied to Latinos in America, including Hispanic, Latin, and Latino American. In addition, specific identity labels apply to national and other subgroups, such as Cuban American, Chicano, Boricua, and *mexicano.* The variety of identity labels for Latinos can be confusing for non-Latinos and Latinos alike, given a number of factors including who uses which labels and in what context.

History

One such factor is history. Although Latinos have not always been referred to as such, they have a long and rich history in the United States. Just as designations for African Americans have changed over time (as from colored, to Negro, to Afro American, to black, to African American), so the accepted name for Latinos has changed (as from Hispanic and Latin to Latino and Latino American). The changes have come about as a function both of choice on the part of Latinos themselves—what the majority of the community has wanted to be called—and of the changing views of other, dominant social groups.

Mexicans have always constituted the largest Latino group in the United States. Today, nearly two-thirds of the Latino community is of Mexican origin. Not surprisingly, therefore, the experience of Mexican Americans with identity labels has been longer and more complex than that of any other Latino group.

The Spanish arrived in what is now Mexico in 1519. At the time, there were between 9 and 25 million Native Americans living in the area, representing different nations and numerous cultures and languages. In what is now Mexico City alone, there were about 200,000 people and fifty-five city-states that made up the Mexica, or Aztec, civilization. When the Spanish arrived, they lumped all these peoples into a single category: *indio* (Indian). The term is still used today to refer to Latinos and Latin Americans—sometimes as an insult, sometimes asserted with pride, especially by certain Chicanos and politically progressive groups.

Confronted with the racial mixing of European, Native American, and African peoples, the Spanish colonial government devised a system of fifty-three *castas* (castes) to which people were assigned based on blood or heritage. Two important casta names are still used widely throughout Latin America and the U.S. Latino community today: *mestizo* or *mestiza,* referring to the child of a white European man and a Native American woman; and *mulato* or *mulata,* the child of a white European man and an African woman. Other, less common casta names that endure today are *coyote* (the child of a Native American man and a mestiza woman); *cholo* (child of a mestizo man and a Native American woman); *jarocho* (child of an African man and a Native American woman), and *zambo* (child of a Native American man and an African woman).

From 1810 to 1821, the colony of New Spain (covering all of contemporary Mexico and areas north) fought and won its independence from Spain. Having the opportunity to define their own identity, the people chose a name for their new country—Mexico—that emphasized their Native American heritage rather than their European domination. "Mexico" comes from the Náhuatl word *mexitin*—what the Aztecs called themselves. Other Latin American countries, most of which gained their independence during the nineteenth century, also chose names that reflected native rather than colonial identities.

In 1848, the Mexican-American War was ended by the Treaty of Guadalupe Hidalgo, in which Mexico turned over half its territory to the United States: what today encompasses all or part of Arizona, California, Colorado, Nevada, New Mexico, Texas, Utah, and Wyoming. About 100,000 Mexicans suddenly became citizens of the United States, and many of their descendants still express resentment toward the treaty and resistance to colonization by calling themselves Mexicans. Throughout the 1800s and early 1900s, however, many people of Mexican descent started referring to themselves as Spanish, Spanish-American, or *Hispano,* emphasizing their European heritage rather than their Mexican or Native American blood, especially following the heavy influx of Mexicans into the United States after the Mexican Revolution of 1910. This was particularly the case in New Mexico, and many New Mexicans still consider themselves Spanish instead of Mexican or mestizo. Even in California, another label was often used for people of Mexican descent: *Californios.* These were mostly Mexicans and mestizos, long-term inhabitants of the area who owned land and had some wealth. However, like Hispanos, Californios were often seen, and saw themselves, as more "Spanish" than Mexican or Native American.

This emphasis on Spanish or European heritage can be interpreted as a response to (and even an expression of) racism in which people of white skin and European culture are seen as superior to those of brown skin and native or non-European culture. Emphasizing this aspect of one's heritage over the other was a useful tool for Mexicans and Latinos to gain acceptance by a white European majority at key historical times, particularly when the Californios were losing economic and political power, and when New Mexico was campaigning for statehood at the beginning of the twentieth century. In New Mexico, identifying as Spanish also helped Latinos distance themselves from the large local population of Native Americans.

In Mexico, meanwhile, the new revolutionary government of 1917 began doing the opposite, by celebrating what it deemed the people's unique indigenous and mestizo heritage and using the old casta word mestizo with pride instead of shame. Philosopher Jose Vasconcelos promoted the idea of *la raza cósmica*—"the cosmic race," alluding to its universality—which celebrated the indigenous heritage of mixed-blood Mexicans and the great potential of Mexican culture because of its unique mixture.

Such pride in ethnic mixture began to be reflected in the United States following World War II. Many people of Mexican descent had fought in the war, proud of their American national identity. At the same time, most also wanted to recognize their Mexican origins, especially as the United States was seeking more positive relations with Latin America. Many began to call themselves Mexican American, sometimes hyphenating the term, as European immigrant groups such as Irish American and Italian Americans had done, in the hope that they could be included in the melting pot and gain more social acceptance and legal rights.

By the late 1960s, however, many young Mexican Americans did not feel that they were any more accepted by American society than they had been before. Despite working hard and fighting for the United States in war, they still suffered from racism, violence (as in the Zoot Suit Riots of 1943), and even mass deportation (as in Operation Wetback in the mid-1950s).

At a pivotal youth conference in Santa Barbara, California, in 1969, the major youth organizations UMAS (United Mexican American Students), MASC (Mexican-American Student Confederation), MAYA (Mexican American Youth Association), and MASA (Mexican American Student Association) consolidated into MEChA—*El Movimiento Estudiantíl Chicano de Aztlán* (Chicano Student Movement of Aztlán). Thus the Chicano Movement was born. Chicanos chose a name that embraced their indigenous roots, highlighting this long-ignored part of their identity. Although there is some disagreement over what Chicano/a means exactly and where it came from, most believe the term is a shortened version of *mexicano,* with the Náhuatl rather than Spanish pronunciation (*x* is pronounced as *sh* or *ch*). Thus, some Chicanos/as spell the word with an *X* (Xicano/a).

The organized Chicano Movement waned in the early 1970s. Meanwhile, new U.S. immigration laws and political turmoil in Central America brought a heavy influx of new immigrants from other Latin

American countries—suggesting to some Americans the need for a single, generic label for Spanish-speaking people. The term Hispanic was adopted as an official government designation to help account for education, health, and welfare programs. The term Hispanic was first used by the Romans in reference to peoples of the Iberian Peninsula—what is now Spain and Portugal. Hispano and Hispanic had been used sporadically in the United States during the eighteenth and nineteenth centuries but did not become prominent until the terms were revived by a handful of Mexican American and Puerto Rican members of Congress. They used it to refer to any person of Mexican, Puerto Rican, Cuban, Central or South American descent, or other Spanish culture of origin, regardless of race.

While Hispanic became the official government designation, the people it referenced began adopting the identity label Latino starting in the late 1980s. Itself an umbrella term that covers a number of culturally diverse groups, Latino was regarded as a term of pride, implying preservation of language and culture and the pursuit of social justice. Many Latinos consider it the most culturally, racially, and gender neutral term available. Unlike Hispanic, which references a European colonial heritage, Latino refers to a broader international community, centered in the Western Hemisphere and including Native American roots.

Country of Origin, Generation, and Age

Aside from history, the names and identity labels of Latinos have also been affected by a variety of factors such as country of origin, generation, age, education level, political beliefs, social class, and region of residence. About 40 percent of Latinos in the United States in the early twenty-first century are first-generation immigrants—born in another country. Latinos come from twenty major Spanish-speaking countries in North and South America, including the Caribbean and Central America. Not included among these are Brazil, Haiti, Guyana, Suriname, and French Guiana, which are not Spanish-speaking countries; nor does it include sixteen additional Caribbean island nations. (Some people from these countries consider themselves Latinos; others do not.) Almost two-thirds of first-generation Latino immigrants are Mexican, as are more than 27 percent of all legally documented U.S. immigrants. In addition, an estimated 5–10 million more Mexican immigrants arrive undocumented.

Latinos often refer to themselves as citizens of their country of origin, or the country of origin of their parents or ancestors, even after living in the United States for many years. In fact, 88 percent of all Latinos sometimes identify themselves by their country of origin, and more than half identify themselves *first* by country of origin (instead of "Latino" or any similar term). More than two thirds of first-generation Latinos identify themselves first by country of origin, while only one third of second-generation Latinos do.

When identifying by country of origin, Latinos often use the Spanish term instead of the English term. Thus, many Mexicans refer to themselves as *mexicanos,* Dominicans as *dominicanos,* and Venezuelans as *venezolanos.* Most nationality names in Spanish end in the plural suffix *–nos* (in the singular, *–no* for a man and *–na* for a woman), but various other endings are used as well: *puertorriqueños* (Puerto Ricans), *panameños* (Panamanians), *salvadoreños* (Salavadorans), *hondureños* (Hondurans), *guatemaltecos* (Guatemalans), *paraguayos* (Paraguayans), *uruguayos* (Uruguayans), *costarricenses* (Costa Ricans), and *nicaraguenses* (Nicaraguans).

Many Latin Americans use nicknames for their own people or those from other countries—such as *ticos* for Costa Ricans, *nicas* for Nicaraguans, *salvatruchas* for Salvadorans, *charrúas* for Uruguayans, and *gauchos* for Argentines. There are also local terms for people from particular cities, states, or regions—such as *tapatíos* for those from Guadalajara, Mexico; *porteños* for those from Buenos Aires, Argentina, or from Valparaíso, Chile; *cariocas* for those from Río de Janeiro, Brazil; and *jíbaros* for rural Puerto Ricans from hill regions. Such terms have their own rich histories; many are indigenous Native American words (jíbaro and charrúa, for example). Finally, Latin Americans may use other slang terms for each other that are derogatory in nature.

Second-generation Latinos, or the children of immigrants born in the United States, may still use country-of-origin terms for themselves, but many identify with U.S. culture and use such hyphenated or dual labels as Cuban American or Peruvian American. Third-generation Latinos (and beyond) prefer identity terms that reflect their identification, at least in part, with their non-U.S. American heritage; still, more than half (57 percent) identify first as Americans.

Age and education level, which are often related to generation, also influence preferences for particular designations. Younger and more educated Latinos tend to prefer the terms Chicano and Latino.

Class, Political Beliefs, and Region of Residence

Social class and political beliefs play an important role in how Latinos identify themselves and how they identify others. This is particularly true of Latinos of Mexican descent. Mexican Americans tend to be middle and upper class, for example, while Chicanos are more often of the working class. By no means is this the case for every individual, however, nor is it the same in every region of the United States. Mexican Americans also tend to be more politically conservative, while Chicanos are typically more liberal or progressive. This is especially the case in California, where Hispanic is considered a politically conservative term. Many Latinos of Mexican descent who identify themselves as Chicanos/as do so in the spirit of the Chicano Movement—that is, they identify themselves with their Native American roots and their common historical experience as an oppressed group.

Similarly, politics is important in the use and understanding of another common Latino identity term: *boricua.* Many Puerto Ricans identify themselves as *boricua* or *borincano* to express their opinion that Puerto Rico should be an independent country rather than a territory of the United States. Like the term Chicano, boricua and borincano are indigenous words derived from the Taíno name for their island, and their use expresses special pride in Native American heritage.

Geographic region plays another important role in determining the identity terms Latinos/as use for themselves and what those terms mean. There are major differences among the terms preferred in California, Texas, New Mexico, and the East Coast. In California, where people of Mexican origin make up one third of the state's population, Chicano is a popular term used with pride by many liberals and progressives of Mexican descent, in various social classes. The Eurocentric label Hispanic is not generally regarded favorably, but Latino is—especially with a growing population of Latinos of Central and South American origin in the state. In New Mexico and Texas, however, few people use the word Latino. Hispanic is an acceptable term, especially in New Mexico, where Chicano tends to have less political meaning than it does in California. During the Chicano Movement of the 1960s and 1970s, some radical New Mexicans began to refer to themselves as *Indo-hispanos* rather than Chicanos—and the concept came to be applied to New Mexican Hispanics in general. In Texas, the label Mexican American is a term of pride and not necessarily linked to upper-class or conservative political values. Chicano is popular there as well, although not as much as in California, and mexicano is also common. *Tejano,* which simply means Texan, is another identity term used with pride by some Texan Latinos of Mexican descent.

On the East Coast, particularly in major cities with large Latino populations like New York and Miami, Latino and even Latin American are the preferred terms for a cultural and racial mix that includes a large population of *caribeños* (Caribbeans) and Afro Latinos (Latinos with African blood), such as Cubans, Dominicans, and Puerto Ricans. Many Latinos in these areas also identify closely with their country of origin (dominicanos, salvadoreños, and the like). Puerto Ricans in New York even have their own label—Nuyorican or *neoyorquino*—for city residents of Puerto Rican descent.

Which Label is "Correct"?

When talking to or about Latinos, it is important to remember the importance people attach to ethnic and national identity and that identity labels are based on a variety of complex factors. A person's preferred designation can also change during the course of his or her life, according to political and historical trends, regional movement, or sheer preference. Indeed, an individual might call herself Chicana, mexicana, or Latina in the same week, depending on where she is, whom she is talking to, and what she wants to communicate about herself. Moreover, the same identity label can mean different things to different people, and Latinos themselves often disagree about identity labels. A Chicano in California may see himself as identifying more closely with Mexico by using this label. On the other hand, a mexicano (born in Mexico) may see this term in a negative light when used for people of Mexican descent born in the United States, whom he does not really consider Mexican at all. Despite the complexity here, more than 80 percent of Latinos report using either "Latino" or "Hispanic" to identify themselves at least some of the time, and Latino is generally the least offensive term for the majority of Latinos in the United States today.

Susana Rinderle

See also: Boricua; Chicano/a; Chicano Movement; La Raza; Latino/a; Mestizo/a; Mexican-American War; Race; Tejanos.

Further Reading

Anzaldúa, Gloria. *Borderlands/La Frontera: The New Mestiza.* 1987. San Francisco: Aunt Lute, 2007.

Brodie, Mollyann, Annie Steffenson, Jamie Valdez, Rebecca Levin, and Roberto Suro. "2002 National Survey of Latinos." Menlo Park, CA: Henry J. Kaiser Family Foundation; Washington, DC: Pew Hispanic Center, 2002.

Chávez, John R. *The Lost Land: The Chicano Image of the Southwest.* Albuquerque: University of New Mexico Press, 1984.

Hayes-Bautista, David E., and Jorge Chapa. "Latino Terminology: Conceptual Bases for Standardized Terminology." *American Journal of Public Health* 77:1 (January 1987): 61–68.

Tanno, Dolores V. "Names, Narratives and the Evolution of Ethnic Identity." In *Our Voices: Essays in Culture, Ethnicity and Communication,* ed. Alberto González, Marsha Houston, and Victoria Chen. Los Angeles: Roxbury, 2004.

Illegal Immigration

Illegal immigration is the act of entering and taking up residence in a foreign nation without the proper authorization of that country's government. People who live in the United States in violation of U.S. immigration laws are referred to as *illegal aliens, illegal immigrants,* or *undocumented immigrants.* It is estimated that approximately 11 million illegal aliens resided in the United States in 2005, living in all fifty states. The exact number of undocumented immigrants is difficult to determine, however, because of flawed statistical estimates, undocumented inflow, and the inability to account for departures from the United States, deaths, or changes in immigrant status. The undocumented immigrant population in the United States consists of virtually every nationality in the world. However, slightly over half are of Mexican origin, comprising an estimated 5.9 million undocumented immigrants.

Illegal immigration is not a recent issue, but it has emerged as an especially controversial political and social topic in recent years as the foreign-born population of the United States increases and large Latino communities have emerged in areas where they previously did not exist. Critics of illegal immigration maintain that undocumented immigrants take jobs from American citizens, do not pay their fair share of taxes, and burden social services, such as education and health care. Cultural conservatives also claim that undocumented immigrants, particularly those from Latin America, threaten the "cultural unity" of the United States by refusing to assimilate into the dominant Anglo social and cultural core. Immigrant rights advocates counter these arguments by claiming that undocumented aliens often take low-paying and menial jobs that American citizens do not want, that illegal immigrants actually do pay social security and federal income taxes, and that all previous immigrant groups to the United States faced a period of social and cultural transition while being incorporated into American life.

Early 1900s

The U.S. Border Patrol was established in 1924 to regulate the entry of foreigners across the U.S.-Mexico and U.S.-Canadian borders and to enforce immigration laws by detaining those who illegally entered the country. The federal government established the Border Patrol at a time when several other immigration restrictions were being put in place. The new restrictions were directed primarily at Southern and Eastern

European and Asian immigrants. In fact, immigration enforcement at the turn of the twentieth century focused on apprehending Chinese immigrants attempting to enter the United States from Mexico rather than on Mexicans attempting to cross the border. During this period, certain theories about "race," which argued that Southern Europeans and non-white peoples were morally and intellectually inferior to those of Northern and Western European descent, gained wide popularity in the United States. Since the vast majority of immigrants at the time were from Southern and Eastern Europe and Asia, these groups became the primary targets of anti-immigrant nativism and immigration control efforts.

Anti-Mexican prejudice flared up throughout the Southwest during the Great Depression of the 1930s. American workers and politicians often viewed Mexicans, whether foreign or U.S.-born, as unwanted competitors for scarce jobs and government relief programs. Throughout the 1930s, the U.S. government, with the support of the Mexican government, repatriated more than half a million Mexicans, including illegal immigrants, legal immigrants, and Mexican Americans who had been born in the United States.

During the 1950s, President Dwight D. Eisenhower and Attorney General Herbert Brownell launched a massive deportation campaign known as "Operation Wetback." The term "wetback" is a derogatory term for Mexicans who enter the United States by swimming across the Rio Grande. Between 1953 and 1954, when the United States experienced an economic recession that nearly doubled the unemployment rate, Mexicans once again became a target and scapegoat for the economic downturn. From 1954 to 1959, the Border Patrol and local police in the Southwest rounded up and sent 3.8 million people back to Mexico, the overwhelming majority of whom did not receive an official deportation hearing.

Late 1900s

The U.S. government has not conducted large-scale deportations of illegal immigrants since the 1950s, although illegal immigration has steadily received increasing attention from the media, the public, and policymakers since the late 1970s. In late 1986, President Ronald Reagan signed the Immigration Reform and Control Act (IRCA), popularly referred to as the Simpson-Mazzoli Bill, after its leading congressional sponsors, Senator Alan Simpson (R-WY) and Representative Romano Mazzoli (D-KY).

IRCA contained two major planks. First, it offered amnesty to illegal immigrants who could prove that they had resided in the United States since 1982. (An amnesty is an official pardon or act of forgiveness by the government for an illegal activity committed in the past.) Undocumented immigrants who qualified were given the opportunity to adjust their immigration status and live and work freely in the United States. Some politicians and immigration control groups opposed granting amnesty to illegal immigrants because, in their estimation, it rewarded those who had violated immigration laws, potentially encouraging further illegal immigration.

The other major provision of IRCA made it a crime for employers to hire undocumented workers. As a result, federal law requires employers to verify that their employees are either American citizens or otherwise eligible to work in the United States. Since 1986, job applications routinely ask individuals if they are a U.S. citizen or legal resident, and employers require applicants to produce a Social Security card, work authorization permit, or other document verifying that an employee is not in violation of immigration laws. IRCA gave the federal government the ability to fine employers who failed to comply with these guidelines.

Since many illegal immigrants come to the United States in search of employment, IRCA's supporters believed that illegal immigration would decrease significantly when undocumented immigrants learned they would not be eligible to find work. Civil rights organizations feared that IRCA opened the door for employment-based discrimination against all Latinos/as and "immigrant-looking" peoples, as employers who sought to avoid criminal sanctions might treat all members of such groups as a suspect class. However, despite some initial success in reducing illegal entry during the late 1980s, IRCA has not thwarted illegal immigration. Relatively few employers have been fined for hiring undocumented immigrants, and the number of illegal immigrants in the United States has grown steadily throughout the 1990s and early 2000s.

In the mid-1990s, illegal immigration once again grabbed national media attention, with California taking center stage. As recession and unemployment took hold in the state, many California policymakers began calling for a crackdown on illegal aliens. Proposals ranged from an increase in the number of Border Patrol agents to denying American citizenship to U.S.-born children of undocumented parents. One member of the California legislature even suggested that all Latinos/as in the state be required to carry a personal identification card to verify legal residency—a clear civil rights violation that illustrates the racial undertones of the immigration debate. In 1994, California voters passed Proposition 187, a referendum that, among other things, called for the denial of nonemergency medical care and public education to adults and children who reside in the state illegally. Although a federal judge blocked implementation of Proposition 187, the debate emanating from California in the wake of voter passage had national reverberations, with lawmakers in other states and the U.S. Congress contemplating how to stem the influx of undocumented immigrants.

Although illegal immigrants in the United States come from nearly every nation in the world, most of the attention given to this matter centers on that from Latin America and the Caribbean—particularly Mexico, Haiti, and Cuba (despite the fact that Cubans have historically been granted political asylum and are therefore permitted to live in the United States legally as refugees). In the mid-1990s, new fences were erected along the U.S.-Mexican border, and Operation Hold the Line and Operation Gatekeeper were implemented in El Paso and San Diego, respectively, to crack down on the influx of undocumented immigrants from Mexico. Meanwhile, interceptions of Haitian and Cuban refugees intensified off the coast of Florida, with those captured often deported to their homelands or placed in detention centers. Less attention was given to securing the U.S.-Canada border and to cracking down on undocumented immigrants who overstayed their tourist or student visas.

On September 30, 1996, President Bill Clinton signed into law the Illegal Immigration Reform and Immigrant Responsibility Act (IIRIRA). Although the main thrust of the legislation was toward apprehending and deporting foreigners who commit

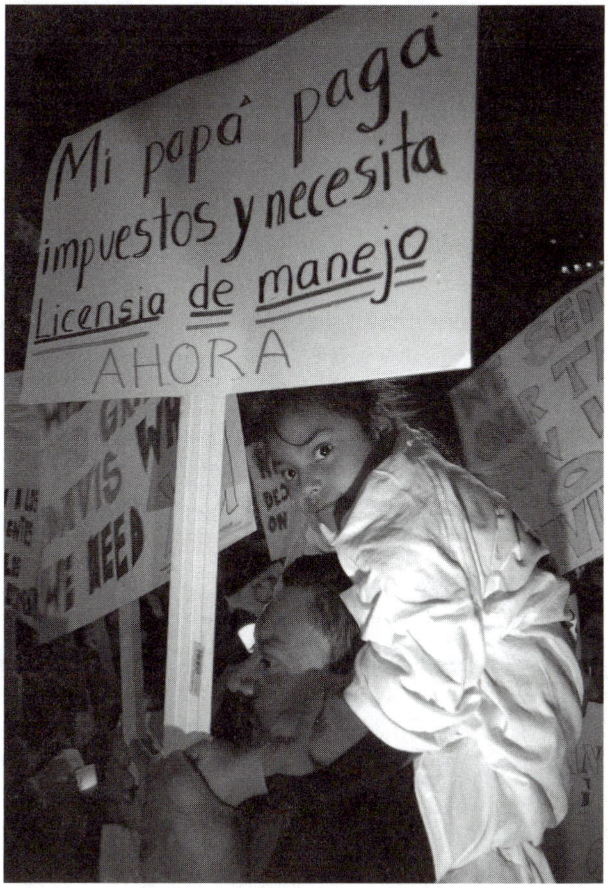

Marchers in Los Angeles rally for amnesty for illegal aliens on May Day—international workers' day—in 2002. The sign reads: "My father pays taxes and needs a driver's license NOW." *(David McNew/Getty Images)*

violent crimes in the United States, it also called for increased border enforcement and placed stricter restrictions on a refugee's ability to obtain political asylum. Under the IIRIRA, undocumented immigrants who lived in the United States for at least six months would be banned from legally migrating for at least three years. The most controversial provision of the original bill—excluding illegal immigrant children from attending public schools—was eventually dropped and did not become part of the law.

Twenty-First Century

At the beginning of the twenty-first century, illegal immigration remains one of the most controversial social policy issues in the United States. However, two recent trends distinguish current illegal immigration and the debate surrounding it from those of the past. First, the geographic concentration of undocumented immigrants has diversified and is no longer confined to the Southwest. During the 1990s and early 2000s, illegal immigration became a hot-button issue in suburban and rural communities in Long Island (New York), Virginia, North Carolina, and Georgia following heavy legal and illegal migration of Mexicans and Central Americans to these regions. Secondly, there was a proliferation of private citizens' groups and grassroots organizations attempting to draw attention to illegal immigration, influence political opinion on the subject, and, in some cases, apprehend undocumented immigrants themselves.

In April 2005, a group calling itself the Minuteman Project began conducting citizen patrols along the southern Arizona border. The purpose of the group, according to its members, was to monitor the U.S.-Mexico border in Cochise County, Arizona, and report suspected illegal immigrants to Border Patrol authorities. The Minuteman Project became the subject of national controversy, however. California Governor Arnold Schwarzenegger expressed support for the Minuteman patrols, while President George W. Bush criticized the group and alluded to its tactics as "vigilante."

Bush himself expressed strong support for a guest worker program, much like the Bracero Program of the 1940s and 1950s, as a method to reduce illegal immigration and provide certain American industries, such as agriculture, with an adequate labor force. Senators John McCain (R-AZ) and Edward M. Kennedy (D-MA) proposed a guest worker bill in 2005 that would require undocumented immigrants to first pay a fine and complete a medical examination and criminal background check and then apply for guest worker status. But guest worker proposals in general faced opposition from hard-line immigration control advocates, who demanded stricter border enforcement and crackdowns on illegal immigration. In December 2005, the House of Representatives passed a bill that called for the construction of new fences along the Texas and Arizona borders and stricter penalties against employers who hire undocumented immigrants. Congress continued to debate a number of measures, but in June 2007 the Comprehensive Immigration Reform Act, backed by President George W. Bush and Democratic leaders, failed to survive a procedural vote in the Senate, effectively killing legislation for that year.

Illegal immigration is a controversial issue and evokes strong emotional reactions from opponents and defenders alike because it represents a confluence of several concerns: business interests, labor interests, law and its enforcement, and issues of racial/ethnic, linguistic, and cultural diversity. These factors ensure that illegal immigration will remain a hotly debated policy issue and social concern in the United States for many years to come.

Justin D. García

See also: Immigration Enforcement; Immigration Reform and Control Act of 1986.

Further Reading

Aguirre, Adalberto, Jr., and Jonathan H. Turner. *American Ethnicity: The Dynamics and Consequences of Discrimination.* 4th ed. New York: McGraw-Hill, 2004.

Chavez, Leo R. *Shadowed Lives: Undocumented Immigrants in American Society.* 2nd ed. Orlando, FL: Harcourt Brace, 1998.

Meier, Matt S., and Feliciano Ribera. *Mexican Americans, American Mexicans: From Conquistadors to Chicanos.* New York: Hill and Wang, 1993.

Sánchez, George J. *Becoming Mexican American: Ethnicity, Culture, and Identity in Chicano Los Angeles, 1900–1945.* New York: Oxford University Press, 1995.

Immigration Act of 1924

The Johnson-Reed Act, officially known as the Immigration Act of 1924, set quotas on the number of immigrants who could enter the United States from any given country. The bill was authored by Republican restrictionists who sought to curtail immigration from Southern and Eastern Europe—an area that, prior to 1924, produced the majority of immigrants to the United States—as well as from Asia. Representative Albert Johnson (R-WA), chairman of the Committee on Immigration, favored immigrants from Northern Europe. His political preferences were heavily influenced by the eugenics movement, which held that persons from Northern Europe are superior to those of other races. Senator David A. Reed (R-PA) introduced the final provision of the bill, which based the immigration quotas for individual nations on the origins of the white population in the United States according to the 1890 census. Reed maintained that immigration quotas favoring Northern Europeans would racially purify the nation and thereby ensure its international standing. The Immigration Act of 1924 also all but excluded people from Asia and established the U.S. Border Patrol to stop the influx of "unwanted" Asians, among others.

The national origins system established by the 1924 legislation shaped U.S. immigration policy until the Immigration Act of 1965. The system set immigration quotas for individual foreign countries based on the number of people from that nation who had come to the United States decades before, and also capped total immigration at 164,000 annually. The Johnson-Reed Act did not establish quotas for immigrants from the Western Hemisphere; unlimited numbers could enter the United States from Canada, Mexico, and Central and South America. Although primarily aimed at immigrants from Southern and Eastern Europe and from Asia, the Immigration Act had dramatic implications for the future of Mexican immigration into the United States. From the end of the Mexican American War in 1848 to the Immigration Act of 1924, no policing of the U.S. border had taken place. As a result, peoples from both nations traveled back and forth without difficulty. With the establishment of the Border Patrol, however, the frontier became a real barrier for people, particularly Mexicans, traveling between the two countries. It can be said that the creation of the Border Patrol alone marked a watershed in U.S.-Mexico diplomatic and labor relations, and the growth of Mexican American communities.

Impact on Mexican Labor

Historically, restrictions on European immigration have led to increased employer reliance on Mexican workers. Labor-hungry employers often assisted Mexican immigrants in circumventing barriers such as fees and literacy tests. The following table illustrates the increase in Mexican immigration following the Johnson-Reed Act, as Mexicans filled the labor void left by European immigrants. If not uniformly from year to year, the number of Mexican immigrants admitted to the United States increased significantly beginning in 1924, especially in comparison with other groups; thus, the percentage of total U.S. immigration accounted for by Mexicans also jumped.

Although large numbers of Mexicans were admitted legally to the United States, after 1924, increasing numbers of Mexican immigrants began to bypass the required paperwork and entered the country illegally.

From Mexican to Mexican American

As a result of this increased border patrolling, Mexican communities became more established. The curtailment of circular migration led immigrants to place an ever-increasing emphasis on family stability and community building. Thus they began a transition from being largely a group of male sojourners following seasonal labor to becoming a community of families seeking a life as Americans.

U.S. Immigration Before and After the Immigration Act of 1924—Mexican and Total

Year	Total Number of Immigrants Admitted	Total Number of Mexicans Admitted	Mexican Immigrants as Percentage of Total
1922	309,556	18,246	5.9
1923	522,919	62,709	12.0
1924	706,896	87,648	12.4
1925	294,314	32,378	11.0
1926	304,488	42,638	14.0
1927	355,175	66,766	19.9

Source: Bloch, Louis. "Facts about Mexican Immigration Before and Since the Quota Restriction Laws." *Journal of the American Statistical Association* 24:165 (March 1929): 50–60.

This has not been an easy transition, however. The historical need for cheap, temporary laborers in the U.S. economy has often conflicted with nativist racial prejudices. Federal government policy has welcomed Mexicans as laborers at various times, but only on a temporary basis. U.S. employers have sought low-wage laborers, but hesitate to welcome these people into the mainstream society. Problems have arisen when guest laborers have sought to become permanent residents. The result has been a community characterized by cultural change yet with limited social acceptance or upward mobility.

Madeleine E. López

See also: Illegal Immigration.

Further Reading

Sanchez, George J. *Becoming Mexican American: Ethnicity, Culture and Identity in Chicano Los Angeles, 1900–1945.* New York: Oxford University Press, 1993.

Vargas, Zaragosa, ed. *Major Problems in Mexican American History: Documents and Essays.* New York: Houghton Mifflin, 1999.

Immigration Act of 1990

Extending the landmark Immigration and Nationality Act of 1965, which abolished the national-quota system in favor of granting visas to those with family members in the United States, the Immigration Act of 1990 increased the total number of legal U.S. immigrants from 500,000 to about 700,000 per year. The legislation further emphasized the need to attract immigrants with specialized job skills and prospective workers in the service sector, adding more than 100,000 permanent and temporary job-related visas. The measure also added 50,000 "diversity visas," to be assigned by a new lottery program, for countries that had been limited under previous legislation; strengthened the Border Patrol; revised the grounds for exclusion and deportation; authorized temporary protected status to aliens of certain countries; and revised nonimmigrant admission categories. For Latino and Asian immigrants in particular, the act's stress on family reunification continued to enhance immigration opportunities. Albeit to a lesser extent, Latinos/as also benefited from the employment-based aspects of the measure.

The family reunification aspect of the 1990 Immigration Act proved especially advantageous to Mexicans seeking legal residency in the United States. An overwhelming number of Mexican nationals applying for visas had a parent, spouse, or other close relative who was a U.S. citizen, and the new law established a first-come, first-served policy for second preference (parental or minor children) visas. Previously, there had been a per-country cap on second-preference visas, which had greatly restricted Mexican immigration.

Indeed the emphasis on family reunification boosted Latino immigration in general. From 1995 onward, about 70 percent of legal immigrant slots were designated for family-based immigrants. The actual number of legal immigrants admitted in the immediate years after the legislation surpassed the 675,000 originally authorized (with increases to accommodate immediate relatives). In 1995, a total of 720,461 immigrants legally entered the United States; the figure rose to 915,900 in 1996 and then dipped slightly to 798,378 in 1997. Of the aggregate from 1991 to 1997, 50.1 percent were immigrants from the Western Hemisphere—most of them Latinos/as.

While the family-based provisions of the 1990 Immigration Act benefited Latino/as inordinately, the employment-based provisions also provided an opportunity for some to come to the United States as temporary workers. H-2A visas, for example, allowed thousands of seasonal agricultural workers from Mexico to enter the United States for temporary hire. Fewer entered the country on H-1B visas, granted to guest workers in specialty professions; these were granted predominantly to European and Asian nationals.

In addition to redefining the U.S. immigration preference system and the total number of legal immigrants admitted, the 1990 legislation also led to reforms in naturalization and refugee policy. Despite widespread anti-immigrant and English-only initiatives across the United States at the time, the measure made it easier for longtime legal residents not proficient in English to become U.S. citizens, which benefited many in the Latino community. The Immigration Act of 1990 further allowed spouses and children of illegal immigrants who had received amnesty under the Immigration Reform and Control Act of 1986 (most of whom were Latino) to remain in the United States. Yet another clause gave the U.S. attorney general the power to grant "temporary protected status" to undocumented immigrants who had fled territories beset by war, earthquakes, or other natural or economic emergencies. Latinos/as from El Salvador and Nicaragua benefited from this part of the 1990 law.

In order to appease lawmakers who wanted tighter immigration laws, other sections of the 1990 legislation imposed harsher U.S. border control measures. The expansion of the Border Patrol itself was included to placate those legislators who feared an influx of illegal immigrants from Mexico. With the demise of the Soviet Union, the end of the Cold War, and the passing of communism as a national threat, illegal immigrants became a growing preoccupation in many political circles and parts of the country—especially the Southwest. While only a relatively minor portion of the Immigration Act of 1990 addressed the threat of illegal immigration, concern over this issue would increase throughout the course of the decade and especially after the terrorist attacks of September 11, 2001.

Lisa Y. Ramos

See also: Illegal Immigration; Immigration and Nationality Act of 1965; Immigration Enforcement; Immigration Reform and Control Act of 1986.

Further Reading

Calavita, Kitty. "Gaps and Contradictions in U.S. Immigration Policy: An Analysis of Recent Reform Efforts." In *The Immigration Reader: America in a Multidisciplinary Perspective,* ed. David Jacobson. Malden, MA: Blackwell, 1998.

Daniels, Roger. *Coming to America: A History of Immigration and Ethnicity in American Life.* 2nd ed. New York. HarperCollins, 2002.

Daniels, Roger, and Otis L. Graham. *Debating American Immigration, 1882–Present.* Lanham, MD: Rowman & Littlefield, 2001.

Tichenor, Daniel J. *Dividing Lines: The Politics of Immigration Control in America.* Princeton, NJ: Princeton University Press, 2002.

Immigration and Nationality Act of 1965

The Immigration and Nationality Act amendments of 1965 (a revision of the original 1952 legislation) reshaped U.S. immigration policy by officially eliminating race and national origin as admission criteria. The measure was introduced by Representative Emanuel Celler (D-NY), passed by the Democratic-controlled Congress, and signed into law by President Lyndon B. Johnson. While the nation's immigration laws have been revised several times since then, the basic framework established by the 1965 legislation remains at the heart of U.S. immigration policy to the present day.

The 1965 amendments replaced a regulatory scheme established during the 1910s and 1920s, which limited immigration from the Eastern Hemisphere to 150,000 individuals per year and established a severe set of restrictions based on race and national origin. Immigration from most Asian and African countries was effectively prohibited, either explicitly or in practice, while a system of quotas divided the 150,000 annual limit among the remaining countries on a pro rata basis, based on the percentage of individuals from each country already present in the United States. This formula conferred approximately 85 percent of all immigrant visas to Northern and Western European countries, since individuals tracing their ancestry to those nations lived in the United States in much larger numbers than individuals from other parts of Europe. Congress declined to extend similar numerical restrictions to the Western Hemisphere, based largely on concerns over the potential effect on relations with Canada and Mexico (which accounted for the vast majority of Western Hemisphere immigration) and the need for agricultural labor. Accordingly, significant numbers of Mexicans, in particular, continued to enter the United States legally facilitated by extensive migration under the Bracero Program—and, due to limited regulation of the southern border, illegally.

After World War II, pressures mounted to repeal the race- and origin-based restrictions. The progression of the civil rights movement influenced reformers, who explicitly drew parallels between domestic racial segregation and the discriminatory classifications embedded in the immigration laws. Like segregation, these classifications were increasingly regarded as incompatible with the principles the United States sought to advance internationally, especially in the wake of the war against fascism in Europe and the onset of the Cold War. More tangibly, the restrictions also excluded many individuals—whom the United States wished to protect—fleeing Communist and totalitarian regimes. At the urging of successive presidents, Congress accordingly eased restrictions on Asian immigration symbolically, if slightly, and authorized the special admission of significant numbers of refugees in the late 1940s and early 1950s.

By the 1950s and 1960s, the quota system itself had become increasingly unworkable. Quotas for Northern and Western European countries often went unfilled, as immigration from those countries declined. Growing numbers of immigrants entered the United States outside the quota system, as Congress enacted special laws and private bills to supplement the 1920s legislation, and successive presidents authorized the entry of refugees by executive order. While support for the original system made reform in Congress elusive for many years, efforts in that regard accelerated after the election of President John F. Kennedy in 1960 and, especially, after Kennedy's assassination in 1963 and President Johnson's landslide election in 1964, which altered the political dynamics in Congress. Both Kennedy and Johnson prioritized immigration reform more than their predecessors had; while other legislative priorities had taken precedence during the early 1960s, the nation's immigration laws finally were reformed in 1965 with overwhelming support of both houses of Congress.

The 1965 legislation represented a compromise: while it eliminated all remaining racial exclusions and origin-based quotas—an outcome reformers had fought for—it imposed restrictions on the overall number of immigrants per year. The new system modestly increased the overall ceiling for immigrants from the Eastern Hemisphere to 170,000 visas per year, with a maximum of 20,000 entries per country. Immigrant visas were to be allocated on a first-come, first-served basis within a set of hierarchical "preference" categories: four family-based categories (comprising 74 percent of all visas), two employment-based categories (20 percent), and a seventh category for refugees fleeing persecution or natural calamities (6 percent). In some instances, the legislation permitted unused visas from higher-preference categories to be reallocated to lower categories within the hierarchy. Above and beyond these preference categories, the 1965 act also authorized numerically unrestricted immigration by "immediate" relatives (spouses, children under age 21, and parents) of U.S. citizens, subject to neither the 170,000 overall nor the 20,000 per-country limitations.

While the act modestly eased restrictions on immigration from the Eastern Hemisphere, it imposed, for the first time, severe numerical restrictions on immigration from the Western Hemisphere—another compromise accepted by the reformers. Western Hemisphere immigration was capped at 120,000 visas per year—a 40 percent reduction from the levels allowed before 1965. This numerical ceiling was instituted on the heels of the elimination in 1964 of the Bracero Program, which had facilitated the lawful entry of hundreds of thousands of Mexican guest workers in the years during and after World War II. As with Eastern Hemisphere immigration, immediate relatives were not subject to this ceiling. While per-country limits and the preference system did not initially apply to Western Hemisphere immigration, new laws enacted during the 1970s extended these provisions to the Western Hemisphere and consolidated the existing numerical restrictions into a single, worldwide ceiling for immigrant visas.

Reformers passionately advocated for the elimination of the race- and origin-based restrictions and the establishment of formal equality between different countries, which were at the heart of the 1965 amendments. While some advocates may have anticipated that the new law would significantly change immigration patterns, many others seemed to suggest that it would not significantly increase the overall number of immigrants or dramatically change the composition of the immigrant pool. In reality, however, the legislation led to dramatic changes. While other economic, political, and social factors played significant roles as well, the new policy facilitated an increase in the overall number of immigrants after 1965. Moreover, "chain migration" under the law's family reunification provisions, reshaped the ethnic composition of the immigrant pool. The growth in the number of Asian immigrants, in particular, was overwhelming: while Asians constituted only 5 percent of all immigrants before 1965, Asian immigrants outnumbered European immigrants by 1971. By the end of that decade, Asians constituted 40 percent of all immigrants in a pool that itself had grown significantly since 1965.

At the same time, however, the act's low numerical ceiling constrained legal immigration from Latin America, especially Mexico. The effect of the new ceiling was particularly severe in light of the discontinuation of the Bracero Program. U.S. agricultural employers, in particular, had become heavily dependent on Mexican labor under the program, which had facilitated patterns of migration to and from Mexico and extensive cross-border social and economic ties that had become well developed and relatively stable. While elimination of the Bracero Program might simply have caused Mexicans to seek entry using immigrant visas, the new ceiling instead rendered those existing migration patterns illegal. Accordingly, the number of Mexicans entering the United States without legal authorization increased sharply after 1965.

Anil Kalhan

See also: Bracero Program; Illegal Immigration.

Further Reading

Chin, Gabriel J. "The Civil Rights Revolution Comes to Immigration Law: A New Look at the Immigration and Nationality Act of 1965." *North Carolina Law Review* 75:1 (November 1996): 273–345.

Massey, Douglas S., Jorge Durand, and Nolan J. Malone. *Beyond Smoke and Mirrors: Mexican Immigration in an Era of Economic Integration.* New York: Russell Sage Foundation, 2002.

Ngai, Mae M. *Impossible Subjects: Illegal Aliens and the Making of Modern America.* Princeton, NJ: Princeton University Press, 2004.

Reimers, David M. *Still the Golden Door: The Third World Comes to America.* 2nd ed. New York: Columbia University Press, 2002.

Tichenor, Daniel J. *Dividing Lines: The Politics of Immigration Control in America.* Princeton, NJ: Princeton University Press, 2002.

Immigration Enforcement

Primary responsibility for protecting America's borders and enforcing federal immigration laws lies with U.S. Immigration and Customs Enforcement (ICE), an agency of the Department of Homeland Security (DHS). ICE was established on March 1, 2003, as part of the reorganization of federal security and intelligence in the aftermath of the September 11, 2001, terrorist attacks. As the largest investigative branch of DHS, the agency is responsible for identifying and dismantling "criminal activities and eliminating vulnerabilities that pose a threat to [the] nation's borders." ICE also works in collaboration with a sister agency in the DHS, the U.S. Bureau of Customs and Border Protection (CPB), which is responsible for enforcing U.S. trade laws, regulating foreign trade, and collecting import duties.

The roughly 16,000 members of the U.S. Border Patrol constitute the law enforcement arm of the CPB. ICE, which combines the law enforcement divisions of the former Immigration and Naturalization Service (INS) and the former U.S. Customs Service, seeks to protect the American people and support public safety in part by targeting "illegal immigrants: the people, money, and materials that support terrorism and other criminal activities." Despite the circumstances of its creation and its primary mission of national security, ICE extends its authority in the enforcement of immigration law for broader interests and purposes. Its Office of Detention and Removal (DRO), for example, seeks the removal of illegal aliens; uniformed Immigration Enforcement Agents (IEA) seek to "interdict, apprehend, and remove criminal aliens," including ones found in prisons and jails.

Under ICE and predecessor agencies beginning in the 1890s, the U.S. federal government has conducted ongoing campaigns and a number of special programs to enforce the nation's immigration laws. Practices range from frontier patrols and the apprehension of illegal border crossers to the more recent construction of physical barriers and deportation of undocumented people who have been residing inside the United States for up to several decades. Aside from federal and state laws on employment, customs and rules barring access to social welfare benefits, and other measures to limit the influx and perceived social costs of illegal immigrants, "enforcement" efforts have also devolved to citizen action groups that resort to vigilante tactics.

Federal Efforts

Although the agencies of U.S. immigration enforcement, their authority, and their tactics have changed through the course of the nation's history, one constant has been the increasing difficulty of attaining citizenship and, therefore, the growing need for protection against those seeking illegal entry. With the exception of African slaves, immigration was not restricted by race or nationality by federal policy until the Act of February 19, 1862, which outlawed the transport of Chinese male laborers, called "coolies," on American ships. This measure was a precursor to the Chinese Exclusion Act of May 6, 1882, which drastically altered national immigration policy by suspending immigration from China completely for a period of ten years. The heavy influx of Chinese in previous decades had led to concerns over economic competition with Anglo-Americans in the West and an outbreak of nativist sentiment. The Chinese exclusion was extended another ten years in 1892 and indefinitely in 1902. A series of Alien Contract Labor Laws in the late 1880s and early 1890s barred any immigrants from entering the country to work under contracts signed before their arrival, measures again aimed at reducing job competition from low-wage foreign laborers. Still other federal laws excluded convicts, those suffering from disease, and persons deemed likely to become dependent on public financial assistance. Such measures gave rise to the first federal agencies charged with implementing and enforcing national immigration policy.

The Immigration Act of 1891 established the Office of the Superintendent of Immigration (precursor to the INS), an office in the Department of Treasury charged with admitting or rejecting those seeking entry into the United States and with administering the admission process. Immigrant Inspectors, as they were called, were deployed at major ports of entry, including the Ellis Island immigrant station opened in New York Harbor in 1892. Reorganized and renamed the Bureau of Immigration in 1893, the agency expanded its efforts in administering national immigration policy and was transferred to the Department of Commerce and Labor in 1903. It was renamed again in 1906, as the Bureau of Immigration and Naturalization, after passage of federal legislation that standardized the naturalization process. Administering immigration and naturalization policy were combined, later separated, and finally united again in 1933 under the Immigration and Naturalization Service (INS).

In the meantime, as early as 1904, mounted federal agents were patrolling the U.S. border in the Southwest and California to curb the flow of illegal immigrants. Congress, in 1915, granted arrest authority to federal immigrant inspectors, whose patrolling efforts were bolstered by the U.S. Army and Texas Rangers. In May 1924, Congress formally established the Border Patrol as an agency of the Department of Labor to bar illegal crossings of the U.S.-Mexico frontier. Staff and funding were increased for deportation as well, and interdiction operations were expanded to the Gulf Coast in the 1920s to protect against illegal arrivals by ship.

The Bracero Program, based on an agreement between the U.S. and Mexican governments that brought hundreds of thousands of guest workers into the United States during World War II and the years that followed, brought a relative lull in immigration enforcement. Yet even as legal border crossings under the program continued until 1964, the INS ten years earlier quietly initiated a major campaign—called Operation Wetback—to identify, apprehend, and deport the many illegal immigrants who had settled in the American Southwest. Deploying more than 1,000 border patrol agents, along with state and local police, the crackdown led directly to the removal of nearly 150,000 Mexican nationals in one year. According to the INS, more than a million others, fearing arrest, fled voluntarily back across the border.

INS arrests and detentions along the southern border remained heavy in succeeding decades. In 1975, INS Director Leonard Chapman issued a warning, declaring that there would be "a vast and silent invasion of illegal aliens" if the efforts and resources of the Border Patrol and the INS were not increased. In 1976, the number of people arrested and detained along the border surpassed 1 million for the first time. Thus, the efforts of these two organizations came to focus heavily on Latino immigrants during the 1970s and 1980s.

Federal immigration enforcement underwent a significant strategic shift in the mid-1990s under the administration of President Bill Clinton. Because the vast majority of border arrests took place in two narrow stretches of the frontier—near San Diego, California, and near El Paso, Texas—it was decided that traditional apprehension methods should give way to a strategy of deterrence and the use of technology and infrastructure to limit illegal border crossings. Thus, under Operation Gatekeeper in the San Diego sector, Operation Hold-the-Line in the El Paso sector, and Operation Safeguard in the Tucson sector, billions of dollars in federal funding were allocated to surveillance technologies (such as cameras), information systems, and physical infrastructure (fences and other barriers) in some locations to stem illegal immigration and the drug trade. Also in the mid-1990s, Congress mandated that the Border Patrol strategically reallocate its agents from apprehension and deportation in the nation's interior to deterrence efforts in borderlands.

The terrorist attacks of September 11, 2001, brought another major shift in strategic purpose as well as organizational restructuring. National security and the interception of terrorist weapons became the overarching concerns, and the realigned immigration enforcement agencies brought to bear all means of both apprehension and deterrence in their efforts. The Border Patrol alone created several specialized units—dedicated to air and marine operations, mounted guard, search and rescue, special response, and a mobile tactical support team, among others—coordinated by an Operations Group established in 2007. Similarly, ICE today includes offices of investigation, intelligence, detention and removal, protective services, legal advice, and professional responsibility. Meanwhile, federal lawmakers introduced legislation in 2005 calling for the construction of a full, reinforced barrier that would extend the entire length of the U.S.-Mexico border. While supported by the administration of President George W. Bush and Republicans in Congress, Mexican officials and many

A U.S. border agent patrols the fence between the United States and Mexico near Ciudad Juarez, a well-traveled crossing point for illegal immigrants into west Texas. Physical barriers have become a centerpiece of U.S. immigration enforcement. *(Chip Somodevilla/Getty Images)*

Americans condemned the proposal. The Secure Fence Act of 2006, passed in both houses of Congress and signed into law by President Bush that October, guaranteed $1.2 billion in border security funds, but the incoming Democratic majority in Congress announced in January 2007 that the fence plan would be revisited. Public opinion polls showed that a majority of Americans support expansion of the Border Patrol and its apprehension efforts over the construction of a 700-mile (1100-kilometer) physical barrier.

State Initiatives and Citizen Patrols

Federal legislation—from the Chinese Exclusion Act and the Alien Contract Labor Law of the 1880s, to the national quota system instituted in the 1920s, to Operation Wetback in the 1950s and post-9/11 border security measures—has historically sought to limit immigration and curb the flow of foreign nationals coming to American illegally. So, too, local governments and private individuals have taken steps to stop the influx of undocumented aliens and remove those who have already settled inside the United States. Notable efforts in recent decades have included California's Proposition 187, a 1994 ballot measure—dubbed the "Save Our State Initiative" by supporters—that called for the denial of health care, public education, and other social services to illegal aliens; some 59 percent of voters favored the measure, but it was later overturned in federal court. Similar proposals found support in other states. In Arizona, 56 percent of voters in 2004 cast ballots in support of Proposition 200, which required proof of citizenship to qualify for state benefits or to register to vote. While subject to legal wrangling for the next several years, the initiative carried the weight of law into 2008.

Legislative efforts at the federal and state levels notwithstanding, a number of citizen groups in the border states of the Southwest have felt that government has failed to protect the nation's southern border and have taken it upon themselves to organize patrols—often armed and resorting to vigilante tactics. Among the most notable of these private groups is the Minuteman Project, which organizes patrols along the Arizona-Mexico border and reports illegal immigration to the U.S. Border Patrol. The Minutemen openly declare their fear that the uncontrolled flow of immigrants entering the United States through Mexico threatens the culture, economy, and future of the United States. A similar group, calling itself the Civil Homeland Defense, began operations in Cochise County, Arizona, in 2002. Volunteers patrol the border to protect America against the influx of Latino immigrants.

Thus, much as the nation's immigration policies have shifted and evolved through the centuries, reflecting changes in social values, prevailing ideologies, economic trends, and international relations, so efforts at enforcement have waxed and waned, have spawned new organizations and tactics, and have had greater or lesser degrees of success. Nevertheless, for at least the last several decades, the unchecked arrival of millions of undocumented aliens has swelled the ranks of "illegal" residents whose denial of rights and services—or outright deportation—strikes many Americans as unjust, inhumane, and simply impractical in many respects.

Jessica Hulst

See also: Illegal Immigration; Immigration Reform and Control Act of 1986.

Further Reading

Daniels, Roger. *Guarding the Golden Door: American Immigration Policy and Immigrants since 1882.* New York: Hill and Wang, 2004.

Graham, Otis. *Unguarded Gates: A History of America's Immigration Crisis.* New York: Rowman & Littlefield, 2004.

Guskin, Jane, and David L. Wilson. *The Politics of Immigration: Questions and Answers.* New York: Monthly Review Press, 2007.

Miller, Debra. *Illegal Immigration.* San Diego, CA: Greenhaven, 2006.

Smith, Marian. "Overview of INS History." In *Historical Guide to the U.S. Government,* ed. George Kurian. New York: Oxford University Press, 1998.

U.S. Citizenship and Immigration Services. http://www.uscis.gov.

U.S. Customs and Border Protection. http://www.cbp.gov.

Immigration and Nationality Act of 1952

See **McCarran-Walter Act (1952)**

Immigration Reform and Control Act of 1986

Enacted after extensive debate over illegal immigration in the 1970s and early 1980s, the Immigration Reform and Control Act of 1986 (IRCA) established a system of immigration enforcement in the form of civil and criminal penalties for employers who knowingly hire non-citizens residing unlawfully in the United States. Along with that system of employer sanctions, IRCA also provided for the legalization of millions of undocumented migrants and dramatically expanded the resources devoted to border enforcement.

Background and Political Context

IRCA was enacted following many years of debate concerning illegal immigration, which became an increasingly prominent issue during the late 1970s and early 1980s. From the 1940s until the 1960s, immigration from Latin America (and in particular from Mexico) had been tolerated to a considerable extent. Unlike immigration from the Eastern Hemisphere, legal immigration from the Western Hemisphere was not subject to the per-country quotas and overall ceiling of the Immigration Act of 1924; between 1942 and 1965, the Bracero Program facilitated the recruitment and migration of millions of Mexican citizens to work lawfully in agriculture and the railroad industry. Agricultural employers also recruited significant numbers of unauthorized migrants from Mexico during this period, either to supplement the pool of workers available through the Bracero Program, which failed to fulfill completely the demand for labor, or to avoid the costly formalities of the program's recruitment process. Enforcement of the southern border during this period was limited, and employers did not face any liability for hiring unauthorized migrants. (The so-called "Texas Proviso" under federal immigration law explicitly protected employers from prosecution for hiring undocumented workers.) Immigration officials were lax in searching for and apprehending undocumented workers throughout the country so as not to antagonize growers, who wielded considerable political clout. Approximately 5 million individuals came to the United States from Mexico during this period.

Following the elimination of the Bracero Program in the mid-1960s and the establishment of severe numerical restrictions on legal immigration from the Western Hemisphere, the number of illegal immigrants from Latin America increased dramatically. Despite the changes to the immigration laws, the pattern of migration from Mexico continued along much the same trajectory as before, developing into what some have called a "de facto guest worker program." The demand for low-wage immigrant labor in the agricultural industry remained, and many Mexican citizens, faced with their country's increasing population and declining economic performance, looked to the United States as a source for work. As a result, Mexican workers continued to come to the United States in significant numbers. Given the shrinking opportunities for lawful entry, unauthorized migrants came to dominate the flow of Mexican migrants during this period. Approximately 28 million Mexicans entered the United States without authorization between 1965 and 1986; since much of this migration was temporary and circular, the net migration from Mexico during this period has been estimated at between 4 and 5 million.

Despite some measure of stability in these migration patterns, illegal immigration steadily became a more salient political issue during the 1970s and 1980s, especially in the face of economic difficulties confronting the United States. The prominence of immigration as an issue was heightened by the increase in the overall numbers of immigrants from all countries in the wake of the Immigration and Nationality Act of 1965 and the increasing visibility of migration from Latin America. While earlier generations of Mexican migrants working in agricultural settings were largely invisible to most Americans, over time increasing numbers of Mexican migrants, having gained English-language skills and familiarity with life in the United States, sought and found better, higher-paying jobs in non-agricultural, urban settings. At the same time, unrest and civil war in Central America during the 1980s caused refugees to flee to the United States in large numbers. In this context, many political figures fostered a sense of panic about illegal immigration and a border that was supposedly "out of control," at times seeking to link immigration to the issues of drug trafficking and national security.

In 1981, a bipartisan commission established by Congress, the Select Commission on Immigration and Refugee Policy, recommended a compromise response to the issue of illegal immigration. On the one hand, employers would be penalized for hiring workers who were unlawfully present in the United States; on the other hand, undocumented migrants already in the United States would be permitted to legalize their immigration status. Members of the Select Commission advocated legalization for a variety reasons; they noted, for example, that most undocumented migrants were hard-working individuals who had paid taxes and contributed to the U.S. economy, that scarce enforcement resources were best directed toward future flows of migrants, and that the United States had some responsibility for the presence of undocumented migrants in the country given the lack of any laws prohibiting employers from hiring them.

Soon thereafter, several members of Congress sponsored legislation based on these recommendations. The ensuing political debate continued for several years and cut across party lines. Many advocates of employer sanctions and increased border enforcement vigorously opposed legalization, deriding it as a form of "amnesty" for individuals who had broken the law. Indeed, the House of Representatives ultimately voted to include legalization in IRCA by a very narrow margin. On the other hand, many advocates of legalization opposed employer sanctions, concerned that they would cause employers to discriminate against legal immigrants and citizens on the basis of race, national origin, alienage, or citizenship status. Sensing a political imperative to act, however, members of Congress accepted the compromise, even as many of them candidly acknowledged what they regarded as the bill's imperfections. IRCA was passed by Congress in October 1986 and signed into law by President Ronald Reagan the following month.

Provisions

IRCA's enforcement provisions required employers to verify that new employees are eligible for employment in the United States, albeit without requiring them to determine the authenticity of documents presented to them. The law imposed civil penalties upon employers who knowingly hired undocumented migrants and criminal liability upon employers found to engage in a "pattern or practice" of doing so. IRCA also increased the resources available for immigration enforcement at the border and in the interior of the country, significantly increasing the Border Patrol's budget and making new funds available to the Department of Labor to conduct workplace inspections. Acknowledging concerns over potential discrimination, IRCA prohibited discrimination against qualified, legal immigrant job applicants and imposed fines for violations. The statute also mandated Congress's General Accounting Office (GAO) to investigate whether employer sanctions were resulting in discrimination, providing for the repeal of employer sanctions if GAO concluded that widespread discrimination was occurring.

IRCA included two separate legalization programs, one conferring legal status upon undocumented individuals residing in the United States since 1982, and another conferring legal status to undocumented individuals who had performed at least ninety days' worth of agricultural work between 1985 and 1986. However, legalization was neither automatic nor simple. Within an eighteen-month window beginning in early 1987, applicants were required to pay an application fee and submit extensive documentation—including a lengthy application form, photographs, fingerprints, and other documents—to establish their identity, residence, employment history, and financial responsibility. Applicants also had to undergo a medical examination by an approved doctor and appear for a personal interview. Successful applicants were granted temporary legal status and, after one year, would become eligible to become lawful permanent residents upon showing minimal proficiency in English and knowledge of U.S. history and government—requirements that previously had been required only for applicants for U.S. citizenship, not new immigrants.

While broader immigration policy concerns also were part of the debate leading to IRCA's enactment, the law did not significantly change the overall number of legally authorized immigrants or the allocation of immigrants among different countries and preference categories that had been established under the Immigration and Nationality Act of 1965. IRCA did, however, seek to account for the demand for agricultural workers by authorizing additional temporary, non-immigrant visas for short-term agricultural labor. The law also established a lottery allocating 10,000 immigrant visas to individuals from countries underrepresented in the post-1965 immigration flows.

Impact

Despite the hopes of its backers, IRCA failed to significantly curtail illegal immigration. Approximately 3 million individuals obtained legal immigration status under IRCA, more than 75 percent of whom were of Mexican descent. In addition to gaining the right to sponsor relatives seeking to migrate legally, these newly legalized immigrants increased the overall social capital available in the United States for other Mexicans seeking to migrate, whether lawfully or unlawfully—including many who might not previously have sought to migrate to the United States. Moreover, Mexico's entry into the General Agreement on Tariffs and Trade (GATT) in 1986 initiated an extended process of integrating the Mexican and U.S. economies; the integration of markets for capital and goods made it increasingly difficult to preserve a rigid separation between Mexican and U.S. labor markets. Since IRCA did not account for this future flow by significantly increasing opportunities for Mexicans to immigrate legally, the numbers of unauthorized migrants grew significantly over the course of the 1990s.

Employer sanctions proved largely ineffective as an enforcement measure, even as they raised business costs for employers and rendered millions of employees vulnerable to discrimination. The economic and social factors causing migration were stronger and more powerful than the costs to employers and employees associated with employer sanctions. Since employers were not required to verify the authenticity of identification documents presented by job applicants, a black market in fraudulent documents quickly emerged. Moreover, evidence gathered by GAO and community organizations indicated that the employer sanction provisions resulted in significant levels of discrimination. In 1989, GAO found that the statute directly caused about 10 percent of employers nationwide to discriminate on the basis of national origin and 9 percent to discriminate on the basis of citizenship status—resulting in discrimination against approximately 2.9 million individuals on the basis of national origin and 3.9 million on the basis of citizenship status. While these findings did not lead Congress to repeal employer sanctions, Congress did attempt to strengthen some of the law's antidiscrimination provisions in the Immigration Act of 1990. During the course of the 1990s, government resources devoted to enforcement of employer sanctions dropped considerably, and many groups—including some that previously had advocated their enactment, such as organized labor—increasingly urged their repeal.

Anil Kalhan

See also: Bracero Program; Illegal Immigration; Immigration and Nationality Act of 1965; Immigration Enforcement; Migrant Workers.

Further Reading

Hing, Bill Ong. *Defining America Through Immigration Policy.* Philadelphia: Temple University Press, 2004.

Massey, Douglas S., Jorge Durand, and Nolan J. Malone. *Beyond Smoke and Mirrors: Mexican Immigration in an Era of Economic Integration.* New York: Russell Sage Foundation, 2002.

Ngai, Mae M. *Impossible Subjects: Illegal Aliens and the Making of Modern America.* Princeton, NJ: Princeton University Press, 2004.

Zolberg, Aristide R. *A Nation by Design: Immigration Policy in the Fashioning of America.* Cambridge, MA: Harvard University Press, 2006.

Indigenismo

The term *indigenismo* (from the Spanish word *indigena,* meaning "native") refers to an intellectual, cultural, and political movement in Latin America during the nineteenth and early twentieth centuries that denounced the exploitation of indigenous peoples and advocated their unity in the population at large through social integration and acculturation. The influence of indigenismo was particularly strong in Mexico, as well as in Andean countries with a large population of indigenous people, such as Peru, Ecuador, and Bolivia. Although some scholars argue that indigenismo had been a coherent philosophy since the Spanish Conquest of the early 1500s, most scholars refer to it as a movement that arose in the latter part of the nineteenth century and gained ascendancy in the 1920s and 1930s.

Early Expressions

The concept of indigenismo played a vital role in the consolidation of the nation-states founded at the end of Spanish colonialism in the late 1800s. According to Dutch historian Michiel Baud, the indigenous element became a symbol for many of the emerging republics of Latin America, which sought roots outside of Spain. As a result, these founding ideologies exalted native culture and history even though ethnic and social rejection of Indians continued. In order to avoid such contradiction, many intellectuals and politicians of the region joined the indigenista movement, which consisted of the search for a national identity among the Latin American indigenous populations as well as a desire to improve the substandard living condition of the native populations.

Attitudes regarding indigenous cultures have varied widely through time. For European colonizers, native peoples of the Western Hemisphere were generally viewed as brutish, inferior, and morally despicable as well as merely alien. Indeed it was common for the political elites of nineteenth-century Latin America to regard the indigenous element as backward, the antithesis of progress for the region. In Mexico, for example, as part of a series of reforms aimed at propelling the national economy, Indians were dispossessed of vast communal lands they had occupied since colonial times.

The process of modernization in the late nineteenth and early twentieth centuries continued the exclusion of native people that had begun with colonization. As exclusion increased, Latin American intellectuals such as the Mexican philosopher and politician Jose Vasconcelos began to write about ethnic and cultural *mestizaje* (mixing) as the ideal means by which to integrate native populations into the modern world. Vasconcelos defined mestizaje as a synthesis of Spanish and indigenous traits that would make it possible for a new identity—different from both—to be forged.

Despite these new ideas, there remained a widespread dilemma over whether to integrate or assimilate native peoples into the rest of society. Generally, *integration* is defined as the incorporation of ethnic subgroup peoples into society at large while preserving their cultures and traditions; *assimilation,* by contrast, is the absorption of individuals from separate groups into a standard "national" culture, with the consequent loss of indigenous cultures. Faced with such a choice, Latin American politicians and intellectuals of the period generally opted for the integrationist approach, which called for the gradual inclusion of Indians into the rest of society while avoiding the imposition of a dominant Latin culture.

Mexican anthropologist Alfonso Caso, one of the best-known representatives of the so-called integrationist current, thus suggested that the state launch policies to foster the development of indigenous communities. Such initiatives would allow Indians to contribute to their own progress and to that of the country as a whole. Caso emphasized the importance of safeguarding what he described as the "positive values" of indigenous cultures, among which he pointed to the solidarity between the individual and the community, as well as to the production of handicrafts with artistic value. Caso also warned, however, that it was necessary to eliminate "inefficient aspects" to solve the problems of indigenous communities and avoid their extinction. Among the elements to be eliminated were speaking only the native language, which limited the ability to communicate with the rest of the national population, and attributing medical ailments to magical causes, thus resorting to magical remedies.

Twentieth-Century Manifestations

Ideas communicated by scholars and writers like Caso began to have considerable influence on the governments of several Latin American countries. In Peru, the administration of President General Augusto Leguía (1908–1912 and 1919–1930) adopted indigenismo as its official doctrine and fostered the education of Indian communities. In Ecuador, under the governments of President Eloy Alfaro (1895–1901 and 1906–1911), several laws were passed to protect the indigenous; among them was a decree to abolish enslavement due to debt, a condition under which many native peoples were subjected.

In the aftermath of the Mexican Revolution (1910–1920)—which resulted in legislation that addressed historic problems of Mexico's indigenous peoples, including underdevelopment, land possession, and exploitation—indigenismo became an integral part of the official state ideology. During the government of Lázaro Cárdenas (1934–1940), for example, lands were returned to indigenous communities as part of agrarian reform and a broad campaign for Indian rights. Cárdenas sponsored the First Inter-American Indigenist Congress (often referred to as the Pátzcuaro Congress), held in Pátzcuaro in the state of Michoacán in 1940. Bringing together intellectuals (such as anthropologists, sociologists, and historians) and high government officials from North and South America, the congress raised consciousness about indigenous issues and considered specific measures to improve the lives of the represented countries' native populations. The Congress led to the formation of the Inter-American Indigenist Institute in 1948, an official body charged with administering state policies for indigenous groups.

The popularity of indigenismo also brought about a growing interest in the patrimony of native peoples. Archeological sites were restored in Teotihuacán and Palenque in Mexico, and Machu Picchu in Peru. Conversely, the indigenous past became a major source of inspiration for the muralism movement in Mexican painting, as exemplified by the work of Diego Rivera, José Clemente Orozco, and David Alfaro Siqueiros. These and other artists used their work—painted on the sides of buildings and in other public spaces—to comment on contemporary social and political issues, help forge a common national (or pan-American) identity, pay homage to pre-Columbian society, and dramatize both the devastation and the contributions of the Spanish conquest.

The early decades of the twentieth century also saw the rise of so-called Indigenismo, or Indianista, literature—novels, poetry, and short stories that vividly communicated the oppression and poverty of native peoples. It began as an urban-based literary movement that profiled the exploitation and marginalization of various indigenous societies, advocated on their behalf, and portrayed them sympathetically to national reading audiences. Among the writers associated with this literary movement are Miguel Ángel Asturias of Guatemala, Jorge Icaza of Ecuador, Ciro Alegría of Peru, and Alcides Arguedas of Bolivia. The works of the Paraguayan Agustín Roa Bastos, of the Peruvian José Maria Arguedas, and more recently of Manuel Scorza, also of Peru, discuss the plight of the indigenous peoples in their regions and exhibit a highly advanced knowledge of the indigenous reality.

Criticisms

Most contemporary scholars acknowledge that indigenismo contributed to a greater worldwide consciousness of the subordinate lifestyle to which many native peoples of Latin America were subjected, as well as to a deeper appreciation of native influences on national cultures in the region. Nevertheless, the movement has also been the object of severe criticism. Scholars such as Michiel Baud have pointed out that even some of the most vocal proponents of this movement were less than knowledgeable about the reality in which native peoples lived. Such ignorance, he maintains, has led to the attribution of a kind of isolation to Indian communities, an isolation that hasn't really existed since before colonial times; indeed many indigenous peoples and communities have been exposed to constant contact with Western cultures since colonial times.

Indianista writer José María Arguedas, who distinguished himself in the mid-twentieth century for his vast knowledge of the native cultures of Peru—he spent his childhood and youth in an indigenous region and was able write texts in the Quechua language—criticized proponents of indigenismo who called for the preservation of aboriginal "purity," that is, for the isolation of indigenous peoples so that they could preserve their cultural identity. Indeed many scholars have come to criticize the paternalistic attitude of many non-natives toward indigenous peoples—a patronizing view that borders on racism, presupposing the inability of natives to overcome obstacles on their own.

Given the limitations of indigenismo in improving the living standards of indigenous peoples without undermining their culture, a new political movement emerged in the late twentieth century called *indianismo*—the product of indigenous peoples themselves, emphasizing the preservation of cultural identity. Although indigenous resistance movements have existed since the Spanish Conquest, indianismo constitutes a recent cultural phenomenon whose distinguishing feature is its opposition to an integrationist type of indigenismo.

The marginalized conditions in which a large number of indigenous peoples of Latin America continue to live, as well as the growing recognition of the rights of original peoples, have given rise to new indigenous movements in the region. Among these is the revolutionary movement headed by the militant Zapatista National Liberation Army (Ejército Zapatista de Liberación Nacional) in Mexico's southern state of Chiapas. As well, the rise to power of Evo Morales as president of Bolivia—the nation's first native leader since the Spanish Conquest—underscores the resurgence of indigenous power and influence in Latin America.

Alberto Hernández-Lemus and Juan Carlos Hernández-Lemus

See also: Conquest of the Americas.

Further Reading

Arguedas, José María. *Deep Rivers.* New York, Longitude. 2002.

———. *The Fox from Up Above and the Fox from Down Below.* Pittsburgh, PA: University of Pittsburgh Press, 2000.

———. *Yawar Fiesta.* New York: Longitude, 2002.

Friedlander, Judith. *Being Indian in Hueyapan: A Study of Forced Identity in Contemporary Mexico.* New York: St. Martin's, 1975.

Lockhart, James. *The Nahuas after the Conquest: A Social and Cultural History of the Indians of Central Mexico, Sixteenth through Eighteenth Centuries.* Palo Alto, CA: Stanford University Press, 1992.

Internal Colony

The term "internal colonialism" refers to a series of theories that describe the conditions and circumstances of Latinos/as living in the United States as essentially colonial in character. Thus, according to this perspective, the economic and political inequality that has defined the U.S. Latino experience amounts to a colonial situation—regardless of residency status, law, or constitutional principles—in which Anglo institutions constitute a colonizing force. Over time, these theories have come to be used not only to explain the circumstances of Latinos/as in the United States, but also as the rationale for important struggles for identity and equality.

The internal colony model has offered Latinos/as in general, and Chicanos/as in particular, a compelling conceptual framework with which to analyze, understand, and call attention to their unique history of oppression—a history marked by U.S. territorial expansion and dispossession, economic exploitation, and racism. Sociologist Robert Blauner, in particular, has identified four key components, some of which demanded modification to apply fully to Chicano/as. First, internal colonialism requires forced entry. As he wrote in 1968: "The colonized group enters the dominant society through a forced, involuntary, process." The U.S. annexation of the Southwest and the subsequent abrogation of its obligations outlined in the Treaty of Guadalupe Hidalgo (1848) mark the clear beginning of such involuntary absorption in the case of native Mexicans. Subsequently, economic underdevelopment facilitated by policies such as the North American Free Trade Agreement (NAFTA) has forcibly incorporated migrant workers from Latin America, providing a massive labor reserve to be exploited.

Second, according to Blauner's defining elements, internal colonialism has a profound cultural impact: "The colonizing power carries out a policy which constrains, transforms, or destroys indigenous values, orientations, and ways of life." For centuries, to be sure, Latinos/as have faced a grinding process of Americanization that has eroded, or intentionally stripped them of, their distinctive culture, heritage, identity, and language.

Third, says Blauner, internal colonization depends on external administration. "Colonization involves a relationship by which members of the colonized group tend to be administered by representatives of the dominant power. There is an experience of being managed and manipulated by outsiders in terms of ethnic status." Again, the Chicano population in America clearly meets this criterion, as U.S. lawmakers and police, city planners and social workers, schools, media, and other institutions and organizations have defined and ruled the Chicano experience, often in segregated barrios.

Finally, racism anchors and animates the internal colony: "Racism is a principle of social domination by which a group seen as inferior or different in terms of alleged biological characteristics is exploited, controlled, and oppressed socially and psychically by a superordinate group," writes Blauner.

The four features of an internal colony as defined by Blauner mirror the analysis of scholars like Rodolfo Acuña, who has referred to the Chicano experience as one of living in an "occupied America." Importantly, recognition of the underlying concepts has also energized efforts to redefine and reassert identity, equality, and autonomy.

The internal colony model was always more than an academic idea. Indeed, its greatest influence was within social movements of the Chicano community. Perhaps the earliest effort to link the Chicano experience to colonialism occurred in 1964, when Roberto Rubalcava and Luis Valdez, then student activists at the San Jose State University, in California, traveled to Cuba as part of the first Venceremos Brigade, a group that visits the island annually in support of Cuban socialism. That summer, the two young activists suggested that Mexican Americans shared a similar condition with their comrades in Latin America, because the exploitation faced by both the Cuban and Chicano peoples were byproducts of U.S. imperialism. A few years later, Rodolfo "Corky" Gonzalez began arguing that the conquest of the American Southwest paralleled European imperialism and likewise had resulted in underdevelopment and racist oppression. Similarly, during the Poor People's Campaign in 1968—an effort spearheaded by the Reverend Martin Luther King, Jr., and the Southern Christian Leadership Conference to highlight the plight of America's poor—Gonzalez and Reies Lopez Tijerina, who fought vigorously to restore the land rights of New Mexico Latinos/as, highlighted the disastrous effects of colonialism for Mexican Americans. Such colonialism, they argued, robbed Mexican Americans of their land, stripped them of their cultural heritage, and forced them into menial jobs. And El Plan de Santa Barbara, a 1969 manifesto that sought to improve the Chicano student experience and bolster their access to higher education, famously lamented the colonized position of Chicanos/as: "The result of this domestic colonialism is that the *barrios* and *colonias* are dependent communities with no institutional power of their own."

As articulated in these and many other speeches and activities, the internal colony has been more than a theoretical model for analysis and insight. Instead, internal colonialism has provided a lens through which activists have reimagined what it means to be Mexican American and, in the process, has helped them map new paths toward liberation. To begin with, they have invoked internal colonialism to help identify themselves as a bounded, recognizable people, possessing a unique experience and identity. In fact, it is within this broader movement that Chicano identity was first named publicly and articulated collectively. Furthermore, the internal colonial model allowed activists to link their histories and conditions to those of other colonized peoples in a global context. Rather than seeing themselves as landless workers, activists and intellectuals came to identify themselves as a people who originated from a particular homeland—the invaded and occupied territory of Aztlán. Redefining themselves, their origins, and the impact of power in this manner in turn enabled them to identify decolonization as a viable political strategy.

The notion that Chicanos/as and Latinos/as in America were living in an internal colony began to fall out of favor in the 1980s. Although the exact reasons for the demise remain unclear, the discrepancy between the model and the lived experience of many Mexican Americans, who enjoyed increasing economic success and political integration, may have been an important factor. In addition, the challenges advanced by feminist, gay and lesbian, and critical racial theories provided more nuanced understandings of identity, society, and power, and exposed the limitations of domestic colonialism theory and the forms of Chicano nationalism it supported. Nevertheless, the notion of an internal colony remains entrenched in both academic and activist debates to the present day. For some, the model remains useful because Chicanos/as and Latinos/as have continued to be subjected to colonial-like conditions in many ways. For others, the rise of globalization, the resurgence of nativism, and the persistence of American imperialism have contributed to the enduring relevance of the theory.

C. Richard King

See also: Acuña, Rodolfo; Chicano/a; Gonzales, Rodolfo "Corky"; Identity and Labels; Plan de Santa Barbara, El; Race; Tijerina, Reies López; Treaty of Guadalupe Hidalgo (1848).

Further Reading

Acuña, Rodolfo. *Occupied America: A History of Chicanos.* 6th ed. New York: Pearson Longman, 2007.

Almaguer, Tomás. "Historical Notes on Chicano Oppression: The Dialectics of Race and Class Domination in North America." *Aztlán* 5 (1974): 27–56.

Barrera, Mario, Carlos Muñoz, and Charles Ornelas. "The Barrio as an Internal Colony." In *Peoples and Politics in Urban Society,* ed. Harlan Hahn. Beverly Hills, CA: Sage, 1972.

Blauner, Robert. "Internal Colonialism and Ghetto Revolt." *Social Problems* 16 (1969): 393–408.

Gutiérrez, Ramón A. "Internal Colonialism: An American Theory of Race." *Du Bois Review* 1:2 (2004): 281–95.

J

Jones Act (1917)

The Jones Act, also known as the Jones-Shafroth Act or the 1917 amendments to the Organic Act of Puerto Rico, was signed into law on March 2, 1917, by President Woodrow Wilson. Named for its congressional sponsors, U.S. Representative William Atkinson Jones (D-VA), chairman of the House Committee on Insular Affairs, and Senator John Shafroth (D-CO), chairman of the Senate Committee on Pacific Islands and Puerto Rico, the measure amended the Foraker Act of 1900. The Jones Act granted U.S. citizenship to the citizens of Puerto Rico, established on the island a three-branch system of government like that of the United States, and conferred all rights guaranteed under the U.S. Constitution, except trial by jury, to island residents.

The new civil government consisted of legislative, executive, and judicial branches. The legislature was bicameral, consisting of a Senate and a House of Representatives. The Senate was made up of nineteen members elected from each of seven senatorial districts, with two members per district and five at-large members. The thirty-nine members of the House of Representatives were elected from thirty-five representative districts—one member per district plus four at-large members. For the first time in the island's history, all members of the legislature were elected—by men only—rather than appointed. Terms were four years.

The vested power of the legislative branch was balanced by that of the executive branch. All bills passed by the legislature were subject to the power of veto of the governor, the head of the executive branch, appointed by the president of the United States. The Jones Act called for the creation of six executive departments: Education, Finance, Health, Interior, Justice, and Labor and Agriculture, each responsible for overseeing the necessary social and political programs in Puerto Rico and protecting the rights newly conferred to all Puerto Ricans. Finally, according to the Jones Act, the executive branch would include a resident commissioner to the U.S. congress—an executive position to be elected by the people of Puerto Rico, although his salary was to be paid by the U.S. federal government.

The Puerto Rican Bill of Rights established by the Jones Act generally mirrors its U.S. counterpart as well, guaranteeing, among other things, that no law shall be passed that will impinge on the liberty or freedom of the individual; that no title of nobility can be conferred; that individuals charged with a crime have the right to a fair trial and counsel; and that there shall be no state-funded church. The Bill of Rights also provided protections for labor that had been unavailable to the working masses of Puerto Rico, and an open-trade system between the United States and Puerto Rico that cemented bilateral industrial ties.

Finally, the Jones Act conferred upon Puerto Ricans the right of free movement. After 1917, just as Americans could move freely between states, so Puerto Ricans could move freely between the island and the mainland. The movement between island and mainland brought with it a new set of complications for Puerto Ricans in both locations. While Puerto Ricans on the island could participate only in local elections and had virtually no representation on the federal level, they were able to maintain cultural distinction, including the use of Spanish. Conversely, Puerto Ricans living on the mainland, while able to participate fully in both local and federal elections, found themselves on the receiving end of institutionalized discrimination, as the racial ambiguity and linguistic difference of Puerto Ricans marked them as unassimilable "others" in the eyes of many Anglo-Americans.

While the Jones Act established a more democratic political structure for Puerto Rico, it continued to limit sovereignty. The U.S. Congress and U.S. President retained the power to veto any laws passed by the Puerto Rican legislature; all cabinet positions in Puerto Rico were subject to U.S. congressional approval; and all decisions by the Puerto Rican District Court were subject to review by the U.S. Supreme Court. Nevertheless, it represented a fundamental change to the political structure of the island, serving as a precursor to the establishment of a free, associated commonwealth, the status that Puerto Rico has officially held since 1952.

Lorna Perez and David J. Leonard

See also: Circular Migration; Puerto Ricans.

Further Reading

Burnett, Christina Duffy, and Burke Marshall, eds. *Foreign in a Domestic Sense: Puerto Rico, American Expansion, and the Constitution.* Durham, NC: Duke University Press, 2001.

Grosfoguel, Ramón. *Colonial Subjects: Puerto Ricans in a Global Perspective.* Berkeley: University of California Press, 2003.

Malavet, Pedro A. *America's Colony: The Political and Cultural Conflict Between the United States and Puerto Rico.* New York: New York University Press, 2004.

Justice for Janitors

Justice for Janitors (JfJ) is a movement organized and run by the Service and Employees International Union (SEIU), which was founded in 1921 to improve the working conditions of janitors throughout the United States. Since its inception in 1985, Justice for Janitors has brought together more than 200,000 primarily immigrant workers, who have successfully secured family health insurance, livable wages, full-time work, and better working conditions.

JfJ was founded in Denver, Colorado in 1985, but soon spread throughout the United States, in part because of innovative strategies borrowed from Latin American labor unions. From its inception, for example, workers and union organizers formed close working partnerships with community organizations and churches, and the JfJ has conducted organizational activities in the dominant language of the workers. In addition, the JfJ has sought to capitalize on multi-city actions, signing or renewing contracts on the same day throughout the United States as a means of regaining critical bargaining leverage from corporations who preferred to answer to their contractors alone. At the local level, strategies have been equally dedicated and creative. Often with grassroots community support, workers have taken over building lobbies, marched with drums, and stopped traffic during rush hour.

The Justice for Janitors campaign grew out of what the SEIU regarded as a crisis in working conditions and compensation. Throughout the 1980s, janitorial wages fell and workers lost medical benefits as businesses began to utilize subcontracting practices that left workers with limited bargaining power. As companies hired under contracts, they no longer had to answer directly to workers, resulting in a common situation seen in other trades known as "the race to the bottom." In the process, each contracting company is encouraged to pay lower and lower wages in an effort to win contracts with a city's largest companies. Thus, for example, janitors in Los Angeles saw their wages fall from an average of $7 an hour to less than $5 an hour due to contract hiring. Business after business laid-off workers and signed on with contractors who underbid their competition and passed losses onto their employees.

At a time when many unions, including the SEIU, faced declining membership and shrinking bargaining power, JfJ succeeded in revitalizing the parent union, and winning both increased wages and medical benefits for its membership nationwide. Under the slogan, "One Industry, One Union, One Contract," the campaign coordinated efforts both nationally and internationally to return bargaining leverage to janitorial workers. In many areas of the country, Latinos/as formed both the foundation of the worker-activist movements and the campaign leadership of JfJ. Exemplifying the new style of union leadership was Rocio Saenz, who worked for more than ten years to build a successful campaign in Los Angeles, helping organize janitor strikers in 1990 and 2000. In 2001 she moved to Boston, where she was instrumental in revitalizing Local 254. In cooperation with a coalition of Latino and African American workers, the campaign succeed; and in 2003 she would be elected the president of Local 254. Meanwhile, in 1996, another prominent Latino in the SEIU, Eliseo Medina, gained distinction, becoming the first Latino to hold a leadership position in the 1.8-million-member union when he won election as international executive vice president.

The JfJ campaign came to the attention of the larger American public through the popular movie *Bread & Roses* (1994), which dramatized the struggles of janitorial workers and the differences between the rights of American workers and those of immigrants. Ironically, the story is told with a white male—rather than Saenz—as the primary organizer of the LA campaign. Before popular culture drew attention to the struggles of workers in downtown Los Angeles, JfJ workers in the Century City district paid a high price for their organizing efforts. In 1990, while workers and supporters occupied high-rise office buildings in Century City and blocked traffic, members of the Los Angeles police beat them mercilessly, leaving sixteen people with broken bones and resulting in one woman having a miscarriage. While the publicity associated with the beatings helped SEIU win new allies, it took five more years before the district was fully unionized. SEIU workers and allies have since celebrated an annual Justice for Janitor's day in remembrance of the struggles of the Century City workers.

By 2000, JfJ began to shift the focus of its energy to the need for health care benefits. With the cost of health coverage rising steadily, SEIU workers succeeded in maintaining or winning full benefits in Orange County, San Francisco, and San Jose, California. In cities such as Denver, where a majority of janitors had lost their health insurance, JfJ successfully pressured various employers to provide their workers family health benefits. In this case, as in others, JfJ and the SEIU have demonstrated that unions can succeed in the twenty-first century if they address the real needs of workers, engage in creative protests, and build coalitions across race, class, and community lines. They have also demonstrated that the support of Latino immigrants, residents, and citizens is critical to the strength of unions in contemporary America.

Linda Heidenreich

See also: Unions, Industrial and Trade.

Further Reading

Merrifield, Andy. "The Urbanization of Labor: Living-Wage Activism in the American City." *Social Text* 62 (2000): 31–54.

Service Employees International Union. http://www.seiu.org.

Wunnava, Phanindra V., ed. *The Changing Role of Unions: New Forms of Representation.* Armonk, NY: M.E. Sharpe, 2004.

K

Kahlo, Frida (1907–1954)

The twentieth-century Mexican painter Frida Kahlo was little known in her native country during her lifetime and was the subject of only three solo exhibitions. Recently, however—more than fifty years after her death in 1954—she has become the most recognized woman artist of Mexico, where she is considered a national treasure. The majority of her oeuvre of approximately 200 surviving works consists of vivid self-portraits, which capture the physical and psychological pain she experienced as a woman living in postwar Mexico.

She was born Magdalena Carmen Frida Kahlo y Calderón in Coyoacán, a suburb of Mexico City, on July 6, 1907. (She later claimed 1910 as her birth year in solidarity with the outbreak of the Mexican Revolution). Her father was German, a photographer by trade, and her mother was an uneducated Mexican. Her mixed heritage gave Kahlo much to draw from as she formed her personality and aesthetic. Stricken by polio at the age of six, Kahlo spent months in bed recovering. Immobilized, she turned to painting as a way to endure her convalescence. Throughout her life, Kahlo spent months at a time confined to bed or restricted by plaster corsets and wheelchairs as a result of more than thirty corrective surgeries to repair damage to her pelvis and spine sustained in a streetcar accident in 1925.

Kahlo entered the elite National Preparatory School in Mexico City at the age of fifteen. As one of the first young women to study at the school, she focused her painting on portraits in the nineteenth-century Mexican tradition. During this time, she adopted the traditional Tehuana style—brightly colored clothes, native jewelry, and braided hair worn on top of her head—which became her lifelong signature. In 1928, she showed her work to the up-and-coming Mexican painter Diego Rivera, whom she had met years earlier when he was painting murals at her school. The two artists bonded immediately and were married a year later.

Initially drawing upon both European and Mexican techniques and traditions, Kahlo developed her own blended style of painting. She eventually came to reject Western European influences in favor of pre-Columbian and contemporary folk art, as part of the *Mexicanidad*—a nationalistic art movement whose goal was to free Mexico of its European colonial traditions and to realign the country's cultural identity with its ancient, indigenous heritage. Kahlo's signature style is characterized by a surrealist blend of fantasy and fable, as well as by her depiction of animals, including deer, monkeys, and dogs.

Kahlo and Rivera spent four years in the United States beginning in 1932, when the Detroit Institute of Arts commissioned Rivera to produce several murals. Much of Kahlo's own work during this time depicts her antipathy for capitalism and the cultural divide between Mexico and the United States. The personal trauma of a miscarriage became the subject of a notable work in 1932: *Henry Ford Hospital,* in which a naked Kahlo lies in a pool of blood on a hospital bed surrounded by various surreal images, including an orchid, a fetus, a snail, and pelvic bones. In his autobiography, Rivera said of this time, "Frida began work on a series of masterpieces which had no precedent in the history of art—paintings which exalted the feminine qualities of endurance of truth, reality, cruelty, and suffering. Never before had a woman put such agonized poetry on canvas as Frida did at this time in Detroit."

After their return to Mexico, Kahlo and Rivera actively supported the Mexican Communist Party—she became a party member twice, in 1928 and 1948—and revolutionary politics. When Leon Trotsky was exiled from Russia for leading the socialist resistance to Communist leader Joseph Stalin, he found refuge in Mexico in 1937—and a romantic relationship with Kahlo. Although her affairs with Trotsky and others (many of whom were women) have been characterized as a response to Rivera's notorious womanizing, it was during her marriage to the great muralist that Kahlo produced some of her most riveting self-portraits, albeit reflecting her physical and psychological pain. These include the oil paintings *The Broken Column* (1944)—which shows her partially naked body strapped with bands and pierced by nails, her split torso revealing a shattered Greek column—and *The Wounded Deer* (1946), which depicts her head positioned on a doe's body that is pierced with arrows.

Kahlo had her first solo exhibition at Julian Levy Gallery in New York City in 1938. After a successful exhibition in Paris the following year, the Louvre bought and mounted its first work by a twentieth-century Mexican artist, her painting *The Frame.* Kahlo appeared on the cover of the popular French fashion magazine *Vogue,* which featured photographs of her in native Tehuana attire. The style captured the attention of the fashion world and was so popular that the influential clothing designer Elsa Schiaparelli designed a dress inspired by Kahlo.

Mexican artist Frida Kahlo, often pictured in colorful native costume, became well known after her death for self-portraits characterized by Mexican folk themes and a prescient feminist sensibility. *(Hulton Archive/Stringer/Getty Images)*

A retrospective of her work was finally mounted in Mexico in 1953, a year before her death. By this time, Kahlo was bedridden, and attended the event carried on a stretcher and then lifted onto a four-poster bed. She died on July 13, 1954, in Coyoacán, Mexico. Although the official cause of death was blocked heart arteries, her diary entries and final sketches suggest she may have been contemplating suicide.

Outside of Mexico, knowledge of Kahlo's work and life remained limited for years. In the 1970s, Chicano artists in California began incorporating her image in murals celebrating their cultural heritage, but the community of scholars and critics generally did not "discover" Kahlo until the publication of Hayden Herrera's book *Frida: A Biography of Frida Kahlo* in 1983. During the 1990s, Kahlo's work generated a cult following, especially after the pop musician Madonna's widely publicized purchase of *My Birth* (1932), in which an adult Kahlo is seen being birthed from her mother's womb, and the publication of Kahlo's diary, which had been stored in a bank vault in Mexico City. Although heavily confessional in subject matter and style, focusing on personal experiences and identity, Kahlo's work appeals to feminists, bisexuals, and the disabled, many of whom consider her a role model for her endurance in the face of lifelong physical suffering and victimhood. Her paintings began selling at auction for up to $1 million, and prices have increased at least tenfold since then. The works of Frida Kahlo have become part of the contemporary art canon.

Rebecca Tolley-Stokes and Gina Misiroglu

See also: Chicano Art; Mural Art.

Further Reading

Drucker, M. *Frida Kahlo: Torment and Triumph in Her Life and Art.* New York: Bantam, 1991.

Herrera, Hayden. *Frida: A Biography of Frida Kahlo.* New York: Harper & Row, 1983.

Jones, Jonathan. "Portrait of the Artist." *Guardian Unlimited,* February 14, 2003. http://www.guardian.co.uk/.

Rivera, Diego, with Gladys March. *My Art, My Life: An Autobiography.* New York: Citadel, 1960.

Kennedy, Robert F. (1925–1968)

The prominent politician and civil rights activist Robert "Bobby" Francis Kennedy—born on November 20, 1925, in Brookline, Massachusetts—served as U.S. attorney general in the administration of his brother, President John F. Kennedy, beginning in 1961. After his brother's assassination in November 1963, Bobby Kennedy left his cabinet post to run for the U.S. Senate as a Democrat from New York. Taking office in January 1965, Senator Kennedy became more heavily invested in the burgeoning civil rights movement. Although he is often associated with the Latino community for his highly publicized relationship with César Chávez and the United Farm Workers (UFW) movement, Kennedy's motives for eventually taking up the cause of civil rights remain hotly debated by historians; some maintain that it had less to do with concerns for social justice than with a desire for political success.

Although Robert Kennedy is perhaps best remembered for his civil rights activism, at first he was not publicly supportive of social justice in the streets. In 1961, he advocated a "cooling off" period for the civil rights movement in hopes of avoiding the issue altogether. Waging the Cold War and dealing with Communist Cuba were higher priorities in the Kennedy administration.

In April 1961, shortly after his appointment as attorney general (at the age of thirty-six), Kennedy was thrust into the Bay of Pigs crisis, in which a CIA-trained army of Cuban exiles was sent to overthrow the regime of Fidel Castro. In a profound embarrassment to the U.S. administration, however, Castro's forces thwarted the plot. Of the 1,300 Cubans used in the invasion, 114 were killed and 1,189 taken prisoner, left behind by retreating U.S.-operated troop transports. Eighteen months later, in October 1962, the Kennedy administration was thrust into the midst of the Cuban Missile Crisis, which put the United States on the brink of nuclear war with the Soviet Union. Robert Kennedy's advice during the thirteen-day standoff was critical to the peaceful resolution of the conflict. He retained his position as attorney general upon Lyndon Johnson's assumption of the presidency in November 1963 but resigned shortly thereafter.

It was only after he became a U.S. senator that Kennedy firmly established himself as a proponent of civil rights. He had never given it primary importance as attorney general, although he did push for a comprehensive Civil Rights Act and enforced the desegregation of the University of Mississippi and University of Alabama in 1962 and 1963, respectively. After his election to the Senate, civil rights became his professional passion.

In the mid-1960s migrant workers in California were enduring some of the worst working conditions in the country. Forced to live in shanties next to pesticide-soaked fields, paid less than the minimum wage, and facing racial violence and discrimination on a daily basis, these workers sought to organize a labor union under the leadership of César Chávez. Wealthy growers sought to discredit Chávez by painting him as a Communist and enlisted private security forces, along with local law enforcement agents, to harass and disrupt any efforts to organize on behalf of the migrant workers.

In these desperate conditions, many farmworkers reached out to Kennedy to help them in their plight. "Dear brother Kennedy," a typical letter began, "I am a farm worker from Delano, Cal., and I am writing to you to ask for help, because we know you are familiar with our [efforts] . . . to win justice for all farm workers in our country." In March 1966, Chávez and the United Farm Workers UFW received global media attention when Kennedy convened the Senate Subcommittee on Migrant Workers in Delano, California, the heart of the migrant workers' struggle. In a blistering critique of local labor conditions, Kennedy warned the growers to recognize the UFW and cautioned local sheriffs not to make unconstitutional arrests of union organizers. Kennedy and Chávez quickly became friends and political allies. "Senator Robert F. Kennedy," Chávez stated later, "is a man whose many selfless acts on behalf of struggling farm workers have been expressions of love. . . . We know from our experience that he cares, he understands, and he acts with compassion and courage."

Over the next two years, Kennedy called for the extension of National Labor Relations Act protections to all migrant workers and pushed for state and federal electoral reforms that would grant Spanish speakers the right to vote. In February 1968, Chávez, an advocate of nonviolent civil disobedience, went on a hunger strike in response to the increasingly violent character of the UFW movement. On March 10, Kennedy traveled to Delano and attended a Catholic mass with Chávez, where they broke bread together, ending his hunger strike in front of hundreds of news cameras from around the globe. "I was pleased to go to Delano," Kennedy wrote after the trip, "to honor a great man, a heroic figure of our time, César Chávez. His nonviolent struggle for the rights of the migrant worker is a great achievement which will afford Americans of Mexican descent the full participation in our society which they deserve."

A week after Kennedy officially announced his candidacy for president in March 1968, Chávez rallied to his support, organizing campaign efforts among California's Latino communities. Chávez later recalled, "For every man we had working for John Kennedy [in 1960], we had fifty men working for Bobby. It was electrifying. The polls will show you." Other Latino leaders who came forward to help the Kennedy campaign included Bert Corona of the Mexican American Political Association and Professor Ralph Guzmen, head of the Mexican American Study Project at UCLA, who wrote, "We need Senator Robert F. Kennedy and he needs us."

In the early morning hours of June 6, 1968, after a surprise win in the California primary made him the Democratic front-runner, Kennedy was gunned down by Sirhan B. Sirhan, a local Los Angeles resident, in the crowded kitchen of the downtown Ambassador Hotel. His untimely death robbed the Latino community of a powerful political ally in the quest for civil rights. Robert Kennedy had dedicated his life's work to relieving human suffering and fighting the racist institutions that produced it. In his relatively short political career, he helped Chávez, the UFW, and, by association, the entire Latino community make important strides in the ongoing struggle for political and social equality in the United States.

Bretton T. Alvaré

See also: Chávez, César; Migrant Workers; United Farm Workers of America.

Further Reading

Palermo, Joseph A. *In His Own Right: The Political Odyssey of Senator Robert F. Kennedy.* New York: Columbia University Press, 2001.

Schlesinger, Arthur, Jr. *Robert Kennedy and His Times.* Boston: Houghton Mifflin, 1978.

Thomas, Evan. *Robert Kennedy: His Life.* New York: Simon and Schuster, 2000.

King, Martin Luther, Jr. (1929–1968)

A central figure and preeminent voice of the African American civil rights movement of the 1960s, the Reverend Martin Luther King, Jr., fought for the rights of racially oppressed and economically disadvantaged peoples—including those in the Latino community. Although his work in the first half of the decade focused primarily on Southern racial segregation and Northern slums, his activism expanded at mid-decade to the general issue of Latino, Native American, and other minority rights as well as the anti–Vietnam War movement.

His initial focus was largely a function of geography. While King's activism ultimately became national in scope, his origins were unquestionably Southern. He was a second-generation Baptist minister born (on January 15, 1929) and raised in Atlanta, Georgia. As a young preacher and community organizer, he spent a great deal of time in Alabama, where the basic objective of black enfranchisement had to be achieved in order for black citizens to gain the political power needed to advance their cause. As the movement gained strength, Dr. King and other civil rights leaders expanded their efforts to cities in the North with large African-American populations—most notably Detroit, Chicago, and New York. By September 1966, King's activism focused as much on the ghettoes of the North as it did on the rural poverty of the South.

With the escalation of the Vietnam War and the burgeoning protest movement, King also became increasingly vocal on U.S. foreign policy issues. On April 4, 1967, at New York's Riverside Church, he delivered a rousing sermon on the Vietnam War and other aspects of U.S. Cold War foreign policy in which he condemned the America's "alliance with the landed gentry of Latin America." He declared that, "because of comfort, complacency, a morbid fear of communism, and our proneness to adjust to injustice, the Western nations that initiated so much of the revolutionary spirit of the modern world have become the arch anti-revolutionaries." In his posthumously published essay "A Testament of Hope," King expounded further on U.S. policy in Latin America: "The American marines might not even have been needed in Santo Domingo," he wrote (in reference to the 1965 deployment to restore order after the outbreak of civil war), "had the American ambassador there been a man who was sensitive to the color dynamics that pervade the national life of the Dominican Republic."

On September 22, 1966, one month to the day after César Chávez cofounded the United Farm Workers Organizing Committee in California, the Reverend King sent a telegram to the labor leader congratulating him on his work. Calling Chávez and other UFW activists "brothers in the fight for equality," King wrote: "I extend the hand of fellowship and good will and wish continuing success to you and your members." And, he continued, "The fight for equality must be fought on many fronts—in the urban slums, in the sweat shops of the factories and fields. Our separate struggles are really one—a struggle for freedom, for dignity, and for humanity."

The communication was important in several respects. Lest there was any doubt, it represented King's explicit endorsement of the farmworkers' movement—hardly surprising coming from a man who had most often described the struggle for civil rights in universal, multi-ethnic terms. Moreover, it clearly left an impression on Chávez, who had been deeply influenced by King's philosophy of nonviolent resistance and would quote the telegram many times in speeches over the following decades. And perhaps most significant of all, at least from a historical perspective, is the phrase "[o]ur separate struggles."

Especially during the final months of his life, King worked to unite the campaigns for justice and equality by diverse ethnic communities in what he referred to as the "second phase" of the Southern Christian Leadership Conference's (SCLC's) civil rights activism. Whereas the first phase had focused primarily on segregation and the legacy of Jim Crow in the South, the second phase would take up broader institutional problems that affected low-income communities throughout the country. In November 1967, King met with SCLC leaders to begin organizing the Poor People's Campaign, which, he said, "must not be just black people. . . . We must include American Indians, Puerto Ricans, Mexicans, and even poor whites."

In early 1968, while working on behalf of the Poor People's Campaign, King met privately with Bert Corona and other leaders of the Mexican American Political Association in an effort to better understand specific issues pertaining to Latinos/as. Corona would later recall that King "exhibited a sensitivity to the needs of Mexicanos" and "stressed that we needed to struggle together to correct common abuses."

King was assassinated only weeks later—on April 4, 1968—and his vision of a powerful multiethnic civil rights movement has remained largely unrealized to this day. Yet his belief in the common cause of African Americans, Latinos/as, and other disadvantaged minorities, along with his calls for coalition building and organized community action, offers a compelling counternarrative to the widespread media coverage of purported tensions between blacks and Latinos/as in later years.

Tom Head

See also: Chávez, César; Corona, Bert; United Farm Workers of America; Vietnam War.

Further Reading

Cárdenas, Jaime. "A Latino Leftist and the United States in the Twentieth Century." *American Quarterly* 49:1 (March 1997): 215–20.

Etulain, Richard W., ed. *César Chávez: A Brief Biography with Documents.* New York: Palgrave, 2002.

Vargas, Zaragosa. *Labor Rights Are Civil Rights: Mexican American Workers in Twentieth-Century America.* Princeton, NJ: Princeton University Press, 2004.

L

La Raza

The term *La Raza*—Spanish for "the race" or "the people"—has been used primarily by Chicanos/as in the United States since the 1960s to invoke a sense of ethnic unity and identity. The concept is roughly synonymous with that designated by the phrases *el pueblo* or *la gente,* literally "the people." In the United States, La Raza gained resonance as a political and social identifier during the Chicano civil rights movement of the 1960s and 1970s, when Mexican Americans—the younger generation especially—began forging a new sense of cultural pride and political empowerment.

Along with such concepts, rallying cries, and terms of identity as brown power, Aztlán, and chicanismo, La Raza has continued to empower a community that had remained on the margins of mainstream American society for over a century. Moreover, such identities have promoted an individual and collective sense of belonging, and have allowed activists to create more inclusive agendas by easing tensions among subgroups. In this sense, the concept of La Raza has enabled activists in the United States not only to consolidate their efforts for the good of the community, but also to establish a sense of solidarity with people in other countries, especially Latin American, engaged in similar struggles. La Raza promised the possibility of breaking down imagined and imposed borders within the United States and beyond.

Before Chicano activists began using La Raza as a politically unifying concept, the Mexican philosopher Jose Vasconcelos had advanced the idea of *la raza cósmica* (the cosmic race) in the early part of the twentieth century. Vasconcelos introduced the term and concept to unify and uplift the downtrodden Mexican people in the aftermath of the Mexican Revolution (1910–1920). La raza cósmica, according to Vasconcelos, was the creation of one race "with the treasures of all previous ones." In this sense, Vasconcelos sought to establish a national identity that united all racial groups into one, the mestizo. *Mestizaje* or "racial mixing," argued Vasconcelos, lay at the heart of the Mexican identity, in which la raza cósmica, a blending of Spanish and indigenous blood, would become the prototype. While the idea of the cosmic race provided a conceptual basis for a unified national identity in Mexico, at the heart of Vasconcelos's argument was a call for assimilation discourse that would have all groups renounce their respective ethnic identities. For Chicano activists in 1960s America, by contrast, the concept of La Raza implied a strong sense of unity and community identification rather than one of assimilation. As part of the daily vernacular of Mexicans, in both Mexico and the United States, La Raza thus took on new meaning at the time.

The association of La Raza with community has remained largely intact for half a century, but the concept inevitably has been transformed as well. For one thing, as the Latino population has diversified and spread throughout the United States, La Raza has become a more inclusive concept, encompassing other, non-Chicano, groups and individuals. Indeed, it has resonated beyond national borders, allowing Latinos/as in the United States to maintain and solidify a shared sense of identity with the people of Latin America.

Moreover, the concept of La Raza is now invoked in a variety of modern contexts, including popular culture (music lyrics, television programs, and the like); academic programs and publications (such as Raza Studies at San Francisco State University and Berkeley's *La Raza Law Review Journal*); as well as groups and organizations that strive to improve the well-being of Latino communities. Several organizations established during the Chicano Movement continue to use La Raza as a unifying concept and designation. The National Council of La Raza, for example, is a civil rights advocacy organization

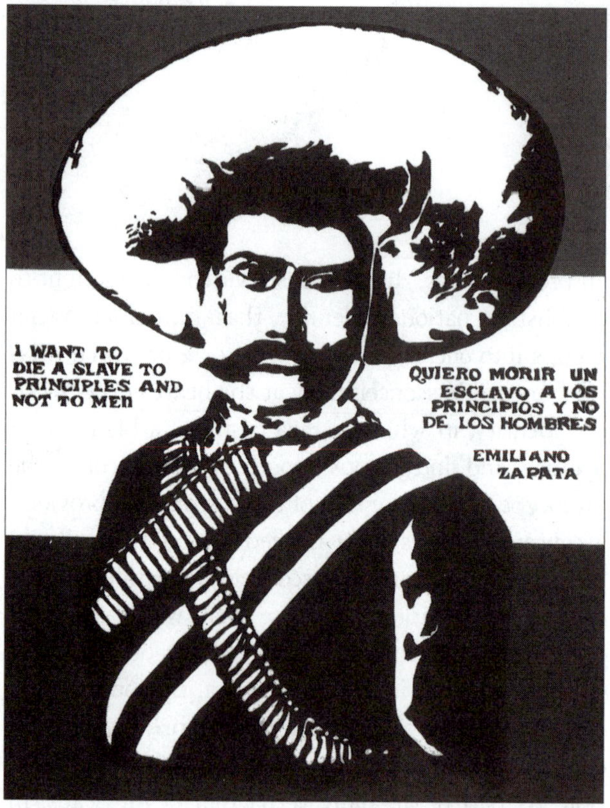

The proud spirit of La Raza, a unifying concept for Mexicans and their descendants since the post-revolutionary period of the 1920s, is captured in the words of peasant guerrilla leader Emiliano Zapata: "I want to die a slave to principles and not to men." *(Library of Congress)*

founded in 1973 and based in Washington, D.C., that works to improve economic and social opportunities for Latinos/as. La Raza Unida Party, founded in Texas in 1970 to bring the plight of Mexicans, Mexican Americans, and all Latinos/as into the political arena, continues to operate chapters in the Southwest. And the national student organization Movimiento Estudiantíl Chicano de Aztlán (Chicano Student Movement of Aztlán), commonly known as MEChA, likewise continues to invoke La Raza as a concept of unity and empowerment.

In recent years, certain conservative commentators have attacked organizations that advance the concept of La Raza for implying racial superiority. In particular, MEChA has faced criticism in the mainstream media for its motto, *Por la Raza Todo, Fuera de la Raza Nada* (For my race everything, outside my race nothing.) The literal translation of La Raza as "the race," however, carries a false implication. The term does not refer to "race" in the conventional American sense, with all of its historical and cultural implications, but to an identification with people, culture, and shared experience. Thus, the phrase *Por la Raza Todo, Fuera de la Raza Nada* refers to the daily struggles of ordinary Chicanos/as to improve the life and fortunes of their community. It implies a unique sense of empowerment, unity, and commitment that cannot be reduced to a single word or phrase in a foreign language, and that extends far beyond imposed and imagined borders.

Aidé Acosta

See also: Chicano/a; Chicano Movement; Día de la Raza; Identity and Labels; La Raza Unida Party; Movimiento Estudiantíl Chicano de Aztlán; National Council of La Raza; Race.

Further Reading

Mariscal, George. *Brown-Eyed Children of the Sun: Lessons of the Chicano Movement, 1965–1975.* Albuquerque: University of New Mexico Press, 2005.

Vasconcelos, Jose. *La Raza Cósmica—Misión Iberoamericana—Notas de Viaje a América del Sur.* Barcelona, Spain: Agencia Mundial Ibrería, 1925.

La Raza Unida Party

A Chicano political organization founded in 1970 to challenge the dominance of the Democratic and Republican parties, La Raza Unida Party (LRUP) grew out of the activism of the Mexican American Youth Association (MAYO), a student group that emphasized direct action demonstrations to protest racism. MAYO, whose leaders José Angel Gutiérrez and Mario Compeán had grown weary of Anglo politicians who made promises to the Mexican American community that went unfulfilled, saw political power as the next logical step in the quest for social equality and influence. Establishing LRUP on January 17, 1970, in Crystal City, Texas, Gutiérrez and Compeán sought to create a national third party that would improve the social and economic prospects for Chicanos/as, increase Chicano political power, and develop a cadre of political leaders who would be responsible for, and accountable to, the Latino community.

The initial focus of LRUP was the local elections in Crystal City. In 1963, five Latino candidates had won election to city offices because of strong Mexican American voter turnout. The Anglo community elite, which had controlled the city government for generations, struck back and succeeded in unseating all five Mexican American officials in the 1965 elections. José Angel Gutiérrez, who had worked on the 1963 campaigns, joined with other local Chicanos/as in late 1969 in the hope of re-creating those victories.

LRUP fielded a whole slate of candidates for the Crystal City elections, with Gutiérrez—along with local businessmen Mike Pérez and Arturo Gonzáles—running for seats on the school board; Ventura Gonzáles and Pablo Puente running on the LRUP ticket for seats on the city council; and other candidates seeking at-large positions in the four surrounding counties. Inspiring voters and capitalizing on a successful grassroots campaign, a total of fifteen LRUP candidates won election in Crystal City, Carrizo Springs, and Cotulla.

With the success of LRUP's first mass campaign, the party emerged as a significant voice in the Chicano community, inspiring activism and organizing throughout the Southwest. By late 1970, the LRUP had spread to Colorado, with statewide campaigns resulting in the election of two party candidates to the state House of Representatives. LRUP leaders then planned for state and local elections in several southwest Texas counties, but ran into difficulty when voting registrars disqualified its candidates for filing irregularities. A massive write-in campaign was largely unsuccessful in garnering LRUP the votes it needed; the party won only one of the fifteen seats it had vied for. The defeat forced Gutiérrez, Compeán, and other LRUP leaders to reevaluate the party's strengths, weaknesses, priorities, and strategies. Ultimately, they decided to reorganize and rededicate the party, focusing on statewide election campaigns in Texas.

Cofounder José Angel Gutiérrez (left) and Chicano youth activist Corky Gonzales stand before the 1972 national convention of La Raza Unida Party in El Paso, Texas, after Gutiérrez was elected chairman of the party's executive committee. *(AP Images/Ferd Kaufman)*

The reorganization of the LRUP at the state level helped establish a more sophisticated political machine. Party leaders created a system of local caucuses to publicize LRUP, orchestrated a statewide publicity campaign, and announced a candidate for the 1972 Texas gubernatorial election. Ramsey Muñiz, a Waco attorney who was not the first choice of many Chicanos/as in the party, turned out to be an energetic and surprisingly viable candidate for a third party. As his running mate, the LRUP selected Alma Canales, another prominent MAYO activist. At the end of the campaign, when the votes were tallied, LRUP candidates had garnered an impressive 219,127 (or 6.43 percent of the overall vote), enough to force a runoff between the Democratic and Republican candidates.

Amid the activity of the gubernatorial race, LRUP leaders called a meeting in El Paso to discuss the organization of a national party. The meeting, attended by nearly 2,000 Chicanos/as, resulted in the formation of the Congreso de Aztlán, which would administer the national LRUP. The LRUP leadership next concentrated its attention on state offices in Texas, Colorado, and California. Its efforts proved unsuccessful in California, however, with failed runs for the state assembly in 1972 and for the governorship in 1974. In Texas, LRUP ran Muñiz for governor again in 1974, but party infighting undermined his chances. While the LRUP secured a number of local victories, including Gutiérrez's successful campaign for Zavala County judge, Muñiz was once again defeated (receiving 190,000 votes).

The statewide losses in Texas and California further fractured the party. Specifically, Muñiz's defeat and subsequent arrests on drug possession charges seriously damaged LRUP's credibility among voters in Texas, and Chicano clashes with police in Colorado took their toll on the party in that state. Amid these controversies, the LRUP began to lose seats that had been gained in southwest Texas in the mid-1970s.

Although La Raza Unida Party had lost much of its political clout by 1978, chapters remain active today in California, Arizona, and New Mexico. Their fundamental goals, if not the militant nationalism of the original party, remain essentially the same: to fulfill America's democratic ideals for a group that has been historically underrepresented in the political process and elective office.

Brian D. Behnken

See also: Crystal City, Texas; Gutiérrez, José Angel; La Raza; Mexican American Youth Organization; Politics.

Further Reading

García, Ignacio M. *United We Win: The Rise and Fall of La Raza Unida Party.* Tucson: University of Arizona Mexican American Studies Research Center, 1989.

Navarro, Armando. *The Cristal Experiment: A Chicano Struggle for Community Control.* Madison: University of Wisconsin Press, 1998.

———. *La Raza Unida Party: A Chicano Challenge to the U.S. Two-Party Dictatorship.* Philadelphia: Temple University Press, 2000.

Rosales, F. Arturo. *Chicano! The History of the Mexican American Civil Rights Movement.* Houston, TX: Arte Público, 1996.

Santillan, Richard. *La Raza Unida.* Los Angeles: Tlaquilo, 1973.

Shockley, John Staples. *Chicano Revolt in a Texas Town.* Notre Dame, IN: University of Notre Dame Press, 1974.

Labor

See Unions, Industrial and Trade

Latinidad/Latinaje

Latinidad or *latinaje* ("Latin-ness" in Spanish) expresses the shared cultural and/or historical characteristics that unite disparate Latino communities in the United States. Ongoing controversy surrounds this umbrella term: Is it one that has been negatively imposed on these communities or one that offers a cultural unity that increases the political and economic power of Latinos in the United States? Many Latinos/as embrace the notion of a shared latinidad that connects their various communities—from the largest and oldest ones, with ties to Mexico, Puerto Rico, Cuba, and the Dominican Republic, to newer ones from Central America and South America, whose populations are also growing and dispersing across the United States. Although the perceived need for a shared identity and culture is both politically pragmatic and socially appealing, notions of latinidad have also been used to stereotype various Spanish-speaking communities and to target them as a "new" and uniform market or demographic for various enterprises, including advertising, government and education policies, and electoral politics.

The term "Latino" was originally coined as an alternative to the U.S. Census Bureau's designation of "Hispanic" (introduced during the administration of President Richard Nixon). The Latino community regarded the latter as an arbitrary category to mark them simultaneously as part of the American multicultural melting pot and as separate from mainstream society. The cultural characteristics associated with latinidad include a history that links the person or community to Latin America; present or past use of Spanish as the primary language; national origins in Central America, South America, or the Spanish-speaking Caribbean; cultural traditions in food, art, and music; strong religious traditions, including Roman Catholicism and Afro-Caribbean Santería; and the central role of the family. The term also emphasizes a collective feeling of belonging and identity as expressed in performance art, visual art, traditional and contemporary music, literature, and film. Popular manifestations of latinidad include the music of Latin pop stars Ricky Martin and Shakira, for example, as well as in Mexican, Puerto Rican, Cuban, and "Latin fusion" cuisines.

Hybridity and New Identities

As these examples suggest, latinidad is marked by a mixing, or "hybridity," of Latin American traditions in a U.S. cultural and geographical context. Although the term has gained popularity in segments of Latin American society, its reference to pan-American Latino cultural sensibility and identity is most pertinent to the U.S. experience, where the historic and ongoing mix of Latin American and Caribbean migrations has had a profound economic, political, and cultural impact. Proponents of latinidad as a category of cultural cohesion and collective belonging note that the realities of U.S. immigrants, both recent and second- and third-generation, exert pressure on these communities to participate in American consumer society and political culture in new ways. The nationalist identities of mid-twentieth century immigrants, such as anti-Castro Cuban exiles, gradually give way to increased participation in U.S. society. Issues such as access to public services, neighborhood activism, education (including bilingual education), working-class economic concerns, and political visibility all generate new opportunities for political and social behavior.

Likewise, these communities exert pressure on mainstream society to bring a higher level of understanding and appreciation to relations with other Latin American countries. The visibility of Latinos/as expressed through latinidad thus draws attention to the political, economic, and labor issues that bind the United States to Latin America, including immigration reform, the war on drugs, trade, the political status of Puerto Rico, and the foreign relations policy on Cuba. In this way, latinidad fulfills the promise of Latino unification announced in the United States by the Cuban writer, poet, and revolutionary José Martí in the late nineteenth century. Martí was one of the first Latin American promoters of a shared political and cultural identity, which he articulated in his famous essay *Nuestra América* (*Our America,* 1891). At the time, Latin American intellectuals such as Martí were especially concerned that the United States would come to dominate their emerging democratic societies economically and culturally. At the same time, however, the publication of Martí's landmark essay in New York City in Spanish (1893) reflected the participation of Spanish-speaking Latin communities in U.S. political and cultural life. Moreover, Martí's differentiation between Anglo America and Latin America at the turn of the twentieth century foretold the emergence of latinidad.

By the end of the twentieth century, the "split state" affiliation of many Latinos/as—such as Dominicans and Mexicans, and others who shuttle back and forth between the United States and their "home" countries—illustrates the complex reality of citizenship and identity for Latinos. The resultant media outlets, means of communication, and commercial goods are often characterized by a shared sense of latinidad. Thus, as long as U.S. citizens and residents with links to Latin America feel the need for a cultural and political identity that joins them together, latinidad will remain a useful identity marker. In the twenty-first century, latinidad is key to both political and cultural expression, and it plays a large role in attempts to create a coherent and powerful U.S.-based political movement of Latinos/as. The appeal of latinidad across diverse communities in the United States also echoes Martí's sense of regional and cultural pride and his critique of the negative stereotypes associated with Latin America and its peoples.

Questions and Controversies

According to some cultural critics, however, the extreme heterogeneity of Latino groups and their respective histories in the United States often makes the concept of latinidad seem more ideal than practically useful. Because it threatens to erase historical and national differences, such as those between Mexicans and Puerto Ricans, many insist that latinidad is a fantasy of marketing executives and political pollsters who see Latinos/as as a population to be manipulated, even created, for the economic or political gain of others. In the realm of politics, for example, observers note the differences in voting pattern, lifestyle, and social behavior between Mexican Americans in California and Texas (rural, conservative, and tradition-bound) and urban, working-class Puerto Rican communities in such eastern cities as New York; Patterson, New Jersey; and Hartford, Connecticut. Others contend that the differentiation of ethnic and national subgroups can be just as artificial and subject to stereotype as those that used to join these communities under one umbrella term.

So while latinidad has grown in popularity and acceptance as a political and social marker of cultural identity for Latinos/as, it remains controversial.

Some commentators suggest that it threatens to become a cultural identity marker that allows the public at large to ignore the political and social struggles of the communities that the term encompasses, such as Chicanos/as or Puerto Ricans. Others caution Latinos/as to remain aware and critical of any attempt to group them together and take advantage of their political and economic clout.

Katherine Sugg

See also: Identity and Labels; Latinization.

Further Reading

Aparicio, Frances R., and Susana Chávez-Silverman, eds. *Tropicalizations: Transcultural Representations of* Latinidad. Lebanon, NH: University Press of New England, 1997.

Dávila, Arlene. *Latinos Inc.: The Marketing and Making of a People.* Berkeley: University of California Press, 2001.

De Genova, Nicholas P., and Ana Yolanda Ramos-Zayas, eds. *Latino Crossings: Mexicans, Puerto Ricans, and the Politics of Race and Citizenship.* New York: Routledge, 2003.

Flores, Juan. *From Bomba to Hip-Hop: Puerto Rican Culture and Latino Identity.* New York: Columbia University Press, 2000.

Flores, William V., and Rina Benmayor, eds. *Latino Cultural Citizenship: Claiming Identity, Space, and Rights.* Boston: Beacon, 1997.

Latinization

Latinization is alive and vibrant in today's U.S. cultural landscape. It is the process whereby people, activities, media events, commercial products, and social phenomena become more Latino in character or more inclusive of Latino culture. It occurs everyday in the literal, tangible spaces of large and small cities, and symbolically in various forms of popular culture, ranging from food to fashion to music. Latinization operates at two levels: the demographic and the representative. On the demographic level, the Latino population of the United States has increased exponentially (almost 150 percent) in the last quarter century. According to the 2003 U.S. Census, there are currently approximately 38 million Latinos in the United States, making them the largest minority group in the country. Latinos actually outnumber Anglos in Southwestern cities such as Los Angeles, Houston, Texas, and San Antonio, Texas. At the level of cultural representation, there are countless examples of Latinization. In the case of food, for example, salsa outsells ketchup in U.S. supermarkets, and Nuevo Latino restaurants—serving a gourmet fusion of Latino cuisines from different national groups—are proliferating in major cities across the country. Fashion has also witnessed a pronounced Latinization, epitomized by the popularity of *guayaberas,* button-down men's shirts with collars and embroidery, traditionally white and usually associated with the Spanish Caribbean. In short, Latinization is an ongoing process seen in many facets of everyday life.

Urban Spaces

Latinization is prominently enacted and highly visible in the everyday life of major American cities. The growing Latino business sector in major cities represents one vital form of urban Latinization. Recent decades have seen a substantial growth in the number and success of businesses owned by Latinos across the country, with an especially high concentration in Miami and Los Angeles. According to *Hispanic* magazine, there are more than 1.5 million Latino-owned businesses in the United States, or 40 percent of all those owned by minorities. These businesses are generally in the service industry and range from small grocery stores to chain restaurants to beauty salons.

The increasing number of public murals by Latino artists, particularly in cities such as Los Angeles and Chicago, is further indication of the Latinization of urban areas. Mural artists literally carve out a space within the boundaries of urban communities for Latino culture. Cultural icons, such as the Virgin of Guadalupe, are indices of particular Latino cultures and are inscribed into the everyday surroundings of major U.S. cities. Another example is the creation of *casitas* in New York City, in which Latino neighborhood residents, particularly Puerto Ricans, erect small houses with architecture reminiscent of the nineteenth-century Spanish Caribbean in abandoned lots. The casitas are then made into cultural centers where Latino communities come together and partake in food and folkloric music, along with other cultural and educational activities. Latinization in the form of murals and casitas is an alternative to the costly purchase of residences and businesses. As such, Latinos/as without access to a great deal of capital are able to create their own cultural domains within the confines of the city. Even with these processes under way, however, it is important to note that Latino neighborhoods in many cities are increasingly at risk of gentrification (the process whereby a neighborhood changes from working-class to more affluent). As such, while many of the physical spaces are becoming more Latino, the soaring cost of living in cities such as New York, Chicago, and San Francisco are displacing Latino communities to other neighborhoods, boroughs, or even outlying locations.

While the focus in Latino scholarship has been on cities with high concentrations of Latino residents, recent years have brought an increase in Latinos/as in both rural and suburban areas. Many of these areas are located in states not typically associated with a Latino presence, such as North Carolina and Minnesota. Rural areas in states such as California, Illinois, and New York continue to see a growing Latino population, often including ethnic enclaves in small towns. Finally, both gentrification and a growing Latino middle class have contributed to the Latinization of the suburbs, where Latino ownership of homes and businesses has grown. The process is exemplified by the suburbs of Chicago, particularly Aurora, Cicero, and Joliet, which have had an increasingly visible Latino presence since the 1990s.

Popular Culture

Within popular culture, Latinization is especially evident in the arena of music, where Latino artists labeled as "crossover" stars have increasingly emerged from the Spanish-language market and reached iconic status in the English-language industry. The trend became prominent in the Latin explosion of the late 1990s, in which artists such as Ricky Martin, Marc Anthony, and Shakira dominated the U.S. charts. Other musical artists in the years since, such as Paulina Rubio and Thalia, have also crossed over into the English-language market, though perhaps not as successfully. Indeed, not all artists categorized by the media as crossover stars actually make the transition from the Spanish-speaking to the English-speaking market. The enormously popular Jennifer Lopez, for example, has often been described as a crossover star, but has never worked in the Spanish-language entertainment industry. Marc Anthony, by contrast, did release an English-language freestyle dance album early in his career, prior to his success as a salsa singer and later success as a U.S. pop singer. The Latinization of music worldwide is also apparent in the growing popularity of salsa in local bands, dance classes, and dance clubs as well as on commercial recordings.

Mainstream English-language television has also been no stranger to Latinization. *The George Lopez Show,* a sitcom with an all-Latino cast, began airing on the ABC network in 2002. It became the first show in U.S. television history with a Mexican American protagonist that was able to survive as a network broadcast. In the news media, meanwhile, anchors and reporters of Latin American descent have become more visible. Cable television has become even more Latinized, as the Lifetime Television Network and Nickelodeon both have featured original drama series starring Latino protagonists—*Strong Medicine* and *The Division,* respectively. Nickelodeon aired two Latino family sitcoms for its young adult audience, *The Brothers Garcia* and *Taina,* along with a highly successful bilingual animated series, *Dora the Explorer,* for preschoolers. The Cartoon Network has featured *Mucha Lucha,* a popular animated series about children who are Mexican wrestlers.

Much of the Latinization of entertainment media is linked to the creation of the Latino market by the advertising industry of the 1980s. According to Arlene Dávila in her book *Latinos, Inc.: The Making and Marketing of a People* (2002), the Latino advertising industry began in the mid-1960s by Cuban immigrants in New York City, many of whom had worked in advertising in Cuba. They produced advertising with an emphasis on Spanish Caribbean culture—a "tropicalization" of Latino identity still dominant in today's Latino advertising. However, it was not until the 1980s, popularly referred to as the "Decade of the Hispanic" (because of a heavy influx of Latino immigrants), that Latino marketing became a full-fledged niche. While tropicalization remains the main trope in Latino advertising, the industry has encompassed other local markets, such as South Florida, California, and Texas, with a growing emphasis on marketing to Mexican Americans. Nonetheless, in constructing the Latino market, advertising continues to represent a homogeneous view of Latino identity—Spanish-dominant, olive-skinned, without specificity to national origin, and working-class—that ignores the racial, ethnic, and class diversity among Latino communities in the United States.

Language is yet another cultural realm that has undergone Latinization. More and more media and services are available in Spanish—from Spanish-language newspapers in every major U.S. city to a wide variety of social services. The increasing visibility of Spanish in everyday life has led the language to become part of the dominant U.S. culture. In this context, "mock" Spanish—the use of Spanish words or phrases by Anglos, usually in an attempt to be humorous—is more frequently heard. Examples of mock Spanish include popular culture references that have made their way into daily life, such as Arnold Schwarzenegger's line in the film *The Terminator* (1984), "Hasta la vista, baby," and Taco Bell's Chihuahua demanding, "Yo quiero Taco Bell." The use of mock Spanish in the mass media has often been contested by Latino audiences, who contended that it denigrates both Mexican and Latino culture, as well as the Spanish language. Meanwhile, they observe, true bilingualism is increasingly attacked as a public policy requirement and educational priority.

Latinization and Latinidad

Latinization is sometimes conflated with or used interchangeably with the term *latinidad.* In fact, they represent different phenomena. Latinization comes from the verb "latinize" and refers to a process, whereas latinidad (or Latino identity) is a noun that defines a state of being. Latinidad stands for a complex cultural landscape in which many terrains coexist. On the one hand, latinidad is a pan-ethnic umbrella under which different Latino national identities are grouped; the concept represents a potential source of solidarity in coalition building for social and political causes. In this sense, Latinos/as form political alliances based on parallel colonial histories, as well as their present struggles for social justice. Felix Padilla, in his book *Latino Ethnic Consciousness: The Case of Mexican Americans and Puerto Ricans in Chicago* (1985), is one of the first scholars to describe this use of latinidad, which he calls "Latino ethnic consciousness," or *latinismo,* in the particular context of Chicago. On the other hand, when latinidad is co-opted by the mass media and other large social institutions, Latino identities are often homogenized. Thus, the term runs the risk of placing Latinos/as into a single undifferentiated group without recognition of the particularities of each nationality.

Further, latinidad can be used to represent the intragroup relations between Latino/as, which, like any other group relationships, are not always simple. They are often fraught with contradictions and struggles over spaces and resources. In Chicago, for example, Mexican Americans and Puerto Ricans have existed at various times in tension and solidarity, depending on historical circumstances. During the 1940s and 1950s, for example, the two groups were highly contentious, while during the 1960s and 1970s they formed a variety of coalitions based on common experiences of discrimination in education, housing, employment, and other realms of society. Thus, within the spaces of latinidad, there can exist strands of discord as well as solidarity.

Moreover, some cities have historically experienced more latinidad than others, as in the case of Chicago and New York. Chicago was the home of both Mexican Americans and Puerto Ricans—along with many other Latino groups—long before many other cities such as Los Angeles and Miami gained a prominent Latino presence. New York differs from Chicago, however, in that it has experienced more of a Caribbeanized latinidad. Due to the heavy influx of Puerto Ricans, Dominicans, and Cubans, followed by the arrival of more immigrants from South America and Central America, New York has been transformed by a Latino presence. Similarly, while a city such as Los Angeles has an increasingly growing Central American population (particularly Salvadoran), it has more of a Mexicanized latinidad due to the historical and contemporary Mexican presence within the Southwest. Ultimately, latinidad can be practiced in different ways depending on the history and demographics of a particular space.

Implications

Latinization is a process visible in many cultural, social, and political aspects of everyday life in America today. In many ways, it is an extension of the ongoing cultural exchange between Anglos and Mexicans/Mexican Americans for more than two centuries in the U.S. borderlands. Some argue that the process will lead to the increased political and economic power of Latinos/as. Indeed, Latinization has helped break the focus in U.S. race relations on Anglos and African Americans by making latinidad more visible. Other observers, such as Coco Fusco in her book *English Is Broken Here: Notes on Cultural Fusion in the Americas* (1995), argue that the celebration of any culture, in this case latinidad, through commodification and mainstreaming represents an acceptance of cultural products but not necessarily a people. Given the broader social context, in which anti-immigration sentiments, a backlash against bilingual education, and wide-ranging discriminatory practices exist simultaneously with the ongoing process of Latinization, the future of social justice for Latinos/as in the United States is yet to be seen.

Jillian M. Báez

See also: Film; Foods and Beverages; Latinidad/Latinaje; Mural Art; Music; Popular Culture; Spanglish; Spanish Language; Television.

Further Reading

Dávila, Arlene. *Barrio Dreams: Puerto Ricans, Latinos, and the Neoliberal City.* Berkeley and Los Angeles: University of California Press, 2004.

———. *Latinos, Inc.: The Making and Marketing of a People.* Berkeley: University of California Press, 2001.

De Genova, Nicholas P., and Ana Yolanda Ramos-Zayas, eds. *Latino Crossings: Mexicans, Puerto Ricans, and the Politics of Race and Citizenship.* New York: Routledge, 2003.

Flores, Juan. *From Bomba to Hip-Hop: Puerto Rican Culture and Latino Identity.* New York: Columbia University Press, 2000.

Fusco, Coco. *English Is Broken Here: Notes on Cultural Fusion in the Americas.* New York: New Press, 1995.

Laó-Montes, Agustín, and Arlene Dávila. *Mambo Montage: The Latinization of New York.* New York: Columbia University Press, 2001.

Negrón-Muntaner, Frances. *Boricua Pop: Puerto Ricans and the Latinization of American Culture.* New York: New York University Press, 2004.

Padilla, Felix M. *Latino Ethnic Consciousness: The Case of Mexican Americans and Puerto Ricans in Chicago.* South Bend, IN: University of Notre Dame Press, 1985.

Ricourt, Milagros, and Ruby Danta. *Hispanas en Queens: Latino Panethnicity in a New York City Neighborhood.* Ithaca, NY: Cornell University Press, 2003.

Latino/a

The term "Latino/a" (male form and female form, respectively) refers to any individual or ethnic group who can trace their ancestry to the Spanish-speaking countries of the Americas and Europe. Latinos/as are descended predominantly from Argentina, Bolivia, Chile, Colombia, Costa Rica, Cuba, Dominican Republic, Ecuador, El Salvador, Guatemala, Honduras, Mexico, Nicaragua, Panama, Paraguay, Peru, Puerto Rico, Spain, Uruguay, and Venezuela.

Latino/as can be of any race, and their diverse origins comprise a multitude of different ethnicities. The dynamics of Latino identity have also been fluid throughout the course of history, influenced by Spanish, African, Asian, and Amerindian culture and by both the Spanish and English conquests. Some Latinos/as have a European, primarily Spanish, ancestry, particularly apparent in South American countries—including, but not limited to, Argentina, Chile, Uruguay, and Venezuela. Likewise, indigenous peoples such as the Taíno, Ciboney, and Carib are the ancestors of many Caribbean-based Cubans, Puerto Ricans, Dominicans, and South Americans. Many Mexicans and Central Americans can specifically trace their roots back to the Maya, Aztec, and Inca, who dominated these territories before the Spanish colonized Central and South America. In addition, people of Asian descent settled in various parts of Latin America through both voluntary migration and indentured servitude. Asian settlement and ancestry is particularly apparent among descendants of Cuba, Ecuador, and Peru, as well as in people of Central American descent. Through slavery and settlement in various parts of Latin America, many Latinos/as also have African ancestry. These roots are especially apparent in the Caribbean islands of Cuba, Puerto Rico, and the Dominican Republic, and the mainland nations of Honduras,

Panama, and Colombia. Although Spanish language and culture proliferate throughout Latin America, the language is not the only one spoken and the culture is hardly the exclusive influence. The combination of indigenous, Ibero-European, African, and Asian cultures thus constitutes the diverse and distinctive pan-ethnic group broadly referred to as "Latino."

Expanding Population

Because of Latin America's close proximity to the United States, Latino immigration is one of the principal causes for the changing U.S. population. Latino immigration has increased especially since 1965, after sweeping amendments to the Immigration and Nationality Act reunited immigrants who resided in the United States with family members from their native countries. Since 1965, Latino migration has expanded steadily; the pan-ethnic population is now the largest and fastest-growing minority group in the United States, comprising about one-seventh of the nation's total population. Approximately one in eight Americans is of Latino origin, about half of whom are under age twenty-five. By 2050, according to projections, Latinas will make up one quarter of all women in the United States.

The dramatic increase of the Latino population in the United States is the result of both higher fertility rates among Latinas and substantially higher rates of immigration from Latin America, with the heaviest migration coming from Mexico. According to the U.S. Census Bureau, there were nearly 42.7 million people of "Hispanic or Latino origin" living in the United States in 2005. This total does not include the estimated population of 12 million undocumented Latinos/as, of which 6 million have migrated from Mexico alone. Thus, the total current population is closer to 55 million people. According to one projection, Latinos/as will make up one quarter of the total U.S. population by 2050. Latinos/as in the United States comprise a large and diverse ethnic group; as of 2002, the leading countries of origin were Mexico (66.7 percent), Puerto Rico (9 percent), Cuba (3.7 percent), Dominican Republic (2.2 percent), and Central and South America (14.3 percent). Although Latinos/as reside in all fifty states, the majority are found in New Mexico, California, and Texas; Mexicans comprise the largest number of Latinos/as in all three states. Many Latinos/as also live in Arizona, Florida, Illinois, New Jersey, and New York. In recent years, with strong employment demand in the agricultural sector and other seasonal work opportunities, there has been a heavy influx of undocumented migrants in Southern states with historically low Latino populations, such as Georgia and North Carolina. Some have seen a threefold increase in the number of known Latino residents in just five years.

Social Construction of the "Latino" Label

Although the economic, educational, occupational, and situational experiences of this pan-ethnic group vary considerably, it does share some general characteristics in culture, language, and even immigration patterns—similarities generically identified by the term "Latino." As an ethnic and racial identifier, however, "Latino" is a distinctly—and often destructively—arbitrary label. Yet it is the widely preferred designation among those who embrace a pan–Latin American identity, with less negative connotations than the official government term "Hispanic." The latter, many argue, excludes the various subpopulations whose ancestry does not derive from Spain, such as those with stronger indigenous, Asian, or African roots, and implicitly celebrates the colonial history of Latino communities. The U.S. Census Bureau, in fact, has conflated the two terms, reporting the population of people of "Hispanic or Latino origin."

In the United States and elsewhere, it has been found, Latinos/as prefer to identify themselves first according to their countries of origin, or "nationality," and only second by the all-inclusive term "Latino." Yet while group members tend to identify themselves as "Puerto Rican," "Colombian," or another nationality, self-identification is a fluid and contextual matter as well. For example, if a self-identified Puerto Rican, born and raised in the United States, were to visit another country, that person might first identify him- or herself as an American to a native of that country, and then identify his or her ethnicity as Puerto Rican. Within the United States, however, the same person might not acknowledge American citizenship or identity at all. The fluidity of self-identification thus confirms that the term "Latino" is what scholars refer to as a "social construction."

A wide variety of socioeconomic, citizenship, and cultural settlement experiences differentiate one "Latino" experience from another—often with significant consequences. For example, many Cubans have arrived in the United States as political refugees from a Communist homeland, while other Latinos, such as Salvadorans, have fled civil war in their homeland; yet many thousands of Cuban refugees have been granted asylum status while Salvadorans have not. The different political statuses under which these two groups have been admitted to the United States in turn affect their current political, economic, educational, and situational realities. Cubans are known as one of the most economically successful Latino migrant groups, while Salvadorans are largely confined to low-wage service sector jobs (in hotels, restaurants, and the like). The generic term "Latino" thus conceals fateful differences in official status, economic opportunity, and social standing.

The term also carries racial undertones, further separating those who identify as white, black, or other. In the social and historical context of racial hierarchy in the United States, "Latino" implies nonwhiteness—automatically conferring "minority" or inferior status. And because the term "minority" historically refers to a pattern of inequality and not just numerical minority, the racial undertones have been profoundly consequential.

The term "Latino" thus also reflects a "social constructiveness" of identity. Social forces both inside and outside this pan-ethnic community influence the need or desire for an inclusive, unified category that encapsulates general conditions and experiences of this immigrant "group." This arbitrary label has relegated Latinos/as into the ethnic category and identity of "other," distinct and separate from any specific racial or ethnic category.

The "other" status has influenced the life chances of various generations within this pan-ethnic group. As a categorical "other," Latinos/as have collectively, historically, and routinely been victims of marginalization and unequal treatment in American society, especially among undocumented, poor, and darker-skinned members. Cases of racial profiling are widely documented in the treatment of Latinos/as, whether in the criminal justice system or in the enforcement of U.S. border and immigration policies. Discrimination against Latinos/as also persists in areas such as housing, where the percentage of home ownership remains relatively stagnant; employment, where the majority of Latinos/as work in the low-wage service sector and relatively few hold white-collar positions; in health care, with many Latino children in the United States remaining uninsured; and especially in education. Statistics reveal that 15 percent of Latino youth drop out of high school each year, double the national average of white students. College graduation rates have yet to exceed 15 percent nationally for Latinos/as, while the percentage of those who obtain an advanced degree is well below the national average.

The most damaging effects of the "otherization" of Latinos/as pertain to the use of Spanish language. Approximately one out of ten U.S. residents can speak Spanish, and the United States is the fifth largest Spanish-speaking country in the world (surpassed only by Mexico, Spain, Argentina, and Colombia). The popular perception is that all "Latinos/as speak Spanish," yet studies have shown that not all Latinos/as in the United States are fluent. Some, especially those in younger generations born and raised in the United States, do not speak Spanish at all. With each new generation, more and more Latinos/as are growing up in predominantly English-speaking households. Still, the pervasiveness of Spanish in public life remains a highly charged issue with strong negative perceptions among many non-Latino Americans. The controversy has been highlighted by ongoing debates over the use of the Spanish language in schools and government.

Additionally, the distinctiveness of Latino-ness in the dominant culture reflects other pervasive stereotypes, such as the domesticated or exoticized Latina, or the criminal, drug, or gang-related Latino commonly portrayed in the media. Other cultural stereotypes commonly attributed to Latinos/as—that they are uneducated, poor, patriarchal, hot-tempered, and overly family-oriented, among others—have helped prevent many from achieving what most immigrants who relocate to the United States aspire to: the American Dream.

Judith A. Pérez

See also: Identity and Labels; Immigration and Nationality Act of 1965; Race; Spanish Language.

Further Reading

Gonzalez, Juan. *Harvest of Empire: A History of Latino/as in America.* New York: Penguin, 2000.

Morin, Jose-Luis. *Latino/a Rights and Justice in the United States: Perspectives and Approaches.* Durham, NC: Carolina Academic Press, 2005.

National Council of La Raza. http://www.nclr.org.

Novas, Himilce. *Everything You Need to Know About Latino/a History.* New York: Plume, 2008.

Oboler, Suzanne. *Ethnic Labels, Latino Lives: Identity and the Politics of (Re)Presentation in the United States.* Minneapolis: University of Minnesota Press, 1995.

Rodríguez, Clara E. *Changing Race: Latinos, the Census, and the History of Ethnicity in the United States.* New York: New York University Press, 2000.

Latino Studies

Latino studies is an academic field comprising multiple disciplines and methodologies with the purpose of analyzing the history, culture, community life, politics, and everyday experiences of people of Latin American descent in the United States. Latino studies was institutionalized as an academic discipline beginning in the late 1960s, with such other ethnic studies disciplines as black (or African American) studies and Native American (or American Indian) studies. By the early 2000s, there were Latino Studies Departments or degree programs at more than a dozen universities around the country. Some operate in conjunction with related disciplines, such as Chicano studies or Puerto Rican studies. The core curriculum in Latino studies programs typically covers such areas as Latino history—in both the United States and nations of origin—Latino immigration, Latino art and literature, representations of Latinos/as in the American media, issues of cultural identity, and the social construction of the Latino subject.

Like other ethnic studies disciplines that originated out of the social upheaval on American university campuses in the 1960s and 1970s, many Latino studies programs—including ones at such presitigious institutions as Columbia University, Cornell University, and the University of Notre Dame—were formed in a bottom-up process, as a result of a campaign by Latino students and faculty. Such individuals advocated for the new discipline as a way of validating their own cultural identity, as a way of expanding the orientation and curriculum of the academy, and ultimately as a way of helping the United States become more understanding and tolerant of its minority population.

For the academic community, the challenge of the field is to design conceptual tools for studying the multifaceted and diversified cultural forces represented by Latinos/as; to educate the population at large; and to create curricular initiatives that enable Latino students to know and enhance their own experience. Central to any program is an emphasis on what makes Latinos/as unique in American society, what they have in common with other ethnic and cultural groups in the United States, and what differentiates the experience and identity of the many diverse national and ethnic subgroups among Latinos/as.

As the field has grown and matured on college campuses, influential professional societies have emerged as well—notably the National Hispanic and Latino Studies Association and the Latino studies section of the Latin American Studies Association. Likewise, several scholarly journals have been established to publish research and commentary in the field—among them *Latino Studies,* published by Palgrave Macmillan, and *JOLLAS,* published by the University of Nebraska. These journals work to sustain the tradition of activist scholarship by engaging critically in the study of local, national, transnational, and hemispheric realities that continue to influence the Latino presence in the United States. They also seek to bridge the academic and nonacademic worlds and to foster mutual learning and collaboration among all Latino national groups.

One issue that has been a source of confusion is the relation of Latino studies with the broader discipline of Latin American studies (LAS). In simplest terms, Latino studies focuses on Latinos/as in the United States, while LAS focuses on the peoples, cultures, and nations south of the border. In reality, however, the distinction has become increasingly ephemeral and uncertain as migration patterns—back and forth between the United States and far-flung homelands, as well as between diverse Latino communities across the United States—have continued to evolve. Likewise, institutions and curricula in the two fields have tended to merge.

All in all, Latino studies is likely to remain one of the most dynamic and vibrant areas of academic inquiry for the foreseeable future, as Latinos/as continue their transition from a people of uncertain identity, grim history, and modest political influence to one of rapidly increasing numbers, with an expanding role in society and growing cultural pride. As more young Latinos/as continue to attend college and assume faculty positions, the field of Latino studies is likely to reinforce the trend and benefit from it.

Bernardo Aguilar-González

See also: Latino/a; Puerto Rican Studies.

Further Reading

Darder, A., and R. Torres, eds. *The Latino Studies Reader: Culture, Economy and Society.* Malden, MA: Blackwell, 2004.

Novas, Himilce. *Everything You Need to Know About Latino History.* New York: Plume, 2003.

Poblete, J., ed. *Critical Latin American and Latino Studies.* Minneapolis: University of Minnesota Press, 2003.

Stavans, Ilan. *The Hispanic Condition: The Power of a People.* New York: HarperCollins, 2001.

League of United Latin American Citizens

The League of United Latin American Citizens (LULAC) is the largest and oldest continually active Latino civic group in the United States, committed to securing educational, political, social, and civil rights for American citizens of Latin American descent. The league was founded in Corpus Christi, Texas, in 1929 and quickly spread throughout Texas, the rest of the Southwest, and eventually the nation. Originally organized in response to political disenfranchisement and racial segregation among Mexican immigrants, today LULAC works to advance the economic condition, political influence, health, and civil rights of all Latinos/as through community-based programs operating at more than 700 councils nationwide. In addition, LULAC councils (affiliated volunteer units) provide more than $1 million in scholarships to Latino students each year, conduct citizenship and voter registration drives, develop low-income housing units, conduct youth leadership training programs, and seek to empower the Latino community at the local, state, and national levels.

Origins

Mexican American leaders in Texas founded the league shortly before the start of the Great Depression in response to changing demographics in the state. An influx of Mexican immigrants between 1920 and 1930, perhaps numbering greater than 1 million people, presented American-born Latinos/as with several problems. First, the immigrants provoked anxiety among Anglos, who feared that Mexicans would overrun the state. Second, most Anglos could not distinguish between a Mexican and a Mexican American. Since native-born Mexican Americans hoped to win these Anglos as friends and benefactors, they came to believe that they should take responsibility for assimilating Mexicans into American society. By helping the immigrants become productive American citizens, Latinos/as could counter Anglo fears that the state was being overrun by Latinoa/as. One of the first organizations formed to achieve this goal was the Orden Hijos de America (Order of the Sons of America, or OSA), founded in a San Antonio barbershop in October 1921. This fraternal society, composed of the community's elite Mexican Americans, operated like a mutual aid society to benefit recent immigrants. The OSA also fought for Mexican American rights, including the right to serve on juries, sue Anglos in court, and have access to all public facilities.

The OSA became increasingly powerful during the course of the 1920s, but the influx of Mexican immigrants continued unabated. OSA leaders began to fear that Mexican nationals would dilute the growing political strength of elite Latinos/as, which pushed the organization to fight more forcefully for the rights of Mexican Americans. Other groups had similar agendas. The Order of the Knights of America (OKA),

Vice President Lyndon B. Johnson (far left) and First Lady Jacqueline Kennedy attend a convention of the League of United Latin American Citizens in Houston, Texas, in November 1963. President John F. Kennedy, a beloved figure to the group, was murdered days later. *(Art Rickerby/Stringer/Time & Life Pictures/Getty Images)*

a splinter group of OSA, formed in San Antonio in the early 1920s and fought for similar goals. The OSA and the OKA, which attempted to reconcile their differences at a 1927 meeting in Harlingen, instead founded a third organization, the League of Latin American Citizens. With the separate groups vying for the same members, utilizing similar organizational structures, and fighting for the same goals, Mexican American leaders tried once again to unite in one central body. Called together by Ben Garza, Jr., a prominent OSA leader, chapter heads of the OSA, OKA, and League of Latin American Citizens met at the Salón Obreras y Obreras in Corpus Christi in 1929 to try to reconcile their differences. On February 17, 1929, they founded a new organization, the League of United Latin American Citizens.

LULAC differed from its antecedent groups in promoting a pro-American civil rights agenda. During its first decade, the league concentrated on formulating its ideological foundation, while its first order of practical business was attracting members and its primary goal was the eradication of segregated Mexican schools. Typically, members were skilled laborers and small-business owners, and to expand its membership rolls, the league appealed to the patriotic sentiments of Americans of Mexican descent. It openly championed the ideal of American democracy, promoted the use of English and the disuse of Spanish, and encouraged Mexican Americans to participate in traditional American holidays such as the Fourth of July. This ideology appealed to the Latino upper-middle class, who throughout LULAC's history have tended to hold leadership positions and work to build the Latino middle class, both economically and as a voting bloc.

LULAC's exaggerated patriotism had little impact on racism in Depression-era Texas, as the constriction of the American economy exacerbated conflicts between Latinos/as and Anglos. Racist fears that Mexicans would take jobs away from "white" citizens resulted in a repatriation effort in which more than 500,000 Mexicans were forcibly relocated south of the border; approximately half were American-born Latinos/as. Despite such actions, the outbreak of World War II prompted the league to vigorously encourage Mexican Americans to join the

U.S. armed forces and fight for democracy. Large numbers volunteered, depleting LULAC's membership ranks and leaving many councils vacant.

Postwar Victories

In the postwar period, LULAC succeeded in winning a number of legal victories. One of its first triumphs came in the case of *Mendez v. Westminster School District,* under which Mexican schools in Orange County, California, were ordered desegregated in 1946. The case involved Gonzalo and Felícitas Méndez, whose children had been denied admittance to the elementary school near their home. The parents filed suit, and the California court ruled in the family's favor, arguing that segregation denied children of Mexican ancestry their constitutional rights. The victory prompted other cases. In 1948, LULAC members attempted to eradicate Mexican schools in Texas. LULAC attorneys filed suit on behalf of Minerva Delgado and twenty others against the Bastrop school district for segregating Latino children. In *Delgado v. Bastrop ISD,* the U.S. District Court, Western Division ruled segregation of Mexican-origin children unlawful. LULAC scored another major victory in 1954 in *Hernandez v. State of Texas.* In this case, LULAC lawyers attacked jury segregation in Texas after an all-white jury convicted Pete Hernandez of murder. The U.S. Supreme Court overturned Hernandez's conviction and confirmed that Latinos/as could not be denied service on juries.

These and other legal victories help popularize LULAC and enabled the league to expand its membership during the 1950s and 1960s. Councils spread throughout the Southwest and into the Midwest, and state chapters began to fight more vigorously for Mexican American rights. One of the organization's most important programs was the Little School of the 400, a preschool English instruction program that began in Texas in 1957. LULAC National President Felix Tijerina initiated the idea, which taught Mexican American children 400 basic words of English before they entered elementary school. Tijerina believed that if children could learn a few words of English at a young age, they could proceed through grade school with fewer problems, thus reducing the high dropout rates among Spanish-speaking students. The state government eventually funded the program with an annual budget of more than $1 million. The Little School program was a precursor of Head Start, a federal program established in 1965 to provide comprehensive education, health, nutrition, and parental involvement services to low-income children and their families. As part of its mission to combat poverty, LULAC in 1964 created Operation SER (Service, Employment, Redevelopment, and also the Spanish verb "to be") to provide Latinos/as with employment assistance and job training. The federal government began funding the program in 1967 and extended its reach throughout the Southwest.

While engaged in grassroots organizing with such programs, the league soon found itself out of step with the burgeoning Chicano civil rights movement of the 1960s. Many Chicano activists came to regard LULAC as too pro-American and conservative, considering it opposed to more radical Chicano tactics such as student walkouts and labor strikes. LULAC members in Texas responded by supporting Chicano school boycotts and walkouts in Houston, Austin, and Crystal City, as well as supporting the work of labor leader and organizer César Chávez by participating in the Austin farmworkers' march in 1966.

That year in Albuquerque, New Mexico, LULAC joined other Mexican American groups, including the Political Association of Spanish-Speaking Organizations (PASO), in staging a walkout during meetings with the U.S. Equal Employment Opportunity Commission (EEOC). The incident took place after LULAC and PASO leaders attacked the EEOC for having only one Mexican American on its Washington, D.C., staff and for not taking action against the more than 800 major corporations in the Southwest that did not employ Mexican Americans. The walkout signaled the first time that Mexican American middle-class leadership participated in an act of collective protest against the U.S. government.

Twentieth-Century Gains

From the days of its founding, the league pushed for an end to segregation and discrimination by arguing that Latinos/as are white. It urged state and federal governments to classify Mexican Americans as white on census and medical forms, in city directories, and on traffic citations. The *Delgado* and *Hernandez* cases also frequently made reference to Latino whiteness. Victories in these cases and the effort to classify Latinos/as as white for census purposes were successful in eliminating some aspects of anti-Latino racism. But the strategy also distanced the league's efforts from those of African American groups like the National Association for the Advancement of Colored People (NAACP). For some LULAC leaders, Mexican American whiteness meant not only a disassociation from black people, but also more overt forms of anti-black racism.

While LULAC's overall strategy of uplift may have been conservative and assimilationist, it was also successful. Additionally, the organization was able to moderate its ideology and agenda as the more conservative 1950s gave way to the more radical 1960s and 1970s. Today, LULAC maintains councils in all fifty states with thousands of active members. In addition, programs for women are carried out at the local level through the efforts of state coordinators. Among the league's most popular programs have been its two-day conferences on education and employment held in various states, and a national women's conference, all of which enjoy high attendance. LULAC has also spawned many active and lasting national organizations, including Operation SER; the Mexican American Legal Defense and Education Fund, a leading nonprofit Latino litigation, advocacy, and educational outreach institution; and the LULAC National Educational Service Center, a financial aid and college admissions outreach program designed to assist academically gifted but disadvantaged, low-income youth gain admission to college.

Brian D. Behnken

See also: Chávez, César; Crystal City, Texas; *Del Rio Independent School District v. Salvatierra* (1930); Education; Identity and Labels; *Mendez v. Westminster School District* (1946); Repatriation; Vietnam War.

Further Reading

Kaplowitz, Craig A. *LULAC: Mexican Americans, and National Policy.* College Station: Texas A&M University Press, 2005.

Kreneck, Thomas H. *Mexican American Odyssey: Felix Tijerina, Entrepreneur and Civic Leader, 1905–1965.* College Station: Texas A&M University Press, 2001.

Márquez, Benjamin. *LULAC: The Evolution of a Mexican American Political Organization.* Austin: University of Texas Press, 1993.

Lemon Grove Incident

The first successful court case pertaining to school desegregation in the United States—*Roberto Alvarez v. the Board of Trustees of the Lemon Grove School District*—originated in the town of Lemon Grove, California, a few miles east of San Diego, during the 1930s. The Lemon Grove Incident, as it is commonly referred to, led to the first judicial prohibition against school desegregation in the United States, more than twenty years before the famous *Brown v. Board of Education* decision by the U.S. Supreme Court in 1954.

On July 23, 1930, the Board of Trustees of the Lemon Grove School District met to discuss the increasing number of Mexican children attending the local school. The school board and Parent Teacher Association (PTA) decided that a separate school was needed for children of Mexican descent so they could be properly Americanized. Endorsed by the Chamber of Commerce, the plan was made without the input of any of the Mexican parents. Although there was some disagreement among board members as to the propriety of a plan reached without the input of all parties involved, it was finally agreed that the construction of a new school for Mexican students, an adapted barn on Olive Street, would be carried out in secret.

On January 5, 1931, as children returned to school from winter break, Jerome T. Green, the principal of the Lemon Grove Grammar School, stood in the main entryway, preventing Mexican students from entering the school. He instructed the seventy-five enrolled Mexican students that they were no longer students at the school and instead were to attend the Olive Street School. Upon hearing the news, the parents of the Mexican students agreed that their children would not attend *la caballeriza* (the stable), choosing to boycott both schools. Town police and the school's truant officers quickly informed the parents that they were violating the law and subject to arrest. This and other tactics of intimidation, including threats of deportation, were invoked to silence the parents and thwart their effort to derail the segregation plan. Not to be stopped, the parents and other community members organized the Comite de Vecinos de Lemon Grove (Lemon Grove Neighbors Committee) and, with the help of Enrique Ferreira, the Mexican consul, were able to retain lawyers Fred Noon and A.C. Brinkley.

Sensing a defeat in the courts, the supporters of racial segregation in California schools turned to the legislature. On January 19, 1931, State Assemblyman George R. Bliss of Carpinteria introduced a bill that called for the legalized segregation of children of Mexican, Chinese, Japanese, or Mongolian ancestry in California's public schools. Indeed, the proposed legislation called for the redefinition of Mexicans as Indians, so they might be legally segregated in any circumstances. The Bliss Bill met with defeat in the state legislature, but only after the concerted efforts of activists and organizers.

On February 13, 1931, the parents of Lemon Grove's Mexican students petitioned the Superior Court of California in San Diego to reinstate the children, claiming that the school board had violated the U.S. Constitution and the Equal Protection Clause of the Fourteenth Amendment by segregating the students.

The case went to court on February 24, 1931, and marked the beginning of a massive grassroots campaign that included rallies, demonstrations, and letter-writing campaigns. On January 25, 1931, *La Opinión,* the largest Spanish-language newspaper in California, published an article on the Lemon Grove incident entitled "No admiten a los Ninos Mexicanos" ("Mexican Children Refused Admission"), which documented the events and called upon Mexicans and sympathizers throughout the state to act in support of the plaintiffs. Members of the Comite de Vecinos de Lemon Grove appealed to the community to put pressure on the school district and government at all levels to reverse the policies of racism, bigotry, and segregation: "We are not in agreement, which is very natural, nor do we consider just, the separation of our children, without any reason, to send them to another establishment that distinguishes Mexican Children from children of other nationalities." On March 30, 1931, amid public protest and media coverage, Judge Claude Chambers ruled in favor of lead plaintiff Robert Alvarez and the other Mexican children. Finding that the plan of the Lemon Grove School District violated California law, he ordered the school to reinstate the children immediately.

In 2007, the school district honored Roberto Alvarez by dedicating the auditorium of the Lemon Grove Middle School to him.

David J. Leonard and Rachel Sandoval

See also: Education.

Further Reading

Alvarez, Robert R., Jr. "The Lemon Grove Incident: The Nation's First Successful Desegregation Court Case." *Journal of San Diego History* 32:2 (1986): 116–35.

West, Gail, Navarre Perry, Doug Jacobs, et al. *The Lemon Grove Incident.* VHS. New York: Cinema Guild, 1985.

Lesbianas Unidas

Lesbianas Unidas (LU) is a lesbian organization based in Los Angeles, formed in 1984 as a task force of the Gay and Lesbian Latinos Unidos (GLLU). The latter organization, established three years earlier, was founded by a group of gay Latino men specifically to address the needs of this population; its "primary goal . . . was to raise consciousness in both the Latino community and the gay and lesbian community about the special needs and issues of gay Latinos." Among the GLLU's subcommittees, which included others on AIDS education, media relations, and culture, was one to encourage Latina participation in the larger group. The mission statement of Lesbianas Unidas reflects its emphasis on community and collective history, with a focus on education and direct action: "Lesbianas Unidas seeks to be a grassroots organization that empowers Latina lesbians. LU shall promote a unique culture that honors our diversity and creates a sense of community by preserving our unique herstory, honoring our accomplishments and organizing educational and other projects that build pride."

The group originally offered a wide range of services and programs: rap and support groups, a program about the Latina lesbian experience, national and international networks dedicated to social and financial development, and cultural events and educational work in the community. Since its founding in 1984, the group has sponsored an annual retreat that includes cultural performances and organizational workshops and has worked directly with local, national, and international Chicano/Latino organizations, feminist groups, Latina and Latin American women's organizations, and lesbian of color groups.

Like many other women of color groups, Lesbianas Unidas arose out of members' frustrations with white feminist groups, straight Latina groups, and male-dominated gay Latino groups that often neglected or ignored the specific concerns and issues facing Latina lesbians. LU faced internal tensions and uncertainty over goals and strategies, divided between members who advocated direct activism and those who urged the group to focus on empowerment and support. As a result, in 1994, Lesbianas Unidas separated from Gay and Lesbian Latinos Unidos and became an independent group. Since that time, its most visible work has been the production and publication of lesbian oral histories. Under the guidance of Yolanda Retter, a founding member and librarian, the organization has sought to compile an extensive archive of lesbian history in print and on the Internet. In 2003, LU received a grant to gather the history of Latina lesbians in Los Angeles, resulting in a collection of videotaped oral histories of twenty Latina lesbians active in the community from 1969 to 1979. With the death of Retter in August 2007, however, the status of the project was uncertain.

Ellen M. Gil-Gómez

See also: AIDS/HIV; Gay and Lesbian Organizations.

Further Reading

Anzaldúa, Gloria. *Borderlands/La Frontera: The New Mestiza.* 1987. San Francisco: Aunt Lute, 2007.

Chávez Leyva, Yolanda. "Listening to the Silences in Latina/Chicana Lesbian History." In *Living Chicana Theory,* ed. Carla Trujillo. Berkeley, CA: Third Woman, 1998.

Ramos, Juanita. *Compañeras: Latina Lesbians.* New York: Routledge, 1994.

Levins Morales, Aurora (1954–)

Aurora Levins Morales is a Puerto Rican Jewish writer, poet, historian, feminist, activist, and educator most famous for the book *Getting Home Alive* (1986), a collection of short stories, essays, prose poems, and poetry that she wrote with her mother. Her work is acclaimed for its exploration of memory and experience in the construction of social identity, and the sense of fragmentation and alienation resulting from identification with multiple cultural groups. Thus she has emerged as one of the leading Puerto Rican writers in the United States.

She was born to Rosario Morales, a Puerto Rican woman from Spanish Harlem, and Richard Levins, a Russian Jew from Brooklyn, New York, in Castañer, Puerto Rico, on February 24, 1954. Her father, an environmentalist, and her mother, an intellectual and artist, directly influenced her life's work as writer and cultural activist. In 1967, Levins Morales and her family emigrated to Chicago, where she lived until entering Franconia College in New Hampshire in 1972.

After taking a break from school to pursue her interests in radio, writing, and activism, she returned to school at Mills College in Oakland, California, in 1989 where she wanted to pursue a degree in Latina studies and writing. Mills did not accept this course of study, which it regarded as too narrow. At the time, she and her first husband, Jim Otis, had a six-month-old daughter, Alicia, and Levins Morales did not have much free time. Since she already had success as a writer, a professor at Mills, Gabriel Melendez, recommended that she not devote her time and effort on pursuing a conventional BA, as she could potentially find a school willing to give her credit for life experience. In 1991, therefore, Levins Morales was accepted and enrolled into Union Institute in Cincinnati, Ohio, under the direction of Minnie Pratt, subsequently earning her MA and PhD. Levins Morales's dissertation was a long theoretical essay, portions of which would later appear in *Medicine Stories: History, Culture and the Politics of Integrity* (1998). Levins Morales's marriage to Jim Otis did not last through graduate school, ending in 1995.

Much of Levins Morales's written work explores the meaning of cultural identity, a subject that touches her own experiences as a Puerto Rican Jewish American. Inspired by writers such as the Chilean poet Pablo Neruda and Uruguayan journalist Eduardo Galeano, who have explored notions of biculturalism or biraciality, Levins Morales has written extensively on her own experiences growing up in a racially and culturally mixed family. Indeed, her career has been defined by a creative search for language that captures her experiences as a Latina Jewish female.

Levins Morales made her short-story debut in *This Bridge Called My Back: Writings by Radical Women of Color* (1981) and *Cuentos: Stories by Latina* (1983). Her work has also appeared in such noted anthologies as *Puerto Rican Writers at Home in the U.S.A.* (1991) and *Reconstructed American Literature* (1990), as well as *Ms.* and other magazines. In *Remedios: Stories of Earth and Iron from the History of Puertorriqueñas* (1998), a work of both fiction and nonfiction, she blends a feminist view of history with an exploration of her own ancestry, describing the "remedies" of herbal lore used by women; she also re-imagines and offers alternative narratives to Latina legends. *Medicine Stories* (1998) is a collection of essays that explores the difficulties faced by multiracial/multicultural people in the United States and the rewards of cultural activism.

Until 1998, Levins Morales taught a wide range of college courses on Puerto Rican and Jewish cultural history, social activism, and writing at such institutions as the University of California, Berkeley, the University of San Francisco, the University of Minnesota, and Pacifica Graduate Institute in Carpenteria, California. In 1998, she shifted her focus primarily to museum work and public speaking. For the next three years, she served as lead historian for the Oakland Museum's Latino History Project, helping create a major exhibit, Web site, and educational posters, and training young people to record oral histories of community elders. She also completed an unprecedented, decade-long study of the history of Puerto Ricans in the San Francisco Bay Area, likewise creating a museum exhibit with oral histories, portraits of elders, and historical photos from family collections. During this project, she worked with Barry Kleider, a professional photographer. (Although now divorced, the two had once been married.) As a lecturer and workshop organizer, Levins Morales traveled around the country to address such issues as racism and anti-Semitism in America, Latina feminism, and the importance of historical understanding in pursuing social change.

From the time Levins Morales was very young, she experienced health issues; as a social activist, she decided to make these issues part of her public persona. As a child she began suffering from fatigue. She has also suffered from epilepsy and had her first epileptic seizure at the age of twenty-three. She believes her epilepsy may have been caused by pesticides her parents used on their farm. As she has gotten older her symptoms of fatigue have worsened, causing her to collapse at times, and the seizures have become more frequent, especially since the birth of her daughter. One episode occurred at Smith College in Northampton, Massachusetts, in September 2005. Levins Morales believes that toxins in the environment may be contributing factors to the worsening of her symptoms.

While she no longer travels, the emotional, medical, and financial support of friends and professional colleagues across the United States and Puerto Rico has enabled her to continue her efforts as a full-time activist, writer, and editor, with several new publications said to be forthcoming.

Nicole Martone

See also: Identity and Labels; Puerto Rican Literature.

Further Reading

Garcia, Elizabeth. "The Making of a Curandera Historian: Aurora Levins Morales." *Centro Journal* 17:1 (2005): 184–201.

Lauter, Paul. "Aurora Levins Morales." In *Heath Anthology of American Literature.* Boston, MA: Houghton Mifflin, 2006.

LLEGÓ

LLEGÓ—the National Latina/o Lesbian, Gay, Bisexual and Transgender Organization—was established in 1987 by a group of California and Texas activists who sought a national voice for the Latina/o lesbian, gay, bisexual, and transgender (LGBT) communities in the United States and Puerto Rico. Initially focused on AIDS/HIV prevention in the Latino community, it filled a void on the local and national levels. At its height, LLEGÓ worked with a group of 172 LGBT community organizations. The group would eventually shift its focus to general advocacy for LGBT Latinos/as, concentrating on issues ranging from civil rights to health and social services.

According to its mission statement, "LLEGÓ is a national organization formed to effectively address issues of concern to Latino lesbian, gay, bisexual, and transgender men and women at local, state, regional, national and international levels." Specifically, the organization's priorities are to make the Latino LGBT community visible and understood within all levels of society, to advocate for effective health policies and treatments, to form and sustain networks to share and distribute resources, and to educate Latino and non-Latino communities to combat oppression in all its forms.

As a result of extensive fund-raising efforts and governmental support, LLEGÓ amassed a multimillion-dollar annual budget and employed more than thirty people at its peak. Its financial security and sheer size were unprecedented for a community-based LGBT group. LLEGÓ focused on six main programs, which would eventually become the six main branches of the organization. *ACCIÓN LLEGÓ* (LLEGÓ Action) focused specifically on civil rights activism through community education and advocacy, specifically targeting public policy and media. *AVANZANDO* (Progression) was the coordinating arm and acted as a consultant to other organizations serving Latino communities engaged in HIV prevention. *HORIZONTES* (Horizons) focused on developing the leadership skills of gay and bisexual men and encouraging individual work in preventing HIV in the community. *¡BASTA!* (Enough!) included training for social service workers involved in domestic violence and sexual assault prevention; its primary purpose was to educate community workers on cultural contexts for Latinas in order to increase program success. *PROYECTO FÉNIX* (Phoenix Project) focused on tobacco prevention among Latino youngsters. And *FUTURO AQUÍ* (The Future Here) served primarily as an educational group focused on developing leadership skills within LGBT Latino youth communities. The hope was to train future leaders, who in turn would educate their own communities on the range of issues affecting their daily lives and future opportunities.

While a number of LLEGÓ campaigns proved successful, providing an important public presence for the LGBT Latino community, the group ceased operation in 2004 due to financial mismanagement and controversy. The group did much to educate the community about AIDS/HIV for its seventeen-year existence and lasted longer than many other similar LGBT organizations.

Ellen M. Gil-Gómez

See also: AIDS/HIV; Gay and Lesbian Organizations.

Further Reading

Guide to the National Latino/a Lesbian and Gay Organization (LLEGO). Division of Rare and Manuscript Collections Cornell University Library, Ithaca, NY, 1996.

Lopez, Jennifer (1970–)

The multitalented Puerto Rican dancer, singer, and actor Jennifer Lopez is an inspiration to many Latinos/as, and other young men and women, who are pursuing a career in Hollywood. For her breakout role in *Selena,* the 1997 film about the slain Tejano pop star, Lopez received professional accolades and became the first Latina actress in a lead film role since 1940s movie star Rita Hayworth. She is also the highest paid Latina actress in Hollywood history. In addition to her successful entertainment career, Lopez—popularly nicknamed J. Lo—heads successful clothing, accessories, and perfume lines. According to *Forbes,* she is the richest Latin American in Hollywood, and according to *People en Espanol,* she was the most influential Hispanic entertainer in 2007.

Born in the Bronx, New York, on July 24, 1970, to middle-class Puerto Rican parents, Lopez imitated their strong work ethic, which resulted in her rare success crossing multiple entertainment genres. Her parents also stressed assimilation into American culture, including speaking English, which they felt would help her succeed in the sphere of popular entertainment. Both of Lopez's parents loved music and encouraged family performances. Lopez began taking dancing lessons at the age of five, going on to practice ballet, jazz, and flamenco.

Dancing was Lopez's ticket to fame. After graduating from Holy Family School, a Catholic high school in the Bronx, she enrolled briefly in New York City's Baruch College before dropping out to pursue a dancing career. She divided her time between working in a legal office and dancing at Manhattan nightclubs. She intermittently danced in stage musicals, performing in a European tour of *Golden Musicals of Broadway,* a Japanese tour of *Synchronicity,* and local productions of *Oklahoma* and *Jesus Christ Superstar.* In 1990, Lopez joined the Fly Girls, a group of dancers who performed between skits on the Fox television show *In Living Color.* Leaving New York to settle in Los Angeles, she quickly gained visibility on other television shows and in music videos, including Janet Jackson's "That's the Way Love Goes" (1993).

Her movie career took off in 1995, when she landed a role in the feature film *My Family,* winning an Independent Spirit Award nomination for her portrayal of Maria the Mexican immigrant. She followed that success with a starring role as femme fatale Grace McKenna in director Oliver Stone's *U-Turn* (1997). But it was her performance as singer Selena Quintanilla Perez in *Selena* that cemented her film career later that year. When she signed the $1 million contract for Selena, Lopez became the highest paid Latina actress in history. In 1998, she received a Golden Globe Award nomination for best performance by an actress in a motion picture for the role, as well as several other awards, including the 1998 American Latino Media Arts Award (ALMA) for best actress. On the heels of the success of *Selena,* Lopez won critics' praise for her role as Federal Marshal Karen Sisco opposite George Clooney in *Out of Sight* (1998).

Lopez spent much of 1998 on the recording and production of her CD *On the 6*—a reference to the subway line she used to take growing up in her Bronx neighborhood—which ignited her musical career when it was released in June 1999. A mix of pop and rhythm and blues, the CD sold 2 million copies before the end of its first year of release, reached the Top Ten on the Billboard 200, and featured the platinum hit single "If You Had My Love," which topped the charts for five weeks. The album also featured the Spanish-language, Latin-influenced duet "No Me Ames" (Don't Love Me), with her future husband Marc Anthony, which reached number one on the U.S. Hot Latin Tracks.

Her second album, *J. Lo,* released in 2001, was number one on the charts at the same time that her movie *The Wedding Planner* was number one at the box office. Lopez thus earned the distinction of being the first actress/singer to stand atop both charts simultaneously. Her songs "Love Don't Cost a Thing" and "Play" were top-five hits in 2001, but "I'm Real" and "Ain't It Funny" were her biggest successes, each spending several weeks at number one.

Her next album, *J to tha L-O!: The Remixes* (2002), also went platinum. *This is Me . . . Then,* released later that same year, reached number two on the Billboard 200 and produced three hits, "Jenny from the Block," "All I Have," and "Baby I Love U!" Also in 2002, Lopez starred in two films, the drama *Enough,* in which she played a battered wife, and the romantic comedy *Maid in Manhattan. Rebirth,* her fourth album, debuted at number two upon its release in spring 2005, but quickly fell off the charts. By early 2008, Lopez had sold more than 50 million records worldwide.

Lopez's longtime interest in fashion led her to expand her creative and business interests, developing the highly successful clothing and accessories line, JLO by Jennifer Lopez; the brand earned more than $300 million in sales in 2004 alone. She has also released several signature fragrances, Glow by J. Lo, Live by Jennifer Lopez, and Desire. Events of 2005 included the introduction of her high-end clothing line Sweetface and a starring role in the film *Monster-in-Law* with Jane Fonda, for which she was paid $15 million.

In 2007, she officially released her first full Spanish-language album, *Como Ama una Mujer,* produced by her husband Marc Anthony. At the 2007 American Music Awards, Lopez won favorite female artist in the Latin music category. To top off her long list of accomplishments, in 2007 Lopez received the Artists for Amnesty International Award in recognition of her work as producer and star of the thriller *Bordertown,* in which she played a reporter investigating the murders of factory women in the border city of Juárez, Mexico. Nobel Peace Prize winner José Ramos-Horta presented the award to Lopez at the Berlin International Film Festival.

Rebecca Tolley-Stokes and Gina Misiroglu

See also: Film; Music; Popular Culture; Puerto Ricans.

Further Reading

Duncan, Patricia J. *Jennifer Lopez.* New York: St. Martin's, 1999.
Hill, Anne E. *Jennifer Lopez.* Philadelphia: Chelsea House, 2001.

Los Angeles

Los Angeles, California, widely referred to simply as "LA," is the unofficial Latino capital of the United States. The city proper has approximately 4 million inhabitants, but most people think of "L.A." as all of Los Angeles County and other areas of the megalopolis—which includes up to 18 million people. As such, Los Angeles is the second largest metropolitan area in the United States (after New York City) and the ninth largest in the world. It is also the largest city in the nation's most populous state, California, and one of the most Latino. According to the 2000 U.S. Census, about one-third of Californians and more than 45 percent of "Angelenos" are Hispanic/Latino. As of 2006, Los Angeles County was home to the largest Latino population in the United States, at more than 4.7 million.

Los Angeles is a multicultural, multi-ethnic metropolis of dizzying diversity. Its inhabitants come from around the world, many from Latin America. Most Latino Angelenos are Mexican or of Mexican descent. If Los Angeles were still a part of Mexico, it would be the second-largest city in the country; more Mexicans reside in Los Angeles than in Mexico's second-largest city, Guadalajara. Los Angeles is also home to several hundred thousand Central Americans; in fact, it has the second-largest populations of Salvadorans and Guatemalans outside their native countries.

History

Los Angeles was initially inhabited by various Native American groups, most notably the Tongva, also called Gabrielinos by the Spanish. The Spanish explorer Juan Cabrillo stopped briefly in the Los Angeles area in 1542, but the Spanish conquest of Mexico did not reach the region for another 200 years and more, when explorer Gaspar de Portolá and two Franciscan padres, Junípero Serra and Juan Crespi, arrived in 1769. It was not until September 4, 1781, that settlers from as far away as Sonora, Mexico, inhabited an area next to a river and established *El Pueblo de Nuestra Señora la Reina de Los Angeles sobre el Río Porciuncula* (The Town of Our Lady the Queen of the Angels on the Porciuncula River). The name "Porciuncula" came from the place in Italy where St. Francis of Assisi, the founder of the Franciscan order of priests, carried out his religious life; the river, now known as the Los Angeles River, passes through the modern city. The founding families were extremely diverse, comprised of two Spaniards, one mestizo (mixed Spanish and Native Indian), two "Negroes," eight mulattoes (mixed African and European), and nine Native Americans.

Los Angeles quickly became a center of cattle ranching and, after gold was discovered farther north in the 1840s, an attraction to mining interests. It was incorporated as a city in 1850, shortly after California was granted U.S. statehood. By the 1870s, Los Angeles was still only a town of 5,000 inhabitants, but the completion of the railroad that connected L.A. to San Francisco and the East Coast led to a boom in commerce and land, as did the discovery of oil in the early 1890s. The population of greater Los Angeles reached 100,000 by 1900; 577,000 by 1920; and 1.5 million by World War II, when war production and immigration helped make the city an industrial and financial giant. Agriculture, dairy, aerospace, and movie production were other important industries that fueled L.A.'s growth during the course of the century.

The city's Latino population remained relatively small through the 1800s. Many Angelenos fought on the side of Mexico during the Mexican-American War—which included a number of battles near what is today East L.A. The conflict ended in victory for the United States in 1848, and the Treaty of Guadalupe Hidalgo granted half of Mexico's territory—including all of what became the state of California—to the United States. Anti-Mexican sentiment translated into racism and violence toward Californians of Mexican descent, who were now strangers in their own land. Many Mexican landowners (*Californios*) lost their holdings and went bankrupt; they and other Mexicans resorted to banditry and threats of revolt against the "gringos." Many chose to live according to their "Spanish" (white, European) heritage rather than Mexican or indigenous roots. Most Latinos/as (overwhelmingly Mexicans) during this period resided south of the downtown area; displaced by U.S. settlers and European immigrants, they later moved east to Boyle Heights.

The city's demographics underwent a major shift when heavy waves of immigration came after the outbreak of the Mexican Revolution in 1910. Drawn north by employment opportunities, affordable housing, and relative tolerance, the immigrants generally planned to return home once the government and economy stabilized in Mexico. Most ended up staying, however. With the arrival of even larger numbers of immigrants after the revolution ended in the 1920s, the Mexican community moved slightly north into the Belvedere neighborhood. While today the Latino population of Los Angeles is spread throughout the metropolitan area, a few communities are especially important—historically, demographically, and culturally—to Latinos/as. First and foremost is East Los Angeles.

East L.A.

East Los Angeles, also known as East LA or East Los, refers to an unincorporated area east of downtown Los Angeles. It is also a cultural term for this region and its surrounding communities of Boyle Heights, Lincoln Heights, Belvedere, City Terrace, and parts of the cities of Montebello and Monterey Park, which together comprise the "Eastside"—recognized as the largest Latino/Mexican American community in the United States. According to the 2000 U.S. Census, 96.8 percent of the 124,000 residents are Latino, most of them of Mexican descent. A majority of households in East L.A. are families with children, and most are working class. More than a quarter of the population lives below the poverty line.

Politics

Common experiences of discrimination and oppression made East L.A. an important site of the Chicano Movement of the 1960s and 1970s. In 1968, some 30,000 students from five local high schools staged walkouts, or "blowouts," to protest the poor physical condition of their campuses and the quality of education in general. They demanded more teachers and administrators of Mexican descent, a college preparatory curriculum, bilingual education, and courses relevant to their Mexican heritage.

Political demonstrations in August 1970 and January 1971 to protest the Vietnam War ended in violence. Partly sponsored by the Chicano Moratorium Committee, and intended to be peaceful, a rally on August 29 deteriorated as police clashed with the 20,000 demonstrators. While official and community versions of what happened differ, the three days of demonstrations left three people dead, sixty-one injured, and more than $1 million in property damage and theft. Among those killed was Rubén Salazar, the news director of Spanish-language television station KMEX, a former journalist for the *Los Angeles Times,* and a Chicano committed to educating and empowering his community. Accusations of politically motivated assassination led to an official investigation, but no prosecutions were forthcoming, which added to the community's suspicion and anger. To the present day, August 29 is often commemorated with marches and rallies in the neighborhood, and Laguna Park—where the rally began—has been renamed Salazar Park in honor of the fallen journalist.

Many organizations and individuals continue the tradition of political activism in East Los Angeles. Antonio Villaraigosa, elected mayor of Los

Angeles in 2005, is a native of East L.A., where he witnessed street violence, participated in the Chicano Movement, and remained politically active as a student at East Los Angeles College and beyond. The National Chicano Moratorium Committee continues to fight for improved education, better health care, and other rights for Latinos/as. The Mothers of East L.A., formed in 1986 by Juana Beatríz Gutiérrez and her friends to prevent the state of California from building a prison in their neighborhood, remains actively involved in local conservation programs, health education, and fund-raising for college scholarships. The One Stop Immigration and Education Center provides resources to immigrants and advocates for immigrant rights. Father Greg Boyle, a Jesuit priest who for decades has lived and worked with gang members in one of the toughest barrios of East L.A.—the Pico-Aliso housing projects in Boyle Heights—has helped create jobs for local youth and advocates for a more compassionate, preventive approach to addressing the community's problems.

Art and Culture

East Los Angeles is not only a historical and political center for Americans of Mexican descent, but an artistic center as well. Self Help Graphics and Art, founded in the early 1970s, provides education, empowerment, and exhibition opportunities for local Chicano/Latino artists. Plaza de la Raza in nearby Lincoln Park maintains an art exhibition and performance space, which houses the School of Performing and Visual Arts. Founded in 1975, the school touts itself as "the only multidisciplinary cultural arts center serving Latinos in Los Angeles." Many of the youth who attend its classes in music, theater, and visual arts, taught primarily by Latino instructors, are from low-income families. Actors Constance Marie and Edward James Olmos both are natives of East L.A., as is boxer Oscar de la Hoya; actor Anthony Quinn grew up in Boyle Heights.

East Los Angeles also enjoys a reputation as a focal point for Chicano art and murals. Los Angeles, recognized by many as the public mural capital of the world, was one of the first places where Americans of Mexican descent adopted the Mexican artistic tradition of painting murals as a means of cultural and political self-expression in the wake of the civil rights movement. The streets of East L.A.—and housing developments such as Nueva Maravilla, Pico Gardens/Aliso Village, Ramona Gardens, and Estrada Courts—are especially rich in mural art, some more than thirty years old. A group called the "East Los Streetscapers," made up of David Botello, Wayne Healy, and George Yepes, is, individually and collectively, among East L.A.'s best-known Chicano muralists. Thanks to the efforts of the Mural Conservancy of Los Angeles, these murals will be preserved for future generations to enjoy.

Education

Education is also an important value to East Los Angeles residents. The two main secondary schools, rivals Garfield High School and Roosevelt High School, are known not only for their role in the Chicano blowouts of the 1960s, but also for the academic achievements of their students—many with disadvantaged backgrounds. Garfield High and former math teacher Jaime Escalante were featured in the 1988 feature film *Stand and Deliver,* which told the true story of Escalante's role in preparing low-income Latino students to take and pass the Advanced Placement exam in calculus and go on to universities. East Los Angeles College (ELAC), established in 1945, boasts the highest transfer rate for Latinos/as in California. It is a valuable community resource, known for educating Latino students on their cultural heritage and for the general quality of its instruction.

Landmarks and Physical Features

Aside from history, politics, the arts, and education, other features help East Los Angeles stand out as a unique Latino cultural center—physical landmarks that are often alluded to or featured in popular music, television shows such as *American Family,* and films such as *American Me* (1992) and *My Family* (1995). The two main streets are Whittier Boulevard and Avenida César Chávez, both running west to east through the entire community. Avenida César Chávez was originally named Brooklyn Avenue to reflect the area's Jewish heritage, but renamed in 1995 to honor the late labor leader and civil rights advocate. Reflecting the diverse ethnic and religious heritage of East Los Angeles, the area is host to several large cemeteries of various faiths, including Calvary Cemetery (Catholic) and Home of Peace Cemetery (Jewish). Mariachi Plaza in Boyle Heights is a gathering place for traditional Mexican ensembles seeking work, a situation that mirrors similar gatherings in Mexico on weekends. El Mercado (The Market) on First Street and Lorena features murals, restaurants, live music, and vendors selling Mexican sweets, fruits, shoes, ceramics, traditional remedies, electronics, and other goods and services.

While no other neighborhood comes close to East L.A. as the political, social, historical, and cultural heart of Latino Los Angeles, other notable communities include South Los Angeles, Pico-Union, and the San Fernando Valley.

South Los Angeles

Among the neighborhoods of Greater Los Angeles that have seen dramatic demographic change, at least in modern times, is South Los Angeles. Formerly known as South Central L.A., or just "South Central," the area's name was officially changed in 2003 to remove some of the stigma of violence and poverty associated with the old names—but most people still use them.

Once an area inhabited predominantly by European immigrants, South Los Angeles became a predominantly African American neighborhood in the 1950s, when blacks escaping the prejudice and economic oppression of the South began moving in—and the white population moved out. The community has always been marked by cultural diversity. Cheech Marin, the popular comedian, television and film actor, and owner of the largest private collection of Chicano art in the world, was born in South Los Angeles in 1946. Today, what was once the largest African American community in the western United States—featured in such movies as *Boyz n the Hood* (1991) by South Central native John Singleton and the rap music of natives Ice Cube, Dr. Dre, and Easy E—is now about 70 percent Latino and Spanish-speaking. The shift became especially pronounced after the Los Angeles Riots of 1992, when many African American residents moved to other neighborhoods. The change has caused conflict and tension in the community, where competition over housing and jobs has led to cultural misunderstandings, prejudice, and even violence between groups.

South Los Angeles is perhaps a microcosm of the larger shift in U.S. demographics and culture, a shift that had Latinos/as outnumbering African Americans as the largest nonwhite ethnic group in the country for the first time in 2000. Even Watts, Compton, and Inglewood—important communities within the history and culture of African Americans in Los Angeles—are now mostly Latino (Watts at 62 percent and Compton at 57 percent in 2000). Efforts to create a Latino-black alliance did pay off when a majority of African American residents in South Los Angeles voted for Villaraigosa in the 2005 Los Angeles mayoral election, playing a key role in securing his victory.

Pico-Union

Pico-Union is so named because it is a neighborhood centered at the intersection of Pico Boulevard and Union Avenue in downtown Los Angeles. One of the poorest sections of Los Angeles—42 percent of residents live below the poverty line—Pico-Union is 92 percent Latino and the heart of the city's Central American population. The district is home primarily to immigrants from Oaxaca, Mexico; El Salvador; Guatemala; and Honduras. A few gangs with international connections were started in Pico-Union—notably the 18th Street gang and Mara Salvatrucha—but it is also a thriving neighborhood with many ethnic restaurants and other businesses, many of which are Korean-owned. Pico-Union is also known for its colorful community murals, landmark church buildings, and atttractive older homes.

San Fernando Valley

The San Fernando Valley, located northwest of downtown Los Angeles and just north of Hollywood, separated by the Santa Monica Mountains, includes about fifteen cities and unincorporated areas, the largest of which are Burbank, Glendale, Van Nuys, and North Hollywood. When the area was annexed by Los Angeles in 1915, the mostly rural area doubled the geographical size of L.A. The northern part of "The Valley" has the highest concentration of Latinos, especially in Pacoima, San Fernando, Sylmar, and parts of Van Nuys, Reseda, and North Hollywood. Much like South Central L.A., the San Fernando Valley has seen dramatic change in recent decades; Latinos make up about 40 percent of the almost 2 million residents of The Valley, an exemplar of the "white flight" phenomenon during the 1960s.

Latino L.A.

Despite its history and present challenges, Los Angeles is regarded by many as a city of the future, not only because of its economic and political power, but also on the strength of its cultural diversity and uniqueness. A major aspect of its new role may be to advance the rights and equality of Latinos—America's largest and fastest-growing minority group. The election of Antonio Villaraigosa in 2005 by a Latino and African American majority is seen as potentially a major step forward in that regard. The first Latino elected to that office since the 1800s, Villaraigosa was seen as a sign of hope, inspiration, and empowerment not only to the residents of Latino L.A., but to Latinos in California and throughout the United States.

Susana Rinderle

See also: Blowouts; Chicano Movement; East Los Angeles; Education; Film; Gangs; Latino/a; Mexicans; Mural Art; Salazar, Rubén; Treaty of Guadalupe Hidalgo (1848); Villaraigosa, Antonio.

Further Reading

Acuña, Rodolfo. *A Community Under Siege: A Chronicle of Chicanos East of the Los Angeles River, 1945–1975.* Los Angeles: Chicano Studies Research Center, University of California at Los Angeles, 1984.

Macias, Reynaldo F. *A Study of Unincorporated East Los Angeles.* Los Angeles: University of California Press, 1973.

McCawley, William. *The First Angelinos: The Gabrielino Indians of Los Angeles.* Banning, CA: Malki Museum, 1996.

Normark, Don. *Chávez Ravine, 1949: A Los Angeles Story.* San Francisco: Chronicle, 1999.

Pearlstone, Zena. *Ethnic L.A.* Beverly Hills, CA: Hillcrest, 1990.

Pitt, Leonard, and Dale Pitt. *Los Angeles from A to Z: An Encyclopedia of the City and County.* Berkeley: University of California Press, 1997.

Romo, Ricardo. *East Los Angeles: History of a Barrio.* Austin: University of Texas Press, 1983.

University of Southern California. *Los Angeles: Past, Present, and Future.* 1996. Adopted by the El Pueblo de Los Angeles Historical Monument.

Lowriders

An expression of Chicano youth counterculture that gained prominence in the barrios of Los Angeles during the post–World War II period, lowriders are cars that have been modified to drive as low to the ground as possible. A symbol of independence, creativity, and "coolness," these colorful vehicles were a statement of resistance to mainstream Anglo culture, whose youth of the era were driving muscle cars that emphasized speed and power. Unlike the more expensive souped-up models, lowriders made a statement of attitude and style in which cruising at slow speeds, low to the ground, was an expression of pride and self-assured flamboyance much like the zoot suit and *Caló* dialect (a mix of Spanish slang and English) popular among Chicano young men in the 1940s and 1950s. Lowriding spread quickly among Latino communities in California, the Southwest, and throughout America, re-emerging by the 1990s as an element of urban hip-hop culture.

Adapted from older models affordable to Chicano youth—standard Fords, Buicks, and Chevrolets usually—the cars were originally lowered by placing cement bags or bricks in the trunk. Owners with mechanical know-how achieved a lower ride by shortening the springs to lower the chassis. Eventually, hydraulic lifts controlled manually by the driver were used to lower and raise the front and rear ends of the car. By whatever means, the object was to ride as close as possible to the ground without scraping the bottom of the car.

As a reflection of cultural pride and artistic taste, the vehicles were often painted and decorated in native motifs, such as lace designs, pinstripes, and murals depicting ancient Mayan scenes or Mexican religious icons such as the Virgin Mary. As a cool reinvention of the *paseo* courtship custom, traditional in Mexican village life, twentieth-century urban drivers would cruise down the street at a slow speed, showing off and attracting attention. Eventually, the pastime of cruising became as much a part of modern Chicano youth culture as it did of the upscale Anglo high school set.

In modern socioeconomic terms, car ownership itself became a symbol of success for young Mexican Americans, some of whom found jobs in the burgeoning economy of Southern California and looked for ways to spend their money and leisure time. Also prominent among lowriding enthusiasts were returning GIs, whose veterans benefits enabled them to buy cars. *Veteranos* especially admired the 1939 Chevy for its gangster look, including suicide doors and front headlights and fenders that came together to form a "V." Mixing cultural pride and a desire to see parts of metropolitan Los Angeles beyond the confines of the barrios, lowriders ventured outside East L.A. to other parts of the city, such as Olvera Street, Old Chinatown, and Lincoln Park, with a sense of defiance and entitlement.

Likewise, lowriders themselves spread beyond the barrio and became a mainstream cultural phenomenon. The self-proclaimed "King of the Kustomizers" was Navy veteran George Barris, who, with his brother Sam in Los Angeles, set up a shop in the 1960s that specialized in lowering chassis and otherwise retooling standard stock cars in distinctive styles; he built a thriving business. Meanwhile, car clubs also emerged as part of the lowrider cruising scene of the 1960s. In the Chicano community of Southern California, prominent clubs included the Dukes, the Imperials, and the Lady Bugs (an all-Chicana Volkswagen group). Indeed the cultural marker of lowriding was not even limited to cars, as young people who could not afford true lowriders began fixing up their bicycles in the same style. Inevitably, the bicycle trend went commercial, as Schwinn came out with a new model in 1963, called the Stingray, which featured a low-slung "banana"

Lowriders—standard car models customized to cruise as low to the ground as possible—originated in the barrios of Southern California, then spread to Chicano youth culture in the Southwest and across the country. *(Gordon Gahan/National Geographic/Getty Images)*

seat and "sissy bar." By the 1980s, the appearance of *Lowrider* magazine perpetuated the phenomenon and attracted yet new adherents. Once confined to the barrios of Los Angeles and Southwest, lowriding—and the collection of vintage lowrider cars—is now a global phenomenon, with adherents as far away as Europe and Japan.

Paul López

See also: Hip-Hop; Los Angeles.

Further Reading

Doeden, Matt, and Pete Salas. *Lowriders.* Minneapolis, MN: Lerner, 2006.

Genat, Robert. *Lowriders.* Minneapolis, MN: MBI, 2001.

Mendoza, Ruben. "Journey to Aztlán: An Anthropologist among the Lowriders." *Q-vo Magazine* 3:2 (1981): 18–19.

———. "The Low Rider Ritual: Social Mobility on Wheels." *Minority Notes* 2:1/2 (1981): 10–11, 30.

Penland, Paige R. *Lowrider: History, Pride, Culture.* Minneapolis, MN: MBI, 2003.